HILLFORTS

Later Prehistoric Earthworks
in
Britain and Ireland

Frontispiece: St. Catharine's Hill, Winchester, from the south-west.

HILLFORTS

Later Prehistoric Earthworks
in
Britain and Ireland

edited by

D. W. HARDING

1976

ACADEMIC PRESS

London · New York · San Francisco

A Subsidiary of Harcourt Brace Jovanovich, Publishers

ACADEMIC PRESS INC. (LONDON) LTD.
24/28 Oval Road,
London NW1

United States Edition published by
ACADEMIC PRESS INC.
111 Fifth Avenue
New York, New York 10003

Copyright © 1976 by
ACADEMIC PRESS INC. (LONDON) LTD.

Library of Congress Catalog Card Number: 74 17993
ISBN: 0 12 324750 0

PRINTED IN GREAT BRITAIN BY
WILLIAM CLOWES & SONS, LIMITED, LONDON, COLCHESTER AND BECCLES

Notes on Contributors

MICHAEL AVERY is Lecturer in Archaeology at the Queen's University, Belfast.

SARA CHAMPION is currently engaged in research on the European Iron Age; her husband is Lecturer in Archaeology in the University of Southampton.

DAVID COOMBS is Lecturer in Archaeology in the University of Manchester.

PHILIP DIXON is Lecturer in Archaeology in the University of Nottingham.

G. C. DUNNING was formerly an Inspector of Ancient Monuments for England and Wales.

JAMES DYER is Head of the Department of Archaeology and History at Putteridge Bury College of Education, near Luton. His published works include *Southern England, an Archaeological Guide* (1973).

GRAEME GUILBERT is currently engaged in excavation on behalf of the Rescue Archaeology Group.

D. W. HARDING is Lecturer in Archaeology in the University of Durham. His published works include *The Iron Age in the Upper Thames Basin* (1972) and *The Iron Age in Lowland Britain* (1974).

CHRISTOPHER HAWKES was Professor of European Archaeology in the University of Oxford, 1947–1972; his published works include *St Catharine's Hill, Winchester* (1930) (with J. N. L. Myres and C. G. Stevens,) *Archaeology in England and Wales, 1914–1931* (with T. D. Kendrick) (1932), *The Prehistoric Foundations of Europe* (1940), *Prehistoric Britain* (with Jacquetta Hawkes) (1943), and *Camulodunum* (with M. R. Hull) (1947). He is an Honorary Fellow of Keble College, Oxford, and Fellow of the British Academy.

GEORGE JOBEY is Reader in Archaeology in the University of Newcastle-upon-Tyne.

EUAN MACKIE is Assistant Keeper at the Hunterian Museum, University of Glasgow.

C. R. MUSSON is currently engaged in excavation on behalf of the Rescue Archaeology Group.

BARRY RAFTERY is Lecturer in Archaeology at University College, Dublin.

H. N. SAVORY is Keeper of Archaeology in the National Museum of Wales. His published works include *Spain and Portugal: the Prehistory of the Iberian Peninsula* (1968), *Dinorben* (with W. Gardner) (1964), and *Excavations at Dinorben, 1965–1969* (1971).

W. J. VARLEY is well-known for his excavation of hillforts in Cheshire and Yorkshire. His published works include *Prehistoric Cheshire* (1940) and *Cheshire before the Romans* (1963).

BERNARD WAILES is Associate Professor in the Department of Anthropology in the University of Pennsylvania, Philadelphia, U.S.A.

Preface

No other class of prehistoric monument has been regarded as so representative of its period as the hillfort has been for the British Iron Age; the history of hillfort studies has been virtually synonymous with the development of Iron Age studies as a whole. That this should be so is scarcely surprising. Fortified enclosures, ranging in size from less than an acre to several hundred acres, and in structural complexity from simple univallate earthworks to vast multivallate fortresses, are among the most numerous of all our surviving prehistoric monuments—nearly 1500 were listed in the Ordnance Survey's *Map of Southern Britain in the Iron Age* alone—distributed in a density which is unknown on the Continental mainland. Such prominent landmarks naturally attracted the interest of antiquaries and pioneers in archaeology from earliest times, an interest which has been amplified rather than abated by the advent of scientific field techniques and modern methods of excavation.

With the increasing effort which has been devoted to hillfort research in recent years, two issues in particular have come to the fore. The first concerns chronology. Once assigned to a relatively late third century B.C. horizon for the most part, it has become evident that hillforts throughout Britain were being built and occupied over a much longer span of time; indeed, the accumulation of radiocarbon dates which underline the late or even middle Bronze Age origins of these fortifications involves a fundamental reappraisal of the later prehistoric period in these islands. Looking back over half a century of hillfort research, Professor Hawkes is able to observe with a wry smile the irony of the apparent vindication of Williams-Freeman's assumption that these were "Bronze Age camps".

The second problem has been one of definition, considered by Michael Avery in our opening chapter. Is it legitimate to bracket under the umbrella heading of "hillforts" earthworks which may be sited on hill-slopes, promontories, or even in valleys as well as on true hill-top locations? Can we properly include enclosures, like the Irish sites at Rathgall, Dún Ailinne and Emain Macha, where a military function, if not absent, may have been of secondary importance only?

Fundamental as hillforts are to later Bronze Age and Iron Age studies, few reports of hillfort excavations have appeared in monograph form, and for both students and local fieldworkers alike it is not easy to follow up the results of key excavations without access to a wide range of periodical literature. The object of the present book, therefore, has been to present within the compass of a single volume summaries of a number of outstanding sites and excavations which will prove central to a balanced understanding of the subject. A number of these relate to recent or even current excavations, though by no means all; we have chosen to include also reappraisals of sites first dug many years ago, such as Traprain Law or St. Catharine's Hill. Only one such summary became, in the event, a final report, that on the excavations carried out between 1931 and 1934 at Salmonsbury in Gloucestershire. Like the Lambton Worm, Dr. Dunning's contribution "growed and growed" until it had become the definitive report of his fieldwork: that it stands to no disadvantage beside other reports of contemporary excavations is a remarkable measure of the standard of his excavation, and we welcome it warmly. In addition to contributions on individual sites, we have included also more general summaries of progress in regional hillfort studies, by Dr. Savory for Wales, by Euan MacKie on the "vitrified" forts of Scotland and by Barry Raftery on the problems of Irish hillforts. To introduce the whole, Michael Avery traces the development of hillfort research from its beginnings in the later nineteenth century to the present day, and presents a synthesis of current knowledge of hillforts, their structural components and their role in the growth of later prehistoric society.

Excavation and research continue apace. No book could ever hope to achieve a final or definitive statement on a subject so broad or with so many different facets as hillforts. But excavation can never be exactly repeated, and however interpretations may change, the excavator's records retain their importance as primary data. Only if those contemporary excavations here described are themselves in turn capable of reinterpretation can we be confident that our field techniques have attained some measure of adequacy.

D. W. Harding

Contents

3. *Salmonsbury, Bourton-on-the-Water, Gloucestershire*

G. C. Dunning

4. A Summary of the Excavations at Castle Hill, Almondbury, 1939–1972

W. J. Varley

5. Blewburton Hill, Berkshire: Re-Excavation and Reappraisal

D. W. Harding

6. Excavations at Mam Tor, Derbyshire 1965–1969

7. Ravensburgh Castle, Hertfordshire

James Dyer

13. Excavations at the Breiddin 1969–1973

C. R. Musson (On behalf of the Rescue Archaeology Group)

14. Moel y Gaer (Rhosesmor) 1972–1973: An Area Excavation in the Interior

Graeme Guilbert

15. Dún Ailinne: An Interim Report

Bernard Wailes

16. Rathgall and Irish Hillfort Problems

Barry Raftery

1 | *Hillforts of the British Isles: A Student's Introduction*

Michael Avery

". . . the hillfort, in one form or another, becomes the typical field monument of the Celtic world . . ."
(*Piggott, 1965, p. 207*)

Hillforts have always fascinated students of the Iron Age, and a massive and specialised literature has grown up around the subject over more than a century. In one sense, information on hillforts is easy to come by. In the Ordnance Survey *Map of Southern Britain in the Iron Age*, and its Gazetteer, published in 1962, are lists and distribution maps of almost all hillforts and small earthworks in that area which were then generally accepted as of Iron Age date—some 1400 of them. For Scotland, Rivet (1966) presented maps of hillfort sites, and gave an extensive bibliography. Only in Ireland does this basic information still need to be published in an accessible form; B. Raftery (1972) has recently made a start by collecting together some forty examples. For a student wise enough to wish to visit sites himself, as well as read and look at illustrations, Thomas (1960), Feachem (1963) and Evans (1966) provide useful guides to England, Scotland and Ireland.

It is when one seeks to go deeper that major problems arise. Individual sites have been studied in very varying detail: for some, there is no adequate plan published; for others, there are extensive excavation reports; for many, there are brief or long notes in a bewildering variety of journals. There is no comprehensive bibliography published. A beginner is reduced to reading what is said in passing about hillforts in general studies of the Iron Age or Roman periods, or studying a few "classic" excavation reports. This outline of what is known and surmised about hillforts of the British Isles may therefore help the student to approach the serious work of more specialised discussions with a clearer idea of the general framework into which these contributions fit.

I. What is a Hillfort?

All over the British Isles are large numbers of sites which have one feature in common, that they were deliberately built with man-made fortifications, constructed of earth, timber or stone; many are additionally placed in tactically defensible positions, for example, on hills. The central aim of the construction of these sites was to provide a fortified place that would be defensible against human attack. As soon as written history provides administrative documents relating to such sites, it becomes possible to call some of them by names which interpret their function in the light of these documents. Thus some of these fortified places are Roman towns, or Saxon burghs, or feudal Norman castles[1]. The residue, consisting of prehistoric sites fortified against human attack, are now all usually called "forts"[2]. In this context, prehistory broadly ends in England with the Roman Conquest in A.D. 43, in Scotland with the twelfth century introduction of feudal castles and in Wales and Ireland only with the Norman conquest of these areas in the twelfth century A.D.[3].

This prehistorian's use of the word "fort" should be clearly distinguished from its later use to mean a site built and garrisoned by professional soldiers, such as a Roman fort, or an artillery fort, or a star-shaped fort. The word "fort" is applied to many prehistoric sites which were not manned by professional soldiers but were apparently built to protect occupants who spent most of their life in the normal activities of agricultural and manufacturing industries. For prehistoric sites, the term "fort" is used simply to mean "a site fortified so as to be defensible against human attack". Conclusions as to the livelihood and social structure of its occupants have to be deduced from the evidence of excavation and field survey.

There are many thousands of such prehistoric fortified sites in the British Isles, and it is first necessary to draw a crucial distinction within them. This is the distinction between the tiny sites which enclose less than $\frac{1}{4}$ acre (or $\frac{1}{10}$ hectare, in metric terms) and all larger sites. These tiny sites seem to be a distinct phenomenon, for several reasons. Firstly, although their defences may be impressive, they enclose only enough space for one or two houses. They contrast with the hamlet or village settlements which apparently occupied the larger sites. Secondly, they exhibit structural peculiarities which are not found in larger sites, such as the complete raising of the interior with artificial mounding, or the extreme thickening of wall or the raising of walls to extra

[1] For Roman towns, see Collingwood and Richmond (1969, pp. 95–132). For Saxon burghs, see Radford (1970).

[2] Many names of forts, as given on maps, often include the word "Castle": this is usually merely a misnomer. Sites surrounded by a wall or fence that seems too slight for deliberate defence against humans, even though it might have served as a defence against animals, are usually termed "enclosures", not forts.

[3] A distinction should be drawn between fully historic periods and what are sometimes called protohistoric periods. In fully historic periods, there is administrative documentation which allows us to interpret the function of sites in the light of their society, and thus provides us with interpretative names for different types of site. In protohistoric periods, heroic legends, legal codes and travellers' tales may throw some light on the society, but satisfactory administrative documentation is absent. In Southern England, the Dark Ages between the Roman and Late Saxon periods were protohistoric rather than historic, as were Wales, Scotland and Ireland prior to the feudal or Norman periods. Much of Ireland remained outside the area of feudal society even longer than this, and continued to be protohistoric. For an archaeologist, protohistoric periods have at present to be treated very largely as if they were purely prehistoric periods.

height. Thirdly, where these tiny sites occur, they tend to abound in very great density. There are very large numbers of them in Ireland, where they appear in general to be a later feature than the larger fortified sites[4]. In Northern and Western Scotland, they occur in areas which apparently lack the larger sites[5]. It seems clear that these tiny sites are quite different structurally, socially and economically from the larger fortified sites. No all-embracing name has apparently hitherto been given to them: I propose to class them all together under a name of their own, and to call them all "fortlets". I shall restrict the term "fort" to the larger sites, that is, those enclosing more than $\frac{1}{4}$ acre[6].

Now not all forts can be correctly termed "hillforts". A hillfort is a fort which not only has artificial man-made defences raised to protect it, but also exploits the natural terrain so as to give defenders an advantage of height over those approaching the site. We shall see later that this may be done in various ways.

The word "hillfort" has a long history, extending back at least as far as the middle of the nineteenth century. It was then used to emphasise the military nature of these sites, against those who saw them as temporary camps of refuge or even as Druids' circles[7]. An important milestone in the term's acceptance was the classic article "Hillforts" by Hawkes in 1931. The word was originally developed for the forts of Central Southern England. Here the majority form a relatively homogeneous group: most have artificial earthen defences all round them, and these defences exploit the terrain by being sited where the hill-side starts to drop away more steeply. Once one looks more closely, however, problems emerge. Even within the Southern English hillforts, a number of different categories of siting can be distinguished. Outside Southern England, not only can hillforts be subdivided, but a variety of other forts become prominent which are not necessarily sited in strong defensive positions; these may also have stone or wooden defences, rather than

[4] Those with earthen banks and ditches are known as "forts", "raths" or "ringforts"; those with stone walls are termed "cashels"; similar sites which are defended islands, using water as a defence, are termed "crannogs"; these are three environmental adaptations of the same idea, using whatever materials the terrain provides. Estimates of their numbers in Ireland range to 50,000, but there is no full listing of them published; many appear to date from the period around A.D. 500 and later, although some may be earlier (Proudfoot, 1961; 1970). In South-western Wales, sites known as "raths" also occur, but some at least are pre-Roman (Hogg, 1972a, pp. 16–17; Wainwright, 1971a, p. 98).

[5] In Western and Northern Scotland, these sites were first clearly isolated by Childe (1935a, pp. 197–206), under the name of "castles": they are built in stone, and come in two distinctive varieties, called "duns" (Feachem, 1963, pp. 175–177; Rivet, 1966, map at back; Maxwell, 1969) and "brochs" (Feachem, 1963, pp. 162–163; Rivet, 1966, map at back; Mackie, 1965). The date of these Scottish structures is still rather obscure. Comprehensive survey of these tiny sites has never yet been attempted, and what little excavation there has been in Scotland and Ireland has hardly scratched the surface of the problem. In Southern England, such tiny fortified sites are notably absent.

[6] I should make it clear that this is a new terminology, and that others have used the term "fort" to include fortified sites of all sizes, even fortlets: see, e.g., Mackie (1965, p. 98). This seems to me, however, to confuse together sites which are sufficiently distinct to merit separate names.

[7] See, for example, Turner (1850) and Lane-Fox (1869a). The word "hillfort" has taken a long time to oust the earlier word "camp", but "camp" is now very rarely used by archaeologists. The spellings "hill-fort", "hill fort" and "Hill Fort" are all found, but are really all synonymous with "hillfort".

earthen ones. Thus we have on the one hand a general category of forts, which all seem very broadly of the same date, function in society and economy. On the other hand, when looked at in detail, both hillforts and other forts break up into a multiplicity of conflicting categories. This problem of terminology has been dealt with in two main ways. On the one hand, specialists have tended to drop the word "hillfort", and refer instead to "forts"; they then qualify this with an adjective to state which detailed category they are referring to[8].

On the other hand, some authors have extended the word "hillfort" as a general term to cover all forts, until the "hill-" part has lost almost all its force. Thus "hillfort" is sometimes used as a synonym for "prehistoric fort", to distinguish these forts from Roman forts and professional military forts[9].

In general, it seems best to restrict the term "hillfort" to those sites which are defended not only by man-made fortifications but also by a deliberate exploiting of the terrain to give at least some advantage from height. It is clear that the builders of such sites were often prepared to sacrifice convenience to a considerable degree, in order to obtain defence. Although other sites with man-made fortifications clearly have some of the defensive characteristics of hillforts, it is likely that there is something anomalous about those which did not place a sufficiently high priority on defence for them to have made such use of the terrain. These other sites should be called simply "forts".

Clearly, some of the descriptions of hillforts are also applicable to other forts. In particular, descriptions of surface morphology, rampart structure and entrances do seem to be widely applicable to all forts. Descriptions of interiors, economy and place in society, however, are very much more difficult to apply so widely, since the evidence we have for these aspects at present has come overwhelmingly from hillforts. The student should bear this distinction firmly in mind when considering how widely to apply descriptions of hillforts.

II. Surface Morphology

Since there is no complete published set of plans of forts, a detailed classification of them according to their local position and surface features is not possible. Useful collections of detailed modern plans of forts have, however, been published for certain areas by the Royal Commissions: a bibliography is given in Appendix 1.

Unexcavated forts show a variety of features, for which a number of technical terms have been coined. The defensive structures usually consist of a bank (often termed a "rampart") or banks, built including material dug out

[8] Classifications may be based on siting and position (e.g., "plateau fort", "hill-slope fort", "contour fort"), or on layout (e.g., "nuclear fort", "univallate fort", "bivallate fort"), or on date (e.g., "Bronze Age fort", "Iron Age fort", "Dark Age fort") or on the material of which the defences were constructed (e.g., "earthen fort", "stone fort", "timber-framed fort"). I shall outline some of these classifications in later sections.

[9] It is often found in this sense in the titles of articles and in introductory paragraphs; later in their articles, authors usually abandon the word "hillfort" and replace it with more specialist terms like "plateau fort", "timber-framed fort", etc.

of a defensive ditch or ditches in front of the bank(s). Sometimes, a small amount of upcast from the ditch has been thrown out also on the outer side of the ditch, opposite to the defensive escarpment of the main bank, and this material may form a low bank termed a "counter-scarp" bank. Sometimes, the natural surface of the ground forms a flat ledge, a metre or so wide, between the edge of a ditch and the foot of a bank beside it: this ledge is termed a "berm". Old-fashioned terms (from the Latin) occasionally used are *"vallum"* for the rampart and *"fosse"* for the ditch. The inmost bank is normally the strongest and highest defence: not infrequently, quarrying for material for an inner bank may have taken place behind the site of the bank, when traces may show on the surface of the interior of the fort; this internal "quarry ditch" may be visible on the surface as a series of scoops (e.g., Hod Hill and Hambledon Hill). A limited number of earthwork forts were apparently abandoned unfinished. Surface study of them has suggested that a variety of temporary markers, and "marking-out" banks and ditches, were used to lay out the line of the defences, and that the erection of the final earthwork was allotted to "gangs" of construction workers, each gang being responsible for one stretch of the perimeter. Occasionally, internal walls have been found within the structure of an excavated rampart, which may reflect division of the construction work amongst different gangs[10].

The number of lines of bank (excluding counter-scarp banks) enclosing the interior of a fort is a major feature in classification. Usually, a simple distinction is drawn between univallate sites (with one bank) and multivallate sites (with more than one bank). Within multivallate sites, however, it is possible to note the existence of bivallate forts, with two lines of bank; trivallate, with three lines; quadrivallate, with four lines; and very rare examples with more than four lines. In many cases where more than one line of bank is found, these extra lines have been added only around part of the perimeter where, for example, the natural slope of the ground allows a gentle, easy approach to the inner banks from a certain direction. In such cases, the site should be classified as univallate, bivallate, etc., according to the number of lines visible all the way round the perimeter (exercising care, of course, over the problems caused by such things as removal of surface traces of banks by ploughing), with a note that extra lines make the site bivallate, trivallate, etc., at specified points.

The location of the banks and ditches is also significant. In most sites of Central Southern England and the borders of Wales, these concentric lines of defence are "close-set", that is, there is little space left clear between the outer edge of a ditch and the inner edge of the next bank. Sometimes, there is enough space for a human to run easily along a berm behind the outer bank, but rarely more. Elsewhere, however, a quite distinct feature is found of "wide-set" lines of defence, where the distance between a ditch and the next bank outwards may be up to several hundred metres. Often, of course, the outer bank and

---

[10] For unfinished forts, see Feachem (1971) and Piggott (1931). For evidence of gang-work within a finished rampart, see Maiden Castle, Dorset, site H (Wheeler, 1943, Pl. LXXIX and Pl. XIX).

ditch may be earlier or later than the inner ones. Such "wide-set" defences can be divided into two sorts. In some, the outer works are continuous around the perimeter and in strong, defensive positions. Here one should suspect that a refortification took place with new defences on a new alignment. In others, however, the outer works are not continuous round the whole perimeter. The latter occur particularly in South-western England. Here, interpretation of their function can be puzzling: the aim evidently is to demarcate or provide some defence for an extra area outside the main fortified enclosure[11]. A limited number of forts have "appended enclosures" outside the main defences. These can be subdivided into: (a) "dependent enclosures", where an outer bank and ditch remains close to an inner bank and ditch for most of the perimeter, but diverges in part to enclose an area outside the inner defences, usually at the entrance (when the dependent enclosure may be termed a "fore-court" or "barbican", p. 18 below); (b) "annexed enclosures", where the outer enclosure is built on to the inner so that the outer earthwork abuts against the inner one. The date and function of these appended enclosures is often uncertain[12]. Occasionally, inner enclosures are found: these, however, have a nasty habit of turning out on excavation to be either earlier or later than the main defences (e.g., Crickley, Chapter 8, p. 161ff.). One form of visible internal subdivision of a fort's area results from extension or shrinkage of the main defended area. Normally, this leaves traces in the form of degraded banks enclosing an area different from that enclosed by the best preserved banks. Evidence of a change of plan may show in abrupt changes of alignment in the plan of the main (later) banks, as at Maiden Castle and Hambledon Hill, Dorset. In cases where the plan of the fort shows more than one concentric line of defensive structure, one may usually suspect that the site is multi-period, normally with outer bank(s) added after the inner one.

The defences of a fort are usually a bank and ditch, but there are many forts defended only by a stone wall, without ditch. Good examples occur in North Wales. Here they are usually termed "walled forts"; these should be distinguished from "wall ramparts" (see below, p. 11). Elsewhere, in Cornwall and Armorica, are found defensive structures which have only a very shallow ditch in front of a stone bank or wall. In both of these variants, where the effective defence is clearly the wall, without any serious ditch, the cause may

[11] For discontinuous wide-set outer earthworks in South-western England, see Aileen Fox (1958) and Whybrow (1967). The use of such outer lines of earthwork may be related to the idea of demarcating the boundaries of certain areas of land with sizeable ditches, not necessarily intended primarily for defence (e.g., on the Chilterns: see Dyer, 1961). These outer areas are usually interpreted as corrals for flocks and herds (see below, p. 28). For wide-set outer defences which suggest refortification, see Feachem (1966, pp. 77–81: Traprain Law and Eildon Hill North) and R.C.A.H.M. (Wales and Monmouthshire), 1964, pp. 69–72, Carn Fadrun. For close-set outer lines of defence, with a berm behind the outer bank, see Maiden Castle, Dorset (Wheeler, 1943, p. 5 and Pl. LXIX) or Rainsborough phase 2a (Avery et al., 1967, p. 213).
[12] For the terminology and illustrations from South-western England, see Aileen Fox (1958, pp. 37–42). For Scottish examples, see Feachem (1956b, p. 77, Dumyat) and R.C.A.H.M. (Scotland), 1956, p. 111, Penchrise Pen.

possibly be the difficulty of carving a deep ditch out of hard rock[13]. On some sites, a quite different technique of creating a defence was used, for which Rivet (1958a, pp. 31–32) coined the term "downward" construction. In these cases, the defences are set part way down a slope, and the hillside has been dug into so as to form a flat ledge, with a very steep inner slope; material from this "ditch" has then all been thrown *down*hill so as to widen the ledge and create a steeper slope below it.

The builders often paid considerable attention to designing complex entrances, and excavators have concentrated considerable effort on uncovering entrances. The surface traces seen before excavation can often be misleading, so I have chosen to discuss entrances below, in the context of excavated examples (Section V).

III. Size, Siting and Layout

Forts, as I have defined them, enclose areas ranging from $\frac{1}{4}$ acre to over 100 acres. Several proposals have been made to draw subdivisions within this enormous span of size. The best known, and probably the most illuminating, is a division of forts into those enclosing less than three acres and those enclosing more than three acres. I shall call these respectively "minor forts" and "major forts"[14]. When one inspects the distribution of these two size categories, it is clear that they are not universally distributed over the British Isles (see Figs 1 and 2). Minor forts are normal only in Cornwall, South-western Wales, Northern England and Southern Scotland. In these areas, however, they are very much more common than are major forts. In Cornwall, minor forts are known as "rounds"; many are clearly not hillforts, but are sited in less defensive positions. In Northern England and Southern Scotland, minor forts are more defensively sited, that is, they are hillforts[15]. Major forts on the other hand, occur particularly densely in a band from the Dorset coast to the Mersey Estuary, with another concentration in the Cotswolds. They thin out rather as one moves away from these regions, even in areas where tempting hill-tops exist. It is clear, then, that availability of suitable hill-tops is not the only factor involved in the general distribution of either major forts or minor forts. The nature of the terrain does, however, have a decisive effect on the layout or plan of individual hillforts.

The ground plans of most hillforts are overwhelmingly determined by

[13] For North Welsh walled forts, see Hogg, (1964, p. lxxiv) and Savory (below, p. 237ff.). For shallow ditches, see Gurnard's Head, Cornwall (Gordon, 1940, Fig. 2, facing p. 100) and in Armorica, see Erquy, Côtes-du-Nord (Giot *et al.*, 1968, Fig. 2, facing p. 73).

[14] This division is that drawn by Rivet for the Ordnance Survey *Map of Southern Britain in the Iron Age* (1962). Other, complementary divisions have been suggested for certain regions of the British Isles. See, for example, Feachem (1966, p. 78) for Scotland, and Hogg (1972b, p. 295) for Wales.

[15] For Cornish rounds, see A. Fox (1964, pp. 125–126) and Thomas (1966b, pp. 87–91). Considerable numbers of new sites (certain, probable and possible) are still being found: see, e.g., Russell (1971, pp. 41–47 and 56–60). For minor Northern forts, see Feachem (1966, p. 67), Jobey (1965) and plans published in R.C.A.H.M. (Scotland), 1956.

defensive factors inherent in the location chosen, and, therefore, in effect, by the underlying solid geology. One may distinguish three main groups based on siting[16]: (1) hillforts which rely on natural defences, in the form of cliffs or steep slopes, for most of their perimeter, with only short stretches of man-made defences; (2) hillforts which are completely enclosed by man-made defences which follow the contours of the terrain and improve its natural advantages; and (3) forts where man-made defences extend around the whole perimeter, but the siting does not seem to exploit natural advantages for tactical strength very effectively.

The first group can be subdivided into three classes: (a) "cliff-edge forts", where round much of the site there may be steep slopes, or river courses, without man-made defences, but there remains a considerable extent of the perimeter which is fortified by artificial bank and ditch defences (e.g., Crickley, below); (b) "promontory forts", where a natural promontory is joined to a scarp or plateau only by a narrow saddle or ridge, and the man-made defences are limited to a cross-bank and ditch barring the way across this saddle with the rest of the perimeter unfortified by man; and (c) "ridge forts", where a fort is sited on top of a narrow ridge, with steeply sloping flanks, and fortification was necessary only to delimit the two ends of the fort, thus producing a roughly rectangular, elongated plan[17].

In hillforts of this first group, the extent of reliance on natural strength alone, without the use of man-made banks and ditches, varies considerably: some sites (e.g., Hambledon) were provided with artificial defences strengthening—apparently unnecessarily—steep slopes which were already tactically strong. Forts of this first group are particularly prominent in regions where the geomorphology, reflecting differential erosion of the underlying geological strata, offers locations to be exploited. For example, inland promontory and cliff-edge forts cluster along the Northern scarp of the Cotswolds; while sea-edge and promontory forts of the Cornish coast show the same two types of siting, and are termed "cliff-castles" (Cotton, 1959).

The second group of hillforts can all be called "contour forts"; they can be subdivided into two classes: (d) "low eminence forts", where a low hill, standing a little above the surrounding countryside, provides some natural tactical strength which is exploited by the enclosing defences (e.g., Maiden Castle, Dorset; Danebury, Hampshire); and (e) "high eminence forts", where long and steep natural slopes provide good tactical strength, but artificial defences were added (e.g., The Caburn, Sussex). With this last class, high eminence forts, it is not unusual for the man-made defences to take the form of "downward" construction. At all contour forts, it is common for the entrance to be on a side which has a more gentle slope leading up to it; the entrance then sometimes has outer works, to create a defence in depth.

[16] For other general discussions of siting, see Rice-Holmes (1907, pp. 135–138), Allcroft (1908) and the scheme proposed in the early 1900s by the Earthworks Committee (Balcarres, Allcroft *et al.*, 1910).
[17] Feachem (1966, pp. 67–68); R.C.A.H.M. (Scotland), 1956, Vol. 1, p. 18.

All these hillforts, of both the first group and the second group, tend to have an irregular ground-plan, following the natural contours of the ground. The emphasis is very heavily on tactical defence. This normally implies location in a relatively inaccessible position, and also the absence of a source of continuous ground water supply within the defended area.

The third group includes a number of relatively unusual types of siting, where the layout does not seem to have been so heavily determined by tactical considerations[18]. The identification of the following six classes has very largely been the result of detailed regional field-work in the 1950s: probably other distinct categories will eventually be defined. Class (f), "plateau forts", are sited in high positions, but where the natural lie of the land provides little tactical defensive strength (e.g., Rainsborough). A number of these can be classified as (g), "polygonal plan forts", on the grounds that they are defended by relatively straight stretches of bank and ditch, often forming a four-sided plan; where polygonal plan forts are sited on hills, this plan is not imposed by the shape of the hills, and indeed does not seem to exploit the terrain at all well in the tactical sense. Examples have been suggested in Sussex and Wiltshire. In Scotland is found a class (h) of "oblong forts" which also seem to have been built to a preconceived plan, not determined by the terrain[19]. In class (j), "hill-slope forts", the banks are sited on the slope of a hill, so that the interior of the fort is definitely overlooked by higher ground outside the defences; this position seems tactically weak to defend, and must reflect a choice determined by factors other than solely defensive tactics. Hill-slope forts occur in South-western England and Western Wales, and are often provided with "wide-set" banks and dependent or annexed enclosures[20]. Class (k), "valley forts", are rare, since most forts are sited at least on a low eminence[21]. The final class (l), "nuclear forts", consists of very unusual sites in Scotland. These sites appear in plan as a small central defensive structure, some 30 m by 40 m, with a number of relatively small annexed enclosures (usually each delimited by a wall without ditch, running along a line where a change in surface level creates craggy outcrops). These annexed enclosures were added successively around the central structure to create a cluster of enclosures[22].

[18] With some of them, one might hesitate before calling them "hillforts". In this article, however, I shall include as hillforts all except hill-slope forts and valley forts.

[19] For polygonal plan forts in Sussex, see Curwen (1937, p. 202; 1954, p. 227–228), followed by Cunliffe (1966, pp. 118–119); Cunliffe (1973, p. 410) extends the idea to Wiltshire. The term "polygonal plan" is my own. For oblong forts in Scotland, see Feachem (1966, pp. 67–68).

[20] For hill-slope forts, see A. Fox (1952; 1958) and Whybrow (1967).

[21] One example, however, is Cherbury, Berkshire.

[22] For nuclear forts, see Stevenson (1951, pp. 190–195) and Feachem (1956b, pp. 78–83: Dalmahoy, Dunadd and Dundurn). Nuclear forts are not easy to distinguish from other, more normal Scottish sites which have a small central, defensive structure; these more normal sites are usually multivallate forts which have annexed or dependent enclosures outside the main defences (Feachem, 1956b, pp. 73–83: Turin Hill, Dunearn, Dumyat and Moncrieffe Hill; Feachem, 1966, p. 83, Carman, and p. 74, Brown Caterthun). The terminology here is a little confusing. In both types of site the small central defensive structure has usually been termed a "citadel", although Feachem (1966, pp. 82–83) suggests replacing this with the term "defensive enclosure" (which should not be confused with the clustered enclosures which constitute the outer parts of a nuclear fort). Nuclear forts and other

IV. Excavated Structures: Ramparts and Ditches

The bank, covered with grass, bushes or trees, which is often all which now marks off the area of a fort, is of course the result of collapse followed by centuries of weathering. Buried within these banks are often the traces of what were once much more complex structures of stone, timber, rubble and earth. Excavators have devoted by far the largest part of their time and attention to digging ramparts, and we have therefore a fairly clear idea of what the original structures envisaged by the builders were like. On many sites, the ramparts were reconstructed or rebuilt, at intervals over the centuries, to form a complex succession of structures. Fundamental distinctions in methods of construction can be drawn between (1) wooden palisades; (2) dump banks; and (3) ramparts built as walls (whether with a stone facing or merely with a timber frame filled with a rubble or compacted earth core). Illustrations of what some ramparts looked like, and how they were built, are given in Fig. 3. It is the third class, wall ramparts, which provide the clearest and most interesting evidence of how fort architects tackled the constructional problems in civil engineering involved in creating impressive defences for their sites.

Wooden palisades took the form of stout vertical timbers, usually embedded in a continuous trench dug into the ground, rather than in individual postholes; the wooden superstructure has, of course, rotted away, but presumably the timbers were braced or lashed together to form a stockade. In Southern England, all surface traces have usually been ploughed away or buried by later building. Such palisades were sometimes demonstrably only the first stage before more impressive wall or bank structures were built; it is possible that many settlements which later became forts were initially protected only by such a wooden fence. In Northern England, however, wooden palisades were often not succeeded by earth or stone ramparts, and the palisade trenches are sometimes still faintly visible on the surface of the ground. A number of these Northern sites are encircled by both an inner and an outer defence of wood, separated by some 10 metres. In some cases, both inner and outer defence each consist of a double, or "twin", palisade: the trenches which were dug for these "twin palisades" are some one to three metres apart. In Southern England, palisaded enclosures are usually thought of as primarily non-defensive, and are not termed forts; in the North, they are sometimes thought of as minor wooden hillforts[23].

---

forts with a citadel have sometimes been grouped together as "citadel forts". On close inspection of both nuclear forts and other citadel forts, however, the central citadel appears to have been a fortlet built later than the outer works; the citadels are apparently post-Roman, though the other structures on these sites constitute forts which could be pre-Roman (Feachem, 1966, pp. 83–84; 1956b, pp. 73–76). Nuclear forts, therefore, have a distinctive type of layout but other citadel forts are more normal forts with a distinctive type of later reuse.

[23] For a hillfort with an initial phase consisting of a palisade, see, for example, Hollingbury, Sussex. A list, and brief discussion, of palisaded sites in Northern Britain is given in Ritchie (1970). For wooden forts in Northern England and Southern Scotland, see also Feachem (1966, pp. 62–65) and Jobey (1966b, pp. 89–95; 1965, pp. 22–24).

Dump banks inevitably exhibit few structural features of any complexity. Material dug from a ditch is piled to form a bank, and the material settles at the natural angle of rest. This technique is sometimes termed *glacis* construction. It was often used to save time and effort in refurbishing the collapsed remains of an earlier rampart (e.g., Blewburton, below, pp. 135–136), and many dump banks were topped by a stout wooden stockade along the crest. Some dump banks are particularly high, with a wide, flat-bottomed ditch, and apparently never had a palisade along the crest, but rather a capping of stones; these are sometimes termed "Fécamp type" banks, after the site in Northern France dug by Wheeler[24]. A limited number of very high dump banks were built with rear stone facings either visible or hidden within the body of the bank; the function of the walls presumably was to restrain the bank material from collapsing on to houses immediately behind the bank (Wheeler, 1943, Pl. IX, facing p. 101).

Wall ramparts are the most complex of the defence structures found in forts. The fundamental aim of their construction was to present to those approaching the site a front which was vertical or near-vertical. This task was tackled by constructing a high front facing backed and supported by a "core" either of loose stone rubble or of closely packed earth and softer rocks such as chalk; often a steep rear facing was added to keep the core clear of interior houses[25]. Such constructions clearly posed two problems: how to construct the facing; and how to stop the relatively unstable core from sliding and collapsing. The methods used by the builders reveal a marked administrative ability in assembling supplies and considerable skill in exploiting local resources for civil engineering projects. The designers evidently had a grasp of the principles of reinforcing unstable earth and stone mounds against collapse.

The front face was given its steepness either by a front facing wall of stone (creating a "stone-faced" rampart) or by vertical timbers supporting a facing of timbers or turfs (creating a "timber-framed" rampart). The distinction very largely reflects an adaptation to environment, stone walls being used where building stone was available (e.g., on the Cotswolds) and timber where building stone was difficult to obtain (e.g., on the Southern English chalk downs). Architects were, however, sometimes prepared to import suitable building stone in sizeable quantities from a considerable distance (e.g., Maiden Castle, Dorset: Wheeler, 1943, p. 34).

The stone wall facings of a stone-faced rampart are always of dry-stone, build, never mortared, and are usually of relatively small stones, normally only one skin in thickness. Where the rock breaks naturally into larger pieces, these may be included either horizontally or as upright slabs[26]. The facing walls

[24] Wheeler and Richardson (1957, pp. 8–11 and 62–75); Cotton (1958, p. 65); Ward Perkins (1944, pp. 139–141).
[25] "Wall ramparts" should be distinguished from "walled forts". Walled forts are those without ditches (see above, p. 6); wall ramparts can, however, occur with ditches.
[26] For the inclusion of larger slabs, see e.g., Bathampton (Wainwright, 1967,b); Dinorwig, Caernarvonshire (R.C.A.H.M. (Wales and Monmouthshire) 1960, no. 1170); Tre'r Ceiri and Garn Boduan, Caernarvonshire (Hogg, 1960).

appear never to have been set in foundation trenches: very rarely did the build-ers even cut a trench through the ancient top-soil to found the wall on bed-rock. They are in fact merely a facing, and can have had little value as retaining walls. On rare occasions, the facing was strengthened at its base by a thicker banking of carefully laid stones[27]. Sometimes, vertical timbers were set at intervals to support the front face of the core, and the spaces between the timbers were then filled in with a stone facing; this has been named the "Preist" type of construction, after a hillfort in Germany[28]. Usually, one suspects, the wall was built with a batter, that is, built so that the top was several feet behind the bottom[29].

The timber structures which were used in a timber-framed rampart to create a steep front face leave evidence in the form of sizeable individual post-holes. These are found in line usually at about three metre intervals, either at the edge of the ditch (e.g., Ivinghoe) or set several metres back from the edge of the ditch (e.g., Grimthorpe): often there is also a second line of post-holes at or near the rear of the rampart. The distance between these two lines of post-holes may vary from stretch to stretch of the same rampart (e.g., Ivinghoe). The core which filled the space between these two lines of vertical frame timbers has usually collapsed badly or even been ploughed away. These ramparts are sometimes described as of "box-type" construction, or named "Hollingbury type", after an early discovery of one in Sussex. Sometimes the rear frame timbers were buried by a sloping ramp or "tail" of earth and rubble behind them. The front facing, however, presents more difficulties, since there is as yet nowhere any direct evidence known to me of how it was built, only inference. The normal reconstruction suggests a stockade of horizontal timbers lashed to the vertical frame timbers, to form a wooden facing; sometimes the structure is reconstructed with horizontal or sloping beams lashed to verticals and running back into the core of the rampart. This raises problems, since forts were very often burnt during or after capture, but the quantities of charcoal and burnt core material which one would expect the burning of such a wooden wall to produce in the ditch have not been found by excavators. The alternative is to suppose that a front facing wall or cladding of turfs was built, either between the front frame timbers and the ditch edge, to hide the timbers entirely where there was room; or to fill in the spaces be-tween the frame timbers, leaving these timbers visible, as is done in stone in the Preist construction. Turf revetments were used effectively in Roman forts, though they have only rarely been noted at pre-Roman forts. Again, no evi-cence of such turf facings collapsed into the ditch has, to my knowledge, been claimed by excavators[30].

[27] See, for example, Rainsborough, section T (Avery et al., 1967, Pl. XXA.)

[28] For vertical timber and stone facing, see, e.g., Maiden Castle, Dorset (Wheeler, 1943, Pl. XC and XCI). For the fort at Preist, see Cotton (1954, pp. 64–65).

[29] See examples from Leckhampton (below, Figs: 4, 5 and 6).

[30] For Hollingbury, see Curwen (1932). For a rampart with a tail, see Wandlebury, Cambridgeshire, inner rampart (Hartley, 1956, Fig. 2 and pp. 8–9). For timber-framed ramparts reconstructed with a wooden stockade on the front, see Bindon, Dorset (Wheeler, 1953, Pl. IIIb) and Hollingbury

Timber-lacing (that is, laying horizontal branches or beams within the core material to stabilise it) was commonly used in stone-faced ramparts; evidence for it is less frequently found in timber-framed ramparts, but probably only because of the different character of the core material, as we shall see[31]. The wood may be laid either transversely (i.e., at right angles to the wall faces) or longitudinally (along the rampart). Transverse timbers, which are by far the commonest in the British Isles, apparently occur normally in layers, but the precise character of the timber constructions is difficult to determine in excavation. Such information as we have comes mainly from sites where a rampart was burnt: this was evidently a common occurrence, and indeed Caesar describes the use of fire as a standard method of attack in Gaul. Where the core consisted of compacted earth or rocks like chalk or sand, access of oxygen to the burning timbers was severely restricted, and the wood did not burn away completely to ash, but can be traced as charcoal. Where the core was originally formed of loose rubble blocks, the air spaces allowed access to oxygen which burnt the wood to ash, sometimes creating extreme heat. Under these temperatures, the material of the core sometimes became calcined and soft or partially melted. This procedure has resulted in ramparts in Southern England where lime produced by the heat has been slaked by rain-water, and become a solid, hard mass of mortar. In Scotland, the partial melting of the rocks has fused individual stones together to form a vitrified mass, giving the name "vitrified forts" to these sites[32]. The scarcity of such vitrified forts in Wales and Cornwall perhaps suggests that adequate timber was not available. More recently and rarely, evidence has come to light of the position of unburnt timbers, in the form of air-holes left in a core of close-packed earth or chalk when the timbers rotted: either the rampart was not burnt or else the close-packed core restricted the flow of oxygen so much that the buried wood did not even char[33]. Many cores, of course, collapsed when the timbers rotted, and such evidence is therefore difficult to trace.

The function of these timbers clearly was to stabilise the rampart core against collapse, particularly if the front facing was weakened or collapsed through frost or rain or enemy attack. Horizontal branches, especially transverse ones, would restrain the core from slumping and sliding into the ditch to form a

(Curwen, 1954, p. 242). For a front cladding, hiding the timbers, see Wandlebury (Hartley, 1956, pp. 5–7). For turf revetment in a Roman fort, see Hod Hill, Dorset (Richmond, 1968, p. 68 and Fig. 38) and in a hillfort, see Buckland Rings, Hampshire (Hawkes, 1936a, pp. 146–147 and Fig. 8, facing p. 143).

[31] Mrs. Cotton (1954) has gathered together and analysed many of the earlier records of timber-lacing in stone-faced ramparts. Her analysis places much emphasis on differences in technique of timber-lacing which probably do not reflect differences in function.

[32] (See below, pp. 205, ff.). For Caesar's description of use of fire, see Rivet (1971, pp. 189–190). For a distribution map of vitrified forts, see Rivet (1966, map at back). This effect was for long the subject of controversy (see Cotton, 1954, pp. 94–101). It was finally shown experimentally by Childe and Thorneycroft (1938) that the effect would be produced by burning of a loose rubble-cored rampart.

[33] For examples of air-holes, see the Camp d'Artus, Finistère (Wheeler and Richardson, 1957, Pl. III and Pl. XI); Blewburton, below, p. 138; Ranscombe, Sussex (Burstow and Holleyman, 1964, p. 58).

scaleable breach. Longitudinal timbers are not commonly found in the British Isles, though they are a feature of the distinctive "*murus gallicus*" rampart which Caesar described at Avaricum in Gaul in the fifties of the first century B.C. True *murus gallicus* constructions have transverse and longitudinal beams in alternate layers inside the core and fixed together at their crossing points[34].

The methods used to fix lacing timbers to the facings are of course obscure. Where timber-framing was used, or a stone facing of Preist type (with vertical slot in the facing for a vertical timber), some of the horizontal lacing timbers may have been lashed or jointed to the verticals, although the undressed branches which were sometimes used as horizontals were presumably not fixed to verticals at all. Other stone-faced ramparts had holes left through the stone facing, through which transverse timbers protruded from the core: these timber-laced stone-faced ramparts are sometimes termed "devolved Avaricum type"[35]. Such ramparts presumably used dressed baulks of timber.

Alternative methods of constructing all-stone wall ramparts are occasionally found in Northern Scotland, North Wales, Cornwall and Ireland. These are stony areas where timber was perhaps scarce, and methods of stabilising loose rubble and stone wall ramparts without timber had to be devised. These ramparts are usually termed "composite" ramparts. They were built by two methods: (a) "shell-construction" and (b) "deck-construction". A shell-construction rampart was built by constructing a stone-faced rubble-cored wall rampart, with its stone facings resting upon the old land surface, then adding an extra "shell" of rubble (with an outer stone facing) which leant against either the outer or the inner wall face of the original rampart, partly hiding it. Where this extra shell was added on to the interior face of the original wall, it was often not as high as the original wall, and created a "stepped" rear to the rampart. The idea behind this construction seems to have been that a collapse of the stone facing and loose rubble of a shell would still leave the original wall standing, and not cause serious collapse of the whole structure. Deck-construction ramparts were built by constructing first a low wide platform of rubble along the line where the rampart was to be built, to prepare a level deck. Upon the secure foundation of this deck was then raised a normal stone-faced rubble-cored wall rampart. The wall rampart was sometimes narrower than the platform or deck, and was sited along the front edge of the

[34] See Cotton (1957) for detailed discussion of Caesar's text and archaeological evidence on *murus gallicus*. It is unfortunate that the English translation, "Gallic wall", was rather loosely applied by Childe (1935a, p. 193) in Scotland to any stone-faced timber-laced wall rampart. It is often taken as distinctive of *murus gallicus* ramparts that their timbers are nailed together at their crossing points, and indeed many Continental examples are so nailed. Strictly speaking, however, Caesar's words, though often mistranslated, mean "fixed together", not necessarily "nailed together". No nailed *murus gallicus* wall is known in the British Isles: the fort at Burghead, Morayshire, was for long thought to be one (Cotton, 1954, pp. 56–57), but recent excavation suggests a date in the middle of the first millennium A.D. (Small, 1969).

[35] For "devolved Avaricum" ramparts, see Cotton (1954, pp. 57–59). The true Avaricum rampart is a true *murus gallicus*, and thus also necessarily has longitudinal timbers in the core fixed to the transverse timbers. The "devolved Avaricum type" has only transverse timbers.

deck; the rear of the deck then projected and formed a low step at the rear of the rampart. Thus both types of composite rampart often have at their rear such steps, which are sometimes termed "terraces" or "banquettes"[36].

On occasions, naturally, different techniques of building a wall rampart are combined, and stone facings are used with vertical frame timbers or composite ramparts with a timber palisade; in general, however, it is clear that wall ramparts reflect the variety of ways in which the builders used the resources of their area to overcome the problem of the stability of their structures.

The defensive function of both dump banks and wall ramparts was clearly aided by a sentry walk along the top of the rampart. Evidence for this is rare, since rampart crests have usually been eroded fairly severely, but probably one should guess that it was a fairly common feature of wall ramparts. An example of such a rampart walk was revealed in the excavations at Rainsborough, Northamptonshire. Maiden Castle, Dorset, ramparts 4 and 6 show what might be expected for a dump bank, with the post-holes of a palisade along the crest[37]. Elsewhere, one should perhaps regularly assume that the front verticals of a timber-framed rampart were carried up to support a wooden breast-work to protect sentries, or that a wooden breast-work was placed on the top of stone-faced ramparts. In some bivallate and multivallate sites, an opportunity for defenders to move easily along outer ramparts, to mass at any spot where an assault needed to be repulsed, was given by a pathway, or wide berm, left between an outer rampart and the ditch behind it.

V. Entrances

Entrances are designed to stop a rush attack from getting into a fort. Simple entrances provide either merely a narrow gateway through the rampart or a gateway with attached quarters for guards who could shut the gates in an emergency. More complex entrances use a variety of devices to detain an attacking party in a cramped and vulnerable position, where defenders would have the advantage of height and freedom of action.

These entrances are often remarkably complex and sophisticated structures: they reflect the concentration of defensive ingenuity in an area where attack also would be concentrated. The provision of more than one entrance is a common feature, and sites may have a main entrance and also a simpler side entrance, or "postern".

There are obvious problems in knowing what was originally present at

[36] For a shell-construction wall, see Worlebury, Somerset (Dymond and Tomkins, 1886, Pl. V). For deck-construction walls, see Gurnard's Head, Cornwall (Gordon, 1940, Fig. 2) and Kercaradec, Finistère (Wheeler and Richardson, 1957, Pl. XXVII). Shell-construction walls are also sometimes called "*murus duplex*" ramparts (i.e., "double wall" ramparts), after an obscure use of this term by Caesar (*de bello gallico*, 2.29.3). The terms "shell-construction" and "deck-construction" are my own new ones. For previous discussions, see Wheeler (1943, pp. 41–42), Gardner and Savory (1964, pp. 90–91) and Hamilton (1968, pp. 45–52).
[37] Rainsborough: Avery *et al.* (1967, p. 214 and Pl. XXA). Maiden Castle: Wheeler (1943, Pl. XI, facing p. 107).

entrances which now often appear merely as grass-grown gaps in ramparts. It seems wiser to suggest a terminology for entrance features which is based on the results of excavation (see Fig. 4 for these terms)[38]. Entrance features are, of course, often modified in detail to suit particular sites.

The main function of an entrance is to provide a gap through ditch and bank by which people may enter and leave a fort by a route which follows an even gradient. This route is constricted to form a relatively narrow, defensible passage, usually crossing banks and ditches at right angles to their line, but quite often set askew, so that people entering tend to turn towards their left, and thus present to the defenders their right-hand side, carrying a weapon and therefore unprotected by a shield. This passage was usually wide enough for at least a cart to enter, and was often cobbled, or metalled with slabs of stone. The gap through one bank and the original causeway across the ditch in front of it, together with any superstructures upon the bank on either side or over the passage, is usually termed a "portal". One entrance may have several portals, if there are several lines of bank or one bank has more than one passage through it.

The simple portal form of entrance has merely a main passage, between the rampart ends (e.g., Blewburton, below, p. 140 ff.). It is across this main passage that one normally expects to find the gate. Occasionally, double gates, or a twin carriageway are found. One may also expect, on *a priori* grounds, that a bridge over the passage, to link the two adjacent stretches of rampart, was a common feature here: the superstructure was, of course, of wood, and has therefore perished, but suggestive evidence has occasionally been found (e.g., Rainsborough phase 2: Avery *et al.*, 1967, p. 240). It is often difficult, however, to ascertain the exact location of gate-posts and possible bridge, since the passage is nearly always lined with a timber (or timber and stone) facing to retain the rampart core; the lining is constructed with vertical timbers, usually set each in its own post-hole, and these holes are often very large and deep, to take the sizeable timbers required to withstand the sideways thrust of the rampart core; for the sides of the passage were presumably built as nearly vertical as possible. Thus commonly there are several places where bridges of various designs, or gates, could have been set on sizeable vertical timbers. The method of hanging gates is equally unsupported by excavated evidence: presumably the commonest procedure was the pintel and socket method (where one side member of a wooden door frame projects above and below the door panelling and pivots in socket holes at top and bottom)[39]. On some sites, a post-hole in the centre of the passageway suggests that double gates met at this point; clearly, however, double gates could be hung without needing such a central post.

[38] Classification of entrances on the basis of surface morphology has been attempted by, for example, Hawkes (1931, pp. 72–74) and Varley (1948, p. 53).

[39] The nearest approach to evidence on this seems to be the iron objects from Hembury, Devon (Liddell, 1935a, p. 156 and Fig. 11, p. 145) and South Cadbury, Somerset (Alcock, 1971a, p. 4), which may be shoes for the bottom of pintels.

Most modifications of this simple portal entrance form are designed to lengthen the distance which anyone wishing to enter the fort would have to traverse along a route of restricted width while overlooked by the defenders. This can be done (1) by lengthening the passage through a portal; or (2), more elaborately, by defence in depth, extending the entrance defences with outer earthworks, normally on bivallate or multivallate sites; or, more rarely, (3) by outer obstacles, creating a long approach way overlooked by the defences, or setting up *chevaux de frise*, outside the defences.

Lengthened passages can be constructed either by extending a "rearward passage" inwards into the fort or by extending the main passage outwards, with a short "forward passage" to the causeway of a portal. The rearward passage was created by building twin ramparts into the fort, to flank an elongation of the main passage. The sides of the passage were usually faced with a timber or timber-and-stone-wall construction. Either the main gate, or a subsidiary second gate, was placed at the inner end of this rearward passage, to bottle up attackers in a narrow passageway where they could be slaughtered by defenders standing above and behind them on the main ramparts and on the ramparts flanking the passage. This type of portal is regularly found in major forts; it is sometimes called the "Bredon entrance", since elongated rearward passages are a feature of the portals at Bredon Hill, Gloucestershire. This type of portal seems to be a particular feature of forts on the borders between England and Wales, though found elsewhere in England[40]. The construction of a forward passage extending to the ditch causeway of the portal, by the extension outwards of the main passage, is a modification which is rarely found; perhaps because it occurs in a part of the portal which is more rarely excavated. A forward passage may have at its outer end fencing which flanks the passage where it crosses the causeway; the function of this fencing may be partly to prevent humans and stock from falling into the ditch, but it would also inhibit attackers from clambering unnoticed from the causeway up the outer face of the rampart beside the portal. Rarely, also, there is evidence that the ramparts themselves may have been carried forward, in slight bastion-like out-turns, to flank a short forward passage. The unusual feature of a more marked forward passage, flanked by definite out-turns of the main rampart and visible on the surface, is seen at the East entrance of Battlesbury, Wiltshire[41]. Crickley (below, p. 167) presents the very unusual feature of a bank thrown forward from the main rampart to form a "horn-work" and a forward passage

[40] See below, Fig. 5 (Blewburton) for an example. For the Welsh borders, see Chitty (1937). An alternative term often used to classify surface indications before excavation is "inturned entrance", but this term can be misleading. Bredon portals have a distinctively long rearward passage or "inturn", and long inturns should be distinguished from the shorter inturns created by guard-rooms, which have a different function in defence (see below, p. 19). Continental parallels for this idea have been illustrated and discussed by Dehn (1961), who uses the term "Zangentor" (= "scissors entrance") for them. His dates are probably too late for the Welsh and English examples.

[41] For "bastions", see Rainsborough (Avery *et al.*, 1967, p. 240, Fig. 15, and Pl. XXII) and Dinorben (below, Fig. 17 (Savory) and Gardner and Savory, 1964, p. 20). Battlesbury: Allcroft (1908, p. 197, Fig. 68).

with a definite bend in it; in this case, the portal has an outer gate at the outer end of the forward passage and also, apparently, an inner gate in the main passage. Again, the function of the forward passage is to restrict attackers to a narrow space where defenders above can kill them off.

Defence in depth can be created (a) by building an outer portal through the outer bank; or (b) by joining the passages of inner and outer portals into one long passage; or (c) by constructing outlying banks of various designs. The construction of an outer portal as well as an inner portal, is obviously an adaptation to bivallate and multivallate construction. The outer portal may, of course, be a simple one, with only a main passage, or may have the passage lengthened with forward or rearward passages (e.g., Bredon Hill, Gloucestershire; Eggardun, Dorset, eastern entrance). Commonly, the outer bank and ditch swing outwards away from the inner defences at the entrance, so that the distance from the outer portal to the inner portal is lengthened; the area between the two portals is then sometimes termed a "forecourt" or "barbican". The outer portal may be placed either directly in front of the inner portal, or offset to one side. As an extension of this, the distance between the outer and inner portals was sometimes converted into one long continuous passage by the building of ramparts flanking such a passage. From the top of these, the defenders would have assaulted attackers in the narrow passage below them; this tactic, like the Bredon portals, was designed to give the defenders the advantages of height and freedom of movement over a massed rush of attackers. The best example is perhaps that at Blackbury, South Devon. In the most complex and sophisticated design of entrance, outlying banks were thrown up, which may be placed in front of the portal of a univallate fort, or added within the forecourt of a multivallate fort. These banks normally provided defence in two ways. Firstly, they were designed to split up the attackers, either by providing more than one route to the inner portal (as at Maiden Castle, Dorset, phase IV), or by providing "blind" routes, which did not lead to the inner portal at all (as at Danebury, Hampshire, east entrance). Secondly, these banks provided vantage-points, from which defenders again had the advantage of height and freedom of movement over attackers. Such complex and sophisticated defences as this are rare, and occur at a relatively late stage of hillfort design. They were sometimes combined with the provision of platforms and hoards of sling-pebbles, so that "suicide squads" of slingers could take up position on these platforms, outside the inner portal, and create confusion amongst attackers in the confined space of the forecourt with a barrage of stones.[42]

Outer obstacles were sited outside the outermost defences of the fort. The creation of a confining approach road, overlooked by the defences, was a particular adaptation, where terrain permitted, of the common tendency to have a demarcated approach road leading to the entrance. Such an approach road is sometimes sufficiently worn down by traffic to be termed a "hollow

[42] For Maiden Castle, see Wheeler, 1943, especially p. 46; Fig. 3 (p. 17); Fig. 9 (p. 46). For Danebury, see Williams-Freeman (1915, p. 370); Cunliffe (1971a).

way"[43]. *Chevaux de frise* are blocks of stone embedded upright in the ground at fairly close intervals over an area outside the defences, in such a way as to obstruct and slow down any massed charge by attackers, or any attack on horseback. Sites known to have used *chevaux de frise* are very rare. Examples using stone are found in areas where the rock breaks up into suitable fragments, in Ireland, North Wales and Scotland. The idea is also found in Portugal and Spain. It is possible that the idea was more widely used with wooden stakes: excavation has very rarely been carried out just outside the ramparts of hill-forts[44].

An entirely different approach to the strengthening of a simple portal is the use of guard-rooms or guard-huts. These are small rectangular or circular buildings, usually placed one on each side of the passage immediately behind the main rampart, with entrances facing one another; guard-rooms are those built integrally with the rampart structure, while guard-huts are free-standing structures. In this case, the aim is to establish a permanent watch on those who pass through the entrance: at Rainsborough, there was clear evidence that a fire was built in the centre of both guard-rooms, and meals were apparently eaten inside. The small size of the guard buildings found suggests that the guards were no more than a few persons who would be able to sound the alarm and close the gates. It is possible that such a permanent watch was kept even where no guard buildings have been found, but that the facilities provided were less comfortable. The gates of the portal are normally sited forward of the guard-rooms: a gate at the inner end of the passage, to the rear of the guard-rooms, would act like the gate at the inner end of a Bredon portal, and bottle up the attackers, but a sloping guardroom roof is not a good position from which to hurl things at attackers battering in the gates, and gates were apparently not sited to the rear of guard-rooms. Guard structures are visible even without excavation in a number of North Welsh forts, but have also occasionally been revealed during the excavation of entrances in Southern England[45].

Besides these commonly recurring themes, entrances show a large variety of adaptations to particular siting and a considerable degree of ingenuity, particularly in the placing of outer banks to protect weak spots or to check rush attacks.

VI. Interiors

Most hillforts were lived in by communities of hamlet or village size; apparently, the same fort was often successively occupied, abandoned and

---

[43] Approach roads overlooked by defenders on the ramparts are well exemplified at Hambledon Hill, Dorset, south-eastern entrance (R.C.H.M. (England), 1970, part 1, plate facing p. 82); and Garn Boduan, Caernarvonshire, south entrance (Hogg, 1960, Fig. 2).

[44] The British, Irish and Continental examples of *chevaux de frise* have been well summarised by Harbison (1971b).

[45] See Gardner and Savory (1964, pp. 87–90).

reoccupied several times over the centuries. Recently, detailed surveys and excavations have begun to throw a little hesitant light on the layout of these settlements. The portable finds throw considerable light on the activities carried out inside hillforts, at least in Southern England.

Evidence of structures in the interior often comes to light only through excavation, and there has been far too little excavation of interiors. There is good evidence that forts were intended by their builders as sites for permanent human settlement, although in some major forts this settlement may not have occupied the whole of the interior area, and may not in fact have lasted for very long. The settlement seems always to have had the character of a defended village, not the stronghold or castle of a military caste. Evidence for wooden houses and other buildings takes the form of post-holes, narrow foundation trenches or "gullies", and sod walls. Occasional finds of burnt clay with impressions of wattling show that the walls were of wattle and daub construction; the roofs were presumably thatched. Within the Highland Zone (Wales and Scotland), traces of stone-built huts or houses are common; in forts on the steeper hills, traces of "hut platforms" occur, in the form of levelled areas cut out of a hill slope. The occupation of the interior was not normally continuous from the first building of a defence to the very latest use of the site. It consisted instead of intermittent reoccupations. Each reoccupation was probably intended to be permanent, but reoccupations were sometimes separated from preceding and succeeding occupation by a considerable lapse of time. Since the soil cover of most sites has remained thin, all post-holes and foundation trenches have been dug down from the same level. This has turned some of the more densely inhabited interior areas into a palimpsest of successive buildings. Successive phases of reoccupation are sometimes to be distinguished by different types of building (e.g., Crickley, below, p. 172ff.), but more often by changes in associated artifacts. There is sometimes evidence that a building was reconstructed during one single phase[46]. Successive reoccupations may alter the use of a particular part of the interior, for example from living quarters to storage pits and vice versa. Particularly useful information on the succession of artifacts can often be gained from excavation immediately behind an inner rampart, where successive occupations may have built up material in a quarry ditch or successive periods of erosion of the rampart may be interleaved with renewed occupations[47]. This allows the construction of a "key sequence" of artifact types for a hillfort, using the evidence of direct vertical stratigraphy provided by the successive stratified layers; into this key sequence it is then possible to tie in artifacts recovered from pits, postholes and trenches in other parts of the interior, and thus to construct a picture of the occupation of the fort in successive phases.

Excavation has rarely been extensive enough to find clear evidence of the layout of the settlement inside a fort. Three types of pattern do, however,

[46] For a palimpsest of successive buildings, see South Cadbury, Somerset (Alcock, 1972c, pp. 82–83). For reconstructed buildings, see Credenhill, Herefordshire (Stanford, 1970, pp. 98–105).
[47] See, for example, Maiden Castle, Dorset, site D (Wheeler, 1943, Pl. VIII, facing p. 93).

seem to be emerging from recent excavations. The first pattern is one of apparently random and disordered scattering of individual houses over a large part of the interior. The great majority of the evidence consists of plans of unexcavated house sites: it is probable that not all of the houses were in occupation together, so that calculation of the density of occupation is difficult[48]. Many hillforts do, however, seem to have had a moderate sized population living more densely packed together than people apparently did outside hillforts. Many individual small farmsteads outside forts, each housing only perhaps one or two families, seem each to have had their own land around them (see § VII, below).

The second pattern is of regular and ordered streets of houses, reported from Croft Ambrey, Danebury and Crickley. There are hints here of what can only be called town planning; clearly, however, extensive work is still needed in order to establish whether this regular arrangement normally covers the whole or only part of the interior of hillforts where it occurs.

As a third pattern, other sites show large areas without evidence of structures, with buildings and occupation apparently concentrated in a small area. It has been claimed that these sites may be cattle enclosures, depending on a different economy from other forts, that is, pastoral rather than arable. This also needs more investigation[49].

There is some possibility that the disordered arrangement of the first pattern is normally composed of round houses, while the town planning of the second pattern is made up of square or rectangular buildings, but too few sites have yet been dug to prove this. The round houses appear usually to be of the smaller, single-ring design, though they are sometimes of the double or multi-ring type. The rectangular buildings come in a variety of sizes, from sheds to aisled halls[50].

The portable finds excavated from hillforts throw considerable light on the activities carried out inside them, and on the level of material culture possessed by the inhabitants. This is true at least of Southern England. When, however, one moves to Wales, Northern England and Scotland, the number of finds discovered is generally very low; this is partly because fewer excavations have taken place, but partly also it seems to reflect a lower level of material prosperity[51]. One has of course to remember that much of the perishable organic evidence from both Southern and Northern sites will not normally be found by excavation. The detailed chronology of these finds is much too

[48] Examples are Hod Hill (Richmond, 1968, Fig. 2); Garn Boduan, Caernarvonshire (Hogg, 1960, Fig. 2); Eildon Hill North, (Feachem, 1966, p. 81; R.C.A.H.M. (Scotland), 1956, Vol. ii, pp. 306–310). Hogg (1960, pp. 22–23) and Stanford (1972a, b) have based population estimates on theoretical assumptions about the very small amount of evidence at present available.

[49] See, for example, Balksbury, Hampshire (Wainwright, 1969) and Bathampton Camp, Somerset (Wainwright, 1967b, pp. 56–57).

[50] Stanford (1970) contains a useful list of suggested examples of rectangular buildings, to which should be added Crickley, the Breiddin and Moel-y-Gaer (below, p. 172ff., p. 298 and pp. 310–311). For round houses, see Musson (1970b).

[51] What evidence there is from Scottish forts has been presented by Childe (1935a, pp. 236–255) and Stevenson (1966).

complex to present here, though the pottery is outlined in § IX below. Taking the finds all together, however, three categories of activity can be distinguished : firstly, the preparation of food, for which we have a great deal of evidence; secondly, manufacturing industries, including clothing, iron, bronze and pottery production, where we have in general very little evidence except in the case of clothing; and thirdly, the possession of tools and trinkets of metal, glass, shale, etc., which were clearly not common, but for which there is a certain amount of evidence.

Firstly, there is considerable evidence of the activities connected with food. The inhabitants of hillforts relied on both corn and animal flesh. The evidence for corn consists of discoveries of charred grain and discoveries of objects and structures used to store and prepare it. The corn was probably mostly wheat and barley, and the wheat at least seems to have been harvested, stored in the ear in underground storage pits, taken out to be roasted to loosen grain from chaff, thrashed, and ground with stone querns to prepare what was presumably bread or gruel. The evidence for animal flesh consists of quantities of animal bones found in pits and occasionally in other refuse tips : the animals kept were mainly cattle, sheep and pigs. We have no clear idea of the proportions in which these animals were kept, nor do we know from the archaeological evidence whether the average inhabitant's diet would have been mainly meat or mainly grain products[52].

For the second category, manufacturing industries, our most extensive evidence is for the manufacture of clothing, by weaving and probably the preparation of skins into leather. This evidence consists mainly of bone and antler implements ("weaving-combs", boring tools and needles), which were probably used for weaving, sewing and/or leather working; there are also stone and bone weights for spinning thread ("spindle-whorls") and baked clay weights perhaps for weaving-looms. There is occasional evidence for iron smelting, in the form of slag and cinder, and very occasional evidence for the manufacture of bronze tools and decorative bronzes; but there is no evidence that the forts were major centres of these industries. I know of no reliable evidence for the manufacture of pottery in any fort; pottery, however, was probably fired in a bonfire, not in a specially constructed kiln, and thus no trace would usually be left. There is considerable evidence of the use of pottery,

---

[52] The evidence of pits, roasting or baking ovens and querns is particularly clear at Maiden Castle, Dorset (Wheeler, 1943, pp. 51–55). The use of pits as storage pits, later filled with refuse, has been well established by the work of Bersu (1940, pp. 60–64), Reynolds (1967) and Bowen (1967). Much of the grain evidence has been collected together by Helbaek (1952) and Godwin (1956, pp. 262–273). There are certain distinct problems with the grain evidence, in that the identifications are mostly of charred grain; this will, therefore, mostly be of grain types which needed roasting before thrashing. Grains which could be thrashed without roasting (e.g., most barleys) are probably seriously under-represented. The statistics of animal bones have rarely been thoroughly examined, to determine how many animals were kept and how much meat of the various animals was eaten; I know of no general study which collects together even the evidence there is, although Jewell (1963) and Hodgson (1968) have gathered some. Much light is thrown on the sort of information about diet which may be obtained from study of animal bones by, for example, Cram (1967, p. 79) and Jarman et al. (1968).

but we have no clear ideas of the function of various vessels, since we do not know what part was played by wooden and leather containers. The main value of pottery lies in its use to establish a chronology within a single site.

Manufacture of wooden objects was probably common, but the products have of course nearly all perished. The evidence from bone and antler implements suggests that saws, spoke-shaves, chisels, gouges, drills and compasses were all available, although they can rarely be identified in the excavated remains.[53]

For the third category, possession of metal tools and trinkets, there is some evidence from most hillforts which have received much excavation. In general, however, such objects were common only after the middle of the first century B.C. (i.e., in la Tène 3, or Hawkes' C); as we shall see, this now appears to be very late in the occupation of many sites. Prior to this date, metal objects are notably rare in most forts, as they are in most occupation sites of the first millennium B.C. There is evidence of the presence of bronze tools at a few sites; it is not yet quite clear whether they were contemporary with the fortified period of the settlement; they may have been connected with earlier occupation on the same site. There is evidence of a few iron tools and weapons at many sites; their scarcity may result from the accidents of survival (since iron corrodes badly in the ground), or from the scarcity and high value of the metal at the time of the main occupations of the forts. Occasionally, trinkets of bronze and iron are found, especially *fibula* brooches, and "ring-headed" dress pins. Items of horse and cart or chariot harness are widely but thinly spread across the country; again, they are probably mainly of the first, or possibly the second century B.C. Other trinkets of shale and glass beads are occasionally found[54].

[53] All aspects of clothing manufacture are well exemplified at Maiden Castle, Dorset (Wheeler, 1943, pp. 294–310); the most extensive evidence comes from Meare and Glastonbury in Somerset (Bulleid and Gray, 1911, pp. 266–399, 340–341; 1917, 404–479, 568–579, 582–601; 1948, pp. 61–105; Cotton, 1966, pp. 295–356). Although the "weaving-combs" were probably used in connection with thread, no one has yet worked out exactly how they were employed (Roth, 1918, pp. 124–315). There is very little evidence for the nature of weaving looms, and very little evidence for the character of any leather goods. Evidence for iron slag and cinder has been claimed from, for example, Hunsbury, Northamptonshire (Fell, 1936, p. 95). Decorative bronzes may have been manufactured at, for example, South Cadbury, Somerset (Spratling, 1970), and bronze tools may have been manufactured at Rathgall, Co. Wicklow (Raftery, B., 1971). The evidence for both bronze and iron urgently needs further study. The procedures of firing pottery in a bonfire are discussed in Shepard (1956, pp. 74–92). The use of pottery to establish an internal chronology within a site is exemplified at Maiden Castle, Dorset, and at Rainsborough, Northamptonshire. Much of the evidence for the technology of small artifacts of wood, bone and antler comes from Meare and Glastonbury; I have profited from reading the study by Penney (1974).

[54] Bronze tools are exemplified at Ivinghoe (Cotton and Frere, 1968). Iron tools and weapons can be seen from Maiden Castle, Dorset (Wheeler, 1943, pp. 270–274) and Bredon Hill, Gloucestershire. Manning (1972) has collected together records of nine Iron Age ironwork hoards, of which seven come from hillforts: most are probably not earlier than the first century B.C. Allen (1967) has listed and discussed other hoards, of iron "currency bars", many from hillforts; these also are probably not earlier than the second century B.C. Apart from these objects, iron is rarely found in hillforts, but I do not know of any thorough list of known examples. For brooches and ring-headed pins, see again Maiden Castle, Dorset (Wheeler, 1943, pp. 267–270) and the study by Dunning (1934a). For general

VII. Hillforts and their Environment

The study of the relationship of hillforts to their environment is the study of the economic and political pattern of a society. Three aspects must be considered: firstly, the spatial relationships of the forts themselves one to another; secondly, the relationship of forts to unfortified occupation sites; and thirdly, the use of available resources by the inhabitants of forts, especially for food. All three aspects are bedevilled by two acute problems. The first is the absence of a complete record of sites, particularly in the large areas of the British Isles where prehistoric monuments have been removed by later agriculture: a near complete record even of major forts exists only for Southern Britain. The second problem is that of chronology. It is now clear that forts, other occupation sites and also agricultural monuments such as Celtic fields and boundary ditches were in use over a much longer period than previously thought; this use, however, was not necessarily continuous, but often intermittent, at least in the case of forts and other occupation sites. These two problems mean that plausible views as to the relationship of forts to their environment can be formed only for Southern England, and even there only the broadest conclusions can be suggested. These views should certainly not be extended to cover the minor forts of the North and West.

In general, what evidence there is suggests that each hillfort may have had its own political territory, but that hillforts do not seem to have been centres of greater economic power whose inhabitants dominated an impoverished and subject peasantry. Economically, all occupation sites, both fortified and unfortified, were apparently largely self-sufficient in the production of clothing and tools, and hillforts do not produce larger quantities of trinkets and luxury goods than other sites. The occupants of forts, like others, apparently had their own arable and pasture lands, where they produced their own grain and meat for food.

The relationships of hillforts one to another have for a long time been interpreted in terms of their imposition, by an invading aristocracy, as castles to hold down the countryside militarily. Studies have been published of, for example, the Welsh borders, West Wales, Cornwall and Sussex[55]. More recently, the tendency has been to see forts in more static and less military terms, and to investigate the possibility of attributing a territory to each fort and arranging them into a hierarchy of importance. Perhaps the most convincing approach is to assume that the size of fortified area bore at least some

studies of horse-harness and bits, see C. Fox (1946), Ward Perkins (1939a) and Haworth (1971). For la Tène 1 brooches, see Fox (1927), which has now been brought up to date by Miss Wardman (1972); for la Tène 2 brooches, see Dunning (1932b) and Dudley and Jope (1965). There is no published corpus of la Tène 3 brooches, but examples can be seen at Camulodunum (Hawkes and Hull, 1947). For Irish la Tène brooches, see Jope (1962).

[55] An early study of the borders of Wales was Chitty (1937), followed by Varley (1948) and Stanford (1972b; 1970, pp. 122–124). For other regions, the same approach has been adopted by Hogg (1964; 1972a) on West Wales, discussed for Cornwall by Mrs. Cotton (1959) and adopted by Thomas (1966b, p. 81).

relationship to the effort involved in constructing the defences and, therefore, to the area controlled by the builders[56]. Even this approach raises many problems about the extent to which the area enclosed was determined by local terrain at each hillfort site, and also about the relationship of major settlements outside forts to the forts themselves: did unfortified settlements have territories independent of those belonging to forts? Like most other approaches to these questions, it suffers from the fundamental problem that it assumes that all forts being considered were contemporary. Mrs. Cotton (1962) has attempted to analyse the forts of Berkshire on the probably much more accurate assumption that different forts were used at different times, and that they were never all in occupation together: her work shows clearly how difficult it is to offer dates. There is some evidence that stable boundaries between territories may have been achieved by the immediately pre-Roman period, but we do not know whether we should assume that these boundaries also existed in earlier periods. Another approach has been to distinguish between forts used for different purposes. The evidence is not yet enough for us to see whether different forts had different manufacturing industries. In food producing, however, distinctions have been suggested between forts which were built to be occupied by grain producing communities and a few forts which may have been cattle enclosures[57].

The overall pattern of distribution of major and minor forts suggests some speculations which may deserve closer examination (see Figs 1 and 2). There seem to be four distinct patterns of settlement, which may reflect societies differing in their use of forts. Firstly, in the East of Southern England is an area with very few forts. This was presumably therefore more settled and less turbulent than elsewhere. Secondly, in Southern England east of the main concentration of hillforts from Dorset to the Mersey, and also in North-western Wales, are two areas where major forts are moderately frequent, but minor forts are uncommon. These are also areas where hillforts seem to have been occupied only relatively infrequently, at wide intervals of time. One may perhaps imagine that these were relatively peaceful areas, of fairly centralised government, subject to only occasional upheavals. Such upheavals may have been widespread or more localised[58]. Thirdly, in a band from the Devon and Dorset coast to the Mersey Estuary, and in the Cotswolds, come many major hillforts. This is an area within which a number of sites seem to have been occupied and reoccupied relatively frequently, even if they were not in continuous occupation through the centuries. This is the hillfort zone par

[56] See, for example, Hogg (1971, pp. 114–124) and Stanford (1972b, pp. 310–313). See also Atkinson (1972).

[57] Other discussions of hillfort distributions can be seen in Clarke (1968, pp. 508–509), Newcomb (1970), Forde-Johnston (1962a), Cunliffe (1971c, p. 60). Possibly pre-Roman boundaries which may have lasted into later periods in Wiltshire and Dorset are discussed by Bonney (1972, pp. 181–183). For forts as cattle enclosures, see J. Hawkes (1940, pp. 344–345), Wainwright (1967b; 1969) and A. Fox (1952, pp. 17–20; 1958).

[58] For the infrequency with which forts in these areas were re-occupied, see Avery et al. (1967, p. 252) and Hogg (1964, pp. lxxiii-vi).

excellence. One may suspect that it was a region of sizeable population and fairly centralised government, but of considerable turbulence for a large part of the last millennium B.C.[59]. Fourthly, Cornwall, South-western Wales, Northern England and Southern Scotland are areas where a few major forts are found with many minor forts, forming a dense distribution of fortified sites. It is not yet clear whether we should construe these forts of differing sizes as contemporary features of one society. It may be that they are of different dates[60]. The pattern does, however, suggest that societies in these areas were, at any rate at certain periods, more fragmented in their government and more turbulent than elsewhere in Britain, with many small communities each feeling the necessity for a separate fort.

The relationship between hillforts and unfortified settlements does not, on present evidence, seem to be one of rich hillfort occupants and poor peasant farmers. The character of the unfortified settlements which were contemporary with hillforts is still obscure. There may have been both fenced settlements, or "enclosures", and also completely open settlements, which appear as groupings of storage pits. Few of either sort have been extensively excavated in detail, and we do not yet know how many houses we should assume there were in any given enclosure or how many pits it takes to imply the presence of one house. On present evidence, fenced enclosures seem rarely to have housed more than three or four families. One would have expected there also to have been larger settlements, or villages, but it is difficult to produce convincing examples outside the forts. Nucleated settlements of village size seem to have continued in occupation into the Romano-British period, and it is very difficult to know how large they may have been in the pre-Roman period[61]. There is, however, in any case little evidence for any concentration of particular economic activities in forts rather than in unfortified sites. All types of settle-

[59] Sites where repeated occupation seems to have taken place include Maiden Castle, Dorset; Croft Ambrey, Herefordshire; South Cadbury, Somerset (Alcock, 1969, p. 34).

[60] In Cornwall, Thomas (1966b, pp. 77–78) has suggested that minor forts, or rounds, should be thought of as a relatively late introduction, and that major hillforts are an earlier feature. Unfortunately, there is as yet very little evidence for the date of hillforts in Cornwall. In Southern Scotland and Northern England, Feachem (1966, p. 80) and Steer (1964, pp. 15–16) have suggested that minor hillforts precede major hillforts; Jobey (1965, p. 56) is more cautious. Again, the absence of dating evidence is a stumbling block.

[61] See Perry (1969) for types of fenced enclosures in Central Southern England. For extensively excavated enclosures, see Little Woodbury, Wiltshire (Bersu, 1940), Tollard Royal, Dorset (Wainwright, 1968) and Gussage All Saints, Dorset (Wainwright and Spratling, 1973). See Bowen (1966 and 1969, pp. 32–34) for "villages" attributed to the Romano-British period, admittedly on the evidence of surface finds only. There are some hints of larger settlements, but it is not easy to be sure that they are contemporary with hillforts: see Hog Cliff Hill, Maiden Newton, Dorset (Rahtz, 1961) and Dartmoor (Radford, 1952). Such large areas of pits as that on Boscombe Down West, Wiltshire (Richardson, 1951) must imply settlements of some sort, but the nature and size of these settlements are not clear: they could be nucleated villages or could resolve into such "closely dispersed" individual farms as those planned by Harding (1972, Pl. 28) in Oxfordshire. The old view that the settlement at Glastonbury "Lake Village", Somerset, was a village of some 90 close-set huts (Bulleid and Gray, 1911, p. 45; Bulleid, 1958, Pl. II, facing p. 12; Tratman, 1970; Clarke, 1972) can be shown by careful examination of the stratigraphy to be almost certainly an error, based on the conflation of some 6 or 7 periods into one: in reality, the settlement seems to have had only 12 huts at its maximum extent.

ment seem to have the same evidence for preparation of food and clothing, and the same rare evidence for smithing of iron and bronze. Tools and trinkets of iron and bronze occur apparently universally, and even the manufacture of expensive decorated metal-work occurred not only inside forts but also in other settlements[62]. Thus it does not look as if other settlements provided grain for hillforts in barter for manufactured goods. It is more difficult to know whether food came to a fort as "tribute" from surrounding farming settlements. The answer to this depends on the relationship between hillfort dwellers, and their king or chieftain, and those living outside the forts. This relationship is almost impossible to sort out in the absence of documentary evidence. Although we know that leaders and followers were connected together by mutual obligations, sometimes called "clientship", we do not know what this may have meant in peacetime practice[63]. On the whole, such evidence for storage pits inside a fort and "Celtic" fields immediately outside it as that from Fosbury, Wiltshire, does suggest that inhabitants of hillforts must have been largely, if not entirely, responsible for producing their own grain, as well as for processing it. It seems likely that farms outside forts each had their own fields around them, perhaps delimited from those of their neighbours by boundary banks. We may, therefore, probably imagine that hillfort occupants also had their own farming area, near to the fort and distinct from any larger political or tribal area[64].

[62] Examples of excavated settlements which may be compared with excavated forts are: Little Woodbury, Wiltshire (Bersu, 1940; Brailsford, 1948), Tollard Royal, Dorset (Wainwright, 1968), Gussage All Saints, Dorset (Wainwright and Spratling, 1973), Boscombe Down West, Wiltshire (Richardson, 1951), Stanton Harcourt, Oxfordshire (Hamlin, 1966; Harding, 1972, Pl. 28), All Cannings Cross, Wiltshire (Cunnington, 1923) and Allard's Quarry, Marnhull, Dorset (Williams, 1950). Good drawings of a selection of objects are given in Cunliffe (1973, p. 415 and 418): the date and function of these is not always precisely established. It may be that detailed statistical analysis would show up differences between hillforts and other sites, but this has not yet been done. For smelting and smithing of iron, see Tylecote (1962, pp. 192–201) and Schubert (1957, pp. 15–33). For manufacture of fine metal-work, see South Cadbury, Somerset (Spratling, 1970) and Gussage All Saints, Dorset (Wainwright and Spratling, 1973, p. 125). It is only certain types of decorated pottery which so far show clear evidence that they were manufactured in specialised production centres and then marketed to the consumer (Peacock, 1968 and 1969); a similar suggestion has been made for glass, but less confidently (Newton, 1971); even with these, there is no evidence that they were manufactured in hillforts or in locations under their special control.
[63] The difficult question of the relationship of hillforts to surrounding farms has been approached from early Welsh legal documentary evidence by Jones (1961), opposed by Alcock (1965); see also Alcock and Jones (1962). Stevens (1966) has also attempted to compare settlement layouts with documentary terminology relating to post-Roman land tenure. A major problem in Central Southern England is the extent to which Roman land law and practice may have modified earlier customs: see Rivet (1969a, pp. 178–185) for discussion of the marked legal changes which one might expect in the particular case of Roman villas.
[64] For Fosbury, Wiltshire, see Bowen (1969, Pl. 1, facing p. 8). Boundaries between "Celtic" fields belonging to different farms are, of course, difficult to trace, in their present damaged state: a good example is on Kingston Down, Corfe Castle, Dorset (R.C.H.M. (England), 1970a, part 3, p. 631). One may, of course, question whether such boundaries reflect land tenure and use, except at the unknown date of the initial enclosure. For "Celtic" field systems in general, see Bowen (1961) and R.C.H.M. (England), 1970b, part 2, pp. 318–346; 1970a, part 3, pp. 622–633. Published plans of field systems near forts are not very common: for examples, see Cunliffe (1971c, p. 63); Rhodes (1950, Pl. 5); Bowen (1972, Pl. V, p. 45).

The food on which hillforts depended came mainly from two sources: grain and pasture animals. The agricultural economy of Southern England appears to have been mixed, based on a rotation of arable and pasture, with certain areas retained for pasture, and animal manure used for the fields[65]. The importance of grain is very evident from the frequency of storage pits and "Celtic" fields, but there has always been a strain of archaeological thought which has emphasised the interpretation of certain banks and ditches as "ranch boundaries", and of some fortified sites as "cattle corrals". More recently, with the increase in publication of good plans of field systems and "boundaries", it has become clear that some areas near to hillforts were probably delimited as pasture areas or areas for corralling herds and flocks. The idea was either to bring animals under the protection of a nearby fort or else to keep them off crops growing in adjacent "Celtic" fields. It is not clear whether we should think of such pasture or corral areas as the property of hillfort occupants alone or as used in common by nearby farms[66]. The importance of animals in the diet should not be underestimated[67]. Bank and ditch boundaries delimiting possible pasture areas of downland have been identified in several areas of Southern England. There have also been suggestions that certain hillforts developed from earlier "ranch boundaries"[68]. It is clear that references to extensive meat-eating in the Classical and Old Irish descriptions of life should be taken seriously (see below, § XIII).

VIII. Chronology I: The History of Hillfort Dating

It is impossible at present to offer a bald list of dates for individual hillforts or styles of building. For it is only relatively recently that a system which had

[65] These are the conclusions come to by Applebaum (1954) and Bowen (1969). The importance of fruits such as berries and nuts, and of wild fowl, fish and animals in the diet is unknown: tools of antler are common enough to suggest that deer were a frequent source of meat. The impact of possible changes in climate during the first millennium B.C. (Dewar and Godwin, 1963) has been only partially explored (Godwin, 1956, pp. 262–273).

[66] Plans of field systems and "cattle enclosures" around forts can be seen in Crawford (1928), Applebaum (1954), Cunliffe (1971c, pp. 54 and 63), Hawkes (1939a, Fig. 2, facing p. 151), A. Fox (1958). They are not all necessarily contemporary with the forts.

[67] The relative importance of grain and flesh as sources of food is extremely difficult to estimate: datable finds from sites are obviously only a partial record of what was once present; plans of "Celtic" fields and boundary ditches may one day enable us to estimate what food input an area might have produced, but such monuments are amongst the most difficult to date. Farming experiments, such as those now being started at Butser Hill, Hampshire, will eventually accumulate evidence. The usual approach has been to emphasise the dependence of Southern England on grain crops, interpreting Celtic fields and storage pits as evidence of an arable economy, and distinguishing this from a pastoral economy in West and North, where fields and pits have not been found (Piggott, 1958; Trow-Smith, 1957, pp. 29–34; Bowen, 1969). The absence of pits may, of course, mean only that grain was stored in a different fashion, above ground, but at present only very few field systems have been found in Northern England, Scotland, Wales and Ireland, and the date of these is usually debatable: lists of some are given in Bowen (1961, pp. 73–75); see also Feachem (1973).

[68] For bank and ditch boundaries on downland, see Cunliffe (1971c, p. 56), Dyer (1961) and Fowler (1964). For hillforts developing from such boundaries, see Bradley (1971c, pp. 72–73; 1971): one could wish that both evidence for date and evidence for a distinctively pastoral economy were a little stronger.

grown up gradually since the 1920s has collapsed, and a new system is now slowly being built up, based on the skeleton of a few radiocarbon determinations. It used to be thought that hillforts were of the Iron Age (indeed, characteristic of the Iron Age) and that they did not start, according to some views, until as late as 250 B.C.; now, however, it is clear that some were built well before 600 B.C., and probably as early as 1000 B.C., and are, therefore, really of the Later Bronze Age. This dramatic lengthening of the possible time-span has rendered out of date almost all views on chronology expressed in excavation reports and general discussions. A student who wishes to assess the value of a date offered for a fort in the literature must be familiar with the different doctrines and methods used over the past century to arrive at datings. Thus a first approach to a very thorny problem is to outline the history of thought about the dating of forts. Six main stages can be identified.

A. 1850–1907: "British Camps"

During the late nineteenth century, workers like Pitt-Rivers (born Lane-Fox) and Arthur Evans established the "British", pre-Roman date of the introduction of hillforts in Southern England, arguing against earlier attributions to the Romans, Danes and Druids. Although the distinction was drawn early between Bronze Age and Iron Age, no clear dates were envisaged for these Ages, and the question of whether hillforts should be attributed to Bronze Age or Iron Age was at first left for later research[69]. Soon, however, it was recognised that certain classes of wheel-thrown cordoned pottery and certain classes of curvilinear-decorated pottery were late pre-Roman, "Late Celtic", and distinct from earlier, "ruder" pottery, which was envisaged as a form of Bronze Age pottery. Excavations had produced from hillforts not only Late Celtic pottery but also, in stratigraphically earlier positions, pottery "of the coarser kind". Thus it was possible for Rice-Holmes to argue in 1907 that hillforts were indeed used in the Late Celtic period, but that many had been built and used earlier, in the Bronze Age[70].

B. 1907–1932: The Growth of the Iron Age Hypothesis

The twenty-five years from 1907 were a period of steady abandonment of the Bronze Age hypothesis. Three factors were involved. Firstly, a developing

[69] For recognition of pre-Roman date, see Lane-Fox (1869a, commenting on Harcourt, 1848, Turner, 1850, and Irving, 1857); Lane-Fox (1881, pp. 424–425, 429, 446, 464, 475, on the subject of the Caburn, Sussex), and Evans (1890, p. 335, about Danes Camp, Hunsbury, Northamptonshire and commenting on Dryden, 1886). An accurate contrast between "Roman camps" and "British posts" had been drawn nearly a century earlier by Roy (1793, pp. 205–206), but had not become established antiquarian doctrine. For uncertainty as to Bronze or Iron Age date, see Lane-Fox (1881, p. 464); Lane-Fox himself had earlier proposed a Stone Age date (1869b).

[70] For recognition of Late Celtic pottery, see Evans (1890, pp. 350–356). For stratigraphy of pottery of "the coarser kind", see Lane-Fox (1881, pp. 452–453, 462–463). For the two-period use of hillforts, see Rice-Holmes, 1907 (pp. 255–260, Late Celtic; pp. 132–139, Bronze Age). This Bronze Age attribution by Rice-Holmes was to some degree controversial (1907, pp. 134–135, footnotes). Christison (1898, pp. 352 and 381) had earlier argued firmly for an Iron Age date for Scottish forts, but in his context "Iron Age" finds meant post-Roman finds, many of which were probably derived from reoccupations of the sites.

recognition on the Continent that hillforts, even though they included Bronze Age and late la Tène examples, were also occupied in Hallstatt times[71]. Secondly, a clearer recognition of the character of British Bronze Age pottery, following the publication of the *corpus* of Abercomby (1912). Thirdly, the recognition at Hengistbury Head and All Cannings Cross that there was "Hallstatt" pottery to be found in England distinct from both Bronze Age pottery and Late Celtic pottery. This third factor led to the attribution of much of the "ruder" pottery from British forts to the Hallstatt period, and with it the forts themselves were dated to the Iron Age[72]. This stage also saw the wider spread of the collection of data by excavation and the development and improvement of techniques of stratigraphical excavation[73].

In 1930–1932, these developing views were codified by Hawkes, who at that time plumped firmly for an Iron Age date for the introduction of hillforts (see below, p. 62). He argued that forts were common on the Continent first in the Hallstatt period, although not unknown before; that the pottery and other material of All Cannings Cross, Hengistbury and other sites should be distinguished firmly from Late Bronze Age material, and should be seen as initiating, during the late Hallstatt period, a new, "All Cannings Cross" culture in Southern Britain; and that British hillforts should be attributed at earliest to this All Cannings Cross culture, and, therefore, should not start prior to 600 B.C.[74]

C. The 1930s: The Classic Phase

The next ten years saw the general acceptance of this *terminus post quem*, and also an enormous increase in collection of excavation evidence, concentrating on rampart sections and chronology[75]. In Scotland, some order was introduced into the native, pre-Roman Iron Age by Childe, who distinguished clearly between five types of defensive structure, and grouped these into three major cultures. (1) The Abernethy Complex included (a) "gallic forts" (with alleged *murus Gallicus*, for example at Abernethy) and (b) vitrified forts (e.g., Finavon). (2) The Castle Complex included (a) "castles" (a term used by Childe to denote small stone forts with massive walls, including brochs) and (b) "small forts".

[71] For Bronze Age and late la Tène forts, see Déchelette (1910, Vol. II, i, pp. 121–131; Vol. II, iii, pp. 945–996); for Hallstatt occupation, see Déchelette (1913, Vol. II, ii, pp. 693–713).

[72] For Hengistbury Head, Hampshire, see Bushe-Fox (1915, p. 33); for All Cannings Cross, Wiltshire, see Cunnington (1923, pp. 17–19). For the attribution of British forts to the Iron Age, see Fox (1923, pp. 94–96 and 134–140) and Smith (1925, p. 132); the attribution to the Bronze Age still remained in the background as a possibility (Smith, 1925, p. 138).

[73] See, for example, the work in Wiltshire of Mrs. Cunnington (1908, 1909, 1912, 1913, 1917, 1925, 1932, 1933) for the spread of excavation. Important improvements were introduced at Lydney Park, Gloucestershire by the Wheelers (1932) and at St. Catharine's Hill, Hampshire by Hawkes, Myres and Stevens (1930).

[74] Continental Hallstatt forts: Hawkes *et al.*, 1930, pp. 67–79. "All Cannings Cross" culture introduced: Hawkes *et al.*, 1930, pp. 140–161. British forts not prior to 600 B.C.: Hawkes (1931, p. 60) and Kendrick and Hawkes (1932, pp. 161–167).

[75] See, for example, the volumes published during the 1930s and early 1940s of the *Sussex Archaeological Collections*, the *Proceedings of the Hampshire Field Club*, the *Proceedings of the Devon Archaeological (Exploration) Society*, the *Antiquaries' Journal* and *Archaeologia Cambrensis*.

(3) "Hill-Top Towns" were large structures like the normal large hillfort of Southern England; Childe defined these sites as enclosing 10 or more acres. Childe was very tentative about absolute dates, but concluded that the Abernethy Complex was introduced suddenly into Scotland "by 200 B.C."; the Castle Complex also started suddenly, "in the first century B.C."; while Hill-Top Towns were gradually developed by the indigenous people who had lived in Scotland in Bronze Age times[76].

In Southern England also, people tried during the 1930s to date the introduction of hillforts more closely than simply "between 600 B.C. and A.D. 43". Much of the detailed work centred on the classification and dating of Iron Age pottery, which I shall not discuss, but around 1940 two major contributions started a new stage in the views on dating.

D. 1939–1958: *The Late Datings, 250 B.C. and 56 B.C.*

Firstly, Hawkes (1939a) presented a complex argument, of which the major conclusion was that a horizon when forts were first built could be seen in Sussex; they were started as a defence against invaders, who arrived from the Continent around 250 B.C. The argument was that the forts of central Sussex were all very similar in methods of construction, and should, therefore, have been built at the same time, against invaders. A shift in the location of settlement could be seen at the site of Park Brow (from Park Brow I to Park Brow II, some distance away). A further site, Findon Park, was first occupied at the time of this shift of settlement at Park Brow. This shift could be dated by a few metal trinkets with Continental parallels which were found at Park Brow and Findon Park. These movements of population were all traced by Hawkes to one major political event, an invasion from the Continent around 250 B.C. The invaders, he suggested had come from the Marne region of France. Strictly, this argument was applicable only to the South Downs, for which it was propounded; but Hawkes presented apparently cogent arguments for a very precise date, and thus gave his work an impact far outside that area[77].

Secondly, Wheeler in 1943 made three contributions: (a) he provided some support for Hawkes' dating, by concluding on independent grounds that the fort at Maiden Castle, Dorset was first built around 300 B.C. (Wheeler, 1943, pp. 187–192); (b) he suggested that bivallation and multivallation were a defensive tactic introduced to make use of a new style of warfare, using

---

[76] See Childe (1935a, pp. 190–211, 236–255, 266–267). To date the start of the Abernethy Complex, which he concluded was introduced by invaders from Gaul, Childe used three types of object found at sites of this complex: "safety-pins", ring-headed pins and finger-rings (1935a, p. 236). To date the start of the Castle Complex, which he concluded was introduced by invaders from South-western England, he used three types of object: "weaving-combs", bone dice and "dart-heads" made from sheep bones; all three have good parallels at the Glastonbury "Lake Village" and at All Cannings Cross, to which he drew attention (Childe, 1935a, pp. 238–241). Continuity in the Hill-Top Towns was evidenced by Late Bronze Age objects and iron objects of Late Bronze Age design found at Traprain Law (Childe, 1935a, pp. 249–250).

[77] This impact was partly due to the popularisation of these conclusions by Childe (1940, pp. 212–227). See also Varley (1948, p. 56), writing on the forts of the borders of Wales.

slingstones (1943, pp. 39–40, 48–51), and that the first introduction of multi-vallation in England should be ascribed to invaders fleeing to Maiden Castle from Caesar's suppression of the Breton tribes in 56 B.C. (1943, pp. 55–57); and (c) he used this date of 56 B.C. as a peg on which he hung the dating of various types of portable find[78]. Wheeler's views had a major impact on hillfort studies outside Dorset both directly and indirectly. They led to a doctrine that multivallation did not start until 56 B.C., and to a tendency to accept for some Iron Age objects later datings than had previously been propounded[79].

Thus, there was established a theory that hillforts were first built about 250 B.C., as a defence against "Marnian invaders"; and that in the fifties of the first century B.C. a new style of fortification, using multivallate defences, was first introduced by refugees fleeing from North-western France to Dorset. After 56 B.C., some older forts were rebuilt with the new style multivallate defences, and some new forts were built from scratch in the new fashion.

Such views had an important impact also on the dating of Scottish forts, for in 1946 Childe returned to this subject. This time, he offered rather later dates than he had suggested in 1935. The Castle Complex (or "broch culture" as he rechristened it) was introduced to Scotland by refugees from South-western England at the time of the "Belgic" (or Hawkes "C") invasions of South-eastern England, which he now dated to the early first century A.D. For the Abernethy Complep, Childe accepted the later dates, around 100 B.C., proposed at Maiden Castle for la Tène 1 brooches and ring-headed pins. He drew attention to the fact that some of the Abernethy Complex forts were bivallate and, therefore, on Wheeler's dating, later than 56 B.C., though he did not accept that all of the Abernethy Complex was necessarily later than 56 B.C. The Hill-Top Towns he did not now try to date. Six years later, Mrs. C. M. Piggott offered an even later date for the start of Abernethy Complex forts, around the turn of the first centuries B.C. and A.D.[80]

These two very precise dates, of 250 B.C. and 56 B.C., and the theories which Hawkes, Childe and Wheeler based on them, were not replaced, or seriously challenged, until the 1960s[81].

[78] Wheeler suggested, for example, that la Tène 1 brooches were still in use in Britain in the first century B.C. (1943, p. 253), and that the introduction of la Tène 3 brooches, wheel-thrown pottery and coins (the "C" or "Belgic" phase at Maiden Castle) should be dated to the early decades A.D., since these objects were found at Maiden Castle only at stages definitely later than the long "B" phase which started in 56 B.C. (1943, p. 209).

[79] For multivallation not earlier than 56 B.C. see, for example, Rivet (1958b, p. 36 and 41). For the introduction of later datings, contrast Wheeler's date in the early first century A.D. for the introduction of wheel-thrown pottery with the date of c 75 B.C. propounded for the same thing by Hawkes and Dunning (1930, p. 246) and by Evans (1890, p. 382).

[80] For Childe's redating, see Childe (1946, pp. 128–130). Mrs. Piggott (1952, pp. 129–133) argued that, besides the la Tène 1c brooches and ring-headed pins (for which she, like Childe, accepted Wheeler's late date), the objects associated with these forts included also a particular type of rotary quern, found elsewhere in contexts of the first and second century A.D., and spiral finger-rings, dated at Maiden Castle by Wheeler to the period from 25 B.C. to A.D. 50 (Wheeler, 1943, pp. 266–267).

[81] See, for example, Kenyon (1953, p. 29), R.C.A.H.M. (Scotland) (1956, Vol. I, pp. 18–19), Rivet (1958b, pp. 35–36), Alcock (1961, p. 129), Rivet (1962, pp. 9–10), Hogg (1964, p. lxxxi), Simpson (1964a, p. 209).

E. 1958-1962: *The Collapse of the System*

After the Second World War, and particularly during the 1950s, came a considerable increase in accurate field observation and recording, particularly outside the classic areas of Central Southern England. This, coupled with other work on chronology, led to a great increase in data, which was bound to lead to the modification of established views. The next stage of rethinking about the date of hillforts was introduced by Hawkes in 1958, at a C.B.A. conference. Here he proposed minor modifications, changing his original 250 B.C. to 300 B.C., and changing Wheeler's 56 B.C. to 100 B.C. At the same conference, Wheeler's 56 B.C. was more radically challenged by Rivet, on the general grounds that "multivallation is a better form of defence whatever form of warfare is in vogue"; this view allowed bivallation and multivallation to be considerably earlier than 56 B.C. or 100 B.C. Rivet's challenge had the support of new evidence presented by Wheeler himself. For in 1957 Wheeler and Richardson had published Wheeler's Northern French excavations of 1939 and 1940. These excavations showed that the forts which were sacked by Caesar in the fifties of the first century B.C. were already using wheel-thrown pottery like that of Hawkes C (see especially le Petit Celland), not the bead-rimmed round-bodied vessels of Hawkes B which precede the C style (see below, p. 39). Wheeler thereby provided the evidence to controvert his own earlier theory (Wheeler, 1943, pp. 56–57) that it was Armorican refugees displaced by Caesar who had brought Hawkes B pottery into Dorset and introduced multivallate ramparts at Maiden Castle; he thus made it possible to date such B pottery, and the multivallate ramparts associated with it, earlier than the fifties B.C. At the same C.B.A. conference also, Allen used the evidence of the coin hoard discovered in 1957 at le Catillon in Jersey to redate, to the decades immediately after 50 B.C., the coins found stratified at Maiden Castle in the Hawkes C phase, between the roadway levels of the inner portals. Frere immediately pointed out that the preceding B phase at Maiden Castle, with its multivallate ramparts, should, therefore, be dated earlier than 56 B.C. The value of the date 56 B.C. was thus called seriously into question[82].

As regards Hawkes' date of 250 B.C., Hodson (1962) was able to suggest a more accurate dating of the Continental-style metal-work found in Sussex. He showed that uncertainty generated by imprecise stratigraphy and assoction in the Sussex excavations made it implausible to see these forts as initiated by a single horizon at either 250 or 300 B.C. More crucially, the implied conclusion, that building of forts could start earlier than 300 B.C., came at a time when opinion was on other grounds ready to accept it. In 1959, Margaret Smith working closely with Hawkes, had shown that much of what had been thought of as Late Bronze Age in date was really Middle Bronze Age in date, and thus

---

[82] For Hawkes' modifications, see Hawkes (1958, pp. 12–15). For Rivet's discussion of multivallation, see Rivet (1958a, pp. 30–32). For the stratified coins at Maiden Castle, see Wheeler (1943, pp. 117–118 and 329–334), redated by Allen (1958, pp. 106–107); see also Allen (1968). For earlier dating of multivallation to accord with these views, see Frere (1958b, pp. 86–90).

opened up a large vacuum in the Late Bronze Age. Work in the 1960s has suggested that much of this must be filled by dating to the period from 1000 to 600 B.C. a good deal of what had, since the 1920s, been thought of as Iron Age material, that is, later than 600 B.C.

F. The 1960s: Starting Afresh

Almost immediately, dates earlier than 300 B.C. were suggested for the foundation of hillforts. An example is the site at Rainsborough, published in 1967, when a date in the late fifth century B.C. was suggested. Attention was drawn by bivallation at this early site to Rivet's suggestion nearly 10 years earlier that bivallation need not all be as late as 56 B.C. At the same time, much greater credence began to be attached to evidence that hillforts were occupied in the Late Bronze Age: perhaps such sites as Ivinghoe were genuinely built in the seventh century B.C. (Cotton and Frere, 1968, p. 212–213) or the sixth century B.C. (ibid, p. 200). Into this new situation, where there was now no universally accepted starting date for the building of hillforts, C-14 determinations began to introduce some new data. Their value was first demonstrated by Mackie (1969b), who saw that the absence of easily datable artifacts from Scottish forts created a situation where dates derived from C-14 might be invaluable: using C-14 determinations, he proposed a radically new, and much earlier, date in the seventh century B.C. for some Scottish hillforts, which Childe had suggested pre-war should have started "by 200 B.C.". This has led to increasing use of C-14 determinations in more southerly regions, and to the proposal of much earlier dates than 300 B.C. for the introduction of hillforts in Southern Britain, ranging to dates earlier than 1000 B.C.[83].

The present situation, therefore, is that the published literature contains a great many estimates of the date of hillforts which are based on two theories: (1) that hillforts were not built until the Iron Age, i.e., after 600 B.C.; and (2) that hillforts in general were not built until after 250 or 300 B.C., and multi-vallate forts not until after 56 B.C. These two theories are now known to be wrong, but the evidence on which to construct an alternative scheme is not yet available. It is clear that hillforts were built and occupied at dates which stretch over a much longer range than used to be thought, probably starting well back in the Bronze Age, earlier than 1000 B.C.; but to fill in reliably the details of this long story we shall need a lot more work, and particularly a lot more C-14 determinations.

IX. Chronology II: Towards a New System

In the present situation, therefore, any attempt to propose a new system of dating must be premature, tentative and subjective. One can, however, offer a few guidelines to aid the student in assessing for himself the date of a given hillfort.

[83] See Savory (1971a), Stanford (1971, pp. 41–45), Burgess (1970).

There are three kinds of evidence for date to which the student should pay attention: C-14 determinations, stratigraphical succession of common structural features, and datable artifacts.

A. Radiocarbon Counts

These are still relatively few, and the precise stratigraphical context of a number of them has not yet been published. The Council for British Archaeology's *Archaeological Site Index to Radiocarbon Dates for Great Britain and Ireland*, published at regular intervals since 1971, is a most useful guide in a rapidly changing situation. To demonstrate the potential, Fig. 5 shows those determinations known to me in September, 1973, converted to calendar years[84]. There is, of course, still uncertainty and even controversy surrounding the conversion of C-14 counts to real years. The two most recent studies are broadly in agreement with one another, but both depend entirely on the dendrochronology of the South-western United States[85]. These conversions must at present be applied rather tentatively in Europe.

Although these determinations are few in number, some broad conclusions can be tentatively drawn. Firstly, that hillforts were undoubtedly being built considerably earlier than used to be thought; the date of first construction of the majority so far dated probably lies within the period 750 to 500 B.C., but others started probably as early as 1000 B.C. Secondly, that construction of some new forts in the North does, however, seem to have continued well after 500 B.C., as well as the refurbishing in other areas of ramparts originally constructed before 500 B.C. Thirdly, that hillfort building may possibly have started in North-eastern Wales, then spread to Southern England, Yorkshire and Central Scotland, and only later to Northern England and Southern Scotland; this seems to be suggested by both pre-rampart samples and those associated with a rampart.

Some hillforts, therefore, were broadly contemporary with Later Bronze Age hoards and settlements (for which some C-14 dates are emerging), although most were occupied or reoccupied during the Iron Age. Comparison of the dates for Rainsborough and Dinorben does, however, show the difficulties still present in seeking to attribute any particular constructional feature to the same date over a wide area. For there is, at present, a clear conflict

---

[84] Some of those associated with ramparts come from rebuilt ramparts, not the first construction of the fort. I have omitted samples of which the published stratigraphical position is not clearly related to the rampart, and also (a) Birm-144 (Croft Ambrey), since this seems to conflict with Birm-185a and 185b; (b) BM-444 (Cullykhan), since the source material for this seems to be stratigraphically later than BM-446 and 639; (c) BM-17 (Hod Hill), which is presumably contaminated. There are some doubts about the earlier Grimthorpe sample (NPL-137): see Stead (1968, p. 190). The Rainsborough samples were both from wood probably used in constructing the guard-room roofs in EIA phase 2a (Avery *et al.*, 1967): UB-737 in the North guard-room; UB-853 in the South guard-room.

[85] Damon, Long and Wallick (1972) and Michael and Ralph (1972). See also Switzur (1973), Burleigh and Switzur (1973), Ralph, Michael and Han (1973).

between the date of guard-rooms at Rainsborough (apparently around 600 B.C.) and their date at Dinorben, where they are later than Period II, and, therefore, probably later than the fifth century B.C.[86].

B. Stratigraphical Succession of Structural Features

This is a form of evidence on which it is difficult to base a precise chronology, since we do not in general know whether successive features are separated by a long or a short period. There is, quite clearly, a distinction to be drawn between forts on the Welsh–English border, such as Croft Ambrey, Dinorben, Midsummer and Ffridd Faldwyn, with a sequence of many reoccupations (even though these may not amount to continuous occupation), and easterly forts such as the Trundle, Rainsborough, St. Catharine's Hill and Blewburton, with only two or three successive occupations (apparently separated by long intervals of abandonment). Forts in Caernarvonshire, similarly, show evidence of only two or three fortifications. Since the character of constructional features must have been heavily dependent on local terrain and resources in men and materials, it is probably unwise to treat similarities in construction as in themselves evidence of close contemporaneity, particularly on sites which are widely separated in space. Nevertheless, some tentative suggestions can be made, although the evidence is by no means strong enough to prove them true[87].

There is increasing evidence that many hillforts were built on sites where less defensive occupation had taken place earlier. Some hillfort sites had evidently been used during the Neolithic as causewayed camps (e.g., Maiden Castle, Dorset; Crickley), but such occupation, of course, precedes the hillforts by perhaps 2000 years. More interesting are those sites where the pre-fort occupation came within the last few centuries before the fortifications were built. These sites may throw some light on the social and economic changes which led to the construction of hillforts. A number of sites have produced evidence of pre-fort occupation sealed under the rampart (e.g., Bathampton, Caburn, Chalbury, Rainsborough). At others, the evidence is a little more uncertain, since it consists of finds and structures not in direct stratigraphical relation to the rampart, but interpreted as preceding the rampart (e.g., Ivinghoe, South Cadbury). In some cases, the pre-fort settlement appears, on our present evidence, to have been completely open and undefended; in other

---

[86] Dinorben period II is dated by V-124, V-176 and V-175: see Savory (1971a, pp. 252–256).

[87] The suggestion has frequently been made that there were stages during the first millennium B.C. when numerous forts were built or refurbished simultaneously: see, for example, Hawkes (1939b) for Sussex and, following him, Varley (1948, p. 56); Hogg (1960; 1964, pp. lxxiii–vi) for Caernarvonshire and Hogg (1965, especially pp. 116–117) for Wales; Thomas (1966b, p. 78) for Cornwall; Avery *et al.* (1967, p. 252) for the Eastern part of Central Southern England. These stages of hillfort building have usually been envisaged as times of invasion and unrest. The new long chronology, however, makes it clear that fortifications and refortifications may come at the same stage of the history of two forts without being closely contemporary. Our chronology must be considerably more precise before we can even establish such countrywide stages of hillfort building, much less interpret them.

cases, palisades or minor ditches evidently preceded the first major fortification (e.g., Hollingbury, Sussex; Ram's Hill, Berkshire). Palisaded enclosures of apparently the same type occur elsewhere without later hillforts overlying them; such palisaded sites appear in general to be settlements of people engaged in arable or mixed farming, and probably many of them date to the first half of the first millennium B.C. Thus, some hillforts were not started "from cold" with the construction of the first rampart and ditch defence, but continue a tradition of occupation on the site and of farming near it. Usually, of course, we still do not know whether there was a hiatus, or period of abandonment, between the pre-fort occupation and the building of the hillfort[88].

Within hillforts themselves, there is some stratigraphical evidence that wall ramparts are earlier than dump ramparts. Within the several types of construction generically called "wall ramparts", there are clearly variations, not only of timber versus stone, but also of size and shape; but it is not yet clear how far these variations have a chronological significance[89]. It is necessary to be a little cautious and not assume that all vertical-fronted ramparts are early, for they were certainly common at a late date in France, where the *murus gallicus* ramparts observed by Caesar in the fifties B.C. are only a specialised version of a wall rampart. Similarly, bivallation and multivallation are normally the later stages of construction, adding outer defences to what usually starts as a univallate fort; but this is not always what happened. Bivallation can also appear in a stratigraphically early context[90].

Simple portals are probably the earliest entrance structures. From the evidence at both Dinorben and Croft Ambrey, guard-rooms are not likely to belong to the very earliest phase of the building of forts. At the same time, Croft Ambrey, Rainsborough and St. Catharine's Hill suggest that they are not a particularly late development. Similarly, the elongation inwards of the entrance passage of a portal, by providing an inner passage, seems to be a feature that first occurs in a middle stage of the development of entrance architecture, to judge from Croft Ambrey[91]. Complex entrances, such as those at Maiden Castle, Dorset and Danebury, Hampshire, are almost certainly a late development, although they may well overlie earlier entrance structures.

[88] For Bathampton, see Wainwright (1967b); for Caburn, Hawkes (1939b, pp. 229–230); for Chalbury, see Whitley (1943). For South Cadbury, see Alcock (1969, pp. 33–34); for Ram's Hill, see Piggott and Piggott (1940). For Northern palisaded sites preceding hillforts, see Jobey (1965, pp. 22–24) and Ritchie (1970, p. 54). For other palisaded sites, not succeeded by hillforts, see Staple Howe, Yorkshire (Brewster, 1963); Little Woodbury, Wiltshire (Bersu, 1940; Brailsford, 1948); Longbridge Deverill Cow Down, Wiltshire (Chadwick, 1958); Pimperne Down, Dorset (R.C.H.M. (England), 1972, pp. 54–55). Some hillforts have also been interpreted as in some way developing from earlier, possibly pastoral, activity which may have taken place nearby (Bradley, 1971a; 1971c).

[89] For wall ramparts earlier than dump ramparts, see e.g., Avery *et al.* (1967, p. 251). For variations within wall ramparts, and suggestions of chronological significance, see Stanford (1971, p. 50).

[90] See Rainsborough (Avery *et al.*, 1967, p. 216). See also Jobey (1966b, pp. 96–97) for probably early bivallate wooden forts in Northern England.

[91] For Croft Ambrey, see Stanford (1967; 1971, p. 42). The definitive publication of the recent excavations at Croft Ambrey (Stanford, 1974) appeared after this paper had been submitted.

C. Pottery

This is the commonest artifact found in hillforts. It is found, however, almost exclusively in Southern Britain. The study of pottery is a highly specialised subject in its own right. Here, it is possible only to outline a broad general scheme which will enable the student to use pottery as a rough guide to the dating of hillforts[92]. In broad outline, the ABC classification proposed by Hawkes forms the best approximately chronological classification of pottery styles[93]. Each class, Hawkes A, B and C, comprises both a number of specialised and distinctive styles ("fine wares") which are probably short-lived (but are not yet closely dated), and also a range of commoner, generalised and long-lived styles. The longer-lived styles will, perhaps, be enough here to provide a broad chronological framework.

The earliest styles, Hawkes A, comprise a variety of unburnished, thick-walled, hand-built vessels, usually showing distinct surface irregularities and marks of the building, and fired in an uncontrolled atmosphere which has left them with distinct patches of light and dark colour. The addition to the clay as non-plastic temper of quantities of large lumps of shell or stone is common. The profiles of these vessels usually show them to be relatively tall, shouldered jars, commonly with a neck constricted above the shoulder and then becoming vertical or flaring out at the rim. The commonest decoration is by pressing, jabbing, slashing or scoring marks and lines on the clay while it was still fairly moist and plastic, to produce rather crudely executed simple patterns; use of finger-nail and finger-tip impressions in lines around rim and shoulder is common, sometimes on separate, applied fillets of clay. Probably the examples of Hawkes A decorated in this fashion are earlier than undecorated examples[94].

One particular style of pottery is extremely important for absolute dating. This is the "carinated" pottery, or "sharp-shouldered" vessels, sometimes interpreted as the latest A and sometimes as the earliest B. Carinated pottery has long been interpreted as pottery distinctively of the fifth century B.C.

[92] There is no published corpus of the pottery of the first millennium B.C. There are, unfortunately, few clear definitions published of the distinct classes of pottery which can be isolated, and few reliable distribution maps. There is no coherent analysis published of the stratigraphical evidence for succession of techniques and styles, and there are few C-14 determinations which would help date various styles. From the author's own detailed studies of the methods of construction and decoration of pottery of the first millennium B.C., it is clear that the most satisfactory way of distinguishing broad chronological groupings is to use technological groupings based on methods of production. Unfortunately, excavation reports tend to concentrate on the shape of the profile of the vessels found, and publish few technological data. Harding (1972) presents a selection of good drawings of some of the more notable classes of relevant pottery, particularly those found in the Oxford region.

[93] For the original classification, see Hawkes (1959) and Kendrick and Hawkes (1932, pp. 153–208). It should be emphasised that I am using Hawkes' ABC system as a *pottery* classification, not as a classification of *cultures*. Originally, Hawkes proposed this ABC system as *Iron Age* ABC: there is now, however, a distinct possibility that C-14 determinations will show that some of the earlier pottery is really Late Bronze Age. I shall, therefore, refer to the system as "Hawkes ABC".

[94] For a discussion of the regional variation in the profiles of these styles, illustrated with examples, see Kenyon (1952).

Parallels are drawn with Continental pottery, especially from the Marne region of France. Much of the dating of other A and B pottery has been based on attempts to demonstrate that the style to be dated is either later or earlier than carinated pottery[95].

The middle styles, Hawkes B, are also handbuilt, but usually with the surface much more carefully even and regular, so that some could almost have been thrown on a wheel (though the "striae", or horizontal rilling, usually produced by the fingers on the inner surface of wheel-thrown pottery are missing). Vessel walls are usually thinner, and the clay normally contains rather finer particles added as non-plastic temper. The even surface has nearly always been carefully burnished (and the marks of the stone or bone tool commonly show clearly in oblique light); the surface is often glossy. The firing commonly leaves the vessel a homogeneous black or dark grey in colour. The term "smooth dark ware" is sometimes used of this fabric. The profiles of the vessels usually show them to be relatively squat and round-bellied (though with flat bases or low pedestals). The rims are emphasised by being thickened by the careful addition of extra clay around the inside lip, or everted, or rolled over into a slight external "bead", or given a short vertical neck. Decoration is found on some vessels, and is normally of rectilinear and curvilinear patterns, formed by lines and dots and use of a cog-wheel to form rouletted lines; almost all such decoration is shallowly impressed into the relatively firm, burnished surface of "green-hard" clay before firing, and is executed with markedly greater care than Hawkes A decoration[96].

Hawkes C pottery, introduced sometime apparently in the first century B.C., and often termed "Belgic", is quite distinct from earlier styles in being very largely wheel-thrown. This pottery often shows striae on the inside surface from this process. A variety of thin-walled shapes is produced, mainly variations of shouldered bowls, with an upstanding neck. The technique of manufacture lends itself readily to the production of vessels with cordons or rilling on the exterior, and with pedestal bases; some vessels show signs of burnishing as well. Decoration often consists of very shallow burnished lines, zig-zag or criss-cross, made on unburnished zones. The clay usually has fine inclusions of temper, and normally is fired to an even grey or brown[97].

In Western England and the Welsh borders, a rather different pottery classification has been propounded (Peacock, 1968). As I write, the final report on the Croft Ambrey excavations is not yet available, and the chronological significance of this pottery classification is difficult to assess.

[95] See Savory (1937; 1939) for early and cautious exposition of the argument that this pottery was used in the fifth century B.C. Other discussions of the same question include Hawkes (1962; 1958, pp. 12–13) and Clark and Fell (1953, pp. 37–38). Useful sources for drawings of pottery from the Marne are in Bretz-Mahler (1961; 1971, Plates 101–130). For arguments which use carinated pottery as a horizon by which to date other pottery, see Wheeler (1943, pp. 189–90), Avery *et al.* (1967, pp. 263–266), Harding (1972, pp. 86–96), Saunders (1972, especially p. 3).
[96] See Avery (1973); Peacock (1969).
[97] Good examples of the shapes of these vessels can be seen in Hawkes and Hull (1947) and Birchall (1965).

X. Oppida

Among the larger communal sites which were defined earlier as major forts, are a small number of very large sites, found mainly in South-eastern England, which are sufficiently distinct from other major forts to have been given a separate name: they are called "oppida". *Oppidum* in Latin means merely "walled town" (plural *oppida*), and the Romans would probably have used the term for any sizeable occupied hillfort. In the German, Czech and English language literature, however, the word has become a technical term (although not in French, where *oppidum* is normally used in the Latin sense). The term is applied to sites which, taken as a group, have a number of features which distinguish them from hillforts. These features seem mostly to arise from the nature of oppida as town sites, with a semi-industrialised economy; thus the locations and structures of oppida reflected the demands of industry, trade and commerce rather than solely the demands of tactical defence.

These sites were occupied at a relatively late stage, mostly during la Tène 3 times, that is, from about 100 B.C. or a little earlier; in Britain, none can yet be shown to be even as early as 50 B.C. Partly as a result of this late date, they reflect a more developed industrial and trading economy than was previously in existence: this economy was dependent to a large degree on semi-industrialised production of pottery, iron, glass, small bronze objects, etc., and on trade for which coinage had to some extent superseded barter as the medium of exchange; such an economy contrasts with that of a normal hillfort, which was apparently overwhelmingly dependent on agriculture and on barter. In Britain, the archaeological evidence for this developed economic basis usually takes the form of wheel-thrown pottery, la Tène 3 brooches and coins, sometimes in considerable quantities. An oppidum is often envisaged as a capital town for a sizeable tribal area, with tribal coin mint, and a complex layout of streets and industrial quarters. As might be expected, oppida differ from hillforts also in siting and layout. Oppidum defences enclose a much larger area than do most hillforts. The defences of oppida often appear as discontinuous stretches of bank and ditch, usually wide-set bivallate or trivallate, with apparent gaps between one stretch and the next, or with adjacent stretches joining at a marked angle; the site is often not completely surrounded with such defences. Although oppida may enclose high, defensive positions, their outer line of defence usually also encloses a considerable area of lower ground and a source of water: Bagendon, for example, is really a partly defended valley, not a hill. In Britain, the defences apparently take the form of a Fécamp type of rampart, though on the Continent wall and *murus gallicus* constructions were apparently used. Such siting and layout contrasts markedly with the defences characteristic of hillforts, which almost always provide a continuous perimeter of natural or artificial defences sited to produce clear tactical superiority for defenders all the way round the site (see §§ II and III above).

The classic site of an oppidum is Manching, in Southern Germany[98]. Within Britain, it is rare for the features of this classic site to be well reproduced: the nearest approach is Camulodunum (pre-Roman Colchester). Other sites where layout, siting and the results of excavation seem to justify the use of the term are Bagendon, Gloucestershire, and Verulamium (Prae Wood) at St. Albans, Hertfordshire[99]. The best simple concept for the student of hill-forts to grasp is probably that an oppidum is a "defended town with an economy largely dependent on semi-industrialised manufacturing and trade". The features which consequently distinguish oppida from hillforts, such as size, population, political importance, siting, layout, date and the nature of the portable finds, serve as symptoms to diagnose a site as an oppidum. The student should however, exercise caution in assessing the value of these various features when found alone. Thus, size has been used in Scotland and Northern England to apply the term "oppidum" to some sites which would probably be better described as large major forts[100]. The Chichester entrenchments in Sussex, and the sites at Wheathampstead in Hertfordshire and Minchin-hampton in Gloucestershire, have all been suggested as oppida; a small amount of Hawkes C pottery dates these earthworks late in the pre-Roman period, and their layout is not like that of a normal hillfort. More extensive excavation here would be very desirable. The presence of large numbers of pre-Roman coins at Selsey Bill in Sussex, and the political importance of the vast site at Stanwick in Yorkshire, have been used to diagnose the presence of oppida. In each case one may perhaps call for more evidence. Great caution is necessary about interpreting as oppida all earthworks which are late pre-Roman and cover extensive areas. Very large areas were apparently demarcated by certain earthworks built at this date; the function of these earthworks is very unclear, but they do not seem to have enclosed defined pre-Roman towns. Good examples are the several series of works all called "Grim's Ditch", in North Oxfordshire and South Oxfordshire[101].

There has also grown up a tendency, of which students should beware, to describe or define oppida as "Belgic" town sites[102]. The term "Belgic" used

[98] See Krämer (1958b), Krämer and Schubert (1970). Plans of other German examples are also given in Dehn (1962).

[99] Camulodunum: Hawkes and Hull (1947). Bagendon: Clifford (1961). Verulamium (Prae Wood): Wheelers (1936, pp. 10–16, 22–24, 40–49, 151–180).

[100] This use of the term "oppidum" was started by R.C.A.H.M. (Scotland), 1956, p. 18, and has been followed by Feachem (1966, pp. 77–82) and Jobey (1966b, p. 97). It arose because in Scotland the term "hillfort" has been applied to minor forts enclosing well under three acres, and a need was felt for a different term for the few really large sites in this area. These sites, however, although large, are sited in tactically defensive positions like the Southern English hillforts, and do not seem to have had a population markedly larger than recent work might suggest for some Southern English forts (see § VI). Scottish "oppida" do not form a homogeneous group in other respects (Steer, 1964, p. 15). Evidence for the economic basis of these Scottish sites is extremely slight.

[101] Chichester entrenchments: Bradley (1971b). Wheathampstead: Wheelers (1936, pp. 16–22). Minchinhampton: Clifford (1937; 1961, pp. 155–159) and Rennie (1959). Selsey Bill oppidum: Cunliffe (1971b, p. 15) and Allen (1958, pp. 289–290). Stanwick: Wheeler (1954). South Oxfordshire Grim's Ditches: Bradley (1968). North Oxfordshire Grim's Ditches: Harden (1937) and N. Thomas (1958).

[102] See, for example, Rivet (1958b, p. 44); Frere (1967, p. 24).

in this way has become a common shorthand for "with an economy using wheel-thrown pottery, la Tène 3 fibula brooches and coins". It does, however, of course, still carry the tribal or racial overtones, implying origin with invaders from *Belgium*, which were given to the term by its initial use. These overtones are misleading, particularly in view of evidence that the Belgian tribes which invaded South-eastern England settled only in the area south of the Thames; counties north of the Thames, where oppida are found in Essex and Hertfordshire, were never conquered by Belgic invaders[103]. Use of the term "Belgic" should be avoided, and two concepts should be clearly distinguished: "of Belgian racial stock" and "with an oppidum economy". Two other problems may occasionally cause trouble. Firstly, that an earlier hillfort may be surrounded, at a later date, by an oppidum: German examples of this have been suggested, though I do not know of a British example, except possibly Stanwick. Secondly, on a very few British sites, earlier hillforts appear later to have developed an oppidum economy, although the defences were not physically altered from their earlier form[104].

XI. Roman and post-Roman Occupation

In line with the chronological system in vogue before 1960, with late datings and a compressed chronology, it has often been assumed that Southern English hillforts were in continuous occupation until the Roman Conquest in A.D. 43, and therefore were defended against the Romans[105]. With the new datings, we need to modify this a little. It is clear that some areas with hillforts did resist the invasion of A.D. 43: the Roman historian Suetonius tells us that, in the conquest of Britain, Vespasian (later to be Emperor of Rome, but at this stage only commander of the Legion II Augusta) "fought thirty battles with the enemy; he brought about the submission of two very powerful tribes, more than twenty towns and the Isle of Wight, just off the coast of Britain". We know also that the initial Roman advance Westwards across Southern England halted at the Fosse Way, roughly along the Eastern border of Somer-

---

[103] For the initial use of "Belgic", see Hawkes and Dunning (1930, pp. 240–262) and Hawkes (1958, pp. 14–15). For Belgian invaders only south of the Thames, see Avery (forthcoming). Briefly, the argument is that Caesar (*de bello gallico*, 5.11.8–5.12.4) says that Britain was divided into two parts: firstly, a coastal area, invaded by the Belgian tribes; secondly, an inland area, where the inhabitants said that they were native British, not foreigners. Cassivellaunus, king of the Catuvellauni of Hertfordshire, had a frontier with the coastal tribes, and maintained constant warfare with them; this frontier lay on the River Thames. It seems clear that Caesar thought of Cassivellaunus as king of an inland area, and therefore native; and thought of Kent as the area of foreign, Belgian penetration, extending northwards only as far as the Thames. Detailed examination of the Gallo-Belgic coin evidence shows no good reason to suppose that there was an invasion from Belgium into the area of the Catuvellauni, North of the Thames, between Caesar's time and the Roman invasion of A.D. 43.

[104] For hillfort surrounded by oppidum see, e.g., Dehn (1962, pp. 356–358). For earlier hillfort developing an oppidum economy, see the promontory fort and port at Hengistbury Head, Hampshire (Bushe-Fox, 1915).

[105] See, for example, Collins, 1952, p. 57, for Blewburton; Rivet, 1968b, pp. 40–41 for a general statement; Frere (1967, pp. 73–74).

set[106]. Before Vespasian reached this limit, it is clear that his soldiers had to overcome widespread resistance. It seems likely that a number of hillforts were refortified against him, but what little evidence there is suggests that people in each locality merely retreated hastily to a fort which was no longer being maintained as a defensive site, and were quickly over-run[107]. The best evidence comes from Maiden Castle, Dorset, where the defensive ditches had been allowed to silt up, and houses had been built over them in the shelter of one entrance; as the Romans advanced, the entrance ditches were hurriedly deepened a little, so that the legionaries were forced to mount an attack and kill a few defenders. British resistance, although widespread, cannot have been difficult for Vespasian to overcome in a couple of seasons of fighting[108]. As the Romans advanced further West and North they met stiffer resistance, and here also forts clearly may have played some part which is not yet entirely clear[109].

The most plausible picture, probably, is that of a period of peaceful occupation in and around some Southern English hillforts, in the latter part of the first century B.C. and the early part of the first century A.D., as a pale imitation

[106] See Frere (1967, pp. 72–76), Dudley and Webster (1965, p. 110) and Webster (1970) for the Roman forts which mark the line of the Fosse Way. For Vespasian, see Suetonius, *Divus Vespasianus*, 4: for "towns", Suetonius used the word "oppida"; in this context, he probably meant hillforts (see above, p. 40).

[107] Cunliffe (1971c, p. 67) claims 25 forts which may have been defended against Vespasian, unfortunately without presenting evidence. Looked at in detail, the evidence from some sites is more shaky than one would like. At Hod Hill, Dorset, various apparently unfinished refortifications have been claimed as constructed against Vespasian, on the basis of ballista bolts found inside the fort and interpreted as part of a Roman attack (Richmond, 1968, pp. 31–33). Evidence to date the refortifications is slight, consisting of one rather obscurely stratified sherd (Richmond, 1968, Fig. 26, no. M5, and p. 38). At the Caburn, Sussex a sizeable refortification, consisting of a new bank overlying an earlier ditch (Wilson, 1938, Plates I and II, rampart 3, which is the same as Wilson 1939, Fig. III, rampart 2 (p. 200)), took place at some unknown time between the immediately pre-Roman period and the twelfth or thirteenth century A.D. (for crucially stratified pottery which appears to give a *terminus post quem*, see Wilson, 1938, p. 174, "Q" and Hawkes, 1939b, p. 261; for *terminus ante quem*, see Wilson, 1938, p. 183, and Dunning in Wilson, 1939, p. 209). At Oldbury, Kent, the second phase of the defences (a partial reconstruction near the entrance, associated in some fashion with the pottery published as Ward Perkins, 1944, Fig. 13, nos 5–19 and Fig. 14, nos 1–9; Fig. 14 is apparently miscaptioned, see Ward Perkins, 1944, p. 160 and 1939b, p. 172), has been dated to the time of the Roman Conquest by "a few fragments of imported pottery, including two sherds of Roman mortaria" found "stratified in the body of the rampart and of the outwork" (Ward Perkins, 1944, p. 139). Unfortunately, no further description of the character or stratification of this crucial pottery was given: it is now clear that some pottery was being imported from the Continent well before the Roman Conquest: see Clifford (1961, pp. 210–211) and Hawkes and Hull (1947, pp. 202–204).

[108] With the redating to the period around 25 B.C. of the roadways, which form part of the last major refortification of the eastern entrance at Maiden Castle (Allen, 1968, p. 52), a considerable period of such non-defensive use may be postulated. See Wheeler, 1943, Pl. XI for the stratification of the "Belgic hut-floor", over the silted ditch and cut by the latest slight refortification; see also Pl. XVI for a plan of this hut and of other Belgic huts in this area through which the "War Cemetery" of A.D. 43 was cut. Similar hasty refortification and easy Roman assault may be implied by the evidence from Spettisbury, Dorset (R.C.H.M. (England), 1970b, part 2, pp. 246–247). See Eichholz (1972, pp. 156–157), on the period of time which Vespasian spent in Britain.

[109] For example, at Stanwick in Yorkshire (Wheeler, 1954, pp. 17–23). See also Frere (1967, pp. 96–101) and Dudley and Webster (1965, pp. 98–103, 147–149, 153–159, 177).

of the contemporary *oppida*. Finally, Vespasian's army surprised the inhabitants or gave them time only to construct a hasty last-minute defence.

Although most forts do appear to have been constructed in pre-Roman periods, occupation of them did not cease abruptly in A.D. 43. The general picture is of sporadic occupation of some sites at various times after that, but no extensive use of many of them as refortifications. There are four categories of evidence to be considered.

Firstly, at some sites within the conquered area, occupation continued well into the later first century A.D., although modified in various ways. At Hod Hill, a Roman fort was built in a corner of the prehistoric fort. At Maiden Castle, Dorset, quite extensive occupation continued until the founding of Roman Dorchester. In the more Romanised areas of Central Southern England, this sort of occupation seems to have petered out during the first century A.D. Elsewhere, it continued later: in Cornwall, the occupation of minor forts continued in some cases into the second century A.D., long after the area was evidently under a Roman military garrison; in Northern England, hillforts were occupied in some fashion at an even later date, under Roman rule[110]. At *oppida*, the situation may be rather different: Verulamium and Camulodunum show clear evidence of the growth of late pre-Roman townships into developing Roman towns. *Oppida* were already sites better adapted than hillforts to the economic character of Roman town life.

Secondly, there is considerable evidence of sporadic occupation, apparently in the form of small-scale, non-military settlement, in the later Roman period. Roman temples were sometimes built inside hillforts, and late Roman finds in a number of forts suggest that occupation took place at least intermittently; the nature of the occupation is usually very obscure. In Wales, the situation seems to have been the same, although earlier theories (based on late datings) had suggested that Welsh hillforts were in continuous defended occupation by natives against the Romans[111].

Thirdly, certain sites were definitely reoccupied after the end of the Roman occupation. Some were definitely refortified, in various ways at various times, sometimes being used even for Medieval castles[112]. Others show evidence of immediate post-Roman occupation in the form of imported pottery[113].

[110] For Maiden Castle, Dorset, see Wheeler (1943, pp. 66–68). For a minor fort in Cornwall continuing in occupation, see Murray-Threipland (1956); for the Roman military garrison of Cornwall in the first century A.D., see Fox and Ravenhill (1972). For Northern England, see Steer (1958, pp. 98 and 101–105) and Jobey (1964, pp. 52–54; 1965, p. 58; 1966b, pp. 101–107).

[111] For Roman temples, see Maiden Castle, Dorset (Wheeler, 1943, pp. 131–135); Lydney, Monmouthshire (Wheeler and Wheeler, 1932, pp. 22–39); and Lewis (1966, pp. 132–133). P. Fowler (1971) has drawn attention to a number of Southern English sites where late Roman or immediate post-Roman occupation may have taken place. For Wales, see Simpson (1964a).

[112] See, for example, South Cadbury (Alcock, 1970a, p. 46); Cissbury, Sussex (Curwen and Williamson, 1931, pp. 32–33); Garn Boduan and Carn Fadrun, Caernarvonshire (R.C.A.H.M. (Wales and Monmouthshire), 1964, pp. 69–70; Hogg, 1960, pp. 8–10 and 21–22); Old Sarum (Rahtz and Musty, 1960, pp. 364–365); perhaps Dover Castle (Colvin, 1959); High Peak, Sidmouth, Devon (Pollard, 1966).

[113] See Cadbury Congresbury, Somerset (Fowler, *et al.*, 1970, pp. 30–35), and also Rahtz and Fowler (1972) for Somerset, and Alcock (1963b, pp. 294–302) for Wales.

Fourthly, in Scotland and Ireland, areas outside Roman Conquest and occupation, there is no clear Roman horizon to aid the dating of forts for which C-14 determinations do not yet exist. Here, there seems to have existed a "Roman Iron Age", contemporary with the Roman occupation of Southern Britain, and it is possible that some hillforts continued in use as defended military structures well into this period. On the other hand, there is some evidence that in Scotland normal forts, as well as the rather abnormal nuclear forts, were succeeded by tiny "citadels" in the post-Roman period, possibly partly as Pictish strongholds. Similarly, in Ireland, Clogher, Co. Tyrone, and Freestone Hill, Co. Kilkenny, appear to consist of major forts succeeded by Early Medieval raths. There is, therefore, in these areas no good evidence as yet for the continued use of major forts unchanged into the post-Roman period, and their initial construction certainly should pre-date the Roman Conquest of Britain[114].

XII. Continental Parallels

Continental forts are, of course, a study in themselves. The number of Continental excavations and discussions which have had an impact on the British and Irish studies is, however, small.

Foremost in impact has been Wheeler and Richardson (1957), with its pre-war survey and excavation of forts in Armorica and the North coast of France. The work is important for its primary evidence of the structures and finds from hillforts adjacent to the English Channel, and for its presentation of drawings of much other pottery from Armorica. The impact of this work on British studies of chronology was very important (see above, p. 33). Here also is to be found the basic description in English of the *murus gallicus* type of rampart structure, and the description of the Fécamp type of dump bank[115].

Equally important has been the light thrown on the oppidum type of settlement by the Manching excavations[116]. Work on other sites has had a more limited impact, mainly because of the absence to date of really close parallels in the British Isles. The excavations at the Heuneburg, in Southern Germany, and at Vix, in France, have emphasised the importance of at least some hillforts as the reflection of an aristocratic society; but comparable evidence for

[114] For "citadels", see Feachem (1966, pp. 83–84; 1956b, pp. 78–86). Clogher: Warner (1973). Freestone Hill: Raftery (1969). For Roman finds in Scotland, see Robertson (1970) and in Ireland, see Bateson (1973).

[115] For *murus gallicus*, see Cotton (1957); for Fécamp banks, see Wheeler and Richardson (1957, pp. 8–11). The decorated pottery published by Wheeler has, of course, been more comprehensively reviewed, and a new dating proposed, by Schwappach (1969). Other excavations on forts in Armorica during Wheeler's pre-war campaign are published in Murray-Threipland (1943). Later work includes that at Erquy, Côtes-du-Nord (Giot *et al.*, 1968; Giot and Briard, 1969).

[116] For a general survey of Manching, see Krämer (1960). For plans, see Krämer and Schubert (1970). For the excavators' view of the date, see Krämer (1962, pp. 308–317). For other volumes in the Manching series, see Collis (1973). Surveys, which make it clear how widely scattered are generally similar sites, include Dehn (1961; 1962), Bren (1971) and Filip (1962, pp. 120–133).

such an aristocracy in the British Isles has been mainly restricted to stray finds, not associated with hillforts, such as iron swords and daggers. There is, as yet, no good evidence from hillforts in the British Isles that they were inhabited by a rich aristocracy (see § VII, above)[117]. The Wittnauer Horn, in Switzerland, dated by Bersu to the eighth century B.C., has for a long time been a warning of the potentially early date of hillforts, while the Goldberg in South Germany has been an example of what settlement plan might be found in a hillfort; excavations in the British Isles have only recently been on a large enough scale to make comparison worthwhile[118]. The plans of some forts in the Iberian peninsula have been compared with wide-set multivallate sites in Britain and Ireland, and examples of *chevaux de frise* in Spain and Portugal have also been used to suggest a Continental origin for such features in the British Isles[119].

XIII. Hillforts in Peace and in War

To understand the role of hillforts, we must first find out what kind of society existed in the British Isles in the first millennium B.C. Our evidence comes from three sources: (i) descriptions in Greek and Latin by Classical authors; (ii) early epic sagas in Irish; (iii) archaeology. The Greek, Latin and Irish sources show a surprising degree of agreement, and tell us much about the political structure of the society, and the way its armies behaved in war, as seen by the people themselves and by Mediterranean foreigners. Archaeology offers much confirmation of the existence of objects and customs referred to in the texts, despite many problems of detail; archaeology also provides some warnings. From this evidence, we can construct some plausible views as to how hillforts functioned in peace and in war.

The Greek and Latin descriptions do not tell us directly very much about the British Isles. They tell us, instead, about the Celts, meaning primarily the inhabitants of Gaul, i.e., what is now France. The information which they give us consists, firstly, of the experiences which the Romans had from the time when Celtic tribes crossed the Alps and attacked and burnt Rome in 390 B.C., until the Celts were massively defeated at Telamon in 225 B.C. and ceased to be a threat to Rome; secondly, of the experiences which the Greeks had when the Celts invaded Greece and eventually passed through to Turkey, to settle in Galatia, in 270–269 B.C.; thirdly, of the observations made by Mediterranean travellers in Celtic lands, particularly Posidonius, who lived from 135 B.C. to 51 B.C. and visited Gaul, and whose ethnography of the Celts seems to have been a main source for later authors; and fourthly, of the observations

---

[117] For the Heuneburg, see Dehn (1958), Kimmig and Gersbach (1971). For the rich burial at Vix, see Joffroy (1954); for references to more recent discussions, see Megaw (1966). For the hillfort of Mont Lassois, close to the Vix burial, see Joffroy (1960).

[118] For the Wittnauer Horn, see Bersu (1946; 1945). For the Goldberg, see Piggott (1965, p. 200).

[119] For forts with wide-set ramparts, see A. Fox (1958, pp. 51–55) and B. Raftery (1972, pp. 49–51). For *chevaux de frise*, see Hogg (1957a), B. Raftery (1972, pp. 50–51) and Harbison (1971b).

of Julius Caesar, in Gaul and Britain between 60 B.C. and 50 B.C., who described his experiences in fighting Celts, although some of his descriptions of Celtic society in peace-time life may owe a lot to Posidonius[120]. The problems with this information obviously are that it relates to Gaul after 400 B.C., and mostly after 150 B.C., whereas hillforts in the British Isles probably started as early as 1000 B.C.; we therefore have to be careful about anachronisms and Gaulish customs which were different from British, especially those related in Caesar[121].

The various early epics in old Irish which form the "Ulster Cycle" tell us about the heroic exploits of legendary Irish heroes. They seem to be stories originally transmitted by word of mouth for an unknown period of time, then written down first in the seventh and eighth centuries A.D. Since, however, no manuscripts of such an early date survive, we have to rely on twelfth century manuscripts, in which the original text has often been altered and added to by the scribes; there is often more than one version of the same story. These alternatives and interpolations create problems even for specialist linguists, and the Irish evidence must be used with caution (see, for example, Greene, 1972). Ireland was not conquered by the Romans, so that it is very likely that pre-Roman political and military fashions lasted on in Ireland into the early centuries A.D. But almost certainly they did not continue completely unaltered, for much had changed in Ireland by the seventh and eighth centuries A.D. Thus details in the epics may be anachronistic, or may be distinctively Irish, not British[122].

[120] Tierney (1960) gathers together and translates the passages in later authors which certainly or possibly derive from Posidonius, whose original text has not been preserved. Tierney (1960, pp. 193–197) also outlines what we are told about Celts by authors before Posidonius. Caesar's *de bello gallico* has information scattered throughout the text, but especially describes life in Gaul at 6.11 to 6.20 and in Britain at 5.11.8 to 5.14.5. The Gaulish information is extensively made use of in Grenier (1945, Chapter 6, pp. 179–231) and Jullian (1926, Vol. 2, *passim*).

[121] For example, Caesar tells us about chariots only in the British Isles (*de bello gallico*, 4.33), where he was apparently surprised to see them used in war. He does not mention chariot warfare in Gaul. Posidonius, on the other hand, seems to report their use in Gaul only some 50 years before Caesar was there (Frere, 1958b, pp. 84–85). We do not know whether this means that chariots went out of use in Gaul between 100 B.C. and 50 B.C. or whether they were just not used in war against Caesar. The heroic warfare between opposing champions, for which chariots were apparently used in the style which Caesar describes in Britain, would, of course, have been useless against Caesar's legions.

[122] We shall need a much more reliable chronology and more detailed archaeology for Ireland, in the first millennium B.C., before we can exploit the Irish legends fully: contrast, for example, J. Raftery (1972) with Champion (1971c) for some of the problems. Chariots, swords and hillforts pose notorious problems in interpreting the Irish legends. There is little archaeological evidence for chariots or use of pairs of horses in Ireland before the first century A.D. (Jope, 1955); horses were commonly used, but perhaps only for riding (Haworth, 1971). Chariots were, however, apparently commonly used in Scotland in the first and second centuries A.D. (Childe, 1935a, pp. 228–231; see Tacitus, *Agricola*, 35.3 and Dio Cassius, 77.12). It is possible that the chariot of Irish legend owes something to seventh or eighth century A.D. use, for chariots are depicted on Early Christian crosses, though other evidence is rare (Harbison, 1969, p. 54; 1971a, pp. 172–174). Such Irish Early Iron Age swords as we know of are quite different in size from the long la Tène iron sword: they are only about 50 cm long, and considerably too small for us to take literally the feats of Irish legendary heroes (Jope, 1954). Irish Late Bronze Age swords are similarly small (Eogan, 1965). Hillforts were apparently no longer used by the seventh century A.D. (Raftery, B., 1972, pp. 53–54), but instead the much smaller ringforts or raths, a type of fortlet, were in use. We do not, however, know when hillforts went out of use.

In so far as Classical texts and Irish legends agree, however, it is certainly proper to use the Irish evidence[123].

Archaeology offers us confirmation of the existence of many objects and customs referred to in the texts; Classical statuary confirms the appearance and dress of the Celts. We can confirm, for example, the existence of torcs, long swords, shields, helmets, headhunting, chariots and nakedness in battle[124]. There is archaeological support for the existence of social stratification, and the contrast between king and peasant can be well exemplified by careful selection of examples[125]. Such contrasts between rich and poor should not, however, be exaggerated: they may reflect, very largely, differences between regions or between different periods of the first millennium B.C. Within the British Isles, there is no sharp contrast in material culture between forts and other settlements during the Iron Age: both appear very poverty-stricken in metal and luxury goods when compared with, for example, Mont Lassois, the hillfort beside Vix (Joffroy, 1960) or with the cemetery at Münsingen in Switzerland (Hodson, 1968). Trinkets such as brooches, and high quality weapons such as iron swords are rare in the British Isles before the first century B.C. The difference between king and poor man in much of the British Isles may have been one of status, reflected only faintly in non-perishable material possessions before the first century B.C.

Where the Irish and Classical texts corroborate one another, we get a picture of the political and military fashions of a society which we can call "Celtic" and fairly plausibly assume existed in one guise or another not only in Ireland and Gaul but throughout the British Isles in the first millennium B.C. In peacetime society, each tribe had a hereditary king at its head, who evidently had some judicial and religious authority, as well as powers in calling assem-

[123] Many useful translations are published in Cross and Slover (1973), though they cannot be relied on in every detail: the first edition, published in 1936, used old translations and editions, but the 1973 edition adds a list of more recent editions and translations of the texts (appended in a Bibliography), although republishing the original English translations. The parallels between Classical and Irish descriptions were pointed out by Hull (1907) and the parallels between Classical and Irish texts and archaeology were emphasised by Jackson (1964). The chapter on Celtic Life in Powell (1958, pp. 65–89) is based very greatly on the Irish information. Binchy (1970) authoritatively discusses the very relevant subject of the nature of early Irish kingship.

[124] For torcs, see Snettisham, Norfolk (Clarke, 1954; C. Fox, 1958, pp. 46–47), the statue of the Dying Gaul (Grenier, 1945, Pl. II), Bretz-Mahler (1971, Pl. 23–51) and Déchelette (1914, pp. 1207–1217). For long swords, see Piggott (1950) and de Navarro (1972). For shields, see C. Fox (1958, Pl. 13–17) and Piggott (1965, Pl. XLIII). For helmets, see Jacobsthal (1944). For headhunting, see the pillars from Enserune in Southern France with holes for skulls (Piggott, 1965, Pl. XXXVIIIb) and similar features at Roquepertuse, also in Southern France (Benoit, 1945, Pl. XXV). See also Rainsborough (Avery *et al.*, 1967, p. 302). For chariots, see Greene, D. (1972), Fox (1946), Stead (1965b) and Wainwright and Spratling (1973). Chariots, i.e., two-wheeled vehicles, should be distinguished from carts or waggons, i.e., four-wheeled vehicles. The latter are perhaps less likely to have been used in war. Waggons are known from Hallstatt graves, but chariots only from la Tène graves (Harbison, 1969, with references). The date of the changeover must be around 500 B.C. For nakedness in battle see, for example, the two statues of defeated Celts in Grenier (1945, Pl. I and II, and p. 27).

[125] For general support of social stratification, see Filip (1962, pp. 28–59). We may contrast Vix (Joffroy, 1954) or Snettisham, Norfolk (Clarke, 1954) with Little Woodbury, Wiltshire (Bersu, 1940, and Brailsford, 1948) or West Harling, Norfolk (Clark and Fell, 1953).

blies, and declaring war or pacts of peace and friendship. Minor kings and tribes often owed some allegiance to major kings, pledged with tribute and hostages, usually through fear of war. A king's chief subjects and advisers formed an aristocracy, comprising two groups: young warriors and older learned men. The learned men, who in the Irish legends sometimes appear also as warriors, included druids (teachers of morals and perhaps priests and possibly jurists), bards (singers and poets) and seers (interpreters of omens). Young men of good family might well be trained in fighting by being brought up in the king's entourage, partly, of course, as hostages for their family's good behaviour. Each of the important aristocratic families had a following of clients; clients and aristocrats supported one another's interests for their own mutual advantage and protection in a society where formal justice was slow and ineffective. Quarrelling and faction fighting between aristocrats, each supported by his clients, was always a problem. These quarrels often arose from the great feasts at which each warrior hoped to be voted the honour of the most sumptuous portion of meat, and would sometimes fight if this was given to a rival he despised, or if the boasting which was characteristic of these feasts turned nasty. In such an heroic society, the services of bards were often in demand to sing the praises of past or present heroes, and visitors of good family had a right to expect treatment as honoured guests of the house. Meat is described as the staple diet, and sheep, pigs and especially cattle formed a major part of the economy and were highly prized; the Irish legends are full of raids for cattle.

In war, the society was equally an heroic one. The king was commander-in-chief, but most of the personal fighting was done, eagerly, by his warrior champions. It was normal for a battle to be started by the champions on one side coming out in front of their army; there, they would dance and shout and boast of warriors they had killed and taunt their enemies, to provoke the champions of the other side to come out and fight on behalf of their army. Following single combats between champions, the rest of the army would attack, to press home their champion's advantage or to save him from death. The set-piece battle then degenerated into a melée. Many warriors went into battle stark naked except for shield, long sword and spears, and sometimes a helmet. A major component of a battle between Celtic armies was evidently the individual contests of warrior champion against warrior champion. Champions were regularly brought to the battle in chariots, and the chariot stood by to move them from place to place, seeking an opposing champion whom they would gain honour by defeating. To demonstrate this honour and their prowess, victorious champions cut off the heads of champions they had killed, and hung them from the necks of their horses; after the battle, these heads, especially those of notable champions, were embalmed and kept as trophies by the victor. The other ranks were evidently of much less account, though champions boasted of the vast numbers of unnamed soldiery they had killed. The disciplined and relatively well-armoured Roman armies, with their light short swords, and fighting without such reliance on individual champions, eventually learnt to overcome with relative ease the naked Celts, wildly swinging their unwieldy long swords. Clearly, the concept of individual honour and prowess was all pervasive in Celtic warfare. Classical authors tell us how the Celts were eager to join battle, seeking honour, intolerable in victory, with their head-hunting, but totally despondent and submissive in the dishonoured humiliation of defeat.

Hillforts are almost never mentioned in the Classical accounts of Celtic peace-time life and rarely in the Irish ones. Accounts of their place can only be informed speculation. At present, we can form only a generalised picture of the place of a fort in peacetime. As we learn more, we shall probably conclude that some of the later uses of these sites would have astonished their original builders. They must evidently have been tribal centres of some sort. The effort and skill involved in erecting impressive defences, and the thought and expertise which have gone into the positioning of ramparts and entrances, show that able leaders with power and influence were responsible for many forts. We do not know whether each king or tribe had a fort, nor whether aristocratic but non-royal families also maintained forts. We do not know if minor kings, with hillforts, owed allegiance to other kings as overlords. The large areas, which eventually became the tribal territories of, for example, the Dobunni or Durotriges, include many hillforts. Probably, the concept of an overlordship over the many petty kings of the region is the background from which these larger tribal areas developed. In any event, petty kings and aristocratic families evidently felt themselves quite entitled to wage war against one another if they could get away with it. Thus, tribal boundaries and allegiances will have fluctuated rapidly, probably involving the destruction and abandonment of old forts and the reoccupation of others, or the construction of entirely new ones. Wholesale replacement of an old aristocracy by a new invading one seems much less likely than the replacement piecemeal of individual kings by ambitious members of their own royal kin, who often called on armed assistance from other tribes, but could rarely be held in check by these patrons once a rebellion had been successful. The evidence of permanent guards kept at some forts clearly agrees with the evidence that young men of good family served a military training in the king's entourage. It is not so clear who else lived inside them. Permanent occupation, particularly by women and children, seems to be implied in the Irish legends: though some women were queens or learned persons, wartime society was predominantly masculine. Permanent occupation, and hard agricultural labour, is implied by the archaeological evidence. Hillforts may also have been the centres for feasting, councils, assemblies, judicial functions and even religious rites: we have, of course, rather little evidence of what structures might have served for such rites (see Ross, 1967, pp. 19–60).

If one may interpret the maps, Figs 1 and 2, in terms of political structure, a pattern emerges in which the East of England seems to have had curiously few forts; Central Southern Britain had many major forts, presumably implying a power structure at least partly centralised, but into many tribes;

South-western England, Western Wales, Northern England and Southern Scotland had fewer major forts, and many minor forts, presumably implying a power structure more dispersed and fragmented. Northern and Western Scotland have many fortlets, presumably implying a yet more fragmented society. Ireland forms a peculiar case, where major forts exist as well as many fortlets; the fortlets appear to be later than the major forts, but there are too many obscurities about their chronological relationships for one to venture an interpretation as yet.

As regards hillforts in battle, we have a little more evidence from Classical authors, though I do not know of any from the Irish legends. Unfortunately, most of our Classical evidence comes from Caesar: Rivet (1971) has collected it together, and cogently pointed out that many of the tactics were learnt from Caesar. Caesar does, however, tell us that the normal method of attack in his day was to shower the defences with stones, to denude them of their men, then approach and set fire to the gates. In practice, it is not easy to see how hillforts can have functioned in the heroic style of Celtic warfare described above. On the face of it, this seems to relate more to pitched battles in open country: both chariot warfare and single combat of champions seem better adapted to such terrain. The entrance defences of forts seems to be designed against surprise and mass attack, using guard-rooms, lengthened passages and outworks with or without slingers. This fits with a picture where the hillfort would be attacked either by surprise or when its defence was already depleted by the defeat of its army in a pitched battle. The aim of an attack on a hillfort was not to take and garrison it, but to sack and burn it. Inside the fort would have been women and children, many probably refugees from outside the fort, and a battle for a hillfort was not a heroic combat, but a scene of desperation pitted against ruthlessness. Ramparts were apparently successful in repelling attack, for it is clear that entrances were felt to be the really vulnerable point. Here, the defences were clearly designed to create confusion in relatively poorly disciplined ranks, and to provide defenders with the maximum advantage of height and freedom of movement over massed and confined attackers. The number of forts which were burnt is melancholy evidence of the inadequacy of this policy when once the warrior army had been defeated and the way lay open for an enemy to plunder a fort.

XIV. Who built Hillforts, and Why?

The hillforts of the first millennium B.C. constitute a phenomenon unparalleled in the history of these islands. Perhaps never before, nor since, did such a large proportion of our population huddle in sizeable communities on relatively inaccessible hilltops and fortify itself so laboriously for the defence of these separate communities. What brought this about?

The visible and excavated remains of hillforts are the material expression of a social custom, that of placing a very high priority on the physical defence of farming communities. The custom itself should be carefully distinguished from the various techniques which were employed to obtain this defence. These techniques include the design of entrances and rampart construction, and the particular locations chosen for particular sites. If we ask why the social custom grew up, the answers must be at least partly social ones. The custom of seeking community defence developed and spread in the British Isles apparently first during the period from around 1000 B.C. to about 500 B.C., if recent calibrated C-14 dates are representative. The custom has obvious connections with warfare. We have, in effect, to postulate a time of unrest and warfare in the first half of the first millennium B.C., and to seek a reason for this.

Most explanations to date have postulated invasions from abroad. Now, invasions are very difficult to demonstrate conclusively from strictly archaeological evidence alone. We have to be rather careful what evidence we accept as relevant. Many of the techniques used in building hillforts in the British Isles may have originated abroad, but this does not demonstrate that invasions took place. These techniques are merely a means to an end, that of obtaining community defence. If the need for such defence was already felt, successful techniques would rapidly be adopted very widely, and the spread of these techniques need not require the arrival of more than a few individuals with architectural and constructional interests and expertise. It is, therefore, again a social phenomenon which needs an explanation, the unrest and warfare. Now, the hillforts themselves constitute some of the main evidence which we have for such warfare, and "invasionist" theories have largely been built on interpretations of their military function. Some have viewed hillforts as weapons of aggression used by invaders to "hold down" a hostile countryside; some have viewed them as defences against invaders[126]. There are two main arguments which throw some doubt on the value of these interpretations. Firstly, if we try to view hillforts as weapons of defence against invasions, we have to explain why hillforts were not apparently built against Beaker period settlers, "Belgic" settlers and Anglo-Saxon settlers[127]. We have to probe deeper than the view that hillforts were defences against invaders, and ask why invasions in the early first millennium B.C. should have produced different responses from other invasions. Secondly, the whole of the argument that invasions took place at this time depends in the end on the view that new features in the British Isles cannot be explained as indigenous developments, but must have been introduced by foreign invaders[128]. Thus, before accepting that foreign

---

[126] Hawkes (1939b) is a classic statement of the case for hillforts as a defence against invaders in one area. Elsewhere, they have usually been seen as aggressive weapons, and views have been developed about the routes by which the invaders arrived: see, for example, Hogg (1972a; 1972b), Stanford (1972a, pp. 33–34; 1971, p. 50), Varley (1948, p. 59), Chitty (1937).
[127] For Beaker period settlers, see Clarke, D. L. (1970, Vol. I, pp. 276–280).
[128] The reason is that invasions from abroad require mobile forces of armed foreigners, and these foreigners are very elusive. The best evidence for them, physical anthropological evidence of racially distinct settlers, we do not have for the early first millennium B.C. As a second best, we might deduce that a group of people were of foreign race or birthplace from their artifacts, if we found them using foreign-made objects in quantity for commonplace purposes. These groups have not been found. It is still very difficult to locate sources of manufacture for most prehistoric objects

invaders are needed, we must first show that indigenous development alone cannot account for the new features. In the last few years, therefore, attention has been turned to explanations which avoid invasions. This approach to hillforts is still new, speculative and uncertain, and relatively little has been published. Clearly, however, this will be an important theme in the future.

One approach draws attention to the necessity for some form of centralised political control to plan and carry out the construction of hillforts. The likelihood is that this centralised government took a royal or aristocratic form, even though there is little material evidence that the inhabitants of hillforts were richer than other people. There is, however, clear evidence that individuals or certain families had emerged much earlier than this as in some sense leaders of their communities. The organisation required to construct long barrows or Stonehenge is evidence of this, and the wide personal contacts shown by Wessex culture graves is evidence of social stratification. We must again ask why community leaders spent their energies on community defence in the Later Bronze and Iron Ages, but not earlier.

A second approach sees in hillforts a stage on the way towards urban settlement and a step towards specialisation in function by the people of the British Isles. According to this view, palisaded enclosures would lead on to hillforts, and hillforts would lead on to *oppida* and Roman towns, with their concentration of more specialised manufacturing, marketing and administrative functions. A little caution is, perhaps, necessary about this. The material from hillforts prior to 100 B.C. does not show much evidence of any industrial specialisation differentiating hillforts from other sites. We have very little evidence on which to base speculations about the political function of hillforts. A hillfort's economy was basically farming, but what evidence we have about the farming activities associated with hillforts is not yet sufficient to show either that hillforts played a special role in agriculture or that different agricultural functions were divided up amongst the inhabitants of a single hillfort. *Oppida*, Roman towns and the specialisation of manufacturing, marketing and administrative functions are really a feature mainly of Eastern England, where there are few hillforts. Hillforts are, therefore, not a necessary prelude to these developments, and may be very largely out of the main stream of such a process of specialisation. The highly defensive siting and function of hillforts might suggest that other factors were important in the development of hillforts, at least in a contributory form.

Another approach places emphasis on indigenous developments in warfare.

as precisely as this without geological help (for which see, for example, Evens *et al.*, 1972; Peacock, 1968; 1969), but recent studies have tended to show that true imports are rare in the British Isles, and probably best explained by trade. Most British and Irish objects show distinctive insular characteristics, and are similar to Continental objects and customs only in general technological and stylistic features (for details, see, for example, Jope, 1961; Avery, 1973; Stead, 1965a, pp. 84–88 and 1967, pp. 48–49; Hodson, 1964b). As a third best, therefore, it is usually argued that these general features themselves demonstrate that invasions took place, because these features are novel in the British Isles and cannot be explained as the result of indigenous development. This, of course, is just what first needs to be proven.

The new, longer chronology for hillforts has taken their origin back in time to a period when there is evidence that warfare must have been undergoing decisive changes. From around 1100 B.C., increasing numbers of increasingly effective bronze swords were being produced in the British Isles. The swords and their chapes are thinly distributed at first, but reach a particularly wide distribution in the late eighth century B.C.[129].

Once available in adequate numbers, these new weapons offered a way to kill or maim an opponent that was much more effective than spear, bow, axe, club or dagger. This change in warfare must have had dramatic repercussions. For, firstly, swords are a weapon of attack and aggression, which need to be countered by improved defence. Secondly, they confer enormous powers of patronage on any man whose abilities as leader enable him to persuade others to fight for him. The introduction of effective swords provides, in fact, the ideal immediate cause for an increase in warfare (whether indigenous or invasive), for the consolidation of an aristocracy and royalty in martial form, and for the introduction of new forms of collective defence by predominantly farming communities.

We may, of course, probe deeper, and ask why the metal industries devoted so much time to manufacturing of weapons rather than to other products. Some people must have wanted to use these weapons. Is there any special reason why people should have wished to attack their neighbours in the early first millennium B.C.? Here, we reach what are still the realms of speculation, but some possible reasons may be dimly seen. It seems likely that there was a deterioration in climate between 1000 B.C. and 500 B.C. It is possible that population had increased to a critical point. These economic forces may have led to a scarcity of good agricultural land and pasture[130]. Many features of the first millennium B.C., such as "Celtic" fields and their crops, and "ranch boundaries" and their grazing stock, seem to have originated well before 1000 B.C. These features had, of course, an agricultural function, but it is worth noting that they also act as enclosures, a mark of possession. They therefore fix territorial boundaries more clearly and create barriers against pressure by one community on its neighbour which make aggression more patent, more serious and more controversial. We need a clearer idea of their chronology. We also need a better understanding of the economic development of areas outside Central Southern England, for at present it seems that hillforts perhaps developed first on the Western fringes of the English lowlands; this is where

[129] See Burgess (1968a) for distribution maps of successive types, from Ballintober swords in the eleventh century, succeeded by Erbenheim/Hemigkofen, Wilburton, Ewart Park (late eighth century), Carp's Tongue and finally Gündlingen types in the seventh century. It is probably best to interpret the distributions after excluding the numerous examples from the Thames, since that much-dredged river is responsible for many peculiar distributions of metal-work (see Jope, 1961, p. 322; Cowen, 1967). To the same general period may also belong the development of horse-riding, starting perhaps with the Wilburton hoard, of the ninth century (C. Fox, 1923, Pl. X), but more evident in the eighth century, with the Heathery Burn hoard (Britton and Longworth, 1968) and the Parc-y-Meirch hoard (Hawkes and Smith, 1957, p. 154; Burgess, 1968a, p. 42).
[130] For climatic deterioration, see Pennington (1969, pp. 78–85), and details in Dewar and Godwin (1963) and Turner (1965). For speculations about population, see Bradley (1971c, pp. 77–78).

hillforts are commonest, and where the earliest of our few C-14 dates come from. Ecological and economic pressures may have been more critical here; swords, though fewer than in Eastern England, may have spread disproportionately greater fear. It is the history of these marginal areas which perhaps holds the key to the development of hillforts.

In summary, therefore, no single explanation can alone account for the development of a phenomenon as significant as the introduction of hillforts. The building of these monuments resulted from the complex interplay of climatic, economic, social and military developments which make up the history of several centuries on either side of 1000 B.C.

XV. Future Work

After forty years of regular excavation, it is now possible to stand back and assess fairly reliably the methods by which the builders of forts consciously exploited the terrain, coped with the problems of constructing viable bank and ditch defences and protected their most vulnerable point in tactical defence, the entrances. Less reliably, one can form some views as to who lived inside and what their economy and society was like. Future work obviously has to divide into three aspects.

(1) We need the comprehensive collection of past data on both major and minor forts, in the form of abstracts or bibliography, and complete modern survey plans of individual forts showing them with their surrounding areas. Further precision can then be given to our understanding of choice of siting and of the builders' response to the challenge of tactical defence; and a clearer idea can emerge of the strategic, economic and social implications both of major forts and of minor forts. Particularly important will be the clearer definition of regional characteristics of hillforts.

(2) We need the construction of a new and viable chronological system, which must obviously rely heavily on precisely stratified C-14 and thermoluminescence samples. These techniques are, however, both inherently imprecise and also vulnerable to field sampling techniques of any but the highest quality; finance is certainly likely to prohibit the obtaining of enough determinations to overcome these problems completely. Thus, the results of these techniques will need to be controlled by the independent construction of stratified sequences of artifacts and structural changes.

(3) We need the exploration of the interiors of both major and minor forts, and also the exploration of nearby settlement sites, on a scale large enough to throw light on the population, social structure and economy of these sites. In this, Ireland is clearly an area of crucial importance to the whole of the British Isles, because of the tantalising glimpses which the legends give us of a pre-Roman society. Just as no two sites reflect identical approaches to tactical defence, so all sites will vary in social structure and economy. The task of the next forty years must be to create sound data, and a sound chronology, as the basis for an understanding of these aspects.

Appendix 1   Surface Plans of Forts

Plans of hillforts, unfortunately, nearly always show only the hillfort site itself, and detailed plans of hillforts in their surroundings of other sites and "Celtic" fields are still very rare.

For England, useful selections of good plans of major forts can be found in some of the County Inventories of the Royal Commission on Historical Monuments (England), particularly those on Herefordshire and Dorset. Both of these counties contain numerous examples of important major forts. Good plans can be found in Herefordshire Vol. 2 (Herefordshire East, H.M.S.O., 1932) and Vol. 3 (Herefordshire North-west, H.M.S.O., 1934) and in Dorset Vol. 1 (West Dorset, H.M.S.O., 1952), Vol. 2 (South-east Dorset, part 3, Prehistoric and Roman, pp. 483–501; H.M.S.O., 1970), Vol. 3 (Dorset Central, published in two parts, H.M.S.O., 1970) and volume 4 (Dorset North, H.M.S.O., 1972). Except in the volume on South-east Dorset, sites of all types and periods are, unfortunately, arranged in these volumes on the parish system, so that forts must be sought under the name of their parish.

For Wales, good plans can be found in the County Inventories of the Royal Commission on Ancient and Historical Monuments (Wales and Monmouthshire), in the three volumes on Caernarvonshire (Vol. 1, East Caernarvonshire, H.M.S.O., 1956; Vol. 2, Central Caernarvonshire, H.M.S.O., 1960; Vol. 3, West Caernarvonshire, H.M.S.O., 1964, with discussion at pp. lxx-lxxviii). Plans are also published in the County Inventory for Anglesey (H.M.S.O., 1937), and in the History of Merioneth, Vol. 1 (Bowen and Gresham, 1967). All of these are also published on the parish system.

For Scotland, the Royal Commission on Ancient and Historical Monuments (Scotland) has published good plans in four Inventories: Roxburghshire (in two volumes, H.M.S.O., 1956: pp. 16–19 and then plans by parishes), Selkirkshire (H.M.S.O., 1957: see pp. 18–20 and pp. 88–108), Stirlingshire (Vol. 1, H.M.S.O., 1963; see pp. 26–32 and pp. 69–87) and Peebleshire (Vol. 1, H.M.S.O., 1967: see pp. 26–28 and pp. 101–157). Plans can also be found in the Inventories of Fife, Kinross and Clackmannanshire (H.M.S.O., 1933: see pp. xxxiii-iv for list) and Mid-and-West Lothian (H.M.S.O., 1929: see pp. xxi-iv for list).

For many counties of England, a number of plans at a small scale (usually drawn up before the First World War) can be found in the Victoria County History volumes, in Vol. 1 or Vol. 2 for each county, under "Ancient Earthworks".

Unfortunately, few archaeologists adopt the useful practice of superimposing a scale grid on their plans, and even the practice of adding a one-acre square to plans is regular only with the English Royal Commission. Students, therefore, often need to compute the areas enclosed for themselves. One acre = 4840 sq yd, i.e., the area covered by a square approximately 60 yd by 70 yd or a circle approximately 80 yd in diameter. In metric terms, one hectare (= 2·47 acres) is 10 000 m², i.e., a square 100 m by 100 m, or a circle approximately 110 m in diameter. One-tenth of a hectare = 1000 m², i.e., a square approximately 33 m by 33 m, or a circle approximately 35 m in diameter.

Appendix 2   Excavated Hillforts

This booklist contains only main references for some important sites: it makes no pretence to be comprehensive. The sign † means that the site has received reasonably extensive modern excavation, competently published. A student will find some even of these reports tough going, but taken together (and in conjunction with the outline of chronology in sections VIII and IX) they will introduce him to a reasonable understanding of past excavations.

There is no comprehensive bibliography available on hillforts. Bibliographical help of varying quality does, however, exist for the period before 1910 and for the period after 1940. For all publications prior to 1891, some use may be made of the massive bibliography compiled by G. L. Gomme (1907), although unfortunately this has no subject index. For 1891 to 1910 inclusive, this work was continued in the *Index of Archaeological Papers*, published annually under

the direction of the Congress of Archaeological Societies in union with the Society of Antiquaries; these annual issues do have subject indices. The period from 1940 to 1949 inclusive is
covered by the Council for British Archaeology's *Archaeological Bulletin for the British Isles*
(published at intervals between 1949 and 1952). From 1950, the C.B.A.'s annual *Archaeological
Bibliography for Great Britain and Ireland* has been published regularly, and since 1967 the same
Council's *Archaeological Abstracts* have been published regularly. The Hill Fort Study Group
now (1973) has under way a scheme for abstracting in detail all publications about hillforts:

†Abernethy (Castle Law), Perthshire (NO-37-183153): Christison and Anderson (1899) and
Childe (1935a, pp. 193–195, 236–237 .
Balksbury, Hampshire (SU-41-351446): J. Hawkes (1940), Wainwright (1969).
Bathampton Camp, Somerset (ST-31-774650): Wainwright (1967b).
Bindon Hill, Dorset (SY-30-835802): Wheeler (1953).
†Blackbury Castle, Devon (SY-30-187924): Young and Richardson (1955).
Bredon Hill, Gloucestershire (SO-32-958400): Hencken (1938).
Buckland Rings, Hampshire (SZ-40-314968): Hawkes (1936a).
Bury Wood, Colerne, Wiltshire (ST-31-818740): King (1961; 1962; 1967; 1969).
Caburn, Sussex (TQ-51-444089): Lane-Fox (1881), Wilson (1938; 1939), Curwen and Cur-
wen (1927), Hawkes (1939b).
Chalbury, Dorset (SY-30-695838); Whitley (1943).
Cherbury, Berkshire (SU-41-373963): Bradford (1940), Harding (1972, pp. 52–3 and 140).
†Dinorben, Denbighshire (SH-23-968757): Gardner and Savory (1964), Savory (1971a;
1971b), Alcock (1972d).
†Finavon, Angus (NO-37-507557): Childe (1935b; 1936).
†Ffridd Faldwyn, Montgomeryshire (SO-32-217969): O'Neil (1942).
Garn Boduan, Caernarvonshire (SH-23-310393): Hogg (1960).
Grimthorpe, Yorkshire (SE-44-816534): Stead (1968).
Gurnard's Head (Treen Dinas), Cornwall (SW-10-397220): Gordon (1940).
Hambledon Hill, Dorset (ST-31-845126): R.C.H.M. (England) (1970b, part 1, pp. 82–83),
Crawford and Keiller (1928, pp. 44–55).
Hembury, Devon (ST-31-112031): Liddell (1930; 1931; 1932; 1935a).
Hengistbury Head, Hampshire (SZ-40-170908): Bushe-Fox (1915).
†Hod Hill, Dorset (ST-31-857106): Richmond (1968).
Hollingbury, Sussex (TQ-51-322078): Curwen (1932).
†Hownam Rings, Roxburghshire (NT-36-790194): C. M. Piggott (1950).
Hunsbury, Northamptonshire (SP-42-738583): Fell (1936).
Ivinghoe Beacon, Buckinghamshire (SP-42-960168): Cotton and Frere (1968).
Lydney Park, Gloucestershire (SO-32-616027): Wheeler and Wheeler (1932).
†Maiden Castle, Dorset (SY-30-669885): Wheeler (1936; 1943), Grimes (1945), R.C.H.M.
(England) (1970a, part 3, pp. 493–501).
†Oldbury, Kent (TQ-51-582566): Ward Perkins (1944; 1939b).
Quarley Hill, Hampshire (SU-41-262423): C. Hawkes (1939a).
†Rainsborough, Northamptonshire (SP-42-526348): Avery, *et al.* (1967).
Ranscombe Camp, Sussex (TQ-51-438092): Lane-Fox (1881), Burstow and Holleyman (1964).
†Saint Catharine's Hill, Hampshire (SU-41-484276): Hawkes, Myres and Stevens (1930).
Sutton Walls, Herefordshire (SO-32-525464): Kenyon (1953).
Tre'r Ceiri, Caernarvonshire (SH-23-373446): Hogg (1960).
Trundle, Sussex (SU-41-877110): Curwen (1929; 1931).
Wandlebury, Cambridgeshire (TL-52-493534); Hartley (1956).

Oppida and suggested oppida:
†Bagendon, Gloucestershire (SP-42-017062): Clifford (1961).
†Camulodunum, Essex (TL-52-987253): Hawkes and Hull (1947).

†Silchester (Calleva Atrebatum), Hampshire (SU-41-639624): Colton (1947, with bibliography of earlier work at p. 122): Boon (1969).

†Stanwick, Yorkshire (NZ-45-184117): Wheeler (1954).

†Verulamium (Prae Wood), Hertfordshire (TL-52-125065): Wheeler and Wheeler (1936, pp. 10–16, 22–24, 40–49, 151–180).

Interim reports exist for three recently excavated sites, apart from those reported on above. The final definitive reports will clearly be of considerable importance.

Croft Ambrey, Herefordshire (SO-32-445668): Stanford (1967); the final report has now appeared, Stanford (1974).

Danebury, Hampshire (SU-41-323376): Williams-Freeman (1915, p. 370), Cunliffe (1971a).

South Cadbury, Somerset (ST-31-628252): Alcock (1972d), with bibliography of earlier interim reports.

2 | St Catharine's Hill, Winchester: The Report of 1930 Re-Assessed

Christopher Hawkes

Summary

The report when new was the fullest study yet attempted on a British hillfort. The article, after evoking first the conditions and spirit of the time, reviews three principal aspects of its findings.

First, the occupation prior to the fort is confirmed as already of the Iron Age, with material combining older native and newer or Hallstatt elements. The latter, differing from Wiltshire's and better to be matched in downland Sussex, can have issued from Hallstatt Belgium, around 600, and scattered down-Channel. Of the settlement spread on the hilltop, small parts only were brought to light: extensive stripping was impossible, and at the time was not to be expected. The review of the fort supports the belief that the single rampart was dump-built. Affinity with Sussex, and not with Wiltshire, is again now seen in the pottery. The primary date of building is best to be judged from reviewing the Entrance. It resembles at the start, even though pottery seems so different, the eastern one at Danebury (a dozen miles to west), in the second of the stages distinguished for this in the recent excavations by Cunliffe. Professor Cunliffe has drawn (Fig. 7) a fresh interpretation, superseding the old report's, of what the excavators found. Period A (decayed in B) provides the first of the two main phases, giving the Danebury resemblance; period C provides the second. This was a thorough rebuilding, sharply narrowed to an inner barbican, and flanked by the heightened rampart-ends that the old excavation proved. Though the ensuing destruction (D) may afford some questions not yet answered, the heightening in C was done through having the ditch in front recut, and material also scooped from behind the rampart-ends. In the hollowing there thus made, and in a pit near by (the "beehive" R), was new-style pottery with "saucepan" forms: "La Tène II" in the report, and by Cunliffe in 1964 defined as "St. Catharine's Hill Group".

Lastly, comparing this central-Hampshire group of the ware with others, the article focuses attention on its presence in a part of Winchester: the up-hill westerly part where Biddle has now a defended settlement, bigger by far than the St. Catharine's fort and also lasting longer—to be separated only by one more phase from the founding of Roman Winchester. As this was *Venta Belgarum*, the question is raised of who were its Belgae. Superseding thus the 1930 treatment of Winchester's origin, the article ends by saluting the advance to be looked for in a new one now.

I. Introduction

In Hampshire, some 70 m (230 ft) above the river Itchen, and 1600 m (or a mile) to south of Winchester Cathedral tower, St. Catharine's Hill has its summit 328 ft above Ordnance Datum, and around it the single bank and ditch of a hillfort. Three young men had charge of the excavations done in this, in August of 1927 and of 1928. In August of the two preceding years with some friends, at and near to the summit, they had found and excavated all that survived of the hill's medieval chapel, recorded in the sixteenth century as destroyed under Henry VIII, and as dedicated to St. Catharine—whence its name. The manual labour was good experience; it completely achieved its object; and its progress soon became known among leading members of the Hampshire Field Club. An approach made by these to the three young men, of New College at Oxford and all former scholars of Winchester, led to the forming of a committee to promote their working on the hillfort, with the aid of funds from the Club and from a number of its members, and on the Winchester side from many who had been in the school or were on its staff, from others mainly at Oxford, and the two colleges' governing bodies. The total for the two seasons was £411 15s. 3d.; £110 was given by a single anonymous donor (the late Mr. E. G. Royden), £100 by the Club, £20 each by the governing bodies, £15 15s. by bodies of Masons. The Royal Archaeological Institute gave £10 10s., the Society of Antiquaries £5. These figures, in the money of the day, seem to me not without modern interest: at Oxford, the University Archaeological Society (undergraduate) gave £1 1s., at Winchester the school Archaeological Society £1 10s., with £5 from the presiding master (Mr. C. E. Robinson). The headmaster gave £2, and then a guinea; his predecessor M. J. Rendall, in retirement, gave two guineas. All this was munificence. And it shows how in the 1920s what would now be called "the establishment" could support three young pioneers. The three were J. N. L. Myres, the future Society of Antiquaries' President; C. G. Stevens, brother of the future Mrs. Myres; and the present writer (mover of the dig for the chapel—but its finder had been our doughtiest digger, Stevens)[1].

---

[1] Charles Guy Stevens, husband of Joan Stevens, F.S.A., of Jersey, must be distinguished from Oxford's well-known C. E. Stevens, B.Litt., F.S.A., though he too had joined in the dig for the chapel.

Laying out this money on tools and hut, and on engaging good labourers (each year from a dozen to twenty), we felt in truth pioneers. For in the southern English chalk-lands, before 1927, the only hillfort explorers were in Sussex the Doctors Curwen, who had started at the Caburn with a single man, the admirable H. A. Gordon[2], and in Wiltshire Mrs. Cunnington, who had lately dug at Figsbury[3], resuming there her work from before the recent First World War, done at Casterley Camp (and smaller enclosures, Knap Hill and Lidbury). Most of such knowledge of the Iron Age as there was had come from sites without defences, like her All Cannings Cross[4]; Dr R. C. C. Clay's on Fifield Bavant and Swallowcliffe Downs[5]; and in Sussex that on Park Brow (up behind Sompting and close to Cissbury)[6]. One had to go back to General Pitt-Rivers's work at Winkelbury[7] and at Cissbury and the Caburn (done when his name was still Lane-Fox)[8], and to Martin-Atkins at Uffington[9], in the middle nineteenth century, to find any further record of digging in hillfort defences[10]; Bushe-Fox at Hengistbury Head in 1911–1912, had sectioned its double promontory-dykes, but they failed to afford him finds[11]. Yet the surface inspection of sites, made popular first by Hadrian Allcroft[12], had for Hampshire at least been mightily advanced by Dr. J. P. Williams-Freeman[13]; and to his careful plans and profiles, done exhaustively through the county, there was added now air photography, brought into life by O. G. S. Crawford[14]. Which brings us back to St. Catharine's Hill, for Crawford was now at Southampton, established at the Ordnance Survey by its chief, Sir Charles Close; he already knew Myres (through his father, later Sir John) and myself (through Hampshire field-work done as a schoolboy). Williams-Freeman I also had met, when he lectured once in Winchester; he was now the Field Club's President, with Crawford and Close on its Council too; and it was these strong characters who had moved for our committee, with its secretary Frank Warren and another of its pillars, Colonel Karslake.

Magnificently strong they were; but not even Crawford had dug in a hill-fort. The committee's official meeting on the site, before each season, was even at the time distinctly laughable. But we showed them where we believed we ought to dig; they solemnly consented; so what more could we want? As for the Ancient Monuments Inspectorate, its consent came promptly by post; later, the Inspector for England, Bushe-Fox himself, climbed up to inspect us.

[2] And as their adjutant, R. P. Ross Williamson: Curwen and Curwen, 1927.
[3] Cunnington, 1925.
[4] Cunnington, 1923.
[5] Clay, 1924; 1925–1927.
[6] Wolseley and Smith, 1924; Wolseley, Smith and Hawley, each 1926 (though vol. was issued 1927).
[7] Pitt-Rivers, 1888; rampart built above chalk-filled holes (for former posts?), Pl. CXLV.
[8] *SCH*, (note 15), pp. 68–69, with nn. 3–4, refs.; and here pp. 63, 71–74, on Curwen, 1931.
[9] *SCH*, pp. 67–68, with ref.; n. 1 notes sarsen stones disclosed besides his palisading.
[10] *SCH*, p. 69, notes a minor Wiltshire instance of 1910: Oliver's Camp, near Devizes.
[11] Bushe-Fox, 1915.
[12] Allcroft, 1908.
[13] Williams-Freeman, 1915.
[14] Crawford, 1924.

And the crowning glory, of course, was the Club's plenary Field Meeting, held in the midst of the digging and led by Williams-Freeman in person. Mrs. Cunnington was there with her husband; Heywood Sumner, the Curwens, Karslake; Sir Thomas Troubridge of Beaulieu; and the committee heading the crowd. Williams-Freeman, towering above them, made us a grand and weighty speech. "In my book", he said, "I took these British earthwork camps for Bronze Age. Well! I was wrong, and I'm pleased to say so now. After what we've seen today, I'm convinced they're all Iron Age. I congratulate the excavators heartily." There was a crackling burst of applause.

My memory of the scene has in the last few years been sharpened: had the Doctor really, in general, been so wrong about Bronze Age "camps"? We have started to learn that some were in fact just that, or at least began so. The division of Bronze from Iron has started to melt, at any rate sometimes. And that is only one among the many sides of hillfort work, which a book like the present one can demonstrate now, sixty years from the Doctor's work, and forty-five from ours. So what did our work amount to, seen and judged in a modern light? I am choosing three of its aspects, which I think are at present the leading ones, for this essay in reassessment of our findings and our report[15]. The report had a part on St. Catharine's Chapel and related features and finds, and one on the use of the hill for resort and games by Winchester College, for about 300 years from the 1560s. But the Iron Age made its first part (pp. 1–188), and the aspects I am choosing are of course from this. My article on Iron Age Hampshire in honour of Warren (Hawkes, 1956) shows the thought of the time half-way from our work to the present; it is thus superseded here in much, though I think not yet in everything.

II. The Pre-Fort Occupation

The size of the fort with its earthwork, 23 acres (roughly) overall, leaves some 19 acres (7·6 hectares) of space enclosed, verging on oval in conformation but following the hill's contour (Fig. 1). This is straighter along the steep fall to the

---

[15] This was published by the Club, as Vol. XI of its *Proceedings* (pp. i–xvi, 1–310) and in cloth for separate sale (Winchester: Warren, The Wykeham Press); see Bibliography under *SCH*, the abbreviation adopted here for references. Its description and interpreting of the excavations throughout represented the full consensus of the three of us; the final text, using source-material and portions composed by each, was my own but checked by my colleagues in autumn 1929, on their return from the British Association Meeting in South Africa; among the portions that I had added (pp. 1–6, 67–84, comparisons offered for pottery and finds pp. 97–135, and the essays pp. 140–161 (with supporting lists), pp. 169–188 and 248–256), all but the last were on Iron Age matters, and therefore fall to be criticized here. To any one of us singly, however, the report's most signal debt was to Stevens, for his surveys and drawing of the maps and plans, sections and architectural (chapel) elevations, and his drawing of all the pottery and finds; his skill was untiring. Reproductions given here have been made from his originals, all of which I have fortunately been able to keep in safety. Of the photographs by H. W. Salmon and Son of Winchester, specially taken on site and supplying the report with most of its half-tones, those here reproduced are from negatives freshly made at Oxford, from my set of still excellent prints, by Robert Wilkins, F.S.A.: Pl. II and III.

Itchen valley on the west, and more rounded thence in its sweep towards the saddle of land connecting it, between north-east and east, with the main chalk ridge beyond. Its summit, at 328 ft O.D., is along this axis flattish, with slopes that at first are slight on the north-east and again thence right around the south. Dr. Rendall's winter photograph taken from the riverside south-west of it (Pl. I) displays its contour well. So from west and south of the summit round to the entrance built for the fort (north-east beyond the "Labyrinth")[16] all this ground would be good for settlement: with views in all directions, slight shelter from the westerly winds, seclusion given by the saddle on the east, and access down to the river. When the fort was laid out, it included much more: it conformed to the brows of the hill, to command the steeper slopes beneath them: a "contour fort", in fact, as has long been recognised[17]. On plan, it draws the eye away from the area best for settlement; but this had attracted settlers prior to the fort. The area used for settlement then and thereafter, continuously or not, till the whole was at last abandoned, can be estimated best from the plan Fig. 2. This is Stevens's plan, *SCH*, Fig. 36, excluding its western portion with the chapel and attendant features, and with minor indications added accordingly.

In the right bottom corner of Fig. 2, next to the relatively modern Ditch 6[18], is marked the trench that gave our Section 1 of the earthwork (Fig. 5 and p. 70 below): it produced no finds, nor did our trial cuttings close to it. Trial pits were negative too where cut in the north of the area, but Iron Age pottery was found to be scattered from west and south of the chapel, north-east towards the earthwork on either side of the Entrance axis[19]. And near this, in the trench for our earthwork Section 2, such pottery and relics were found beneath the rampart's inner half, and in its body where formed of tips from the inner side. Its middle may thus be a guide here to the edge of the prior occupation[20]. No trace of anything bounding this at the time was anywhere seen, but it was roughly along that line that the ground began its slope to the saddle. Reserving note of the finds here in regard to the earthwork's date, their priority thus proved may send us back to the inward area, in a quest for finds to be recognised as our earliest.

In this, besides the surface scatter, there is aid from our finds in pits. For while surface stripping was beyond our powers, and post-hole planning had hardly been heard of, we did find pits, by luck and from surface indications, though seldom in our limited trial trenching[21]. In Sussex at the Caburn, following Pitt-Rivers (above, p. 61, with nn. 2 and 8), the Curwens had dug 107 pits besides his 40. They were sure that anyhow most were too small for habitation, but were for storage or for refuse; the dwellings had stood on the

[16] On this chalk-cut Maze, see *SCH*, p. 269–280.

[17] *SCH*, pp. 10–12 (Aubrey, Gough, Shore, Williams-Freeman).

[18] Just S. of the modern chalk-cut "Domum Cross", on which see *SCH*, pp. 7, 276–278.

[19] *SCH*, pp. 85–87.

[20] *SCH*, p. 21 with Fig. 4, here Fig. 5.

[21] The grass was too thick for thumping until the ground sounded hollow, a method of finding ditches and pits which some employed elsewhere.

surface, though they never could strip it widely enough for tracing them[22]. Our total was only 10, but we thought their purpose had been more varied: storage (as our Pit Q), merely for rubbish (our Pit X), habitation (our R and A), all passed as credible. Really, of course, they were storage pits of the usual Iron Age sort, with refuse in their chalky fillings of various kinds and amounts[23], all except the somewhat peculiar Pit A, of which I still regard the purpose as uncertain (Fig. 3). A broad oval 13 ft by 12 ft, splayed broader around its top whether by intention or through weathering, it then showed a shelf, flat and 2 to 3 ft wide, at 2 ft down in the chalk, and within it a narrower oval, 10 ft by 4 to 5, with its floor at $5\frac{1}{2}$ ft. The floor was covered with half a foot of sand (available on chalk in fissures from otherwise vanished sandy drift); this had a level surface which we were sure had been a trodden floor, showing charcoal and other traces of burning, while the lower parts of the chalk-cut walls were discoloured, plainly by scorching. We thought it had had inhabitants, lighting fires about the floor; but if all was caused by its having a roof that was burnt and fallen in, the sand floor will still attest the time when the pit was in use— not inhabited, indeed, but used for some purpose quite particular. And in the sand of the floor, underneath the subsequent filling, was the stratified group of pottery Fig. 4, A1–A6. Our sole such stratified group from a pit, it appears of special interest.

Its vessel A1, the upper part of a tall-necked jar, with bulbous body gently bent to evert the neck, which is only once uneven below the lip of its flattish rim, is of fine hard ware, orange-brown with ferruginous surface, darkened in part (through scorching, as a second piece of it shows), and with admixture of fine white grit from pounded flint. In describing it (*SCH*, p. 97) I called its type Hallstatt, and in this was quite right, though the comparisons I had were few. That from the Thames ("Old England" tidal marsh) at Brentford, in Greater London, where the very numerous ancient bronzes include good Hallstatt types[24], was a right comparison; Gerald Dunning gave me another, from Ham Hill in Somerset, whence there is also a Hallstatt razor[25]; the pottery from Castle Hill, Scarborough (Yorkshire), which I drew on for another, is regarded as Hallstatt still[26]. That is, in the British passage to the Iron from the Bronze Age, such pottery was seen as exotic and Continental in its tradition[27]. It is seen so still today, and occurs still seldom far from a sea-coast; vary though it may in its different regions of occurrence, the tradition at the start must be foreign and stand for immigrants. Leaving aside the east and keeping the

[22] Curwen and Curwen, 1927, pp. 4–5.
[23] To our error about Pit R, I return below, p. 73.
[24] Wheeler, 1929, pp. 20–32; Jar, 31 and Fig. 4, 3; Hallstatt scabbard-chape, Pl. II, Fig. 1, 9 = Cowen, 1967, p. 453, 1 ("Sion Reach"); swords, ibid. p. 443, 175, 176 = Pl. LIX, 1, and "almost certainly" 186.
[25] Piggott, 1946, p. 140, no. 91.
[26] Smith 1927; Wheeler in Rowntree 1931 with fresh drawings by Gerald Dunning.
[27] Hence my rather full survey, *SCH*, pp. 140–161. "Deverel-Rimbury" was not yet seen to exist already in the Middle Bronze Age; not everyone had wanted even to distinguish it from Hallstatt. My view of the phase of incomings as seventh century to fifth, though it needs toning down, had I think the right perspective.

South Coast in the forefront, from Sussex to Hampshire and Dorset, we have now the study by Cunliffe, presenting and discussing the finds from his Dorset site of Eldon's Seat[28]. Its pottery assemblage I, though with jars resembling bronze situlas[29], of which the prototype was foreign[30], is essentially Final Bronze Age; assemblage II, on the other hand, shows a regional devolution from an "intrusive influence" entering in the interval of time between them, perceived at Kimmeridge (and elsewhere near) in the material called Kimmeridge II[31]. Less far to west, there could be a similar tale in Hampshire.

Yet we first have to recall that in its north-west and west, its Iron Age culture-sequence long resembled Wiltshire's. And that, all over the chalk-lands there, is famous for its distinctness, shared by those parts of Hampshire (including coastal Hengistbury Head), with an early beginning (still to be published) on Longbridge Deverill Cow Down[32]. In its pottery, as at All Cannings Cross (Cunnington, 1923), many of the finer jars and bowls have a bright red haematite coating, the jars often with ornament incised and punched and filled with white, the bowls (whether red or black) most frequently with horizontal furrowing. Both traditions, in France, belong to the Later and Final Bronze Age; and though the transmission is still unclear, they distinguish the Wiltshire-centred group very sharply[33]. Beside the latest furrowed bowls, too, and soon superseding them, it took to bowls with segmented profiles, having cordons around their angles, usually with fine decoration cut through the haematite coat after firing. Probably a reaction to developments along the Thames, beyond our present scope, they reinforce the group's distinctness[34]; seemingly adopted first before 400 B.C., they continued in the fourth century leaving the furrowed bowls superseded. And though in Dorset slightly touching the distinct and coastal tradition, seen in the Kimmeridge II and then the Eldon's Seat II assemblages[35], that of Longbridge and All Cannings Cross must differ, in its origins, from both that and the related forms of Hallstatt culture farther east. It is with these that our jar A1 declares affinity; and an early affinity too, as we may next judge from Sussex.

Of the other pieces from the same Pit A (besides fourteen that were too small to be considered), the form of A3 with its pinched-up knobs seems rare but

[28] Cunliffe, 1968, map, 194; site is in Purbeck, South-east Dorset.
[29] Same work, pp. 208, 212, Figs 10, 2 and 6.
[30] Hawkes and Margaret Smith, 1957, on bronze buckets and cauldrons Continental "Kurd" buckets were both imported and locally modified here, as "Irish-British" buckets (central date, seventh century), so that simple pottery versions could precede the Tessin and Rhine situlas, essentially fifth century. Studied by Kinning, then by Primas, then by Pauli.
[31] Cunliffe, 1968, pp. 231–233 (Kimmeridge II, with Fig. 23), 201–204, 206–208, 210–211, 218–226 (Eldon's Seat II, with Figs 16–18), 233–234, 234–237 (discussion).
[32] Ministry of Works excavations, to 1960 (Sonia Chadwick Hawkes).
[33] Map of furrowed bowls in Harding 1972, Pl. 3; text 75, 79–81, list 144, where for the last three sites in Hampshire and the two in Sussex, see pp. 68–69, n.48, below.
[34] Map of cordoned (segmented) bowls, ibid. Pl. 4; text 80, 92–95, 127, list 145, where for Winchester see p. 68, n.47, below.
[35] Cunliffe, 1968, pp. 210, 219, Fig. 17, 140–143 furrowed, 148–153 incised and punched.

widely scattered: Eldon's Seat II[36] besides All Cannings Cross[37] and my other two cases, Grime's Graves (Norfolk) and Fengate (Peterborough)[38]. A2, with the inwardly-slanted flange of its rim, must be related to the often flatter such rims, from Upper Thames sites, discussed by Harding (1972, pp. 77–78 with Pl. 45) who sees them as pottery renderings of the rim of a bronze cauldron: almost certainly then of a cauldron of the Atlantic class A, formed in the Late Bronze Age from Eastern prototypes brought past Spain (in the article cited n. 30 I said through France, which was surely wrong). As Harding has also rims that suggest the slightly later class B (pp. 75–77 with Pl. 44), of which the best, from Colroger in Cornwall, has a bulging body with finger-tip impressions, just where the cauldron could have a double row of rivet-heads, there seems good reason to guess that the knobs on our A3, and the scattered similar vessels, render such rivet-heads themselves; a further Dorset vessel that he cites, from Purbeck near Eldon's Seat (Gallows Gore), makes the likelihood certainly stronger. The rim like A2 that I cited from Hunsbury, the hillfort at Northampton, which was subsequently published[39], has beneath it an applied band that opens out into a circular ring; the vessel was red, and its rim-diameter huge, so cauldron-like certainly, with the ring as a simplified version of what on the Cornish vessel are copies in clay of the cauldron's bronze ring handles. All these vessels are more or less coarsely gritted in the native manner, passed on from the Late Bronze Age just as in the Eldon's Seat period I; and there I notice rims resembling each of Harding's forms, several body-sherds with bosses, and one with loop as though for a handle[40]. From the turn of the eighth and seventh centuries when both the forms in bronze would be current, it is nowadays no long stretch to reach the Iron Age; either or both could be passed to this adapted into pottery, in the tradition of native inhabitants whom the Hallstatt newcomers met. My parallels for A4, 5 and 6 can today be disregarded, being only due to the paucity of even vaguely similar pieces; calling them "Hallstatt-La Tène I" was only the language of the time, aping the cautious Reginald Smith: it requires no lowering of the date. So our Pit A group of pottery shows tradition from the Late Bronze Age, lasting to be met by a new one, foreign and Hallstatt.

There remains the comparison I made of A1, the Hallstatt jar, with examples found in Sussex. That eastward quarter, away from Wiltshire, and reached by the South Downs ridgeway (*SCH*, p. 2 with p. 4, map Fig. 3), seems the right one still for comparisons with our pre-fort Iron Age phase. I offered a jar of similar but rather finer ware and surface, similar rim and neck but with a shallow fluting below it, and a shoulder higher in the bulge, from Park Brow (p. 61, n. 6). It had been added, in the second (1926) publication, to a series

[36] ibid. Fig. 17, 173; and Chalbury, Whitley 1943, 115 with Fig. 6, 28; site is in South Dorset between Weymouth and Maiden Castle, but the bowl with a knob thence cited is scarcely similar.
[37] Cunnington, 1923, p. 180, Pl. 42, 1, large ovoid vessel, 4 knobs surviving out of 6.
[38] Where the fresh excavations should check the early dates I claimed.
[39] By Clare Fell, 1936, p. 88 with Fig. 7 (78), C6.
[40] Cunliffe, 1968, pp. 208–209, with Fig. 10, 3 (cauldron A form): Fig. 11, 17 (cauldron B form); with boss 15, 22; Fig. 12, 31; Fig. 13, 52–53, and with loop 54.

in some ways ampler figured in the first (1924); common to both, and finer, with a similar reddish-brown surface, were a jar with a humped-up shoulder and very tall everted neck, and a bowl with a very low base-ring and a rim very slightly everted, having a cover that fitted over it, plainer and lower[41]. The bowl was found with three coarser jars, one with finger-tipping round its shoulder, one with shoulder very slight and one with finger-nail nicking of its rim[42]; only the first was repeated in the later publication, and the other finer vessels in the first include three Hallstatt bowls and a jar, like ours in the rim and somewhat in body but shorter in the neck[43]. That the site produced also an angular bowl, and two bases with pedestal, "Hallstatt" surely no longer but La Tène, and indeed distinctive, was afterwards found vexatious by Dr. (now Professor) F. R. Hodson. He complained at their being compared by me, in 1939, with La Tène vessels from the Marne in France, and at Smith's and my "typological" claims for distinguishing these from the Hallstatt[44]. And on the site, where he expected that any house should be round, "since the round house plan has been recognised so universally", he dismissed the twin straight rows of post-holes found by the excavators (Hawley, 1926, p. 34, with p. 32, Fig. P) as a rectangular plan "construed" from these post-holes. In this he was following Clark, whose words had in fact been rather less sharp[45]. But elsewhere in the present volume, Philip Dixon on Crickley Hill shows such twin straight rows of large-sized post-holes certainly meaning houses: long rectangular houses of distinctly early date (pp. 170–174). Why confusion arose at Park Brow was that the rows there ran through a "working-hollow", like that at Little Woodbury (Wiltshire), dirty in its fill and irregularly scooped[46]. The excavators imagined this the floor of the post-built house; really, it can have only been made when the house was no longer standing. Finds made in the area thus may have been derived from either; they cannot be forced to cohere, and each should be taken on merits of its own. Thus the Hallstatt vessels are not to be mixed with the angular bowl and the pedestals of different ware, in feel and colour, as Hodson himself observed. And neither its Hallstatt nor its La Tène phase matches this Park Brow site with the East-bourne one, which Hodson compared with a phase in France of a date that is intermediate, the "Jogassian" (Hodson, 1962, pp. 140–145). It is the primary

[41] Jar with fluting at neck; Smith, 1926, pp. 16–19, Fig. 6; jar with very tall neck, and bowl with cover, Figs. 5 and 7, from Wolseley and Smith, 1924, pp. 352–355, Figs 2 and 10. Nearly the whole series is in the British Museum.

[42] ibid. Figs 11, 12, 13; the first = Smith, 1926, Fig. 4. Figure 14, a squatter version of 12, was a cremation urn, filled full.

[43] ibid. Figs 4–6 (bowls) and 7 (jar).

[44] Smith, 1926, p. 19, where the pedestal Fig. 10B = Fig. 8 in Wolseley and Smith, 1924. That of Fig. 9 there was not repeated in 1926, but both were re-drawn, and also the angular bowl Fig. 3, by me in the British Museum with ones from the Marne: Hawkes 1939b, pp. 232–235, Fig. G. Hodson cited them from this, ignoring the 1924 publication; he called the first a "freak", the second "another curiosity", and declared that on this Park Brow I site, Smith's Hallstatt area, "all the material was equally associated"; Hodson, 1962, pp. 145–148.

[45] Clark, 1952, p. 163, n. 116 (after discussing a different claim at Maiden Castle made by Wheeler), wrote of Park Brow: "A rectilinear house has been claimed, but not certainly validated".

[46] Bersu, 1940, pp. 64–78.

Park Brow Hallstatt phase that is matched at St. Catharine's Hill, in the jar that accompanied the native sherds on the floor of Pit A (Fig. 3, A1).

In its pottery's general style, this British Hallstatt is like the Belgian. We know little of the time in Artois and Picardy, the parts of France between, but can well believe in incomings over from the Belgian coast direct. Its bringers into Hampshire, west from the Sussex Downs or from coastal landings, of course meeting with natives, will have brought them soon into unified living. I do not intend to consider what was found in the fillings of our pits, nor to guess the further history of the settlement as such. Any attempt at ascertainment must be based on results of stripping, impossible for us, yet still with plenty of terrain available—though disturbed here and there by diggings for chalk to build the medieval chapel. Time for its range of dating is ample too: from around 600 (suitable to Belgium) and on, whether continuously or not, into the period of its enclosing by the hillfort.

III. The Hillfort: Earthwork and Entrance

Our excavations in the hillfort's earthwork (Fig. 2) consisted to two complete sections, 1 and 2 (*SCH*, pp. 13–17, 17–25), through the rampart and ditch and (in 2) the counterscarp bank outside; a third, extended across this too but mainly in the end of the ditch, where its squared-off end against the entrance-causeway, on the southern flank of that, was entirely cleared out (*SCH*, pp. 25–28). The causeway was shown to be of undisturbed natural chalk, about 40 ft wide (=some 12·3 m), crossed only by a small and relatively modern secondary ditch, seen in Fig. 5 (p. 248) inset, and edge marked *e*, which all our three sections found continuing along southward, cut in the silting of the earthwork ditch itself. Near our Section 1 (Fig. 2) we found the small Ditch 6 to have branched from it outwards, as presumably did Ditch 5 and the un-examined 8 and 7; nothing was found inside the fort showing any of them running inwards, and our only likely Iron Age minor ditch was thus Ditch 4 (Fig. 2). It stopped against the earthwork's back and had Iron Age sherds beneath and within its silt, underlying some Roman (*SCH*, pp. 95–96, 227–231, with sections of all these ditches Fig. 25). If Ditch 4 was an area boundary, like the Swallowcliffe Down one cited (Clay, 1926), we could not explain it any further; and I include it in what I am here refraining from any attempt to judge, namely the features and history of the settlement in itself, between our earliest findings (Pit A) and our latest (Pit R: p. 73). Neither plan nor continuity can be assessed without stripping, and the pits intervening in age are only eight, too few to judge from. However, they do show nothing, I think, of the Wiltshire All Cannings pottery, other than features in coarse ware common to all the earlier Iron Age. That group seems too far west for our site. And even if the hill were found to share, like a site discovered in Winchester[47], the mar-

---

[47] Cunliffe, 1964, pp. 1 (no. 4), 2, 20–22 (Figs. 7–8, plans), 33; 54–55, Fig. 12, 1–2, sherds of furrowed bowls; 3, one of an angular bowl showing deep-incised lines; 4, one of a cordoned bowl, the only

ginal scatter of its haematite-coated bowls[48], this would only—as elsewhere—attest its "influence", not its presence. The Stanmore site, on the opposite side of the valley, suggests the same[49]. The lands of the Test and west of it were neighbouring, yet distinctive: on the Itchen here, as in Dorset and Sussex, the Hallstatt modes seem easterly[50]. But after—I would say long after—their implanting, the hill received its earthwork.

A. *Earthwork*

The manner of the rampart's building was an especial concern of Stevens. As Myres with the pits, so he with this found matter for close attention, which

example found; all had got included in a later earth bank, behind the old Royal Oak inn; there were some furrowed sherds just east of it, under the former Kingdon's Workshop, and west as far as Jewry Street, with a few in a hearth beneath the former George Hotel; coarse-ware pieces, Fig. 12, 5–7 (from the earth bank); scatter over some 80 yards in all, George to Workshop.

[48] Of two scraps from the Trundle hillfort (Goodwood, West Sussex: Curwen, 1929, p. 53, Pl. X, 99–100), both with the fine red coating, furrows may be guessed from 100's rim, but neither actually shows them. At Highdown (near Worthing), over Late Bronze Age occupations, the Iron Age fort explored 1939 and 1947 (built first with a vertical-posted rampart, afterwards re-faced in the dump or "glacis" style) yielded typical Sussex pottery like Park Brow's here noticed above, but its ditch on the south was later re-cut as the small Ditch 3, which did yield haematite-coated pottery: Wilson, 1940, pp. 174, 182 with Pl. IV, 201 and Fig. 4 (194), *d-e-f* (straight rims, as though of bowls really cordoned). This pottery, which I examined with all the rest, was in little fragments, fine but sandy (193) and none with furrows nor with cordons; my explaining it (202) as due to migrants out of Wessex (viz. from the All Cannings group: Hawkes, 1939a, p. 227) was I think certainly wrong; and my taking them farther east to the Caburn (ibid. pp. 227–228, 241), if not Newhaven Castle Hill (Hawkes, 1939b, 276), confused the exporting of Wessex cordoned bowls, most rarely attested—as in the Winchester scrap or another from Maiden Castle (Wheeler, 1943, pp. 195–196, Fig. 56,4)—with the Sussex tradition's own bowls and jars with a reddish surface: as in Highdown's earlier phases, but at times now coated visibly with haematite. What I called Caburn I ware, including this among its various features (Hawkes, 1939a, pp. 217–230), needs no Wessex migration to explain it, was developed sooner than I thought, and may be found not only in the east of the Sussex Downs (as then) but throughout them. This restatement was rightly first advanced by Cunliffe, 1966; the pottery he redrew includes (16 in his Fig. 3, from Curwen and Hawkes, 1931), a piece from Kingston Buci, furrowed but unlike Wessex bowls in its angle and its rim, so that one ought to discount its mapping with them—and Trundle too—by Harding, 1972, Pl. III and 144.

[49] Hooley, 1927; the excavation found a well-preserved oven. Pottery included a bowl with flat-topped rim on upright neck, and prominently rounded shoulder (p. 65, Pl. II, 19), justly called "Hallstatt" and like *SCH*, Mis. 12 (pp. 108–110, Fig. 8); both are within the profile-range of Figs 3 and 7 from Highdown (Wilson, 1940), and go with A1 from our Pit A (Fig. 4).

[50] For metal, besides the pottery, I claimed as Hallstatt the cast bronze bird, 24 mm. long and with a slot across its stomach, *SCH*, Fig. 16, 4 and Pl. IX no. 3, on which I wrote a discursive essay (pp. 127–133), pointing broadly to the Hallstatt Continent: bird-figures frequent, origin sacred. Yet its birds in metal are either fixed by a peg-like leg (Pl. IX, 4–8), or else (9–10) are cast together with the object they adorn. A rib or tongue on it, fitting our slot, would not be upright (10A) but slanted; and Adolf Mahr, when he gave me the notion of a tongue on the foot of a brooch (11), was thinking of the "chariot-fibula" type of brooch in the Eastern Alps, where a tiny chariot and horses are the head and bow, but the foot is a bird. Though normally cast in one with the catch for the pin and the rest of the foot, the bird if imagined separate might have been affixed with a slot like ours. East Alpine bird-brooch and horse-brooch forms do appear among Celts in Spain, and if some bird-adorned bronze (whether brooch or not) can have passed to Britain, it would start from intermediate country, North-Italian or Rhenish or Gaulish. Formerly dismissed as "strays", such cases are slowly gathering attention. Relevance to Britain may grow with any emergence of clearer patterns—which the bird of St. Catharine's Hill should be held in wait for.

his section-drawings convey (Fig. 5)[51]. In both Sections 1 and 2 (Pl. II) the old turf and soil had been dug away, in front for the ditch and behind for a scraping-up of material also from there. The build proceeded by tips (although a single operation): in the first section six, in the second seven. For Stevens' view of the process, see his diagram; it is surely still as convincing now as then, and confirmed by the finds-distribution beneath the rampart and some of the tips (Section 2). Tips 1–3, here with finds, and 4, came first: from the scraped ground within, like 6 shortly after. The clean chalk of 5, meanwhile, and finally 7 (lumpy blocks), came from the ditch as it went on deepening. In Section 1, the ditch first supplied tips 1–3, and then the lumpy 6 after 4 and 5 had come from within; 7 was a final addition thence, to fill a cavity. The ditch here lacked features other than the silting normal in chalk: its recutting in Section 2 will concern the Entrance (see below: for the secondary ditch in this and Section 3, see above).

So I pass straight to the question of greatest interest today, when so many primary ramparts are known that were built (at least on the outer side) like walls, vertical or nearly, upheld by timbers, stone or turves. Such a face could only have had timbers here; and in post-holes, not in a continuous bedding-trench: this much, the sections show. But were there post-holes that we missed, through their interval being too wide both for our 4-ft section 1, and even for our 8-ft section 2? The alternative is that the rampart was built from the start as a dump, with body sides sloped. Such "glacis-type" works seem normally later than the "wall-type". Would ours be abnormally early, making a "wall-type" build more likely? We were sure it was always a dump. We did the best we could to check this, by trenching on the very steep slope on either side of the Entrance; but we found nothing of post-holes outside those of the Entrance itself (Fig. 6). Cunliffe lately at Danebury, only a dozen miles off to westward, where his first-period rampart and its principal entrance both were timbered, and this "wall-type" rampart was held in post-holes along its face, found their interval here was 1·3 m, not more than $4\frac{1}{2}$ ft (Cunliffe, 1971a, p. 245 (with p. 246)). As this entrance in its second stage was closely similar to ours in plan, one would expect our rampart's build, if really with posts, to have given them an interval at any rate less than twice the Danebury figure: less than 9 ft, in fact, or even than 6. How could we have missed them, then, in our 8-ft Section 2, and our trenches beside the Entrance? I believe there were none; and that we rightly trusted Stevens to have given a complete account of the method, of tips piled successively, that our rampart builders had used.

That this should be wrong is I think unlikely. At Maiden Castle (Wheeler, 1943, pp. 31–36, 36–39), where the "wall-type" primary rampart only enclosed the east of the hill (17), the extension to enclose the west as well was carried out in dump construction (pp. 36–37): "glacis-type", which remained the mode thenceforward. By then the primary "wall-type" face had long fallen, through

---

[51] This Fig. 5 is *SCH*, Fig. 4, starting the Section 1 description, pp. 13–17; the Section 2 is pp. 17–25. Section 4 belongs to the Entrance (here p. 72 below).

the posts' mere decay, and been overgrown with turf. It showed itself a model, were one needed, for the dump work; yet the builders of each of the phases had in culture the same tradition, modified only through the lapse of time in unbroken occupation. And modern reckoning of dates would put the extension fairly early, well back in the third century B.C. At Highdown, when the excavation was ended after the war, the conclusions showed that the primary "wall-type" rampart here, too, after similar decay and perhaps at least 200 years, was reconstructed with a "glacis" face. See Wilson, 1950, pp. 176–178: timbers there were, but only behind, protecting a defenders' platform, and after them came nothing but simple dump-work. Wilson dated the first "glacis" face to c 300 B.C., and this would suit more modern opinions. We ourselves had believed our earthwork not prior to the fourth century, but well prior to the second, so within the fourth or third: SCH, pp. 21, 24, 38, 58, 88: towards the end of the neighbouring Continental La Tène I period, taken as c 250, so probably somewhere near 300. Such round figures are guesses, of course; yet dump-construction ramparts of around that time in southern Britain appear entirely credible, even if built in less haste than I judged was Quarley Hill, where the entrance remained unfinished and the rampart incomplete (Hawkes, 1939a).

Of the pottery fragments prior to our rampart, two are important: E2 from beneath it in Section 2, and the rim E28 from its original make-up south of the Entrance (in Fig. 5, Section 4, A1). In the language of Reginald Smith, I called the latter an "incipient bead-rim", which meant a rounded and slightly demarcated lip, approaching in profile what a carpenter calls a beading. In the note below[52] it is shown that this rim has its closest counterparts in Sussex Caburn 1 ware, on angular bowls which in their shoulder correspond to our piece E2, and the similar but grittier E118[53] (see below again with n. 52). Both are among the pieces, in fact (SCH, Fig. 12 has more) which confirm belief in relationships at St. Catharine's Hill with Sussex. This holds in spite of the nearness of the All Cannings group, at Danebury and near by at Meon Hill

[52] Rim E 28: SCH, p. 108, Fig. 12, 2nd in lowest row, described 113, with a bad comparison (Fifield); in its hard brown smooth-surfaced ware, and made so thin, it is certainly from a bowl. If this were cordoned it could resemble Richardson, 1951, pp. 142–143, Fig. 8, 32, from Boscombe Down West (Wiltshire), pits in her Area R; yet that, like all its kind, has the haematite coating which our piece lacks. In fact it appears much rather to resemble the Sussex type of bowl, often with just such a lip, included by Cunliffe in his Caburn I ware: Cunliffe, 1966, pp. 110–111, Fig. 1, 1–6, Stoke Clump near Chichester; pp. 115–116, Fig. 3, 7–14, Caburn (7–8) and 4 other well-known sites. His dating (pp. 117–119), from perhaps sixth-fifth century till even into third, will cover also E2; see following note.

[53] Shoulder E2: SCH, p. 108, Fig. 12, in top row next to E128, which has main feature more pronounced. This feature rather resembles a cordon along the angle, formed in E128 with a groove which is standard for such bowls of the Caburn I kind, in E2 without one—whence my comparing All Cannings Cross. In this (SCH, p. 109) I was surely wrong, for the sherd is fine dark reddish but lacks the haematite coating. Cunliffe, 1966, pp. 110–111, has such shoulders on Fig. 1, 1–4, in the same set of Stoke Clump bowls just cited for our rim E28, and on Fig. 3, 7–14 from Caburn 1 and elsewhere (see preceding note); also his Fig. 2, 57–8, from H. S. Toms's pit in the fort of Hollingbury, Brighton (pp. 112–114), with its classic "wall-type" rampart (Curwen, 1932), befitting the fairly early date which Cunliffe gives this pit-group. Thus both our bowls correspond to the Caburn I or Sussex angular bowl form.

above Stockbridge (Liddell, 1933, 1935), which doubtless explains the haematite-coated sherds found in Winchester (above with n. 47). And as for date, it is still left free to float around 300.

B. Entrance

Professor Cunliffe, to my benefit, has kindly enlarged on the resemblance of his Danebury stage 2 entrance, already remarked on here, to ours. After sketches suggesting revisions in our interpretation of this (*SCH*, pp. 29–57, with Figs 5, 6 and 4, Section 4) and in my resultant scheme of its periods (pp. 58–66, with Fig. 7), he has drawn for me Fig. 6 here, with the points re-adjusted. The recesses or bays on either side, like their Danebury counterparts, will be open ones from the start: in period A no less than in B. And in what we called Pit V and its annexe, at the north (right) flank of the gateway (Pl. III), the "annexe" will have held the three posts of the bay's re-entrant, as on the south did holes 9 and 10. The projecting deep pit, "Pit V" itself, is removed as belonging to Period C, along with our Pits M and T; all three are in fact not pits, but very large post-holes. Thus Period B is simply A left in the interval of decay which we saw had intervened before the rebuilding done in C. This Period C brought the recutting of the ditch, and heightening of the rampart-ends, entirely as we stated. But the collapsed south revetment will now have been replaced on a line thrown forward to the *axis*-line of A: from "Pit M", dug for its innermost feature, opposite the like in "Pit T" on the north, along this line to hole 17, and thence to 16 and its annexe. In these, and along the trench connecting 16 with 9 and 10, were placed the timbers not of a "blocking" but of the new revetment's front. They were encased along their foot in the flint walls, C and B: surely continuous throughout, and turning to follow the old line outwards. Between this and the shorter northern revetment, encased in flint wall A, the passage abruptly narrowed into the corridor, or barbican, with 16 and V at its forward end and M and T at its rear. How much heightened rampart-material really was packed behind its sides, may be questioned in terms of what happened in Period D, when all was burnt, and how much material might (then or thereafter) have been removed. The whole revision requires good heed to our sections, in *SCH*, Figs 4 (4) and 6. But I regard it as thoroughly viable, and I warmly thank its proposer.

As for the dates, it is still to be noted that the interval shown by B seems to have left no pottery in any but the older (A) tradition. A rim sherd closely similar to *SCH*, Fig. 12, E136 (108, described 113), brownish and coarser than E28 but still with the same lip profile ("beading"), which I wrongly compared with Fifield again, was found in the heightened rampart material (*SCH*, pp. 39–40) on the south side (B in Section 4, Fig. 5). And nothing in the whole site's pottery seems to change till Period C. Change in the pottery comes with this (reconstruction of the Entrance), not before. The change brought the new-style ware that we called "La Tène II". It was found in the "Area", as we called the hollow behind the southerly rampart-end, scraped and scooped to get it heightening-material (*SCH*, pp. 13, 17, 92, 113–116 with Fig. 13; here Fig. 7), and in the beehive-shaped Pit R, close within on the opposite side (pp. 91–92, 118–120 with Fig. 14). Wrongly believed by us to have been "intended for habitation" (*SCH*, p. 91), its shape has been long found typical of the phase with the new-style pottery. This is the ware with "saucepan" pots and rounded bowls and jars, some large, very plentiful in Winchester and the neighbourhood, with which occupation appears to start on a number of downland sites, such as Twyford Down, Worthy Down and Owslebury. From Period C of our Entrance to the destruction (D) was not long: so we thought, from the state and initial cleanness of the silting in the recut Ditch (*SCH*, p. 26). And this pottery was not found widespread. So now I have exhausted the second aspect, of the three that I chose to review, and can end with the third.

IV. The Hill and Iron-Age Winchester

Such pottery as that from our "Area" and Pit R on St. Catharine's Hill was called "La Tène II" by Reginald Smith. He noted that at Park Brow (p. 61 above) it came from a new site, at the foot of the hill below the older one (Smith, 1926, pp. 20–21). Sites in Sussex found with it since then, and in Surrey and Hampshire, Wiltshire too, have been numerous enough to allow a degree of regional distinction. For Hampshire it was made by Cunliffe in publishing finds of such ware from Winchester: Cunliffe, 1964, pp. 1–15 (located finds also p. 21ff.). He called this regional form of it "the St. Catharine's Hill Group", and drew and described a representative type-series of its forms and ornament. This makes it needless to do the like here. But I would emphasize its frequency on quite fresh sites, such as Worthy Down (Hooley and Dunning, 1929, pp. 182–185), Twyford Down (Stuart and Birkbeck, 1936, pp. 197–199), Owslebury (Collis, 1968; 1970 and forthcoming), besides such cases as our hill (and seemingly Winchester), where prior occupation was now altered or transcended. In *SCH* I firmly declared (pp. 120–122) that it was "directly developed" from British Hallstatt-La Tène I pottery. But the more that is found, the harder it is to sustain the case for this. The "St. Catharine's Hill Group" forms, and what answers to these in adjoining counties, do seem to appear quite suddenly, as we have seen. Yet in Wiltshire they really come gradually, from an initial phase there, distinguished also by jars with pedestal base. And at Little Woodbury there, this phase was shown from Bersu's excavations (Brailsford, 1948), to enter the story of the site by what appears as an infiltration, while the preceding haematite-coated ware went fairly quickly out. This transition, and the new "smooth dark ware" (as Brailsford called it: Smith's "La Tène II"), will be considered in the report on the site at Longbridge Deverill Cow Down; but in part at least of Sussex there was a transition seemingly similar, represented at Park Brow and elsewhere (Hawkes, 1939b, pp. 230–243) and leading on to the phase with the hillfort (Caburn

II) at the Caburn (p. 243ff.). My claim that the novel element in that was intrusive over the Channel, sharply attacked by Hodson (1962; 1964a and b), has lain awaiting further evidence. But the St. Catharine's Hill Group seems to appear without any prior transition. It is farther, thus, from immediate likeness to anything Continental. But it could have been started from neighbouring regions, on east or on west, which had had transitions of their own; and this remains to be further studied.

Anyhow in central Hampshire, and on our hill and now in Winchester, its presence whets the appetite for what (as I write these words) is awaited from Martin Biddle: an exposition further to Cunliffe's of 1964, and superseding my essay in *SCH* (pp. 169–188) on "St. Catharine's Hill and the Origin of Winchester". Biddle in correspondence has given me plentiful information, with many photocopies of drawings, showing that whereas our hill became abandoned, while this group of pottery was current, just as we said in *SCH*, the Winchester occupation went on until the last pre-Roman phase there. I was therefore wrong (Hawkes, 1936b) when I tried to upset the *SCH* conclusions, and fancied our hill's occupation itself had lasted as late as that. And the Winchester finds, on the western slope running up to Oram's Arbour, come most from the ditch now found to have made this slope a defended settlement (see Biddle, 1970, pp. 279–281), internally as large as 41 acres or more than 16 hectares, an 84 per cent increase on St. Catharine's hillfort (p. 62). In the *Review* for Groups 12 and 13 of the Council for British Archaeology, 1971, we owe to Biddle a plan still fuller. Dating from the pottery as found in the ditch, and as found with fragments of amphoras—Roman but prior to the conquest—leaves a last phase only remaining, before the conquest brought the Romans into Winchester, *Venta Belgarum.*

Who then were Venta's Belgae? Biddle's discoveries sharpen the question. If the folk of the "St. Catharine's Hill Group" were, then how did they come to be Belgic? Should their predecessors, or neighbours spreading from Sussex or Wiltshire regions, onward from around 300, stand among the folk recorded by Caesar, as entering into "maritime Britain" *ex Belgio*? If so, Venta's Belgae would belong to "*the* Belgae" of Britain. And already since 1962, independently of Hampshire work, I had started refuting the belief that I advanced, with Dunning in 1931, that "the Belgae of Britain" entered not here but in Kent, and not in La Tène II but in III, *c* 75 B.C. I am busy refuting it still (Hawkes, 1972; 1973). But it is Hampshire work that may, I think, be decisive now in the end. So I salute the approaching truth that in the past I never yet found for myself: the truth about Winchester's origin—and perhaps much else besides. Digging St. Catharine's Hill, though so well worth while, was too long ago.

3 Salmonsbury, Bourton-on-the-Water, Gloucestershire

G. C. Dunning

Salmonsbury is situated on the eastern margin of the village of Bourton-on-the-Water, on the east side of the Cotswolds[1]. The earthwork occupies the greater part of a large spread of gravel in the angle between the river Windrush to the south and the river Dikler to the east, at a height of about 440 ft O.D. The ground slopes gradually from north to south, and from west to east; in the last direction, close outside the camp, it becomes marshy. The position of the site is thus unusual and contrasts with that of the Cotswolds hillforts, since it lies on almost flat ground in Bourton Vale.

The siting of Salmonsbury should be considered in relation to the trackways or ridgeways in the vicinity which, either certainly or presumably, were in use during prehistoric times. The most important route is the long-distance Jurassic Way, which linked North-east and South-west Britain in the Iron Age[2]. Although the Way kept to the high ground of the Cotswolds, it has been suggested as an alternative that it passed through Bourton Vale, where occupation-sites and finds from the Neolithic period onwards are numerous[3].

In its regional context, Salmonsbury may be regarded as an outlier of the multivallate hillforts on the higher ground of the Cotswolds. Its position in an open valley made it accessible along the ridgeways running southwards to end in Bourton Vale. The use of routes in this direction, such as Buckle Street, goes back to Roman times and cannot yet be demonstrated earlier. Salmonsbury has two entrances; the excavation of that in the north-east side (p. 88) produced ample evidence of its use by traffic in the Iron Age, and the approach to that in the north-west side would be from the west along the gravel. However, as yet no trackway can be connected directly with either entrance.

[1] Nat. Grid Ref. SP 173208. 6in. O.S. Gloucestershire, XXIX, SW.
[2] Grimes (1951b), Fig. 39.
[3] O'Neil (1966), pp. 46–47, Fig. 1.

The name *Sulmonnes Burg* (ploughman's stead) is recorded in a charter of A.D. 779, whereby Offa, king of Mercia, grants four hides of land to the thegn Duddonus[4]. Translated it states: "there is moreover a part of that land adjacent to the city (urbi) which is called *Sulmonnes Burg*, on both sides of the stream which is called *Theodningc* on the west side of the river which is called *Uuenrisc*". The names of the rivers on two sides of Salmonsbury are given, and their relationship. In the course of time, however, the rivers have exchanged names, the first-named becoming the present Windrush and the second the Dikler.

It remains to mention that the name of Salmonsbury was given to the Hundred in which Bourton-on-the-Water lies; later, the Hundred took the name of Slaughter. The Court continued to assemble at the "Salmonsbury Stone" near a gap in the north rampart until the early nineteenth century[5]. The place is recorded by a stone inscribed SF CP 1794, formerly built into the field-wall near the north-east entranee.

I. Description of Salmonsbury (Fig. 1)

The camp is rectilinear, almost a square in plan, but slightly longer on the south side than the north. The interior measures about 1550 ft from north to south, and about 1500 ft (average) from east to west; the banks enclose an area of about 56 acres. The defences were two closely-set ramparts, each with an external ditch. Both banks are present on the north-east and south-east sides; on the north-west side only the inner rampart remains along Harp Lane, its southern part being levelled to build houses and to make Station Road; and on the south-west both banks have been almost entirely destroyed by gravel-digging. Where best preserved on the north-east side, the inner rampart is now about 4 ft high, but even here the outer rampart is much reduced by ploughing.

Two original entrances to the camp are known. The entrance in the middle of the north-east side is in good condition, with the banks on both sides in alignment. The other entrance, towards the southern end of the north-west side, is recorded on a plan of Salmonsbury made by Sir Henry Dryden and W. Lukis in 1840, now in Northampton Public Library. The inner banks, levelled almost flat, of this inturned entrance were observed by Mrs. H. E. O'Neil in 1965 and since in the garden of Camp House. In addition, there is a gap in the south-east ramparts for the exit of the stream passing across the interior of the camp.

On the south-east side of Salmonsbury, a single bank with an external ditch prolongs the line of the ramparts for about 500 ft from the east and south corners. These banks are curved inwards at the ends, and define an annexe of about 15 acres outside the main enclosure; on the east side the annexe is open, and limited by a stream and the marshy ground towards the river Dikler.

[4] Grundy (1936), p. 52; Smith, A. H. (1964), pp. 192–193 and pp. 195–196.
[5] Camden (1789), p. 279; *Trans. Bristol and Gloucestershire Arch. Soc.*, VII (1882–83), p. 16.

II. Excavations in 1931–1934

The excavation of Salmonsbury was initially made possible by the interest and generosity of the late Mr. A. S. Owen of Keble College, Oxford. A local committee was formed to raise funds, with Mr. Owen as Chairman, Miss H. E. Donovan (now Mrs. O'Neil) as Secretary, and Mr. E. W. Kendall as Treasurer. The work was carried out during the Summers of 1931–1934 by the Anthropological Society of University College, London, augmented by students from other London colleges and local helpers. At the invitation of Dr. O. G. S. Crawford and Dr. R. E. M. (now Sir Mortimer) Wheeler, the writer was director of the excavations. The grateful thanks of the committee are due to the owners of the land for permission to excavate; Mrs. H. A. Albino, Lt.-Col. and Mrs. C. Donovan, Mr. F. M. Lodge, and Christ Church, Oxford. With the ready consent of the owners, the finds were deposited in Cheltenham Museum.

The objectives of the work were threefold: (1) to investigate the structural history of the ramparts and ditches (Site I), the north-east entrance (Site V), and the annexe (Sites VI and VII); (2) to locate hut-sites inside the line of the ramparts (Sites I, II and III), and near the middle of the camp (Site IV); and (3) to identify the cultures associated with the periods of occupation of the camp. Although the excavation was on a relatively modest scale, it can fairly be claimed that the three objectives were largely achieved. The structural history and stratification of the site were found to be comparatively simple, so that the results are straight-forward. As a framework to this report, the findings may be summarized as follows.

A. Earlier Occupation

Evidence of pre-camp occupation was found on three sites. On Site I were 9 small pits and a short curved ditch, all filled with stiff red clay. Six of the pits were sealed by the old turf-line under the inner and outer ramparts. The only finds in the pits were a few flint flakes, but a rim of Peterborough ware was a stray find in the Iron Age inner ditch. Another rim of Peterborough ware was in the turf-line under the inner rampart on Site V. On Site IV two ditches were filled with similar red clay, but produced no finds. However, on or in the old turf-line on this site were a leaf-shaped flint flake and a transverse arrowhead of class 2, and a tanged arrowhead was a stray find in an Iron Age ditch. On Site V a barbed and tanged arrowhead was in the turf-line under the Iron Age inner rampart (Fig. 11).

These pits and ditches, and the finds, attest some occupation in the late Neolithic period and the Early Bronze Age. They are to be correlated with the pits near Slaughter Bridge, which contained a large pot decorated in Fengate style and a rim of Peterborough ware[6]; and nearby a beaker burial[7].

[6] Dunning (1932a), p. 280, Fig. 2, 1–2; Smith, I. F. (1968), pp. 26–27.
[7] Dunning (1937), p. 163.

Occupation later in the Bronze Age is now shown by a ring-ditch 96 ft in diameter, with two dogs buried near the centre, recorded by Mrs. O'Neil early in 1972 just outside the north-west entrance of Salmonsbury. The site belongs to the same group as the ring-ditches at Lower Slaughter, which are dated by cremations in collared urns[8].

Finally, Site I produced slight evidence of occupation in Iron Age A. In and on the old turf-line beneath the inner rampart (p. 80) were a few sherds, some with finger-nail decoration, an iron strip and a small bronze loop.

B. Occupation of Salmonsbury

The stratification on Sites III and IV showed that the occupation belonged to two successive periods in the later part of the Iron Age.

(a) *Period I*. Abundant pottery and small finds occurred on the hut-sites and in the storage pits associated with the huts, on Sites I, II, III, IV and V. The pottery has curvilinear, geometric and linear decoration, seldom combined on the same pot. The assemblage belongs to the Western Second B culture, and is provisionally dated to the first century B.C.

(b) *Period II*. This period immediately followed Period I; it was mainly revealed on Site III and to a lesser extent on Site IV. On Site III there were two structural phases: (i) a sub-rectangular enclosure close behind the inner rampart, defined by a palisade-trench and other ditches, (ii) rough paving laid above the filled-in ditches, on which were small round huts and other structures. On Site IV only phase ii is represented.

Period II witnessed the arrival and domination of "Belgic" culture. It is defined by the introduction of wheel-turned pottery of Western Third C, imported Gallo-Belgic and early Roman wares, Dobunnic coinage, and brooches of iron and bronze. This culture was imposed on that of Western Second B, which still continued. The period belongs to the early first century A.D., starting *c* A.D. 30 and terminating *c* A.D. 50–55.

C. Roman Period

The main Roman settlement at Bourton-on-the-Water centred on the Fosse Way where it crossed the river Windrush at a ford. Permanent occupation about here is attested by a posting-station, and by numerous finds along the gravel eastwards in the direction of Salmonsbury[9].

Inside Salmonsbury there is ample evidence of occupation during most of the Roman period. The finds are densest over the western half of the camp and near its centre, where excavation in 1931–1934 and digging subsequently has been most active. The structures comprise a length of wall, rough stone floors, rubbish pits (Sites III and IV), an early straight ditch and late rectangular stone floor (Site IV), and the stone blocking-wall across the north-

[8] Dunning (1932a), p. 279; Smith, I. F. (1972), pp. 162 and p. 165, Fig. 15.
[9] O'Neil (1934), p. 99; (1935), pp. 234–245; (1968), p. 29.

east entrance (Site V), also numerous chance finds of pottery and coins. The range of occupation extends from the mid first century down to the late fourth century. The evidence suggests continuing occupation of Salmonsbury to some extent in the Roman period, possibly intensified as a migration back to the camp from the region of Bourton Bridge in the late fourth century.

D. Anglo-Saxon Period

In the pagan Anglo-Saxon period, occupation in the vicinity is proved by the hut found near Slaughter Bridge[10], and by eight burials of an inhumation cemetery in the make-up of the Fosse Way about 500 yd to the south-west of the hut[11]. These finds indicate Saxon settlement of the region in the sixth or seventh century A.D.

At Salmonsbury, evidence of occupation in this period was absent from all the sites excavated. The only find since is by Mrs. O'Neil in 1963, when grave 480 was dug in the present cemetery inside the south-west part of the camp. A small iron knife (p. 117, Fig. 31, 1) was found with human bones, evidently a disturbed burial.

One burial and two cemeteries are recorded at different places, both on the line of the defences. In 1931 the extended burial of an adult man with head to the west, with a small iron knife (p. 117, Fig. 31, 2) by the right forearm, was found inserted into the outer side of the south bank of the annexe, about 70 yd from the south-east corner of the main defences. This burial may be related to a small cemetery of seven burials laid side by side, found about 1850 some 50 yd north of the south-east corner of Salmonsbury. The only associated object was an iron knife by the right hand of one burial. The cemetery is recorded in Dr. John Moore's notebook[12].

The other cemetery, in the north-west inner rampart, is also recorded by Dr. Moore:

In Harp Lane, forming the west boundary of the camp, in squaring down the bank, which is here about 9 ft high, numerous human bones were found and the skull of a skeleton lying east and west fell into the lane. Much pottery sherds was found here, Roman and Saxon principally the latter, also a portion of a knife about 18 in from the skull; a sword handle had been previously found there by George Gashier.

In the Moore collection in Cheltenham Museum are two iron knives (p. 117, Fig. 31, 3–4) of different dates in the Saxon period, both presumably from Harp Lane. The seax could be furniture from a late seventh-century grave, but the other knife is ninth or tenth century and so too late to have come from a burial.

---

[10] Dunning (1932a), p. 284.
[11] O'Neil (1961). On the bronze spiral-headed pins see K. Pretty in Brodribb *et al.* (1972), pp. 84–85.
[12] MS. notebook no. 1, by Dr. John Moore. In the Library of the Bristol and Gloucestershire Archaeological Society.

III. Description of Sites Excavated: Site I

A section 12 ft wide and about 150 ft long was cut through the middle of the defences on the south-east side. This is the only place where the defences of Salmonsbury, comprising an inner rampart, inner ditch, outer rampart and outer ditch, have been examined by a complete cross-section.

A. *Earlier Occupation* (Fig. 3 and Pl. I)

Occupation previously to the construction of the defences of Salmonsbury belonged to two different periods.

(a) *Late Neolithic*. Nine pits dug in the gravel and sealed by the old turf-line; three pits were inside the line of the defences, four pits under the inner rampart and two pits below the outer rampart. The pits extended for 150 ft from east to west and 40 ft from north to south, but six of them were within the 12 ft wide section through the defences. About 45 ft to the south-west of the pits was a short curved ditch, 7 ft long, 1 ft wide and 1 ft 3 in. deep. All the pits were oval in plan and basin-shaped in section. In size the pits varied from 3 ft 3 in. to 7 ft 3 in. long, 2 ft 6 in. to 5 ft 6 in. wide and 1 ft 4 in. to 3 ft deep. The filling of all the pits and the ditch was uniformly a stiff red clay. A few flint flakes, patinated dull white, were the only finds in the pits. In the lower filling of the Iron Age inner ditch was a rim of Peterborough ware, decorated on top with incised chevrons (Fig. 11, 1); presumably this was derived from a pit destroyed in making the ditch, and so may be used to date the pits.

(b) *Iron Age A*. Slight occupation in this period is shown by a few finds in and on the turf-line beneath the inner rampart; sherds of coarse pottery, some decorated with finger-nail marks, a bent strip of iron and a small bronze loop.

B. *Inner Rampart* (Fig. 3 and Pl. I)

The spread inner rampart is now about 60 ft wide and 3 ft high. It was simple in construction, built of gravel thrown up from the inner ditch to form a bank 24 ft wide and 2 ft high. The tail of the bank was overlaid by occupation-material containing pottery similar to that from the huts and pits inside the defences. The bank covered the old turf-line, a layer of dark red-brown soil up to 9 in. thick, which on the outer side extended for 8 ft beyond the toe of the bank. Presumably this space had been occupied by a revetment-wall of slabs of Oolite, like the wall in this position in the inner rampart to the west of the north-east entrance (p. 89). The mass of loose stones in the lower filling of the inner ditch represents the collapse of the revetment early in the Roman period.

C. *Inner Ditch* (Fig. 3)

The inner ditch was originally 36 ft wide and 12 ft deep; in profile it was an open V-shape. Erosion on both sides had widened the top of the ditch to 40 ft.

The ditch was filled to a maximum depth of 10 ft. At the bottom and on the inner slope was a thin deposit of fine yellow sandy gravel, forming the initial rapid silt from the inner side of the ditch. Above this was a thick layer of light reddish-brown soil and gravel, derived from the inner and outer ramparts but mainly from the former. This layer was both below and above a mass of loose slabs of Oolite, mostly on the inner side of the section. It contained sherds of Iron Age B pottery, but considerably more Romano-British sherds were among the stones and above them.

The upper part of the filling, about two-thirds of the total filling of the ditch, was consistently dark brown soil mixed with gravel and resulted from the later denudation of both ramparts over a long period. In the lower part of this deposit were a few Romano-British sherds and two coins, of Gallienus (A.D. 253–268) and the House of Constantine (A.D. 330–335); the upper part contained numerous sherds of medieval pottery of the thirteenth century and later.

The ditch had not been recut; its filling proceeded without interruption from the Iron Age down to medieval times. No turf-lines had formed at any level in the filling.

D. *Outer Rampart* (Fig. 3)

The outer rampart was levelled almost flat; its gravel make-up had entirely disappeared, and the old turf-line remained only in two patches. The complete reduction of the bank suggests that it was ploughed down in Roman times, since most of the filling of the outer ditch occurred in this period. The maximum width of the bank was about 40 ft.

E. *Outer Ditch* (Fig. 3)

The outer ditch was originally 19 ft wide and 9 ft deep; in section it was a sharp V-shape.

The filling showed the same sequence of three fills as in the inner ditch. Stone slabs were absent, so no revetment-wall had been present in the outer rampart. There were no finds of any period in the two lower deposits.

The dark brown soil and gravel which filled most of the ditch contained a few Iron Age B sherds in the lower part; rather more Romano-British sherds were at all levels, but mainly in the upper part. In addition were four coins, of Claudius II (A.D. 268–270), Tetricus I (A.D. 270–273), Carausius (A.D. 287–293) and the House of Theodosius (A.D. 388–395).

Thus the outer ditch had filled up by the end of the Roman period; the only medieval sherd was in the top soil.

F. *Huts* (Figs 2 and 4 and Pl. III)

A rectangular area 80 ft by 65 ft was excavated on the inside of the inner rampart, and two huts close together were located.

Hut 1. Circular hut, 22 ft in diameter, surrounded by a ring of eighteen post-holes. The majority of the post-holes were 6 to 9 in. in diameter, and 6 to 12 in. deep in the gravel. The entrance, 8 ft wide, was to the south-east between two larger post-holes, both 1 ft 6 in. in diameter and 7 in. deep. At the centre of the hut a group of three post-holes was for a tripod to support the roof. Outside the hut, 12 ft to the south-east, were two stone hearths built over shallow oval pits.

Hut 2. Circular hut, 20 ft in diameter, with a ring of fifteen post-holes similar in size to those of hut 1. The entrance, 5 ft 3 in. wide, was to the east between post-holes 1 ft 6 in. in diameter and 9 in. deep. At the centre of the hut were two post-holes for the roof posts. Two stone hearths were outside the hut, 12 ft and 16 ft to the south.

It should be noted that the two hearths of hut 1 are too close to the ring-posts of hut 2 to be contemporary. Since the hearths were still built up, hut 2 was abandoned previously.

The circular huts on Site I appear to be the usual form of dwelling at Salmonsbury in period I. Similar huts were found on Sites III and IV. The type may be reconstructed as a circle of wall-posts tied by a ring-beam connecting the upper ends. The spaces between the posts could be filled with wattle and daub. At the lower end the rafters of the conical roof rested on the wall, and the upper ends met at the top of the centre-posts. The roof could be thatched with reeds.

A system of drainage ditches enclosed both huts and extended beyond them. The ditches were about 2 ft wide and 6 to 10 in. deep. A continuous ditch encircled the north and west sides of hut 1 and thence passed round the southern half of hut 2. Between the huts a second ditch had been dug outside it, and another ditch dug on the inner side round hut 2. In the southern sector straight ditches led off in several directions, some to end in pits.

G. Pits (Fig. 2)

A large number (22) of pits were associated with the huts. One pit (A) was close to the south side of hut 1, and another (V) in a similar position outside hut 2. The majority of the pits were, however, grouped to the west and south of the drainage ditches, at a distance of 12 to 32 ft behind the huts. The pits were neatly dug in the gravel, accurately circular and mostly straight-sided; they varied from 2 ft 6 in. to 5 ft in diameter and 9 in. to 3 ft 6 in. deep. Although some of the pits were only a few inches apart, none of them overlapped.

Presumably most of the pits were intended for storage purposes, though no traces of lining were observed, and later filled with domestic rubbish. The ashes of a fire were on the bottom of pit A, and burnt stones and ashes in the upper filling of two pits (B and H). Human remains were found in four pits; two infants in pit A, the skull of an adult female (cranial index 76·9) in pit E, and ribs and vertebrae in pits D and H.

IV. Site II

On the north-east side of the camp, about 400 ft west of the entrance, an area 65 ft by 30 ft was excavated inside the inner rampart. The site was chosen because in digging a small gravel pit here a hoard of 147 iron currency bars was found in 1860[13].

The limits of the disused gravel pit were plotted. To the west of it were five circular pits, but the only evidence of a hut in the vicinity was the end of a drainage ditch. One pit (A) was covered by the tail of the rampart, and another (E) had a stone hearth in the upper filling.

In the lower filling of the largest pit (D), 5 ft 9 in. in diameter and 2 ft deep, was the burial of a woman (cranial index 74·6), laid on the right side with head to the east and legs flexed.

Nearby, between pit E and the ditch, a shallow grave contained the burial of a man (cranial index 79·3), lying on the right side with head to the north, in a tightly crouched position with the legs drawn up to the chest. No grave-goods accompanied either of the burials.

V. Site III

On the north-west side of the camp, about 700 ft from the north-west corner, an area 72 ft by 60 ft was excavated inside the inner rampart. This site was occupied in both periods of the Iron Age, and to a less extent in the first and second centuries A.D.

A. Period I

1. Hut

In the south-east part of the site was a drainage ditch for a hut. The ditch, about 1 ft 6 in. wide and deep, was roughly circular and enclosed an area 30 ft by 26 ft. A gap 11 ft wide on the west side probably marks the entrance. On the north side of the gap a ditch 12 ft long ran outwards, and a post-hole here may indicate that the hut had a porch. Very few post-holes were located within the area. The largest, 2 ft by 1 ft 9 in. and 7 in. deep, with a stone laid flat in the filling, was on the south side of the entrance; another was on the opposite side of the area. Near the centre were two post-holes to support the roof. Although slight, the indications are of a hut about 20 to 22 ft in diameter, similar in construction to those on Site I.

2. Ditches

About 16 ft north of the hut was a segment of a large curved ditch, 4 ft wide and 2 ft deep, with a radius of about 20 feet. On the east side it joined another

[13] Allen (1967), pp. 328–329.

curved ditch at right angles. Both ditches continued beyond the area excavated. No post-holes were located on the inner margins of these ditches, so that they do not appear to have enclosed hut-sites.

In the south-west part of the site and 12 ft west of the circular hut was the end of another large ditch; this continued southwards outside the excavation.

3. *Pits* (Pl. IV)

Fourteen pits were found, grouped in different parts of the site. Seven pits (A to G) occupied its western side, in the space towards the inner rampart. The other pits (H to O) were within the circular hut or close outside it.

In the first group of pits, one (B) partly cut into the large curved ditch. On the bottom was the contracted burial of a young woman (cranial index about 66·6), lying on the left side with head to the east; a flat stone had been placed at each end of the body. A small stone hearth was in the upper filling of pit D. In pit G were hearths at two levels; in the lower filling black earth and ashes with a hearth of flat stones, and in the upper filling two burnt layers with stones set upright round the western half of the pit.

In the second group, four pits (H, K, L and M) were inside the eastern half of the circular hut; pit H had a large stone hearth across the top. Two large pits (J and N) had been cut across the filling of the drainage ditch, and pit O was outside the ditch to the south. Clearly occupation on this part of the site had continued in period I after the abandonment of the circular hut and the filling up of its drainage ditch.

Twelve pits were circular; the largest (N) was 7 ft 6 in. in diameter and 4 ft 3 in. deep, but the majority were 4 ft 6 in. to 5 ft in diameter and 1 ft 6 in. to 3 ft deep, Two were oval; pit L was 5 ft 6 in. by 3 ft 3 in. and 2 ft 9 in. deep, and pit K was only 3 ft 3 in. by 2 ft 6 in. and 1 ft deep.

B. *Period II*

The settlement of period I was abandoned; there was no evidence of violent destruction by burning. Since no turf-line had formed over the filled-in ditches and pits, this period was very soon if not immediately followed by period II. Excavation showed that period II was clearly divided into two phases, the first defensive and the second an open settlement.

1. *Phase i* (Fig. 5 and Pl. IV)

On the inside of the inner rampart a rectilinear area defined by straight ditches was cut off, demarcating a small enclosure. The main defence, towards the interior of Salmonsbury, was ditch 1; the trench, a sharp V in section, was 5 ft wide and 4 ft deep, with a slot 1 ft wide in the bottom for a timber palisade. Along part of the inner margin of the ditch was a line of vertical post-holes, presumably for a parapet on the inner side of the palisade. Ditch 1 was parallel to the inner rampart; it ended near the north side of Site III, but continued further south beyond the excavation.

On the west side the enclosure was limited by ditch 2, dug through the inner slope of the rampart into the gravel; it was 4 ft 6 in. wide and 3 ft 6 in. deep, and also had a slot 1 ft wide in the bottom.

Along the north side of the enclosure was ditch 3, about 3 ft wide and 1 ft deep, and flat on the bottom. At one end it joined ditch 1 in a series of enlargements, and at the other end passed towards the inner rampart. The excavation did not include the junction between this ditch and ditch 2.

As defined by the ditches, the enclosure was 40 ft wide from east to west; its length from north to south was 50 ft on Site III, but it extended further south beyond the limit of the excavation.

No hut-sites were present within the enclosure, although occupational debris of pottery and small finds occurred in the few inches of soil beneath the floor level of phase ii. The only structures, near the south side of the site, were two small hearths of baked clay, 1 ft 3 in. and 2 ft in diameter respectively.

The initial phase of period II clearly demonstrates the arrival of newcomers, who defended themselves by a palisaded enclosure on the inner side of the north-west ramparts of Salmonsbury. This period is Western Third C or "Belgic", and is defined by wheel-turned pottery and brooches. It begins early in the first century A.D., not before c A.D. 30.

2. *Phase ii* (Figs 5–6 and Pl. VI)

After the enclosure of phase i had been dismantled and its ditches backfilled, the whole area of Site III was covered by rough stone paving which formed the occupation surface in phase ii. The surface of this paving was only 6 to 9 in. above the ground level in phase i. The stone floor was very irregular in composition and density. In several places flat stones were laid close together to form paving a few feet across, but elsewhere the floor was very patchy and made of small stones.

Only one hut could certainly be identified, and possibly another. Hut 1, in the south-east part of the site, had a few feet of the surrounding stone wall, 2 to 3 ft thick, well preserved on the north-west side; the wall ended on the west side, presumably at the entrance. The rest of the wall was very patchy, or missing. A large post-hole, 1 ft 4 to 6 in. in diameter and 9 in. deep, lined with packing stones, was at the centre for the support of the roof. Its position gave a diameter of about 18 ft for the hut. Numerous pieces of burnt daub scattered on the floor indicate that the hut wall was of wattle and daub construction above the stone footing. Inside the hut was a small stone hearth. A few feet outside the hut to the west were two hearths; the larger was of baked clay, 3 ft by 4 ft, partly built up with stones, and the other was made of flat stones, 2 ft 3 in. by 1 ft 9 in.

The evidence is much slighter for hut 2, in the north-east part of the site. Several patches of stone appeared to belong to a circle about 18 ft in diameter, but no central post-hole could be found.

In the south-west part of the site were five post-holes in an almost straight line 16 ft long; each socket was bedded round with stones. The interior of this structure, possibly a shed, would be to the west where, 9 ft away, the lower part of a large pot containing raw clay was buried flush with the paving.

The remaining structure was 10 ft north of the storage pot, and near the western limit of the site. A double line of closely-set stone slabs, firmly bedded on edge, extended for a length of 5 ft 3 in. At each end and on the same side of the stones were post-holes. At the south end was one hole, 12 to 15 in. in diameter and 12 in. deep, with packing stones; and at the north end were two holes close together, one 10 in. in diameter and 11 in. deep and the other 9 in. in diameter and 9 in. deep, both with packing stones. It is difficult to suggest a purpose for this structure; possibly the post-holes held the firmly bedded uprights of a loom.

The latest feature of phase ii was pit 1, in the north-east corner of the site. It was oval in shape, 7 ft by 5 ft 3 in., and dug to a depth of 1 ft 6 in. below the Belgic paving. The contents comprised five pots of romanized Belgic forms and a sherd of samian form 29 (p. 105).

The dating of phase ii is given by finds of the early Roman period. In the back-filling of ditch 1 were two imported pots, a vessel of *Terra Nigra* (p. 103), and a hemispherical cup made at Lyons (p. 104). These date the beginning of phase ii to Claudian times, *c* A.D. 45. Although stratigraphically later, in pit 1 was a sherd of samian form 29, also Claudian. The latest find on the Belgic paving is a worn bronze coin of Claudius (p. 109); this is a copy probably minted in Britain in the early post-conquest period, and may not have been lost until *c* A.D. 60. Phase ii was thus of short duration, from *c* A.D. 45 down to *c* A.D. 50–55.

C. Roman Period

Subsequent occupation on Site III is shown by a ditch and a rubbish pit.

The ditch ran diagonally across the north-west corner of the site in a slightly curved direction. A length of about 25 ft was excavated, and to the east it passed outside the site. It was 6 ft wide and about 3 ft deep. The filling contained rather indeterminate sherds, probably late first century.

The large pit was in the south part of the site. It was oval, 12 ft by 8 ft, and 1 ft 6 in. deep. The contents included samian form 37, form 18/31 stamped by Suobnus, and form 33 stamped by Masuetus; sixteen pots of coarse ware; and among the objects of iron a knife, sickle and stilus.

Date: mid to late second century.

VI. Site IV

Near the middle of Salmonsbury an area 48 ft by 40 ft was excavated at the east end of the paddock of Camp House.

A. *Earlier Occupation* (Fig. 7)

Two ditches in line crossed the site in a north-south direction, with a gap of 9 ft between them. The north ditch passed across the middle of the Iron Age hut of period I; it had a short branch eastwards at the north end. The south ditch continued beyond the excavation. Both ditches were about 2 ft 3 in. wide and 1 ft deep. The ditches were filled with stiff red clay, but contained no finds. However, elsewhere on the site the old turf-line produced a leaf-shaped flint flake, partly retouched on both faces (Fig. 10, 3), which Dr. Isobel F. Smith suggests could be a rather small plano-convex knife of the Beaker period, and a transverse arrowhead of class 2 (Fig. 10, 4). The tanged arrowhead (Fig. 10, 5) was a stray find in the filling of the drainage ditch (south side) of the Iron Age hut. These finds suggest that the two ditches are late Neolithic or Early Bronze Age in date.

B. *Period I* (Fig. 8)

1. *Hut*

The hut was circular, 26 ft in diameter, with a ring of twelve post-holes round about two-thirds of the circumference. No post-holes were found in the gap 25 ft wide on the western side of the hut. At its centre were three post-holes for the roof posts. The drainage ditch round the outside of the hut was co-extensive with the post-holes; the ditch had been dug in three lengths, which overlapped at the ends. Outside the hut to the south-west were two stone hearths, both about 3 ft in diameter, one with a baked clay floor laid over a shallow scoop in the gravel.

From the middle of the gap in the western side of the hut a ditch ran outwards to the north-west and passed beyond the site. It was 3 ft 6 in. to 4 ft wide and about 2 ft 3 in. deep. In the filling was the skull of a young woman (cranial index 74·2), as well as numerous animal bones, a goat's skull and the lower jaw of a pike.

2. *Pits*

To the west of the hut were five circular pits, of which one cut into another. In two pits were contracted burials, which had been partly destroyed by the Roman ditch crossing this part of the site. The burial in pit B lay on the left side with the head end to the east; that in pit D, an adult woman, lay on the right side facing north, with the head also to the east.

C. *Period II*

Site IV was occupied to a slight extent in phase ii only of this period. Patches of stone paving were found in the south part of the site but no huts could be identified. The only structure was a stone hearth 1 ft 9 in. square. Belgic pottery was found in and near the hearth, and scattered elsewhere on the site.

D. *Roman Period* (Fig. 9)

The site was occupied both early and late in the Roman period.

1. *Ditch*

Running diagonally across the western part of the site from north-north-east to south-south-west was a straight ditch. It was excavated for 45 ft., and in both directions passed beyond the site. In section the ditch was V-shaped, originally 4 ft 6 in. wide, but it had remained open long enough for the upper part to erode to 6 ft wide; it was 2 ft 9 in. deep. The filling contained pottery of the late first century. Subsequently a pit about 8 ft by 4 ft had been dug into the upper filling of the ditch at the north end.

2. *Pit*

About 12 ft west of the ditch was a large oval pit, 9 ft by 5 ft 6 in. and 2 ft 3 in. deep. It contained pottery of the late first and early second centuries. Above the filling was a patch of stone paving on the same level as the stone floor described next.

3. *Stone floor*

Diagonally across the eastern part of the site, 15 ft from the ditch and in a north-east to south-west direction, was a long rectangular stone floor, roughly paved. Only the south-west corner of the floor was within the site, and near it was a large square post-hole, 1 ft 4 in. by 1 ft 6 in. and 1 ft 6 in. deep. The floor was uncovered for a length of 38 ft 6 in., but the north end lay beyond the site. Its width was 14 ft at the south end, and 13 ft at the other.

Beneath the floor were coins of Gallienus (A.D. 253–268) and a barbarous radiate, and third century pottery. On the floor were coins of Constantine I (A.D. 306–337), Constantius II (A.D. 324–361) and two of Valens (A.D. 364–378), and fourth century pottery.

VII. Site V: North-East Entrance

The entrance is in the middle of the north-east defences of Salmonsbury. It is marked by a gap in the ramparts and a causeway between the ends of the filled-in ditches. At each side a stone field-wall runs along the crest of the inner rampart.

An area 55 ft by 34 ft was excavated; it included the two ends of the inner rampart and was enlarged along the inner side of the banks to expose the returns of the revetment-walls.

1. *Inner rampart* (Fig. 10 and Pls VII–VIII)

The abutting ends of the inner rampart were stripped for 12 to 14 ft. They were built of gravel covering the old turf-line. Both ramparts had a terminal revetment-wall, well preserved on the west side but largely destroyed on the east side. The revetment-walls were 3 to 4 ft wide. At the inner ends both walls had a short spur wall projecting about 2 ft into the entrance. Along the inner side of the ramparts the revetment-walls were continued for at least 15 ft. That on the west had six courses remaining to a height of 7 in.; clay was packed between the stone slabs.

It should be recorded that about 100 ft west of the entrance, the revetment on the outer slope of the inner rampart was exposed for a length of 18 ft by Mr. J. Griffith Davies in 1949. The dry-built wall remained to a height of 3 ft 9 in. and had a slight batter; its width at the base could not be determined, but was more than 2 ft 7 in. (Pl. II).

2. *Entrance*

The entrance was 28 ft 6 in. wide between the terminal revetment-walls of the inner rampart. Its structural history is divided into three phases.

3. *Phase i* (Fig. 10 and Pl. III)

The surface of the passageway was formed by the old turf-line, which remained for a few feet on both sides beyond the revetment-walls of the inner rampart. The passage showed evidence of much usage, which had worn down the central part into a hollow in the gravel for a width of 16 to 20 ft and to a depth of 2 ft 3 in. below the original surface. This roadway showed no signs of repair. The southern part of the hollow was faintly grooved longitudinally by wheeled traffic.

The entrance was closed by gates across the inner and outer ends of the passageway. The evidence was more complete for the inner gates.

The post-holes for the inner gates were in the angles between the spur walls and the revetment. At each side of the entrance was a group of three post-holes. The largest was 10 in. in diameter and 6 to 8 in. deep, and close to it was a smaller hole on the inner side; the third post-hole was about 3 ft away towards the spur wall. The gates would be hung from posts in the largest sockets, the other holes being for struts to support the gate-post. The distance between the gate-posts was 24 ft, so that the gates must have closed against a post placed centrally in the entrance.

The outer gates were 16 ft in advance of the inner pair. On the west side the group of three post-holes remained; the largest, 1 ft 3 in. in diameter and 7 in. deep, was set partly into the revetment. On the opposite side of the entrance the largest post-hole was 10 in. in diameter and 6 in. deep, but only one other post-hole was located. The arrangement of the post-holes of the outer gateway showed that its gates opened outwards, and thus would act as barriers on each side of the causeway between the ends of the inner ditch.

The wearing down of the central part of the entrance eventually caused the collapse of the central posts, and thus led to the disuse and removal of the two pairs of gates.

It remains to mention two circular pits on the inner side of the entrance on the west side. Pit A was near the revetment-wall of the rampart, and thus well back from the passageway; it was 4 ft in diameter and 1 ft 8 in. deep. Pit B, about 12 ft from the revetment, was situated just within the edge of the worn-down roadway; its upper part had been removed by traffic. The pit was 5 ft in diameter and 3 ft 6 in. deep. Loose stones filled the bottom, and were covered by a layer of brown soil. The upper 2 ft of the pit was closely packed with stones to bring its top level with the hollow in the roadway.

From its position pit B clearly predates the use of the entrance. However, the form of both pits is precisely that of the numerous pits associated with the circular huts on Sites I, III and IV, and thus they probably belong to period I of the occupation of the camp.

4. *Phase ii* (Fig. 10 and Pl. VII)

The wearing down of the passageway, which caused the disuse of the gates across the entrance, determined the position and nature of the construction across the entrance in phase ii.

The northern end of the hollow was now blocked by a row of six large posts, closely set together. The overall length of this construction was 17 ft. The post-holes were subrectangular in shape, and in size varied from 1 ft 8 in. each way to 2 ft 6 in. by 2 ft 2 in.; the holes were 8 to 12 in. deep in the gravel. The four central holes contained many packing stones.

At each end of the row of posts there was a gap between them and the revetment-wall at each side. On the west side the gap was 6 ft 6 in. wide, and 5 ft 6 in. wide on the east side. The row of posts was in line with the larger post-holes for the outer gates of phase i, which thus probably remained in use and were hung with smaller gates.

The row of post-holes held substantial posts or piers, and though these might be regarded as simply blocking the entrance, a more convincing explanation is that the piers supported a timber bridge between the ends of the inner rampart. There is no evidence as to how the bridge was tied into the rampart at each end. A comparable bridge at least 30 ft in length crossed the inner entrance of Bredon Hill camp, Gloucestershire[14], and the reconstruction of another is published at Crickley Hill camp, near Cheltenham[15].

The date of phase ii is determined only relatively. It appears to belong to the latter part of the Iron Age occupation of the camp, either late in the first century B.C. or early in the first century A.D. In any case, the timber bridge had ceased to function some time before the late Roman period, when the soil above the filled in post-holes had accumulated to a depth of 2 ft above the middle of the hollow in the entrance.

5. *Phase iii* (Fig. 10 and Pl. VIII)

The final phase belongs to the late Roman period. The denudation of the inner rampart filled up the hollow in the entrance with 2 ft of brown soil and stones, on which a turf-line formed right across the entrance between the few remaining courses of the revetment-walls.

The filling contained fourth century pottery and the following third century brass coins; Constans (A.D. 337–342), ? Constantius II (A.D. 330–337), House of Constantine (A.D. 335–342), Constantius II or Constans (A.D. 345–361) and barbarous *Fel. Temp. Reparatio* (A.D. 345–361 or later).

A stone blocking-wall was built about mid-way across the entrance between the revetment-walls of the inner rampart. The footings of the wall were laid in the late Roman turf-line. The wall was about 2 ft wide, single on the west side and double on the east side, where one length may be a replacement of the other.

About 4 ft in front of the blocking-wall was a shorter wall, 12 ft long and 3 to 4 ft wide. The position of this wall corresponded roughly with the underlying row of post-holes of phase ii.

The pottery and coins in the filling of the entrance date the blocking-walls not earlier than the mid-fourth century. There seems to be no adequate context for them at a later date. The walls are thus to be associated with the late Roman occupation of Salmonsbury, for which the most substantial evidence found in the excavations was the stone floor on Site IV.

VIII. Sites VI and VII: Annexe

The rampart and ditch which prolong the north-east defences of Salmons-bury were examined at two places near the ends of the bank. At its western end the bank is in alignment with the outer rampart of the camp, but the relation is uncertain due to a gravel pit at the corner. Air photographs taken by the Royal Commission on Historical Monuments (England) suggest that the ditch was continuous with the outer ditch of the main defences.

[14] Hencken (1938), pp. 45–46, Pl. XXI.
[15] Dixon (1972), p. 50, Fig. 1.

A. Site VI

A section 6 ft wide and about 55 ft long was cut through the rampart and ditch.

1. Rampart

The bank was simple in construction, without a stone revetment-wall on the outer side. It was composed of three successive tips, forming a bank about 32 ft wide and 3 ft high. The first tip, towards the ditch, consisted of mixed clay and gravel dug from the surface outside the bank and partly from the ditch. The next tip overlapped the first on the inner side, and was gravel obtained by deepening the ditch. The third tip, similar in composition to the first, resulted from digging on the inner side of the bank. The first and second tips covered the old turf-line for a length of 22 ft; this was a layer about 3 in. thick of clay mixed with gravel, and overlay a thin black line with decayed vegetation.

2. Ditch

The ditch was 18 ft wide and only 2 ft 6 in. deep, flat along the bottom. It showed no stratification and was entirely filled with black mud, presumably once wet from the stream at present 6 ft beyond it.

No finds of Iron Age pottery were present in the bank or ditch. Only a flint scraper was found in the upper part of the second tip of the bank, and the base of a Romano-British pot just above the mud filling the ditch.

B. Site VII

A section 6 ft wide and 50 ft long, near the east end of the bank, produced results similar to those on Site VI.

1. Rampart

The greater part of the bank, 3 ft high, was made up of two tips of clay covering the old land surface for 22 ft. The larger tip, on the outer side of the bank, was overlaid by a lenticular mass of sandy gravel dug from the lower part of the ditch. The hollow left between the tips of clay was levelled up with more sandy gravel. Finally, a cavity in the inner slope of the bank was filled with clayey gravel derived from surface scraping. The overall width of the bank was thus about 26 ft.

2. Ditch

The ditch, not so well defined as on Site VI, was a wide, shallow scoop in the gravel. It was about 20 ft wide and 1 ft 6 in. deep at the most; again, the filling was black mud.

There were no finds in the bank or the ditch.

3. *Burial*

On the outer slope of the rampart a burial had been made in the brown soil covering the lenticular mass of sandy gravel. The skeleton, in poor condition, was contracted, lying on the right side with head to the south-east. No grave-goods accompanied the burial. In this respect and in its flexed position it conforms with the burials in the pits on Sites II, III and IV, and on these grounds the burial is referred to period I of the Iron Age occupation.

IX. Pottery

A. Period I

The pottery of period I was found in the drainage ditches of the huts and in the pits on Sites I, II, III and IV. It may be divided into three classes: (1) with curvilinear decoration, (2) with linear decoration, and (3) plain wares. In the absence of stratified deposits on any of the sites it would be premature to sub-divide the pottery of period I; in any case it appears that all three classes of the pottery were in use throughout this period.

The pottery belongs to the Western Second B culture, for which Salmonsbury is the type site on the east side of the Cotswolds. It may here be noted that the stamp-decoration (so-called "duck" motif and its derivatives) of Western Third B pottery is entirely absent from period I at Salmonsbury, neither is there any hint of its influence.

1. *Curvilinear decoration* (Fig. 12)

The forms comprise wide-mouthed globular bowls (nos 1–3 and 6–8), mostly with highly burnished surface. The decoration is in shallow lines and girth-grooves, rounded in section, made by blunt-ended tools. The patterns range from simple arcs, sometimes of two lines with hatched lines between (nos. 3–4) to complex interlocking semicircles and swags (no. 1). Usually the decoration is in a single zone, but on one bowl (no. 1) it is arranged in two zones. Dimples are combined with the curvilinear decoration on some bowls (nos 1 and 3), but also occur alone on one bowl (no. 8). In addition, on three pots distinctive in style (nos 5–7), the dimples are surrounded by concentric circles of dots forming a rosette pattern, connected by arcs.

General parallels for the motifs and patterns on the Salmonsbury bowls exist over a wide area of the Iron B culture, from Glastonbury in the south-west to Hunsbury in the north-east. It would, however, serve little purpose to quote parallels extensively but with slight direct relevance.

The form of the globular bowls, without a distinctive neck, is close to those at Hunsbury, on which the curvilinear decoration, though different in character, is also arranged in two or even three zones[16]. More immediately, the interlocking semicircles on no. 1 are matched almost exactly on the globular bowl from Frilford, Berkshire[17]. The technique of the infilled semicircles and swags on nos. 1 and 4 is also comparable with the decoration on another globular bowl from Frilford and that from Yarnton, Oxfordshire[18]. Although less determinate, the narrow hatched band above the curvilinear pattern on no. 2 is also in the same position on the three bowls just mentioned.

It thus appears that stylistically some of the Salmonsbury bowls are most closely linked with the more highly decorated pottery of the Upper Thames region. The motifs and techniques of this region evidently formed a major element of the curvilinear-decorated pottery of the eastern Cotswolds.

The unique saucepan pot (no. 10) is to be associated with this form over a wide area of Southern England and Wessex and, marginally to the main incidence, the Upper Thames region[19]. The panel of symmetrical, waisted curvilinear decoration, outlined by fine dots, could be a simplified or debased version of the patterns on metalwork[20].

It has long been recognised that an Armorican element is present in Western Second B pottery. At Salmonsbury this is strikingly demonstrated by the dimples surrounded by circles of dots on three pots (nos 5–7). For these and the arcs of dots connecting the dimples there are close analogies in Brittany, on the pots from Ploemeur (in the St. Germain Museum) and Bignan, Morbihan[21]. The persistence of this Breton "metal" style as late as the first century B.C. in the Cotswolds is noteworthy.

1. Globular bowl of fine brown ware with sparse shell. Highly burnished reddish-brown surface. Three wide girth-grooves below the rim. The decoration is in two zones. Upper zone: alternating semicircles hatched vertically with dimples in the voids, each outlined by two concentric circles. Lower zone: interlocking semicircles hatched with short lines. Site III, pit L (body) and pit M (rim).

2. Bowl of fine brown ware with sparse shell. Highly burnished reddish-brown surface. Two wide girth-grooves below the rim and between zones of decoration. Upper zone: short hatched lines. Lower zone: curvilinear pattern hatched vertically. Site III, ditch in north-eastern corner of site.

3. Globular bowl of grey ware with pounded stone and shell. Burnished grey surface. Everted rounded rim. Two wide girth-grooves above and one below decoration. Arc pattern with dimple in upper space. Site III, ditch in entrance of hut.

[16] Fell (1936), p. 74, Fig. 6.
[17] Harding (1972), p. 107, Pl. 67, F.
[18] Harding (1972), Pl. 76, E and Pl. 68, F.
[19] Harding (1972), p. 115, Pl. 7 and Pl. 66.
[20] Grimes (1952), p. 170.
[21] Déchelette (1927), p. 976, Fig. 665, 4–5.

4. Sherd of grey ware with sparse shell. Burnished light brown surface. Curvilinear pattern hatched with short lines. Site I, pit Q.

5. Bowl of black ware with shell. Burnished light brown surface. The rim has been broken off and the fracture trimmed roughly level. Six dimples on the shoulder, each outlined by one or two concentric circles of dots, and connected by arcs of dots. Site III, inside ditch on northern side of site.

6. Small globular bowl of brownish-grey ware with much fine shell. Burnished dark grey surface, slightly soapy. Two wide girth-grooves on shoulder, below dimple outlined by two concentric circles of dots. Site I, hut 1, drainage ditch, northern side.

7. Sherd of grey ware with shell. Burnished brownish-grey surface. Large dimple, outlined by two concentric circles of dots, and part of double arc of dots. Site I, pit K.

8. Globular bowl of light grey-brown ware with shell. Burnished surface, grey on upper part, brown to red below shoulder. Rim everted and rounded. The hole in the base was made before firing. Eight shallow dimples round shoulder. Site I, hut 2, drainage ditch, southern side.

9. Sherd of grey ware with sparse large shell. Burnished buff surface. Rim inturned, with finger-nail marks on inner slope. Angular shoulder just below rim. Double arcs of finely incised lines. Site III, pit N.

10. Saucepan pot of fine grey sandy ware. Burnished dark grey surface. Two narrow girth-grooves below rim. Symmetrical, waisted curvilinear decoration, bordered with small dots. Garden of Camp House, chance find.

2. *Linear decoration and handled pots* (Fig. 13)

Small globular bowls, with the rim either vertical and rounded (no. 1) or everted (no. 2). The form of no. 1, though thicker walled and more squat, and the narrow zone of infilled lines below the rim, clearly relate this pot to the globular bowls of finer ware (cf. Fig. 11, 1–2). On the other hand the bowls with geometric decoration of hatched triangles (nos 2–3), very lightly incised, could represent influence from South-Western Second B, or even be derived ultimately from Iron A in Wessex or the Upper Thames region. The everted rim on no. 2 and the wide girth-grooves on no. 3 are perhaps more in favour of the first alternative. The bluntly-tooled girth-grooves and chevrons on no. 4 are evidently the more usual version of this tradition in the Cotswolds.

A number of pots of thicker and coarser ware are of different forms, sub-globular (nos 5–6) or more straight-sided with a distinct angular shoulder (no. 7). On these pots the body is finely striated vertically. The surface treatment of these pots again suggests the survival of a technique derived from earlier Iron Age cultures.

Bowls and jars with pierced handles on the shoulder (nos 8–9) have the rims either everted or thickened internally. The handles are not countersunk on the inside of the pot. This form of handle appears to be characteristic of Western Second B pottery in the Cotswolds.

1. Small globular bowl of thick grey ware with sparse shell. Burnished light brown surface with reddish tones. Narrow incised girth-grooves below rim, hatched in upper part. Site I, hut 1, drainage ditch, western side.

2. Small bowl of grey sandy ware. Burnished brown-grey surface. Rim rounded and everted. Zone of lightly incised shaded triangles. Site I, hut 1, drainage ditch, western side.

3. Small bowl of grey ware with fine shell. Burnished buff surface. Zone of lightly incised shaded triangles, very neatly made, between wide girth-grooves. Site II, unassociated.

4. Large bowl of light brown-grey sandy ware. Burnished dark grey surface. Rim rounded and everted. Zone of bluntly tooled chevrons between wide girth-grooves. Site III, ditch in south western part of site.

5. Large sub-globular pot of coarse grey ware with shell. Rough surface, light red with grey tones. Tooled round rim and striated vertically on body. Site II, unassociated.

6. Small globular pot of coarse grey ware with sparse shell. Upright rim, pinched thin. Grey-brown surface, striated vertically on body. Site III, pit D.

7. Small pot of coarse grey ware with much shell. Rough surface, greyish-brown with light red tones. Rim rounded, with bevel on inside. Well-marked angular shoulder, below which the surface is striated vertically. Site IV, hut, hearth 2.

8. Bowl or jar of coarse grey ware with sparse grits. Light reddish-brown surface. Rim rounded, thickened on inside. Pierced handles on shoulder. Site IV, hut, hearth 1.

9. Bowl of grey ware with fine shell. Tooled brown-grey surface. Rim everted. Pierced handles on shoulder. Site I, hut 2, drainage ditch, southern side.

3. *Plain wares* (Fig. 14)

The plain coarse wares show a range of forms, some but not all represented among the finer decorated pots. Nos 1 and 2 are probably the most frequent shapes; for both there are parallels in the Upper Thames region[22], although of course these rather undifferentiated forms occur over a wider area.

The two bowls (nos. 3–4) both with thin everted rims, and a change in profile between the neck and rounded shoulder, are difficult to parallel elsewhere. They thus appear to be a local form in the Cotswolds.

The form of no. 5 relates it to the striated pot (Fig. 13, 5), though its rim is more inbent and simply rounded.

More conical forms with a high, rounded shoulder are represented by nos 6–7. The rims are pinched thin and rounded (no. 6), or thicker and beaded (no. 7).

1. Pot of grey ware with sparse fine shell. Burnished buff surface, grey

[22] Harding (1972), Pl. 61, G, Pl. 63, R and Pl. 65. E.

toned on upper part. Rim vertical, thin and rounded. The three holes in the base were made before firing. Site IV, hut, drainage ditch, southern side.

2. Tub-shaped pot of coarse black ware with sparse shell. Rough surface, buff with grey and red tones. Rim vertical and rounded. Site IV, hut, drainage ditch, southern side.

3. Small bowl of coarse grey ware with much fine shell. Smooth brown-grey surface. Rim everted, thin and rounded. Upright neck above rounded shoulder. Site III, pit E.

4. Larger bowl of reddish-brown ware with much fine shell. Smooth dark grey surface. Rim as no. 3. Upright tall neck above more pronounced shoulder. Site III, pit O.

5. Large sub-globular or ovoid pot of coarse grey ware with much shell. Rough brownish-grey surface. Rim inbent and rounded. Edge of base slightly projecting. Site III, hut, drainage ditch, northern side.

6. Pot of grey ware with shell. Smooth brown-grey surface. Conical form with high rounded shoulder. Rim thin and rounded. The base was made separately, with an overlapping join on to the side. Site I, hut 1, drainage ditch, northern side.

7. Pot of coarse black ware with shell. Smooth grey-brown surface. Conical form with high rounded shoulder. Rim beaded and angular outside. Site I, pit Q.

B. Period II

1. *Western Second B* (Fig. 15)

At Salmonsbury the Western Second B tradition continued with only slight change into Period II on Sites III and IV. The pottery of native ancestry is still hand-made with burnished or tooled surface. In technique the decorative motifs are carried out, as in Period I, in bluntly tooled girth-grooves and lines (nos 2–3), narrow incised lines (nos 1, 4–5), and very lightly incised fine lines (no. 6). The lattice pattern on no. 3 and the hatched arcs on no. 6 were, however, incised after firing.

Derivatives of the saucepan type persist, with rounded profile and short everted rims (nos 1–2). The zone of arcs and swags on these pots may be compared with examples at Lydney[23], and Llanmelin[24] in South Wales.

The decoration on the other pots is still simple in character, and limited to the upper part of the body; lattice pattern (no. 4), triangles hatched in alternate directions (no. 5), and small chevrons in two zones (no. 7). There is only one example of a dimple in this period (no. 3), in contrast to its greater frequency in Period I (cf. Fig. 12, 1, 3, 5–8).

The plain pot (no. 8), with angular moulding on the neck and recurved profile, probably shows the influence of a metallic form.

[23] Wheeler and Wheeler (1932), pp. 93–95, Fig. 24 and Fig. 25, 19–20.
[24] Nash-Williams (1933), p. 292, Fig. 43, 39.

Pots with pierced handles also continued into Period II. A large example with rim section like Fig. 13, 9 was found in the makeup of the phase ii paving on Site III.

The pots with burnished vertical lines on the body (nos 9–10) are an innovation in Period II and occur in both phases. In style and technique the burnishing compares closely with that on the hand-made Malvernian ware of the first and second centuries A.D.[25]. At Salmonsbury, however, these pots are half a century earlier than the Malvernian counterparts. Moreover the rims, instead of being expanded or beaded as in the later series, are simply everted and rounded as present already in Period I at Salmonsbury (cf. Fig. 13, 4). Dr. D. P. S. Peacock, of the Department of Archaeology, University of Southampton, has kindly examined a rim sherd with burnished lines and other sherds from Salmonsbury and reports as follows. "There is not much to say about the source of the raw materials beyond suggesting a local, that is, Cotswold source. The sherds contain either shell or limestone grits, and of course it is not possible to tie down these materials closely. I can see nothing that resembles the Malvernian wares, but this I would expect anyway, as they do not seem to have travelled further east than the western edge of the Cotswolds."

On stylistic and petrological grounds the Salmonsbury pots with burnished line decoration are thus to be regarded as the late Iron Age prototypes of Malvernian ware. The later series includes debased forms of the saucepan type, and bead-rim bowls which could be derived from the Belgic Dobunnic forms in the Cotswolds (see p. 100). Mention may here be made of an associated group of pots found in the filling of a small pit at Eastington in the south Cotswolds (in the Stroud Museum). The group included three pots with burnished line decoration, in form and rim sections exactly matching the Salmonsbury examples, and a large pot with two pierced handles comparable with those of Periods I and II at Salmonsbury.

Numbers 1–6 and 8 are from Site III, phase i, below paving; and nos 7 and 9–10 are from Site III, phase ii, on paving.

1. Saucepan pot of dark grey ware with sparse stone grits. Burnished black surface. Rim everted and rounded. Zone of deeply incised double arcs between double girth-grooves.

2. Saucepan pot of grey ware with small stone grits. Burnished dark grey surface. Small rounded rim, slightly everted. Zone of bluntly tooled swags between girth-grooves.

3. Squat wide-mouthed bowl of light brown ware with small stone grits. Highly burnished surface, light brown with grey tones. Rim angular outside and hollowed on inside. Two bluntly tooled girth-grooves on shoulder, above widely spaced dimples. Above the grooves is a zone of lattice pattern incised after firing.

4. Bowl of coarse grey ware with small stone grits and shell. Burnished surface, buff with light red tones. The rim was everted. Wide zone of incised lattice pattern between girth-grooves.

[25] Peacock (1967), p. 15, Fig. 1, 1–12.

5. Upper part of bowl of light reddish-brown ware with sparse shell. Burnished black surface. Rim rounded and slightly everted. Zone of lightly incised triangles, hatched horizontally and vertically alternatively, between girth-grooves.

6. Bowl of grey-brown ware with small stone grits. Burnished black surface. Rim everted, angular outside. Narrow girth-grooves bordering hatched arcs, the latter lightly incised after firing.

7. Small bowl of grey ware with sparse shell. Tooled brown-grey surface. Rim rounded and everted. Two zones of chevrons between girth-grooves.

8. Wide-mouthed bowl of coarse grey ware with sparse shell. Burnished grey surface, buff below shoulder, Rim rounded and everted. Angular moulding on neck, above bluntly tooled girth-grooves. Bulging shoulder and profile recurved on lower part.

9. Pot of light brown ware with small stone grits. Tooled grey surface. Rim rounded and everted. Burnished lines horizontally below neck and vertically on body.

10. Pot of coarse black ware with sparse stone grits. Tooled black surface with light brown tones. Rim rounded and everted. Burnished lines as on no. 9, but near vertical on body. A sherd with similar rim section and burnished lines was found on Site III, ditch 1 and another in ditch 3, both of phase i; also on Site IV, near the phase ii hearth.

2. *Western Third C* (Figs 15–17)

The Western Third C pottery found at Salmonsbury on Sites III and IV demonstrates the arrival of Belgic culture, based on the Dobunnic capital at Bagendon, and the expansion of that kingdom in a north-easterly direction along the eastern side of the Cotswolds (Salmonsbury is 13 miles north-east of Bagendon). At Salmonsbury this occupation is characterised by an abundance of wheel-turned pottery of Belgic forms; imported Gallo-Belgic *Terra Nigra* and early Roman wares (pp. 103–104); brooches of Belgic types (p. 105); and by two Dobunnic silver coins (p. 108), one of Class C in a ditch of phase i, and the other of Class G inscribed ANTED found above the paving of phase ii, and thus stratified in the right chronological order.

As yet Salmonsbury is the major site in the Cotswolds to produce evidence of settlement in the Belgic Dobunnic period. It is important, therefore, to define the chronological relationship with Bagendon. The occupation of Bagendon is divided into four periods[26]. The initial date is uncertain, but is placed *c* A.D. 10, and in any case within the first two decades of the first century A.D. The lower terminal date is late Claudian to Neronian, *c* A.D. 50–60. At Salmonsbury, judging by the brooches and the scarcity or absence of the later imported pottery at Bagendon, Period II appears to start rather later than Bagendon and to terminate slightly earlier. The Belgic occupation of Salmonsbury is therefore provisionally dated from *c* A.D. 30 down to *c* A.D. 50–55; that is, in round terms to cover the second quarter of the first century A.D.

[26] Clifford (1961), pp. xvii-xix.

At Salmonsbury the most frequent form of Belgic Dobunnic pottery is the necked bowl with a low foot-ring, usually decorated with cordons and girth-grooves (Fig. 16, 3, Fig. 17, 1–4 and Fig. 18, 6). Examples were found on Site III, phases i and ii, and on Site IV, phase ii. This is form 122 at Bagendon[27], where on the whole the bowls have less elaborate cordons. A variant of this type with plain rim and high shoulder (Fig. 16, 4) corresponds with form 126 at Bagendon[28].

Another leading form is the carinated bowl or cup, present in various sizes, with one to three cordons above the angular shoulder and a slight foot-ring (Fig. 16, 1–2, Fig. 17, 8 and Fig. 18, 4). This also occurred on Site III in phases i and ii. Form 107 at Bagendon[29], but not numerous there.

The bead-rim bowls (Fig. 16, 6 and Fig. 18, 9) have a well-developed rim and a high rounded shoulder. Examples were on Site III, phases i and ii, and on Site IV, phase ii. Forms 146 to 152 at Bagendon[30], where it is abundant, sometimes in Romanized grey ware as in phase ii at Salmonsbury.

Native butt-beakers (Fig. 16, 5 and Fig. 18, 1–3) were found on Site III, phases i and ii, and on Site IV, phase ii. The only rim is simple and everted. The form is distinctly globular, with large cordons, and the body is rouletted or striated horizontally. Forms 58 to 62 at Bagendon[31].

Pedestal bases are uncommon (Fig. 17, 5–6), and occurred only on Site III, phase ii. The bases are of the flat type, sealed at the lower end, and apparently belonged to tazzas rather than pedestal urns. The high cylindrical form of no. 5 is, in fact, exactly paralleled on the globular tazza dated c A.D. 30–40 at Hurstbourne Tarrant, Hampshire[32].

The tankard (Fig. 16, 7) on Site III, phase i, is apparently not represented at Bagendon. This is primarily a Durotrigian form[33], present in the Belgic period at Maiden Castle[34]. The side of the Salmonsbury tankard is, however, incurved and so more akin to one at Colchester[35].

Wide-mouthed jars with striated surface (Fig. 17, 10–11) were only on Site III, phase ii. One rim, no. 10, is rounded and everted in the local tradition, and no. 11 is thickened and angular outside. The type is not represented at Bagendon; the closest parallels, with more emphatic combing or rilling, are at Prae Wood, Verulamium[36], and form 260A at Camulodunum[37].

A small biconical cup (Fig. 18, 5) was on Site III, phase ii. It resembles form 96 at Bagendon[38], but without the foot-ring.

[27] Fell (1961), p. 237, Fig. 66, also Figs 52–53.
[28] Fell (1961), p. 238, Fig. 66, also Fig. 60.
[29] Fell (1961), p. 235, Fig. 65, also Figs 52 and 60.
[30] Fell (1961), p. 240, Fig. 67, also Figs 54 and 60.
[31] Fell (1961), p. 224, Fig. 63, also Fig. 50.
[32] Hawkes and Dunning (1930), p. 306, Fig. 32, 1.
[33] Brailsford (1958), pp. 104 and 118, list.
[34] Wheeler (1943), p. 233, Fig. 72, 185 and Fig. 74, 227.
[35] Hull (1958), p. 282, Fig. 118, 121.
[36] Wheeler and Wheeler, (1936), p. 166, Figs 19-21.
[37] Hawkes and Hull (1947), p. 270, Pl. LXXXII.
[38] Fell (1961), p. 232. Fig. 65, also Fig. 52.

The only example of a platter (Fig. 18, 7) was found on Site IV, phase ii. The vertical rim and the profile are paralleled by one of the native platters, form 17, at Bagendon[39].

The large jar with wide cordon below the neck (Fig. 18, 8) was also on Site IV, phase ii. It is comparable with cordoned pots at Verulamium[40], and form 232 at Camulodunum[41].

Finally, the only sherd certainly of a jug (Fig. 20, 3) was on Site III, phase i. It is probably from a two-handled jug, copying form 163 at Camulodunum[42] and represented by form 72 at Bagendon[43].

In the range of types the pottery at Salmonsbury is thus closely comparable with the native Belgic wares at Bagendon, mainly in Periods II to IV there. It seems reasonable that the bulk if not all of the native Belgic pottery at Salmonsbury was imported to this site, and not made in the locality. At Bagendon it is considered that "the pottery was made somewhere close by or on the site", since some of it shows defective potting[44]. It is therefore suggested that the kilns, not yet located, that supplied pottery to Bagendon also sent their products to Salmonsbury. This would be a rational economic connexion between the two sites. However, at Salmonsbury there are differences, both in fabric and in the details of the forms, that point to another source within the Dobunnic kingdom which did not supply the capital. It may be added that one other Cotswold site, Hawkesbury, near Chipping Sodbury (20 miles south-west of Bagendon), has produced Belgic pottery. This is a chance find, the upper part of a necked bowl similar to Fig. 16, 4 (in the Gloucester Museum).

Apart from Bagendon, the nearest parallels for the Salmonsbury pottery are at the Belgic settlements in the Upper Thames region. In this area the necked bowl with a low foot-ring is the most frequent type, and the assemblage, although somewhat limited in range, includes carinated and cordoned bowls, bead-rim bowls or jars, butt-beakers and platters[45]. The pottery of Belgic character has been found on sites almost exclusively to the north of the Thames and to the west of the Cherwell in Oxfordshire. The distribution suggests that this region formed a corridor between, on the one hand, the Catuvellauni to the east, and on the other hand, the Belgic Dobunni to the west. It may be noted that in this area late Belgic kilns existed at Hanborough, Oxfordshire, for the supply of local needs.

C. Site III, phase i (Fig. 16)

1. Carinated bowl of black ware. Concave sided, with two narrow cordons. Burnished surface above and below cordons, matt between. Ditch 3.

---

[39] Fell (1961), p. 218, Fig. 61.
[40] Wheeler and Wheeler (1936), p. 163, Fig. 16, 45–46.
[41] Hawkes and Hull (1947), p. 263, Pl. LXXIX.
[42] Hawkes and Hull (1947), p, 248, Pls LXIV–LXV.
[43] Fell (1961), p. 229, Fig. 63, 72.
[44] Clifford (1961), p. 152.
[45] Harding (1972), pp. 118–123, Pls. 8–9 and 69–72, and Fig. 9.

2. Carinated bowl of grey ware. Burnished black surface. Concave sided, with three narrow cordons. Ditch 1, upper filling.

3. Necked bowl of grey ware. Burnished black surface. Three girth-grooves on lower part. Ditch 3.

4. Necked bowl of grey ware. Burnished black surface. Beaded rim on straight neck, and high shoulder. Ditch 3.

5. Butt-beaker of grey ware. Burnished surface with red slip outside and inside. Rim rounded and everted. Two wide cordons on side. Ditch 3.

6. Bead-rim bowl of light grey ware. Darker grey surface. Ditch 1, upper filling.

7. Tankard of grey ware. Burnished light brown surface. Wide girth-groove below rim. Slightly concave sided. Ditch 1, lower filling.

3. Rim of light grey ware. (Fig. 19). Dark grey surface. Large flange, under-cut below. Two girth-grooves on outside of flange, and one on inner slope of rim. Probably from a wide mouthed jug with two handles. Ditch 1, lower filling.

D. Site III, phase ii, below paving (Fig. 17)

1. Necked bowl of light grey ware. Burnished brown surface. Rolled rim. Cordon below neck, carinated shoulder with recessed cordon, and two girth-grooves on lower part. Low foot-ring.

2. Necked bowl of grey ware. Burnished grey surface. Expanded rim. Wide and narrow cordons below neck, and two zones of shallow girth-grooves on lower part.

3. Necked bowl of grey ware with red slip outside. Burnished black surface. Offset below neck, wide girth-groove on shoulder, and two matt zones on lower part.

4. Necked bowl of grey ware with light brown slip outside. Cordon below neck, and four girth-grooves on lower part. Low foot-ring.

5. Pedestal base of light grey ware. Burnished light brown surface. Cylindrical foot, sealed at the lower end. Spiral groove on underside of base. The completed drawing suggests that the base belonged to a globular tazza.

6. Pedestal base of grey ware. Burnished brown-grey surface. Girth-groove above the foot-ring.

7. Conical bowl or cup of brown ware with light red slip. Burnished surface, striated horizontally.

8. Carinated cup of grey ware. Burnished black surface. Concave sided, with one cordon. Low foot-ring. Two similar cups were found at the same level.

9. Wide-mouthed jar of grey ware with shell. Light brown surface. Rolled rim, grooved on top.

10. Wide-mouthed jar of light brown ware. Rim thickened and angular outside. Offset below neck. Surface lightly striated horizontally.

11. Wide-mouthed jar of coarse grey ware with sparse stone grits. Rim rounded and everted. Surface lightly striated horizontally.

1–6, Site III, phase ii, on paving; 7–9, Site IV, phase ii. (Fig. 18).

1. Butt-beaker of buff ware with light red slip. Angular cordons and zones of rouletting.

2. Butt-beaker of light grey ware with light red slip. Rounded cordons and zones striated horizontally.

3. Butt-beaker of light grey ware. Dark grey surface. Large rounded cordons and zones of rouletting. The upper part of the pot had been broken off, and then reused by smoothing the edge above the upper cordon.

4. Carinated bowl of light grey ware. Burnished black surface. Two cordons on upper part. Below the marked carination the surface is matt, with three girth-grooves.

5. Small biconical cup of black ware with sparse stone grits. Burnished brown-grey surface.

6. Necked bowl of black ware. Burnished black surface. Cordon and girth-grooves below neck. Four zones of narrow girth-grooves on lower part. Low foot-ring.

7. Platter of light grey ware. Burnished grey surface. Vertical rim above angular moulding. Two girth-grooves on lower part. Girth-groove and rouletting on inside of base.

8. Storage jar of light grey ware with black stone grits. Moulded rim, vertical outside. Wide angular cordon below neck. Zone of lattice pattern made by a serrated tool, between girth-grooves.

9. Bead-rim bowl of light grey ware. Matt grey surface, burnished below rim. Other examples were found on Site III, phase ii, below and on paving.

3. *Imported Gallo-Belgic Terra Nigra.* (Fig. 20, 1 and Pl. IX. Site III, ditch 1, on bottom)

Vessel of fine grey ware with highly burnished grey surface. The pot has a thin rounded rim and a conical neck with a band of fine rouletting. The body is defined above by a cordon and below by an offset. The surface of the body is fluted vertically; along the upper side is a line of incised dots as setting-out marks, and the decoration was then made by paring down the surface in parallel grooves. The base is a low pedestal, with moulded edge undercut on the upper side.

Mr. Kevin T. Greene, of the Department of Adult Education, University of Newcastle, has kindly commented as follows:

Direct parallels for the vessel are not forthcoming, but it may be suggested that various features indicate an origin in Gallia Belgica or the Lower Rhineland. By continental standards it falls within the definition of *Terra Nigra*; the term is more freely applied there than in Britain, where it is restricted to platters or occasionally to bowls[46]. Thus, jars or beakers in related fabrics have been rather overlooked in this country. An obvious *Terra Nigra* beaker form is the biconical Camulodunum form 120A[47], with its plain mouth and moderately

[46] Behrens (1912), p. 101, abb. 10 gives a good idea of the range of *Terra Nigra* vessels.
[47] Hawkes and Hull (1947), p. 241, Pl. LVIII.

elaborate base, sometimes stamped. The smoothly curving neck without any rim moulding, the foot-ring, and the highly burnished surface relate this form to the Salmonsbury vessel in general terms. An example from Nidmegen has a particularly similar profile[48].

The technique of the decoration on the body of the Salmonsbury vessel is difficult to parallel, but the vertical flutings recall many Rhineland vessels in *Terra Nigra*, where they are executed *en barbotine*[49]. The form of the base, sometimes undercut on the upper side, is also known on Gallo-Belgic vessels in the same region[50].

Thus it is suggested that the three main features of the Salmonsbury vessel—the smoothly curving neck, the vertical flutings on the body, and the low pedestal base—point to a continental origin, most probably in the Lower Rhine or its hinterland. These cannot be paralleled together on single vessels there, it is true; but considering in addition the distinctive fabric and probable Claudian date, an alternative origin is difficult to envisage.

4. *Imported cup made at Lyons* (Fig. 20, 2. Site III, ditch 1, upper filling)

Hemispherical cup of pale cream ware with a faint greenish tinge. Both surfaces have a greenish-brown colour-coating; the inside has rough-cast sand. On the outside is a small cordon below the rim. The side is decorated *en barbotine* with a running design of leaf-buds on stems, isolated leaf-buds, and lines of dots.

Mr. Kevin T. Greene has also identified this cup and commented on it:

The fabric and surface coating of this cup place it among the products of an industry located at Lyons, probably at a site named La Butte, which made drinking cups, beakers, and moulded volute-lamps[51]. Elsewhere I have discussed the products of this industry and their dating; the production period seems to have been *c* A.D. 40–70[52].

However, the decoration of the Salmonsbury cup cannot be paralleled on any other Lyons cups. Moreover it is unusual in being executed *en barbotine,* in contrast to the applied technique used for such decoration as the scales, berries, etc., that are commonly found on cups in this ware. But the decoration is paralleled on colour-coated drinking vessels made in the province of Baetica, Southern Spain. These are characterized by free-hand barbotine designs of leaves, tendrils and dots. An identical use of pointed leaves on stems combined with lines of dots occurs on several vessels[53].

The Spanish ware is not precisely dated, but its period of production certainly overlapped that of Lyons ware. In the Claudian-Neronian period it dominated the fine ware market of Gallia Narbonensis. The trade also reached some forts on the Rhine and Danube, presumably by way of the Rhône corridor. Spanish vessels were thus familiar to potters working at Lyons, the great centre for trade from the Western Mediterranean to the Rhine-Danube area.

Apart from the Salmonsbury cup, I know of only three other vessels which imitate Spanish types; two come from Vindonissa and one from Lyons itself. All three copy a cylindrical beaker, both in form and simple decoration of large conical points[54], neither of which formed part of the normal range of Lyons products. The Salmonsbury cup differs in that its form is perfectly normal for Lyons[55]; whereas Spanish cups have different rims, with

[48] Stuart (1962), Pl. 18, 277.
[49] Ritterling (1913), taf. X, 113; Behrens, 1912, abb. 10, 19.
[50] Göse (1950), types 313–316.
[51] Lasfargues (1972), p. 17.
[52] Greene K. T. (1972), pp. 1–2, Figs 1–4.
[53] Greene, K. T. (1972), pp. 7–9, Fig. 8, in particular No. 6.
[54] Greene, K. T. (1972), Fig. 8, No. 9.
[55] Compare with profiles in Greene, K. T. (1972), Fig. 1, Nos 1.4, 2.4, 3.1 and 4.1.

girth-grooves but no cordon[56]. Furthermore, the more elaborate barbotine patterns do not occur on small cups, but on larger bowls or cylindrical beakers; the cups usually have simpler decoration of scales, dots, or other recurrent motifs.

5. *Contents of pit* 1 (p. 86) (Fig. 19 and Fig. 20, 4)

Figure 18. Nos 1 to 4 are of types which occur earlier in Period II at Salmonsbury. However, in two respects they differ slightly from the main series. The fabric is uniformly grey and fired harder, and the foot-rings (nos 1 and 3) are low and devolved. These differences point to another source for some of the pots of phase ii and to some degree of Romanization, both in fabric and form. No. 5, not represented earlier, is early Roman in character.

1. Necked bowl of grey ware. Burnished buff surface. Devolved foot-ring.

2. Carinated bowl of grey ware. Burnished light red surface, tooled below shoulder. Upper part incurved, with wide angular cordon.

3. Cup of grey ware. Light red surface, burnished on upper part. Low foot-ring.

4. Bead-rim bowl of coarse grey ware with stone grits. Matt grey surface, burnished above shoulder.

5. Small jar of light grey ware. Dark grey surface. Wide girth-groove on shoulder.

Figure 20, 4. Sherd of early South Gaulish samian, form Dr. 29 with good matt gloss. Upper frieze with scroll decoration. The scroll terminates in small double circles, which are repeated in the field.

Dr. Grace Simpson kindly reports as follows:

Although I know of no exact parallel to the design, there are three features in the decoration which support an attribution to the Claudian period, rather than to any other time:

1. The beads on either side of the central moulding were impressed over a guide-line. This is very uncommon, but see Knorr (1912), taf. 2, 7, with similar small beads, possibly in the style stamped by SENICIO, A.D. 30–55; and *ibid.*, taf. 3, 9 which is the same as Knorr, 1952, taf. 52A. Aislingen was a Tiberian-Claudian fort.

2. The scroll is a simple, bold design. Earlier scrolls tend to be irregularly curved, and later scrolls are often overfull of small details, or are incomplete[57].

3. Most important of the three are the small double circles, which are of an early type. The references below[58] are all to the Claudian or earlier periods, on Dr. 29s; and double circles like this are not on any Neronian or later Dr. 29 known to me. There is a later type which is slightly different.

In conclusion, the sherd has several distinctive features which suggest that it belongs to the Claudian period, A.D. 43–54.

X. Brooches

Although excavations were made at four places (Sites I, II, III and IV) inside Salmonsbury, on all of which were circular huts of Period I and ample

[56] Greene K. T. (1972), Fig. 8, Nos. 3 and 4.

[57] Hermet (1934), Pl. 104, 27–33.

[58] Knorr (1952), taf. 2A (Vindonissa), 4D–E and 52C (Aislingen), 52D–E (Hofheim), 65F (Aislingen) 65J (Kempten,) 72B (Colchester), 78A (Mainz) and 79B (Bregenz).

evidence of occupation, it is remarkable that not a single brooch of this period was found. Brooches of the first century B.C. are, in any case, peculiarly scarce in Gloucestershire. It may be suggested that if brooches of Period I were to be found at Salmonsbury, they would be of the collared La Tène II type and of forms transitional between these and La Tène III, with vestigial decoration on the bow[59], like the bronze brooches from Maiden Castle[60]. That brooches of the latter type continued into the early first century A.D. is shown by the contexts of those at Maiden Castle and, more relevantly here, by the iron brooch of this type (Fig. 21, 1) of Period II at Salmonsbury. This brooch is thus, typologically, the earliest of the series of brooches from the site.

Sites III and IV at Salmonsbury, both occupied in Period II, produced no less than 13 brooches, of which nine are of iron and four of bronze. The short duration of this period, provisionally dated from c A.D. 30 to c A.D. 50–55, makes the range of types of particular interest for the last decades of the Iron Age in this region. Comparison with the longer series of brooches from Bagendon[61] shows that the Salmonsbury types B, C and F occur there also. At both sites, however, are types of brooch not represented at the other. In any case, it seems that the occupation of Bagendon lasted rather longer than Period II at Salmonsbury.

Copies of the drawings of the brooches and a draft of the text were sent to Mr. M. R. Hull, to whom I am greatly indebted for his comments and for supplying references.

The Salmonsbury brooches have been divided into seven types, A to G, described as follows:

1. *Brooches of Iron* (Fig. 21)

A. No. 1. Brooch with strongly arched bow, rectangular in section, with two narrow mouldings at head end of the bow as vestigial decoration representing the collar on the La Tène II type; solid catchplate.

B. Nos 2–3. Plain brooches with the bow curved in a flat arch. In section the bow is either round or a pointed oval. The catchplate is solid and continues the line of the bow.

C. No. 4. Plain brooch with the bow meeting the head at right-angles; round in section. The large catchplate is solid, and joins the line of the bow at an open angle.

Types B and C are variants derived from the Nauheim type, as discussed by Mr. Hull at Camulodunum[62] and Bagendon[63].

D. No. 5. Plain brooch with arched bow, flat and rectangular in section; small solid catchplate. The pin is hinged.

[59] Fowler, M. J. (1953), pp. 96–102, Figs 4 and 8.
[60] Wheeler (1943), p. 258, Fig. 83, 8–10.
[61] Hull (1961), pp. 167 ff.
[62] Hawkes and Hull (1947), pp. 309 and 312, type VII.
[63] Hull (1961), pp. 167–168, Fig. 29.

Mr. Hull regards this as a hinged Nauheim derivative. In Britain it is almost limited to the south-west; the bronze form he calls the Maiden Castle type[64].

E. No. 6. Plain brooch with long straight bow, round in section, which expands into a flat plate-like head. The catchplate is pierced by a large opening and continues the line of the bow. The pin is riveted or brazed into the head, but the coiled spring covered by the head-cap is missing.

Mr. Hull comments that this is a type well-known on the Continent, but seldom found in Britain (see below, type G). As a close parallel he cites an iron brooch from Ober-Gurina, Carinthia[65]. Several examples of bronze and iron are from the Hradischt of Stradonitz, Bohemia[66]; at Raab, Hungary, of silver and niello; several variants in the Nauheim cemetery[67]; at Xanten[68]; Flavion (in the Namur Museum); and at Châlons-sur-Marne (in the St. Germain Museum, no. 13633).

The area of distribution of these brooches is thus fairly wide, and there are several variants of the form, even on the same site. As regards the dating, they may be placed approximately in the middle of the first century B.C., probably lasting down to the beginning of the Empire. Because this brooch was developed no further in Roman times, it is always to be considered as pre-Roman.

2. *Brooches of bronze* (Fig. 22)

F. Nos 7–9. Brooches of the Colchester type III[69]. The bow is either arched in a continuous curve from head to foot (nos 7 and 9), or flatter and more sharply bent at the head (no. 8). In section the bow is D shaped, with a tendency to flattening along the sides near the head. Two brooches have plain bows, the other (no. 9) has two fine longitudinal lines enclosing a few oblique lines. All the brooches have a spring of eight turns, with an external chord held by a hook. On two brooches the catchplate is complete and is pierced; no. 7 has an elaborate step-pattern, and no. 9 a single small round hole. The foot of no. 8 is much smaller than the others, and incomplete.

At Bagendon the eight brooches of Colchester type III well represent this form for a site so far west[70]. The type is frequent on Belgic sites over a wide area of Britain, from Kent in the east to Gloucestershire in the west, and from Dorset in the south as far north as Lincolnshire[71]. Thus it is found over the entire Belgic regions to the limits reached by this culture in the west and north of the country. In addition, brooches of this type occur in two other tribal territories; that of the Belgicized Coritani in the east Midlands, and that of the non-Belgic Durotriges in Dorset.

[64] Wheeler (1943), p. 261, Fig. 84, 18, (bronze) and 262, Fig. 85, 35 (iron).
[65] Meyer (1885), p. 23, taf. VI, 1.
[66] Pič and Déchelette (1906), p. 33, Pl. III, 23–28.
[67] Quilling (1903), p. 99, No. 15.
[68] Houben, (1839) p. 56, taf. IX, 8.
[69] Hawkes and Hull (1947), p. 308, Pls LXXXIX–XC, 6–24.
[70] Hull (1961), p. 169, Fig. 30, 3–10.
[71] Dunning and Ogilvie (1967), p. 223.

G. No. 10. Brooch with arched bow and the curve reversed near the foot; plain catchplate, comparatively long and narrow. At the head end the bow expands into a wide flat plate, decorated with straight and curved longitudinal grooves, each with an engraved zigzag line. The front part of the bow also has two incised lines joined by cross-cuts. The hinged pin (mostly missing) was of iron, and it is held by a bar, also of iron.

Mr. Hull regards this brooch as a magnificent example of the "Banjo type", a variant Nauheim derivative, which he would class together with the iron brooch of type E, no. 6. Among the eight examples found in Britain, the Salmonsbury brooch is only exceeded in size by one from Sudbrook camp, Portskewett (in the National Museum of Wales), which has no reversed curve but an open foot. Smaller examples are from Desborough, Northamptonshire[72]; two from Cold Kitchen Hill, Brixton Deverill, Wiltshire[73]; Filkins, Oxfordshire[74]; Meare[75]; and ? London (in the British Museum). All of the above examples have a spring; the Salmonsbury brooch is the first with a hinged pin.

Incidence of the brooches according to type

A. Site III, below paving (no. 1).
B. Site III, ditch 1, lower filling, and on paving (no. 2); Site IV (no. 3).
C. Site III, ditch 1, lower filling; Site IV (no. 4).
D. Site III, below paving, and on paving (no. 5).
E. Site III, below paving (no. 6).
F. Site III, below paving (no. 7), and on paving (no. 8); Site IV (no. 9).
G. Site III, on paving (no. 10).

Type	Site III			Site IV	Totals
	Ditch 1	Below paving	On paving		
A		1			1
B	1		1	1	3
C	1			1	2
D		1	1		2
E		1			1
F		1	1	1	3
G			1		1
	2	4	4	3	13

XI. Coins

A. Dobunnic (*Fig. 23*)

Identified by the late D. F. Allen, F.B.A., F.S.A.
1. Base silver, uninscribed, Class C[76].

[72] Smith, R. A, (1909b), p. 345, Fig. 13.
[73] Nan Kivell (1926), p. 390, Pl. I. F–G.
[74] Akerman (1857), p. 142, illus.
[75] Bulleid and Gray (1953), p. 207, Pl. XLV, EE 19.
[76] Allen (1961), p. 104.

Obverse: head to right, pellet in circle for eye, cross and pellet for chin, row of pellets and fine beads for hair.

Reverse: triple-tailed horse to left; above, two pellets in circles; below, three petals on a stalk representing the cock's head ornament on Class A. Site III, ditch 1, lower filling.

2. Base silver, inscribed, Class G[77].

Obverse: head to right, long nose joined in a single curve to the lower lip; cross between pellets in circles (O X O pattern).

Reverse: ANTED, realistic triple-tailed horse to left; below, annulet. Site III, above paving.

B. *Republican Roman* (*Fig. 22*)

Identified by the late B. H. St. J. O'Neil, M.A., F.S.A.

3. Denarius of VIBIUS (49 B.C.)[78].

Obverse: head of Bacchus to right.

Reverse: VIBIVS. C.F.C.N. Ceres walking to right. Site III, ditch 1, upper filling.

4. Denarius of M. VOLTEUS (*c* 78 B.C.)[79].

Obverse: bust of Attis to right.

Reverse: M. VOLTEI M.F. Cybele in chariot drawn by lions. Site IV, in Roman rubbish pit.

C. *Roman* (*Fig. 23*)

5. *As* of CLAUDIUS I (A.D. 41–54)[80].

Obverse: T CLAVDIVS CAESAR AVG P M TR P IMP. Head to left.

Reverse: S C. Minerva fighting to right. Site III, on paving.

This coin, originally identified by Mr. O'Neil, has recently been examined by Mr. G. C. Boon, Department of Archaeology, National Museum of Wales, who kindly comments as follows:

The coin is one of the series of copies of the orthodox Claudian bronzes, probably struck in Britain in the early post-conquest period. The legend is complete and ends with the title IMP(erator). The later issues of Claudius, from *c* A.D. 50, had the additional P(ater) P(atriae). The end of these issues came with the appearance of Nero's bronze and copper coins from the Lyons and Rome mints in the years after A.D. 64, principally *c* A.D. 65–67. Thus between A.D. 43 and 64, or at farthest 70, is the widest dating for the Salmonsbury coin irrespective of its state of wear.

The opportunity to check the rate of devolution in the size and weight of copies during this period has arisen only recently, with the series from the Neronian fort at Usk, which was founded not much later than *c* A.D. 55. Here there is a large proportion of Claudian copies, mostly rather small, in the 20 to 22 mm size.

---

[77] Allen (1961), p. 108.
[78] British Museum, *Coins of the Roman Republic*, I (1910), p. 510, No. 3976 ff.
[79] *Ibid.*, I (1910), p. 390, No. 3179 ff.
[80] Mattingly and Sydenham (1923), p. 129, No. 66. Boon (1974), p. 103, Pl. III, 29.

The Salmonsbury coin measures 25 mm across and weighs 6·91 grammes. I would therefore judge that it was struck in the later forties; and its condition of wear suggests a few years' circulation. It might well be that it was lost *c* A.D. 55, or possibly somewhat before, but obviously this latter deduction is less valid than the first.

Since this coin is the most closely datable find of the Claudian period on the paving on Site III, it is used to define the lower terminal date of Period II as *c* A.D. 50–55.

XII. Small Finds

A. Period I (*Fig. 24*)

Objects of iron, bronze, baked clay, antler and bone, and one glass bead were found in the drainage ditches of huts and in the associated pits on Sites I, II, III, IV and V. Compared with the abundance of contemporary decorated pottery, the paucity of ornament on the small finds of metal and other materials is surprising in Period I at Salmonsbury.

1. Iron sickle with flat tang and rivet hole. Site III, pit B.
2. Iron sickle with riveted socket. Site III, pit A.
3. Iron gouge with burred-over head. Site II, hearth over pit E.
4. Part of iron latch-lifter with ring at end of handle. Site III, pit D. A similar but larger example is from Site I, pit U[81].
5. Iron plate, pierced by four holes. The branched ends are incomplete. Use uncertain. Site I, hut 2, south ditch.
6. Annular bead of blue glass. Site IV, pit J.
7. Reel-shaped object of grey baked clay. Site I, pit Q. Similar objects are from Glastonbury[82] and Scarborough (Iron Age A)[83].
8. Bone "toggle" with single perforation through side. Incised with double-line lattice pattern. Site I, south ditch. Similar objects of bone were found at Hunsbury[84].
9. Antler weaving-comb with oval enlargement of the butt, type 2. Cross hatched incised decoration below the butt. The comb is illustrated here since it is the only example from Salmonsbury. Chance find in the Moore collection, in the Cheltenham Museum. For the types of weaving-combs see Glastonbury and Meare[85], and Maiden Castle[86].
10–11. Artifacts made from the metatarsal bones of sheep, with the condyles complete. No. 10 has a central perforation on one side only, type A; and no. 11 is pierced obliquely at the proximal end, type D. Site III, pit J. For the types

[81] Bulleid and Gray (1917), p. 375 ff.
[82] Bulleid and Gray (1917), p. 559, Pl. XC, D 48.
[83] Smith (1927), p. 183, Fig. 11.
[84] Fell (1936), p. 72, Pl. IX, 2–3.
[85] Bulleid and Gray (1911), pp. 266 ff.; (1948), pp. 61 ff.
[86] Wheeler (1943), pp. 297 ff.

of these objects, numerous on Iron Age sites, and discussion see Glastonbury[87] and Maiden Castle[88].

12. Bone tool, carefully made and smoothed, possibly for decorating pottery. The butt is slightly enlarged and spherical, decorated with two lightly incised lines, and the other end is chisel-shaped. Site IV, hut, north-west ditch. Not illustrated. Spindle-whorl of stone. Site III, pit N. Sling-bullets of baked clay. Site I, pit P and Site III, pit N.

B. Period II, phase i (Fig. 25)

1. Iron penannular brooch with spiral terminals in the same plane as the ring. Site III, ditch 1, upper filling. Fowler's type B[89].

2. Bronze penannular brooch, also type B. Site III, below paving.

3. Iron tankard handle, semicircular in section. The terminal plates are shaped differently at each end. One bronze rivet remains. Site III, below paving. No close parallel among the various classes of British tankard handles of bronze[90].

4. Bronze strip with rounded end, decorated with line of punch-marks along both sides. Two rivet holes near end. Site III, below paving.

5–6. Iron knives with curved blades. Site III, below paving. Similar knives are from Belgic levels at Maiden Castle[91].

7. Iron bracelet or armlet, rectangular in section. Site III, below paving.

8. Iron currency bar. The socket and part of the blade, found 4 ft apart, have been drawn together, though they may belong to different bars. Site III, below paving. As Mr. D. F. Allen has remarked, the finding of these pieces of bar in the make-up of the paving is no evidence that currency bars were in use in a Belgic context[92].

9. Dome-shaped boss of dark blue glass with disc of opaque yellow glass set in the top. Site III, below paving. Probably a gaming-piece, comparable with the more elaborate set from the Belgic burial at Welwyn[93].

10. Bone ring, oval in section, carefully worked and polished. The ring widens downwards from the top, which shows signs of wear. Possibly a pendant or an ear-ring. Site III, ditch 1, on bottom.

11. Cheek-piece of antler tine. The upper end is perforated by a round hole and an elongated slot at right angles. Site III, below paving. Not paralleled among the types of cheek-piece at Glastonbury and Meare[94].

12. Part of triangular crucible of baked clay, with traces of bronze slag

[87] Bulleid and Gray (1917), pp. 421 ff.
[88] Wheeler (1943), pp. 306–307.
[89] Bulleid and Gray (1911), p. 205, Pls XLII and XLIV: Wheeler (1943), p. 264, Fig. 86, 5; Fowler, E. (1960), pp. 157–159.
[90] Corcoran (1952), p. 85 ff.
[91] Wheeler (1943), p. 274, Fig. 89, 10–11.
[92] Allen (1967), pp. 328–329.
[93] Stead (1967), pp. 14–17, Fig. 10 and Pl. Ia.
[94] Bulleid and Gray (1917), p. 440 ff; Cotton (1966). p. 328 ff.

adhering to the inside. Site III, below paving. The most frequent type at Glastonbury and Meare[95].

C. Period II, phase ii (*Fig. 26*)

All from Site III, on paving.

1. Object of iron plated with bronze. In shape it is globular with a moulding at each end. Possibly the head of a linch-pin.

2. Iron tool with curved cutting-edge and flat tang. Dr. W. H. Manning has identified it as a leather-worker's lunette knife; the type is not very common in Roman contexts.

3. Bronze spiral finger-ring. Type as in Belgic contexts at Maiden Castle[96].

4. Bronze finger-ring decorated with incised line and dot.

5. Small bronze bracelet, elliptical in section, tapering at the ends.

6. Bronze tubular binding decorated with incised chevrons. One rivet hole at each end.

7. Part of iron ox-goad.

8. Lead spindle-whorl. Type as at Glastonbury[97].

9. Stone spindle-whorl with edge slightly faceted.

10. Boar's tusk pendant, perforated at middle.

11. Bone toggle for a strap, with mouldings at each end.

12. Bone ring, grooved round outside.

13. Part of Kimmeridge shale bracelet. Oval in section, flattened on the inner side, like bracelets from Belgic levels at Maiden Castle[98].

Pl. X. Bronze toilet set, comprising nail-cleaner, tweezers and ear-scoop on a ring. A similar toilet set formed part of a Belgic burial-group at Deal[99].

Not illustrated. Iron sickle with socket, similar to Fig. 23, 2. Stone spindle-whorls. Part of triangular loom-weight of baked clay, pierced across the angle; two complete loom-weights of this type from Salmonsbury are in the Cheltenham Museum.

XIII. Decorated Pyramid of Stone (Fig. 27)

In 1956 Mrs. O'Neil carried out an excavation in the garden of Avilon house, on the east side of Cemetery Lane, about 100 ft south of the inturned entrance on the north-west side of Salmonsbury. The site revealed the ditch of a large circular hut of Period I, with entrance to the east. The Iron Age occupation continued into the first century A.D., as shown by a few imported Roman wares. Outside the hut to the north was a laid gravel surface at a higher

[95] Bulleid and Gray (1911), p. 300 ff. (1963), p. 253 ff.
[96] Wheeler (1943), p. 266, Fig. 86, 12–16.
[97] Bulleid and Gray (1911), p. 250, Pl. XLV, L 19.
[98] Wheeler (1943), p. 313, Fig. 107, 18.
[99] Birchall (1965), p. 306, Fig. 12, 101.

level, apparently the courtyard of an early Roman dwelling. The finds in the
brown soil on this floor include Iron Age pottery, early samian and coarse
wares. In the same layer was a stone object of exceptional interest, which Mrs.
O'Neil has kindly given permission to be included here; it is dated about the
middle of the first century A.D.

The object is complete and made of Lower Lias limestone. In shape it is a
tall four-sided pyramid, with inward curvature to the base, which is slightly
convex. The apex is domed, and defined by a stepped edge. Height 3·5 in.;
base about 2·5 in. square; weight 16 oz. The decoration is incised on the pyramid and the base. Round the conical sides are four lines of vertical marks,
triangular in shape. The topmost line, immediately below the apex, is inter-
rupted by a hole, 0·25 in. in diameter, bored transversely through the summit.
The lowest line is just above the edge of the base.

The decoration on the base consists of four triangles, each hatched with
lines of short marks. The points of the triangles meet at the centre, and their
bases are outwards near the corners of the stone, forming a saltire pattern.

The only comparable object is the cone of Liassic limestone found at Barnwood, near Gloucester[100], now in the British Museum. This is curved in
profile, slightly incurved to the flat base, and not quite circular in plan. It is
decorated in incised technique, partly linear and partly curvilinear. Round the
cone are three triskeles in panels between vertical bands of hatched triangles,
and on the base is another triskele. The formalism of the patterns on the
Barnwood cone points to a date in the mid-first century A.D.[101].

The similarities between the Barnwood and Salmonsbury objects are
remarkably close in many respects. They are the same height and made of the
same stone, and both have incised patterns on the side and base. Moreover,
both belong to the same period, at the end of Western Second B; a source in
common is thus certain.

As Sir Cyril Fox commented on the Barnwood cone: "an object so shaped
and so small can have no purpose other than in magic or ritual". Reginald A.
Smith pointed out, in the original note on this cone, that its character brings
it into close relationship with the stelae and betyls of the Armorican Iron Age.
The ritual significance of these stelae is emphasised by their inclusion in late
Gaulish cremation cemeteries in Brittany, sometimes as the nuclei round
which the burials were grouped[102].

The association of stelae with burials is not yet demonstrated in Britain.
However, the Barnwood cone came from a site occupied during the Iron Age,
which also produced the contracted burial of a young woman accompanied
by a Western Second B pot[103]. The site continued to be used for burials by

[100] *Antiq. Journ.*, XIV (1934), 59. It may be noted that the triskele motif occurs four times on the
bases of pots at Meare; Bulleid and Gray (1948), p. 19, Pl. VIII.
[101] Fox, C. (1958), p. 112.
[102] Giot (1952); (1960), pp. 178–182.
[103] Clifford (1930), pp. 224–226.

cremation in Western Third C and into the Romano-British period, and "can be said to have belonged to Belgic Dobunni of the second generation"[104].

The context of the Salmonsbury object is quite different, since it was found on a dwelling site. Its pyramidal shape, square in section, recalls that of the larger stelae in Brittany; but a slightly different interpretation may be suggested, which explains the hole through the top. It may be compared with loomweights of baked clay, in shape a truncated pyramid and pierced by a single hole near the top, such as those dated about 25 B.C. at Maiden Castle[105]. If this analogy is valid, then the Salmonsbury pyramid may be regarded more as a symbol of the domestic occupation of weaving. Possibly it was suspended from the roof, so that the decoration on the base would be visible.

In support of the identification of the stone pyramid as a cult object. Dr. Anne Ross has kindly pointed out the significance of the saltire motif or St. Andrews cross decoration on the base. This occurs on several small altars of Mars in south-west Britain, e.g. at Chedworth, Glos., which pertain to native rather than to classical cults in the Roman period.*

XIV. Querns (Figs 28–30)

In the excavations of 1931–1934 querns were found only on Site III, all in stratified contexts. On this site saddle querns only were represented, in both Period I and Period II. In Period I there were two rubbers for saddle querns, found in pits L and M. In Period II all the querns belong to phase ii; two rubbers were in the make-up of the Belgic paving, and two rubbers and a broken lower stone on the surface of the paving. Since the lower stones are so poorly represented, Mrs. O'Neil has kindly allowed me to include a complete saddle quern of Period I found near Camp House (Fig. 27).

Thus at Salmonsbury the use of saddle querns continued throughout the Iron Age occupation, right down to the middle of the first century A.D. The preponderance of this primitive type of quern agrees with the evidence from Meare, where the proportion of saddle querns to rotary is eleven to one[106]. On the contrary, at Glastonbury the ratio is reversed, with twice as many rotary as saddle querns[107].

Although no rotary querns were found on any of the sites excavated at Salmonsbury, their presence here is attested by a complete upper stone in the Cheltenham Museum (Fig. 30).

At Bagendon one complete lower stone of a rotary quern, and more than a dozen pieces of others of this type were found[108], but apparently no saddle querns. It is evident that in the late Iron Age both types of quern were in use,

[104] Clifford (1961), p. 155.
[105] Wheeler (1943), p. 297, Fig. 100, 2. *Antiq. Journ.*, XV (1935), 474, Pl. LXXIII.
[106] Cotton (1966), p. 380. *Ross (1967), pp. 156 and 185.
[107] Bulleid and Gray (1917), p. 609.
[108] Clifford (1961), pp. 151 and 196.

but that great diversity existed in their relative frequency. This applies even between two contemporary sites so close together in the territory of the Belgic Dobunni as Bagendon and Salmonsbury.

I am grateful to Dr. J. S. W. Penn, Lecturer in Geology, Kingston Polytechnic, for kindly identifying the stones.

1. *Saddle quern* (Fig. 27)

Complete lower stone of a saddle quern found by Mrs. O'Neil in 1965 after removal of a tree for an electric boosting unit, adjoining the north wall of Camp House garden. The site is about 20 ft inside the line of the inner rampart and immediately north of the inturned entrance, on the north-west side of Salmonsbury. The quern was associated with pottery of Period I.

Length 20·5 in.; width 13·9 in.; maximum thickness 6·6 in.; weight 104 lb. The quern is exceptionally large, and roughly rectangular in shape. The milling surface does not extend the whole length, but reaches nearer the edge at one end than the other; depth of concavity 1·75 in. Stone: coarse-grained sandstone.

2. *Rubbers for saddle querns* (Fig. 29)

1. Complete upper stone. Length 16·7 in.; width 7·4 in.; thickness 2·1 in.; weight 14 lb. 3 oz. The milling surface is worn to a depth of 0·6 in., leaving a transverse boss at each end as a grasp for the hands; it is convex transversely. Stone: medium-grained sandstone, probably from Shropshire. Site III; Period I, pit L.

2. Complete upper stone. Length 9·9 in.; width 6·75 in.; thickness 2·35 in.; weight 7 lb. 15 oz. The milling surface is convex in both directions. Stone: medium-grained sandstone, probably from Shropshire. Site III; Period I, pit M.

3. Complete upper stone. Length 13 in.; width 6·1 in.; thickness 2·9 in.; weight 10 lb. 8 oz. The milling surface is convex in both directions. Stone: Old Red Sandstone, from the Midlands. Site III; Period II, phase ii, in make-up of Belgic paving.

3. *Rotary quern* (Fig. 30)

The only rotary quern from Salmonsbury is in the Cheltenham Museum (no. 1915/121); no details of its exact provenance are known. Complete upper stone. Diameter at base 11·5 in.; height 6·75 in. Beehive-shaped, with slight moulding round the mouth of the hopper. The socket hole for the handle connects with the lower part of the hopper. The milling surface is slightly concave. Stone: medium-grained sandstone.

XV. Evidence of Cannibalism (Pl. XI)

It is well-known that in addition to formal burials on Iron-Age settlements, broken and disjointed human bones are of common occurrence. Often complete skulls or fragments of skulls, single limb bones, vertebrae, and bones of the hands and feet are scattered about and found indiscriminately. Finds of both categories were made at Salmonsbury. Crouched burials of Period I occurred in pits near the circular huts on Sites I to IV. These raise no particular problem in the present context, since the burials were clearly intentional and ritualistic in character.

In addition, parts of skeletons and separate bones, both of infants and of adults of both sexes, were found in the filled-in ditches of the huts and in the adjacent pits, again of Period I on Sites I to IV. These remnants of humanity are not easy to explain and could result from various causes. Possibly some of the skulls and limb bones represent burials that had been disturbed and the bones scattered; or it may be that certain bones, or parts of bones, were removed from burials and made into amulets, such as the cranial roundel found at Glastonbury[109]. No evidence of this practice was found at Salmonsbury.

A different interpretation is required for a number of human bones found on Site III. All of these bones were found at the same level and in one deposit, in the make-up below the paving of Period II, phase ii, of the Belgic period. It is therefore certain that all the bones are strictly contemporary, and reached this position at the same time. The bones comprise the following parts of the skeleton:

1. Skull; right and left parietals, left temporal and left malar.
2. Shafts of right radius and ulna, and shaft of left radius.
3. Shaft of right femur.
4. Left patella.
5. Complete left fibula.
6. Left talus and calcaneum, and one metatarsal.

When assembled and examined together, it was evident that all the bones had belonged to one and the same individual, a young adult female aged about 20–25 years at the time of death. The age is estimated from the cranial sutures and the fibula. The sutures of the parietal bones are open and show no signs of closure, which commences about the thirtieth year. The epiphyses at both extremities of the fibula are united with the shaft; in the female, fusion at the lower and upper ends is in the fifteenth and seventeenth year respectively[110]. Thus at the widest limits, the individual was over 17 and under 30 years of age.

It should be noted that only a relatively small part of the skeleton was recovered, though the skull, both forearms and both legs are represented. The greater part of the cranium and face, the lower jaw, any bones of the vertebral

[109] Bulleid and Gray (1917), p. 405, Pl. LXIII, B 59.
[110] Gray's *Anatomy* (35th edn., 1973), pp. 312 and 373.

column and pelvis, both humerii, the left femur, and both tibiae (all substantial limb bones), were not found on the area excavated, which extended considerably beyond the smaller area where the bones occurred. The bones were scattered over an area of about 18 ft by 30 ft. The dispersal is well shown by the distance between the four bones of the skull. The two parietal bones, which articulate, were 15 ft apart; the left temporal was 22 ft and the left malar 18 ft from the left parietal bone. This displacement of the bones implies that the body was completely dismembered before the various parts were discarded.

The special feature of this skeleton is the condition of the three forearm bones and the femur. Both ends of the forearm bones are smashed obliquely, and the breaks are from 0·8 in. to 2 in. long. The thicker shaft of the femur is fractured more transversely; at the proximal end just below the lesser trochanter, and at the distal end it is irregularly broken for 0·8 inches. In each case the fractures were made where the compact bone of the shaft becomes thinner and the extremities are filled with cancellous bony tissue. The breaking of the bones, particularly the femur, would require some force, and can only have happened at or soon after the time of death, and after the dismemberment of the body. The bones have been smashed in precisely the same way as numerous bones of ox, sheep and pig found in the excavations. In the case of animal bones, it is accepted without question that the purpose was to extract the marrow for eating. There seems no reason why this explanation should not apply to the human long bones. It may be added that the skull could easily have been broken up to remove the brain, and this would account for so few pieces of it being found.

The evidence appears to be conclusive that the bones of the young woman were smashed deliberately to obtain the marrow from the parts of the limb bones where this is most easily done, that is, the spongy tissue at the ends of the shafts. In that case, the bones from Salmonsbury are the most convincing evidence yet adduced for the practice of anthropophagy in Iron Age Britain[111].

XVI. Anglo-Saxon Finds (Fig. 31)

1. Small iron knife with slender blade. The back is straight and meets the tang at an obtuse angle. Found with the bones of a disturbed burial, in Bourton cemetery inside Salmonsbury in 1963.

2. Small iron knife; width of blade 0·75 in., tang missing. The straight back, parallel to the cutting edge, runs down to the point in a convex curve[112]. Found beside right forearm of burial of an adult man, inserted into outer slope of south bank of the annexe of Salmonsbury in 1931.

3–4. Large iron knives in the Moore collection of finds from Salmonsbury in Cheltenham Museum. Almost certainly these are the "two knives from

[111] Brothwell (1961).
[112] Meaney and Hawkes (1970), p. 43, Fig. 13, for types of knives.

graves on the west bank of the camp" exhibited by Dr. Moore at Stow-on-the-Wo inld 1881[113]. The seax (no. 3) could be from a late pagan burial, but the other knife is too late for grave furniture.

3. Large iron knife or seax; blade length 11·5 in., width 1·5 in., end of tang missing. The back is slightly convex throughout to the tapering point, and meets the tang at a right angle. The cutting edge is straight, with convex curvature near the point. Along two-thirds of the back on each side is a broad groove and a narrow groove below it; a radiograph shows that no inlay can now be detected here, as present on a comparable seax from Northolt[114]. Date: late seventh century.

4. Iron knife; point missing, blade length about 6·2 in., average width 1·25 in., tang missing. The back diverges from the straight cutting edge and turns at an obtuse angle to the point; it meets the tang in a deep right-angled step. Date: ninth or tenth century[115].

Acknowledgements

To Mrs. H. E. O'Neil I am especially grateful for constant advice during the preparation of this report, for reading the text, and for permission to include material from her excavations at Salmonsbury. I should like my report to be regarded as a tribute to her long devotion to the archaeology of Bourton-on-the-Water and region.

My grateful thanks are due to the following for their specialist reports and advice. Dr. Isobel F. Smith (Neolithic and Early Bronze Age finds); Mr. Kevin T. Greene (imported pottery); Dr. Grace Simpson (samian); Mr. M. R. Hull (brooches); the late Mr. D. F. Allen (Dobunnic coins); the late Mr. B. H. St. J. O'Neil (Roman coins); Mr. G. C. Boon (coin of Claudius); Dr. W. H. Manning (iron tools); Dr. J. S. W. Penn (identification of stones); and Miss V. I. Evison (Anglo-Saxon finds). I have also to thank the Curator and Mr. K. W. Brown for permission to include finds from Salmonsbury in the Cheltenham Museum.

The drawings of the small finds are the work of Mr. C. O. Waterhouse, formerly Illustrator to the British Museum. The drawing of the stone pyramid is by Mrs. E. M. Fry-Stone.

It is a pleasure to record my indebtedness to Mrs. Elsie M. Clifford, whose pioneer work on the Belgic Dobunni at Bagendon forms the essential foundation for much of this report.

[113] *Trans. Bristol and Gloucestershire Arch. Soc.*, VII (1882), p. 38.
[114] Evison (1961), p. 226, Fig. 58, 4.
[115] Evison (1964), pp. 30–34.

4 | A Summary of the Excavations at Castle Hill, Almondbury 1939–1972

W. J. Varley

I. Introduction

Castle Hill is the name long attached to a most distinctive plateau dominating the ancient village of Almondbury, a few miles to the south of Huddersfield in the West Riding of Yorkshire (Nat. Grid, SE44: 152140). The site has long been the subject of conjecture amongst historians. Some authorities have regarded it as a stronghold of the Brigantes (Petch, 1923); others as the Roman station of Camulodunum mentioned by both Ptolemy (*Geography* II, pp. 3, 17) and the Ravenna Cosmographer (Richmond and Crawford, 1949, p. 27); but most have seen it only as the site of the motte and bailey castle built for the De Laci Earls of Lincoln and Lords of the Honour of Pontefract and the Manor of Almondbury in the twelfth century A.D.

At the instigation of the Tolson Memorial Museum, Huddersfield, and the Yorkshire Archaeological Society, excavations began in the summer of 1939 and were resumed in 1946 and 1947. It was decided to test the conclusions thus obtained by a second series of excavations in 1969–1970 and 1972, more particularly aimed at obtaining material for absolute dating.

It has now been firmly established that there were three cycles of occupation on Castle Hill, widely separated in time. The first was Neolithic, belonging to the third millennium B.C.; the second concerned a four-fold series of earthworks erected, occupied, and abandoned in the first millennium B.C. and the third related to a medieval castle built in the twelfth century A.D. In the context of this particular volume, the present summary is concerned merely with the second cycle.

II. Physical Setting

The site and its relationship to the present topography are shown in Fig. 1. The watershed of the Central Pennines hereabouts, the land above 1200 ft

O.D., only narrowly separates the river systems flowing westwards to the Mersey and Ribble estuaries from those flowing eastwards to the Humber. Castle Hill overlooks the eastward flowing series from a commanding position near to the Colne (2), the Holme (3), the Fenay Brook (4), south of their junction with the Calder (1) which has long been the principal valley route linking the Lancashire and Yorkshire Plains.

The summit of the hill occupies an area of 3·7 ha., and is composed of a capping of Grenoside sandstone. In the south-west, it attains a height of just over 900 ft above sea level, sloping away steeply to the River Holme 600 ft below on the west, but less steeply in all other directions, particularly towards the north east. Nonetheless, its partially isolated position in the series of escarpments developed in the Lower and Middle Coal Measures which run parallel to the Millstone Grit core of the Central Pennines has given Castle Hill a most distinctive shape and skyline which can be seen and recognised from whatever angle it is approached.

Castle Hill abounds in raw materials ideally suited to the building of earthworks, ranging from Grenoside sandstone which yields admirable walling blocks through the various deposits of the Elland Flagstones with their large flat flagstones, and shales which weather down into a false-clay, a substitute for the boulder clay which is missing from the higher parts of the Central Pennines.

The hill-top may once have supported sessile oakwoods, cleared, as we now know, in the Neolithic period. Despite its soils being thin, cold and acid, and badly-drained in places, cultivation has kept them free from peat formation. The present surface of poor grassland and thorn-scrub is a measure of the deterioration which has occurred since the site was last abandoned, which has been greatly accelerated by the atmospheric pollution produced by the adjacent industrial areas of the Lancashire and Yorkshire coalfields. Until the late Middle ages, the area abounded in game—one of the principal reasons for its choice as a hunting lodge by the De Lacis when they no longer used it as a Castle.

III. Archaeological Context

Although this area of Britain is still too frequently regarded as a cultural backwater, remote from the principal populated areas and centres of cultural innovation, it has, in fact, as long a period of human occupation as any other in Britain. It was hunted over and occupied seasonally throughout the Mesolithic period, especially in the Sauveterrean, and during the post-Mesolithic settlement period from the Neolithic onwards, the Calder and associated valleys were one of the principal routes between the Yorkshire Wolds, the Peak District of Derbyshire and the Mersey and Ribble Estuaries. Miss Chitty's maps of the distribution of axes and bronzes in this region of Britain have long made this clear (Varley, 1963), while more recent work on the Wallingford–Wilburton tradition in the Late Bronze Age reinforces the significance of the routes through the Central Pennines (Burgess, 1968b, Fig. 19), at or about the time when settlers were establishing themselves on the southern end of Castle Hill. As one of the most conspicuous landmarks in an area which has long been regarded as the territory of the Brigantes, Castle Hill has naturally been thought of as a major Brigantian stronghold in the Iron Age.

IV. The Visible Earthworks

The earthworks still visible on Castle Hill are shown in Fig. 3. They comprise (i) Ramparts I and II, complete circumvallations of the summit and upper slopes; III and IV, partial circumvallations confined to the north-east quadrant; V and VI, the Outer Series at the foot of the hill; (ii) the Annexe in the north-east quadrant and (iii) the Hollow Way (HW) which connects Entrance E2 with the bottom of the hill in the north-west quadrant.

As they stand now, these earthworks are composite structures. All that is now visible is what is left of the Medieval earthwork (No. 5), though excavation has now firmly established that this earthwork had four predecessors, all dating to the pre-Roman period.

V. The Stratigraphical Succession as Established by Excavation

The structural sequence is set out in Table 1. Here we are concerned only with Deposits 3–11, Phases Two to Seven, all pertaining to successive events which we have called the First Interregnum, the Univallate Enclosure, the Second Interregnum, the Open Settlement, the Univallate Fortlet, the Bivallate Fort, the Multivallate Fort, and, finally, Burning and Collapse, respectively. This sequence rests upon stratigraphy only. Its validity is not affected in any way by other considerations.

The sequence may now be summarised *seriatim*, as follows.

The *First Interregnum*, meaning thereby the first break in the continuity of human occupation on this site, takes the form of a land-surface developed *in situ* over the remains of the first-known occupation which rests directly on the bed-rock.

The Univallate Enclosure (Phase Three) consists of a single bank without known ditch carried round the southern half of the summit plateau, enclosing some 2·2 ha. The lay-out is shown in Fig. 2, from which it will be seen that, except for the bank which bisects the summit from north-west to south-east, the enclosing *vallum* is placed on the edge of the plateau top in the area which has the steepest slopes. It may always have been slightly higher than the rest of the summit, but the natural contours were not those now to be seen. This end of the hill was given a pronounced face-lift in the late thirteenth century A.D.

The only known entrance to this enclosure lay in the middle of the transverse bank and consisted of a simple gap through the bank with a small enclosure

TABLE 1. *The Stratigraphical Succession, Castle Hill, Almondbury*

Archaeological Deposits		Event	Phase	Stage
16 Existing Land Surface		Final Decay	Nine	
15 Final Rainwash				
14	Debris of final Building	Final Building	Eight	10
13	Debris of Slighting	Slighting		9
12	Remains of Earthwork 5	Castle Earthworks		8
11 Penultimate Land Surface		The Great Interregnum	Seven	
10	Debris of Burning	Fire and Collapse	Six	7
9	Remains of Earthwork 4	Multivallate Fort		6
8	Remains of Earthwork 3	Bivallate Fort		5
7	Remains of Earthwork 2	Univallate Fortlet		4
6	Hut Floors	Open Settlement	Five	3
5 Third Land Surface		Second Interregnum	Four	
4	Remains of Earthwork 1	Univallate Enclosure	Three	2
3 Second Land Surface		First Interregnum	Two	
2	First Occupation Floors	First Occupation	One	1
1 Original Land-Surface				
BEDROCK				
Natural Deposits				

which could have served as a guard-room on the south side (site 9). There was a central hearth, a flagstone set on a fire-reddened clay deposit, inside the guard-room.

The bank now only survives to a variable extent but the foundations which remain are distinctive (Fig. 4). First, there are two rows of flagstones set on edge in narrow slit-trenches 3 m apart. Inside these, on the inner face, there is a low wall faced with blocks outside a rubble core acting as the inner revetment. On the outer face of the bank there is a dry-stone wall resting on flat slabs placed outside the row of flagstones standing on edge. Between the two revetments there is a clay core derived from the weathered upper surface of the bed rock, the Elland flagstones.

Apart from the hearth in the entrance there is now no evidence of occupation within this enclosure.

As noted above, the single bank survives to a markedly varying extent. In some places, only the double row of flagstones is left. A whole series of sections on the eastern leeward side confirm what happened to bring about this state of affairs. First, the site fell into ruin and decay. Second, a land surface developed over these ruins to a depth of several centimetres and for sufficiently long to result in a soil-profile, albeit very immature. In other words, the Univallate Enclosure was abandoned and left to nature in the period I have called the *Second Interregnum* (Phase Four). This was ended by the building of a series of stone-kerbed huts both on the site of the earlier enclosure bank and also beyond it elsewhere on the plateau summit, usually under the ramparts of the Bivallate Fort. All that now remains of these huts are their flagstone-kerbs set in slits in the land surface below or sometimes, as at Site 6, in specially laid false-clay floors. Inside the hut kerbs, roughly circular, eight metres in diameter, there were charcoal spreads radiating from a central point, though no hearth now survives. Since these huts partly overlay the earlier bank, and in the north western and north eastern corners protrude beyond it, and since they also extend to areas completely outside either the preceding Enclosure or its ultimate successor, the Univallate Fortlet, they are taken to represent a period of Open Settlement (Phase Five).

This gave way to the *Univallate Fortlet* (Phase Six) which marks the first stage in a progression of earthworks which embody more and more complex ideas of what constituted a defensive lay-out (Fig. 2, 2). Like its predecessor, the second earthwork encloses 2·2 ha., the southern half of the plateau top, within an inner rampart erected nearly, but not quite exactly, on the site of its predecessor at all points, including a gap-entrance in the middle of the transverse sections which bisects the hill top. The style of that rampart was changed to some extent. Similar double rows of large flagstones set on edge within slit trenches three metres apart were dug into whatever surface lay below (Fig. 4). Inside the inner edge of these flagstones, a dry-stone inner revetment was built of quarry-dressed Grenoside blocks. The outer revetment, more strongly built of similar blocks was laid on large horizontal slabs outside the flagstones laid on edge. The core between these two revetments was internally braced with stretches of undressed blocks supported centrally by a pillar of undressed boulders so as to create a series of internal cells filled with false clay. Occasionally, prepared timbers (posts, rails and planks), had been inserted into the clay core as if to stiffen it. These timbers were not tied together in any way, nor did they protrude into or through the stone revetments; nor were they tied into them. Finally, the core was topped-off with a layer of flagstones or blocks except where, at roughly three metre intervals, flag-lined post holes have been inserted as if to support timber posts originally standing vertically. Outside the inner rampart, there was usually a narrow berm, sometimes gently, sometimes steeply, sloping down to a round-bottom ditch, 3 m wide and 2 m deep, which had upcast thrown up on its outer lip so as to form a very low bank, revetted by a single row of stones on the outer edge. The transverse banks were of identical construction, and stood on the inner edge of a deeper V-shaped ditch with a narrow, flat bottom; a natural causeway led through the rampart and ditch at the only known entrance (E.1). The earlier guard-room may have been retained, but was not rebuilt so far as the foundations were concerned.

Behind the inner revetment of the inner rampart there were a series of occupation floors, presumably used by those who manned the defences.

The Univallate Fortlet of Phase Six, Stage 4, was transformed into the *Bivallate Fort* of Stage 5 in the following manner. Both ends of the transverse ditch were blocked off by large boulders, and new ramparts, identical in structure with their immediate predecessors, were carried across the blockings and continued round the northern half of the summit plateau so as to double the area enclosed. The original entrance was abandoned and a new entrance was created at the north-eastern end of the hill-top, overlooking the easiest approaches (E.2). Elsewhere, the defences of the Univallate Fortlet were retained, but were reinforced by the addition of rampart II (Fig. 3). Once more, there were hut floors, stone-based in some cases, defined by stone slabs laid on edge immediately inside the inner rampart. There was also evidence that vertical post-holes front and rear were contemporary with this period of the defences, and presumably supported the timbers of some kind of shelter attached to the rampart. Elsewhere, neither excavation nor resistivity surveys[1] yielded any evidence of structures within the interior, except in one possible instance at Site A.

The Bivallate Fort was next superseded by a vast reconstruction which turned the site into a *Multivallate Fort* in Stage 6 of Phase Six. In this reconstruction, the following were the major items. First, the Inner Rampart was widened and heightened by using the berm and half the ditch to carry a new outer revetment (Fig. 5). Second, a new ditch, deeper and distinctly V-shaped, was cut outside the final version of the Inner Rampart throughout its extent. Third, a short length of a third rampart (III), built as a *glacis* of small shale, was built parallel to the counterscarp of the Bivallate extension on the east side, where a lower shelf permitted such an extension. Fourth, a longer stretch of similar construction was built on the outer edge of this shelf and carried

---

[1] Carried out by Mr. Arnold Aspinall of the University of Bradford.

round it continuously to link up with a similar, lower bank on the east side of the revised entrance (IV). Fifth, the external ditch to this fourth rampart near the entrance was shared with the southern end of the quadrilateral Annexe, enclosed within its own bank and ditch on a still lower shelf to the north east. The *Annexe* had a small two-roomed hut-foundation cut into the bed rock and defined by flagstone walls.

From the revised north eastern entrance, the natural causeway lying between ramparts and ditches was prolonged north eastwards as a sunken or *Hollow Way* which was protected on both sides by banks until opposite the south western corner of the Annexe, it swept round through a right angle and descended north westwards sharply to the bottom of the hill. Here the low earthworks which define the Hollow Way, linked up with an extension which crossed a flat shelf between the inner and outer banks of the outer series (Fig. 3, V and VI). The latter as they now stand are not necessarily pre-Roman, but the shelf between them is, and it carried an outer bank which completed the final circumvallation of the Multivallate Fort.

There is evidence to the effect that the shelters built in the Bivallate Fort stage were retained in use in the succeeding Multivallate stage. In all such cases, except for the hut-floor in the Annexe, these shelters occurred where the inner revetment of the Inner Rampart of the Bivallate Fort was shared with the corresponding feature in the Multivallate Fort.

Finally, the Multivallate Fort suffered a catastrophe induced by burning of the inner and second ramparts in part, followed by substantial collapse and decay (The Burning and Decay of Stage 7 of Phase Six). They were never rebuilt in pre-Roman times. Instead, there formed over the ruins a continuous land surface, the product of natural agencies operating on whatever lay below, and most emphatically sealing the pre-Roman defences from their ultimate successors, the defences of the Medieval earthwork. This land surface constitutes the *Third or Great Interregnum* (Phase Seven). Everything above this seal is evidently Medieval, everything below is demonstrably pre-Roman. There are no signs of any structures of protracted occupation belonging to this phase.

VI. Chronology

Any attempt to place the foregoing succession of events on any kind of time scale, archaeological or absolute, has always foundered in the past because of the inadequacy of the data. I trust that in their charity, readers will forget what I and others have said on this subject.

Since 1969 the situation has been partly remedied in our case. We now possess a more complete stratigraphical record which provides a more accurate guide to the relative chronology of the various events for which we have stratigraphical evidence. Secondly, we now possess archaeological evidence in the form of pottery with recognisable characteristics which permit of comparison with their counterparts elsewhere. Next, we have a series of samples of timber taken from sealed rampart cores for which conventional carbon dates have been provided. Finally we have a date obtained by thermoluminescence for the final destruction of the multivallate fort by burning.

The table sets out the relevant data. Columns 3 and 4 give the figures arrived at in terms of the Libby convention (Half-life = 5568 years, 0 = 1950). Though the Libby half-life is still generally used for convenience, subsequent research has resulted in various modifications which have been proposed since 1950. I have therefore included in column 5 the calendar-date equivalents based on the revised half-life proposed by Dr. Suess in 1970, and in column 6 the single values for bristlecone pine corrections based upon the work of Damon, Long and Wallick.

It will be noted that the sequence of radio-carbon dates, plus the thermo-luminescence date, correlates well with the stratigraphical succession. Attractive though this sequence may be, we must remember that the timbers from which the samples were taken could conceivably have been derived from earlier structures, such as the palisade timbers of the Univallate Enclosure or the huts of the Open Settlement. Purely statistically—given the range of dates and the deviations quoted—one cannot exclude the possibility that all the timbers came from trees cut down at the same time. There are indeed similarities between the first and later earthworks in lay-out and details of structure which make it likely that they belong to the same tradition.

I now turn to consider the evidence provided by the pottery. The majority was derived from hearths lying immediately inside the inner revetment of the inner rampart and was sealed by the debris of the collapse which followed the burning, which was itself sealed by the land surface of the Great Interregnum and the tail of the Medieval shale banks. Stratigraphically, therefore, the pottery could be contemporary with the Bivallate Extension or the multivallate fort.

The fabric of the Castle Hill pottery is dark-grey in colour and is copiously stiffened with grits. Most of these are fragments of chalk, but there are others that can be matched from the post-glacial and late glacial deposits of the Yorkshire Wolds and the Humber Basin. In fact, in *form*, though perhaps not necessarily in *fabric*, the Castle Hill pottery most closely resembles sherds from Salthouse Road, Hull and Faxfleet on the Humber (excavated in 1964 and 1962)[2]. It belongs to the family perhaps best represented by the collection from Atwick on the East Coast of Holderness.

Until recently, no one has ventured an opinion on the date of this pottery, beyond calling it "Early Iron Age" or "Late Bronze Age", largely because the fabric was believed to have had a very long life, being native to the area from Neolithic to late Roman (Huntcliffe) times. It is now becoming evident, however, that our forms do occur in pre-La Tène contexts in the East Riding, as at Grimthorpe, Cowlam, and Burton Fleming (Stead, 1972, 21ff). If we follow the general view that the La Tène square ditched barrows, crouched

---

[2] I am obliged to Mr. J. Bartlett, formerly Director of the Hull Museums, for confirmation of this view.

TABLE 2. *Castle Hill, Almondbury: Absolute Chronology*

1	2	3	4	5	6	7
	Burning (Site 30) (T.L.)					431 ± 180
	Multivallate Fort Site 30	2400 ± 130 2410 ± 130	450 ± 130 460 ± 130	525,670,780 525,670,780	585 B.C. ± 130	
Six	Bivallate Fort Site 30 28(†) 40	2470 ± 110 2505 ± 95 2480 ± 110	520 ± 110 555 ± 95 530 ± 110	540,620,780 660 545,625,780	645 ± 140 660 ± 120	
	Univallate Fort Site 35(†)	2545 ± 95	595 ± 95	810	731 ± 180	
Five	Open Settlement					
Four	Second Interregnum					
Three	Univallate Enclosure					
Two	First Interregnum					
One	First Occupation Site 40	4060 ± 130	2110 ± 130	2530 ± 2750	2680 ± 154	
Phase	Event	Radio Carbon (Libby)	Calendar (Libby)	Calendar (Suess)	Calendar (D.L.W.)	T.L. (Oxford)

Dates marked (†) in Column 2 provided by Teledyne Isotopes; the remainder by N.P.D. Harwell.
Thermoluminescence dates (T.L.) by Research Laboratory for Archaeology and History of Art, University of Oxford.

inhumations on north-south axes, Danes' Graves pottery, cart burials and linear earthworks which we collectively refer to as the Arras Culture (Stead, 1965a), start with Cowlam sometime towards the end of the fifth century, then our pottery would appear to be pre-Arras. As such it accords with the C-14 Libby calendar date of 690 b.c. for Grimthorpe and our own of 555 and 520 b.c. The significance of such pottery in the West Riding remains problematical, but the chronological implications seem to be confirmed by the thermoluminescence date of 431 B.C. ± 180 for the burning observed in the Inner Rampart of the multivallate fort, for that burning brought to an end the occupation of the site in the pre-Roman phase of its history.

The other pottery objects found in the same stratigraphical context were salt-pot lids and fragments of side and base of shallow rectangular salt pots; these are not closely datable, nor has their source of production been traced, but there were pre-Roman salt workings on the east coast as at Ingoldsmells in Lincolnshire. In short, the available evidence suggest that the pre-Roman earthworks at Castle Hill can be assigned to the first half of the first millennium B.C. As such, they are broadly contemporary with some Scottish sites (Finavon, 590 b.c.), Craigmarloch Wood (590 b.c.) and Dun Lagaidh (490 b.c.), Northumbrian palisade enclosures (Huckhoe 510 b.c.), the settlement at Longbridge Deverill, Wiltshire, (630 b.c.), South Barrule in the Isle of Man (523 b.c.), Navan, Armagh, (680 b.c.) and nearer at hand, Grimthorpe, Staple Howe and Scarborough. It is now evident that the sequence of earthworks on Castle Hill, Almondbury, came to an end at or about the beginning of the hegemony of the bearers of the Arras culture in East Yorkshire, and not with the Roman Conquest, as I once believed. Indeed, it is conceivable that the two events were connected, in view of the fact that the people who manned the Castle Hill defences apparently had some affinity in ceramic tradition with the pre-Arras culture of the Wolds. Be that as it may, the end at Castle Hill was brought about by the burning and collapse of Stage 7, whereafter the defences were not repaired or re-erected until the twelfth century A.D.

VII. The Burning of the Stage 6 Defences

Since at least the time of Camden, the burnt ramparts of Castle Hill have been a subject of comment. His own remarks are an accurate description of the visible effects of that burning: "But when Cadwall (sic) the Briton, and Penda, the Mercian, made sharp war upon Edwin, the king of these countries, it was set on fire by the enemy, as Bede writeth, which the very dust and burnt colour as yet remaining upon the stone doth testify" (1587). The time is now ripe for a re-consideration of what caused the effects observed. Excavation and the use of a sensitivity meter[3] have enabled us to show that such burning as there is, is

[3] I am indebted to Mr. Arthur Bailey of the Department of Electrical Engineering in the University of Bradford for help in field survey; and to Mr. Dougherty of the Physics Department of Huddersfield Polytechnic for laboratory experiments.

confined to the Inner and Second ramparts as they existed in Stage 6, Phase Six of the pre-Roman period. The burning varies in intensity within the ramparts in which it occurs. There are parts of these same ramparts which are not in the least affected only a few centimetres from other sections which were intensely affected. There are some parts of the Inner and Second ramparts which are not affected at all in their entirety from top to bottom, even though they stand up vertically against rampart cores which were burnt to a cinder, or to brickdust.

Experiments with identical materials obtained *in situ* have shown that the colour changes observed in the field can be reproduced in the laboratory within the temperature range 400° to 800°C. Experiments have shown that the purple slag of the most intensely affected areas can be produced at a temperature of 700°C + applied for varying lengths of time, culminating in as little as ten minutes at 800°C. These temperatures are considerably lower than Thorneycroft required to reproduce the effects observed at Rahoy (Childe and Thorneycroft, 1938b). Even so, all our attempts to produce such temperatures inside the rampart core by the application of heat to the outer face of either front or rear revetments without changing both their colour and their mechanical strength, have failed. The revetments in one of the most intensely affected sections (Site 30) are not even faintly discoloured. The suggestions made by Thorneycroft, that vitrefaction at Rahoy was achieved by burinng piled up brushwood next to the outer face, and by Hamilton that the rampart at Clickhimin was affected by the burning of a range of lean-to buildings inside, therefore, evidently cannot apply to the phenomena observed at Castle Hill. Evidence from the same section (30) shows that the heat engendered within the rampart-core left both clay, stone blocks and timbers at the base of that section totally unaffected. Officials of the Yorkshire Division of the National Coal Board, who examined that section in the field, were of the opinion that the effects they saw resembled those they were familiar with in coal waste-tips and which were attributed to spontaneous combustion. Oddly enough, Professor Robert Newstead held a similar view of the ramparts I excavated at Maiden Castle, Bickerton and the Castle Ditch, Eddisbury. In both these cases, there was visual proof that the heat had not been applied outside the revetments of Triassic sandstone within which the affected cores were encased. At Maiden Castle, Bickerton, the rampart core was interlaced with trunks and branches of sessile oak. At Eddisbury, the timbers in the inturned entrance in the north west were unmistakably fabricated, and had a structural function.

The inference, is therefore, that pieces of timber, green or fabricated, though not necessarily pre-seasoned, heated up inside the rampart to the required temperatures. This explanation could well account for the irregular distribution of heat-effects within all three series of ramparts and if it is acceptable, it appears to suggest that those effects were the result of a catastrophe induced by natural causes rather than by the deliberate attempt to fire the rampart.

The only alternative suggestion I am able to make, admittedly unsupported by objective experimental evidence, is that the posts inserted in the centre of the crest of the rampart, for which there is some evidence, took fire, or were fired, and that thereafter the heat travelled downwards and was transferred to timbers inside the rampart and thence to the clay core in the areas around those timbers, as visual impressions suggested. This latter possibility does hold out the chance that the burning could have been induced by human action aimed at destroying the external palisade; if such, it had the possibly unexpected bonus of causing the core of the rampart to burn, then collapse. This view, offered very tentatively, is based on the fact that in Section 30, the area of rampart most intensely affected, to the right of the median section shown in Plate II, was a crater carried down almost to the base of the rampart containing the charred remains of a large oak post, now lying on its side in the bottom of that crater. One further complication must be introduced. The inner rampart of the Bivallate Extension of the west, windier side, was burnt to brick dust but appeared to contain little or no timber inside the stone revetments, which were unaffected on their outer faces. Clearly the matter will remain unresolved for the time being.

VIII. Conclusions

What is undisputed is that the affected ramparts were never repaired and that the land surface of the Great Interregnum developed over the ruins. The latter event took place, apparently, before the Roman Conquest, since a piece of Arretine ware (an import dated by Dr. Felix Oswald to midway in the first century A.D.) lay on this land surface at Site 3 and a second sherd of Roman coarse ware of a kind familiar at Roman Slack, and presumably dated 80–120 A.D., was found on a similar land surface overlying the abandoned guard-room inside the entrance of the Univallate Enclosure. These two fragments and a piece of an amphora reputedly found in the cutting of a cable trench from the Castle Hotel to the bottom of the hill, are the only evidence of Roman contact with the site. On all other counts, the Romans can be acquitted of the charge of deliberately destroying the pre-Roman defences of Castle Hill.

So if Almondbury ever was Camulodunum (Richmond, 1925, pp. 83–84), it can only have been given its name as a tribute to that Celtic god of war whose stronghold it had been, at least in legend, and whose ancient ruins could have been a place of excursion for those stationed at Slack, from which it was all too plainly visible. On present evidence, Castle Hill could not have been a stronghold of those Brigantes who finally joined their leader Venutius in open revolt against his former queen Cartimandua for her continuing pre-Roman sympathies in A.D. 69 (Tacitus, *Histories*, III, 45). The lack of archaeological evidence for an immediately pre-Conquest occupation at Castle Hill further reinforces Allen's reappraisal of the numismatic evidence. Allen argued that the so-called "Almondbury Hoard" arose from a confusion in provenance of coins which in reality all came from a single hoard from Lightcliffe in the Calder Valley, and that these, together with the Honley hoard, were to be attributed not to the Brigantes, but to the neighbouring Coritani (Allen, 1963, pp. 22–28). A further consequence of Allen's survey was the abandonment of the identification of the unique silver coin from Honley, inscribed VOL-ISIOS-CARTIVEL, with Cartimandua herself and either her husband Venutius or her subsequent consort Vellocatus. When Richmond proposed the equation of Camulodunum with Castle Hill, Almondbury, in 1925, he insisted that only excavation could demonstrate occupation on the site in the Roman period; as yet, our excavations have yielded no such proof.

5 | Blewburton Hill, Berkshire: Re-Excavation and Reappraisal

D. W. Harding

I. Introduction

The excavation of the hillfort on Blewburton Hill in Berkshire is incomplete, and, for the present, has no prospect of completion. The 1967 season was planned as a continuation of the programme of work carried out under the auspices of Reading Museum, and under the field direction of A. E. P. and F. J. Collins, between 1947 and 1953. (Collins, A. E. P., 1947; 1952; Collins, A. E. P. and F. J., 1959). The re-excavation of the site was sponsored by Reading Museum in collaboration with the Department of Archaeology in the University of Durham, and volunteer labour was provided by the Oxford University Archaeological Society, Durham University and several local educational organisations and institutions. Additional financial support was received from the Leverhulme Trust and the British Academy in 1967. A further season's work in 1968 was cancelled through insufficient funds, and in consequence the present summary is less a report than the salvage of the report that should have been.

Blewburton Hill is a northern outlier of the Berkshire Downs, situated between the parishes of Blewbury and Aston Upthorpe (Berkshire 21 NE SU 544861). Prior to excavation, an early Iron Age occupation of the site had been indicated by the quantities of pottery recovered from the interior of the camp, and especially in its south-western sector (Bradford, 1942). It was here that excavation had been directed initially, in the 1947 season, with the opening of Cuttings A–E. These cuttings exposed the palisade trench of the primary, stockaded settlement, but of the defences of the hillfort proper less could be inferred at this point, since the earthworks had been substantially reduced by ploughing. In consequence, work in 1948 and 1949 was concentrated on the western end of the hillfort, where two major rampart sections (F and G) revealed the main structural sequence of the defences. In addition, a substantial area of the western entrance was opened, exposing a metalled roadway and the foundations of successive gateway structures (Cuttings H and

J). In the course of excavating these trenches, several Anglo-Saxon graves were uncovered, and it was to the more extensive exploration of this cemetery that the 1953 season was devoted.

In retrospect, a number of outstanding problems required clarification. Though the basic stratigraphic sequence of the earthworks had been established by Collins' excavation, the structural details of the defences were still lacking, in particular for the first rampart which appeared to be of box-construction. Second, Collins' interpretation of the gateway structures in the western entrance as a two-phase system (Collins, 1952, Figs 9 and 10) seemed inconsistent with both the three-phase sequence of the defences and with the evidence of the 1949 excavation, which itself could justify three successive passage-ways. And finally, in spite of the quantities of pottery recovered from the southern side of the camp, no evidence for settlement had yet been traced in the form of buildings or ancillary structures within the precincts of the hillfort. The 1967 season of excavation was aimed at the resolution of these problems. In the event, the complexity of the features revealed in the defences and in the entrance prevented a more extensive examination of the interior, and internal buildings have still to be located.

Four cuttings were opened, two across the defences, one in the entrance and one in the interior. Each will now be described in detail.

II. The Defences

A. *Cutting 1*

The initial objective of the 1967 season of excavation was to verify and clarify the structural sequence of earthworks which had been suggested by Collins' Cuttings F and G in particular, and if possible to assign the principal phases of construction to their chronological horizons on the strength of associated artefactual evidence. The area selected for this major section was a well preserved length of earthwork on the northern side of the camp, which promised to give a more complete vertical sequence than the southern ramparts, which Collins' Cutting B had shown to have been much reduced by ploughing, and which had not been subjected to such intensive excavation in the earlier campaigns as the earthworks on either flank of the western entrance. In terms of its structural evidence, the choice was amply justified.

The cutting measured 3 m in width and 35 m in length (Fig. 2), and extended from a point well behind the tail of the main rampart to the second cultivation terrace below it. No trace was found within this cutting of the stockade trench which represented the earliest fortification of the site: its absence here, and the inward turn which it displays in Cutting 4, argue strongly that the camp in this primary phase occupied only the western half of the hill-top. The first structural period represented in Cutting 1, therefore, was the hillfort proper with box rampart. Coincidentally, the major revetment posts of this rampart were exposed exactly in the western face of the cutting, confirming that the original width of the defensive wall from front to back had been 4 m. Subsequent excavation in Cutting 2 showed that this corresponded exactly to the spacing of the vertical timbers along the front, and presumably therefore also along the rear of the rampart. The box-rampart was evidently constructed methodically as a symmetrical unit, separated by a narrow berm from its ditch. At the time of excavation, no sign was found in Cutting 1 of the horizontal braces which were clearly traced as hollow cavities in the front face of Cutting 2, and which must surely have been an essential element in any timber-framed rampart. In retrospect, at the time of drawing the final site sections, a series of faint silty streaks were noticed in the western face of Cutting 1, which could have been the last vestiges of such horizontal timber-lacing. It is conceivable, of course, that this method of construction was not used exclusively throughout the perimeter works of the camp, but on balance I suspect that lack of site experience led us to overlook in this first cutting the very faint traces which are all that survive of such a system. The eastern face of Cutting 1 could be instructive in this respect. It will be seen that the layers which constitute the core of the main rampart have here taken on a marked internal dip, an effect which could be simply the result of flinging up baskets of rubble in construction, but which equally could result from the sagging and decay of the timber framework at the point where it was weakest and unsupported in the middle of the rampart. Behind the box-rampart was a low ramp of turf (layer 6), a feature which has been found consistently in every rampart section on the site, and which invites comparison with a similar backing of the stone revetment at Rainsborough Camp, Northamptonshire (Avery *et al.*, 1967). Its purpose was evidently to buttress the timber revetting against the weight of the rampart, and perhaps to afford an additional facility for defenders mounting the parapet.

One respect in which the stratification of Cutting 1 proved to be typical of the entire site was the clarity with which the turf line (layer 10) buried below the first rampart stood out from the old humus level beneath it (layer 11). It was in these layers that the vertical post-holes associated with the box-rampart most clearly showed, since their filling was invariably white chalky rubble which had collapsed into them from the rampart core when the timbers themselves had decayed or been removed. Unlike the usual pattern on chalk-down settlements, where post-holes are generally recognised as dark intrusions in the natural bedrock, the Blewburton defences introduced the concept of "negative post-holes", recognised as white patterns in the former ground surface.

In the course of time, the timber-laced box-rampart fell into decay, its collapsed debris (layer 5) spreading like a tail back from the crest of the bank over the turf backing. Here again, the turf-line which grew over this layer of earth and rubble was very distinct (layer 4), and likewise corresponds to a comparable feature noted in Collins' Cuttings F and G. When the defences were eventually reinstated, the ditch was evidently cleaned out and probably (on the basis of evidence from Collins' Cuttings B, F, and G) redug to make it deeper and wider, the upcast being used to heighten the bank as a simple dump or *glacis* (layer 3). It is presumably to this phase that we should attribute the construction of the counterscarp bank with its close-set palisade, and the partial attempt at bivallation. In Cutting 1, the evidence for the outer bank was unequivocal, and quite contrary to the impression of sterility given by the section drawings and photographs of Collins' Cutting F, the nearest adjoining section to our own in the north-west sector of the fort (Pl. 3). The counterscarp bank must clearly be considered in conjunction with the pit or partial ditch revealed below it at the end of Cutting 1. If these features do represent an attempt at bivallation, it was one which apparently did not embrace the north-western corner of the defences spanned by Cutting F. In the south-west sector on the other hand, bivallate defences are still witnessed by extant earthworks, tested by Collins in his Cutting G, which evidently extended formerly along the southern perimeter at least as far as Cutting B. Unfortunately, the problem could not be resolved by geophysical means. A survey with the aid of a magnetometer not only failed to trace the line of this latter ditch, but also failed to register the position of the intrusion at the northern end of Cutting 1 when a traverse was conducted immediately prior to excavation. We can only conclude therefore, that the filling of this ditch contains insufficient magnetic material to give a reliable result by this method and excavation alone can confirm or refute its effective existence as a secondary feature. Whether or not this attempt at refortification was stimulated by a period of political unrest, and overcome by events before its completion, we can only speculate.

When the Iron Age camp lay derelict, a further accumulation of humus grew up over the collapsed tail of the rampart, and above this two worn Roman coins were found, lost by passers-by or squatters sheltering in the lee of the earthworks. The depth of humus washed down from the summit of the hill was clearly increased by medieval agriculture, which not only created the lynchet system along the north and west of the hill, but evidently skimmed the top of the dump of the main rampart, leaving it levelled with the interior as it stands today.

In our second endeavour, to obtain a stratified sequence of datable artefacts, the location of Cutting 1 was, in retrospect, less happy, since only a very small number of significant sherds of pottery was recovered from its excavation. Hillfort ramparts are not noted for their productivity in this respect, but it has to be admitted that the choice of a cutting across the north-facing defences, probably remote from the domestic habitation sites from which pottery refuse would naturally be derived, did not enhance the chances of success. Enough material was recovered, however, to make one observation, namely that the layers of accumulation or collapse *between* the principal structural layers produced much more material than the layers of the ramparts themselves, and hence one is attempting to reconstruct not so much a sequence for the major structural phases as one for the intervals of occupation between them. Whilst it may seem obvious that very little pottery, relatively, will be broken during the actual construction phase, and hence incorporated into the layers of the bank, nonetheless, the fact that the pottery from the collapsed debris of the box-rampart and the turf above it, and from the humus deposit behind the dump rampart was not particularly abraded should warn us against interpreting these phases as periods of "abandonment". They may represent nothing less than a period of peaceful occupation when the defences were not required, and were allowed to fall into a state of disrepair.

The small quantity of pottery which was recovered from Cutting 1 at least affords a consistent pattern. In the humus deposit which accumulated at the back of the dump rampart (Fig. 2, layer 2) two distinctive Iron B forms occurred, a worn fragment of "saucepan" pottery (Fig. 7, 2), and two sherds of globular bowls of the kind which is particularly associated with the later Iron Age site at Frilford, Berkshire (Harding, 1972, Pl. 67). One of these displayed the characteristic "wall-paper border" ornament below the rim, and a double-lined swag dependent from an impressed circlet (Fig. 7, 1). The dump rampart itself (Fig. 2, layer 3) contained a single sherd with quasi-rouletted ornament, which should belong to approximately the same chronological horizon. From the turf-line over the collapsed box-rampart (Fig. 2, layer 4) downwards, the pottery was totally devoid of Iron B forms. Immediately beneath the turf-line was a small rim with angular neck profile, while the body of the collapsed box-rampart contained another small shoulder fragment of a carinated vessel. Neither were especially characteristic of early La Tène angular pottery in the region, however, and they might well belong to an earlier chronological context. The uppermost layer of the rampart itself—or the deposit which filled the hollow when the box-framework sagged—(Fig. 2, 5a), produced three sherds, including an indeterminate rim, in that leathery grey/brown burnished ware which is especially characteristic of the early Iron Age pottery series in the Upper Thames. The fragments of "saucepan" pottery and globular bowls from layers 2 and 3 certainly suggest a date for the dump rampart phase somewhere between the later second and mid-first centuries B.C. The evidence for the earlier structural phases is perhaps slightly more contentious. Some additional light was thrown on the chronology of these earlier levels by the excavation of two further rampart sections in Cutting 2.

B. Cutting 2 (North and South)

From the excavation of Cutting 1, it was clear that sufficient new evidence was forthcoming from the defences to merit an additional section across the earthworks on the western side of the hillfort, and nearer the 1948–1949 cuttings, in order to establish whether the construction of the hillfort defences really did differ markedly along different sectors of its perimeter. In the event, the discoveries made in the main rampart in this area were such that time did not permit the further examination of the ditch and counterscarp at this point.

Two parallel trenches were opened in Cutting 2; 2 South measured 4 m wide and 15 m long, 2 North was 1 m longer, the two being separated by a baulk 3 m wide. The main structural sequence encountered in Cutting 1 was repeated, and further stratified pottery of value was recovered. Beneath the earlier rampart the palisade trench of the stockaded camp was located once again, in accordance with its last recorded position in the 1947–1953 excavations (Pl. 2a). The major importance of this area, however, was that it provided confirmation that the first rampart proper had been contained within a complete timber framework. In essence this comprised a line of vertical timbers along both the front and back faces of the bank, which were probably braced by horizontal rails to form a continuous revetment, parallel to the alignment of the rampart on both its sides. In order to prevent their collapse under the weight of the chalk core, these vertical revetments had been tied together by at least three levels of horizontal cross-braces, which thereby lent rigidity to the entire structure. The position of these horizontal timbers was betrayed by a series of hollow cavities, located initially by chance in the front face of the rampart, which in some instances were all that survived after the wood itself had decayed (Pl. 4). Evidently the weight of the compacted chalk had encased the timbers like a plaster mould, so that, long after the timber had perished, its form was retained in the chalk core of the rampart. Some cavities had collapsed nonetheless. Others still contained traces of the horizontal braces in the form of charcoal stains. The circumstances at Blewburton are reminiscent of the Caburn, where Wilson found horizontal cavities within the puddled chalk, hollow for a length of over 4 ft, and containing only the slightest sprinkling of "dark powder" (Wilson, 1938, p. 174). Horizontal cavities of this kind could easily be destroyed by an excavator working quite properly downwards layer by layer, since he would never recognise in the absence of charcoal filling a hollow pipe in the chalk once it had collapsed beneath his feet. In consequence, relatively few sites are known where the horizontal timber-lacing has been recognised, and more often we have to be satisfied with examples like Ranscombe, Sussex, where a few short lengths of timber were all that survived of what must have been a system as complex as that now verified at Blewburton (Burstow and Holleyman, 1964, p. 57 and Pl. IIA). Once recognised in the front face of the rampart, it was naturally an easier matter to locate the position of horizontal timbers from above (Fig. 3, plan).

Cutting 2 produced further information concerning the vertical posts of the timber framework. The location of two pairs of revetment post-holes, one pair in each trench, enabled the spacing between uprights to be calculated at almost exactly 4 m. Furthermore, it appeared that these vertical posts had been squared off, since the rear post-hole in Cutting 2 North preserved the position of the post itself as a hollow cavity of rectangular cross-section for a depth well over a metre within the chalk core of the rampart. The posts used at this point apparently measured 18 cm by 14 cm. No information was recovered to indicate the method of jointing the timbers. As in Cutting 1, the filling of the remaining post-holes associated with the timber-laced rampart was a fine chalk rubble, which clearly distinguished post-holes of this phase from those of the pre-fort occupation. For instance, the post-hole adjacent to the rear revetment post in Cutting 2 North on its south-west side contained a chalky fill, whereas the post-hole which was contiguous with it on its north side was fillep with a uniformly dark chalk-speckled humus, and therefore must ante-date the rampart. The composition of the core of the box-rampart was not absolutely uniform in both trenches (Fig. 3, layers 7–9; Fig. 4, layers 8–9), but in both the rear face of the rampart was buttressed by a low turf ramp, as in Cutting 1 (layer 6). Above this, the sequence of layers corresponded exactly to that of Cutting 1, the collapsed debris of the box-rampart (layer 5) with its turf-line above (layer 4) being superseded by the dump rampart (layer 3), over which lapped a layer of dark humus (layer 2) and finally the post-Iron Age deposits (Figs 3, 4).

By comparison with Cutting 1, Cutting 2 produced far greater quantities of pottery. For this reason, the relative paucity of material from the layers associated with the dump rampart occupation is the more significant, suggesting a shift in settlement in the later period away from the western end of the camp. In fact, one fragment of "saucepan" pottery from the humus layer (2) at the back of the dump rampart in Cutting 2 South (Fig. 7, 3), together with a rim of Iron B ware from the comparable layer in Cutting 2 North (Fig. 7, 4) confirm the pattern established in Cutting 1, but otherwise little pottery of any value was recovered from the later Iron Age levels. The majority of the pottery came from the collapsed debris of the box rampart, with additional sherds from the rampart itself, its turf backing, and the old ground surface beneath it. In Cutting 2 North, the thin turf-line over the collapsed box rampart contained a number of small sherds, including two small expanded-rim fragments and one worn sherd with haematite slip. Otherwise, pottery with finger-tip or plastic ornament was absent, but equally there were no later wares or forms included in this assemblage. Even in the collapsed rampart itself, layer 5, there were only a few very worn sherds with finger-tip decoration (Fig. 7, 9). There were, however, in this layer many fragments in coarse shelly fabric, so characteristic of the earliest Iron Age in the region, and a number of vessels with expanded rims (Fig. 7, 12), a form which likewise belongs to an early phase of the Iron Age in the Upper Thames region (Harding, 1972, p. 73ff; Pls 44, 45). Two other vessels from this level deserve comment. One, represented by rim and body sherds bearing traces of haematite coating, was a round-bodied bowl with tall, slightly flaring rim (Fig. 7, 11); the other comprised a jar with tall S-shaped neck in Hallstatt tradition, with signs of external burnishing, and decorated on the shoulder with a small dotted rosette (Fig. 7, 8). Slightly expanded rims—certainly not the heavily expanded variety—in coarse ware were also found in the turf backing behind the primary rampart (layer 6), together with a fragment of a round-bodied bowl in burnished brown ware. The only layer of the rampart itself to produce any diagnostic pottery was the uppermost (layer 5A), in which was found a single coarse ware rim with diagonal slashed decoration (Fig. 7, 15). Finally, from the old ground surface below the rampart was recovered a curving body sherd with chevron ornament (Fig. 7, 17) and a number of sherds of coarse gritty ware.

Cutting 2 (South) yielded an equal quantity of pottery from the earlier levels. The thin turf-line over the collapsed box-rampart included a variety of small bowl fragments (Fig. 7, 6 and 7) including one with very worn haematite slip (Fig. 7, 6), as well as a fragment of a vessel in coarse shelly fabric with an inward expansion of its rim and faint finger-tip decoration. Below this the collapsed debris of the rampart (layer 5) produced at least two vessels with expanded rims, one with quite a pronounced outward flange, and both bearing heavy cabled ornament about the rim (Fig. 7, 13 and 14). A similar sherd was found embedded in the top of the turf backing of the rampart (Fig. 7, 16). Less pronounced was the expansion of the rim of a jar from the old turf line below the box rampart (layer 10) which displayed a series of shallow dimples around the shoulder (Fig. 7, 18).

The significance of the pottery from the rampart cuttings will be discussed later in this report. For the present we need only remark that the sherds from contexts associated with the primary rampart and the later dump rampart each formed entirely homogeneous and independent groups, and were strongly indicative of a period of abandonment between the two phases. Between the stockade phase and the primary rampart, on the other hand, there was little evidence to suggest any such break in occupation.

III. The Western Entrance (Cutting 3)

The excavation of the western entrance of the Blewburton hillfort was very largely accomplished by Collins in 1948 and 1949. He successfully located the causeway across the ditch, and showed it in its final phase to have been a little over 8 m in width. From the inner lips of the ditch terminals, he excavated an area some 27 m into the interior of the camp, and uncovered a complex series of entrance structures, including the post-holes which supported the earlier timber passageways, and the stone flanking walls of the latest Iron Age entrance. The surface of the entrance passage was cobbled, and evidently this street had been patched or even remetalled completely on more than one occasion. Unfortunately, Collins' interpretation of the Blewburton entrance (Collins, 1952, Figs 9 and 10) provided for only two structural phases, and seems curiously at variance, not only with the three-fold sequence which he had plainly demonstrated in his rampart sections, but also with the information afforded by his own plan of the area (Collins, 1952, Fig. 7). From the composite plan (Fig. 5) two major features are apparent, the parallel revetment walling on the latest entrance passage, and the narrower passage which preceded it. The latter comprised a double line of substantial post-holes, including half split-timbers reminiscent of those at Rainsborough Camp, Northamptonshire (Avery *et al.*, 1967, Pl. XXII), and terminating at its inner end in a pair of massive holes which presumably sustained the gate itself. In addition, a number of smaller post-holes were located, of which five on the northern side of the entrance form a fairly convincing line, which could be matched by an opposing line to the south of the southern revetment wall. These three phases of entrance structures would seem to correspond quite satisfactorily with the three principal periods of occupation, namely those represented by the dump rampart, the box rampart and the stockade trench respectively. Collins' interpretation omits one of these three phases altogether, the omission being *not* the admittedly unsubstantial early phase, which he adopts as his Phase 1, but the substantial post-holes of Phase 2. Several of these he incorporated instead into his latest phase, the alignment of which is in any case at a different angle from its predecessor. In consequence of this reduction of three phases into two, his Phase 1 entrance passageway is absurdly orientated in respect to the causeway across the ditch, being much too wide on the south, and a little too narrow on the north side. This situation is remedied by the revised phasing, since the hillfort ditch would not yet have existed when the entrance to the stockaded camp was built.

Even so, several outstanding problems are posed by the Blewburton entrance. At what point did the palisade trench of the earliest camp adjoin the entrance post-holes? Excavation of the Anglo-Saxon cemetery in 1953 certainly traced it north of Cutting G, and therefore presumably to within a few metres of the entrance. Unfortunately, the exact relationship of this excavation to the Iron Age entrance is hard to establish, since the former is not shown on any of Collins' overall site plans, which in any case are reproduced at an unusable scale. It is conceivable that the palisade abutted directly on to the Phase 1 entrance passage; the failure to excavate below the street cobbling may account for its apparent absence at this point (Collins, 1959, p. 3). The street itself presents problems since it apparently extends laterally well beyond the width of the hillfort entrance passages, and slightly beyond even the greater width of the entrance to the stockaded camp. For the timber phases, at least, we might wonder whether guard-rooms or sentry boxes, so far unlocated might account for the spread of cobbling beyond the limits of the street itself.

Excavation in 1967 has added a further complication to the interpretation of the gateway structures, in the form of a ditch, some two metres in depth, which was found to extend across the back of the entrance, and approximately at right angles to it. The proportions of this feature argue against its association with the stockaded camp. Though there is the suggestion of a small external ditch some three to four metres outside the palisade trench in Collins' 1953 cutting, nowhere else on the site is there any suggestion of earthwork in conjunction with this phase of occupation. On the other hand, the deep pits which marked the end of the revetment wall of the latest Iron Age entrance, and which presumably were the terminal posts to support a timber gate at the inner end of the passage, showed quite clearly in the filling of the cross-ditch, and were evidently constructed at a stage when the latter was no longer in use and had been completely backfilled. By elimination, therefore, unless this feature belonged to another hitherto unsuspected building period, there remains only the second phase entrance, that represented by the narrow alignment of substantial post-holes, in which to incorporate this extraordinary ditch. The apparently excessive gap between it and the inner end of the timber passage could again be explained by the failure to excavate below the latest roadway surface. Some interval would presumably have been necessary in any case, to permit access to the interior of the camp. Unless we imagine that the cross-ditch was normally spanned by a timber bridge, traffic entering the fort must have been diverted to one side once it emerged from the entrance passage. This arrangement could certainly account for the extension of cobbling on the northern side of the excavated area. As a military feature, the function of the ditch is self-evident; it would have impeded any direct assault upon the interior through the gateway, and would have exposed the assailants' flank to cross-fire from defenders lined up behind the ditch. In fact, there was no sign of a bank on the inner edge of the cross-ditch, though this could well have been levelled by the same medieval agricultural activity which reduced the dump rampart itself on the western and northern sides of the hill. Alternatively, the post-holes located in 1967 behind the cross-ditch could conceivably have retained the timbers of a breastwork to provide cover for the defenders. The possibility raised above, that this ditch belonged to a hitherto unsuspected structural phase should not be totally dismissed, however. Among the material from its filling was a much-abraded Langdale axe, and though the few sherds of pottery appear to be of Iron Age, rather than Neolithic fabric, we may recall the discovery of causewayed camps within the precincts of later Iron Age fortifications elsewhere in Southern England (see Dixon, below p. 161). The previous discovery of worked flints, and other fragments of polished stone axe (Collins, 1952, pp. 48–49; 1959, Fig. 6, 20) certainly suggests some Neolithic activity in the near vicinity.

Though it seems reasonable to correlate the sequence of gateway structures at Blewburton with the sequence revealed by the defences, independent dating evidence might well have been recovered by the careful excavation of the roadway levels in the middle of the entrance passage, where there was apparently a greater depth of stratigraphy than at the extreme eastern or western ends of the excavated area. The lack of a section across the roadway at its deepest point, and the absence of associated artefacts from the post fillings of the successive gateway structures is particularly unfortunate, since these deficiencies cannot be made good by further excavation. There seems little doubt that a final phase of the gateway with its stone flanking walls belongs to the later pre-Belgic Iron Age; Collins' discovery of a "saucepan" pot with curvilinear ornament (1952, Fig. 12, 3; Harding, 1972, Pl. 66, B) on the upper roadway surface is certainly consistent with the association of similar pottery with the humus deposit which lapped over the dump rampart in Cutting 1. From the 1967 extension, a substantial fragment of a globular bowl (Fig. 7, 5), undecorated except for a faint panel below the rim, but otherwise comparable to those from Frilford (Harding, 1972, Pl. 67) was recovered from the filling of the post-pit which marked the inner end of the revetment wall on the northern side of the entrance passage. The evidence suggests, therefore, that the camp was refortified at some time towards the end of the second century B.C., or perhaps even later, at the beginning of the first century, as a protective measure against Belgic expansion from the south-east. The virtual absence of Belgic material itself argues strongly against Collins' alternative view that the occupation of the site was prolonged into the first century A.D., until it was brought violently to an end by the advancing Roman legions. Indeed, we may seriously question whether there is any evidence for destruction of the hillfort, accidental or with intent. First, the collapsed masonry of the gateway passage showed no sign of fire-reddening, and could equally well have tumbled from the weight of the rampart behind it after the abandonment of the camp. Second, the distribution of the horse-skeletons in the entrance in pairs, and in particular the situation of another buried in its own pit behind the cross ditch, seems far too orderly to be regarded simply as the "corpses of animals strewn about the street" (Cotton, 1962, 34). Quite clearly, we are here dealing with a deliberate ritual of horse-burial (cp. Müller-Wille and Vierck, 1971), in which the pairing of animals presumably reflects their use as two-horse teams for drawing wheeled vehicles (Pl. 5). And finally, in the 1967 extension to the entrance excavation at any rate, traces of charcoal were few, and certainly no more than could result from normal occupation. From this it does not necessarily follow that Blewburton was not abandoned abruptly as a result of pressure by hostile invaders; but the hillfort itself was not apparently the scene of any battle or sack, nor was it systematically dismantled afterwards by intruders.

IV. The Interior (Cutting 4)

Within the interior of the camp, and centrally situated just within its southern perimeter, an area of 440 m² was stripped in the hope of locating buildings and ancillary structures of domestic occupation. In this objective, the excavation was unsuccessful. Although the area contained numerous post-holes, none formed a coherent plan or regular pattern of any kind. The only significant structural feature exposed in Cutting 4 was the continuation of the palisade trench of the primary stockaded camp. From its general direction (Fig. 6) it is clear that the stockade swung northwards at this point, encompassing the western half of the hill only, and an area approximately half that enclosed by the subsequent 11-acre hillfort. Within the smaller of the two squares opened, a second short length of gully was revealed, terminating in a disturbed area which included at least one substantial post-hole. The function of this gully, and its relationship to the palisade trench in the main cutting can only be clarified by further excavation, but it seems possible that there was here an offset entrance into the south-east corner of the stockaded enclosure.

The proximity of the entrance might well account for the quantities of pottery, including a high proportion of early forms and fabrics which could have been contemporary with the stockaded camp, recovered from Cutting 4. None of this material had any significant stratigraphic context, however, since the natural bedrock lay immediately below the ploughsoil. Some of the post-holes produced pottery in their filling, principally the larger holes in the south-east quadrant of the major cutting. Though there is no guarantee that earlier rubbish survivals could not have been scraped up and incorporated in the post-packing at the time of construction, nonetheless the homogeneity of the material, and the fact that substantial fragments of coarse ware jars not excessively abraded were included, may suggest that in this instance the pottery could be regarded as a contemporary association. Most evidently diagnostic of an early date was a sherd bearing deep-punched and scored ornament in the Wessex tradition of the earliest Iron Age, and two fragments from separate post-holes of coarse ware with diagonal as well as horizontal finger-tipping, for which we might postulate later Bronze Age antecedents. Among the unstratified pottery from Cutting 4 was a large number of coarse ware sherds with finger-tip decoration, several haematite-coated fragments including one with deep-scored linear ornament, and one haematite-coated bowl fragment with horizontal furrowing in the Wessex fashion. Elsewhere, in the topsoil, late material was still in evidence, including swag-ornamented pottery and an iron currency bar of Allen's sword-shaped category (Allen, 1967, pp. 308–310 and footnote 1).

The excavation of Cutting 4 revealed one further piece of information worthy of record. In the north-west corner of the major trench, a natural fissure in the chalk was found to be filled with glacial sand and gravel to a depth of 20 cm or more. An auger survey conducted along the east-west axis of the hill demonstrated that this was part of a hitherto unplotted outcrop of pleistocene gravel, comparable to those known on Moulsford Down and at Wittenham Clumps.

V. The Anglo-Saxon Cemetery

The first indication that Blewburton Hill had been the site of a cemetery in the Anglo-Saxon period was the discovery of an inhumation burial of a young girl at the western end of the hill-top in 1945. Collins' excavations in 1948, 1949 and 1953 revealed 18 more inhumations and one cremation burial aligned along the lee of the south-western rampart, adjacent to the Iron Age entrance on its southern side. Various ages and both sexes were represented in the burials, which included both supine and flexed attitudes. Most of the graves contained grave-goods, mainly brooches of circular, disc or penannular type. A late sixth or early seventh century date was suggested for the cemetery.

Extension of the gateway excavation (Cutting 3) in 1967 revealed two further graves of the Anglo-Saxon period (Fig. 5). In Grave A, a shallow depression in the chalk of irregular outline, the skeleton of an adult male was orientated approximately west–east. Its grave-goods comprised small bronze belt-plates at the waist, and an iron-bound wooden bucket by its head. The second burial—Grave B—was that of a child of six to eight years. Here, the skeleton, like its nearest neighbour to the west, was aligned approximately south–north; no trace of an excavated grave-pit survived in the surface of the chalk. The only grave-goods which accompanied this burial were a small iron knife, and an iron belt-buckle.

In a small trial trench, excavated prior to the 1967 season by Mr. R. A. Rutland, formerly of Reading Museum, to the north of the western entrance to the camp, a further cremation burial was uncovered some metres from the main concentration of burials, perhaps indicating that the cemetery was more extensive than has been supposed hitherto.

VI. Chronology and Conclusions

The basic structural sequence of the Blewburton defences has been fairly reliably established by excavation: the threefold pattern of palisade/box-rampart/dump-rampart has emerged with a fair degree of consistency in most of the sections excavated across the defences. This sequence correlates well with the revised sequence for the western entrance, a reinterpretation based largely upon the excavated evidence of 1947–1953.

If the relative sequence of structural phases is clear enough, the absolute dating which should be assigned to these structural horizons remains very subjective. Insufficient financial resources in 1967 precluded the use of radio-carbon dating, though adequate samples for the primary rampart could probably have been obtained from the decayed remnants of its timber-lacing. It is, in fact, for the earlier periods that dating is most problematical. Among the pottery from the box-rampart in Cutting 2, or from the layers immediately related to it, two forms were outstanding, the round-bodied bowl and the coarse ware jar with expanded rim and cabled ornament. The round-bodied bowls—essentially a Hallstatt form—include examples with haematite coating or deep-scored ornament for which a sixth century dating would seem appropriate, and others with rosette or even incipient (dotted) swag ornament which should belong to a later—perhaps even early La Tène–context. On the other hand, the relative absence of angular wares of the kind which characterised Long Wittenham and the early La Tène settlements of the Thames Valley at present argues against a later fifth century date for this phase of construction, though occupation could have continued elsewhere in the interior of the camp. Ceramically, it is scarcely possible to see a significant distinction between the material associated with the timber-laced rampart and the preceding stockaded phase: rubbish survivals from the latter could in any case have been incorporated in the construction of the rampart. There is, nonetheless, a certain amount of earlier material from the interior of the settlement, including odd sherds of furrowed bowls and a couple of coarse ware fragments with random or diagonal-with-horizontal finger-tip decoration which could indicate an ultimate Bronze Age occupation, transitional into the earliest Iron Age, on the site. Provisionally, therefore, we might suggest a seventh–sixth century dating for the construction of the stockaded camp, and a sixth–fifth century date for its replacement by the first hillfort proper.

The distinction between this earlier occupation and the phase represented by the refortification with dump rampart, on the other hand, is very clear. The two outstanding pottery forms representative of this period are the globular bowl, frequently with pendant swag ornament, and the "saucepan" pot. Both would be consistent with a re-occupation of the hillfort at the end of the second, or beginning of the first century B.C., continuing until the site was abandoned before the end of the century, at a time of political unrest consequent upon Belgic territorial expansion from the south-east. To this period, rather than to the first century A.D., should we now assign the final abandonment of the Blewburton hillfort, which lay derelict through the Roman period, until its prominence as a local landmark commended it as a cemetery-site to the early Saxon settlers of the Blewbury region.

6 | *Excavations at Mam Tor, Derbyshire, 1965–1969*

D. G. Coombs

Mam Tor[1] is by far the largest and most imposing of a small group of hillforts situated in the Peak District at the southern end of the Pennines (Fig. 1). It is built on the highest point of a long hog backed ridge of shale and sandstone with steep slopes on three sides. Its height of 1696 ft O.D. gives it commanding views on all sides especially dominating the Edale and Hope valleys.

The area (*c* 16 acres) defined by the rampart is tongue shaped (Fig. 2). The defences consist of a single rampart and ditch, 1·1 km in circumference which follow the contours of the hill. Preston (1954) suggests that an inner bank and ditch are present behind the main rampart in the south and east; the fort is classified as multivallate on the O.S. *Map of the Iron Age in Southern Britain*. The greater part of the interior stands well above the defences. At its southern end the fort is subjected to landslides; consequently the defences are incomplete. It appears that this process had already begun before the defences were built. The weakest part of the fort is at its northern end where a ridge joins it to Loose Hill, where there are indications of a double inturned entrance. A semi-inturned entrance occurs on the south side.

A stream rises just within the rampart on the north-western slope and flows through marshy ground across the line of the defences. The present rampart height is *c* 7–9 m above the surface of the ditch and the visual effect is of a *glacis* rampart.

At the southern end of the site, near the highest point are two Bronze Age round barrows. Bateman (1848) states that one was opened some time in the

[1] I would like to thank the National Trust as the owners of the site, and the Department of the Environment for granting permission to excavate, my colleagues at Manchester, Prof. G. D. B. Jones and Dr. J. P. Wild for help in organising the excavations, Prof. F. W. Shotton of Birmingham University for arranging the C-14 dates, Dr. S. E. Ellis, British Museum (Natural History) for analysing the stone axe, Dr. A. Challis, Durham University, for discussion on the pottery, Mr. F. H. Thompson for allowing me to study the results of his excavations and to use his map as Fig. 1, and my wife for drawing the pottery and help in preparing this article.

The main references to the site are; Bateman (1848), Coombs (1967) and (1971), Gould (1902), Jones and Thompson (1965), Pennington (1877), Preston (1954), and Tristram (1915).

nineteenth century and that a "brass celt and some fragments of an unbaked urn" were found.

Any study of hillforts and the first millennium B.C. in the Southern Pennine region is hampered by the lack of hillfort excavation and the dearth of open sites of this period in the area. Hence there is no local sequence of ceramic development for the period and other aspects of prehistoric life such as economy or trade are unknown. It is because of this lack of knowledge in the area that the results of the excavations on Mam Tor are so interesting and important.

In 1950 Mrs. C. M. Piggott found a small fragment of a rounded and slightly inturned rim (now in Sheffield Museum) within the rampart on the eastern side of the fort. Pennington (1877) mentions that "arrowheads and other articles of flint have been picked up on Mam Tor and especially along the line of the fort". However, no excavations were carried out until 1965 when the site was used as a training excavation by Manchester University.

Before excavation began a proton magnetometer survey was carried out by Dr. M. Tite in the north-east sector of the fort. Where tested, each anomaly produced evidence of occupation in the form of pottery, post-holes and construction gullies. Numerous depressions occur on the surface of the fort and indicate the positions of hut platforms.

The first two seasons work was carried out by F. H. Thompson, who cut two sections through the defences on the north-east side and excavated Hut 1.

From the sections (Fig. 3) it can be seen that the rampart survives to a height of 3 m and is 6 m wide at its base. The rampart was found to rest on an artificial platform cut into the hill slope, its core being made up of stones mixed with clay and loose rubble. Turf lines appeared at 30·5 cm and 2 m above the natural but according to Thompson (Jones and Thompson, 1965) do not indicate separate phases in the building of the rampart. The 1966 section shows stepped stone revetting at the front of the rampart and a single line of stones at the back. There are indications that an earlier smaller rampart had been cut away, except for its tail, during the construction of the present bank. A single post-hole (1966 section, Fig. 3) was found sealed by the rampart and pre-dating it. Without further excavation it is impossible to understand the exact nature of this feature but it is possible that it formed part of an earlier timber palisade. The defences are completed by a vertically sided, flat bottomed ditch cut c 2 m wide and deep into the bed rock.

Inside the hillfort the excavated huts all show the same basic construction details; platforms were cut into the hillside and huts were constructed on these artificial terraces. Evidence for the huts consists of semi-circular gullies immediately in front of the escarpment, large stone packed post-holes and smaller stake holes. It is possible that originally the huts were circular in plan but the outward facing parts may have eroded away. Only one internal hearth was found.

Test trenches were excavated in nine surface depressions and in every case revealed evidence of huts. Four huts were more extensively excavated. The plans of Huts 3 and 4 will serve as a general pattern.

Hut 3 (Fig. 4) was almost completely excavated and consisted of a gully at the back of the platform with a scatter of stake holes set outside and inside the gully. Three post-holes were set on the platform, 1 m from the gully and following its line. All of these post-holes had stone packing. A single post-hole set well inside the platform could have served as a central post support. Excavation of Hut 4 (Fig. 5) showed the extent of the level platform. Evidence for the construction of the hut, however, only amounted to a gully at the back of the platform and a line of stake holes outside. No definite post-holes were found on the platform, but towards the front were three large pits, one of which appears to have contained a burnt organic container. Pottery was found in all of the huts; scattered about the floor, in small gullies, on the slopes outside the huts and, in the case of two pots (Fig. 7), in a pit at the front of Hut 4.

Of the prehistoric sites in the Peak District Mam Tor is unique in producing such a large volume of pottery. The vast majority of the sherds belong to large plain vessels of the general bucket and barrel shapes. Decoration is extremely rare and is only found on five sherds. Colour ranges from buff, red to black and many of the pots are poorly fired. Clay inclusions include sandstone, chert, flint and grog. The following sherds deserve to be mentioned prior to the full publication of the pottery.

Five sherds are decorated with raised arcs or circles. These sherds are smoother and finer than the majority of the pottery from Mam Tor and in places show a red coating on the surface. The profile of the pot is a large barrel shape with everted rim (Fig. 6, 1.2). As the decoration is incomplete and only an arc remains, the full extent of the raised area is unknown. Therefore both alternatives have to be discussed. If an arc, then the decoration is reminiscent of some of the strap handles seen on some biconical urns during the earlier part of the Bronze Age (Forde-Johnston 1966). Equally they could be linked to the pottery with "eye brow" decoration of the Iron Age (Wheeler, 1943, Fig. 69) although this decoration is more often incised. Pottery with raised circle decoration is known from the Late Bronze Age site at Minnis Bay, Kent (Worsfold, 1943, Fig. 8, 8) and the Early Iron Age sites of Ballevullin, Tiree (MacKie, 1963, Fig. 4, 77) and Tigh Talamhanta, Barra (Young, 1966, Pl. 2a, 6–8). Another possibility is that the shape and decoration is copied from a bronze cauldron with ring handles. A ceramic copy of a bronze cauldron was excavated at Lannvréon en Peumerit, Finistère (Cowen, 1971, Fig. 5). The site at Castle Pit Hill, Melbourne, Derbyshire (Manby, 1963, Fig. 19.1) also produced a sherd with incised circle decoration.

A situlate shaped vessel (Fig. 6, 5), once considered to be a characteristic form of Early Iron Age A is represented by a sherd from Hut 2. The fabric is very fine and the pot has extremely thin walls, unlike the majority of the vessels from the site. A similar vessel with more rounded shoulders was found at Harborough Rocks, Derbyshire (Ward, 1889, Fig. 4).

A vessel (Fig. 6, 7) with sharp internal bevel and holes below the rim was found on the slope outside Hut 4. Although pots with perforations below the rim are known in England from the Neolithic, late Bronze Age/Early Iron Age examples are known from Eldon's Seat I, Dorset (Cunliffe and Phillipson, 1968, Fig. 13, 46), and the Heathery Burn Cave site (Britton and Longworth, 1968, 190). Locally this feature also occurs at Ball Cross hillfort (Stanley, 1954, Fig. 3, 4).

The pot with straight neck and everted rim (Fig. 6, 6) of hard black fabric is close to one from Grimthorpe hillfort, Yorkshire (Stead, 1968, Fig. 6, 6). Enclosed mouth forms are common during the Late Bronze/Early Iron Age and in the North have been found at Grimthorpe (Stead, 1968, Fig. 6, 8) and Ball Cross hillfort (Stanley, 1954, Fig. 3, 1). Besides the raised arcs or circles, the only other decoration known is finger pinching and this only occurs on one pot (Fig. 6. 3), of a globular shape. The site at Brassington Common, Derbyshire (Radley and Radford, 1969) also produced a pot with similar decoration. The vessels illustrated in Fig. 7 were found together in a small pit at the front of Hut 4.

Apart from the pottery, Mam Tor produced an interesting collection of small finds.

A. Polished stone axe (Fig. 8, 6)

The axe was found at the bottom of a small gully in Hut 3, which also produced pottery. The axe was analysed by Dr. S. E. Ellis of the British Museum (Natural History) who reported that the rock was a much altered fine grained quartz dolerite. However, its exact area of origin is a mystery, and the closest comparison that could be found is with the rock on the summit of the Breiddin Hills, Montgomery, though it is not identical with this mineralogically. It bears no resemblance to any of the numbered types established by the South-western Museums axe petrology group.

B. Bronze axe fragment (Fig. 8, 5)

A number of fragments from the central portion of the body of a bronze socketed axe were found just outside Hut 4. The axe can be reconstructed as having a narrow body and decorated with three, long thin, vertical ribs. Although not enough of the axe remains to be able to establish its type exactly, it does not belong to the Yorkshire or South Welsh ribbed forms. Bronze socketed axes, although the most common bronze type of the late Bronze Age, are extremely rare among the finds from settlement sites. Besides Mam Tor they are only known from the hillforts of the Breiddin (information kindly supplied by C. Musson), Traprain Law (Burley, 1956) Beacon Hill (Evans, 1881, Hoard no. 54) and Portfield (Blundell and Longworth, 1967).

C. Whetstones (Fig. 8.4)

Four stones best described as polishing stones or whetstones on account of their wear patterns were also found. Three of these are of hard stone; the fourth is of shale and has been cut to shape.

D. Shale bracelets (Fig. 8. 1, 2, 3)

The three fragments of shale bracelets from Hut 3 all have different cross sections and thicknesses and represent three different bracelets. Simple circular bracelets of shale make their appearance during the Late Bronze Age and continue into the early Iron Age.

Charcoal fragments collected from the floors of Huts 2 and 3 gave the following C-14 dates ($\frac{1}{2}$ life 5568 years); 1180 ± 132 b.c. (Birm. 202) and 1130 ± 115 b.c. (Birm. 192, Radiocarbon, 1971, Vol. 13, no. 2 pp. 143–154). Unfortunately it is impossible to date the defences and the C-14 dates only relate to the two huts in question. Hut 4, with its different pottery types and bronze socketed axe, would seem to be of a later date than that indicated by the C-14 dates for Huts 2 and 3. If the two C-14 dates from Mam Tor are accepted as valid for their contexts, then the occupation represented by the two huts is almost contemporary with that at the Deverel-Rimbury settlement at Shearplace Hill, Dorset (Rahtz and ApSimon, 1962) with an amalgamated date of 1180 ± 108 b.c., and is not too far removed from the recent C-14 dates for Wessex culture graves (*Current Arch.* 32, 1972, 238–244).

Summary

Excavations at Mam Tor have provided evidence for possibly three phases in the construction of the defences; (1) timber palisade or revetment, (2) earlier rampart, (3) later rampart. Within the enclosure, the huts have produced large quantities of pottery and small finds, all of which seem to date from the first half of the first millennium B.C. The exact relationship between the defences and the occupation is unknown at present.

Mam Tor and the Hillforts of the North

Of the 18 hillforts at the southern end of the Pennines, only four[2] have been excavated. Besides Mam Tor, only Ball Cross has produced pottery in any quantity, although the pottery from this site is of a different fabric and only a few of the shapes are shared.[3]

Little help is given by recent excavations of three hillforts in the north-west. Castercliff, Nelson, was devoid of finds, although it produced evidence of an outer rampart of narrow timber revetted box construction and a vitrified inner one. Very few sherds were found at Portfield, Whalley, and Skelmore Heads produced no cultural material. Similarly excavations on the Cheshire hillforts have not been very helpful in the study of Mam Tor.

[2] The four hillforts are: Almondbury, Yorkshire: Varley, this volume, pp. 119–32 above. Ingleborough, Yorkshire: a small private excavation at the end of the last century. Castercliff, Nelson, Lancashire. Excavated by Rev. J. A. Plummer, 1958 and 1960, D. G. Coombs, 1970 and 1971, as yet unpublished. Portfield, Whalley, Lancashire, a number of excavatoins by the Bury Archaeological Group, P. Beswick and J. S. Hallam, 1970 and D. G. Coombs, 1972, as yet unpublished.

[3] Two sherds from Markland Grips promontory fort (Lane, 1969) were described as resembling the fine wares at Mam Tor by the excavator.

To the south the nearest hillfort that has produced pottery in any quantity is Breedon Hill, Leicestershire (Kenyon, 1950; Wacher, 1964) but the pottery bears no relationship to that from Mam Tor. The conclusion is that while the pottery from Mam Tor seems to belong to the late second/early first millennium, it is impossible to find good parallels for it on neighbouring sites. Excavation has shown the archaeological importance of the site, but without further excavation many of the problems will remain unsolved.

7 | *Ravensburgh Castle, Hertfordshire*

James Dyer

I. Introduction

Ravensburgh Castle lies 1 km south-west of Hexton Church on the borders of Hertfordshire and Bedfordshire (National Grid: TL: 099295). The traditional route of the Icknield Way lies $1\frac{1}{2}$ km to the south. The fort, which encloses almost 6·5 hectares (exclusive of fortifications) is the largest hillfort in eastern England and the Chilterns. It is situated on the lower chalk and covers the western half of a plateau which is surrounded on all sides except the east and north-western corner by deep, steep-sided dry valleys (Pl. I). On the eastern side a gentle slope down to a small stream and spring, the Burwell, has been strengthened by a great rampart still 5·1 m high, and a ditch which has been filled-in and levelled. The rampart is considerably lower on the other sides where the steep hillside reduces the danger of attack. On the north side the main rampart appears to have been formed from internal quarry scoops, and is separated by a wide berm from a small ditch and outer bank. There is a small outer bank and ditch on the east, south and west. The main entrance faces the level approach across the peninsular neck in the north-western corner. It is slightly oblique, and may once have had outworks since destroyed by ploughing. A second entrance in the south-east corner is of simple straight-through type and probably provided access to the spring at the foot of the hill. A third gap midway along the eastern side may be fairly recent in date. The whole of the site, which had previously been open downland, was planted with trees about 1908.

The earliest description of Ravensburgh is in the manuscript history of Hexton written by Francis Taverner about 1640 and now in the British Museum:

Of Ravensburye Castle

... It is probable that here hath anciently been a fort of earth, both in the times of the Romans, Saxons and Danes, for Mr Camden says that the Romans had such like summer standing camps. This had, like theirs, a treble rampart of earth, and it was near the military Roman way, for that famous highway called Ickle is near adjoining to this place . . . I have in my keeping a copper pike, likely to be the pike of a copper target digged out of a pit near this fort . . . It containeth about a dozen acres of ground within the walls. The fort was strongly situated by nature, being almost rounded with exceeding deep bottoms and mountains, which we call Lynces, but no question the upper walls were made by art. . . . This fort being upon the brow of the hills, did overlook the vale country, and did discover much ground, neither is it improbable but that it might be watered by the spring at Burwell, running at the foot of the Castle.

William Stukeley visited the fort in 1724 and drew a fine picture of it from the west (Pl. II). His text described it as

a square Roman camp upon a lingula, or promontory, just big enough for the purpose. It is very steep quite round, except at a narrow slip where the entrance is; double ditched and very strong, but land-locked with hills every way, except to the north-east, and that has a good prospect: under it is a fine spring: it seems made by the Romans when they were masters of all the country on this side, and extending their arms northwards. (Stukeley, 1776, 77)

The first plan of the site was produced for Clutterbuck's *History of Hertfordshire* (1817) and was made long prior to the tree planting, whilst another important survey with useful profiles of the earthworks was conducted by E. A. Downman in April 1907 (Downman, 1910). Although based on the 25-inch O.S. map of 1879 it shows added detail particularly relating to the counterscarp banks. S. E. Winbolt (1932, p. 32), noted that "the ground inside the banks has been made a sorry jumble by quarrying".

A large number of trial holes were dug at Ravensburgh during the winter of 1940–1941 by the late W. Percival Westell of Letchworth Museum, but no record of his discoveries has been found. On the strength of a sherd of wheel-thrown Belgic pottery found on the surface, the Ordnance Survey identified the fort as Belgic on their *Map of Southern Britain in the Iron Age* published in 1962.

The first of the present seasons of excavation at Ravensburgh was undertaken in July and August 1964 by John Moss-Eccardt and James Dyer on behalf of the Letchworth Museum and Art Gallery. Further work was undertaken for two weeks in June 1970 and July 1972 by the Archaeology and History Department of Putteridge Bury College of Education under the direction of the writer, and has continued annually since.

II. The Pre-Hillfort Occupation

The old turf line below the rampart sections clearly represents a buried plough soil, and we may therefore assume that most of the hilltop was under cultivation prior to the construction of the fort. Grains of carbonised wheat and barley were obtained from the surface, which were identified by Dr. A. M. Evans and Mr. Andrew Bowman of the Department of Agricultural

Botany at Reading University as emmer wheat, spelt wheat, two-rowed and six-rowed barley.

III. The History of the Defences

A. Period 1

Excavation has confirmed that an initial Hollingbury-type rampart was present on the west, south and east sides of the fort (Pl. III). This consisted of two parallel vertical rows of posts, some 2·1 m apart. The individual posts in the outer row were about 2·0 m apart, but the separation of the inner row has not yet been established. Although the wood had decomposed the hollow impression of some of the posts survived. Linking the posts were horizontal tie-beams running from back to front, and along the length of the rampart. Vertical facing timbers probably ran along the outer face of the stockade, their lower ends bedded in a shallow footing trench. Chalk rubble had been packed between the two rows of posts on the east side of the fort, whilst on the south and west turves had been piled in this area. The fort remained in use long enough for the rampart timbers to have been renewed at least twice.

Associated with the Hollingbury-type rampart was a flat-bottomed ditch averaging 3·0 m deep, 6·7 m wide at the top and about 2·0 m wide at the bottom. On the south the bank and ditch were separated by a substantial berm some 3·6 m wide, but this was not present on the east or west. The stratification in the ditch indicated that it had taken many years to fill up before it was recut in Period 3.

B. Period 2

A long period of neglect and disuse followed during which the rampart became overgrown and the ditch silted completely.

C. Period 3

The eastern rampart was cleared of brushwood which was burnt in piles on the inside of the defences. This firing burnt the outside of a surviving squared upright post and burnt another horizontal timber that lay along the length of the rampart. At the same time some surviving uprights were pulled out of the ground. A new V-shaped ditch was cut into the silted-up Period 1 ditch. This averaged 6·1 m wide and 2·4 m deep. The material removed was apparently dumped on top of the denuded Period 1 rampart to produce a loose glacis-type rampart. On the south this material, largely chalk rubble, was placed on the wide berm outside the rampart (Pl. III). There were indications of quarry scoops which may have provided additional material on the inner western side of the fort when the Royal Commission plan was made prior to 1910 (R.C.H.M., Hertfordshire, 1910, 114), but these have not been tested by excavation. Certainly chalk from this recut ditch was also piled on the outer downhill side of the western rampart to create an outer or counterscarp bank along that side of Ravensburgh, and this seems to be present around part of the southern side.

D. Period 4

On the eastern side the rampart appears to have been slighted and deliberately pushed down into the ditch, where the filling was found to be rapid and uneven. Low in this filling beside the south-eastern entrance was a wheel-thrown pedestal base. This is the only piece of Belgic pottery so far excavated on the site.

E. Period 5

At some later period, at present undated, a second outer ditch and bank of minor proportions were cut. The ditch is 1·5 m wide, 1·2 m deep with a flat bottom 0·9 m wide. Its inner bank is constructed of clean chalk rubble and measures 2·4 m wide and stands 0·5 m high. This feature runs along the whole of the eastern side of the fort outside the Period 3 ditch, and cuts completely across the south-eastern entrance. It turns the south-eastern angle and merges into the southern counterscarp bank. A similar bank and ditch are present along the western side of the fort, though they do not cut across the north-western entrance. At the south-western corner this ditch and bank swing away from the fort and run down to the valley bottom. It may be significant that the Bedfordshire–Hertfordshire county boundary follows it.

IV. The Entrances

The earliest known plan of Ravensburgh (1809) which is reproduced by Clutterbuck (1817, 5) shows three entrances to the fort: one at the north-west corner, another half way along the eastern side and a third near the south-east corner. There is no doubt that that at the north-west was the major entrance. It is slightly oblique, with the northern rampart end curving into the camp, and the southern side curving outwards. Immediately north of the entrance the rampart end becomes much higher and wider and clearly forms an observation post at the highest point of the fort, from which it is possible to survey the whole of the interior; without this extra height dead ground within the fort on the south-east would not have been visible (Dyer, 1962, 77).

The entrance at the centre of the eastern side appears to be of comparatively recent date, and to be associated with a farm track that runs up the valley. A proton-magnetometer survey indicated that the fort ditch was continuous across the entrance and that there was no causeway at that point. In the light of the excavation of the south-eastern entrance, however, this eastern gap will need to be tested by excavation before a final judgment can be made.

At the south-east is a small entrance of simple, straight-through type, at present 6·0 m wide (Site D). It is planted with pine trees, which have made excavation difficult. The causeway crossing the ditch is quite distinct and rises steeply to enter the fort. On the analogy of Maiden Castle it was decided to excavate this smaller and apparently weaker entrance. Work is still in progress, but it can be tentatively recorded that the entrance is a Period 3 or 4 feature. The original Period 1 Hollingbury-type rampart ran right across the entrance gap, and at that time the ditch in front of it was continuous. At a subsequent date the rampart was pushed down into the ditch and the causeway of chalk rubble constructed (Pl. IV). There is no indication that a gate was ever hung across the opening created, and until the entrance causeway blocking the ditch is excavated, its place in the time sequence cannot be certainly established. An entrance at this point would give valuable access down to the Burwell spring, but the rough and untrampled nature of the causeway suggest that it was never used, and might possibly be part of the Period 4 slighting.

It was on the surface of the side of the causeway as it dipped into the adjoining ditch that the wheel-thrown pedestal-urn base was found. This tends to suggest that the causeway and entrance are of pre-Roman construction. The minor outer bank and ditch (Period 5) run across the end of the entrance causeway without a break.

V. The Interior (Site B)

Due to the wooded nature of the site little work has been possible inside Ravensburgh, although 0·1 hectares ($\frac{1}{4}$ acre) were stripped in 1964 close inside the south-eastern entrance. Here some 44 large post-holes each averaging 45 cm deep and 40 cm wide were found in irregular and approximate lines. They seem to have supported timbers for an extensive series of cattle stockades or pens. Some of the holes had been recut two or three times. There was little sign of human settlement in this area and pottery was sparse and weathered, indicating that it had long been exposed on the surface.

VI. Dating

The pottery is almost entirely attributable to Period 1 and dates from the beginning of the fourth century B.C. extending to the third century B.C. A wide range of southern A types are present. The material is particularly notable for its angular bowls, often with internal as well as external decoration, some of which is inlaid in white. Associated with one of the angular bowls was a magnificent bronze eight-coil spring brooch of La Tène 1b type and almost certainly of insular construction. The bow, plate and spring are decorated with incised dots, and the bow also has incised oblique hatching. Professor Jope has suggested a date for it of about 350 B.C. No other metal work has been recovered from the fort, with the exception of a Roman coin of Crispus (A.D. 317–326) found high in the Period 4 ditch silt.

All the pottery associated with the Period 3 rebuild is clearly weathered surface material derived from Period 1. Absence of obviously late pottery suggests no domestic settlement in the limited areas examined. The single wheel-thrown pedestal base from the edge of the south-eastern entrance causeway is the only clue to a possible early Belgic occupation.

VII. The Function of the Hillfort

In Period I Ravensburgh fits securely into place as one of the headquarters of territories separated by triple-dykes that ranged along the Icknield Way in the Early Iron Age (Dyer, 1961, 32). How long the fort was unoccupied before its refortification in Period 3 is a subject for speculation. It was clearly long enough for the original ditch to silt completely and for the fort to have become sufficiently overgrown to warrant timber clearance and massive bonfires. On the slender evidence of the pedestal base it may be possible to date Period 3 to early in the first century B.C. and the initial period of Belgic penetration into Hertfordshire. The extensive cattle pens and apparent slighting of the defences in Period 4 might lead, with further excavation, to a consideration of Ravensburgh as the site of the Catuvellaunian *oppidum* attacked by Caesar. For some time Sir Mortimer Wheeler's choice of Wheathampstead (Wheeler and Wheeler, 1936, 20) has been criticised; firstly on the grounds that the site is neither a hillfort nor *oppidum*, since it is demarcated on one side only by a humanly constructed fortification, the Devil's Dyke. The Slad earthwork to the east is a natural feature of no great strength and the 90 to 100 acre enclosure that it was claimed to enclose did not exist. Secondly, there is nothing in the pottery from Wheathampstead datable to the first half of the first century B.C.

Physically Ravensburgh fits Caesar's description rather better than Wheathampstead, and it could have been easily reached by the Lea valley and along the Icknield Way:

> The *oppidum* of Cassivellaunus, which was protected by woods and marshes, was not far off, and a considerable number of men and of cattle had assembled in it. The Britons apply the name of *oppidum* to any woodland spot, difficult of access and fortified with a rampart and trench, to which they are in the habit of resorting in order to escape a hostile raid. Caesar marched to the spot indicated with his legions, and found that the place was of great natural strength and well fortified: nevertheless he proceeded to assault it on two sides. The enemy stood their ground a short time, but could not sustain the onset of our infantry, and fled precipitately from another part of the *oppidum*. (Caesar, *de Bello Gallico*, V, 21)

To reach Ravensburgh from the Lea valley would have entailed crossing the extensive Lea marshes at Leagrave as well as the minor marshes around the Burwell east of the fort. There is little doubt that the clay-capped hills south of the camp were forest covered, and no one can deny the great natural strength of the hillfort which cannot be matched by any other in the Chilterns. For

Caesar to have assaulted the fort on two sides, and Cassivellaunus to have escaped on a third would seem to suggest that the oppidum was of no mean size, and again few other sites in eastern England fortified with a rampart and trench could compare in size with Ravensburgh. It would also have been natural for the Romans to have made some attempt to slight the earthworks, perhaps in the manner apparent on the eastern side. As the excavations continue new light may be thrown on these interesting possibilities.

VIII. The Burwell

Mention may also be made of the Burwell, the spring which rises in a miniature natural amphitheatre some 360 m east of the fort, which must have formed the main source of water supply for the fort, and may also have served as a Celtic sanctuary. It is perhaps significant that close to a Romano-British habitation site 0·8 km downstream at Hexton, another spring (now piped underground) was dedicated during Christian times to St. Faith, where

> People that come to offer did cast some thing into the well, which if it swamme above they were accepted and their petition granted, but if it sunk, then rejected, which the experienced Priest had arts enowe to cause to swymme or sinke according as him selfe was pleased with the Partye, or rather with the offring made by the partie. (Taverner, 1640)

Acknowledgement

We are most grateful to Mr. James Ashley Cooper, the owner of the site, for his permission, kindness and continued interest.

8 | *Crickley Hill, 1969–1972*

P. Dixon

The steep westward-facing scarp of the Cotswolds is divided by small valleys into a series of flat-topped spurs which dominate the Severn Valley. About 4 miles to the south of Cheltenham and a mile north of the line followed by the Roman road between Cirencester and Gloucester, one of these spurs, Crickley Hill, has been cut by a rampart about 300 m long, which separates the end of the hill from slightly higher ground further to the east. At its southern end the rampart overhangs a cliff produced by relatively recent quarrying. Similar quarrying on the northern side of the hill has truncated at least some of the contours, but there are surface indications that the rampart turned here to run for a short distance above the steepest part of the slope.

About 120 m within the first rampart a second, much eroded bank is clearly visible on air photographs (see Fig. 1); at its southern end this inner bank is cut by a cluster of early modern surface quarries, and appears to be earlier than a long low mound, of uncertain purpose and date, which runs in a hollow across the hill.

On behalf of the Committee for Research into the Iron Age in the North West Cotswolds, and with the generous support of the Gloucestershire College of Art and Design in Cheltenham, a total of 20 weeks has been spent in excavations during the summers of 1969–1972. These excavations are still continuing, and the present report is an account of the interim conclusions reached after four seasons work on the site, with particular stress on the phasing and constructional technique of the rampart.

These conclusions may be briefly summarised: excavation of the inner bank uncovered three concentric rings of banks and ditches belonging to a multi-phased Neolithic causewayed enclosure. The outer bank contained ramparts of three periods. The first of these was timber-laced and had been destroyed by fire: this rampart stood in front of long rectangular houses, arranged on either side of the road from the entrance. After a period of rebuilding, perhaps a preliminary stage in the refortification of the hill, the defences were massively reconstructed, using the burnt rampart as a core. During this rebuilding a large roundhouse, perhaps associated with less substantial huts, was erected behind the entrance passage. The new rampart and the roundhouse were in their turn burnt, and the site was abandoned at a date which present evidence suggests was very early in the Iron Age.

I. The Inner Bank (see Fig. 2)

In the area of the inner bank three ditches, all of which contained Neolithic material, ran parallel to the outer rampart, and cut off the end of the hill. The bank and ditch of which surface traces were visible proved on excavation to be the later of two adjacent ditches: the earlier ditch, subdivided by small causeways, had been filled in and its bank levelled before the digging of the later, so far continuous ditch. Slightly behind the crest of the second bank a line of burning indicated the presence of a palisade. About 25 m further east a third ditch, a series of shallow scoops, ran parallel to the inner pair and, like them, had a bank on its western edge. One of the causeways across the third ditch was matched by a break in the bank behind it. A large gull, a structural weakness in the hill, crossed this area, and the soft crumbly limestone which had been washed into it was pitted by post-holes and stake holes, not all of which are shown in Fig. 2. The latest structure here was an irregular, apparently flimsy hut with a central hearth and a hard-packed floor, which sealed more substantial post-holes of what was perhaps a rectangular house built later than the Neolithic bank, which itself sealed several post-holes belonging to a pre-enclosure phase. The dating of these structures is not certain, but the hut with the hearth probably belonged to the Iron Age occupation of the site.

Cut partially into the infill and partially into the edge of the later ditch, two rows of post-holes held the supports for a ten-post house with a central hearth, which sat astride the ditch, apparently taking advantage of the shelter of the bank; this was comparable to, and presumably contemporary with the long houses uncovered in the interior of the fort. To the north west, behind the crest of the bank, four post-holes dug into the Neolithic later bank may have formed an outbuilding; beyond lay three hearths and groups of post-holes, none of which can confidently be dated.

II. The Outer Bank

A. Pre-Rampart Occupation (Period 1)

To the north of the entrance passage the earliest rampart sealed four shallow post-holes which appeared to form two sides of a rectangular structure at least 2·8 m in width (for plan, see Dixon, 1969, Fig. 4). The posts themselves were unburnt and had decayed within the post-holes. About 1·8 m to the south a curving slot, perhaps a drain, led to a natural joint in the limestone. No evidence for date was found in association with these post-holes, but 2 m to the north-east sherds of a Beaker were also sealed in the old ground surface below the rampart. Six other post-holes may belong to the first period. Stratigraphically they antedate the hornwork and the "counterscarp" of Period 3b, and may belong either to Period 1 or 2, or to neither: F50 and 68 could be survivors from a fence on the outer lip of the south Period 2 ditch; in other parts of the excavated area the lip was quarried away during Period 3b. The other four post-holes (F1, 8, 38, and 40) were well beyond the ditch edge in Period 2, and predated the low Period 3b bank outside the latest ditch. They may thus belong to a pre-rampart structure.

B. The Period 2 Rampart

The first rampart (see Fig. 4) consisted of a front and rear wall built of slabs of limestone on average 30 cm square; the intervening space between the walls was filled with smaller limestone rubble and the structure was strengthened by a lacing of timbers which passed through both the front and the rear walls. Beyond a berm which varied in its width from 0·5 m to 1·75 m lay a ditch cut from 1·6 m to 2 m into the bedrock. The ditch was crossed at the entrance to the fort by a causeway 5 m broad. To the north of the causeway the ditch was about 5·6 m in width; to the south much of its outer lip had been removed during the building of the last rampart: in a surviving stretch the ditch width was 7·5 m.

C. Rampart Construction

Within the core of the rampart the timber lacing was supported by vertical posts. Two parallel rows of post-holes were uncovered. To the south of the entrance the front row was represented by post-holes 37, 35, 21 and 22, which were from 0·8 m to 2·0 m within the line of the front wall. About 2·5 m to the west ran a corresponding series (post-holes 36, 34, 59 and 9), which were from 2·0 m to 2·8 m within the line of the rear wall. To the north of the entrance the rear alignment was formed by post-holes 33 and perhaps 20. The front row was represented by post-holes 71, 95, 96, 97, 83 and 98, and it may be assumed that post-holes parallel to 33, 95–98 and 83 lie in the unexcavated parts of the rampart in this area. All these post-holes were from 30 to 40 cm in diameter and varied in depth from 25 to 35 cm below the old ground surface. Where they survived the posts themselves were 25 to 35 cm in diameter; posts 34, 36 and 37 were well preserved, and they at least had been dressed with five faces.

Little remained of the front wall south of the entrance. To the north, however, the wall was preserved to a height of 1·8 m and sockets for three tiers of horizontal lacing were visible in its elevation (see Fig. 3). The burning of the rampart and subsequent collapse of its core had disturbed the lacing above the level of the old ground surface, but traces of charcoal survived to confirm the general direction of the individual timbers. Not all were aligned on the post-hole settings: of the eleven lacing timbers in this area at least three cannot have been joined to a vertical post in the front row; the only surviving joint, that between post-hole 59 and its horizontal, appeared to be lashed rather than half-lapped, and the alignment of the other horizontals tends to confirm this method of construction. Some traces of charcoal and a slight settlement in the core suggested that the vertical posts were joined by at least one transverse timber, running parallel to the front wall at a height of about 1·5 m; if this is so, the "floating" lacing timbers could have used this as their front support.

The rear wall was badly damaged and reduced in places to its lowest course. In the face of the front wall, however, two clear building breaks were visible. Behind them, below the burnt core, bonding into and therefore contemporary with the front wall, low walls were found to run from front to back of the rampart. The first of these "joint walls" lay 5·8 m to the north of the entrance, and the second 5·9 m further northwards. Horizontal timbers overlay and thus postdated them, but one of the walls partially obscured the edge of post-hole 97 (though not its post), and thus was laid later than the cutting of the post-holes.

With some probability, therefore, the order of building can be reconstructed.

Stage One

Post-holes were cut in two rows about 2·5 m apart, perhaps at the same time as the quarrying of the ditch. On either side of the entrance passage low mounds of earth and small stones ran from front to back of the rampart and appeared to delimit the area of the entrance. These banks were unburnt, and were overlain by the burnt timber-lacing. It seems reasonable to identify them as topsoil removed from the ditches.

Stage Two

The lowest courses of the front and rear walls, including the joint walls, were laid in stretches. The upper 75 cm of the bedrock lifts easily as slabs from 3 to 5 cm in thickness. Below this level the rock is harder and blocks up to 50 cm thick have been obtained. It is therefore of interest to note that the length of walling immediately north of the entrance (see Fig. 3)—length 1—clearly showed a horizontal break at a height of 40 cm above the old ground surface: below this point the courses averaged 4 cm in thickness; above it lay three courses, each about 12 cm thick, which appeared to have come from the middle or lower parts of the ditch. Northwards, length 2 presented a similar but less clearly marked division at the same height: the lowest courses were built of slabs from the middle or bottom of the ditch. Above the break the rubble included blocks up to 30 cm thick, presumably from the very bottom of the ditch, among stones of various sizes. Similar large blocks formed the lowest courses of length 3; above these, at a height here of about 60 cm above the old ground surface, lay a few courses of much thinner slabs. At this point the ground surface was dipping; the break in construction of all three lengths formed an approximately horizontal line immediately below the first tier of timber lacing. It may thus reasonably be suggested that length 1 was built using the first stone available, the upper *laminae* of the ditch, to a height of

40 cm; length 2 was then built using the middle stone in the ditch sequence. The lowest courses of length 2 increased markedly in size at its northern and southern ends: here, then, were blocks from the bottom of the ditch. Length 3, with similarly large blocks, was built next, and the rampart wall was thus begun at the entrance passage and built, in stages, northwards. Only length 1 was built with the upper *laminae*; elsewhere, perhaps, the thin slabs, less stable for building, were used as core material in stage five.

Stage Three

Above the old ground surface a raft of small timber (up to 10 cm in scantling) and brushwood was laid within the walls, which had thus been built free-standing as far as the first horizontal break.

Stage Four

The uprights may have been erected at any time during stages one to three; they must at any rate have been placed before stage five.

Stage Five

Small stones (the upper ditch levels) and rubble were piled into the core of the rampart, levelling off at the top of the first horizontal break.

Stage Six

The first tier of horizontal lacing was laid across the rampart and lashed to the uprights. The walls above the horizontal building break were built around the lacing, and so at each level the lacing must predate the courses of the front wall at that height. Both length 1 and length 2 showed another horizontal break at a height of 1·2 m, immediately below the third tier of lacing, and it seems therefore that the upper parts of the ramparts were built in stages in the same way as the lower.

At the end of Period 2 the rampart was destroyed by fire. The burning of the timber lacing reduced the rubble of the core to quicklime and this in turn was slaked by water action to form a hard white concretion in which badly disturbed fragments of charcoal and very hard white streaks where the fire had been hottest remained to show the position of the lacing. The rear wall was badly burned and nowhere survived more than five courses high: the amount of tumble, indeed, suggested that it may always have been considerably lower than the front. To the north of the entrance the front wall was barely scorched, despite the reduction of much of its core. It is therefore apparent that in this area at least the rampart was fired from the back, perhaps after the demolition of the rear wall. Experiments in 1970 with a replica of the rampart showed how difficult it would be to ignite the structure; but once it was alight wind action through the rampart would swiftly increase the blaze. No traces of timber buildings have yet been uncovered immediately behind the rampart; in their absence it is unlikely that the Crickley rampart was burned so thoroughly by an accidental brushfire, and a deliberate slighting of the defences, after capture or abandonment, appears the most plausible solution.

D. Period 3a

To the south of the entrance the Period 2 front wall may have collapsed; at any rate refortification here involved stripping back the external face of the rampart to accommodate a new wall which revetted the burnt core (see Fig. 5). Clearance, however, was not complete and the lowest 30 cm of the old wall remained as a footing. In front, a mass of silted slaked lime, washed from the core, had built up before Period 3a. Analysis of this stratum confirmed its origin, but indicated that the period of its deposition—the span between the end of Period 2 and the beginning of Period 3a—was not considerable (Dixon, 1970, p. 9, sample 4).

The new front wall incorporated many obviously reused stones, burnt at the end of Period 2 and reassembled in an order which placed unburnt and heavily burnt stones in contact. Its lowest course, immediately above the burnt footings, was a line of square-dressed unburnt lias blocks; certainly at some date imports to Crickley Hill, these may have played some decorative role in the Period 2 wall[1]. But that they were now specially quarried is possible; in their excavated position they appeared, like a foundation stone, to be a deliberate indication of the new building.

The rear wall of the rampart was rebuilt in this phase or in the subsequent 3b. Above the ruins of Period 2 a series of lenses of washed lime and of humus formation considerably thicker than that at the front suggested that the rear of the rampart during Period 3a was allowed to slope towards the interior of the fort without a rear wall.

To the north of the entrance passage the Period 2 front wall, though burnt, was still sufficiently formidable to be retained. To judge from the height of burning of the core, the old wall presumably needed some reconstruction of its upper parts in Period 3a; all this had collapsed. It should therefore be noted that for a length of at least 6 m the rampart showed evidence of only Period 2, and, in view of the regular practice of making rampart cuttings 3 or 4 m broad, a cutting here over 6 m in width would have revealed only Period 2 structures, and would surely have led to the interpretation of the site as of a single phase.

E. Period 3b

The end of the Period 3a wall immediately south of the entrance passage was demolished, and a roughly semi-circular solid bastion was built encasing the stub, as a similar bastion enclosed the end of the Period 2 wall to the north

[1] Fragments of similar stone in the burnt core may have come from the dressing of the blocks.

of the entrance (see Fig. 7). The lowest course of both bastions included huge weathered boulders, the largest weighing perhaps half a ton. These showed considerable abrasion and weathering not only on their outer sides, but also on the faces within the bastions, and had clearly been exposed to water action. Whatever their origin, they had not been obtained from the ditch, and a reuse from some earlier structure is likely (for the Crickley Hill barrows, see Burrow, 1919, 64); their purpose was to carry the bastion walls across the Period 2 ditches, whose ends were filled by rafts of rubble, 5 m broad south of the entrance and nearly 9 m broad to the north.

The northern defences had been built in three stages: first was the ditch infill raft, second the north bastion, and third a small rectangular projection, the inner hornwork, which abutted the end of the bastion and ran north-eastwards from it across the infill platform to the outer edge of the old ditch. The southern bastion complex matched this sequence; here, however, the outer face of the south hornwork was flush with the edge of the ditch infill and not stepped back from it, but a horizontal break in the walling marked the top of the infill and the lowest course of the hornwork itself. The hornwork post-dated the south bastion, which itself overlay and was later than the infill platform. But since the design of the platforms assumes both the second and the third stages of the defences, all three stages formed part of the same plan.

The outer hornwork, after crossing the ditch, turned northwards across the old entrance approach. An earthmoving machine on test in 1967 accidentally removed the final segment[2]; part of its return, however, was visible, and its approximate location is indicated in Fig. 7. The gap between the hornworks was about 2·7 m, and was presumably closed by a gate held on posts in post-holes 80 and 81. Both hornworks were built with construction breaks in exactly the same way as the Period 2 rampart: from the south bastion the lengths measured 6·5 m, 5·5 m, 2·7 m, 2·2 m, and about 3·3 m, assuming that none lie in the unexcavated areas. The three short lengths may have been due to the turning of the hornwork at this point: the inner hornwork ended in a length of only 1·5 m. The larger units are presumably more representative of construction lengths, and correspond to those used in the Period 2 rampart. Traces of some timber were found in the core of the hornwork, and it is clear that the difference between the timber lacing of Period 2 and the solid dry-stone construction of later phases need not be due to any supposed variation in the cultural tradition of their builders, but to the extreme difficulty of inserting timbers into the Period 2 rampart core.

Material for both hornworks was quarried from a new ditch dug outside the outer hornwork. Further south the old ditch was widened to 12 m by quarrying for the final stage in the Period 3b defences, in which a wall, still surviving to a height of 3·3 m, was built to revet the inner edge of the Period 2 ditch. The presence of this revetment wall has given a characteristically flattened profile to the bank in the entrance area. About 60 m to the south of the entrance the

[2] I am grateful to Mrs. Helen O'Neil for photographs taken in 1967, and for a sketch of the original contours made by the late B. H. St. John O'Neil.

profile of the rampart steepens considerably, and it is thus possible that the revetment was a special arrangement near the entrance. Behind the revetment wall a packing of unburnt stones encased the Period 3a front wall; whether the new wall entirely replaced the 3a wall as a breastwork or not is uncertain, for it is possible that the rampart was stepped. (For a reconstruction drawing, see Dixon, 1972, p. 51.)

About 10·8 m south of its junction with the outer hornwork the outer face of the revetment wall obscured the face of a second wall. The walls were demolished over a length of 3 m to investigate the meeting point of the two faces, and it appeared that the revetment wall was built, within a foundation cut, at first up to 1 m closer to the inner lip of the ditch. After a wall 1 m in height had been built and packed with stones and earth, a second line of walling was begun outside the footings of the first, resting on a stratum of earth and small stones which filled the foundation cut and may have been spillage from the infill of the first wall. Above a height of about 1 m the two walls were bonded and continued as a single wall above the line of the *outer* footings. Immediately south of the hornwork the face of the revetment wall was not removed; it too, however, rested on 10–15 cm of earth and small stones at the bottom of the ditch, and therefore is likely to have been the outer of the two walls. Clearly, then, at an early stage in the construction of the revetment wall the stretch near the hornwork was thickened; whatever the reason for the change of plan, the new line of the wall served to buttress the hornwork at an unstable point where it crossed the centre of the old ditch.

A low bank lay outside the recut ditch, and can be traced intermittently across the hill. Only a short length of this has so far been available for excavation; here it proved to be later than all the post-holes in the area and was composed of earth and very small stones, with a capping of slightly larger stones below the modern ground surface. There were no traces of any structure in the bank, which may represent merely the topsoil and frost-shattered top of the bedrock removed by the workers quarrying the ditch extension in Period 3b.

The structure of the entrance passage in all phases is discussed separately below. In Period 3b, behind the entrance, the bastions joined the line of the rear wall of the rampart not by a straight length of walling but by a series of lobes; a similar constructional technique, perhaps thought more stable than right-angles in dry-stone walling, was noted in the exterior of the outer hornwork.

F. *The Phasing of the Entrance Passage*

The walls of the Period 3b bastions in the entrance passage had removed all trace of earlier structures above bedrock level. Identification of the earlier features thus depends on the analysis of strata in the post-holes (see Fig. 6 and Plate 1). The post-holes themselves were cleanly cut in the rock with nearly vertical sides and fell into three groups. Four (F10, 6b, 25 and 27) were approximately circular and more than 80 cm deep; two (26 and 28) were irregularly rectangular and under 20 cm deep, shallowest at their eastern ends; the remaining ten (F73, 72, 20, 11, 24, 23, 17, 16 and 74) were post sockets up to 80 cm deep cut into two pairs of parallel slots, 30 to 40 cms in depth, which ran on either side of the entrance passage.

G. *Stratification in the Post-holes*

At the bottom of the large post-hole, F10, layer (5) was a packing, presumably the lower packing for the post, of large unburnt stones in a heavy limestone silting; above it layer (4) contained large and small burnt stones and patches of slaked quicklime, apparently the collapse of the packing around the post after burning. Layer (3) was similar, but included among the slaked lime patches of yellow-brown silt, a mixture of burnt material and soil washed into the post-hole. Into this was cut post-hole 10a, which contained large pieces of charcoal; its infill, layer (2), was a loose yellow silt, apparently material washed from the burnt core of the Period 2 rampart. Layer (1) was another post-hole, F12, cut into layer (2) and containing brown soil with small stones and a rectangular setting of packing stones burnt around their edges.

To the east of F10 three post-holes (F14, 64 and 62) contained yellow-brown silt and quantities of charcoal. All were cut through layers of earth and stones, burnt stones, and slaked lime deposited in the south eastern slot. At the bottom of the slot a layer of unburnt limestone silt, like F10 layer (6), appeared to be the primary deposit in the slot before the burning.

A similar stratification was found in F6b. Here the original lower packing, layer (11), corresponded to F10 layer (5), and was covered by a yellowish silt and small stones which contained no burnt material and seemed to be rubble which originally filled the post-hole behind a vertical packing, subsequently removed, around a post or posts in the southern end of the post-hole. Layer (9), burnt stones and slaked lime, was a packing around layer (8), the infill (burnt earth and stones with quantities of charcoal) to post-hole 6c. Washed slaked lime, layer (3), had built up against this post before a much larger post-hole (F6a) was cut in the southern end of F6b. This new post-hole extended to the bottom of 6b, removing half of the original lower packing, layer (11), and being itself packed by a mixture of burnt and unburnt stones, layer (6). A horizontal layer of burnt stones, layer (2), overlay post-hole 6c and appeared subsequent to layer (6), but had been placed in contact with the post itself. Above it layer (1) was a mass of slaked lime and stones filling in the top of the large post-hole, and compressed by the weight of the Period 3b north bastion, from which it was separated by a layer of dark silt. Post-hole 6a was filled with light brown soil and stones, probably washed from the adjacent road surfaces, and contained considerable quantities of charcoal.

The walls of the 3b bastions showed vertical burnt streaks on the lines of post-holes 6a, 12, 62, 64, 14, 66, 63 and 65, and had been recessed around some of them; the posts in these post-holes may therefore be ascribed to Period 3b. Post-holes 10a and 6c were overlain by the 3b bastions and were cut into debris clearly derived from the burnt core of the Period 2 rampart, and were thus of Period 3a. The remaining post-holes were sealed by 3b road surfaces and filled with burnt debris and thus date to Period 2.

H. Interpretation of the Period 2 Entrance

The two large post-holes 6b and 10 may reasonably be seen as sockets for the gates. Recutting and collapse had obliterated evidence for the shape of the posts, but from the size of the holes and the trefoil shape of their inner edges, together with the packing of their outer halves (F6 layer (10); to the south of the drawn section F10 layer (5) rose to a maximum thickness of about 40 cms) they may each have held three posts, perhaps central gateposts flanked by supports for an upperwork above the gate. Between these post-holes a slot about 10 cm deep was probably a sill beam for the gate. The slots on either side of the entrance passage marked the edge of the ramparts and, as the post sockets within them show, some form of fence ran here to revet the rampart core. Even to hold a series of separate posts it might have been easier to dig palisade trenches rather than individual post-holes, but the fact that none of these trenches preserved packing, and were open at the end of Period 2 when they were filled by slaked lime and silting indicates that they held sleeper beams tying the feet of vertical posts. At the back of the entrance the rear walls of the rampart had been removed before the building of the 3b bastions; surviving lengths of the wall aligned on the post-holes at the western ends of the slots. 1·5 m further westwards, behind the rampart, post-holes 25 and 27 seem too large simply to mark the end of the fences, and they narrow the passage to about 2 m. They should probably be interpreted as sockets for a rear gate (compare Avery *et al.*, 1967, 242), supported perhaps by diagonal braces set in the shallow sockets F26 and F28. In the limestone silting and small stones which is identified as the primary packing of the four gateposts (F10 layer (5); F6 layer (10); F25 layer (2), and F27 layer (3)) were found skulls of animals: in F6b and F25 articulated skulls of goats and in F10 and F27 the lower jaws of boars. No such skulls were found in any other post-holes and the coincidence of these deposits in each of the gateposts makes it difficult to avoid the suggestion that some purpose such as the conferring on the gates of the vitality of the animals was here intended.

The front walls of the rampart aligned on two post-holes set in the centre of the eastern palisade slots, F72 and F74, which may mark the end of the main palisade; beyond this point, F73 at the end of the north east slot, and perhaps a corresponding post-hole at the end of the south east slot (which lay below a 3b structure which was not removed), formed a subsidiary, perhaps lower, fence which cut off the berm.

No evidence for guard-chambers was uncovered. The damage caused by the 3b bastions prevented this from being conclusive, and one may see the breaks in the continuity of the palisade slots immediately to the west of the main gateposts as possible sites for the guard-chamber entrances. In the absence of internal supports one would have to explain, *ignotum per ignotissima*, that the guard-chamber roof rested on dry-stone walls which were completely removed in Period 3b; the likelihood of this should not be considered great.

I. Interpretation of the Period 3a Entrance

Only two post-holes, F10a and F6c, certainly belong to Period 3a, and are identified as sockets for gateposts. The attribution of post-holes 62–66 and 14 to this period is only tentative, and the posts without doubt formed part of the 3b entrance. The slight change in the alignment of the entrance passage between Periods 2/3a and 3b made the post settings, within the Period 2 palisade trenches, sit awkwardly against the sides of the 3b bastions, and a reuse of the post-holes from Period 3a is possible; but there were no signs of a recut. To the west of the gateposts no trace of the 3a rampart survived: the evidence of the infill of the Period 2 palisades and rear post-holes indicates that little more than clearance of debris from the back of the passage need have been undertaken at this period.

J. Interpretation of the Period 3b Entrance

Of all the 3b post-holes in the inner entrance the most likely candidate as a gate support was the large F6a, whose post was about 50 cm in diameter. Immediately to the west a vertical slot in the walling of the north bastion had held a post, perhaps intended to brace the gatepost. The much less substantial post-hole 12 seemed too feeble to carry a gate. The passage at this point was 2·8 m wide and could have been closed by a single-leaf door, which swung on F6a and was stopped by F12; the span, 2·6 m (about 8 ft 4 in.), is not excessive. The gate would then open inwards, as the projection of the bastion east of F12 would not allow clearance for an outward-opening leaf. The 3a gate would be better seen as two-leaved: despite the disparity in size of the post-holes a single leaf of 3·5 m here seems implausible. Equally implausible, perhaps, even though the post-holes were of equal size, would be the provision of a two-leaved door in Period 2; here the maximum span was barely 2 m. No trace of metal gate fittings from any phase was uncovered. As ready objects of salvage their absence is not surprising, but other methods of support would be possible for even a heavy door: unlike most Period 2 post-holes no 3b road surfaces covered the sill beam slot, and a horizontal brace probably thus extended between the 3b bastions. With a similar brace above the gate it would be easy to hang the door on pintles at top and bottom.

A bridge, part fighting platform and part for communication at wall-walk level across the entrance, is a necessary component of any serious defence. The Period 2 entrance, with its numerous vertical posts, could be reconstructed with a bridge 3 to 4 m broad across the front or across the back half of the rampart, or, indeed, as a complete covering to the entrance passage. Objections can be made to all: unless some form of *meutrière* were admitted, a bridge supported on F72, 74, 6b and 10 would prevent close-range defence of the outer gate; similarly, a bridge spanning the western palisade trenches would thwart assaults on opponents within the "pen" between the gates. Perhaps, therefore, it would be better to reconstruct with a narrow bridge over the gate itself, to allow lateral attack from the rampart ends overlooking the passage. The six post-holes (F62–6, 14) in the 3b entrance were probably supports for a 3b bridge about 1·5 m wide, perhaps with a gap for defence between it and the outer face of the door[3]. On these settings the bridge would be placed askew over the passage, but exactly parallel to the odd positioning of the gate (F6b–F12), a situation perhaps to be explained by the survival of the bridge supports from the 3a entrance, which was differently aligned, and by the construction of the gate to match the bridge.

After the building of the walls of the 3b bastion, but before the first road surface was laid against them, a large block of limestone, nearly 70 cm square and 35 cm high had been set against F65 within a slight recess in the bastion. The exposed angles of this block had been worn and were slightly glossy. Unlike the block in a similar position at Rainsborough (Avery *et al.*, 1967, 233 and Pl. xxii) it stood too proud of the road surface to form a safe base for a ladder; its purpose, ladder base, mounting block, or even a seat, sheltered below the bridge, for a sentry, is conjectural.

Behind the entrance passage three Period 2 post-holes, 20, 11 and 16 showed recutting in their upper layers. The reuse of F16 is probably to be associated with the Period 4 occupation south of the entrance, but F11 and F16 may have formed supports for the side wall of a small lean-to within the re-entrant of the bastion. The rear of the entrance passage was covered by a layer of crushed charcoal up to 5 cm thick and the bastion walls were burnt red, apparently by the burning of this structure.

III. The Interior

The soil cover in the interior of the fort is shallow; on the top of the slight rise behind the entrance no more than 5 cm separates turf from bedrock, and even where eroded material has built up at the bottom of depressions a depth greater than 20 cm is seldom encountered. But the hill has never been ploughed, and evidence of at least two phases of construction was uncovered (see Fig. 8 and Pl. 2).

The post-holes of these phases fall into three groups:

(1) Post-holes from 60 to 90 cm in diameter, and on average 60 cm deep. Almost all formed pairs from 2·5 m to 3·3 m apart, with similar spacing between pairs. Where packing survived the posts were of about 40 cm scantling.

(2) Twenty-six post-holes on average 40 cm in diameter and 50 cm deep, which formed an almost perfect circle directly behind the entrance passage, the posts being about 20 cm in diameter.

[3] The presence of timber works in this area was suggested by considerable quantities of charcoal in the entrance passage.

(3) Post-holes about 25 cm wide and deep, which clustered to the north and south of the excavated area. For these there was little dating evidence, and they might belong to a number of phases: the groups to the south of House 4 may be seen as for the supports of two structures, outbuildings or flimsy huts with central hearths; absence of subsequent disturbance suggests occupation during Period 3.

Stratigraphic relationship between groups (1) and (2) was preserved immediately behind the entrance. Here the cobbled road surface associated with the Period 3b entrance overlay eleven post-holes of group (1) but turned to run around the south eastern quarter of the group (2) circle. Within the circle a packed layer of small stones, through which some of the group (2) post-holes had been cut, sealed seven more of the group (1) post-holes. These earlier post-holes formed three structures, House 6 and House 2 which were completely sealed, and House 1, one post-hole of which was covered by the house platform of the group (2) circle. No stratigraphic evidence survived in the cases of Houses 3, 4 and 5, but the similarity of construction and the correspondence in alignment of all six houses are good grounds for assuming that they are contemporary. The alignment, furthermore, was that of the Period 2 entrance passage, and the hollow roadway of this period continued beyond the rear gate to run between House 1 and House 2. The settlement of rectangular houses, including the similar one uncovered across the Neolithic ditch, is therefore ascribed to Period 2.

To view the structures not as long houses but as contiguous groups of four- or six-post houses would not be demonstrably false, except in the cases of House 1 and the inner bank house, where centrally placed hearths prevent such subdivision. But the general regularity in spacing of post-holes in individual houses and the slight changes of alignment and gaps between each of the "Houses" shown in Fig. 8 is good evidence for the longhouse interpretation. All may have had hearths; that in House 1 survived erosion merely as a circle of scorched bedrock, and small areas of burning in other houses may have been remains of other hearths.

Where the roadway from the entrance passage ran between Houses 1 and 2 it narrowed to a width of 3 m, coming no closer to the lines of post-holes than 1·5 m. It therefore seems likely that the post settings formed internal support for the houses, which could then be reconstructed as aisled halls, the roof trusses and rafters extending across aisle plates laid on the top of the aisle posts. The width of the houses would then be about 7 m; the outer walls themselves would be non-structural, perhaps screens of wattle-and-daub framed between the eaves and sleeper beams on the ground surface. Between Houses 1 and 3 five post-holes, one of which was cut by a group (2) post-hole, are identified as supports for a small square structure, perhaps with a central post for a raised floor, whose southern side continued the line of the postulated outer walls of the longhouses.

After the burning of the longhouse settlement, presumably during the destruction of the Period 2 defences, a large roundhouse, represented by the group (2) post-holes, was built across parts of Houses 1 and 2. On the north of the post circle the hut platform was about 3 cm higher than the bedrock around it; this shelf, caused by traffic wear around the house ran from 1·7 m to 2·4 m beyond the post circle, and is taken to represent the position of the outer wall; the overall diameter of the house would then be about 14·8 m. No outer ring of holes survived, but the shelf was continued around the house by a burnt streak on the bedrock, and by clusters of burnt daub, and ran to the edge of two large post-holes for the supports of the porch. In the centre of the house the hearth survived as a circular patch of burning. Small post-holes within the post-circle are likely to have supported partitions; there was no trace of more substantial roof supports, and the exact form of the roof is problematic. (Similar problems are encountered elsewhere: see Hawkes, 1958, pp. 18–19; Harding and Blake, 1963, pp. 63–64). The roundhouse postdated the Period 2 longhouses, and was avoided by the cobbled road laid after the building of the Period 3b bastions. It may therefore have been built in either Period 3a or Period 3b: at any rate it was standing in the final phase of occupation of the fort.

IV. The Pottery

Pottery so far recovered from the outer bank and the interior falls into two distinct groups. From the infill of the latest rampart and its ditch sediment, and from the post-holes of the roundhouse, all deposits of Period 3, come sherds with incised linear decoration, generally in the form of chevrons, but including less regular slashed ornament infilled with white paste. Most are too small to show form, but some came from small carinated bowls. From the same layers come fragments of two bag-like vessels with expanded rims, probably best seen as cauldron derivatives (compare Harding, 1972, 76–78). Finger-tipping, on round shouldered or slightly angular jars, has so far been confined to the latest levels of Period 3b[4].

Almost all the material from Period 2 post-holes, on the other hand, consists of sherds of coarse fabrics with sagging shoulders and irregular rims; the only decorated sherd, a fragment of an angular bowl with linear decoration, comes from a post-hole of the five-post structure between Houses 1 and 3. Found in the infill of the post-pipe, it presumably was deposited after the removal of the post and should be associated with the demolition rather than the construction of this Period 2 structure.

To judge from the presence of small fragments of the later pottery in the construction levels of the Period 3b defences, this break in the ceramic tradition on the site should be placed between Period 2 and Period 3a. No radio-carbon dates are so far available, and parallels for the pottery should be treated with caution in view of the paucity of the material. But comparison with Wessex and with the Upper Thames suggests that on present evidence Period

[4] For drawings and some suggested parallels, see Dixon (1971), pp. 10–12 and Fig. 8.

3a should not be dated later than the late sixth or early fifth century, and may indeed be considerably earlier.

The Period 4 Reoccupation

After the abandonment of the fort at the end of Period 3b the evidence is consistent with intermittent scattered occupation over a considerable period. Above the burnt debris of 3b the entrance passage was choked with piles of domestic rubbish. Two small clay crucibles had been placed in a crevice of the south bastion, whose walls were reddened at this point, and quantities of charcoal were mixed with occupation debris. Further to the west a line of upturned stones and fragments of burnt clay, perhaps daub, may have marked the edge of a screen or flimsy shelter; to the south a roughly reconstructed length of the rear wall of the rampart sealed a small Samian sherd. In the centre of the entrance passage the collapse of the bastion walls had crushed a small pig in the middle of a rubbish-heap; elsewhere the collapse sealed sherds of Samian and of Oxford colour-coated ware. Delapidation should have been piecemeal: the internal wall of the outer hornwork sealed Roman sherds, while its external, and presumably less stable wall in falling into the ditch overlay, and was overlain by occupation deposits which contained sherds of the very early Iron Age. Finally, deep cart ruts across the wall tumble and a considerable topsoil scatter of iron fittings (including a waggon plate of 1913) were associated with the recent pit quarries within the fort.

9 | *Leckhampton Hill, Gloucestershire, 1925 and 1970*

Sara Champion

The excavations of the hillfort on Leckhampton Hill, near Cheltenham, in 1925 (Burrow *et al.*, 1925), were remarkable for their time on account of several features, both of excavation and of publication, which seem commonplace in the 1970s. In the words of one of the excavators, E. J. Burrow: "It will be observed from the photographs, drawings and plans which accompany this report that great care was taken to keep an accurate record of everything the spade revealed." (Burrow *et al.*, 1925, p. 90). Up to this time, the normal standards of excavation required no more than a narrow section, sometimes only through the ditch, with an attempt to produce a plan of the entrance by means of surface surveying and perhaps a few trial holes. The sampling of the rampart and ditch at three points, as was the case at Leckhampton, and the recording of levels of both features and finds, were unusual for the 1920s; and although it cannot be determined exactly how much of the entrance was actually excavated, and in cuttings of what size, an appreciably larger portion than was normal was planned in detail. If the excavation was thorough, then the recording and publication were even more so: plans of the fort with the sections marked, scale drawings of the sections, and a detailed plan of the entrance area were provided, and the individual reports on pottery, flint, metalwork, animal bones, charcoal and mollusca, and a useful geological survey of the area, were almost unparalleled in previous work. It is true that as early as 1881, Pitt-Rivers had published a measured section of Ranscombe camp (Lane-Fox, 1881), but that was the exception rather than the rule. The poverty of the information yielded by the more usually accepted standards of both excavation and publication can clearly be seen from Hawkes' survey in 1931 of the state of hillfort research as it then was (Hawkes, 1931). This review formed the basis for an extensive campaign of hillfort excavation during the 1930s, especially in Sussex, Hampshire and Dorset, for which a new standard had been set by Hawkes, Myres and Stevens in the publication of their own work at St. Catharine's Hill (Hawkes *et al.*, 1930). The reports of that decade show a more general appreciation of the necessity for meticulousness in excavation, recording and publication which had been so admirably anticipated by Burrow and his colleagues at Leckhampton in 1925.

In view of the obvious care which had been taken with the recording and presentation of the evidence as excavated at Leckhampton, it is not surprising that the report was assumed to contain accurate and reliable evidence for structure and probable date of the monument, and was widely used in the discussion of hillforts from 1931 until as recently as 1971. Some of the arguments for which Leckhampton provided much of the evidence will be discussed below; but it will perhaps be useful here to present briefly the results of the 1925 excavations.

Burrow, Knowles, Paine and Gray undertook an investigation of the square-ramparted barrow located outside the original entrance to the fort (Fig. 1) in response to a quarrying threat which has fortunately never been realised. They discovered evidence of several previous disturbances of the barrow, and were disappointed "as nearly a week had gone by without adequate return for our labour and expenditure". It was this disappointment which led them to explore the nearby hillfort.

Three sections were taken across the Eastern and Southern ramparts. There is a little difficulty in locating them on their plans, for in Fig. 2 Trench A and Trench B are located *c* 30 ft and *c* 65 ft respectively from the entrance passage, whereas in Fig. 1 Trench A is placed nearly 200 ft from the entrance, and Trench B does not appear at all. In view of the detail with which Fig. 2 is drawn, it is most likely that this is the correct one. Fig. 1 also shows the position of Trench C, across the Southern rampart some 350 ft round from Trench A on the same plan. Descriptions of the excavation of these sections are contained in two parts of the report, the foreword by Burrow, and Knowles' more detailed exposition in Part II. The results are recorded in the section drawings, Fig. 3. The main points to note are the 5 ft of turf and soil on the inside face of the rampart, the triangular core of stone, and the "filling" between the stone core and the remains of the front wall, described by Knowles as "of soil gravel and loose stones which at the bottom in rear of the wall had coalesced into a clayey mass". The ditch in section A and B was rock-cut, deep and narrow near the rampart, becoming wider and shallower after a step cut some 8 ft from the inner face. In Trench C the ditch was apparently not rock-cut, but scooped out of the soil, and there was no evidence of a step. One of the most important conclusions drawn by the excavators from the evidence of the ditch is contained in a footnote (Burrow *et al.*, 1925, p. 98, N. 5).

> Strangely at the higher rock level at O (Fig. 3) there was discovered the earliest of the potsherds of Halstatt (*sic*) date, whilst at the lower rock level (P) were Romano-British fragments. Is it possible that the lower rock level was a later work, and if so is the dry rubble wall on its western edge contemporary with it, together a second period work. The first period comprising a cored rampart and a shallower trench.

These last two sentences formed the basis for the ensuing discussion of Leckhampton Hill.

The excavators also mention burnt material in the core of the rampart, and "large quantities of charcoal and burnt wood" at the bottom of the ditch. Burrow (1925, p. 90) mentioned that there were signs of this also at Crickley Hill.

The front wall seen in all the sections was followed round to the entrance presumably from Trench A, and was found to enclose "a bastion like projection", a "great mound" of material unspecified, but noted on the plan (Fig. 2) in the same convention as the filling between the rampart core and the front wall. It is doubtful whether the bastion, or its pair on the other side of the entrance was ever excavated in any detail.

It is difficult to establish how much of the entrance was actually excavated; the 1925 plan shows the entrance passage and three chambers exposed, but the 1970 excavations suggested that the whole area was not laid open (see below). The points of importance on the entrance plan are chamber J, 10 ft across inside and without any apparent entrance, the D-shaped chamber H, and chamber K to the west of chamber H. There is no explanation in the key of the plan for the broken hatched lines forming the walls of chambers J and K, but the text suggests that they signify "rough foundations".

The pottery report is divided into two parts, describing finds from the sections across the Eastern rampart separately from those found in the entrance and adjoining guard-chambers. From the sections, 51 sherds were considered as Romano-British, and 61 early Iron Age. Included among the latter were two sherds of fingerprinted ware, labelled "Hallstatt". All the pottery from the entrance and chambers "appears to belong to the Early Iron Age". Among the total of 127 sherds were 57 of "very soft thin red ware", a type which was found in some quantity in the same area in 1970, considered then to be Romano-British. An important sherd to come from this area, found in chamber H, was decorated with incised geometric ornament, perhaps the only reasonably datable sherd from either the 1925 or the 1969–1970 excavations. An important point to note about the location of the pottery, in view of the later re-excavation and reinterpretation of the entrance, is that more than 40 sherds were found in chamber K. Also interesting was the appearance of seventeenth century glass, and clay pipe stems, in the entrance area.

The pottery led the excavators to date the hillfort's first phase to about 500 B.C., and they suggested that it continued to be occupied until after the Roman conquest. The first date is also remarkable in its way, for the suggestion that hillforts might be as early as this was far ahead of its time, and was not accepted by some for many years.

In the "Geological Notes", which contain details of a possible Northern rampart marked on an early Ordnance Survey map, Gray refers to a sentence in Buckman and Newmarch's *Illustrations of Corinium* (1850) mentioning "at Leckhampton, a true Roman well still existing in the centre of the camp on that hill". Further reference will be made to this in the description of the 1970 excavations below.

Hawkes' 1931 article on hillforts already mentioned above discussed only those sites for which there was more than just surface information available. Some 66 sites were listed, of which Leckhampton was one of those with a reasonable amount of evidence for structure and date; he reproduced one of the sections and a plan of the entrance. In his discussion of Iron Age A hillforts, he said of Leckhampton:

> it underwent improvement in a late stage of Iron Age B, but the original wide shallow ditch is dated by pottery to the earlier phase, and must be correlated with the stone-cored earthy rampart behind the later rubble wall.

This picked up and emphasised the tentative suggestion in Knowles' footnote as mentioned above; another interesting point was the reference to the "earthy" rampart, possibly referring to the 5 ft of earth on the inner face of the stone core as well as the material between the core and the front wall.

In the section on Iron Age B hillforts, Hawkes returned to Leckhampton in his discussion of the appearance of invaders from the South West,

> so far here only . . . certified at Leckhampton Hill, where they refortified the Iron Age A fort . . . with a coursed rubble wall in front of the old rampart and deepened nearly half the width of the old shallow ditch. There is no Iron Age C here, and their pottery is unmistakable; the entrance . . . perhaps suggests a late date, if not Roman influence.

In the section on entrances, Hawkes elaborated on the one at Leckhampton:

> the passage (10 ft–12 ft wide) was flanked by semicircular projecting bastions, consisting apparently of great mounds enclosed by the rubble facing-wall described above as Iron Age B work. At H and J were two guard-rooms flanking the passage, of one build with the bastions, and at K beyond on the North was an additional chamber. Post-holes and indeed anything to suggest provision for gates or barriers were absent. The remarkable guard-rooms are features already known in Iron Age A at St. Catharine's Hill period A, but appear here in improved form. Though this may owe something to Roman influence, the work is undoubtedly a pre-conquest one of Iron Age B, which is thus seen fully to anticipate the extreme developments of entrance fortifications to be seen in the Welsh hillforts of the Roman period.

This description of the Leckhampton fort as being a two-period structure is clearly understandable in view of the sections as published, and the parts of the structure which belong to each phase are ascribed on the basis of the stratigraphical evidence provided by Knowles. The ascription of the guard-chambers to the later pre-conquest part of Iron Age B was accepted for a long time, and was tentatively revived as recently as 1971 by MacKie (1971a, p. 64): "so far we do not know whether they (guard-chambers) were in use in Iron Age B times, except perhaps at Leckhampton, near Gloucester." This is in support of an argument showing Southern influences in Atlantic Scotland in the first century B.C., and the Leckhampton Hill guard-chambers are the only ones MacKie can claim as possibly late enough in Iron Age B for his argument, as those in the hillforts of the Welsh marches and at Rainsborough are, he admits, too early.

Between 1935 and 1937, Mrs. Hencken excavated at Bredon Hill, geologically an outlier of the main Cotswold range, but in sight of many of the forts which lie along the Western scarp of the Cotswolds. Here the fortifications were apparently of two periods, the earlier being the inner bank of "dump" construction (though see below), ascribed to invaders from the South West in *c* 100 B.C., bringing "duck-stamped" pottery; the second was the outer bank, a wall and berm construction of "native" tradition, dated by pottery and other artefacts to the first century A.D. Mrs. Hencken suggested that this second rampart was built by refugees fleeing from "Belgic peoples fighting their way into South West Britain" (Hencken, 1938, p. 20), perhaps on their way to Herefordshire, and she cited Leckhampton as possible supporting evidence:

> Here very much the same sequence of events is traceable. An original Iron Age "A" camp was suddenly refortified, the bank with dry-stone walling and a deepened rock-cut ditch; a most distinctive inturned entrance was also added, which is of a more elaborate type than that at Bredon and recalls Welsh examples. The associated material for these alterations is "B", and a date just pre-Roman has been suggested . . . it is possible that the sequence of events which were responsible for the founding of the Western Hill towns around 1 A.D. were also the cause of the great refortification of the Gloucestershire camps.

Thus Leckhampton's second phase is here not linked with the South Western invaders who are presumed to have built Bredon's first phase, but with the refugees from the Belgae fleeing North West around the turn of the era.

The first mention of the possibility that Leckhampton had a timber-laced rampart seems to occur in Savory's discussion published in the Dinorben report of 1964 (Gardner and Savory 1964). At the time of the St. Catharine's Hill publication Hawkes had to say that "the use of any kind of timberwork in Early Iron Age fortifications has in this country hardly been attested at all". By 1954, Mrs. Cotton (1954, pp. 26–105) had collected a sizeable list of examples, including the large number of vitrified forts in Scotland, but she was concentrating on those from the later part of the Iron Age which might have derived from Continental *muri gallici*, and was not concerned with those, like Maiden Castle, Dorset and Hollingbury, Sussex, which belonged to Iron Age A. Thus the 1925 report of burnt material in rampart core and ditch at Leckhampton was not mentioned because of the placing of the first rampart here in Iron Age A. Savory (Gardner and Savory, 1964, p. 82), in discussing bastions, said:

> such bastions had a later development in Western Second B: at Leckhampton Camp near Cheltenham some form of timber-laced rampart was later given a dry-stone revetment and the gateway provided with a pair of flanking bastions or platforms with curving fronts and rectangular guard-chambers behind them.

Here again the Leckhampton entrance was being assigned to the later part of the Iron Age, and this tentative dating was repeated later in the same discussion, when in the study of the Dinorben period III guard-chambers, dated to the first century B.C., the Leckhampton examples were quoted as a parallel, though outside the region suggested by Savory as central to the development—the area of the Cornovii and the Deceangli. Savory's views on the Dinorben guard-chambers were revised in the 1971 publication of his own recent excavations at that site, as a result both of C-14 dates, and of excavations at Croft

Ambrey, Midsummer Hill and more particularly at Rainsborough, North-amptonshire. In view of the Dinorben box-rampart construction with dry-stone revetments, presumed earlier than the Croft Ambrey "dump" ramparts, Savory suggested that the North Welsh guard-chambers were part of the Rainsborough Early Iron Age A complex, and were thus removed from the end of the Iron Age to the beginning. He did not mention whether Leckhampton should go back as well.

In the Rainsborough report itself (Avery et al., 1967), Avery looked again at the Leckhampton report, and suggested a reinterpretation of the strati-graphy. This, indeed, was the first time that anyone had attempted to review the Leckhampton evidence in any way other than that suggested by the original excavators. He suggested that the Rainsborough structural sequence, of a stone-built rampart and deep ditch followed by a dump rampart and wide, shallow ditch, might be paralleled at Leckhampton. He reversed the Knowles stratigraphy, pointing out with reason that the present turf line dipped over the centre of the wide shallow ditch (Avery et al., 1967, p. 250, n. 1), showing that this was perhaps the later ditch to be filled (Fig. 3). He attached the rubble core *and* the front wall to the deep ditch, and again reading from the 1925 section drawings, classed the 5 ft of earth on the back of the rampart as a dump rampart going with the wide shallow ditch. It should be stated here that the pottery from the ditch at Leckhampton was in very small pieces, was, in most cases, not distinctive in type, and did not necessarily present contrary evidence to such a reversal of the stratigraphy.

To summarise, the results of the 1925 excavations have led to the fort being cited as a certified example of an Iron Age A hillfort refortified in Iron Age B by South Western invaders; as a possible example of even later refortification by refugees from the Belgae; as a parallel to the sequence of construction at Rainsborough; and as an example of a fort with Iron Age B paired guard-chambers that might affect broch builders in the first century B.C. in Atlantic Scotland.

In 1968 the idea of initiating a research programme into the hillforts of the Cotswold scarp in the Cheltenham region was conceived by Richard Savage, lecturer in Archaeology at the Gloucestershire College of Art and Design. This group of hillforts lie so close to each other along the scarp that it was considered important to try and assess, by means of partial or total excavation of a number of them, their relative chronology. Some had, of course, already been sampled, including Leckhampton Hill, Bredon Hill, The Knolls, Oxenton and Danes Camp, Conderton. There had also been a little excavation on Cleeve Hill, though not within the area bounded by the semicircular rampart on that site. An interesting point about these excavations was that all the sites apart from Leckhampton had produced duck-stamped pottery (Champion, 1971a, p. 21). In view of the use made of the earlier Leckhampton excavations in archaeological arguments as reviewed above, and especially with the recent reversal of the stratigraphy by Avery, it seemed reasonable that the series of excavations should start there, with the immediate aim of checking the stratigraphy in the ditch and rampart, and of re-examining the oddities of the entrance plan. It was also hoped that more dating evidence might be gained, and the question of possible timber-lacing be resolved. At the same time excavations were started on nearby Crickley Hill, of which the interim results are published elsewhere in this volume.

Although the interim report on the 1969–1970 excavations on Leckhampton Hill has now been published (Champion, 1971b), it will be useful here to present the results in brief so that they may be immediately compared with those of 1925.

Five cuttings were opened in the two three-week spring seasons of excavation; three were rampart sections, one lay over the entrance area, and the fifth was a small sondage over a proton-magnetometer anomaly of 110 gamma.

The rampart sections

Cutting 1, 1969, 3 m × 24 m
Cutting 2, 1969, 3 m × 18·50 m
Cutting 5, 1970, 5 m × 17·75 m

Cuttings 1 and 5, which were across the Eastern rampart, may here be taken together. They were opened as near as could be judged to Trench B of 1925 in order to check the previous results as closely as possible. Underneath the turf and soil cover, which was never more than 20 cm thick and was in some places much less, was a layer of red burnt earth and limestone, confirming the 1925 excavators' report of burnt material in the core. Below this, and forming the main bulk of the rampart, was an extensive deposit of a white conglomerate material, identified as slaked lime, and possibly to be equated with the "clayey mass" described in 1925. Slaked lime occurs as a result of the action of water on quicklime (limestone heated to about 1000°C), and in the case of Leckhampton was possibly caused by natural precipitation on burned or burning ramparts. This burning was certainly uneven, for in several places the required intensity to change the limestone to quicklime was not attained: the South face of Cutting 5 (Fig. 4) shows a considerable amount of separate stones underneath a layer of slaked lime, while the North face of the same section (Fig. 6, lower), only 5 m away, has slaked lime right down to the base of the rampart. Below the slaked lime, lying on a thin layer of burnt soil immediately above the bedrock, was a substantial amount of burnt timber, much of it in the form of branches of varying sizes. Many of these branches had crumbled into small pieces of charcoal, presumably because of the weight of collapsing rubble from the rampart, and in the areas where they lay immediately below the slaked lime they were set solid into it, making it impossible to remove or even plan properly. Such details as we were able to plan may be seen on the plan of Cutting 5 (Fig. 4), where near the Southern face clearly recognisable branches were discovered. The timber ran from front to back of the rampart— no definite traces of wood running along the rampart could be found, and though extra care was taken in Cutting 5 to locate uprights after their appearance was recorded at Crickley Hill in 1969, none was found. The transverse timbers ran into the front and rear walls, but did not seem to run through to the outer face, at least of the front wall. Where a burning timber entered the wall it sometimes caused enough heat to change the wall stones to quicklime, and hence slaked lime—this can be seen quite clearly in both the front and rear walls of Cutting 5. The timber must have been present higher up in the rampart to have caused such a high degree of conflagration, but any holes left by the burning of these would probably have filled in during the slaking process. Streaks of a grey shiny material found in the slaked lime are at present being analysed to see if they might be a timber derivative.

The slaked lime had spread over the remaining portion of the front wall in much of the area uncovered, and also over the fragmentary remains of a rear wall, which seemed to have been deliberately destroyed before the fire. Only the foundation stones of the rear wall were burnt, whereas the front wall stones were burnt to varying degrees of redness.

The ditch in both sections was rock-cut, about 4 m wide and 1·5 m deep. It was flat-bottomed, and was filled with stones, presumably from the collapsed front wall. The stones at the bottom and at the far side of the ditch were less burnt than those higher up and nearer the inner face. There was at no point any trace of the step in the ditch mentioned by the 1925 excavators and recorded in their section drawings. There was some charcoal in the ditch, much of it near the inner face; the size of the fragments suggested thinner timbers than those found at the bottom of the rampart, and they were probably of a different type of wood.

Cutting 2 was placed across the Southern rampart, not as near to the 1925 Trench C as we would have liked because of trees. The results were substantially the same as in Cuttings 1 and 5, although the burning was slightly less: the front wall was hardly burnt, and the stones in the ditch were in many cases completely unburnt. The ditch was deeper than on the East, but was similarly rock-cut (Fig. 5), thus conflicting with the 1925 evidence. The parts of the plan marked as "unexcavated" are where it was impossible to cut back the faces of the rampart section to the line of the cutting—the slaked lime in many places was like concrete. Further details of the structure in all three sections can be found in the published report (Champion, 1971b, pp. 6–11).

The entrance

Cutting 4, 1970, 15 m × 13 m. It was not possible in this Cutting to encompass the 1925 bastions because of the limited time and atrocious weather conditions, but the entrance passage and guard-chambers were uncovered. There was much modern disturbance of the area, for the site had been used in the war as a radar station, and there were remains of concrete fence-posts, cable trenches, and a rubbish tip in 1925 chamber J. Figure 7 shows the features we were able to reveal. The main structure was a post-medieval field wall which ran westwards from the entrance, dated by seventeenth century glass found beneath it. Some of the stones used in the building of this wall were reused burnt stones from the rampart. It will be seen that this wall ran right across the front of the southern guard-chamber, and this area has not yet been excavated. The whole area south of the entrance passage was burnt, but much less so than the rampart further South—there was no slaked lime in the entrance area. North of the passage the rampart was completely unburnt. In the positions of chambers H and J of 1925 were found two semicircular guard-chambers flanking the entrance passage, both showing signs of disturbance in 1925. This disturbance in the southern chamber only reached as far as a straightish line in the rubble as seen in Fig. 7. There was no evidence that the Northern chamber was D-shaped, as the straight wall planned in 1925 on the West side of this chamber did not appear in 1970. There is a tree on the North East corner of this chamber which prevented us at that time from getting the complete plan of it. Investigation of the entrance area of these structures has not yet been undertaken.

The rampart, burnt red, curved around the back of the Southern guard-chamber, completely enclosing two-thirds of it, with the rear wall probably continuing round the end along the entrance passage and linking up with the chamber wall. On the North side also the rampart curved round the guard-chamber, but as it was completely unburnt, the 1925 excavators must have taken the limestone rubble for tumble, and have excavated it as chamber K, with the walls consisting of the revetting wall of the rampart. As for the absence of gate-posts in 1925, there was evidence in 1970 that the entrance passage had not been excavated deep enough; there was not time to do this ourselves in 1970, but already there is a possibility that a post-hole, of which we located the edge, which had been used a number of times for field fence-posts and for one of the radar station posts, was a re-used original gate-post hole.

The interior

Cutting 3, 10 m × 10 m, located the edge of a very large hole filled with small limestone chips. It was only 1 m deep in the part we excavated, which was an arc of the Southern edge, and it was clear that the rest of the feature lay underneath a small clump of trees which had not been surveyed with the magnetometer. Such a shallow feature filled with limestone should not have registered such a high anomaly, and perhaps the fact that the trees are the only ones in the centre of the fort, where the topsoil is only a few centimetres deep, suggests that something deeper lies beneath them. We are immediately reminded of the quotation from Buckman and Newmarch quoted above.

The pottery found in 1969 and 1970 was even less illuminating than that found in 1925. None was found in Cutting 2, and the two sections across the Eastern rampart produced 57 sherds; one lattice-decorated Romano-British piece came from the soil above the rampart, and the rest, probably Iron Age, was found in the ditch and behind the rampart inside the fort. There were no rim sherds, and only one decorated piece which had six shallow grooves across it. From the entrance area there was a total of 210 very small Romano-British sherds of the same type that was found there in 1925, and which was then classed as Iron Age. The 37 Iron Age sherds from this area came from the two guard-chambers and the entrance passage, many of them from the part of the Southern chamber which had not been excavated in 1925. Again there were no rims and no decorated sherds.

If the 1925 results are now compared with those from 1969 and 1970, a number of discrepancies can be recognised. In the rampart sections, the 5 ft of earth on the back of the bank recorded in the 1925 sections does not appear to be present. Possibly the remains of the rear wall, which are scattered along the back of the rampart, and which were not recorded in 1925, were considered as part of the material on the inner face of the bank. The triangular core of stones was not found in the recent excavations; as has been said, the burning in the rampart was uneven, and it may be that in 1925 an area of unslaked rubble was located in all the sections. The photographs in the original report show that their cuttings were very narrow. It is most unlikely that the rampart actually did have a triangular core in view of the timber lacing. The "filling" between the core and the front wall must refer to the alternately crumbly and hard slaked lime.

In 11 m of our excavation of the ditch we were unable to locate the step described in 1925. It is difficult to understand its presence then, for the excavators specify that the profile was identical in both Trenches A and B (Burrow et al., 1925, pp. 96–98). Re-excavation of the original sections may clarify this problem, if they can be located. The soil-cut ditch of Trench C is completely contradicted by the 1969 evidence, but again there may be differences along the length of the ditch. It seems unlikely, however, that there is enough soil on the hill to allow a completely soil-cut ditch.

At the entrance there were errors in 1925 which can only be explained by incomplete excavation. The true nature of the post-medieval field wall would surely have been realised if more than a short length had been exposed; although they found seventeenth century glass and clay pipe stems, which we found underneath the wall as well as around it, they failed to recognise the structure for what it was. Thus the whole entrance passage can never have been open. Their chamber J, rectangular, ten feet across inside and with no entrance, was probably made up of part of the field wall, part of the Western and Eastern walls of the semicircular chamber, and the line of rubble which was found halfway across the chamber in 1970, and which is 10 ft from the field wall. This view is strengthened by the fact that the part of the chamber South of the rubble line did not appear to have been previously excavated. It is not so easy to explain the D-shape of chamber H, for the straight West wall certainly does not exist now. Chamber K is doubtless the unburnt rampart curving round the back of the Northern guard-chamber, with its rubble core removed in error in 1925. All this suggests that the cuttings were smaller than the 1925 plan of the entrance would seem to indicate, for with the whole area open the real plan is quite clear. The finding of pottery in "chamber K" as mentioned above may mean that the sherds belong to a pre-rampart phase of occupation on the hill, which has so far not been recognised elsewhere.

The pottery from 1969 and 1970 is similar in fabric to that from the 1925 excavations, but is even less informative. The 1925 decorated pieces remain as the only finds that are in any way datable.

It can be seen now that the whole structure of the Leckhampton fortifications is of one period. As the slaked lime has spread over the stumps of the front and rear walls, then these walls cannot be later than the core, and there is no evidence of any rampart structure previous to that represented by the slaked lime. The ditch shows no sign of a second phase, and there is no layer of earth 5 ft thick on the back of the rampart. The entrance produced no evidence of rebuilding in the Iron Age, although this cannot be certain yet as the re-excavation is unfinished. The pottery suggested a Romano-British reoccupation of the entrance area, though whether the late cross-walls found in 1925 were connected with this or with even later occupation is at present uncertain.

It is now time to consider the date of the construction of the fortifications in Leckhampton Hill, and to see what effect the new excavations may have on some of the arguments that were discussed above. The positive evidence for date rests on three sherds of pottery from the 1925 excavations, and on the comparison of some of the structural features with similar elements found on other more closely datable sites. The negative evidence is supplied by the absence of certain pottery types.

The three distinctive sherds from 1925 are decorated, two with finger-printing and one with incised geometric lines. This does not constitute a large body of evidence, and the two types the sherds represented are not capable of being tied down to a very accurate date. Both should be considered as belonging to the beginning of the Iron Age pottery sequence rather than to the middle or the end, whatever that should mean in terms of absolute chronology. The other sherds from both excavations, apart from the Romano-British ones, are generally in an "Iron Age" fabric, but even this is a judgement that could be proved erroneous in time. More important, perhaps, is that among the two hundred sherds of probably Iron Age date from the site there are none of any recognisably later type, and particularly none with "duck-stamped" decoration. The interest here lies in the fact that, of all the other Cotswold scarp forts excavated, either extensively or with trial cuttings, only Crickley Hill has not produced "duck-stamped" pottery. Bredon and Danes Camp, Conderton (Peacock, 1968) are well-known for the presence of this type of pottery, and the less extensive investigations at The Knolls, Oxenton (Powell, 1933) and on Cleeve Hill (Gray and Brewer, 1904) also yielded sherds. Certainly the excavations at Crickley and Leckhampton have been more extensive than those at the last two sites, and have together uncovered a greater area than either of the other two, and yet there is not one sherd of "duck-stamped" pottery. The dating of the type has been pushed back since the discussion of it ten years ago

(Clifford, 1961, pp. 37–42) owing to its discovery at Croft Ambrey and Midsummer Hill, sites whose main occupation could, on the basis of C-14 dates, be fourth century B.C. (Stanford, 1971, p. 49). There is no evidence that incised geometric white-infilled pottery, as found at Crickley, with the one Leckhampton sherd, should be later than "duck-stamped", even if the earlier date for the latter is accepted, and the conclusion must be that Crickley and Leckhampton were occupied before the time that "duck-stamped" pottery became widespread in the Cotswolds; the two sites were therefore probably earlier than those other Cotswold hillforts, and date to somewhere before the fourth century B.C. This is consistent with a date tentatively suggested for the Cotswold geometric incised pottery (Champion, 1971a, p. 21) of the fifth or even sixth century B.C., a view strengthened more recently by Harding (1972, p. 75).

The structural features to be discussed are timber-lacing and guard-chambers. There is no longer any need to emphasise that the timber-lacing of hillfort ramparts in Britain has a longer history, and is a more extensive geographical phenomenon than was once thought. Mrs. Cotton's thesis that the majority of timber-lacing in Britain was derived from Continental *muri gallici*, and was therefore late, with one or two exceptions, is no longer tenable in view of C-14 dates from sites like Dinorben (Savory, 1971b, p. 21). The presence of timber-lacing at Leckhampton, then, does not indicate a late date, and on its own can no longer be used as a dating criterion. The guard-chambers, stone-built and semicircular, may be a more sensitive chronological indicator. The pair at Rainsborough, structurally very similar to the Leckhampton ones, belong to Avery's phase 2a, dated by him to the fifth century B.C. This dating is based on the appearance of furrowed bowls, which may be even earlier than Avery suggests—sixth or even seventh century B.C. (Harding, 1972, p. 75). The *terminus post quem* provided for the building of phase 2a by a ring found in pre-rampart contexts need not prevent such a back-dating, as this type of ring can be earlier than was thought in 1967 (Avery, personal communication). Savory's discussion of the Dinorben guard-chambers has already been mentioned, and his suggestion that they should be earlier than those from the hillforts of the Welsh Marches could place them in the fifth century B.C. or earlier. Burnt timbers of the second phase of the guard-chambers at Croft Ambrey yielded a C-14 date of 460 ± 135 b.c. (Birm. 185), so that even if the timber was old or reused, the first phase of guard-chambers at this site could be earlier than the fifth century B.C. These parallels to the stone-built chambers at Leckhampton could supply a date between the seventh and the fifth centuries B.C., and the absence of "duck-stamped" pottery with its new date in the early fourth century B.C. would imply that the fifth century B.C. is the latest likely date for the occupation at Leckhampton. It could, however, be much earlier—at Crickley, the latest Iron Age pottery is the geometrically incised, of which there is one sherd at Leckhampton, and yet it is the earlier of the Crickley ramparts which bears the strongest resemblance to Leckhampton. The reasonable quantity of coarse, undistinctive sherds from Leckhampton could belong to an earlier phase.

The realisation, after the 1969 and 1970 excavations, that Leckhampton has only one phase of construction, and the dating of that phase to somewhere before or around the fifth century B.C., have considerable implications for those arguments concerning Leckhampton which have been outlined above.

The refortification of the Iron Age A fort by South Western invaders in Iron Age B which Hawkes described in 1931 is no longer acceptable because there is no second phase of construction, and there is no evidence in the pottery that the whole structure should belong to any period later than the one he suggested for the first phase. The problem of possible "Roman influence" on the guard-chambers has been resolved by excavations at Dinorben, Rainsborough and the Welsh Marcher forts, to which group the Leckhampton chambers must surely belong.

MacKie's thesis, already described above, was countered in part by D. V. Clarke (1970, p. 220), who pointed out that there were no guard-chambers in Wessex B, that Rainsborough was not in Wessex, and that both it and the Welsh forts were too early. This, as we have seen, left MacKie with Leckhampton, which now must be seen to belong with Rainsborough, and also to be too early. Thus there are no known forts with guard-chambers late enough in the South to have any effect on broch architecture; this is not the place to discuss in what way the removal of the structural parallels might affect the rest of MacKie's thesis.

The supposed link between the refortification of Bredon Hill and that at Leckhampton must also disappear, because of the absence of the second phase at Leckhampton; and, as suggested above, Bredon probably belongs to a later period of hillfort construction than Crickley and Leckhampton. Although here is not the place to look in detail at some of the more puzzling features of the Bredon sequence, it is in order to mention that the sections of the inner bank (Hencken, 1938, Pls XII and VX) reveal some striking similarities to the Leckhampton rampart sections: Pl. XV shows a band of charcoal between the base of the rampart and the bedrock, possibly representing a layer of timber of a similar nature to that found at Leckhampton; and Pl. XII has a "lime cap" which covers loose stone in the rampart and continues down the outside of the bank into the ditch. Could this not be slaked lime caused by the burning of a timber-laced limestone structure? The possibility must be entertained that the inner "dump" bank at Bredon was a timber-laced stone construction similar to other Cotswold forts.

Savory was quite right to suspect that Leckhampton had a timber-laced rampart, and he was also right in considering the guard-chambers as a parallel for Dinorben. His later removal of the Dinorben pair from the end to the beginning of the Iron Age was certainly reasonable in view of his own new excavations at the site and the other factors mentioned above; Leckhampton will now go with them. The relationship of the Rainsborough, Dinorben and Leckhampton guard-chambers with those of the Herefordshire hillforts still remains to be clarified.

Avery's reversal of the Leckhampton sequence was a major cause of the re-excavation of the site. The close parallel that he saw between Leckhampton and Rainsborough is in no way destroyed by the disappearance of the second "dump" phase, for the first phase still shows similarities, especially in the entrance construction. In fact, the recent excavations at Leckhampton served to strengthen the parallel with the discovery of C-shaped guard-chambers set into the rampart.

One further point to be amended in Avery's article is his suggestion that Rainsborough "is perhaps the earliest English Iron Age fort yet claimed in print" (Avery *et al.*, 1967, p. 246), for it was in a local periodical in 1925 that Burrow and his colleagues suggested a date of *c* 500 B.C. for the construction of the hillfort at Leckhampton. In the near half-century since then, many hill-forts have had to be drastically redated; and although the structural evidence from Leckhampton has been re-examined and reinterpreted, altering some long-held views about its place in the sequence; although further excavation on the site in the near future will probably provide the answers to some of the remaining problems, and may change the answers again, yet the initial date suggested by the original excavators is probably not very far wrong. This is perhaps the most remarkable achievement of the 1925 excavators.

10 | *Traprain Law: A Summary*

George Jobey

Traprain Law, a detached outlier of the Lammermuir Hills, rises like some great and now scarred leviathan above the coastal plain of East Lothian at the point of its broadest extent, where the coastal littoral sweeps around from the open waters of the North Sea into the wide estuary of the Firth of Forth (Fig. 1). To the south, the hills unfold in increasing altitude to obscure but by no means to prohibit access to the important expanse of lower Tweed-dale beyond. As with some other early fortified sites of this order in Scotland, such as those on Arthur's Seat, Eildon Hill North and Burnswark Hill, nature has provided an eminence of defensive potential and prestige which is not divorced from good and varied tracts of supporting countryside.

The approach to the summit of the Law itself, which rises some 350 ft from the base, is barred on the south by rocky scarps which continue around the eastern extremity to the yawning gap formed by the present day quarry (Fig. 2). Elsewhere, the slopes although arduous do afford some points of reasonable access, particularly in the north west and west. It is the western flank which forms the most obvious extent of ground for settlement, no area more so than the shelf or plateau below the western crest.

It was here, on the western shelf, that the earliest and most extensive investigations were made from 1914 to 1915 and from 1919 to 1923 (Curle, 1915; 1920; Curle and Cree, 1916; Cree and Curle, 1921; Cree, 1923; 1924). Although in northern terms these excavations provided a wealth of material, the main area examined was restricted by comparison with that enclosed by the defensive lines themselves (Fig. 2, *A–T*). Moreover, the method of excavation by arbitrary levels has left a legacy of difficulty in interpretation which it would be idle to pretend is not still with us. The fact that fragments from one Roman vessel may be found on three different levels in adjoining areas may be a brief yet sufficient warning in itself. Later excavations by Dr. S. Cruden (1940) and Dr. G. Bersu (1948) were, by circumstances, confined to parts of the northern and western defences (Fig. 2, *CI–IV* and *BI*). Dr. Bersu's excavations were published only briefly in interim form and, at the time of writing, the material is not readily available for inspection. Since then, contributions specific to the site itself have been made by Elizabeth Burley (Mrs. Fowler), in a comprehensive corpus of the metal-work (1956), and by Mr. R. W. F. Feachem, on an analysis of the defences based upon a detailed ground survey (1956a). The plans from this survey are here reproduced by kind permission of the Royal Commission on Ancient Monuments (Scotland) and the Society of Antiquaries of Scotland.

I. Pre-Roman Settlement

The earliest artefacts recovered from the hill, two microblades, although coming from two widely separated provenances, in all probability represent no more than the brief activity of small mesolithic bands working the coastal grounds. On the other hand, the neolithic finds can hardly be disposed of as falling necessarily into the same transitory category. In total these consist of some sixteen recorded stone or polished stone axe-heads and as many as thirteen leaf and lozenge-shaped flint arrowheads, as against the one barbed and tanged example. Certain of the flint scrapers recovered from time to time may also be included in this group. All of the arrowheads and fifteen of the axe-heads were recovered in the Curle and Cree excavations on the western shelf, and, with the odd exception, consistently from the lowest level. A further axe-head, found by Dr. Cruden at a point much further to the north, may point to a more extended area of activity than the earlier finds suggest. The occurrence of polished stone axe-heads on otherwise later, Late Bronze Age or Early Iron Age sites in North Britain is by no means rare, but with odd exceptions, such as at Dunagoil (Mann and Marshall, 1915), Bute, these have been mainly limited to single finds. Although there is no recognisable neolithic pottery from amongst the "native" ware from Traprain, nor any occupation level or structural evidence recorded as being associated, the now almost familiar occurrence of neolithic occupation from beneath more southerly hillforts may serve as a reminder of the early potentials of the western flanks of Traprain in this respect. As a collection of mixed lithic equipment of the period it does in fact form one of the larger individual groups from the area.

The earlier part of the Bronze Age in the second millennium B.C. is hardly represented in the record of artefacts. Possible exceptions are the one arrow-head, already mentioned, and a fragment from a bronze ear-ring similar to that in the Migdale hoard (Coles, 1969). However, the precise connotation of the latter must remain unknown. It was recovered from the second lowest level on the western shelf in a year when six rather than four levels were preferred by the excavators. Even so, the early sepulchral as well as ritual attraction of the hill, perhaps broadly during the second millennium B.C., is signified in other ways. On the eminent north-east shoulder there previously existed some inscribed rock-surfaces bearing cup and cup-and-ring marks and linear designs, now unfortunately quarried away (Edwards, 1935; Piggott, 1970, p. 88). Immediately to the north of the trigonometrical station on the summit of the hill there are also the remains of a cairn which, though well robbed, gives the appearance of having been a genuine sepulchral monument. Finally, on a ledge of rock beneath later habitation on the western plateau, there came to light in the 1920 excavations a group of four cinerary urns and one accessory vessel, with the remains of a cremation beneath the largest urn.

It is in the Late Bronze Age that settlement of more permanent nature is again attested, since this can be the only interpretation of the comparative wealth of material from the early excavations on the plateau. This amounts to some forty items of bronze together with a range of clay moulds or portions from them (Burley, 1956; Coles, 1960). The bronzes include socketed axes, both ribbed and faceted, socketed and tanged knives, shouldered chisels, a socketed gouge, penannular armlet, lock-ring and a bifid or maple-leaf razor. Some of the pins, though rather smaller, resemble those from the Heathery Burn Cave Group (*Inv. Arch.* G.B. 55, 10(8)) or others found more recently on the Breiddin hillfort site (Musson, 1970a, p. 217), Montgomeryshire. Among the moulds are those for a lunate spearhead and a native Ewart Park type sword, whilst metal-working in the area is further attested by bronze runnels. A Hallstatt C element, whether introduced by trade or new arrivals, is also represented by a bronze razor with a single loop. Dr. Coles saw this occupation at Traprain as belonging to his Adabrock phase of the Scottish Late Bronze Age in the seventh to sixth century B.C. (Coles, 1960, p. 45 ff.) although some individual pieces might indeed be earlier. Other material from the lowest level of the early excavations, such as some of the amber beads, fragments of triangular cross-sectioned jet or shale armlets and, for that matter, perhaps some of the crude hand-built pottery, occasionally bearing finger-tip decoration, could also belong and so give to the metal-work assemblage an added air of domesticity. Traces of structures associated with this occupation are difficult to substantiate in any certain form. Wattle and daub and odd post-holes are recorded but the latter make little sense, even when the original plans are placed on the same scale and conflated[1]. On the lowest level in area *HA* on the western shelf "some paving surrounded by stones" could have formed the remains of a hut of rather questionable diameter, but this again is not unequivocally associated with the nearby socketed axes, a cache of barley and a saddle quern.

As a whole, this Late Bronze Age material was consistently derived from the lowest level of the plateau excavations over several years, perhaps reducing in quantity towards the north-western periphery in areas *S* and *T*. Although there has been no excavation of comparable extent elsewhere on the hill, it may be significant that no such finds were made in the early cuttings further down the western slopes at *C* and *X*, in Cree's investigation of the water-hole on the top of the hill at *Z*, or the later excavations over various ramparts. It is arguable, therefore, that this occupation was most probably limited in physical extent to the western shelf.

Into this community there was introduced the knowledge of iron, if not its

---

[1] It is necessary to remember that the plans of the original Curle and Cree excavations are not all to the same scale.

working, in the form of an iron socketed axe-head found on the lowest level in area *M*. Of all the British examples this axe-head copies most closely the bronze form of its precursors, however inconvenient this may have been in the new medium. At the moment it almost certainly stands alone in this early context but some of the remaining iron-work from the site could possibly repay further close examination. It has been noted recently, that the spear-head from the palisaded site at Hayhope Knowe, Roxburghshire, may lay some claim to being a Hallstatt C import (Ritchie, 1970, p. 53). Although the parallel once drawn between this spear-head and one from the lowest level at Traprain would no longer seem to be valid, the seeds may have been sown. Be that as it may, the problems of the first introduction of iron-working into Scotland cannot delay us here and, in any event, some of the evidence has been discussed recently elsewhere (MacKie, 1971c, p. 64). It was Mr. Robert Stevenson who rightly commented (1966, p. 20), in the early days of the lengthened North British Iron Age chronology, that both the apparent association of the iron axe-head from Traprain and its early date ought to be accepted, rather than that it should be used as evidence in a prolongation of the Scottish Late Bronze Age as favoured by some earlier writers. At the time a perhaps somewhat conservative date in the fifth century was suggested. Even on this estimate it then followed that the western slopes of Traprain lay unoccupied for a long period before the Roman Iron Age, presumably because there appeared to be little in the way of datable metal artefacts to fill the gap. So far as the metal-work itself is concerned, placed against the background stratigraphy such as we have it at Traprain, a considerable gap in occupation on the western plateau is difficult to deny. Not even a rare La Tène Ic fibula or an Aa penannular brooch appears in the record to act as an obvious intermediate link between the early and later material. Nevertheless, some of the metalwork finds require further comment with respect to this problem. Although a better case has now been made for the early origin of the projecting ring-headed pin (MacKie, 1969b, p. 22) as a possible development from the swan's neck sunflower pin by the sixth or fifth century B.C. this lineage has not gone without challenge (Clarke, D. V., 1971, pp. 28–32). In any event, this increased longevity of the type does not at present deny its continued existence into the first century A.D. and beyond. So far as Traprain is in question, both the bronze and iron examples from the site would seem to occur on levels consistently above the bottom, where it is extremely difficult to wrest them from Roman associations. From amongst the bronze spiral finger-rings which are recorded, at least three come from the lowest level, but two of these in years when only three levels were in vogue, and they were never far removed from Roman material. Whilst they may well denote good pre-Roman connections with southern England they cannot close the breach in themselves and, in this instance, need not necessarily be earlier than the first century A.D. (Jope and Wilson, 1957, pp. 79–81; Clarke, D. V., 1971, pp. 26–28). Some of Mrs. Fowler's type A1 penannular brooches were also found on the bottom levels but would likewise be difficult to push back beyond the first century B.C. at the earliest. A single cast, ring-headed pin of evolved form, whilst probably now capable of carrying a much earlier date than has sometimes been assigned to it on typological grounds, nevertheless had a clearly described provenance on the top and latest level in area *HA*. In this context, whether it be regarded as a stray or an heirloom hardly matters. There is, indeed, other material in the metal-work record from the western shelf which could fall into the pre-Roman period but probably at best hardly before the second to first century B.C. and then again never certainly so. Nor must one forget the few fragments of rotary querns from the lowest level. Whilst they do not have to await the Roman period they can hardly be too far removed and do little towards reducing the interval. In short, Mr. Stevenson's considerable gap in occupation on the western slope, possibly from sometime in the sixth century B.C. until the closing centuries of the first millennium B.C., has to be reckoned with. But this is a gap seen to exist in the metal-work alone and well illustrates one of the perennial problems in North British archaeology, which is the exaggerated part that metal-work and, in particular, the so-called "exotic" types may have to play in deciding between long and long, though perhaps not continuous occupation. Particularly is this so where other basic cultural material may change but little and, as here at Traprain, the ceramic evidence is chronologically insensitive. Now it is far from our purpose to deny continuity of occupation on individual sites elsewhere in Scotland, whether they be Abernethy timber-laced forts of the seventh century B.C., later receiving English exotic bronzes of the third century B.C. (MacKie, 1969b, p. 15), or some of the Tyne-Forth hillforts, where the well known structural history can be used to supplement the often uninformative material culture. Nor is it intended to question those possible pre-Roman cumulative movements into Scotland from the south in whatever direction (Thomas, 1961, pp. 16–20; Piggott, 1966, pp. 1–13; MacKie, 1971a, pp. 60–66; Stevenson, 1966, pp. 21–25). Our problem is concerned with one specific area on a single site. And even if a gap in occupation has to be accepted for the western shelf at Traprain, on the basis of this metal-work, this does not thereby prevent continuity of occupation on the hill itself. Indirectly, however, it may well affect any interpretation of context for the defensive lines, and it is to these that we must now turn.

Except for some minor points which border on the eye of faith, the present plan, together with Feachem's physical analysis, take one as far as it is possible to go without further excavation (Feachem, 1966, pp. 284–289). Only three of the five visible lines are likely to have application to a very early pre-Roman occupation (Fig. 2). The first of these, the most doubtful in nature and context, consists of a rather tenuous line of stone, mainly lying beneath the turf, which runs east and west along the top of the hill. It was suggested tentatively that this line could have turned southwards along the western crest to provide an enclosure some 10 acres in area. Close inspection on the ground reveals that it could be earlier than a possible hut-platform and it would undoubtedly provide a reasonable line for a palisade, but otherwise its function and proposed perimeter both remain quite uncertain. What could then be the earliest recognisable rampart as such was partly investigated by Mr. Cruden (1940) and appears high up on the northern slopes to the west of the quarry. From there it runs sporadically westwards to form the central line in cutting *CII*, was shown to pass beneath the latest rampart on the site in *CIII* to reappear in *CIV*, from which point it continues intermittently along the western crest. The resultant enclosure would be in the region of 20 acres. This line appeared to have been stone-built with some facing stones but it was very denuded and there is no mention of timber-work in its construction. All that can be said directly about its context is that it is earlier than the latest rampart on the site and, in *CII*, was shown to be earlier than a hut-floor which was itself undated. Excavation within the interior of this enclosure has been minimal and is of no help in this respect. It is always possible that this line could have been associated with the first of two occupation levels noted by Cruden in *CI*, but this too was essentially undatable. On the other hand, Feachem's assumption of a primary context for this rampart seems to be a correct interpretation given the overall pattern on the hill, and its earliness may well account for the denuded condition of the remains. As such, it might further be understood as arising in response to a greater and more urgent need for defence on the part of the early inhabitants on the western slopes, whose seventh to sixth century settlement, on this thesis, must have been either open or, at best, surrounded by a lightly constructed perimeter of which no indications now remain on the ground or can be detected in the early excavation reports. In this sense it might resemble somewhat the situation, so far as it is known, at Cullykhan (Greig, 1970), Banffshire, where occupation with an Adabrock-type chisel and iron-slag precedes the vitrified fort; except that at Traprain the fortified line had necessarily to be established in a different place. There would be no reason to delay this event too long at Traprain, since there is at least no evidence to deny occupation commencing within the site of the 20 acre enclosure immediately upon the demise of the early settlement on the western slope. In the absence of any certain knowledge of a palisaded precurser to this first fort such a solution may savour too much of the "miraculously spontaneous, like the birth of a Northern Athena" (Hawkes, 1971). Nevertheless, it is not too much at variance with similar realisations both further to the north in Scotland and in England to the south. In the Border country itself some of the smaller palisaded settlements are from radiocarbon assays running almost contemporary with the early Scottish timber-laced forts of the seventh century B.C. And at a site such as Huckhoe, Northumberland, palisades could well have been replaced by a stoutly built stone wall by the seventh century B.C. (Jobey, 1968). Likewise, at the more substantial hillfort on Kaimes Hill (Simpson, 1971), Midlothian, the second phase stone-faced rampart, assigned by radiocarbon dating to the fourth century b.c., in itself demands an earlier date for the timber-laced phase, whatever may be the nature of even earlier, Bronze Age occupation on that site. Nor, again locally, need the large size of this first enclosure at Traprain deter us from proposing such an early context. From one other large centre in southern

Scotland, Burnswark, in Dumfriesshire, two radiocarbon readings indicate the existence of a 17-acre hill-top enclosure by the seventh to sixth century B.C.[2]. Whatever forces were at work, the fact that such large centres were already showing themselves amongst the rash of smaller forts and related settlements of the area implies some political cohesion, and possibly a more complex economy, at a time earlier than might have been considered possible some years ago. The conditions on the hill-top at Traprain do not lend themselves to the surface-detection of hut-positions, and not all areas may have been suitable for habitation, so that the size of the community within this 20 acre enclosure must remain uncertain. However, for the purpose of comparison, the somewhat smaller fort of 13 acres surmounting Yeavering Bell, in Northumberland, contains one hundred and thirty visible hut-platforms though understandably all may not be contemporary (Jobey, 1965, p. 33, Fig. 7).

The next structural phase in the perimeter at Traprain has been seen to consist of a stone-built rampart, somewhat difficult to disentangle from the first in places on the northern slopes to the west of the quarry. It was investigated by Cruden in CII, where it forms the northernmost line, but was once again well robbed and yielded no secure evidence of context. From this point on the ground it appears to continue westwards beyond the turning point of the first rampart, and it has been suggested that eventually it may have followed much the same line as the later defences on the western slope, thus enclosing an area of some 30 acres. No traces of it seem to be recorded in the early excavations at Y or in Bersu's cuttings at B1. This may not be surprising, for at that time it does not seem to have been recognised as a surface feature elsewhere, and, in any event, its precise course on the west is far from being assured. In his original analysis Feachem was inclined to regard this line as an early extension to the primary 20 acre site, maybe with little interval between the two, designed to include the western slopes. He saw it as being tentatively associated with the few relics to which an "early date" could be assigned, if these were not midden material thrown out from the 20 acre enclosure (1956a, p. 288). In general terms this view has been modified since the days of a short chronology (Feachem, 1963, p. 120). The difficulty is now obvious, since to accept the Late Bronze Age material as evidence of occupation by the seventh century B.C., relate it to this proposed 30 acre enclosure, and yet maintain the proposed physical analysis, would entail at least one and possibly two enclosures being of earlier date. With the current dates from Dinorben hillfort and, indeed, others (Savory, 1971a), anything might seem possible and the Parc-y-meirch hoard may well remind us of possibly similar relationships elsewhere. However, it is not considered that the present evidence from Traprain will support the establishment of a 30 acre Late Bronze Age hillfort. A better temporary solution, for it can be no more than this, would be to retain this 30 acre enclosure as a later extension, related to and intended to enclose some renewed activity on the western slopes. This renewed occupation may not show itself very clearly or concisely in the

[2] Jobey, 1970, 21; there is now an additional date of 525 ± 90 on half-life of 5568 years.

archaeological record although we could be approaching a little firmer ground by the second to first century B.C. As we shall see, whatever the metal-work may indicate, the event can hardly be delayed beyond the first century B.C. and might well have been much earlier. In northern archaeology the extent to which reliance has sometimes to be placed upon the structural history of a site is a hazard still to be accepted (Piggott, 1966, p. 2).

Such extensions in the size of existing hillforts are by no means a regular occurrence in the Border counties. The smaller sites show little if any increase in internal area from the early palisaded phase, where it is known to exist, through various later defensive phases. However, there are some larger sites, amongst them Traprain, where the enclosed area is increased from time to time. Nowhere is this more evident than at Eildon Hill North, Roxburghshire, where successive perimeters lead up to a pre-Roman enclosure of some 40 acres, containing some three hundred visible hut-platforms (Feachem, 1966, p. 81). Near to this in size at this stage could have been Traprain, already a paramount centre in Votadinian territory. One other rampart on the site might well have been first constructed before the arrival of Roman armies in the north, but, as it was almost certainly upstanding in Imperial times, it is best considered under that head.

II. Romano-British Occupation

The broad picture of Romano-British settlement in the Tyne-Forth Province is reasonably well assured. As a symbol of the *pax Romana*, enclosed but essentially non-defensive native settlements can be seen to overlie many of the smaller hillforts and related pre-Roman settlements, perhaps first with huts of timber and later of stone (Jobey, 1966a, pp. 1–13). Initially there may have been some fragmentation of the earlier social groupings, but after that individual settlements often show evident signs of expansion, whether they occupy the sites of abandoned hillforts or cluster on the hill-slopes and lower ground. Elsewhere in the Border area the situation is less clear and other reasons might be sought to account for the continued presence of timber rather than stone-built huts (Fig. 3). It is against this background that Traprain Law must be seen to have continued as a great centre, having achieved its maximum enclosed area of 40 acres and a distinction not confined to size alone. As a native town permitted to retain a substantial rampart, it appears as something unique in the Roman intra-mural zone and, as such, has provided an additional point in the arguments for an early philo-Roman Votadinian state. In this respect, attention has often been drawn to the difference in treatment accorded to Traprain Law on the one hand and Eildon Hill North of the Selgovae on the other, the latter now ostensibly abandoned and surmounted by a small Roman signal station.

The perimeter at Traprain for much of the Roman period has been seen as the great terrace-rampart, commencing now on the lower northern slopes hard by the quarry and a gateway at U (Fig. 2). Thus, for the first time the northern flanks, which carry some hut-platforms, and the so-called lower terrace were enclosed. The rampart continues along the western slopes by Y and $B1$ and so around to the southern scarp. From ground-observation this line would seem to be earlier than the one other remaining rampart on the site. It was considered by Feachem to have been first occupied by about the second half of the first century A.D., from the evidence recovered in the early excavations at the north gateway (U). This is difficult to gainsay, since there are some fragments of Roman pottery of first to early second century date from the bottom level in U and from an unmarked area which was cleared by the early excavators on the terrace further to the west[3]. However, it is as well to remember that this evidence comes from occupation material in the interior and, so far as one can be certain, not from the rampart itself at this point. Records of the early excavations on the western perimeter at Y are confused and not helpful in this respect. Bersu's cutting at $B1$ and a second further to the south, both made over the latest rampart on the site, revealed that this had been built over a "terrace-bank" which he related to the terrace-rampart on the northern flanks. This terrace-bank contained scraped up Roman material which indicated a late third or early fourth century date for its construction. Beyond his cutting to the west, he also noted the indications of an earlier terrace-bank the presence of which allowed Feachem to see reconstructions being carried out to his great terrace-rampart of the first century A.D., the last of these, on Bersu's evidence, presumably taking place about A.D. 300. Without further excavation to establish the proposed lines of these versions of the terrace-rampart this must remain the best tentative solution. There is, of course, nothing to prevent the initial construction of this rampart having taken place before the first Roman advance into Scotland. On the other hand, any attempt to move it too far into the Roman period would involve the assumption that before its erection an open Romano-British settlement had sprung up on the northern terrace and, perhaps, on the lower northern slopes. This northern extension, whilst still maintaining a good line nevertheless loses some of the natural defensive advantages of its predecessors. Perhaps population pressures were a real consideration.

Almost inevitably attempts have been made to fit the material from the western plateau and the structural history of this terrace-rampart, so far as it is known, into the specific contexts of Roman frontier events. In the case of a large native centre in the intra-mural zone, where there is material in some quantity, the exercise is justifiable, even though one may doubt its validity in the case of smaller settlements in the area. The coin series from Traprain contains no specimens between Faustina the Elder and Gallienus, suggesting a gap in supply from the mid-second century A.D. to the mid-third century A.D. This in turn has been related to a presumed break in the record of the

---

[3] I am grateful to Mr. R. B. K. Stevenson for making the Roman pottery available for inspection. Only preliminary examination has been made to date, and Dr. Bersu's material has not been immediately available.

metal-work from the western slopes and so a general abandonment of the site for a generation or more has been suggested, coinciding with that somewhat movable event, the demise of the Antonine frontier and the subsequent Caracallan reorganisation (Feachem, 1956a, p. 288). Such troublesome times could then have provided an occasion for a first reconstruction of the great terrace-rampart. This tentative argument is feasible but, as often, incapable of proof. Mrs. Fowler pointed to changes in form and style of metal-work but was less inclined to speak in terms of a long break in occupation. Whatever interpretation may be put upon the coins, and whether third century coins are generally in short supply or not, the series from Traprain, though long, is far from being numerous. Without further investigation any reconstruction of the terrace-rampart in the late second or early third century can be no more than a tentative deduction from frontier history. Finally, for what it may be worth, the Roman pottery record on preliminary examination can hardly be used to substantiate the long break in the coin series. A similar speculative label must also be attached to the events which were seen to lead up to the final reconstruction of this rampart in *c* A.D. 300, when barbarian raids supposedly brought about the temporary loss of the northern frontier. However, even if such barbarian activity did not actually involve the frontier, that something happened or was impending is suggested by the campaigns of Constantius (Mann, 1971; Breeze and Dobson, 1972), so that this may be as good a time as any to envisage reconstruction at Traprain.

In the final phase of rampart construction on the hill retrenchment takes place and, on the northern flank, the line was withdrawn to the crest of the slope, at once making the approach more arduous and reducing the enclosed area to some 30 acres. Cruden first established this latest rampart as being some 12 ft wide and composed of layered turf faced on either side with local whinstone slabs. A sherd of samian ware from beneath this rampart at *C I* allowed him to place a second century *terminus post quem* on its construction. Bersu, on the strength of his late third to early fourth century date for the last version of the terrace-rampart, attributed to it a probable Dark Age context and was inclined to relate it to the remains of undated rectangular buildings on the summit of the hill. Feachem, perhaps more conscious of Roman frontier history and an apparent paucity of evidence for any extensive post-Roman occupation, suggested that it could as well have been constructed about A.D. 370, when Theodosius was then supposed to have converted the Votadini to a treaty state. Certainly there is nothing amongst the Roman material from the northern flanks of the hill, the only area to be abandoned, which would call for an extension of the life of the 40 acre *oppidum* beyond the Picts' War. This would therefore remain as a reasonable occasion, if not the only one, for replacement and remodelling of the defences, although from the material evidence there is again no reason to think that this involved any substantial period of desertion. From thence, the coins alone, however they may have been obtained, carry one forward to Arcadius and the end of the Roman period. As to the frontier role assigned to the Votadini at this time and the pressures to which the whole area could have been subjected, only one brief point will be made. Some years ago Professor Jackson advised caution in the treatment of some of the evidence behind the theory of the important part played by allied kingdoms in the late defence of the frontier (Jackson, 1955, p. 79). It has also been noted subsequently that some forms of Crambeck and Huntcliff wares which do not seem to appear until after A.D. 369 are absent from areas to the north of the linear frontier, although they may be quite frequent elsewhere (Turnbull, 1963). The preliminary re-examination of the Roman coarse pottery from Traprain would confirm their absence here. If this is not native discrimination at work, then it is difficult to see why these particular types should not have filtered through to the chief centre of a supposedly buffer-state. But this is a matter upon which others must expand[4]; it does not affect the issue of continuity of occupation at Traprain which is attested by the coins.

A discussion of the many facets of the metal-work belonging to the immediately pre-Roman and Roman period cannot be entered into in this summary. Recourse must be made to Mrs. Fowler's work on the subject, where some 600 items are listed and the interplay between Roman and native elements discussed. As often, in precise chronological terms their value may be limited, but when taken together with the analysis of the Carlingwark, Blackburn Mill and Eckford hoards (Piggott, 1953a), they undoubtedly provide an important source of material for the social and economic history of the native peoples of the area. Roman metal objects arrive early as does the pottery. Although never in quantity, Samian ware starts with South Gaulish vessels, possibly as early as the last quarter of the second century and, by the evidence of potters' stamps or decorated sherds, can be seen to continue through to Trier Ware and possibly East Gaulish of the later second and early third century. Roman coarse pottery, whilst it may indeed show the general discrimination of native Scotland against the more mundane fumed and burnished wares (Robertson, 1970, p. 198 ff.), ranges from the first to the fourth century with the exception of the very late types already mentioned. Once again, although the quantity may be small as compared with that from military sites, the supply seems to be reasonably steady. The odd fragment bears a soldier's mark of possession but there would seem to be no reason to regard the material as loot from military installations. Indeed, whether Traprain be Ptolemy's *Curia*, a "hosting-place", or not, its importance as a possible trading centre would seem to continue throughout, for long periods situated in the northern outlands but at others probably more closely linked with the nearby *vicus* type settlements, such as that at Inveresk[5]. Its comparative affluence is probably better appreciated against the general paucity of material from the smaller native settlements of the Border area.

Despite these Roman contacts which eventually, by whatever means,

[4] Dr. J. Mann has a paper in progress on the wider aspects of the northern frontier after A.D. 369.
[5] I am indebted to Mr. Gordon Maxwell, R.C.A.M. Scotland, for information in advance of publication.

brought to Traprain a range of Roman toilet articles or those hesitant steps towards literacy in the form of a scratched alphabet or a Roman stylus, one yet wonders how much of the new culture was really acquired and where the true allegiance lay. The smithing tradition continues and Celtic ornament continues or reasserts itself to produce those metal articles which are part of the common culture of the native peoples of the area. Martial and perhaps flamboyant attitudes are still prominent in the metal-work record alongside the lumbering cart, the labouring oxen, the sheep-shearing and agricultural husbandry. The old beliefs no doubt persisted, perhaps here dimly perceived in the guise of a model antler and raven (Ross, 1967, pp. 142 and 253) and, as a very long shot, one might wish to know more of an elusive well which appears on the old plans but now escapes detection. As has been remarked elsewhere, it is one of those tribal capitals where it may still be possible, however tentatively, to infer the three-fold division of Celtic society (Ritchie, 1971, p. 34)

It might be assumed that amongst all this, even given the nature of the early excavations, there would be a corresponding amount of information about the physical nature of the domestic structures. The evidence is at best disappointing. By analogy, one might anticipate a progression from timber to stone-built huts as seen on the smaller Romano-British settlements in the area (Jobey, 1964, p. 45). The best that can be achieved at Traprain, by superimposing plans of the arbitrary levels on the western shelf, is the possibility of four to five overlying circular stone foundations, only one of them anywhere near complete, in the three lower levels of areas P and L. Whether these are bases for stone or turf walls is not easy to decide. It could well be that frequent references in the early reports to closely set parallel lines of stones on edge indicate remains of construction trenches for timber-buildings, but these make no clear patterns. A better indication of continuous rebuilding or alteration on the western shelf may be gleaned from the numerous hearths, probably of changing style or function, to which the early excavators paid more attention. For example, in the 1921 excavations of areas HA and M a total of twenty-nine can be noted on the various levels. This lack of structural evidence, however, need not be taken as a mark of barbarian squalor, as is sometimes done. Once again the metal-work catalogue can come to the rescue and indicate the possibility of some sophistication in the dwellings, whether this be in the form of tools for the job, or house-furnishings worthy of the obvious care which was taken over the construction of the focal hearths. Mr. A. H. A. Hogg's analysis of the structures on the highest or latest level over parts of the western shelf shows the remains of buildings of semi-rectangular form, which may find some support in the shape of some of the platforms still visible elsewhere on the western slopes. Such an architectural development is difficult to establish on the majority of the smaller, albeit perhaps less sophisticated rural settlements throughout the area, where the round hut appears to continue as the norm until their desertion. It must be confessed that the remains of these semi-rectangular structures at Traprain are somewhat tentative but at least their late Roman context is assured and, as such, it is a possible architectural form which may have to be reckoned with, either at this stage or in the sub-Roman period.

III. Sub- and Post-Roman Occupation

Whether or not Traprain continued as a potential sub-Roman citadel of consequence (Thomas, 1968, p. 104 ff.), at a time when Manau had already retracted northwards to the area of Stirling, is a matter which cannot yet be resolved with any certainty. The coin series from the site, as distinct from those found with the great treasure, takes us to Arcadius and possibly into the fifth century A.D. And, in this connection, it must be recalled that some might still wish to see activity of some sort on the Wall to the south after A.D. 383 (Kent, 1951). Similarly, some of Mrs. Fowler's penannular brooches and pins could tentatively qualify for a sub-Roman or fifth century context (1963, pp. 98–156). On the other hand, the great hoard of Roman silver from the hill (Curle, 1923), whether permanent residents' or transient pirates' loot, lacks a firm context as to when it might have been deposited other than that provided by the coins of Honorius found with it. Whilst it may be interesting to envisage it as part of a wider Christian background of a fifth century Cunedda (Watson, 1968, p. 53), who in fact can say? Likewise, the post-Roman massive silver chain was turned up in isolation from the east end of the hill (Museum notes, *Proc. Soc. Ant. Scot.* **73**, 1938–1939, pp. 326–327), whilst the connections of St. Monenna and Dunpeledur can also be no more than an excursion into possibilities (Hogg, 1951, p. 207).

This problem is not a new one, either at Traprain in earlier periods, as we have seen, or indeed elsewhere in the northern area in the sub-Roman period. It is simply what, in any event, might have constituted a cultural assemblage in the fifth century once the supply of Roman material had ceased? The chronologically sensitive material not being present we could be left with such items as the much maligned, yet basic, gritty pottery, still present at Traprain in the fourth century and, for example, at Chesterholm *vicus* in the late fourth or even fifth century[6].

And if we turn to the broader pattern of native settlement as at present known (Fig. 3) one could perhaps be forgiven for seeing some significance for post-Roman continuity of habitation in the cluster of Romano-British settlements on the northern flanks of the Cheviots around *Ad Gefrin* and the native type gritty pottery from that, even later, Anglian site[7]. Much of this may indeed be entering into the realms of unfounded speculation, but the possibility of some occupation persisting at Traprain into sub- and post-Roman times should not be dismissed too lightly.

[6] I am grateful to Mr. Robin Birley for allowing inspection of material before publication.

[7] Unpublished information from Dr. B. Hope-Taylor.

In a summary of this order one has been greatly dependent upon the work of others. The difficulties are manifold and the conditionals perhaps more frequent than some would wish. Nevertheless, one aspect at least may present itself forcibly—that is of yet another "high place" with a total history stretching over millennia and a continuous or near continuous occupation for over a thousand years.

This paper was written in February, 1972, and does not, therefore, incorporate material discovered or published subsequent to that date—Ed.

11 | *The Vitrified Forts of Scotland*

Euan W. MacKie

I. Introduction

This chapter is arranged in three main parts with an appendix. In the first section the phenomenon of vitrification is described and the evidence for its causes reviewed. The second section describes briefly the results of three excavations on vitrified forts which I have undertaken in recent years, namely *Finavon* in Angus, *Sheep Hill* in Dunbartonshire and *Dun Lagaidh* in Wester Ross. The third section considers some of the more general aspects of the archaeology of the vitrified forts in Scotland, including their absolute dating, their size and distribution, possible development, the structure of their walls and the material culture associated with them. At the end there is an Appendix containing a list of known vitrified forts in Scotland.

It is concluded in the following section that vitrified forts are the burnt remains of hillforts which once had drystone walls with internal frameworks of timber beams and, since the term "vitrified" refers to what happened to these at the time of their destruction by fire, the term "timber-framed forts" is preferable and is used throughout most of the chapter. While it is fairly easy to spot burnt timber-framed forts from surface indications (vitrified rock), unburnt such sites—of which a handful are already known—are unlikely to be revealed except by excavation. There may be many more of these waiting to be discovered and the pattern on the distribution map (Fig. 6) should perhaps be regarded as a provisional one.

In recent years a number of timber-framed forts have been excavated or re-excavated and it has become standard practice to obtain radiocarbon dates for their construction. As a result the chronology of these sites has been given a new precision and been put back as much as five centuries earlier than was supposed when the associated finds provided the only direct dating evidence, (Fig. 7)[1]. While the new chronology has redefined the acceptable range of explanations for the origin of these hillforts and their builders—ruling out the old theories based on first or second century B.C. dates—no fresh finds have been made in timber-framed forts which allow the new explanations to be

[1] MacKie (1969).

visualised in more than dim outline. In other words, while we now know that the earliest of these forts was built in the Scottish Late Bronze Age—and that their appearance must therefore somehow be connected with the other cultural and technological changes visible in the archaeological record of that period—there are still almost no direct links between the two categories of finds concerned, fortified sites on the one hand and hoards of bronzes on the other. Some new site needs to be excavated which both originates in that early period and is far richer in finds than any hitherto explored.

II. Vitrification and its Causes

Scattered throughout the north-eastern and central parts of Scotland are about seventy prehistoric fortified sites—ranging in size from tiny enclosures 60 ft across to large hillforts enclosing thousands of square yards—which are unique in Europe in having large masses of melted and fused stone inside the cores of their stone walls (list in the Appendix). Almost since these sites were first described in the eighteenth century[2] it has been believed that the vitrified stone was evidence that a deliberate and ingenious technique of firing rubble to create a fused wall or rampart of enormous strength was practised by their builders[3]. This might be termed the theory of creative vitrification. Ninety-two years ago on the other hand Joseph Anderson suggested that the melting of the stone might have been due to the *destruction* by fire of dry-stone walls which had been built with wooden beams or logs incorporated inside their rubble cores and he referred to observations that a similar process sometimes takes place during the preparation of material for road-making[4]. This inspired suggestion seems to have been ignored and subsequent writings on vitrified forts have not referred to it. In his synthesising account of Scottish prehistory of 1935 V. G. Childe quoted the suggestion that vitrification was a constructional technique[5] but by 1937 he had obviously considered the alternative view, following continental workers[3]. In that year and in 1938 he carried out two experimental demonstrations that a length of timber-framed dry-stone wall would, if thoroughly burnt, yield masses of vitrified rubble[6]. More recently direct evidence that such a prehistoric timber-framed wall had been burnt and partly vitrified was found at Dun Lagaidh on Loch Broom, Ross and Cromarty (Pl. VI)[7]. Yet in spite of all this the theory of creative vitrification occasionally re-emerges, most recently in the new *Journal of Archaeological Science*[8]. Since the theory seems likely in this way to acquire some sort of scientific respectability—and since, in my view, it can only be held by com-

[2] Anderson (1779).
[3] Cotton (1954), pp. 94–101: Nisbet (1974)
[4] Anderson (1883) p. 280 and fn. 3.
[5] Childe (1935), p. 196.
[6] Childe (1938), Childe and Thorneycroft (1938).
[7] MacKie (1969a).
[8] Brothwell *et al.* (1974).

pletely misunderstanding the nature of the sites—it seems necessary to review again the evidence against that view and in favour of the theory of the destruction (deliberate or accidental) of timber-framed walls.

Brothwell, Bishop and Woolley[8] confine their original work on the problem to analysing chemically samples of vitrified rock from three sites in Scotland. The conclusions drawn from this were that, despite wide differences in the composition of the parent rocks, the "glasses" (vitrified stone) from the three sites were remarkably homogeneous and this is easily explained, it seems, in chemical terms. Rocks contain many different constituents which melt over a whole range of temperatures; the higher the temperature the more of the constituents will appear in the glass. Conversely rocks of most compositions when heated to only say 1000°C will produce fairly homogeneous glasses since only those constituents which melt below that temperature will be present in them.

It must be obvious that the only conclusions which can be drawn directly from this kind of evidence (apart from distinguishing between vitrified rock and metal slag) are (1) that the rock has melted and (2) that the composition of the melt will indicate approximately the temperature reached. The chemical analyses by themselves tell us nothing about *how* the temperature was achieved and even less about the social motives and the activities of the people of the fort at the time of the burning. It is necessary to make these statements because of the broad conclusions which follow the descriptions of the chemical analyses and which the undiscriminating reader may take to be reliable deductions from the laboratory work itself. For example we have an initial statement like "(2) Well vitrified fortifications imply quite a large scale technological commitment. Does the evidence show that there was a single planned project on the part of these first century B.C. intrusive people?" Then, following the description of the laboratory work, come some general conclusions including "(e) Considering the high temperatures that have to be produced, and the fact that possibly 60 or so vitrified forts are to be seen in a limited geographical area of Scotland, we do not believe that this type of structure is the result of accidental fires. Careful planning and construction were needed" and "(f) Vitrification is thus a reflection of a cultural tradition, and of the expertise of these people in the use of timber/rock mixes in relation to strong natural draughts."

Even leaving aside the gross error in the dating of the forts in the first statement (new, much earlier dates based on radiocarbon have been available since 1967[9]) one is forced to conclude that these views simply illustrate that *a priori* assumptions based on incomplete or misunderstood evidence can condition the researches of even the most scientifically trained workers. The authors state that "we hope at a later date to investigate the field aspects of the problem" so it may be useful to summarise here the relevant field and archaeological evidence, none of which supports the theory of creative vitrification and all of which actively opposes it.

[9] MacKie (1969). *Discovery and Excavation in Scotland 1967* (C.B.A.), p. 4.

The theory of creative vitrification must imply that one of three processes occurred to produce a deliberately fused rampart of great strength. (1) The rubble was fused along the line of the intended rampart by having fires lit on either side and on top of it; presumably several successive firings would be required to bring the fused mass up to a suitable height, say 12–15 ft. (2) Rock was melted in large crucibles somewhere else and poured in a molten state over the rubble of the wall core. (3) A rubble-cored stone wall, laced internally with timbers, was built and then deliberately fired. From statement (f) quoted earlier it would appear that the third alternative is preferred by Brothwell but, whichever of these processes is claimed to have occurred, one thing is vital to them all. Since vitrification is held to be a constructional technique the process of firing and fusing must have taken place at the *beginning* of the use of each vitrified fort.

The least likely method of creative vitrification—that involving the pouring of molten rock into a rubble wall core to cement it—is not hard to dispose of. Enormous blast furnaces, capable of reaching temperatures of up to 1500°C and equipped with huge crucibles, would be required to melt the vast quantities of rock which would be needed in this bizarre theory and such furnaces are quite incredible in a Bronze and Iron Age context. Blast furnaces of that efficiency—suitable for producing cast iron—were not developed in Europe until late medieval times[10]. In any case the composition of such completely molten rocks would, for reasons already explained, exhibit marked differences from site to site in contrast to the situation actually prevailing[8].

Efforts to create vitrified rock experimentally by building fires along both sides of and on top of heaps of rubble have been tried in the past without success[11] and this would appear to dispose of the first method suggested. Thus we are left with the burning of a timber-laced wall, or mass of rubble, as the only feasible way of producing the fused rampart required by the theory and the list of objections to this view—most of which also apply to the other two views just mentioned—is formidable indeed.

(1) In the first place vitrification is clearly incomplete at many sites. At Sheep Hill for example the vitrified core adhering to the bedrock remains only in the south-west arc (Fig. 1); elsewhere there is nothing. At Dun Lagaidh the whole of the two long sides of the hillfort were completely stripped of stone for the later dun and no vitrified rock remains. Some would almost certainly be fused to the rock and immovable if these stretches of wall had been thoroughly vitrified. The foundations of the eastern end of Dun Lagaidh, which contain the entrance passage, were found intact under the rubble of the dun and bore no signs of burning. The concept of creative vitrification clearly requires that a continuous and high rampart of fused rubble existed at each site. Since except for a few small forts vitrification is not continuous, and since it is notoriously difficult to move a really large mass of vitrification without dynamite, one must conclude that the theory fails on this count alone.

[10] Singer *et al.* (1956), pp. 6, 73.
[11] M'Hardy (1906).

(2) Moreover even in the most severely vitrified fort, like Rahoy and Inverpolly, the fused mass is never more than 4 or 5 ft high (Carradale). This is quite inadequate as a defensive wall.

(3) Every excavation of a vitrified fort except that of Rahoy has revealed that the lumps of vitrification occur over the ruins of a thick, dry-stone wall with vertical faces; the bottom few courses of the faces are preserved under the fallen rubble. It is ludicrous to maintain that a perfectly good and defensible, thick and massive stone wall should be built and then deliberately wrecked by firing and partly fusing it. In any case the quantity of material actually vitrified is usually minute compared with the immense masses of dry rubble from the wall core, severely heated and reddened but not fused.

(4) The stratification observed in every excavated vitrified fort, and the finds made in them, make it perfectly clear that burning and vitrification have always occurred at the end of the use of the fort, as a process of destruction which caused that end; it did not occur at the beginning of the occupation of any site. At Finavon and Dun Lagaidh I observed that vast quantities of heated, not fused, dry rubble had collapsed on to the occupation layer inside the fort on and in which were the charred timbers of wooden constructions ranged along the inside wallface. Vitrified masses were rare in the parts excavated. The evidence of destruction by fire is overwhelming. At Finavon the remains of the vertical inside wallface were twisted and distorted by heat. At some sites vitrified masses have fallen molten out of the wall on to the already collapsed rubble or on to rock and then cooled[12]. After the fire the walls were ruined and the site abandoned. The excavation of brochs and duns with ordinary dry-stone walls produces exactly the same phenomenon of masses of dry rubble resting on occupation layers and preserving the stump of the wall but always without the evidence of tremendous heating.

(5) The experiments of Childe have shown that a dry-stone wall with an internal framework of timber will, when burnt under the right conditions, produce all the phenomena found in vitrified forts[6].

(6) Unburnt timber-framed dry-stone walls, with the beam-holes preserved, are known as at Abernethy (Pl. V). Since an occupation stratum, with finds, was uncovered inside this fort it cannot be maintained that the wall was prepared for firing at the beginning of its use and then abandoned for some reason.

(7) At Dun Lagaidh the stump of the north end of the hornwork was found still standing 6 ft high under its own debris. It was partly fused—with a vitrified mass projecting through the inner face—and beam slots were visible close by in the same face[7].

(8) Hillforts with timber-framed ramparts and walls form a widespread phenomenon in northern and central Europe and Britain from at least as early

[12] Greig (1971), Fig. 2: this section through the wall of the timber-framed fort at Cullykhan was originally drawn on the site by the writer and should show the severely heated and cracked blocks of the outer (right) wallface heavily shaded like the inner ones. The vitrified mass can be seen to have cooled over this destroyed face.

as the eighth century B.C., as most textbooks mention[13]. In most of them the timber is buried inside cores of earth and stone but even these are sometimes found to have been severely heated, though rarely to the extent of being truly vitrified[14]. Only in Scotland it seems was this kind of stone wall built with a core of pure, dry rubble and it is reasonable to suppose that it was this type of core—containing thousands of air spaces and more vulnerable to draughts when it collapsed—that allowed the abnormally high temperatures capable of vitrifying rock to be reached when the fort caught fire.

There is no doubt that there are still unsolved problems over how exactly a massive dry-stone wall—perhaps 20 ft thick and 15 ft high, and with only the ends of the extensive internal network of timber beams showing in the inner wallface—could catch fire and burn so fiercely and it may well prove that arson involving huge quantities of brushwood stacked against the wall was probably necessary. Yet the evidence that vitrification was caused by the destruction by fire of this timber-framed wall is overwhelming and future workers must face this fact and abandon the fanciful notion that the vitrified rock is the remains of some weird and peculiarly Scottish prehistoric technology. Most of what one sometimes hears referred to as old fashioned "cultural" archaeologists—who dig and study stratification—know this perfectly well and may think this section on the causes of vitrification un-necessarily long and detailed. Yet it is a fact that the theory of creative vitrification does live on, always expounded—in my experience—by those ignorant of the mass of "cultural" evidence from excavations. It seems that the lesson that theories must be derived from the whole of the available evidence and not just, for example, from the technological segment of it still has to be learned.

III. Three Timber-Framed Hillforts

A. Finavon, Angus (NO/507557)

Results from the excavations

This site is a rectangular fort sited on a steep-sided ridge and with a detached hornwork. It measures about 160 by 36 yd and was extensively excavated in the 1930s[15]. No clear beam-holes were observed in the distorted wallfaces exposed at that time but numerous traces of dwellings were found in the interior in the form of post-holes and baked clay hearths. Many fragments of thick, plain, light buff-coloured sherds containing large lumps of gravel were found in the occupation layer under the mass of debris fallen from the wall. Childe's observation that large quantities of charcoal were also found in this layer led the writer to select Finavon in 1966 as one site from which material for C-14 dating might easily be obtained. A week was spent there sinking two trenches against the inside faces of the north and south ramparts[16].

[13] Piggott (1965), Chapters 5 and 6.
[14] Cotton (1954), pp. 85 ff.: Dixon (1972).
[15] Childe (1935b; 1936).
[16] MacKie (1969b).

The section of the deposits on the south side revealed some features of interest, even though the actual wallface was not quite reached (Fig. 4). Childe's earlier cuttings had showed that the inside wallface was actually further out than the crest of the visible rampart[17], indicating that the rubble fallen into the interior was piled higher than that over the stump of the wall itself; possibly stone-quarrying had brought about this result. Obviously it was important to be clear about this otherwise the occupation layer might have been interpreted as running under the hillfort wall and thus ante-dating it.

This occupation layer rested directly on the brownish-pink, gravelly subsoil and varied in thickness from 8 in. at the southern end—where the subsoil was descending (presumably quite close to the inside face of the wall)—to about 2 in. at the other end. At the outer end of the trench (nearest the wall) was a zone of what appeared to be carbonised planks under and in the occupation layer; several of them rested directly on the subsoil and these must therefore have been wood which was laid down during, or immediately after the building of the timber-framed wall. They could either be part of the wooden floor of a lean-to hut built against the wall—suggested by the pattern of the post-holes discovered earlier[15]—or perhaps a wooden walkway along beside the wall. The former seems more probable because occupation material subsequently accumulated over the wood. The planks were dated by radiocarbon as also was a sample of charcoal from the occupation layer. The former date was 590 ± 90 b.c. (GaK–1224) and the latter was 320 ± 90 b.c. (GaK–1223).

The only artefact found in the 1966 excavation was a stone which appears to be a crudely hollowed lamp.

B. Sheep Hill, Dunbartonshire (NS/435744)

1. The site and the excavations (Fig. 1)

This is a small fortified site, about 10 miles west of Glasgow, occupying the summit of a volcanic plug of basalt overlooking the river Clyde. In plan the fort consists of three enclosures, defined by natural terraces with steep rocky faces. The summit of the knoll—a little above the 160 m contour—was apparently enclosed by a dry-stone, timber-framed wall which was subsequently vitrified; the only remaining traces of this are on the south-west. The second enclosure has the same boundary as the first on the north side but includes the lower terraces on the south and south-west, there defined approximately by the 153 m contour (Fig. 1). It is not clear whether the extreme south-west, lowest part of the terrace—extending to the western cliff—was within the defences; probably it was as there are traces of dry-stone masonry in clefts in the cliff face near the fence. On the other hand the rampart could have left out this isolated extremity of the hill-top without much loss of security by running along the 153 m contour on the south-west corner.

There are two entrances into this large enclosure, both by way of natural gullies in the rocky edges of the terraces. The north entrance is approached

[17] Childe (1935b), Fig. 2.

by a steep and awkward path overlooked by high rock faces; traces of the rampart flanking it are visible on both sides. The approach to the south entrance, also flanked by the rampart, is shallower and the natural, sloping terrace below it has been converted into the third and lowest enclosure by a clear but very denuded stone-faced rampart. The entrance into this—the outer-most of the whole fort—is visible in the east wall and is protected from a direct approach along the flank of the hill by a thin traverse wall. The area of the whole fort, including the south-west extremity, is about 7400 sq yd, or $1\frac{1}{2}$ acres.

Excavation revealed that the visible rampart, and therefore the two largest enclosures, belonged to a secondary phase in the use of the site, after the destruction of a tiny timber-framed fortlet on the summit of the knoll. This secondary rampart seems to have been crudely constructed, as a simple bank with a rubble core of stones and earth and with a sloping revetment of blocks forming the outer face. The inner face had a sloping facing of flat slabs. On the south-eastern part of the site, along the inside face of the rampart and running up against it, was an uneven, flat, rubble floor layer. Many artefacts were found on this and in the thick deposit of earth which had accumulated over it. One of the objects on the floor was a tiny blue glass ring bead; the others included fragments of jet armlets, some pieces of unfinished armlets and lumps of raw material.

Nearly all the stones composing the rampart of the second fort and the rubble floor behind it were reddened by intense heat. Pieces of vitrified stone, some quite large, were scattered loose and at random through the rubble core among stones and soil which showed no sign of having been heated. It was clear that the second rampart had been built from the debris of the burnt timber-framed fortlet which had first occupied the site. Support for this interpretation is given by the short length of vitrified wall core which remains *in situ* on the summit of the knoll; this is well within the area enclosed by the later rampart (which ran round the edges of the various flat areas of the knoll). One trench was cut through the rampart on the north side at a point where it was expected that timber-framed wall and later rampart followed the same course. However, the former seems not to have stood there since an apparently undisturbed occupation layer rested on rock and immediately underlay the rubble core of the rampart. The position which was occupied by the timber-framed wall is unclear except where vitrified core remains but presumably it must have enclosed only the very summit of the knoll, an area of about 800 sq yd as opposed to a total area of perhaps 7400 sq yd defended by the later ramparts.

Further confirmation of the two phase history of the site was obtained in a section through the secondary rampart on the southern side (Fig. 4). Here its core and outer face overlay an earlier dark occupation layer or midden lying on subsoil, and this also ran under part of the rubble floor layer. This midden yielded many potsherds and other artefacts which presumably belonged to the inhabitants of the timber-framed fortlet. It also produced a sample of charcoal which gave a radiocarbon date of 5110 ± 1020 b.c. (GaK–2469), obviously much too early. Finds from this early midden included about a third of a complete pot (Fig. 2), fragments of moulds one at least of which was apparently for the blade of a bronze axe (Fig. 3: Pl. I), several other pot rims (Fig. 2), a jet whorl, a fragment of a thin jet disc and two fire-cracked hammerstones. None of the many fragments of jet rings and armlets could be clearly assigned to these deposits of the first fort.

One rim sherd had been severely burnt after it had broken off the parent vessel: it was swollen, had a cokey texture and was partly vitrified. It seems likely that this sherd was incinerated when the timber-framed fortlet was burnt and later found its way to the top of midden below the secondary rampart. A piece of vitrified stone was found nearby in the same level. On the other hand it is possible that the hill-top continued to be inhabited for a while after the burning of the fort and that a few fragments of vitrified stone and pottery accumulated on the midden in this way. However, the great mass of reddened, burnt and vitrified stones were in later levels and had clearly been brought down to the region of the rampart of the second fort when the latter was built, possibly several centuries after the destruction of the timber-framed fort.

Eight fragments of one or more moulds were found, made from a hard-fired, light brown clay which was light grey on what appears to be the surfaces in contact with the metal. Four fragments show significant shapes (Fig. 3). One fragment (not shown) is of a section of a tube or a cylinder about 20 mm in diameter and one seems to be a piece of a pouring funnel (no. 2). The third fragment (no. 3) may be part of a mould for a spear-head while the fourth (no. 1) is of a mould for a wedge-shaped object which might well be the blade end of a socketed bronze axe. This piece, and the possible piece of a spear mould, have flat areas next to the casting surfaces which suggests either that they were parts of two-piece moulds, or that the mould was a single piece one but made in separate halves before being bound together by an outer coating of clay. No traces of the sockets and pegs of a true two-piece mould are preserved.

Half of a mould for a bronze spear-butt was recovered from the broch at Vaul, Tiree, and was datable to the first or second centuries A.D. This was made in two symmetrical halves which were formed into a single piece mould by being covered with an outer coating of clay; there were no pegs or sockets in the mould fragments.

2. Comments

Sheep Hill is important because it is the only vitrified timber-framed fort which may have yielded direct evidence—in the mould fragments—of the possession by its inhabitants of a Late Bronze Age metal technology. The only other Scottish hillfort or hill-top settlement which also seems to have produced such evidence is Traprain Law where Late Bronze Age metal-work was found in the lowest levels[18]. Although the sequence of fortifications at that site has been plausibly reconstructed from surface indications[19] it is not possible to relate the Late Bronze Age settlement to this without further stratigraphical excavation. At Sheep Hill there is admittedly no direct proof of the association between the sub-rampart midden with the mould fragments and the timber-framed dun higher up but the circumstantial evidence in favour of it seems strong.

The other elements of the material culture associated with the mould fragments are the gritty potsherds and the jet disc and spindle whorl. The pottery resembles that found at Finavon in being a thick, plain ware with light brown or light buff surfaces and containing large stone grits which often project from the surface to give the vessels a characteristic knobbly appearance (Fig. 2: Pl. III). The shapes of most of the Sheep Hill pots are simple—barrel- or bucket-shaped urns with plain, flat or rounded rims. A smaller number, including the broken vessel (Fig. 2), are thinner with larger quantities of smaller grits mixed into the clay. Slightly everted rims are found on these and one has finger-nail nicks on its flat top.

C. Dun Lagaidh, Ross and Cromarty (NH/143913)

This site stands on an isolated, hog-backed ridge of rock on the south shore of Loch Broom and about 1 mile south of Ullapool across the water (Pl. IV). It was first identified as a vitrified hillfort—one of the most northerly on the mainland of Scotland (Fig. 6)—in 1948[20]; the ruins of a broch on its eastern end evidently represented a later fortification and had been noted much earlier. Excavations in 1967 and 1968 showed that this broch was in fact a dun—that is it was a low, solid-walled dry-stone fortlet which lacked the specialised high, double, hollow wall of the brochs[21]. This dun had been refortified in medieval times[22]. The hillfort lay underneath it and was, as suspected, much earlier.

Figure 5 shows the layout of the site. The grid is in 10 ft squares and each square is known by the co-ordinates of the peg at its south-west corner. The finds were plotted in feet and tenths of feet from these pegs, first to the east of the numbered northing line and second to the north of the lettered easting line. Thus the full reference for a find spot would be 33M/3871 (the bronze object referred to later), 33H being the square concerned and the find being 3·8 ft east of that peg and 7·2 ft north of it. Although this find recording system, analogous to that of the Ordnance Survey national grid, is thought by Biddle to have been invented in southern England in 1969[23] it was in use at Dun Lagaidh in 1967 and was in fact derived from Wainwright's work on the Angus souterains in the 1950s[24].

[18] Cree and Curle (1922), pp. 204 ff., Burley 1956.   [22] MacKie (1968).
[19] Feachem (1956a).   [23] Biddle, M. and B. K. (1970).
[20] Calder and Steer (1949).   [24] Wainwright (1963).
[21] MacKie (1965, 1971c, 1975).

1. *The hillfort*

(a) *Results of the excavations*: A section through the deposits on the eastern side of the hillfort showed the clear stratigraphical relationship between it and the dun (Fig. 4). The foundation platform for the latter had been planted on the ruined hillfort wall—15 ft thick in this sector and apparently unburnt— of which a little of the face was preserved, mounted on a foundation of a double row of boulders (Pl. VIII). A few feet to the south the foundations of the main entrance into the hillfort were discovered with massive blocks underpinning the outer corners of the passage (Pl. VII). This passage was about 4·5 ft wide and its floor was the rock which rose rapidly towards the interior of the hillfort. From the entrance passage, and wedged under the base of the wall, came the only artefact which could be definitely associated with the timber-framed hillfort. This is a small thin fragment of a perforated polished bronze plate (Pl. II). The original edges are nowhere preserved and there are numerous small straight scratches on both polished faces, aligned in all directions. These scratches appear to have been made before the surfaces were polished. Examination under a binocular microscope confirmed this: the edges of all the scratches were smooth and polished and they could well have been cast into the metal. The central hole certainly was cast: its edges were also smooth and rounded with no trace of fracturing.

Despite the complex appearance of the surface "banks" and "ditches" which, before excavation, seemed to form the outer defences[25], the outwork of the hillfort was in fact a single timber-laced wall 8 ft thick which crossed the promontory in a curve 38 ft in front of the main eastern wall. The hard rock of the promontory precluded ditch digging. A narrow gateway was in this wall at its southern extremity, and its passage rose quite steeply up the sloping rock. Though this hornwork had been almost completely demolished in the centre it was still standing 6 ft high at the northern end. Here a trench exposed the inner face in which could be seen beam-holes and, next to them, a mass of vitrified rubble from the wall core which appeared to have burst through the face. This is a final demonstration—if such is needed—that vitrified forts are nothing but burnt timber-framed stone walls[7]. The face of the hornwork—like that of the main wall (Pl. VIII)—is founded on a row of boulders which were partly sunk into a bedding trench.

The western half of the interior of the hillfort was explored by several trenches but no artefacts were found (Fig. 5). Even an occupation layer on the old ground surface was undetectable except as a thin scatter of charcoal in the north-west corner. Only when the floor of the dun interior was cut through was a substantial hillfort occupation layer reached. This was a short distance behind the main entrance at the eastern end and here the black layer, resting on the whitish subsoil which covered the rock in places, was up to 3 in. thick. It overlay a large paved area which looked like a hearth. Evidently this hearth, if it was such, had been abandoned at an early stage and the occupation layer

[25] Calder and Steer (1949).

then accumulated on top of it. No paving was found anywhere else and there were no artefacts in the parts of occupation layer explored.

A mass of charcoal fragments, evidently the remains of carbonised branches, lay on the hillfort occupation layer in the area behind the main entrance. Evidently these had been on fire and had been covered by masonry falling from the wall before being completely turned to ash. Among these branches was a heap of charred barley which gave a radiocarbon date of 460 ± 100 b.c. (GaK–2492). Presumably this dates the destruction and vitrification of the hillfort.

Two pieces of carbonised branches were found in contexts which dated from the construction of the hillfort. One was under the core of the wall at the western end (5K) and gave a date of 490 ± 80 b.c. (GaK–1121). The other rested on the white subsoil just south of the dun entrance (31J) at a point where the dun wall was founded on the subsoil. It gave a date of 880 ± 90 b.c. (GaK–1948). These dates are discussed further on p. 225 below.

(b) *Comments*: In spite of the large area occupied by the hillfort—the walls of which enclose approximately 3000 sq yd ($\frac{2}{3}$ acre)—very little sign of intensive occupation was found in it except at the eastern end, near the entrance. Even there no artefacts were found in the black occupation layer. The closeness of the youngest C-14 date for the construction of the wall to that dating the destruction could mean that this hillfort was not used for very long, perhaps not as much as a century (but see p. 225 below). The absence of pottery was also a feature of the later levels at this site, and also of Dun an Rhiroy half a mile to the south-east[26], so it very probably indicates a genuine aceramic material culture on Loch Broom in late prehistoric times.

No clear evidence for the design of the timber framing of the walls was discovered except that at least two parallel rows of horizontal cross-beams projected through the inner face of the hornwork, as at Abernethy (Pl. V). Large parts of the main wall, including all that exposed at the eastern end, seem not to have been burnt at all: the exposed fragments of faces were undamaged by heat.

Also, as noted, the dun was founded on the ruins of the eastern end wall which seems to confirm that the latter was not vitrified. It is notoriously difficult to move vitrified masses of wall core which have solidified *in situ* and, unless any such lumps were incorporated in the core of the dun wall and are now invisible, it would seem that none such existed in spite of the fire which raged on the nearby hornwork. On the other hand the basal courses of this hornwork were similarly undamaged even though vitrified matter had solidified a little higher up (Pl. VI), so it may be that only the rubble core of the wall fused in many places leaving the basal courses of the faces intact.

An interesting point emerges from the discovery of the main entrance to the hillfort. It is clear that no wheeled vehicles could have traversed it since, in the small section preserved, it was only about 4·5 ft wide. Also its rocky floor was uneven and rose quite steeply towards the interior (Pl. VII). Moreover no wheeled vehicle could possibly have negotiated the lateral gate in the hornwork,

[26] MacKie (1968, 1971a).

to reach which one had to go some way down the steep southern side of the ridge and then ascend again through another narrow, stone-walled passage (Fig. 5). That wheeled vehicles of some kind were in use in southern Scotland in the Late Bronze Age is shown by the hoard from Horsehope, Peebles-shire[27].

2. *The dun*

A round dry-stone dun was built later on the ruins of the hillfort and gives its name to the site. Brief descriptions of it—and the third and final phase of fortification—are appropriate here to complete the history of the use of this site as a refuge.

(*a*) *Results from the excavations*. Before excavation it was noted that the wall of the hillfort had been extensively robbed of stone, presumably to build the dun which lay on its eastern end[20]. The sections showed that what must have been an enormous mass of fallen rubble and still standing wall foundations–relics of the destruction of the hillfort—were quarried to provide building material for the dun and levelled off to make a flat rubble platform on which to site it (Fig. 4). The lower level of black earth, charcoal and rubble under the dun floor is the remains of the burning and later levelling of the hillfort debris. It seems to have been extensively disturbed, although the hillfort occupation layer under it was intact: several fragments of iron, including a small spear point, were found in it.

The dun itself is a circular structure with a dry-stone wall which contains one or more median faces at certain points. The enclosed area, approximately circular, is 35 ft in diameter along the line of the doorway in the south-east. The overall diameter on this line is about 59 ft, so the wall, at floor level, is some 12 ft thick. The main entrance had two sets of doorchecks though no pivot-sockets for the doors were preserved in its rock floor. An elongated guard cell opened from the right side of the passage (looking in). On the opposite side of the central court, at 10 o'clock (assuming the main entrance to be at 6 o'clock), was the doorway to the mural stair. Fifteen steps of this were preserved, rising to a height of 4 ft 10 in. in a horizontal distance of 7 ft 6 in. an average angle of 33°. No trace of an upper gallery was found on the wallhead, which was presumably flat with a stone parapet or breast-work.

The stratigraphy of the interior of the dun consisted of, from top to bottom, layer 1 of dry rubble, layer 2 of rubble and a brown soil containing many tiny shells, layer 3 of rubble and black earth with many fragments of charcoal, and layer 4, the hillfort occupation layer already described. The top of layer 3 was evidently the floor level of the dun and, although no paved areas were found, a number of undoubted Iron Age artefacts were found on and in this layer.

(*b*) *Finds from the dun floor level*. These include many square-sectioned iron nails from 1–2 in. long, several fragments of thin bronze sheeting, one with "paper-clip" double rivets (Pl. X), a complete bronze ring-headed pin

[27] Piggott (1953a).

with a projecting head and a broken, iron two-link bridle bit (Pl. IX). A boar's tusk implied hunting for sport and a small iron spear-head, although it was embedded in layer 3 below the floor level, suggested the same. There was also a bone pin with an ornamental cylindrical head and a circular bone counter 35 mm in diameter. A bone handle with the iron tang of the snapped-off blade still in it was found tucked between the stones of the wall of the stair lobby and could belong to this phase or to the later one described below.

Some large pieces of charcoal were found at the top of the black layer and seemed to be fragments of wooden planks, or something similar, which had been on fire and which had been buried before being completely consumed. A sample of one of these "planks" was sent for dating and it was expected that the result would date some wooden furniture inside the dun, and perhaps its actual construction. However, the age received was a.d. 840 ± 90 (GaK–1947), clearly far too late for the Iron Age occupation (section (c) below).

(c) *Comments*. This type of round, solid-walled dun is known in Argyllshire, at Ardifuar for example[28]. Several duns in that region have produced fragments of Roman Samian ware and are quite likely to have been built at a late stage in the pre-Roman Iron Age. In spite of the C-14 date (see below) Dun Lagaidh ought to belong to the first century A.D. and the finds do not contradict this assumption. However, the central hearth implies that a single group lived in the dun and the character of the finds provides a clue to what sort of people these were.

The iron bridle bit surely means that an Iron Age chieftain built and in-habited the dun and the fragments of riveted bronze sheeting appear to confirm this. These are clear signs of aristocratic horse-riding on the one hand (no Iron Age bridle bits of either bronze or iron have hitherto been found north of the Tay/Clyde line[29]) and of the patronage of a skilled craftsman on the other. There must have been a sheet bronze cauldron in the dun which needed to be repaired and a craftsman who came or was on hand to do it.

3. *The medieval fort*

Layer 2 in the interior deposits gains its light colour and shelly texture from the numerous powdered fragments of mortar in it. The dun doorway was blocked with mortared masonry and strengthening facings of the same were added to the front wall of the guard cell. Evidently the main wall was rebuilt to a suitable height with mortared faces enclosing a dry rubble core. This secondary construction eventually fell off again, the dry core covering the collapsed mortared face to form layers 1 and 2 respectively. Two radial walls were attached to the dun on the western side and formed a bailey for this simple castle. Entry into the "keep" was evidently down the old mural stairway at this time, and the southern radial wall had a wide gateway in it without door-checks.

[28] Christison and Ross (1905).
[29] Thomas (1961), Fig. 2.

The medieval date of the third and final fortification of Dun Lagaidh was confirmed by a hoard of 15 silver short-cross pennies and 9 similar half-pennies buried under the debris of the collapsed north radial wall. Most of these were datable to the period A.D. 1180–1242, an age which was confirmed by a C-14 date of a.d. 1155 ± 80 (GaK–1449) for charcoal on the reused floor of the guard cell. When calibrated by the tree-ring chronology the centre of this time span falls at about A.D. 1215[30], a truly remarkable correspondence with the age of the coins. Thus Dun Lagaidh may have been turned into a simple castle and bailey in the twelfth century, well illustrating that the strategic value of the geographical setting of the site—at the narrowest point of the longest sea loch in north-west Scotland—and the natural defensiveness of its actual position on an isolated ridge, were appreciated and utilised at intervals over a period of fifteen hundred years.

The radiocarbon date of a.d. 840 ± 90, for charcoal on the old dun floor, is not easy to understand. Presumably the wood concerned must belong to the Medieval castle and could be old, reused material. It seems doubtful whether a mortared keep could have been constructed as early as the ninth century but, on the other hand, had it not been for this date, there would have been no reason to dissociate the charcoal from the other Iron Age artefacts on the same level. The conditions are puzzling.

D. Other Newly Excavated Vitrified Forts

Three other vitrified hillforts have been explored since 1950 and two of them are still under excavation. Though no detailed reports are yet available all three sites have produced radiocarbon dates (Fig. 7).

1. Craigmarloch Wood, Renfrewshire (NS/344719)

Craigmarloch Wood in Renfrewshire was explored in 1959 and 1960 by Miss H. Nisbet and proved to be a two period site. A wooden palisaded enclosure was the earliest structure and associated with it was an occupation layer containing plain, thick, gravelly potsherds, crucible fragments, hammerstones and pieces of jet bracelets. Charcoal from this level gave a date of 590 ± 40 b.c. (GaK–995). The timber-framed, stone-walled hillfort was built on top of this but the dated charcoal of this phase (35 ± 40 b.c. (GaK–996)) was stratigraphically unreliable[31].

2. Cullykhan (NJ/616661)

Troup Head or Cullykhan in Morayshire is currently being excavated by C. Greig[32]. The earliest phase of the fortification of this site, spectacularly

[30] McKerrell (1971), Table 2. Barlow and Robertson (1974).
[31] MacKie (1969), p. 19, fn.
[32] Greig (1970, 1972).

situated on a cliff promontory, seems to have been a wooden palisade as at Craigmarloch Wood; in this case it was probably associated with a massive wooden gate tower on the neck of the promontory, one of the oak post-butts of which gave a date of 397 ± 59 b.c. (BM–639)[33]. The timber-framed stone fort was later but wood from its wall core gave an age of 1186 ± 60 b.c. (BM–444). Charcoal from the main occupation layer, which ran *under* this vitrified wall, gave an age of 387 ± 65 b.c. (BM–446). The history of the use of this site could well start in the seventh century B.C. judging from the Late Bronze Age tanged chisel found in the layer just mentioned[34]; this is similar to the one in the Adabrock, Lewis, hoard[35]. Its use may have continued into post-Roman, early Pictish times, judging from the discovery of Late Roman pottery and a date from the same horizon of a.d. 317 ± 40 (BM–445).

3. *Craig Phadrig, Inverness-shire (NH/640453)*

Craig Phadrig is a Group IV timber-framed hillfort more or less rectangular in plan and enclosing an area of about 2300 sq yd; there is more than one outer rampart, one of which may run right round the fort. The situation is strategically significant, being on high ground on the south shore of the Beauly Firth just before the narrows where it debouches into the Moray Firth at Inverness. It also commands the north-eastern exit from the Great Glen. The Ord of Kessock is opposite, on the north side of the same strait.

Excavations in 1971 and 1972 unravelled the stratigraphy of the inner rampart and the interior of the fort[36]. The wall rested on an old turf line and a sloping rubble layer of building material rested on this and against the lower part of the inner face. On top of this builders' level was a thick black turf layer which must have formed during the use of the fort. The mass of rubble from the wall fell on this when the fort was destroyed.

Three radiocarbon dates were obtained for carbonised wood from below the main rampart. They were 330 ± 100 b.c. (N–112), 270 ± 100 b.c. (N–1123) and 180 ± 110 b.c. (GX–2441). The sample which gave the youngest date could be related to the wall stratigraphy only in that it underlay the layer of construction rubble already referred to. Presumably a date in the fourth or third centuries B.C. for the building of Craig Phadrig is indicated. The width of the main wall is about 22 ft and distorted beam holes were observed in the upper part of the inside face.

The outer wall was examined and appeared to be a revetted rampart, not a

---

[33] Carbon dates issued by the British Museum now have much smaller standard deviations than in the past. This is evidently because it used to be the practice of that laboratory to add up to 100 years to the sigma value—making it up to ± 150—to allow for the uncertainties of the de Vries effect. Now that the de Vries effect has been quantified by the tree-ring calibration of C-14 dates (Libby, 1970) this practice has at last been discontinued and a true idea of the precision of individual B.M. measurements can be obtained.

[34] Greig (1970), Plate.

[35] Coles (1960), p. 49.

[36] Small (1971).

stone wall, made of turf and heated stones, the latter having presumably been quarried from the main wall after it had become vitrified. However, debris from the collapse of the inner timber-framed wall partly overrode this outer rampart at one point so the latter must have been built before the burning of the former. Both walls rested on the same turf-line so presumably the outer one was repaired and added to after vitrification had occurred. A carbonised branch in its core gave a date of 300 ± 105 b.c. (N–1120), and some peat and turf laid between the blocks of its outer revetment gave a date of 370 ± 105 b.c. (N–1124). This sample was from the western end where there was vitrification *in situ*, showing that the outer rampart was at least partly timber-framed at this point.

The deposits in the interior of the fort had been extensively disturbed but two occupation layers were identified. The lower one overlay many animal bones. The upper one gave a radiocarbon date of a.d. 410 ± 85 (N–1119) and also produced some sherds of Dark Age class E ware[37] and a fragment of a clay mould for the escutcheon of a hanging bowl of a type which might belong to the early seventh century A.D.[38]. There is thus good evidence that Craig Phadrig was occupied in Pictish times though this was after its ramparts were in ruins.

IV. General Problems of Vitrified Hillforts

A. *Distribution and Size*

The map (Fig. 6) shows the distribution of timber-framed hillforts in Scotland—both the burnt and the few known unburnt examples—and the symbols indicate the size of the enclosed area. The categories of sizes were determined by what appeared to be natural breaks in the total range of enclosed areas in square yards. A list of the forts, with their grid references and other information, will be found in the Appendix (p. 233).

1. *Range of size*

Some clear patterns can be seen on this map. In the first place it is plain that many of the vitrified sites are really large and can be classed without hesitation as hillforts. The largest vitrified fort known is Ord of Kessock in Easter Ross which encloses an area of probably over 17 000 sq yd (an exact plan is not available). It measures about 300 yd in length and some 65 yd in width. Dunearn in Nairn, unique in being a contour hillfort, is not far below at about 10 000 sq yd. The next category includes four forts of between 5500 and 7000 sq yd, equivalent to linear dimensions of about 50×120 yd; Finavon in Angus, described earlier, is a typical representative of this class. There are seven sites between 3000 and 4500 sq yd, including Dun Lagaidh (p. 214 above), twenty-six between 1000 and 2600 sq yd, including Craig Phadrig, twelve between

[37] Peacock and Thomas (1967).
[38] Stevenson (1971).

500 and 1000 sq yd, eleven between 250 and 500 sq yd, and five between 100 and 200 sq yd. Fourteen further sites have no accurately recorded dimensions.

Thus, by hillfort standards, a large number of these sites are very small, enclosing less than 1000 sq yd. Such an area can be enclosed by a circle 35·5 yd in diameter or by a rectangle measuring 25×40 yd. Some of the really small sites, enclosing less than 200 sq yd, are truly circular: Rahoy, Langwell (currently being excavated) and Caisteal Aoidhe are examples. Rahoy has an internal diameter of c 13 yd and, from its size and shape, is clearly to be regarded as a dun rather than a hillfort. Yet the range of sizes shows that, in the case of vitrified forts, no clear dividing line can be drawn between these two categories and this would appear to be confirmed by the vitrification itself. Since the fused stone is an indication that the structure once had a dry-stone wall with an internal framework of timber beams—a specialised type of defensive construction confined, apparently, to a limited span of time (section D below)—it must surely imply that all the vitrified sites are likely to be the product of a single tradition or school of fort-building, even though this may have lasted for several centuries. Some implications of this view are discussed later (p. 223).

2. *Geographical distribution*

When the distribution of the vitrified forts is plotted by size and against the background of the topography of Scotland some interesting points emerge (Fig. 6). Three major groups can be picked out, each of which seems to have a few large hillforts and a large number of smaller ones. The Northern group seems to be centred on an axis which runs from the Moray Firth down the Great Glen. There are two large hillforts, Dunearn and Ord of Kessock, at the north-east end of the Glen and another, Benderloch, at the south-west end. The other forts along this line—and those on the west coasts of Sutherland, Ross and Inverness—seem to be part of this group. Various long straths and passes connect these north-west coastal regions with the Great Glen and the Moray Firth. It is noteworthy that there are no vitrified forts in the neighbouring territories which were later to be occupied by the brochs, none on the Inner Hebridean islands and none north of the Dornoch Firth and the River Oykell that leads into it.

There is a clearly defined Central region which appears to be centred on an axis running from north-east to south-west along the southern fringe of the highland zone, from north of the Firth of Tay down to the Firth of Clyde. Two large hillforts, Finavon and Monifieth, are at the north-east end of this group while, at the other end, a scatter of tiny forts penetrates into the Firth of Clyde and over to Kintyre. Finally the south-west region seems quite separate and has one large hillfort, Mullach in Dumfries-shire.

It is dangerous to draw too many conclusions from simple distribution maps but one or two points may be made about this one. In the first place, if other evidence favours the idea that the timber-framed hillforts were the strongholds of invading colonists,[39] one might suppose that the pattern represents three primary areas of settlement—around the Moray Firth, the Firth of Tay, and on the north side of the Solway Firth. In this case the large hillforts, adjacent to extensive tracts of cultivable land, could represent the earliest strongholds in each area and the smaller ones would then reflect progressively deeper penetration into the rugged highland zone. In the highlands the cultivable land tends to be in tiny patches along the coast, or in narrow straths and glens.

However, independent evidence would be needed to show that the larger hillforts were older than the small ones—and that the east coast forts were the oldest of all—before such an interpretation could be substantiated (Section 4, below). The distribution of sizes in relation to terrain might show only how there were larger populations—needing larger defended enclosures—in areas with large tracts of arable land and that, conversely, the tiny forts in highland terrain simply reflect the smallness of the units of population which used them.

3. *Development of timber-framed forts*

It has already been noted that the great majority of vitrified forts are either approximately oval or rectangular in plan, or even circular in a few cases. In other words they are not contour hillforts like many elsewhere but were built to a preconceived, regular plan more or less independently of the type of ground on which they were situated. This regularity of plan together with the great range in size makes it probable that the timber-framed forts did go through a typological evolution of some kind. It seems quite reasonable to assume that the tiny timber-framed forts—most of which are situated deep in the highlands and on the north-west coast—represent a late stage in the spread of this type of defence work. It also seems reasonable to suppose, as suggested earlier, that they were small because the units of population in these highland areas were themselves very small.

Thus from the regularity of the plans of most timber-framed forts it is easy to infer that these underwent a steady diminution in size as they were built further and further away from the lowland areas and the large centres of population. This phenomenon of the adaptation of a specialised (and easily identifiable) form of hillfort to the highland zone might be called *miniaturisation* and the process in the timber-framed hillforts may be providing the general explanation for the origins of the hundreds of tiny dry-stone forts which are scattered throughout Atlantic Scotland and of which the finest development was the broch[21]. The smallest circular, and near-circular vitrified forts—like Rahoy, Langwell and the others (Appendix, group VI)—are in fact duns and before they were burnt and vitrified they would have looked exactly like the later dry-stone duns from the outside. It is possible that the duns and brochs are directly derived from the timber-framed duns. Alternatively they may be the result of the miniaturisation at a later date of another class of stone-walled hillfort without timber-framing. All that I would suggest here is that the

[39] Childe (1946).

vitrified forts probably provide an excellent illustration of how tiny, dun-sized stone forts developed from larger hillforts in Scotland in late prehistoric times by being adapted to the needs of the small and isolated units of population of the rugged highland regions. Such a deduction need carry no implications as to who built and used these forts—whether they were for the whole of the local community or just a part of it.

If the miniaturisation of hillforts did occur in the manner outlined above, most of the large forts ought to be early in the sequence. Moreover since most of the large forts are on the eastern side of the country, the idea of the timber-framed stone-walled hillfort ought to have been invented or introduced there (though the group in south-west Scotland might well be considered separately from those further north). Unfortunately, as described below (Section C), the few artefacts found in primary contexts in timber-framed forts cannot be dated exactly enough to be used to infer even the relative ages of the sites concerned. If the mould fragments discovered at Sheep Hill really are for Late Bronze Age implements they will have shown that small timber-framed duns were being constructed on the western side of the country at least as early as the sixth century B.C. This is the century in which the Bronze Age as a technological phase seems to have come to an end[40].

B. Absolute Chronology

1. Radiocarbon dates for vitrified forts

In the last few years a large number of C-14 dates have become available for organic samples found in new excavations in vitrified forts. They are depicted as time spans in Fig. 7; those shown solid black are from samples which could be referred to the construction of the timber-framed wall. Several of the dated samples were from occupation layers which are either earlier or later than the time of the construction of the fort concerned; the open black symbols represent the former and the white symbols the latter. Even disregarding some dates which are obviously too old—like that from Cullykhan which is older than several dates for the preceding phase of occupation of the site—a clear pattern seems to be emerging in which the timber-framed hillforts appear in Scotland at least as early as the seventh century b.c. This would certainly place their first appearance in the local Late Bronze Age and the absence of datable bronzes and moulds from all of them except Sheep Hill is thus striking. The early date might also link the idea of timber-framed walls—which have many Continental parallels[41]—with the only reasonably clear evidence of settlement in eastern Scotland by north Europeans at about 700 B.C. This evidence was found in the Sculptor's cave at Covesea, Morayshire[40] and the lowest level there produced flower-pot-shaped, flat-rimmed, plain vessels together with bronze armlets of north German type and pieces of gold-

[40] Coles (1960).
[41] Piggott (1965), pp. 202 ff.

plated bronze Irish ring money. However, this exotic pottery and metal-work —grouped by Coles into his Covesea phase of the Late Bronze Age[42]—has not so far been found in what now appear to be the contemporary timber-framed hillforts, so the significance of the Sculptor's Cave finds is difficult to estimate except in terms of bronze technology.

The radiocarbon dates are showing that a simple unilinear chronological sequence from early large forts in eastern Scotland to later small forts further west is untenable. Finavon is certainly one of the earliest but Dun Lagaidh on the west coast is not much younger. Craig Phadrig, in the centre of the cluster round the Moray Firth, seems not to have been built until the fourth century b.c. at the earliest and Sheep Hill, a tiny timber-framed dun in the west, may be much earlier than this if its mould fragments are a good chronological guide. The timber-framed fort at Cullykhan apparently followed a palisaded wooden fort on a site which probably had a Late Bronze occupation. Here the vitrified wall may be no earlier than the second or third century b.c. The general process of miniaturisation could still hold good in spite of these dates but it could not be a single, uniform process.

2. *The tree-ring calibration and its significance*

When the radiocarbon dates are adjusted by the tree-ring calibration graph[43] further interesting facts emerge. Radiocarbon dates of later than about 400 b.c. do not appear to be much affected so, for example, the time of the construction of the Craig Phadrig hillfort still seems likely to fall in the fourth century B.C. However, prior to that time radiocarbon dates are progressively and varyingly younger than they should be in terms of real years. Moreover, at some periods, the quantity of C-14 in the atmosphere seems to have fluctuated sharply over short spans of time so that a single radiocarbon date can sometimes have more than one equivalent in real years. The calibrations of radiocarbon dates given here are taken from the tables in the MASCA *Newsletter*[43].

The earliest C-14 date from Finavon was 590 ± 70 b.c. (GaK–1274) and this is equivalent to a similar time span centred on about 790 B.C. The date of the *destruction* of Dun Lagaidh—accurately determined on a heap of carbonised barley—was 460 ± 100 b.c. which should be equivalent to a real year age

---

[42] The original excavation was by Sylvia Benton, 1931: the "flat-rimmed ware" is discussed by Childe (1935a), pp. 171 ff., (1946), Piggott (1959), Coles (1960), MacKie (1970).

[43] Libby, 1970; McKerrel, 1971; Suess, 1970; Ralph, Michael and Han, 1973. The simplest way of comparing a C-14 age with its probable equivalent in real years is to apply a set square and ruler to one of the calibration graphs in the publications cited. Alternatively a table of equivalences may be used. McKerrell's gives these for every half century from A.D. 1900 to 4300 B.C. (radiocarbon years) but more useful now is the one in the *Newsletter* of the Pennsylvania University Museum's Applied Science Center for Archaeology, which is distributed free to interested parties. This gives equivalences between radiocarbon years and real years for every decade from A.D. 1840 to 4750 B.C. (radiocarbon years) and is, moreover, based on the C-14 dated tree-ring chronologies from three laboratories. It is this table which is used here even though the C-14 dates in it are annoyingly given in terms of the 5730 year half life instead of the 5568 one in which most dates are published.

centred on somewhere between 500 and 640 B.C. (this being one of the periods in which the quantity of C-14 in the atmosphere apparently fluctuated sharply, though the reality of these alterations has been doubted[44]). Similarly the two earliest dates from Dun Lagaidh—880 ± 90 b.c. (GaK–1948) and 490 ± 80 b.c. (GX–1121)—should be equivalent to about 1030–1100 B.C. in the first case and somewhere between 530 and 720 B.C. in the case of the second.

On the evidence available at present it seems that even if one dismisses the oldest date from Dun Lagaidh as an aberration (caused by the use of ancient wood for example), both this site and Finavon are as likely to have been built in the eighth or early seventh centuries B.C. as in the sixth or fifth. There are even earlier dates from other kinds of hillforts, in both England and Scotland, which makes an eighth century date seem not too extreme[45]. The lack of direct links between these hillforts and Late Bronze Age metal-work is also becoming slowly less marked. Traprain Law in East Lothian[46] and Dinorben in Denbighshire[47] have both produced some and Sheep Hill, as noted earlier, may have given some suitable mould fragments (Fig. 3).

C. Material Culture

1. Excavated timber-framed forts

Few timber-framed forts have been stratigraphically excavated and few of those have produced pottery and artefacts which could be clearly shown to have belonged to their builders and primary users. At *Finavon*, excavated by Childe in 1933–1934, an occupation layer under fallen wall rubble was found and it yielded many sherds of a plain, thick, light brown or fawn-coloured pottery containing large pieces of gravel, often known as Dunagoil ware. There were also a jet ring (from the dry well and therefore probably deposited soon after the fort was built), several spindle whorls, an iron ring, some flints and a crude stone lamp[48]. As we have seen, this fort may have been built as early as the eighth century B.C. and it was still being used in the fourth century. The tiny vitrified dun *Rahoy* in Morvern, Argyllshire—excavated by Childe in 1936–1937—produced a socketed iron axe and a La Tène Ic bronze fibula[49]. The axe, being a copy of the Late Bronze Age bronze form, seems likely to date from the end of the Bronze Age or a little later—perhaps in the fifth century B.C.[50] The fibula seems to be a little later and a third century date has been suggested for it on stylistic grounds[51]. *Sheep Hill*, excavated from 1966–1970, gave the same gravelly Donagoil ware in a layer which was very probably

[44] Ottaway and Ottaway (1972).
[45] MacKie (1971), Savory (1971a).
[46] Cree and Curle (1922), p. 210; Burley (1956), pp. 145 ff.
[47] Savory (1971a).
[48] Childe (1935a, 1936).
[49] Childe (1938a).
[50] Stevenson (1966).
[51] Stevenson (1966).

contemporary with the use of the small timber-framed fortlet at the top of the hill; the possible Late Bronze Age mould fragments also came from this layer. *Craig Phadrig* has so far yielded nothing clearly belonging to the pre-vitrification phase. *Castle Law*, Glencorse, Midlothian, was excavated by Childe in 1932[52] and again by Piggott in 1948[53]. The latter work showed that the innermost rampart was a timber-framed, unburnt stone wall and from its core were recovered a sherd of plain, gritty pottery, three saddle querns and two small stone balls.

No other timber-framed forts have been excavated according to modern standards but several others, explored many years ago, have provided interesting but effectively unstratified finds. *Abernethy* in Perthshire—a rare example of an unburnt timber-framed fort—was explored in 1899 and the interior produced four sherds of the plain, gravelly Dunagoil ware, a La Tène Ic brooch like that from Rahoy, a bronze spiral finger ring, a segment of an ornamented jet armlet, a deer-horn handle, some corroded iron fragments of which one is a crook-headed pin, and pieces of wooden vessels[54]. The multi-period *Benderloch* fort was turned over in 1873–1874 and a fragment of a tanged iron sword was found within the core of one of the walls. From the enclosed area came an iron penannular brooch, a quern of unspecified type and a bronze disc ornamented with red and yellow enamel[55]. The interior of *Duntroon* at Loch Crinan, Argyllshire, was completely dug-out in 1904 and the finds included flint implements, a fragment of jet, whetstones and 36 saddle querns[56]. The finds made in the *Laws of Monifieth*, Angus—ransacked at various times during the nineteenth century—include material from the later broch as well as from the timber-framed hillfort[57]. From the latter probably came the bronze crook-headed pin of the same type as the iron example from Abernethy. The *Mote o'Mark* in Galloway was partly explored in 1913 by Curle[58] who recovered many finds datable to the eighth and ninth centuries A.D. as well as two fragments of Roman pottery. The latter suggested that the timber-framed hillfort was much older than the Dark Age period, as did Curle's observations on the stratigraphy.

One of the most prolific timber-framed forts was *Dunagoil* in Bute but unfortunately the great array of finds has never been properly published. They were identified and listed by Miss Margaret Leechman (now Mrs. Peek) in her Edinburgh M.A. thesis in 1962 and they show that the site was occupied for a considerable period[59]. The published information about the excavations themselves is practically useless[60]. Potsherds were found of the same plain,

---

[52] Childe (1933).
[53] Piggott and Piggott (1952).
[54] Christison and Anderson (1900).
[55] Christison and Anderson (1899).
[56] Christison and Ross (1905).
[57] Neish and Stuart (1860).
[58] Curle (1914).
[59] Leechman (1962).
[60] Mann (1925), Mann and Marshall (1915).

thick, orange-brown gravelly Dunagoil ware noted from other sites. Among the iron finds were at least two ring-headed pins of the English form (not with the projecting head of the Scottish variety), rings, a shaft-hole axe and an early La Tène Ic fibula. Bronze objects included a cast ring-headed pin of English type and another made of a bent rod, a simple and a spiral finger-ring and a pair of tweezers. Among the many objects of bone were needles, awls or pins, polished counters or discs (some perforated), a whistle, two toothed plaques (or short-toothed combs), a gouge or point and a hammer. Of antler there were rings, bridle cheek-pieces, and various handles, picks and otherwise worked or utilised tines. Stone implements included perforated whorls, rings, discs, pieces of two-handled cups or lamps (one of steatite), a bowl, whetstones, hammerstones, a pebble strike-a-light and a pot lid. There were also several querns, but none are certainly from Dunagoil. These included three saddle querns, three upper stones and one possible lower stone of rotary querns. The rotaries were of the flat beehive form with flat grinding surfaces and wide hoppers; one has the lateral handle-socket preserved. Many pieces of jet or lignite were found including unworked lumps, perforated and plain discs and large numbers of rings and armlets.

Glass objects included a piece of a light blue armlet with cable ornamentation of a late first century A.D. type[61], a ring of dull yellow glass, three small blue ring-beads and a drop of the same colour which might be half a dumb-bell bead. Artefacts of fired clay, beside the pottery mentioned, included several mould fragments for rods and spear-butts and many crucibles, both of the hemispherical type and the triangular form of fine grey ware.

The occupation of Dunagoil evidently began at least as early as the third century B.C. judging from the English ring-headed pins and the fibula and, of course, in the light of the C-14 dates from other sites, it may have begun as early as the seventh or eighth centuries. The glass armlet, spiral finger-ring and the triangular crucibles also show that occupation in some form continued well into the "broch horizon" of the first century B.C. to the second A.D., in spite of the absence of long-handled weaving combs and Roman objects from the site.

2. *Other relevant sites*

The main items of the material culture described above which seem to belong to the primary period of the timber-framed forts—that is before the influx of southern English "B" material in the first century B.C.—have also been found on a variety of other sites. These items include saddle querns, probably handled stone cups, jet rings and armlets, Donagoil pottery, La Tène Ic fibulae of bronze and iron, crook-headed pins of bronze and iron, English ring-headed pins of bronze and iron, iron socketed axes and probably shaft-hole iron axes also. The Scottish ring-headed pin with the projecting

[61] Stevenson (1956).

head should also be included as the evidence from Tiree shows that they were in existence much earlier than had been supposed[62], probably at least as early as the fifth century B.C., and one was found at the Laws of Monifieth. It is not clear whether the extensive bone industry found at Dunagoil goes back to the primary period of the timber-framed forts or is even typical of them. The absence of long handled combs—common on broch sites—perhaps suggests that it does.

A variety of other sites on the north-eastern mainland of Scotland have yielded the non-metallic elements of this material culture. The territory is broadly the Forth/Clyde valley including northern Renfrewshire, the lowlands of Angus and Aberdeenshire and around the Moray Firth, and the counties of Sutherland and Caithness; one might call this zone proto-Pictland. The gritty barrel-shaped vessel of Dunagoil ware was probably found in association with Late Bronze Age metal-work at Traprain Law[46], and one sherd was among the "flat-rimmed" pottery with metal objects datable to about 700 B.C. in the Sculptor's Cave, Morayshire[42]. The ware was also found associated with the palisaded enclosure under the timber-framed fort at Craigmarloch Wood, Renfrewshire[63], in a crannog in Bishop's Loch with a socketed iron axe[64], in the Torwood broch, Stirlingshire with stone cups[65] and with a fragment of a jet bracelet in a complex of stone buildings at Forse, Caithness, which included long-houses[66]. Several other Caithness brochs have produced it and a flower-pot shaped vessel of the gritty ware came from the Midhowe broch in Orkney[67]. However, in the western and northern islands the various styles of smooth-surfaced broch pottery are very much commoner.

The handled stone cups have a distribution which is confined almost completely to proto-Pictland[68]. At least two timber-framed forts have yielded them—Barry Hill in Perthshire as well as Dunagoil[69]. The finds from the earliest fort at Clickhimin, Shetland, included such stone cups, so these had penetrated into the far north probably well before the broch period[70]. These cups provide a striking example of the distinctiveness of proto-Pictland in the Iron Age—markedly separate from the Western Isles and from the country south of the river Forth.

The metal-work—various kinds of pins and fibulae—is geographically more scattered and generally scarcer than the other artefacts mentioned. A recent review[71] placed it all in the third and later centuries B.C. and had it inaugurating

[62] MacKie (1969, 1971c).
[63] MacKie (1969).
[64] The unlooped iron socketed axe is mentioned in *Proc. Soc. Ant. Scot.* **56** (1921–1922), 217, footnote. The crannog was discovered in 1898 (*Trans. Glasgow A.S.* n.s. **9** (1937), 39, map) but no account of it seems to have been published. The plain, thick, gritty pottery is in the Glasgow Art Gallery and Museum but the whereabouts of the axe is unknown.
[65] In the National Museum of Antiquities, Edinburgh: nos. GM 26, 29.
[66] Curle (1941, 1948).
[67] National Museum of Antiquities no. GAM 147.
[68] Steer (1956), Fig. 7.
[69] National Museum no. AQ 22: Leechman (1962).
[70] Hamilton (1968).
[71] Stevenson (1966).

the Abernethy complex together with the vitrified forts (this was before the C-14 dates were available). However, a crook-headed pin came from the Late Bronze Age levels at Dinorben hillfort in Wales and Savory suggested that the type may be an Urnfield import from the continent and date to the seventh century B.C.[47]. The three in Scotland as opposed to one from England and Wales might then become rather significant. A similarly early date for the Scottish ring-headed pin is now demonstrated[72] and its origin in the swan's neck sunflower pin of the sixth century[73], in the final phase of the northern Bronze Age, seems reasonable. Increasingly some of the metal-work, together with the pottery, seems to be better explained as Late Bronze Age in origin and fewer reasons are left for suggesting any major cultural changes between the eighth/seventh and first centuries B.C.[74].

Indirect evidence of the association between Late Bronze Age metal-work and timber-framed hillforts can sometimes be detected. For example, on the mainly barren wastes of the west coast of Ross-shire there are only two tiny vitrified forts and one medium-sized one (Fig. 6). As we have seen, the latter, Dun Lagaidh, may have been built on Loch Broom in the eighth, seventh or sixth centuries B.C.—certainly in the Late Bronze Age. A bronze leaf-shaped sword of Coles' "Minch" type was found at Inverbroom some years ago, about 5 miles from Dun Lagaidh (at c NH/182837) and is dated stylistically to about the middle of the sixth century B.C.[75]. It and the slightly later swan's neck sunflower pin from Loggie, close to the hillfort (NH/137907), are the only Late Bronze Age metal objects known from the whole of the north-west coastal region of the Scottish mainland and one might reasonably conclude that their presence there is linked with that of the hillfort.

D. Conclusions

A good case can be made out for supposing that there was a fairly homogeneous material culture throughout the area of the eastern and north-eastern Scottish mainland (proto-Pictland) from at least as early as the seventh century B.C. down almost to Roman times in the late first century A.D. This re-defined Abernethy culture would include the gravelly Dunagoil pottery, saddle querns, jet rings and armlets and, later, handled stone cups. Timber-framed hillforts were presumably imported somehow from the continent and must have played an important part in the origins of the culture, although their vulnerability to fire when built entirely of stone meant that they were eventually supplanted by other types of strongholds.

The inference is that the population of this region was more or less undisturbed by mass immigration throughout this period though small numbers of perhaps influential people doubtless came in from time to time and brought

---

[72] MacKie (1969, 1971c).
[73] Coles (1969).
[74] MacKie (1969b, Fig. 2).
[75] Coles (1960).

in the various new styles of pins and fibulae. However, these novelties—like the new bun-shaped rotary querns—appear mainly on the southern fringes of proto-Pictland. Presumably the Abernethy culture originally used bronze for tools and weapons, and was subsequently converted to using iron in some unknown way. The collapse of the European and British bronze trading networks at the end of the Bronze Age must have made inevitable a change either to iron if it was available or back to stone (as in Shetland) as local supplies of bronze ingots ran out.

The hillforts themselves fit easily into this scheme. Their size and distribution could be interpreted as showing a primary east coast settlement of fort builders in two areas in the eighth or seventh centuries B.C. followed by a gradual penetration westwards (p. 223 above: how the undated Galloway forts are to be explained is not yet clear). A hypothesis worth considering is that the map of the timber-framed forts in a sense shows only the initial phase of the evolution of Scottish hillforts north of the Tay and west of the Clyde (the conditions in the Tyne/Forth province were different and wooden palisaded enclosures were being built at this early date). At this stage the forts were brought in and multiplied and spread—evolving to the tiny dun-sized forms relatively quickly according to the type of terrain. However, by the fifth or fourth centuries B.C. the vulnerability to fire of the dry rubble wall with timber-framing was well known and later forts were of a different design. The marked absence of timber-framed forts in the areas between and north of the main concentrations round the Firth of Tay and the Moray Firth—where there are plenty of other kinds of hillforts—is striking and may be illustrating the abandonment of the original timber-framed designs in the middle of the hillfort period, long before they had covered the country.

As far as the origins of the whole Abernethy complex is concerned, although our understanding of social and political events in Scotland in the eighth and seventh centuries B.C. is obviously extremely limited, the new coincidence of the innovations in metal-working in the Covesea and Tarves phases of the Late Bronze Age[75], and the possible foreign settlement in the Sculptor's Cave, with the appearance of the first large timber-framed stone-walled hillforts in Scotland is striking. It surely shows that major social changes of some kind were occurring. Moreover there is the added coincidence that these changes were taking place at the time of the well known, marked and permanent deterioration of the European climate as cooler and wetter weather heralded the start of the Sub-Atlantic period[76]. The tree-ring calibration of C-14 dates may have shed some light on this also. Suess has recently pointed out that between 780 and 770 B.C. (in real years) there occurred one of the most dramatic increases in the C-14 content of the Earth's atmosphere that his graph has recorded at any time between the present and 5000 B.C.[77]. This was followed by a sharp decrease until about 580 B.C. and he considers that the cause of this could well also have had an effect on the terrestrial climate.

[76] Godwin (1956), Overbeck and Happach (1957).
[77] Suess (1970b).

These coincidences may be no more than that : on the other hand the phenomena could be interlinked in some way. At any rate it may be a useful reminder
that the explanation of British prehistoric archaeological phenomena may
depend on evidence gathered in fields far removed from the interiors of hillforts, and the contents of bronze hoards. It should be reiterated[78] that
radiocarbon dating, though it may be inherently inaccurate for certain periods,
has provided us with a superb tool of relative dating with which one can build
up complex pictures of the situation in Britain at different epochs in the past.
This is because it will show that sites and phenomena which would otherwise
be quite unconnectable are linked together in time and could therefore be
linked in some other way. The understanding of the appearance of hillforts
in the British Late Bronze Age could well benefit greatly from such a comparative approach.

Acknowledgements

I have to thank Mr. David Tait and Mr. Richard Davis—of the Department
of Geography in the University of Glasgow—for the photogrammetric map
of Sheep Hill in Fig. 1. I am grateful to Miss Helen Nisbet for letting me draw
on the information in her own list of vitrified forts, thus making the
Appendix more complete, and also to the staff of the Archaeology Division,
Ordnance Survey, Edinburgh, for information about the Craig Obney fort,
Perthshire. Gratitude is also due to Mrs. M. Peek for allowing me to mention
the contents of her M.A. thesis and to Mr. L. McL. Wedderburn for information about the C-14 dates from Cairnton, shown in Fig. 7. I am also grateful
to Mr. Alan Small for information about the Craig Phadrig fort. I thank Dr.
Hugh McKerrell of the National Museum of Antiquities of Scotland for the
photograph of the bridle bit after treatment in Pl. IX. The photograph of it
before treatment was taken by Mr. Hugh Forbes of the Hunterian Museum,
University of Glasgow. I have to thank the Society of Antiquaries of Scotland
for allowing the reproduction of the photograph of the Abernethy hillfort in
Pl. V.

Appendix

Most of the Scottish vitrified and unburnt timber-framed forts have already been exhaustively
catalogued and described by Mrs. M. A. Cotton and this appendix simply groups them by
categories of sizes and in the numerical order of their National Grid Reference numbers. A few
other relevant details are included. A star in front of the entry means that the site is not vitrified
but that evidence of timber-framing in the walls has been seen. The number in brackets following
the site name refers to Childe's list of vitrified forts (1946). For those sites marked with an asterisk
the size of the enclosed area is only approximate: dimensions given without plans are usually
confined to the lengths of the maximum internal axes and, in these cases, the area has been worked
out roughly by subtracting a quarter from the total square yards enclosed by a rectangle of the

[78] MacKie (1971c).

given measurements. It will be found that a rough oval drawn inside a rectangle and touching all four sides occupies about three-quarters of the area of that rectangle. Where measurements differ in different sources the latest has been taken and much use has been made of Feachem's gazetteer of prehistoric sites, the compilation of which was based on a thorough knowledge of field monuments gained by work with the Edinburgh branch of the Royal Commission on Ancient Monuments (Feachem, 1963). Sites not asterisked have accurate plans available and I am particularly indebted to Dr. K. A. Steer and Mr. A. McLaren of the Royal Commission for making their plans of unpublished forts available to me for measurement. References to the literature on each site are not given except to Mrs. Cotton's paper, which contains an extensive bibliography, unless the site is not mentioned there.

Sites

Abbreviations. RWF = Feachem (1963): MAC = Cotton (1954)

Group I (*10 000–20 000 sq yd*)

NH 663491 *Ord of Kessock** (5), Ross & Cromarty: *c* 17 250 sq yd: MAC p. 79.
NH 933406 *Dunearn* (12), Findhorn, Nairn: *c* 10 000 sq. yd: RWF p. 140: MAC p. 81.

Group II (*5500–7000 sq yd*)

NM 903382 *Benderloch* (*Dun Mac Uisneachan*) *I* (38), Argyllshire: 5700 sq yd: MAC p. 75; RWF p. 109.
NO 493349 *Laws of Monifieth* (24), Angus: 6600 sq yd: MAC pp. 66–67; RWF p. 106.
NO 506556 *Finavon* (21), Angus: *c* 5800 sq yd: MAC p. 66; RWF p. 106.
NX 929870 *Mullach**, Dumfriess-shire: *c* 6500 sq yd: R.C.A.H.M.S. (1920) no. 339, pp. 122–123; RWF p. 117.

Group III (*3000–4500 sq yd*)

NH 143914 *Dun Lagaidh*, Ross and Cromarty: *c* 3000 sq yd: MAC p. 76; RWF p. 149; pp. 214–217 above.
NH 505585 *Knock Farril** (2), Ross and Cromarty: *c* 4400 sq yd: MAC p. 79; RWF pp. 148–149.
NJ 484293 *Tap o' Noth** (18), Aberdeenshire: *c* 3500 sq yd: MAC p. 82; RWF pp. 106–107.
NO 392314 *Dundee Law** (25), Angus: *c* 3700 sq yd: MAC p. 83.
NS 832973 *Dumyat*, Stirlingshire: *c* 3500 sq yd: R.C.A.H.M.S. (1963) no. 68 and Fig. 7, pp. 69–71; RWF p. 157.
NT 229638 ⋆*Castle Law*, Midlothian: *c* 3000 sq yd: MAC p. 68; Piggott and Piggott (1952).
NX 845540 *Mote o' Mark* (60), Galloway: *c* 3500 sq yd: MAC pp. 69–70; RWF p. 129.

Group IV (*1000–2600 sq yd*)

NH 534428 *Dun Mor* (3), Inverness-shire: 1930 sq yd: MAC p. 80; RWF p. 126.
NH 640453 *Craig Phadrig** (6), Inverness-shire: *c* 2300 sq yd: MAC p. 80; RWF p. 126.
NH 651882 *Dun Creich* (1), Sutherland: *c* 1800 sq yd: MAC pp. 78–79; RWF p. 158.
NH 827475 *Dun Evan* (11), Nairn: 1380 sq yd: MAC p. 81; RWF p. 140.
NJ 003495 *Doune of Relugas* (14), Morayshire: 1330 sq yd: MAC p. 81; RWF pp. 139–140.
NJ 613281 *Dunnideer* (19), Aberdeenshire: *c* 2200 sq yd: MAC p. 82; RWF p. 105.
NM 694794 *Eilean nan Gobhar* (31), Inverness-shire: *c* 1170 sq yd: MAC p. 77; RWF p. 127.
NN 126702 *Dun Deardail** (37), Inverness-shire: *c* 1100 sq yd: MAC p. 77; RWF p. 127.
NN 902158 *Machany* (26), Perthshire: 1630 sq yd: MAC p. 84; RWF p. 146.
NN 906304 *Dun Mor** (27), Perthshire: *c* 1175 sq yd: MAC p. 68; RWF p. 146.

NO 100155 *Forgandenny** (45), Perthshire: *c* 1200 sq yd: MAC pp. 67–68; RWF p. 145.
NO 214316 *Dunsinane* (23), Perthshire*: *c* 1500 sq yd: MAC p. 83; RWF p. 146.
NO 262504 *Barry Hill* (22), Perthshire: *c* 2000 sq yd: MAC pp. 83–84; RWF p. 146–147.
NR 803959 *Duntroon* (40), Argyllshire: *c* 1050 sq yd: MAC p. 74; RWF p. 108.
NR 815364 *Carradale* (42), Argyllshire: 1200 sq yd: MAC p. 73; RWF p. 108–109.
NS 017461 *An Knap* (47), Arran: *c* 2600 sq yd: MAC p. 71.
NS 085530 *Dunagoil* (46), Buteshire: *c* 1800 sa yd: MAC pp. 71–72; RWF pp. 113–114.
NS 202628 *Knock Hill* (53), Ayrshire: *c* 1300 sq yd: MAC p. 71; RWF p. 110.
NS 298074 *Kildoun* (55), Ayrshire: *c* 1250 sq yd: RWF p. 109; MAC p. 70.
NS 344718 *Craigmarloch Wood*, Renfrewshire: *c* 1100 sq yd: MAC p. 84; RWF p. 147–148; *Discovery & Excavation in Scotland* 1963, p. 42; 1964, p. 47; 1965, p. 34; 1966, p. 39. (C.B.A., Scottish Regional Group).
NS 797847 *Braes*, Stirlingshire: c. 1060: sq yd R.C.A.H.M.S. (1963), no. 74, pp. 74–75 and Fig. 13; RWF p. 157.
NS 809959 *Abbey Craig*, Stirlingshire: *c* 1750 sq yd: R.C.A.H.M.S. (1963) no. 69, p. 71 and Fig. 8; RWF p. 157.
NT 141344 *Tinnis Castle*, Peebles-shire: *c* 1400 sq yd: R.C.A.H.M.S. (1967), no. 320, pp. 142–3; RWF p. 144.
NT 546631 *Harelaw* (51), East Lothian: *c* 1670 sq yd: MAC p. 84; RWF pp. 122–123.
NX 295515 *Dun o' May* (58), Galloway: *c* 1370 sq yd: MAC pp. 68–69; RWF p. 159.
NX 720745 *Mochrum Hill*, (81) Kirkcudbrightshire: *c* 2100 sq yd: R.C.A.H.M.S. (1914), unpublished plan.

Group V (*500–1000 sq yd*)

NH 718393 *Dun Daviot* (10), Nairn: *c* 600 sq yd: MAC p. 80.
NH 888514 *Castle Finlay* (13), Nairn: 600 sq yd: MAC p. 81; RWF p. 140.
NM 903382 *Benderloch II* (38), Argyllshire: *c* 800 sq yd: RWF p. 109; MAC p. 75; *sub-rectangular*.
NM 970633 *Lochan Gour* (35), Argyllshire: *c* 630 sq yd: MAC p. 76; RWF p. 109.
NO 183153 ✶ *Abernethy*, Perthshire: *c* 580 sq yd: MAC p. 67; RWF p. 145.
NO 633723 *Finella's Castle (Cairnton)* (20), Kincardineshire: *c* 625 sq yd: MAC p. 83; RWF p. 128. *Discovery and Excavation in Scotland* 1973, p. 4: Wedderburn (1973).
NR 757571 *Dun Skeig* (41), Argyllshire: *c* 660 sq yd: MAC p. 73; RWF p. 108.
NS 178491 *Auldhill* (54), Ayrshire: *c* 500 sq yd: MAC pp. 70–71; RWF p. 109.
NS 433744 *Sheep Hill* (phase 1), Dunbartonshire: *c* 800 sq yd: RWF pp. 118–119; this chapter, pp. 211–214 above.
NX 192962 *Dowhill* (56), Ayrshire: *c* 540 sq yd: MAC p. 70; RWF p. 109.
NX 589560 *Trusty's Hill* (59), Galloway: *c* 500 sq yd: MAC p. 69; RWF p. 131.
NX 793589 *Castle Gower* (61), Galloway: *c* 520 sq yd: MAC p. 70: RWF p. 129.

Group VI (*200–500 sq yd*)

NC 066155 *Inverpolly*, Ross and Cromarty: *c* 300 sq yd: RWF pp. 149–150; *circular*.
NG 802753 *Gairloch*, Ross and Cromarty: *c* 350 sq yd: MAC p. 77; RWF p. 149.
NH 527239 *Dun Dearduil* (7), Inverness-shire: *c* 280 sq yd: MAC p. 78; RWF p. 127.
NM 663702 *The Torr* (30), r. Shiel, Ardnamurchan, Argyllshire: *c* 250 sq yd: MAC p. 76 (wrongly described there as in Ross and Cromarty where there is another river Shiel).
NM 693839 *Arisaig* (32), (Ard Ghaunsgoik), Inverness-shire: *c* 350 sq yd: MAC p. 77; RWF p. 127.
NM 903382 *Benderloch III* (38), Argyllshire: *c* 300 sq yd: *circular*: RWF p. 109.
NN 047005 *Pennymore Point*, Argyllshire: *c* 300 sq yd: *PSAS* xcv (1961–1962), p. 58.
NS 018754 *Eilean Buidhe* (45), Buteshire: *c* 250 sq yd: *circular*: MAC pp. 72–73.
NS 793944 *Mote Hill*, Stirlingshire: *c* 450 sq yd: R.C.A.H.M.S. (1963), no. 80, pp. 79–80.

NX 673630 *Mote, Galloway:* R.C.A.H.M.S. (1914), no. 45, pp. 35–37 and Fig. 32; RWF p. 130.

Group VII (*100–200 sq yd*)

NC 411008 *Langwell*, Creich, Sutherland: *c* 100 sq yd: *circular:* found in 1966 by Ordnance Survey.

NG 899270 ⋆*The Bard's Castle⋆* (28), Wester Ross: *c* 330 sq yd: MAC p. 76.

Group VIII (*no measurements: not all certainly vitrified*)

NG 881258 *Eilean Donan* (29), Kintail, Inverness-shire: MAC p. 76;

NH 472429 *Dun Fionn* (4), Ross and Cromarty: MAC p. 79.

NH 531286 *Castle Urquhart* (8), Inverness-shire: MAC p. 78.

NJ 004590 *Cluny Hill* (16), Banffshire: MAC p. 81.

NJ 838663 *Cullykhan* (Troupe Point), Banffshire: MAC p. 82; C. Greig (1972) and this chapter.

NM 612835 *Eilean Port na Muirach* (33), Arisaig, Inverness-shire: MAC p. 75.

NM 627850 *Eilean na Ghoil*, Arisaig, Inverness-shire: MAC p. 76.

NM 882336 *Dun Beg* (39), Argyllshire: MAC p. 75; "dun" on O.S. map.

NO 023382 *Craig Obney*, Perthshire: information from the Archaeology Division, Ordnance Survey, Edinburgh.

NR 468527 *Trudennish Point* (43), Islay I. Argyllshire: MAC p. 74. No vitrification seen in 1969.

NR 963692 ⋆*Caisteal na Sithe*, Argyllshire: MAC p. 75. No vitrification; stonework suggested beam slots to Childe and Graham.

NS 770089 *Kemp's Castle*, Dumfries-shire: RWF p. 118; R.C.A.H.M.S. (1920), no. 557.

NS 356337 *Kemp Law* (57), Ayrshire: MAC p. 70.

NS 182580 *Cumbrae I.* (52), Buteshire, Ayrshire: MAC p. 72.

   ?   *Ardelve*, Loch Long, Ross and Cromatry: MAC p. 76.

12 | Welsh Hillforts: A Reappraisal of Recent Research

H. N. Savory

I. Introduction

A. Past Work

It has long been known that Wales is a land of hillforts, like other parts of western and southern Britain, although the first specialised map showing the known sites of this type in Wales and the Marches is no more than forty years old (Nash-Williams, 1933). This first map distinguished contour forts from promontory forts, but made no differentiation as to size. It brought out very clearly the contrast between the areas of relatively good farming land near the main river valleys in the Marches and on the lower ground near the southern, western and northern seaboards of Wales, on the one hand, and the wet and windy moorlands of the interior of Wales, where hillforts are few, on the other. From this alone a deduction could be made, that most hillforts were built after the climatic optimum of the Early and Middle Bronze Age, when large numbers of burial mounds were built on the high moorlands, presumably at no great distance from the settlements of their builders. The 1933 map, however, suggested that the south-western peninsula of Wales had more hillforts than any other part of Wales and there was no indication of the small size of the great majority of these sites, or the doubtful antiquity of many of them. The present writer once tried (Nash-Williams and Savory, 1949) to remedy this by producing a map with symbols of two sizes, but this approach was later improved upon in a beautiful Ordnance Survey map (Ordnance Survey, 1962) in which many new sites were included.

In spite of its wealth in sites, however, Wales has lagged behind southern England, and perhaps even Scotland, in their study, partly because of the poverty of such sites as have been explored, at least until recently, in settlement material of types which could readily be compared with those which were already available in considerable quantity from southern English sites by the beginning of the Second World War, and partly because of the influence of somewhat exaggerated ideas of cultural retardation in the Highland Zone, of which Wales as a whole was thought to be a part (Fox, 1959). One of the chief pioneers of hillfort study in Britain as a whole, the late Dr. Willoughby Gardner (1926), spent much of his life surveying hillforts, mainly in North Wales, and excavating certain sites, but had at his disposal so little that could then be confidently ascribed to a time before the Roman conquest that he had perforce to accept Wheeler's interpretation of the role of hillforts in the relations between Roman and native in Wales (Wheeler, 1922), as reflections of the influence of Roman military technology upon the native, at the earliest in the immediate pre-conquest period, and at the latest in the third or fourth century A.D. This state of backwardness was naturally reflected in Professor Hawkes' classic paper on hillforts (Hawkes, 1931), which accepts that hillfort building had hardly reached any part of Wales in Iron Age "A" and had only affected a partial penetration in Iron Age "B". In the south "there is no satisfactory trace of true Iron Age culture before the Roman invasion except on the low hills and the coastal plain along the Severn Sea", while in the north "no really satisfactory evidence of pre-Roman hillfort building and occupation is known". Progress in the south was naturally due to Wheeler's work at Lydney (Wheeler and Wheeler, 1932) and Nash-Williams' at Llanmelin (Nash-Williams, 1933) and in the north Hawkes' own prehistorian's sense told him that the earliest phase at Dinorben must be pre-Roman, and that the same must apply to the fine La Tène metal-work from Moel Hiraddug (Hemp, 1928). Above all, it led to the prophetic remark that the rectangular guard-houses at Pen y Gorddyn, though they suggest imitation of a Roman gate plan "recall the guard-houses of St. Catharine's Hill and Leckhampton".

In the years immediately before the Second World War, Dr. Nash Williams' work on the relatively productive Iron Age "B" forts at Llanmelin and Sudbrook in Monmouthshire (Nash-Williams, 1933 and 1939) was being matched in North Wales by O'Neil's excavation at the Breiddin and Ffridd Faldwyn forts in Montgomeryshire (O'Neil, 1937 and 1942), Varley's work at Maiden Castle, Bickerton and Castle Ditches, Eddisbury in Cheshire and at Old Oswestry in Shropshire (Varley, 1935, 1936, 1940, 1948 and 1952) and Daryll Forde's at Pen Dinas, Aberystwyth (Forde, 1937a and b and 1938). Although finds of precise dating value tended to be rare on these northern sites, there were enough of prehistoric character to suggest, when the lack of Roman finds on most of these sites was considered, that they had gone through successive phases of development before the Roman conquest and that structural features belonging to these phases might be chronologically related to similar ones noted in southern English hillforts being excavated about that time which had produced relatively abundant finds of pottery and metal-work then datable approximately by strictly archaeological methods. O'Neil, moreover, with characteristic independence, was already arguing that the development of closely sited multiple defences at hillforts in the northern Marches must have long preceded Caesar's conquest of the Veneti in 56 B.C.—the dateline that Wheeler at Maiden Castle (Dorset) was then proposing for the adoption of such defences, along with sling-stone warfare, in southern England (O'Neil, 1942, pp. 15–17). The discovery at Old Oswestry of pottery closely comparable with Wessex Iron Age "A" forms later encouraged Varley to push back the appearance of univallate hillforts in the northern Marches to the beginning of the third century B.C. and the appearance of bivallate ones to a century later (Varley, 1948, p. 57).

The difficult financial conditions in the years following the Second World War discouraged large-scale hillfort excavation in Wales, and efforts tended to be concentrated on field-work like that which led to the writer's lists of sites in the south-eastern counties of Wales (Savory, 1949, 1950a and b, 1952a, 1953, 1954a). These surveys, though not very detailed, were based to a considerable extent upon study of R.A.F. air-photographs and visits made to the majority of the sites. Lists of earthworks in Cardiganshire and Pembrokeshire were afterwards produced in similar form, as a continuation of this series, by Hogg (1962) and Crossley (1963). The increasingly complex classifications followed in these lists reflect the need to distinguish the small hill-slope and plateau enclosures so common in south and west Wales from large contour forts and to recognise the prevalence in these areas of sites with widely-spaced, concentric banks, like those to which Lady Fox (1952 and 1958) had called attention in the West Country. This field-work, together with that carried out by the Ordnance Survey's own archaeological branch, was reflected in the fine *Map of Southern Britain in the Early Iron Age* (Ordnance Survey, 1962). At the same time, the official field-work carried out by the staff of the Royal Commission on Ancient Monuments in Wales came to fruition in the volumes of the Caernarvonshire *Inventory* (R.C.A.H.M. (Wales), 1956, 1960 and 1964) and led to personal contributions by the Secretary of the Commission to the general discussion of hillforts in Wales (Hogg, 1958, 1960, 1962, 1965, 1971 and 1972a and b). This tradition of field-survey has been carried on, in Montgomeryshire by Spurgeon (1972) and in north-east Wales and northern Marches by Forde-Johnston (1962a, 1964 and 1965), in Merionethshire by Gresham (1967) and Anglesey by Lynch (1970).

Research excavations in the same period were often carried out on a small scale and with modest results. In the south the writer's own work at Mynydd Bychan, Llysworney (Glamorganshire) (Savory, 1954b and 1955a) was an example of a relatively productive and thorough exploration of a small site, and Probert's gradual excavation over the years of a much larger site at Twyn-y-gaer, Cwmyoy (Monmouthshire) has yielded a wealth of material, so far unpublished. In general, however, earlier experience was confirmed and the results of small-scale excavations in Brecknock, west Wales and north-west Wales have been disappointing to their organisers at the time, however real their cumulative value may have proved to be in the end, when fitted into the picture that has gradually emerged, chiefly as a result of larger-scale excavations carried out on an emergency basis for the Government on a limited number of sites in north-east Wales—Dinorben (Gardner and Savory, 1964 and 1971a, b and c), Moel Hiraddug (Houlder, 1961, Stead and Bevan-Evans, 1961 and 1962, Bevan-Evans, 1963 and 1964, Davies and Bevan-Evans, 1969, Davies, 1970–1971) and the Breiddin (Musson, 1970 a and 1972), and in west Wales—Coygan Camp (Wainwright, 1967a) and Walesland Rath (Wainwright, 1971a). All these excavations have produced material which permits at least partial integration with a new cultural and chronological framework established by recent large-scale hillfort excavation in the West Country and the west Midlands of England as well as in northern England and Scotland; above all, radiocarbon dates obtained at Dinorben (Savory 1971a, b and c) have confirmed archaeological evidence from this and other Welsh sites suggesting that the first hillforts in Wales, as in other parts of Britain, belong not to the Early Iron Age but to the Late Bronze Age.

B. The Problem at the Present Time

The work of the last twenty-five years in Wales, in which as we have seen field archaeology played so large a part, has been bringing out ever more clearly the regional diversity to be found in the earthworks of different parts of the Cambrian Massif. In the days when chronological perspectives, beyond the historically fixed threshold of the Roman conquest, were so short, it was permissible to think of this diversity in terms of the tribal geography of the area, as known from classical sources, and to differentiate between the respective cultures of the Silures in the south-east, the Demetae in the south-west, the Ordovices in the north-west, the Deceangli in the north-east and the Cornovii in mid-Wales. As the perspectives have deepened, however, it has become more and more obvious that the great diversity of earthwork types to be found in any one part of Wales must reflect the vicissitudes of a long process of settlement, everywhere spread over several centuries and in the Marches, at least, filling the whole of the last millennium B.C. As long as it seemed possible to confine hillforts to the Early Iron Age it was theoretically acceptable for Hawkes (1958, Figs 1 and 3) to extend his "ABC" system to Wales at least in outline, with Castell Odo (Caernarvonshire) on the boundary between phase Ia and b, univallate hillforts beginning in Wales during "Second A", and Pen Dinas, Aberystwyth on the boundary between phase 3a and 3b, while a "Western Second B" could be seen at Lydney (Gloucestershire) followed (erroneously, as it proved) by a "Western Third B" at Sutton Walls (Hereford). Now, however, the sequence of hillfort building seems to stretch back, in the Marches at least, through the whole of "Iron Age A" into the Late Bronze Age. Unfortunately a chronological and regional system which was evolved in southern England very largely on the basis of the pottery which was found abundantly, and in great variety, on all types of sites in this area cannot even now be satisfactorily applied in an area in much of which it is now clear pottery was not made locally during a large part of the Iron Age. Here finds, where they occur, depend upon importation from distant centres of manufacture, while such pottery as was made locally for part of the time, outside the southern coastal areas, was coarse, very little varied in form, and to a large extent Bronze Age in tradition.

Until many more sites, and above all productive sites, have been explored in Wales, and the culturally significant finds—metal-work, and objects of bone, and stone as well as pottery—are not only much more abundant but spread more evenly through Wales—through the coastal areas of the west, in fact, as well as the Marches—it is best to lay aside Professor Hawkes' regional system and use only the broadest terms—Late Bronze Age, Hallstatt, La Tène— where they are appropriate. In reviewing the present state of knowledge the writer feels that it will be most useful to consider the evolution of the defended settlement in Wales, from the Late Bronze Age onwards, as part of a cultural process in which the different, well-defined geographical regions of Wales and the Marches were affected, to varying degrees at different times, not only by variously orientated "contacts" and "influences" but by actual movements of people, displaced by the periodical upheavals which we know took place on the Continent during later prehistoric times, however little we may know about such movements historically in Britain. We now know through Stanford's work (1971 and 1972a and b) that the building of numerous large hillforts in the central Marches was the work of a large and well-organised population with a southern British Late Bronze Age substratum but with an influential exotic, presumably Continental, component which had imposed an alien domestic and military architecture. Part of the problem in Wales is to decide by what stages and with what intensity these new traditions made their way from the original centres in Wessex and the west Midlands into Wales itself. One can study this process, to some extent, through the distribution of types of fortification, rampart structure, entrance elaboration etc. which can now be arranged in a rough chronological sequence, but we can also see that in some parts of Wales special types arose, which have links with the south-western peninsula of England, Ireland and Scotland, rather than with regions to the east or south-east. These may represent the reaction of a native population to external pressures, and the house-type which is associated with them lends some support to this possibility; but they do not represent a single community or cultural group because there are considerable differences between the range of settlement forms found in south-west and north-west Wales respectively. One returns, therefore, to the concept of enduring tribal entities, the names of which at the time of the Roman conquest are known.

As far back as 1958 the writer (1958a, p. 49 f.) attempted to relate the four main tribal areas of the first century A.D.—the Silures, the Demetae, the Ordovices and the Deceangli/Cornovii—to four cultural provinces discernible, through implement types, in the Late Bronze Age, in south-east, south-west, north-west and north-east Wales. These four cultural provinces really correspond, however, to natural regions which are arranged around the central moorland areas of Wales and have varying contacts with the outside world. Those on the east inevitably have close contacts with the adjoining lowland areas of England to which they are linked by the valleys and estuaries of large rivers, and they contain most of the best agricultural land in Wales. Those to the west are relatively isolated from the east but were always linked in prehistoric times to some degree or other with Ireland by sea-routes, and have sometimes been regarded as part of an Irish Sea Province (Savory, 1970 and Alcock, 1972a); they have also undoubtedly had their independent sea-contacts with Cornwall and Armorica. Their enduring geographical and cultural personality does not necessarily mean complete continuity of population: in fact, as Hogg has shown (1972a), analysis of settlement types, fortified or otherwise, suggests that in the course of several centuries each district went through a different sequence of historical changes, producing a different overall pattern of earthwork types. These local patterns require analysis to determine to what extent they represent survival of the Bronze Age population, to what extent they have been affected by external "influences" and actual invasions, and to establish the origin of the elements they undoubtedly have in common with Ireland and the West Country. Hogg, indeed, in dealing with this problem some years ago (Hogg, 1958 and 1960, p. 18) invented the phrase "Secondary Iron Age" to describe the reaction of surviving Bronze Age groups of hillfort builders to the immigrants who brought true Iron Age culture to Britain, but now that we know that the building of hillforts began in Britain as a whole well before the end of the Bronze Age, and that large parts of the lowlands of Britain as well as the highlands were for long occupied, during the Early Iron Age, by groups descended from the Bronze Age population rather than from recent immigrants, this phrase is not particularly relevant to the hillfort question in Wales.

Finds of metal-work and pottery suggest that after the initial stages of hillfort building in Wales, during which the dominating factors were centred in the Marches, Wales as a whole was subjected in the third and second centuries B.C. to a stream of influences, of Continental origin, which were independent from the hillfort culture of Wessex and the Marches, and it is necessary to consider to what extent these affected developments in hillfort architecture in Wales during the three centuries immediately before the Roman conquest—not only the multiplication of ramparts, which is most marked on the large sites in the Marches but spreads to the smaller sites, mostly in promontory positions, in the west and involves the construction of a number of entirely new coastal sites in Caernarvonshire, but the appearance in the west of special features like back-terracing and *chevaux de frise*. With the Roman conquest, it is clear that hillforts do not disappear from archaeological considerations as abruptly or as completely as they do in southern England: the abundant evidence from numerous Welsh defended sites for some form of continuing or renewed occupation during the centuries of Roman rule, needs to be evaluated. To what extent should these remains be related to continuing resistance by the natives, to what extent do they represent entirely peaceful occupation of sites which no longer had any military value, and to what extent are they connected with the authorised military reoccupation during the last days of the Empire? While the evidence which relates to these problems is relatively abundant, that which bears upon the final question—were hillforts reoccupied, refortified or built on new sites in Wales after the fourth century A.D., when the old tribal entities of the first century A.D. were in a sense being recreated within similar geographical limits, in the Dark Age sub-kingdoms of Wales?—is still relatively slight. It must, however, be considered at the conclusion of this essay.

II. The Beginnings circa 1000–500 B.C.

A. Late Bronze Age Hillfort Building in Wales

The possibility that some fortified settlements in various parts of Britain, including Wales, were built well before the end of the Bronze Age has now been fairly widely accepted (Burgess, 1968a; Harding, 1970; MacKie, 1969b and 1971c; Stanford, 1971). During the past few years evidence for habitation or construction on hillfort sites from the Late Middle Bronze Age onwards has come from all parts of Britain. In lowland Britain the recent evidence includes that from Ivinghoe Beacon (Buckinghamshire) (Cotton and Frere, 1968), where a contour fort with timber-framed rampart was apparently occupied by people who used a variety of bronze implements referable to the eighth century B.C.; from a similar hillfort at Grimthorpe in the East Riding, where animal bones from the lower ditch-filling yielded two radiocarbon dates which are to some degree suspect but at any rate suggest activity in the Late Bronze Age (Stead, 1968, p. 190); and from the site of a large Early Iron Age hillfort at Norton Fitzwarren (Somerset) which was preceded by a contour earthwork enclosing 5 acres with which Middle Bronze Age pottery and palstaves and bracelets of Late Middle Bronze Age types were associated (Langmaid, 1971). Even in Northumberland and Scotland the recent evidence reviewed by MacKie (1969b and 1971c) suggests that timber-framed or palisaded contour enclosures were being built well before the end of the sixth century B.C. and that the same might apply to some of the small walled forts of the western coasts and islands of Scotland. On the Isle of Man, too, a radiocarbon date suggests that some of the huts in a large settlement enclosed by the inner of two widely-spaced ramparts in South Barrule were in use by the sixth century B.C. (Gelling, 1972). But it should be noted that evidence is accumulating, too, for the occupation of hill-tops, in the Late Middle or Late Bronze Age, by villages which were not apparently at first defended by anything more substantial than a fence; although the site was often occupied in later centuries by a hillfort. This appears to have been the case at South Cadbury (Alcock, 1972b, p. 31 and Cunliffe, 1971c, p. 55); at Mam Tor (Derbyshire), where some of the numerous hut-floors enclosed by contour defences which have not yet been dated, yielded pottery of Middle or Late Bronze Age appearance, as well as part of a socketed bronze axe-head and, in two cases, charcoals yielding radiocarbon dates in the twelfth century B.C. (Coombs, 1971); at Croft Ambrey (Herefordshire) where carbonised grain has given a similar early date (MacKie,

1971c, p. 71); and at certain Scottish sites reviewed by MacKie (1971c) where some phases of occupation have yielded radiocarbon dates much earlier than the defences.

In Wales, direct evidence of Late Bronze Age fortification is confined, at the moment of writing, to two sites, though it is likely to extend to other sites in the near future. At the Breiddin (Montgomeryshire) the earlier excavations of O'Neil (1937) had already suggested Late Bronze Age activity on a site which was later defended by walls (Fig. 1, p. 343) and the more extensive excavations by Musson (1970a, 1971 and 1972 and see below pp. 293–302 or 293 ff.) have yielded an unusually rich assemblage of bronze objects—a socketed axe, a socketed hammer, a Thorndon type socketed knife with bronze rivets, and several pins of Late Bronze Age types—as well as pottery of Middle–Late Bronze Age character. Some of these finds might be regarded, like those of O'Neil, as representing a relatively late transitional phase from Late Bronze Age to Iron Age culture, natural in a peripheral area, but not all: one of the pins, for example, with its swollen neck and small expanded head, resembles pins from Hallstatt "A" and "B" sites on the Continent, and the star-shaped bead of blue faience found in the make-up of the earliest rampart takes one back at least to the early Middle Bronze Age. The earliest rampart at the Breiddin had not, at the time of writing, been dated by radiocarbon, although the presence of a double line of post-holes less than a metre apart, with remains of burnt posts, presented this possibility, and the fact that this rampart had been replaced by another of similar construction before a dry-stone box rampart was built in Middle La Tène times, suggests that it is early. Though the bronze implements are in general not clearly stratified in relation to the defences, some may be contemporary with their first phase, even though early objects incorporated in the first rampart and a thin occupation layer, so far without datable finds, passing under this rampart, suggest that there may have been an open settlement on the Breiddin for a long period before the construction of its first defensive palisade or timber-revetted rampart. The Breiddin, it should here be noted, occupies a splendid position, with great cliffs and precipitous slopes on the north-west and south-west, rising to a height of 1000 ft above the Severn plain, at a point where a broad corridor opens into the heart of Wales from the north-west midland plain of England; the area enclosed by the man-made promontory defences, which simply bar a relatively easy approach from the south-east, is no less than 65 acres—part of it too rough for habitation, it is true.

The other early site, Dinorben hillfort near Abergele on the Denbighshire seaboard, is on a much smaller scale than the Breiddin, but in its earliest stage involves a similar conception of a promontory position on a headland, 560 ft above sea-level (Fig. 4) looking out over the broad and for the most part fertile plain near the mouth of the Vale of Clwyd. Here a section through the western end of the main southern rampart, cut by the writer in 1969 (1971a and b, pp. 7–12, Figs 8–10, Pls V–VI) has clarified the interpretation of the numerous sections cut through the same rampart by Willoughby Gardner in 1914–1922 and provided a series of radiocarbon dates. It is clear from the section (Fig. 6) that here, too, the first rampart, consisting of layers of rubble or clay staged with timber rafts and revetted in front with a palisade bedded in a trench and at the back, probably, with horizontal planks fastened to widely-spaced uprights, rested on an occupation layer which had accumulated for some time and had spread down the slope outside the line along which the first rampart was later built. The associated radiocarbon dates for this section, six in number (1971b, p. 76 f.) suggest that the first rampart was constructed some time after the eleventh century B.C. (the approximate date, after allowing for recent refinements of radiocarbon dating methods, of a sample from the pre-rampart layer) and probably in the tenth or ninth century B.C. (as two samples probably derived from its structure suggest) while two other samples suggest that the second, timber-laced rampart, with dry-stone revetment walls, was built in the sixth or fifth century B.C. The uncertainty about the structural allocation of some of the samples is due to the fact that the timber rafts in the part of the first rampart which was still *in situ* had decayed, unaffected by the fire which burnt the outer edges of the rafts and their revetment while the latter had been disturbed by the collapse of the rampart and the construction, long after, of the second rampart. There is little doubt, however, that most of the charcoal samples, including the second earliest, were derived from structural elements of the first or second ramparts.

It should be pointed out here that a reviewer of my detailed report (Savory, 1971b) is correct in suggesting that the palisade trench of the first rampart at Dinorben should have been marked Period "I" not "O" in my section plan (Fig. 7) and that the rubble foundation of the first rampart should be marked Period "I" and not "II" in the section (Fig. 8), as the text makes clear. He is, however, being unreasonable when he suggests that my reconstruction of a timber-staged rampart is unjustified, and that the radiocarbon dates obtained from charred timbers in the section are irrelevant to this early rampart. The dark-banded clay core of the first rampart clearly rested on a foundation of mixed rubble, clay and occupation earth collected from the Late Bronze Age settlement which is dated by sample V-123 (945 ± 95 b.c.), and by potsherds. A timber-staged clay rampart implies timber revetting and it is reasonable to connect the "gully" and the early post-hole to the rear of the rampart with this; that only one post-hole of a rear revetment should have been found in a section 12 ft wide implies the existence of horizontal timbers which had not survived *in situ* in this section, although sample V-122 (895 ± 95 b.c.) was derived from an horizontal beam lying to the north-east of the dark-banded clay of the rampart core, in red clay which probably also represents a disturbed part of the rampart core. This displaced beam could have been derived from the rear revetment or from the staging itself. But that burnt elements from a revetment of horizontal timbers were in fact present here and there behind the Period I rampart is in fact suggested by Dr. Gardner's records of his sections 14 and 19 (Gardner and Savory, 1964, pp. 36–43, Figs 7–8). Whether or not samples V-125 (765 ± 95 b.c.), V-204 (690 ± 85 b.c.) and V-124 (535 ± 85 b.c.)

can be related to the actual rampart structures of Periods I and II, the positions in which they were found at least show that the timber-staged rampart at Dinorben had been destroyed before the end of the Late Bronze Age. The second, timber-laced rampart is directly dated by sample V-176 (420 ± 70 b.c.) and indirectly dated by sample V-124, which must have reached the position in which it was found after the Period II rampart had been burnt and its ditch filled in with debris from its destruction. My reconstruction sections (Fig. 6) are of course based upon the evidence of Dr. Gardner's numerous sections as well as my own.

At Dinorben, then, a promontory fort had been built quite early in the Late Bronze Age, on a headland which was protected on three sides by crags or steep slopes. The associated settlement material is much less explicit than at the Breiddin, since that which can be related directly to the pre-rampart or early defensive stages consists largely of animal bones and simple objects of stone and antler which cannot be precisely dated. Hut floors in the interior of the fort, however, have yielded a little pre-Roman material of a more definite character. The hand-made pottery consists of small fragments, mostly very coarse, and some of it was incorporated in the fabric of the first rampart, having probably been redeposited from the pre-rampart layer. It can be accepted as Middle or Late Bronze Age in fabric; one sherd (Savory, 1971b, Fig. 15.2) comes from a large vessel with a hollow neck and a rounded shoulder —a form by no means foreign to the British Late Bronze Age. Rather more positive is the fragmentary head of a bronze pin of the crook-headed type which points backward to pins associated in France with an early phase of the Urnfield Culture as much as forward to the iron pins of this form which appear in Scotland (Savory, 1971a, p. 256, Fig. 2). Highly suggestive, too, becomes the old discovery of a hoard of Late Bronze Age horse harness, in 1868, at the foot of the crags on the west side of Dinorben, in the light of the knowledge that there must have been a settlement at the top of the crags when this hoard was deposited. Like the crook-headed pin, some elements in the horse-harness are better interpreted as the result of direct connections with the Hallstatt "B" culture of central France than of a trade route connecting the Baltic with Ireland, through Scotland (Savory, 1971a, p. 258).

It is when we consider structural features at Dinorben, however, that we can see most clearly the possibility of an alien element in the population, able to command the labour necessary to fell great numbers of trees in the Vale of Clwyd, perhaps in the course of clearance for cultivation, and to convert them into the rafts necessary for the multiple staging of a rampart about 300 m long (Savory, 1971b, p. 28f.). For the type of construction involved finds its closest parallel, both in Britain and the Continent, in the inner rampart of the Horn promontory fort near Wittnau, Canton Aargau, Switzerland, which was built in Hallstatt "B" and burnt c 700 B.C. (Bersu, 1945 and 1946). Here, as at Dinorben (Fig. 6), the base of the rampart was staged with timber rafts, piled at vertical intervals of two or three feet with layers of clay in between, as well as limestone rubble, and the combustion of the timber in the upper reaches of the rampart core, where there was much rubble, had produced masses of quicklime. As is now becoming clear, the background to this kind of lavish use of timber by the West Alpine Urnfield people lies in the forts of the Lausitz Culture further east, where massive ramparts could be constructed almost entirely of timber (Hawkes, 1971, pp. 9–11). Between Switzerland and Dinorben, it is true, it is not yet possible to point to any certain cases of timber staging in late prehistoric ramparts, though Dr. W. J. Varley has kindly informed me that he has recently found timber rafts, used in the construction of one of the earlier ramparts at Almondbury hillfort (Yorkshire), and that radiocarbon counts suggest a date in the Late Bronze Age–Iron Age transition (see above pp. 119–131). But it is at least clear, as I have sought to show elsewhere (Savory 1971a, b) that the spread of the successive stages of the Urnfield Culture, during Late Bronze Age and early Hallstatt times, through France to the seaboard of Lower Normandy, brought with it the construction of numerous fortified sites of which the promontory fort, sometimes with some type of timber component in its ramparts, was the usual form. One can but wait for the standards of interpretation and record applied to the sections which are now at last being cut with increasing frequency through ramparts of this type in France to rise to the point where one can compare them usefully with the Swiss, German and British sites.

It would, indeed, be rash to regard all unexcavated inland promontory forts in the Welsh Marches as the work of Late Bronze Age immigrants from across the English Channel: one univallate site of this kind which has been excavated—Poston Camp in Herefordshire—was not apparently built until a late phase of the Early Iron Age (Anthony, 1958) and no evidence of occupation at any earlier date has so far come from any of the numerous small promontory forts on the coast of West Wales. But the suggestion that a number of univallate promontory forts had in fact been built in the Welsh Marches well before the end of the Late Bronze Age, beginning the local hillfort series (Fig. 5), is supported not only by the two major Welsh sites which we have just been considering, but by the very early dates that can be assigned to certain promontory forts in neighbouring parts of England. Thus the first fort at Castle Ditches, Eddisbury (Cheshire) was a timber-framed univallate structure with main rampart cutting across a plateau (Varley, 1952) and Almondbury had a similar lay-out (Varley, 1948, p. 46, Fig. 2). At Portfield Camp, Whalley (Lancashire) occupation seems to have begun during the Late Bronze Age, though the main promontory defences have not been dated (Forde-Johnston, 1962b, p. 26f. and Longworth, 1968). The small promontory fort which overlooks the Roveries Camp, Lydham (Shropshire) is not likely to be later in date than the large hillfort with which it is so closely linked and which certainly had an early beginning (Forde-Johnston, 1962a, p. 87f. and Fig. 5.4). There are a number of other promontory forts in Derbyshire (Preston, 1954 and Lane, 1969), Lancashire and Cheshire (Forde-Johnston, 1962b) which are likely to be early, but there is only space here to consider some outstanding sites in Wales itself, which are likely to have early origins.

The most striking of these are the two adjoining promontory forts of Llan-ymynech hill (Montgomeryshire), which occupy a position commanding the lower reaches of the Vyrnwy and Tanat valley much as the Breiddin commands the Severn valley, on the edge of the Midlands plain (Fox and Hemp, 1926). The largest of these, no doubt with several phases of development, encloses no less than 140 acres—the largest hillfort in Wales—and has a sharply in-turned entrance in the north side, and another inturned entrance on the east side. Crowther's Camp, Guilsfield (Montgomeryshire) is a small multivallate enclosure with natural defences on the side which overlooks the Severn. The stages of its development are of course unknown, but it is worth noting that the important Guilsfield Late Bronze Age founder's hoard was found only 100 yd outside this site on the south (Spurgeon, 1972, p. 331) and may, like the horse-harness hoard at Dinorben, indicate an early occupation of this site. Other sites lying near the borders of mid-Wales which are of interest here are the large single-walled promontory fort on Craig Rhiwarth, Llangynog (Montgomeryshire) (Hogg, 1965, p. 138) and the smaller ones are on Llandegley Rocks (Radnorshire) (Savory, 1952a, p. 77) and at Twyn Llechfaen (Brecknock-shire) (p. 272 below) (Savory, 1961 and 1971b). Looking southwards, the fine large promontory forts which occupy loops of the Wye at Spital Meend and Symond's Yat in Gloucestershire (Fox, 1955) are significant in relation to other evidence, to be considered later (p. 249 below) for the use of the Wye valley for penetration of the Welsh Marches by Late Bronze Age immigrants coming from the south.

Not all the fortified sites in the Welsh Marches which have some claim to be considered among the most ancient are in promontory positions. Caynham Camp, near Ludlow, for example, has lately been referred by Stanford (1971, p. 42) to the eighth century B.C. on the strength of the similarity in ware and form of an unstratified sherd from this site to urns of Late Bronze Age type from the Bromfield (Shropshire) urnfield, one of which has been dated by a C-14 count. There is, however, a possibility that we are dealing here with a settlement which preceded the hillfort proper, as at Dinorben, Breiddin, Mam Tor and possibly at Portfield. Nonetheless, Caynham Camp is a contour fort with what may well be primitive features, and we shall be considering later on (p. 257 below) the possibility of a native tradition of contour fort building which had Middle Bronze Age roots in southern England and co-existed in Wales with the alien one of promontory fort building. The earliest fort at Ffridd Faldwyn, too, has been given an equally early date by Stanford (1971, p. 43) on the strength of somewhat precarious calculation of timber replacement, but this is a timber-framed contour fort with a deep, sharp inturn at the entrance which seems to take us outside of the repertoire of Late Bronze Age hillfort architecture in western Europe as we know it at present, and into the sphere of later Hallstatt "C"–"D" contributions to the British tradition, which we will be considering later (p. 253 below). The promontory sites which we were considering earlier are more securely linked with the evidence which settlement material, hoards, and isolated finds provide for the arrival of an alien element in the population of Wessex and the Welsh Marches during the Late Bronze Age.

The finds at the Breiddin and at Dinorben which have already been mentioned give the impression of a mixed culture in which the ceramic tradition was largely indigenous, while the metal-work reflected the strong infusion of Continental ideas which transformed the British bronze industry at the beginning of the Late Bronze Age, during the ninth century B.C., and included horse harness and dress-pins which probably to some extent represent the personal equipment of a new element in the population, arriving from the Continent at a somewhat later date: the processes which brought about these changes in Britain generally have lately been ably reviewed by Burgess (1968a). This impression is reinforced by consideration of other finds from the Welsh Marches. I have already stressed the importance of the lost material from Merlin's Cave, Symond's Yat, with its maple-leaf razor, bronze pins of Continental Late Bronze Age types (particularly relating to the Fort Harrouard series), slotted reel like that from the Parc-y-meirch (Dinorben) horse harness hoard, and rim fragments which appear to be from flattened rim bucket urns as well as from shouldered jars, as evidence for the route by which new settlers reached north-east Wales during the Late Bronze Age (Savory, 1971b, p. 23) and the proximity of this site to two hillforts—Symond's Yat and Little Doward, of which the former is a promontory site—is surely significant. One might add another bronze pin, apparently of Late Bronze Age type, which is known to have been brought to light by clandestine excavations in the Lynx Cave, Llanferres (Denbighshire), a few years ago. There is no need for me to repeat the reasons I have given (1971a and b) for relating both pins and horse harness to contacts, through Wessex, with Lower Normandy and central France rather than to trade with Scandinavia. But I have also pointed out that the associated pottery not only at Dinorben but at Symond's Yat, Bromfield, Caynham Camp and Rhuddlan reflects the spread of the native British Middle Bronze Age tradition of Wessex northwards from the Severn estuary; similar pottery was found in Ogof-yr-esgryn, Glyntawe (Brecknockshire) (Savory, 1958a, p. 46, Fig. 4) and in the Lesser Garth Cave, Radyr (Glamorganshire) (Savory, 1967, p. 35, Fig. 3). Only one decorated sherd, in Wales, might be thought to reflect the influence of the French early Urnfield Rilled Ware group (Savory, 1971a, p. 256, Fig. 2). This fact, and the absence of any burial of Continental Urnfield type from the Welsh Marches precludes any idea of a mass-movement of invaders from the Continent, but it may well be that the Wessex peasants who spread northwards did so under the impulsion and even the military leadership of a limited number of foreigners, and it may be significant that the sites on the south coast of England which have sometimes been described as invasion bases of the Late Bronze Age–Iron Age transition are large promontory forts e.g., Bindon and Hengistbury Head—and have their counterpart in a vast promontory fort on the north-western corner of the Côtentin peninsula (La Hague Dicke), which to judge by an unpublished C-14 date, may have been first constructed in the Late Bronze Age. However that may be, the two very large promontory forts which command the approaches to the Upper Severn basin—one of them, on the Breiddin, founded in the Late Bronze Age—certainly form part of an enduring tradition of large hillfort building, presumably related to large concentrations of people or of cattle, which characterise the Marches, but in Wales itself only penetrate deeply along the northern seaboard. How far hillfort building on any scale may have spread westwards in Wales, before the end of the Bronze Age, is a question which at present can only be considered in relation to the more general question of Late Bronze Age cultural groups in Wales.

B. The Late Bronze Age Cultural Groups of Wales

When in 1958 I sought to relate the regional implement groups of the Late Bronze Age to the beginnings of the historical tribal units of Wales (Savory, 1958a, p. 49f.) I was concerned not so much with the middle "Wilburton" phase of the southern British Late Bronze Age as the final phase after *c* 750 B.C. during which local types of axe-head emerged and the "Carp's tongue" industry flourished in northern France and south-eastern England. Now, however, the radiocarbon dates from Dinorben suggest that the earliest hillforts of the Welsh Marches were being built by the time the products of the Wilburton industry had reached the area, perhaps even earlier, and that whatever may have been the origins of their builders, most of their inhabitants had a cultural community with the Middle Bronze Age inhabitants of southern England, whose characteristic pottery forms had spread as far as Brecknock while Type II razors and Type III rapiers were still in use there (Savory, 1968a, 34f.). As I showed in 1958 (1958a, p. 32) and Burgess has confirmed (1968a, Fig. 8), Wilburton types did not come into general use in Wales. Almost all the finds are concentrated in a limited area on the north-east centred on Guilsfield (Fig. 2), precisely the area which is dominated by the great Breiddin and Llanymynech promontory forts and is liable to be most affected by trade and folk movement using the Severn valley. Our distribution map (Fig. 1) shows that the Wessex Middle and Late Bronze Age types of pottery have a somewhat wider distribution, but one that is still markedly eastern, and reflects similar origins. It is true, of course, that a few Wilburton types have so far been found at the Breiddin with a socketed axe, but the "Thorndon Park" socketed knife belongs to a later horizon. In the succeeding phase, too, the "Carp's tongue" industry and the contemporary barbed spearheads of Burgess's "Broadward" group (Burgess, 1968a, Fig. 16) have an extremely limited distribution in Wales. As Burgess agrees, one must suppose that most of Wales was served, as before, by local industries which produced the "South Wales" socketed axes or certain later types of palstave which are common in north-west Wales (Savory, 1958a, Figs 13 and 14).

It would, of course, be dangerous to assume that the distribution of the products of a particular Late Bronze Age industry necessarily coincides with a true cultural group and it should be noted that the "South Wales" industry largely developed within the range of distribution of the Wessex biconical urns and related pottery in the Bristol Channel area (Fig. 2). But it may be significant that in the south-western part of the westerly, or Irish Channel area of Wales, which was the least receptive of Wilburton types and their successors, a distinctive class of Late Bronze Age pottery now seems to be emerging— one, moreover which has links across the Irish Channel. This class is characterised by bucket or barrel-shaped jars with multiple perforations immediately below the rim, presumably made to secure some kind of perishable covering. These urns are found at the Culver Hole Cave, Llangennith (Glamorganshire) and Llanarth (Cardiganshire) (Savory, 1958a, Figs 4, 8, 10, 14), and part of the rim of a similar vessel has recently been found in a coastal rock-shelter near St. Govan's Head, Bosherston (Pembrokeshire), for information of which I am indebted to Mr. Melvyn Davies. Jars with perforated rims are now known from a number of Irish sites (Fig. 1) some of which are hillforts, and though their chronological range is not as yet well-defined they seem to belong broadly to the Late Bronze Age and Early Iron Age (Raftery, 1970a). This emergence of an Irish Channel ceramic province in the Late Bronze Age cannot be altogether unconnected with the economic boundary which develops about the same time between the spheres of the Irish, Bristol Channel and "Wallington" metal industries on the one hand and the "Carp's tongue" group on the other and warns us that there may have been political factors as well which would have hindered the advance of early hillfort building groups, organised by foreigners, westwards from the Marches. For Ireland, *pace* G. Eógan (1964), never knew a true Wilburton phase, any more than did most of Wales, and there is little to separate the early "Bishopsland" phase of the Late Bronze Age from the later "Dowris" one, which represents a long development of the Irish metal-working tradition with new types adapted as required from the Continent but essentially local in character. Many "Dowris" types, especially in the field of gold ornaments, did not reach Wales to the same extent as did those of the Bishopsland phase, and it is likely that Ireland and Wales became progressively isolated from each other as foreign influences penetrated Wales more deeply, after the seventh century B.C. But there seems to have been a time, in the eighth and seventh century B.C., when Wales shared a number of metal types with Ireland—notably bronze swords—and was importing such things as cauldrons and socketed sickles from across the Irish Channel, or entertaining the Irish smiths who made them, and this may be the horizon to which the perforated-rim jars belong in Wales, and during which the "south Wales" axe-heads were made. It was brought to an end, as it seems, in most parts of Wales, by a renewed and deeper penetration of Continental influences in Wales.

C. The Hallstatt C–D Phase in Wales

It has long been maintained that the Hallstatt stage of the Continental Early Iron Age had little impact on Britain, but this arises mainly from the failure of well-defined Continental groups with distinctive pottery and metal-work types, known chiefly from well-equipped cemeteries in quite limited areas of eastern France and south central Europe, to appear in Britain—a failure which is almost equally marked, in most parts of Britain, in the ensuing early La Tène phase. In fact, it can now be seen that the spread of Continental forms to Wessex and the Severn basin by the well-trodden routes through Lower Normandy to the Hampshire and Dorset coasts, to some extent as a result of small-scale immigration, increased during the sixth century B.C., but that the immediate sources of these influences in France lay outside the area in which the culture represented by the late Hallstatt inhumation cemeteries of eastern France developed, hence the failure of late Hallstatt forms of brooch to appear in Britain. Moreover, it must have been during this century that the All Cannings Cross ceramic tradition, with its furrowed carinated bowls, often haematited, spread to Wessex and onwards as far as Old Oswestry hillfort, on the borders of North Wales, as well as to the East Riding. By this time, too, the practice of reproducing in coarse pottery the forms of bronze vessels—shouldered "situlae" from the "Kurd" type onwards (Hawkes and Smith, 1957) and, in the Upper Thames basin, "Irish" cauldrons (Harding 1972, pp. 75–77)—had become well-established. Pottery in the latter tradition, shouldered and often with a flattened, expanded rim, now not only spreads through the Marches, appearing at some hillforts, e.g., Croft Ambrey, Breiddin and Moel-y-gaer (Rhosesmor, Flintshire), but is found in settlement sites on the South Wales seaboard as far as Pembrokeshire and in north-west Wales, at Castell Odo (Alcock, 1960, pp. 121–131). At the same time certain Hallstatt "C" and "D" metal forms, notably swords (later daggers), razors and pins, were either imported or locally imitated by British bronze-smiths (Cowen, 1967 and Burgess, 1968a, pp. 26–33). To the exotic bronze pins which in the Marches reflect the influence of the Urnfield Culture of the Continent can now be added swan-necked pins of Hallstatt "C" affinity: an iron one, with cupped terminal to hold an ornamental substance, keyed with an iron septum, is included in the unpublished material from Moel Hiraddug hillfort, Flintshire along with fragmentary ironwork which appears to have eastern French Hallstatt "C"–"D" connections, and another iron one has been discovered more recently at the same site (Davies, 1971). More common in Wales, as in other parts of Britain, is the ring-headed form of pin, made of bronze or iron, which is represented at Dinorben hillfort (Gardner and Savory, 1964, pp. 131–132) at Merthyr Mawr Warren (Grimes, 1951a, p. 711) and Penmaen, Glamorganshire (in the collection of the Royal Institution of Wales, Swansea) and at a promontory fort at Bosherston (Pembrokeshire) (Hogg, 1965, p. 134f.). This type has been looked upon as an insular British invention (Dunning, 1934a, p. 272 and Hodson, 1964b, p. 103) but there are a number of quite closely related pins from Hallstatt "C" sites in Languedoc (Louis and Taffanel, 1958, p. 136, Fig. 116.3; there are many examples from the Cayla hillfort, Mailhac (Aude) and others in Cahors and Albi Museums) which form a link between the British examples and the common Urnfield Culture pins with rolled heads.

In South Wales, the exotic forms in the well-known Llyn Fawr and Cardiff hoards must be related in a general way to the extension of Continental Hallstatt "C" influence to the western side of Britain, mainly by the routes followed by elements of the Urnfield Culture through Lower Normandy. Both hoards contain razors of a Burgundian Hallstatt "C" form (Grimes, 1951a, Figs 66.10 and 72.12) and the former seems to illustrate a blending of Continental Hallstatt "C" (razor, belt-fittings, winged object and iron sword) and Irish (cauldrons, socketed sickles) elements at a time when iron was being used for the first time by metal workers in western Britain (wrought iron spear-head and socketed sickle: compare the iron vase-headed pin from Ffridd Faldwyn (O'Neil, 1942, Fig. 14.3) and the iron socketed axe-head from the Berwyns (Wheeler, 1925). The idea that there was some form of settlement at Llyn Fawr can be discounted and the most reasonable interpretation of the hoard is that it was thrown into the lake—a gloomy spot, overshadowed by the highest upland in Glamorgan—as an offering to the unseen powers of the place by raiders who had issued from the uplands of South Wales to attack some rich settlement on the seaboard of the Bristol Channel or in Herefordshire, comparable to those which preceded the hillforts at South Cadbury or Ham Hill (Alcock, 1972b, c). It has, of course, generally been maintained that the winged objects in the Llyn Fawr hoard, like the belt plaque, with their Belgian analogues, support the theory of a spread of Hallstatt "C" influences from the Low Countries across the North Sea to the Thames estuary and thence west-wards (Alcock, 1961), but the razors at Llyn Fawr and Cardiff are Burgundian, not Belgian, and the swan-necked pins at South Cadbury and Moel Hiraddug, as well as the ring-headed pins just mentioned, support the view that the main source of the Continental influences in Somerset and the Welsh Marches in the sixth century B.C. lay much further south, in the same direction as they had lain in the preceding centuries. As before, the horse harness and weapons hint at the presence of an immigrant warrior class. This time, however, the nature of the deposit at Llyn Fawr probably reflects the opposition to this new element in the population of the Severn basin and the regions to the south of it, coming perhaps from the patrons of the south Wales axe industry, and no doubt it is in this context of tribal warfare that we should see the growth of hillfort building which now takes place in the Welsh Marches.

As in the earlier phases of the Late Bronze Age, the appearance of Continental elements in the final phase of the Bronze Age of southern Britain, in this case Hallstatt "C–D" in character, seems to have been accompanied by the spread of hillfort building. By now, however, hillforts were being built in contour as well as promontory positions and construction with single or double palisades, or timber-laced "box" ramparts, had replaced timber staging of the Wittnau and Dinorben type. Moreover, whereas little can be said as yet about the forms of entrance adopted in the first phase at Dinorben and the Breiddin, a distinctive form of deeply and sharply inturned entrance now appears in the Welsh Marches (Fig. 8) and survives there, in various forms, until the immediate pre-Roman period (Stanford, 1971). In the broadest terms, this tradition must relate to Continental practice, as represented by single-palisaded sites of late Hallstatt date at Koberstadt in Starkenburg (Behn, 1936, Figs 28–33) and Kyberg in Bavaria (Torbrügge and Uenze, 1968, Fig. 85) and the early stages in the development of the entrance at the Trundle hillfort in Sussex (Curwen, 1954, Fig. 78). The earliest sites of this tradition in the Marches, on present evidence, are the first forts at Ffridd Faldwyn (Montgomery) (O'Neil, 1942) and on Titterstone Clee (Shropshire) (O'Neil, 1934). Both have long, sharply inturned entrance passages, without guard-chambers. The latter site had a timber-revetted bank and a bridge in front of the gate, and was replaced by a dry-stone revetted rampart and entrance passage with rectangular guard-chambers. The former had a double palisade for a rampart only 5 ft thick which probably had horizontal timber shuttering for an earthen core (Fig. 7). Similar narrow box ramparts are known at Hollingbury in Sussex and Grimthorpe in the East Riding. The guard-chamber tradition, now so strongly represented in the Marches, will be considered later (p. 265 below); its beginnings, at Rainsborough Camp (Northamptonshire) (Avery et al., 1967), Leckhampton (Gloucestershire) (Champion, 1971b) and Moel Hiraddug (J. L. Davies, 1970) may go back to the sixth century B.C. but they are later than the earliest forts at Ffridd Faldwyn and Titterstone Clee.

From the heavy concentration of inturned entrances in the Marches and their apparent failure to become well-established further west in Wales (Fig. 8) one might conclude that their introduction was due to the foreign element which also introduced timber palisades and timber-framed box ramparts, often used in southern England and on the Marches to enclose very large areas. Within such large hillforts recent excavations by Stanford at Croft Ambrey, Credenhill and Midsummer Camp (1970, 1971, 1972a, b, 1974) and Cunliffe at Danebury (Hampshire) (1972a) have demonstrated the presence of large numbers of rectangular wooden dwellings, sometimes arranged in rows along straight streets, and something of this sort may have existed at Ffridd Faldwyn (p. 262 below). Though the lavish use of timber, already established on a much earlier horizon at Dinorben, relates to the central European traditions of the Urnfield Culture (Hawkes, 1971), and the rectangular house evidently springs from the same context and clearly intrudes on the native British Bronze Age tradition of the circular house, the recent evidence for town planning surely points to an extension as far north as Britain of those Ionian Greek influences, operating from Massalia and other outposts on the west Mediterranean seaboard, which have long been recognised as a powerful factor in the Celtic heartland of the sixth century B.C. The influence of Greek architects on fortification is as apparent at the Heuneburg on the Upper Danube (Dehn, 1958) as it is at the Iberian town of Ullastret which developed from late Urnfield beginnings, not very far from Emporion in north-east Catalonia. At the former site a brick wall with rectangular bastions was built on stone foundations, as was done at the Cayla, Mailhac (Aude) under Greek influence (Information from Mme. Odette Taffanel); at Ullastret a chain of massive trunconic towers with "Cyclopean" walling was built, early in the sixth century B.C., and subsequently connected by curtain walls (Oliva, 1970). What must surely be native settlements of about the same date, defended by walls with rectangular or semicircular bastions, have been recorded in southern Ardèche, at Lussas near St. Privat (Hogg, 1969, p. 268, Fig. 8) and at Dent de Retz, between Vallon and St. Remèze (Viré, 1909, p. 415). It may well be that the trunconic dry-stone tower incorporated in the rampart of the Camp de Bierre, Merri (Orne), where recent excavations have suggested occupation during the Late Bronze Age (Edeine, 1965 and Dastugue, 1971) reflects an extension of this Greek architectural influence as far as Lower Normandy. It is therefore not unlikely that such features as the bastions which flanked the entrance passage of the early hillfort on Crickley Hill (Gloucestershire) (see above pp. 166–172) in its second phase and the bastion which was added to the timber-laced rampart of the second phase at Dinorben are ultimately of Ionian Greek inspiration, along with early examples of sharply inturned entrances at Ullastret and the Cayla and on many British sites, and most striking of all, the attempts at town-planning at some early hillforts in Britain, to which we have referred already; although the connection is less obvious at present, the guard-chambers which are such a striking feature of hillforts in the Welsh Marches may prove in the end to have a similar explanation. But above all, the numerous large and well organised hillforts of the Marches, with their growing evidence for habitation by a comparatively large population, with an influential foreign element, are evidence of an intrusive culture which needed to maintain its occupation of the most fertile land in western Britain against the pressure of hostile neighbours. Those neighbours must surely have lain to the west, and it is the reaction of this indigenous population of upland Wales that we must now examine more closely.

D. The Native Reaction

Beyond the area in the central and northern Marches, where we can be confident of the existence of a hillfort building tradition from the Late Bronze Age onwards, related to large settlements inhabited by an agricultural population which was probably mainly of southern British origin but may have had foreign overlords, lies a vast tract in southern, western and north-western Wales in which no hillfort large or small has yet been shown to have been built as early as the Late Bronze Age, or even the Hallstatt period. It may be that the earliest fort at Pen Dinas, lying as it does at the beginning of a long sequence of development is as early as the sixth century B.C.; its timber-revetted box rampart would not be inconsistent with this (Forde et al., 1963) and the position of this site, between the mouths of the two principal streams of north Cardiganshire and opposite the head of the Severn valley and the main focus of early hillfort building in Wales (Fig. 5) marks it out for early settlement. It is certainly possible that some at least of the numerous small or medium-sized univallate forts in south or west Wales belong to an early phase of the prehistoric Iron Age and one might single out the promontory fort at

Bosherston (Pembrokeshire), with its long sequence of development and ring-headed pin (Hogg, 1965, p. 134f.) and the very large promontory fort on Wooltack Point (Pembrokeshire) (Hogg, 1965, p. 147) from among the so far unexcavated sites as ones which might prove to be early. But the fact remains that none of the various finds so far made, in all these regions, of small quantities of pottery which would be conventionally classed as "Iron Age A" can be shown to be contemporary with a hillfort, and some can be shown to be earlier than one. The latter is certainly the case at Dinas Powys (Glamorganshire) (Alcock, 1963a, pp. 16–19) and Coygan Camp (Carmarthenshire) (Wainwright, 1967a, p. 20), while the sherds from Radyr (Glamorganshire) and Grassholm (Pembrokeshire) (Grimes, 1951a, pp. 719–720), like those from Merthyr Mawr Warren (Glamorganshire) (Savory, 1952b), Marlborough Grange (Glamorganshire) (Savory, 1969, pp. 64–66) and Caldey (Lacaille and Grimes, 1961, pp. 40–44) are not connected with fortified sites. All these Bristol Channel finds seem to be connected with movements affecting the seaboard only and may simply reflect trading like that which linked the small ports of south Wales and north Devon in early post-medieval times.

The one site in north-west Wales which has so far yielded pottery which could be classed as "Iron Age A" is Castell Odo, and here again the settlement with which it was associated was not originally fortified, though the excavator believes that an attempt to defend it with a palisade was made just before the whole settlement was burnt down (Alcock, 1960, pp. 84–93). It may well be that the early settlers here were, as Alcock says, aliens who imported a technique of timber construction, both for houses and for defences, as well as pottery, from some well-wooded area which could equally well be north-east Wales, the central Marches or the lands near Bristol Channel, and have used coastal routes to reach the Lleyn. He may also be right in thinking that the later stone-built huts and rampart revetments at Castell Odo reflect the reaction of the native North Wales culture after the aliens had been overwhelmed or dislodged. But it is important to note that the houses in the first settlement at Castell Odo seem to have been round and that the palisade with which they were to have been defended was the first of a series of small ring-works, like those which are above all characteristic of south and west Wales, with a northern outlier in south Lleyn (Fig. 13). The settlement type here certainly contrasts with that of the stone-built forts, often large, of north-west Wales, as well as the large forts of the Marches, with their tendency to timber-staged, -framed or -laced ramparts and rectangular wooden huts; the affinity rather lies with the small forts and ring-works, hill-top or hill-slope, of central and southern Wales.

Until more evidence has been obtained by excavation, one must be content not to have a very clear idea of the extent of very early hillfort building west of the Marches. But it seems likely that there was some delay in its spread, bound up with the process of acculturation of an independent Late Bronze Age population which was served by local bronze industries in south-east and north-west Wales respectively, and it seems that some relatively large uni-vallate hillforts in south Wales belong to quite a late horizon in the Early Iron

Age, e.g. Castle Ditches, Llancarfan (Glamorganshire) (Hogg, 1972a, p. 14f.). It is also likely that cultural differences, as well as less favourable economic conditions, underlie the marked reduction in size of fortified settlements which is noticeable as one travels westwards into Wales from the Marches, in all areas except the northern seaboard (Fig. 5) (Hogg, 1972b). The smaller size of true hillforts in the west is clearly bound up with the much greater prevalence, in south, west and central Wales, of embanked or walled home-steads. Here was a population which continued, throughout the Iron Age, to be spread about the countryside, as it had, no doubt, been in the Bronze Age, whereas the imported peasants of the Marches were concentrated, very likely for security against the raids of the hill tribesmen to the west, in a relatively small number of towns and large villages (Stanford, 1972b). In this light, once again, one should see the Llyn Fawr hoard. Looking across the Bristol Channel one sees a similar situation, in west Somerset and Devon (A. Fox, 1969), where univallate ring-works like the Cornish "rounds" are numerous, large uni-vallate hillforts are mostly of uncertain date, and pottery of "A" tradition is scarce. We may also yet have to consider the possibility that the shared Irish Channel tendency—in the West Country, Wales and Ireland—to build ring-works, large or small, is connected in some way with the native British Late Neolithic and Early Bronze Age proclivity to enclosures of this form, built for ritual and other purposes (Wainwright, 1969), sites like Norton Fitzwarren being connecting links. The recent evidence from Ireland, which suggests a connection between Late Neolithic or Bronze Age cult centres and later hillforts (Raftery, 1970a and 1972 and Selkirk and Waterman, 1970) is particularly interesting in this respect.

If, however, we are to look upon a tendency to ring-works and fortified homesteads in south and mid Wales as a symptom of the acculturation of a surviving Bronze Age population, what are we to make of the ditchless, stone-walled forts of north-west Wales, with their outliers in the central Marches and in south-west Wales, which Hogg has presented as the work of "Secondary Iron Age" folk? (1958). The larger forts in north-west Wales—Pen y Gorddyn Fawr, Conway Mountain, Pen y Gaer (Llanbedr-y-cennin), Braich y Ddinas, Tre'r Ceiri, Garn Boduan, Carn Fadrun, Caer y Twr and Bwrdd Arthur—some of them with large numbers of "hut circles"—appear at first sight to continue the broad zone of large hillforts which stretches from the middle Severn to the Clwyd along the northern seaboard of Wales to the Lleyn. However tempting it may be to identify their builders with a surviving Late Bronze Age population, it will be necessary to consider, in the next section, the exotic features in their structure which may reflect the influence of new settlers, different from those who built the early hillforts of the Marches. In any case, we are still deprived of any direct evidence for the date when these large forts were first built and the only guidance we have is the fact that some Caernarvonshire walled forts—Dinorwig, Craig y Dinas and Pen y Gaer—had bivallate bank and ditch defences added to them at a later date, presumably before the Roman conquest (Hogg, 1972). For that matter, we have very little evidence for the date of the horizon in mid and south Wales when small homesteads first began to be surrounded with walls or earthen banks. Twyn Llechfaen, near Brecon, probably belongs to an early phase in the Iron Age (Savory, 1971d, pp. 18–22) and small enclosures at Pen y Crug, Brecon, Lodge Farm, Caerleon, Llanmelin (Monmouthshire) and Castle Ditches, Llancarfan (Glamorganshire) were replaced by larger hillforts, of which the first three were multivallate while the fourth, though univallate, had associated with it "Iron Age B" pottery (Hogg, 1972a, p. 14f.). The remarkable ring work at Walesland (Pembrokeshire), with its weak primary defences and peripheral timber structures (Wainwright, 1971a) may have been built as early as the third century B.C. But we are not, as yet, in a position to say that any of these Welsh regional types of fortified settlement began as early as the end of the Bronze Age, or to be sure of where they fit into the cultural sequence. We must be content, in the next two sections, to study the structural types which are represented, their distribution in Wales and their probable sources.

III. The Evolution of Hillfort Architecture in Wales

A. Rampart Structure in the Marches (c 600–300 B.C.)

In the Marches, where we have most information, it is now possible to see that hillfort architecture during the early part of the Early Iron Age went through roughly the same phases of development as it did further south, subject to local geological conditions, and this is understandable in view of the general cultural community between the area and the central part of southern England. This community emerges in the tendency for palisade defences to be replaced by timber-framed box ramparts and for the latter to be replaced by dump ramparts without timber framing, and for single ramparts to be replaced by bivallate and multivallate defences. But there is also a tendency for the two areas to share an alternative construction method for box ramparts, no doubt as a result of local geological conditions, with dry-stone revetment walls laced together with horizontal timbers, which are sometimes supported by vertical timbers in the core of the rampart. At the same time, resort to multiple ramparts, box or dump, was already being made on some sites in the early part of the Iron Age in both areas and in districts where it was convenient, as at Croft Ambrey (Stanford, 1967 and 1971) dump ramparts were already being built at the beginning of the period. At Twyn-y-gaer (Monmouthshire) Castle Ditches, Eddisbury (Cheshire) and Titterstone Clee (Shropshire), as at Blewburton Hill (Berkshire), the earliest defence consisted of a single palisade: at the first site this palisade was preceded by a wattle fence (Information L. A. Probert); at the other sites it was apparently the first defence (Varley, 1952; O'Neil, 1934; Harding, 1967). The double palisade, or more exactly the box rampart with two rows of more or less widely spaced timber uprights which were probably laced together, although the clear evidence for this seems to have been preserved only at Blewburton Hill (Berkshire), Danebury (Hampshire) and Ranscombe (Sussex) (Harding, 1967, Cunliffe, 1970, Burstow and Holleyman, 1964), certainly appears on an early horizon in lowland England and at the Breiddin two lines of posts actually preceded a single line of posts bedded in a palisade trench. These successive lines of defence are certainly early, possibly contemporary with some of the Late Bronze Age metal-work on the site, but the double rows of posts are only about 80 cm apart and are interpreted by the excavator as a revetment for the front of an earthen bank (Musson, 1972); the later single line of posts may then also have revetted the front of an earthen bank, as in the original inner rampart at Castle Ditches, Eddisbury (Cheshire) (Varley, 1952). At Ffridd Faldwyn, however, the two lines of post-holes in the first phase of the original fort ("Period II") (O'Neil, 1942, Fig. 6) are about 2 m apart (Fig. 7), as at Danebury (Hampshire), Hollingbury (Sussex) and Grimthorpe (East Riding). It is on the general evidence for the early date of such structures, and for the evidence on the site itself for a long sequence of structural phases, that one should date this first phase at Ffridd Faldwyn as early as the seventh or sixth century B.C., rather than in the light of Stanford's somewhat precarious arguments from post-renewals, which would in fact push this phase back to the eighth century B.C. (Stanford, 1971, p. 43). Avery may well be right in arguing that the upright posts in ramparts of this kind were masked by piles of turves or other soft material and so were not strictly of "box" type (Avery et al., 1967, p. 249f.). True "box" ramparts, in which timber-lacing, with or without upright posts, is masked by dry-stone revetment walls, are rather better represented in the Marches. Sites like Caynham Camp (Shropshire) (Phase 1), Castle Ditches, Eddisbury (Phase 3) and Maiden Castle, Bickerton (Cheshire) (Varley, 1940, Fig. 12) and Dinorben (Phase 2) (Savory, 1971b) (Fig. 4) have their counterparts in the limestone country of Gloucestershire, at Crickley Hill (Dixon, 1972) and Leckhampton (Champion, 1971b). These last two sites can be assigned on the strength of the associated pottery to the beginning of the local Iron Age (sixth–fifth century B.C.)—to roughly the same horizon, in fact, as Rainsborough Camp (Northamptonshire) with its tiered dry-stone revetment walls and timber-staging. The Welsh examples of this type of construction are Dinorben (Period II) (Fig. 4) and Ffridd Faldwyn (Period III). The first of these lacks the vertical timbers which appear at Crickley Hill, Castle Ditches, Eddisbury and Maiden Castle, Bickerton, but they both resemble these sites in that the ends of the transverse, horizontal timbers were not exposed. But at both these sites, as at South Cadbury (Somerset) (Alcock, 1972c, pp. 122–130), the phase of dry-stone revetment succeeds one of timber-framing or -staging and this must be borne in mind when gauging the chronological range of such construction in the Marches; South Cadbury, indeed, did not see a complete masking of the timber frame with the local limestone slabs in Rampart B and the horizon on which this occurred seems to have been relatively late. The development of massive dry-stone revetment walls, with masked timber-lacing, might appear to be a local British development, spreading from the west Midlands to north Wales, distinct from the Continental "Preist" tradition reflected at South Cadbury, but it must be remembered that Continental parallels to the Crickley Hill-Dinorben type of structure occur at Montauban-sous-Buzenol in Belgian Luxembourg and at the Cap d'Erquy on the northern coast of Brittany (Savory, 1971b, p. 28) and these may prove to be derived from Urnfield Culture ramparts like those of Switzerland (p. 246 above). In the latter case in fact, a radiocarbon count suggests construction in the fourth or third century B.C., while the similar counts relating to Dinorben, Period II suggest a somewhat earlier date. The development of this tradition in the Marches may well have begun by the fifth century B.C., but the question of its duration is bound up with that of diffusion and the growth of regional traditions based largely on geological conditions.

The diffusion of the timber-laced, dry-stone revetted type of rampart in Wales is still somewhat obscure and the relatively heavy incidence of modern, large-scale excavation in the north-east may be somewhat misleading. The presence of some form of timber structure in a rampart, especially when there are no vertical posts, the sockets for which would be revealed by careful excavation, is usually indicated only when a conflagration, deliberate or accidental, has produced large deposits of slaked lime, or vitrified material, according to the nature of the stone employed in the structure. It is in this way that the presence of timber lacing is revealed in the second ramparts at Dinorben and Ffridd Faldwyn, and clinker picked up from the surface at Caer Eini hillfort (Merionethshire) and Castle Bank, Llansanffraid yn Elfael (Radnorshire) has been thought by some to indicate the presence of timber structures which have been burnt (Gresham, 1967, pp. 137–139) and Alcock, 1972b, p. 31). Further north, at Moel Hiraddug, extensive explorations in recent years do not seem to have revealed any traces of timber structures in the body of a massive inner rampart with dry-stone revetment walls and rubble core, even though the first constructional phase of the main gateway through this rampart now appears to be earlier than a hearth in which was found a swan-necked iron pin of Hallstatt "C" type (Houlder, 1961 and Davies, 1971). Small-scale excavations by L. L. Stephen in the large univallate hillfort at Llwyn Bryn Dinas, Llangedwyn about 1955 similarly did not reveal clear evidence of timber lacing behind the dry-stone revetment wall (I am indebted to L. L. Stephen for descriptions and photographs of his sections). In the south, extensive excavations by L. A. Probert at Twyn y Gaer, Cwmyoy (Monmouthshire) have not so far yielded such evidence in the dry-stone box rampart which followed the early palisade defences. Further afield there is very little evidence of any kind of timber structure, whether or not associated with dry-stone revetment walls. Though the original northern fort at Pen Dinas, Aberystwyth, with timber-revetted rampart, was followed by a dry-stone revetted rampart on the south summit (Forde et al., 1963), Spurgeon points out that out of about 80 fortified settlements in Montgomeryshire only three—the Breiddin, Craig Rhiwarth (Llangynog) and Pen y gaer, Llandiloes—can be seen to have had dry-stone revetment walls (1969, p. 12f.). It is therefore not easy to demonstrate that the dry-stone revetted walls at Pen Dinas are due to renewed influence in north Cardiganshire from the hillforts of the central Marches, and they may in fact be part of the walled fort complex spreading through the Irish Channel areas of Wales. That the latter complex is indeed distinct from the group we have just been considering seems to be established by a number of individual features which we shall examine later on (p. 267 below), but their distributions overlap and the dividing line between them must remain debatable. The Breiddin, indeed, has been shown by the recent excavations to have had its second timber-revetted bank replaced by stone-revetted wall, without ditch, at a time when Herefordshire stamped ware and involuted brooches were reaching the site, in the third or second century B.C. (Musson, 1972). On the other hand the southern fort at Pen Dinas, Llwyn Bryn Dinas and Twyn y Gaer are ditched forts and may perhaps because of this be grouped with the timber-laced walled forts of the Marches.

The early box ramparts of the northern Marches, we have seen, cannot as yet be shown to have had many counterparts in the southern Marches. Their place in that region seems to have been taken to a large extent by dump ramparts of earth or rubble, without revetments, dry-stone or timber. At Croft Ambrey Stanford's extensive excavations have shown that these were in use throughout the long history of the site, the first one having been built to defend the first promontory fort on the plateau side, long before the construction of the first dry-stone lined guard-rooms at the entrances of the main fort (Stanford, 1967 and 1971). Even if one hesitates fully to accept the excavator's chronological system in so far as it is based upon assumptions about the frequency of post renewals, the chronological range of the guard-chamber tradition, as indicated by radiocarbon counts as well as ordinary archaeological evidence (see below, p. 265), suggests that the first fort at Croft Ambrey could well be as early as the sixth century B.C. and therefore contemporary with or earlier than many of the dry-stone revetted box ramparts further north. The first fort at the Roveries, for example, no great distance away in Shropshire, had such a rampart and an inturned entrance with rectangular guard-chambers of the classical "Cornovian" type (see p. 265 below). It seems that in Herefordshire dump ramparts were liable to be built where the subsoil permitted the rapid digging of the great ditches necessary for such earthworks, but where it did not, as at Midsummer Hill, dry-stone revetted box ramparts might still be built as late as the fourth century B.C. (Stanford, 1972b, p. 309). This should be borne in mind, when considering the chronology of dump ramparts and revetted ramparts in south Wales (p. 279 below).

Multiple ramparts, too, made an early appearance in the central Marches, at least in the special bivallate form, and the ramparts on the excavated sites have all proved to be of the box, dry-stone fronted type. At Old Oswestry these followed the primary palisade and were associated with pottery of Iron Age "A" character, including the famous unpublished fragments of furrowed, carinated bowls of All Cannings Cross type (Varley, 1948). The similar defences at the Wrekin appear to belong to the same horizon (Kenyon, 1942). In Wales, the timber-laced rampart of Period II at Dinorben was soon reinforced for part of its length by a second rampart and ditch (Gardner and Savory, 1964) and the same seems to have been the case with the timber-laced rampart at Ffridd Faldwyn (O'Neil, 1942, p. 14f.) and the dry-stone-revetted rampart at the Breiddin (O'Neil, 1937). These early bivallate constructions in the northern Marches have their lowland counterparts in the newly discovered circular fort at Mucking (Essex), in the primary fill of the outer ditch of which a bronze pin of Hallstatt type was found, and at Rains-borough Camp (Northamptonshire), the whole history of which falls within the early phase of the insular Early Iron Age (Avery *et al.*, 1967). This evidence warns us against a too ready assumption that bivallate defences at unexcavated sites in other parts of Wales necessarily belong to a late stage in the Early Iron Age. We must agree with Stanford (1972b, p. 309) in distinguishing such sites from ones with three or more glacis-fronted ramparts, which certainly represent the final stage of hillfort development in Wessex, as well as at Old Oswestry and some other large sites in Herefordshire and Shropshire, and account for the appearance of such defences as an addition to primary stone forts in north Wales (p. 279 below).

B. *The Layout and Entrance Features of Hillforts in the Marches* (*c 600–300* B.C.)

1. *Layout*

The outstanding characteristic of the Marches hillforts, taken as a whole, in comparison with those in most parts of Wales, is their greater average size. This has been brought out very thoroughly by Hogg in a series of analytical maps (1972b) but is illustrated sufficiently well by our maps (Figs 5 and 16) relating broadly to the early and late periods respectively. Stanford, moreover (1972b) has brought home to us the evidence for the existence of a large population on many of these sites, occupying large numbers of rectangular timber-framed dwellings which in some cases, at least, were arranged in rows flanking paths—a distant reflection of Greek town-planning due, no doubt, to contacts with southern Gaul. The only site in Wales where the existence of this degree of town-planning has so far been suggested by post-hole patterns is Ffridd Faldwyn (Stanford, 1972a), where the parallel rows of large post-holes inside the inner fort were related by the excavator to his period IV, when the fort was enlarged to enclose 10 acres after having been burnt down and probably abandoned for a considerable time. Stanford may be right in interpreting this post-hole system in the same way as those at Croft Ambrey, Credenhill and Midsummer Hill, and it may be that something similar existed at the very large fort on Moel Hiraddug (Flintshire). Here unfortunately, though the existence of rectangular houses, both timber-framed and dry-stone walled, seems to be established (Davies, 1970 and 1971), the interpretation of the elaborate post-hole system behind the main rampart seems still to be in doubt (see p. 289 below); here, and at Moel y Gaer, Rhosesmor (Flintshire), where recent emergency excavations also appear to have revealed rectangular structures, one must await more detailed publication (but see below, p. 310). At the Breiddin, at least, one can see that though the rectangular tradition was established early in the history of the fort, and continued into the dry-stone phase and the time of stamped pottery and involuted brooches, houses of this type were scattered around as loosely as hut circles further west (Musson, 1972). At Dinorben, too, Stanford has suggested that many of the post-holes could be related to the framework of rectangular houses, but acceptance of this idea would involve the demolition of other structures which are really much more plausible: in fact the large numbers of rounded hut platforms scattered around this site, many of which have been excavated as fully as the conditions on the site allowed, show that houses here were normally circular in the early period (p. 288 below) (Gardner and Savory, 1964, pp. 66–72, Fig. 3). Elsewhere in Wales there is evidence for occasional rectangular dwellings in the Early Iron Age (Fig. 9) but nothing to suggest that these formed part of large systems, or had replaced a long-established local tradition of round house building (p. 271 below). It is the complete dominance of rectangular house building in Herefordshire and possibly parts of Shropshire, in planned lay-outs within very large hillforts, which is most suggestive of an intrusive culture the ramifications of which in Wales require further investigation: at present such evidence as there is suggests only a partial penetration of the upper Severn basin and north-east Wales at the expense of haphazard arrangements of circular dwellings. The most recent season of excavations at Crickley Hill (Gloucestershire) promontory fort (Dixon, 1973), has shown that the rectangular houses of the first (probably Late Bronze Age) phase of activity there were large aisled structures quite different from the small four-post structures of the Iron Age at Danebury and Credenhill, and these may provide the best explanation of the parallel rows of post-holes which flank an open space leading in from the entrance of the inner fort at Ffridd Faldwyn.

The exceptional size of sites like Moel Hiraddug (23 acres), Pen-y-cloddiau (Denbighshire) (52 acres) and Moel Fenlli (Denbighshire) (21 acres) prompts comparison with the larger Herefordshire hillforts and raises the question whether their function was similar, even if, as we know in the case of one of them, they all contained large numbers of round rather than rectangular houses for much of their long history, and the finds made in them suggest that the culture of their inhabitants tended to diverge increasingly from that of the Herefordshire people (p. 277 below). If they did contain a relatively large permanent population, as the excavations at Moel Hiraddug now suggest, the old view that their size reflects use as cattle *kraals* must be very largely abandoned. As we shall see (p. 273 below) the pastoral economy natural to most parts of Wales did bring about changes in the layout of large hillforts which had been characteristic of the Marches in the earliest phase, in the form of the addition of lateral, terminal or concentric enclosures to the original fort (p. 276 below), and this is found both at Moel Hiraddug and at Croft Ambrey itself. But the numbers of circular hut-floors at Moel Hiraddug and, indeed, at Dinorben and Moel Fenlli, can now be seen to indicate that their primary function was not that of cattle *kraals*, and this may apply to many, if not all, of the much more numerous sites, in the border regions of Wales, which fall into the intermediate range in size between 3 and 15 acres and like the larger sites are predominantly contour, rather than promontory forts. Many of these sites are univallate, with ditch and sometimes a counterscarp bank, and Beacon Ring on the Long Mountain in Montgomeryshire is a good example (Fig. 3) (Spurgeon, 1972, p. 336). Here 5 acres are enclosed by a massive rampart which was probably of box form; there are no entrance complications. The lesson of excavations on other sites in the Marches is surely that many of the numerous sites of similar size which now appear to have had multiple ramparts may have started like Beacon Ring, and may have had numerous rectangular or circular dwellings even though nothing is now visible on the surface of the interior. Perhaps, too, even if the culture of the inhabitants was not identical with that of the Herefordshire folk, they reflect much the same type of stable and enduring tribal organisation, ensured perhaps by royal dynasties, which enabled the Herefordshire hillforts to renew their timber structures for centuries without any great change. These were certainly not the foot-loose cowboys of Piggott (1958, p. 25), and Alcock is no doubt right to stress the proximity of the large hillforts of Wales to arable land, as well as to summer pastures (1965, p. 187f.). The conclusions of Cunliffe (1971c) and Bradley (1971c) about the development of pastoral enclosures in southern England hardly apply to Wales and the Marches. Here large and well organised hillforts do indeed tend to have an early origin, in contrast to what Cunliffe says of Sussex, and one must suppose, at least as far as the Marches are concerned, a large population living by mixed agriculture in the early phase.

2. *Entrance features*

The enduring nature of the authority under which hillforts in the Marches were constructed, at least in the early period, and its wide scope, are above all proclaimed by their entrance features, about which we are relatively well informed because exploration has tended to concentrate on them.

Roads. Roads properly metalled with gravel or stone slabs as at Dinorben and Moel Hiraddug, running out through the entrance and sometimes showing signs of repeated repair (Fig. 1), speak for wheeled vehicles, military or civilian, which at least required a firm surface in the area close to the entrance, where traffic would have been most concentrated. How far they went is a fascinating but difficult question, as far as Wales and the Marches are concerned. But the community of military tradition in the other entrance features—bastions, "guard-chambers", bridges and deep inturns—found over a very wide area—may mean that a central authority maintained trackways connecting important centres and arranged for their metalling where particularly important.

The early phase. The earliest box-ramparted forts usually have simple entrances, as at Dinorben II (Fig. 4) and the first phases of the north-west and main inner entrances at Moel Hiraddug; at the former (Gardner and Savory, 1964, pp. 25–27) a slight recess behind the gate, on one side, may have served as a shelter for a guard. These early entrances, like the Period I entrance at Ffridd Faldwyn, had single gates but room for a vehicle to pass through; at Dinorben an outer pair of posts may indicate the presence of a wooden bridge connecting the ends of a parapet walk on either side of the entrance passage, and Dr. Gardner discovered that a solid semicircular bastion had been built in dry-stone walling against the original outer revetment wall of the fort to a total height of at least 11 ft, 20 ft west of the Period II entrance. The ultimate inspiration for such structures lies, as we have already seen, in the areas of southern Gaul which came under Greek influence in the sixth century B.C., but the more immediate parallel is provided by the reconstructed entrance of the Crickley Hill (Gloucestershire) promontory fort (Dixon, 1972), which is also believed to have had a bridge. The evidence for an early date at this site accords with the evidence at Dinorben and Moel Hiraddug already referred to (p. 252 above) for a sixth or fifth century date for the features described.

Guard-chambers. Both at Dinorben and Moel Hiraddug the early entrances and road surfaces were replaced by more elaborate ones; at the latter fort the two entrances through the main rampart were simply rebuilt in the same, or nearly the same position but provided with deep C-shaped recesses behind the gate, the north-western becoming a narrow postern with a single recess or "guard-chamber" and the main entrance having a pair of such chambers (Houlder, 1961 and Davies, 1970, p. 71) although it appears that it had at first only a single sub-rectangular chamber. The C-shaped form of these early guard-chambers recalls those associated with the western inner entrance at Rainsborough Camp (Northamptonshire) (Avery *et al.*, 1967) in phase 2 and at Leckhampton Camp (Gloucestershire) (Champion, 1971b); at the latter site there are entrance bastions rather like those at Crickley Hill. At Dinorben, on the other hand, the south-east entrance in Period III is in a different position, and has a pair of large rectangular guard-chambers set in thickened rampart terminals behind the single gate, which is approached by a sequence of renewed road surfaces, the last coming in from a different direction (Fig. 17). This type of dry-stone lined guard-chamber was once treated by the author as typical of the Cornovian and Deceanglian territory, where indeed it is well represented (Fig. 8)—at the Wrekin (Period II), Titterstone Clee (Period III), the Roveries (Period I), the Castle Ditches, Eddisbury, Moel y Gaer, Rhosesmor (Flintshire), Moel Arthur, Cilcain (Flintshire), Pen y Gloddiau, Nannau (Flintshire), Castell Cawr, Abergele (Denbighshire) and Pen y Gorddyn Fawr, Llanddulas (Denbighshire) (Gardner and Savory, 1964, pp. 87–89 and Forde-Johnston, 1964), but Stanford has since shown it to be characteristic of Credenhill, Croft Ambrey and Midsummer Camp in Herefordshire (1970, 1971 and 1972a and b) and to belong to a horizon defined by gate-post renewals and dated by radiocarbon and archaeological evidence to the late fourth and early third centuries B.C.—a date which would, in fact, accord very well with that suggested for Period III at Dinorben (Savory, 1971b, p. 29). There is also evidence for an initial phase of timber-framed rectangular guard-chamber building at Credenhill, Midsummer Camp and Castle Ditches, Eddisbury (Varley, 1952) and possibly at the Wrekin and Titterstone Clee, which would fall into the early fourth century B.C. It is in any case difficult to resist the conclusion that at some stage in the fifth or fourth centuries B.C. a large area in the west Midlands and the Marches came under the same rule, vested presumably in a royal dynasty and served by men who maintained a standardised tradition of military engineering over a long period. Such men would have had at their disposal local forced labour and would not trouble too much if such labour was better able to build a massive dump rampart, with ditch, in one area with a suitable subsoil, and a dry-stone fronted rampart in another. It is interesting, in this connection, to note that timber-revetted rectangular recesses of a different type, more related to the one found at Dinorben II, are known at St. Catharine's Hill (Hampshire) (Hawkes *et al.*, 1930) and at Danebury (Hampshire) (Cunliffe, 1972a) and are thought to have been first constructed at the latter site about the beginning of the fourth century B.C. In the eastern part of Wessex, at any rate, there are so far no signs of the guard-chamber tradition having evolved to the point we find in the west Midlands. Further west, however, it seems that vestiges of a series of single or paired guard-chambers with curving plank or dry-stone lined walls were found in the south-west entrance at South Cadbury (Somerset) and are dated there from the beginning of the fourth century B.C. onwards (Alcock, 1972c, pp. 130 and 162) and there is a possibility of rectangular guard-chambers in the first western entrance at Maiden Castle (Dorset) (Stanford, 1972a, p. 27).

Bridges. The provision of a bridge across the entrance passage, as at Dinorben II–IV (Fig. 17) and at Crickley Hill, was certainly widespread in the early phase of hillfort architecture in the Marches. It is very clearly demonstrated in Period I at Titterstone Clee, here again before the earliest guard-chambers (O'Neil, 1934) and it has been suggested in relation to the inner main entrance at Moel Hiraddug on the horizon of the C-shaped guard-chambers (Davies, 1969). At Croft Ambrey and Midsummer Hill, Stanford suggests that bridges do not appear until about the middle of the first century B.C., but it would be wrong to draw any general conclusions from this: the practical necessity for such a feature would have asserted itself on military works at all stages of the Early Iron Age.

Inturned entrances. Deeply inturned entrances, which Miss L. F. Chitty once used to trace the movements of invaders passing northwards up the Marches (1937) also seem to have a very long history, beginning in the Late Bronze Age at Ffridd Faldwyn (Fig. 7). For centuries afterwards the sharply inturned type, reflecting the possibility of constructing even a right angle with timber framing or dry-stone revetment walling, was being constructed where materials locally available made this possible, while a more gently curving inturn would be produced when battered dry-stone revetments or dump construction were being used. It would certainly be a mistake to relate all sharp inturns in the Marches to the Continental late La Tène *Zangentore* (Stanford, 1972b, p. 310), or to assume in the case of unexcavated examples that a deep inturn implies the presence of guard-chambers: in fact *Zangentore*, sometimes constructed wholly of timber, with a palisade casing, existed in the Lausitz culture hillforts of central Germany at least as early as the sixth century B.C. (Coblenz, 1966). Undoubtedly the desire to provide a narrow passage outside the gate which could be commanded from the parapet walk or the bridge, or to extend the rampart so as to provide a backing for a guard-chamber behind the gate, would have produced this effect in many cases, but the late Bronze Age inturn at Ffridd Faldwyn II and the sharp inturns at Castle Ditches, Eddisbury and Maiden Castle, Bickerton, in Cheshire, are either earlier than or contemporary with other inturned entrances which have guard-chambers, while at the east entrance at Twyn-y-gaer, Cwmyoy (Monmouthshire) we can see how a deep and sharp inturn was gradually achieved by a series of extensions of a dry-stone revetted rampart which had originally had a simple entrance (Information L. A. Probert). At the latter site, the Herefordshire stamped pottery had already begun to arrive when the first apsidal inturn was added to the entrance, and later phases of development of this entrance and of that through the western cross-bank may be much later, but there were no guard-chambers at any stage. Dating of inturned entrances without excavation is therefore clearly hazardous, but one might suspect that the sharply inturned entrances at Cwm Cefn-y-gaer and Careg-wiber forts in Radnorshire, both of which are univallate and probably had box ramparts, are of early date, and the same probably applies to the fine deeply and sharply inturned entrances at Moel y Gaer, Llanbedr (Denbighshire) (Pl. I) (Hogg, 1965, p. 142). What can, however, be asserted with confidence of the inturned entrances in the Marches as a whole, is that they are more distinctive of this region than any other in Britain, as our map shows (Fig. 8), and were only imitated on a limited number of sites in other parts of Wales.

C. The Walled Forts (c 500–100 B.C.)

A considerable number of hillforts in Wales and the Marches are defended by ramparts built solidly of dry-stone walling, without any sign of timber-framing or lacing, and without any ditches. The absence of ditches clearly has some relationship to the local geology, which in many cases is most unfavourable to the digging of ditches, but in other cases it has proved possible for later occupants of a site to dig ditches in order to reinforce its defences (p. 257 above). The predominance of this type of walled fort in north-west Wales, almost to the exclusion of other types of fort (compare our maps, Figs 5–10) has led Hogg (1960, 1965, 1972a) to see it as a separate cultural group representing the reaction of the Late Bronze Age inhabitants to Early Iron Age invaders, perhaps with the help of a few settlers from the Iberian peninsula. But, as we can now see, the Early Iron Age inhabitants of north-west Wales were far from being the only ethnic group in southern Britain which was mainly of native Bronze Age origin, and the origins of hillfort building in Britain generally lie in the Late Bronze Age. As has already been pointed out (p. 257 above) the size of some of the walled forts (e.g., Carn Fadrun, Garn Boduan, Bwrdd Arthur, Braich y Ddinas) and the numbers of huts within them is such as to suggest that they represent a continuation, in some respects, of the belt of large fortified settlements which runs from the lower Severn valley to north-east Wales. Moreover the walled group has out-liers which partake to some extent of the character of the normal early hillforts of the Marches. Moel Hiraddug in its early phase, for example, with its numerous rectangular houses and its sequence of guard-chamber entrances, was a walled fort without ditches, and so were Titterstone Clee III and Pen y Gorddyn Fawr, and for that matter, the Breiddin in its middle phase. Obviously it is difficult to be sure, in the areas where timber-laced ramparts occur, that a rampart built like a wall was not timber-laced: only where extensive burning has taken place, and widely distributed deposits of clinker or slaked lime can be demonstrated by excavation or surface collection, can one establish the presence of timber lacing in dry-stone fronted ramparts, in cases where timber uprights were not used. But the fact remains that so far not a single case of timber-lacing has been demonstrated in Gwynedd by traces of burning or other-wise with the possible exception of Craig y Dinas, Llanllyfni (Caernarvon-shire) (R.C.A.H.M. (Wales) 1960, No. 1281), and the walled forts of this area, taken as a whole, present a number of characteristics which differentiate them from the typical timber-laced sites of the Marches.

One obvious difference between the north-western walled forts and the early forts of the Marches is the simplicity of their entrances. These are usually plain gaps, without deep inturns, guard-chambers or other complications. In the whole area, in fact, there now appears to be only one certain case of an inturned entrance with a rectangular guard-chamber on at least one side, built during a second phase of construction—Pendinas, Llandegai (Caernar-vonshire) (R.C.A.H.M. (Wales) 1956, No. 345), although there may have been C-shaped guard-chambers at Moel Offrwm in Merionethshire (Gresham, 1967, p. 142). A few small sites in west Merionethshire have gently inturned entrances and Craig y Dinas, Llanllyfni (Caernarvonshire) appears to have had, in its sec-ond phase, a semicircular bastion added to the rampart a little to one side of the entrance, as at Dinorben II (R.C.A.H.M. (Wales) 1960, No. 1281). On the other hand there are recurring features at the Gwynedd forts which are hardly ever found in the Marches and must be derived from another direction. The most obvious is the predilection for back-terracing of the walls, relatively well-preserved at Conway Mountain, Tre'r Ceiri, Caer y Twr, Pen y Gorddyn and Caer Drewyn. This arrangement which produces two or more terraces or *banquettes* at the back of the rampart, seems to relate closely to what is found at Gurnard's Head in Cornwall (Gordon, 1940), Kercaradec in Brittany (Wheeler and Richardson, 1957, pp. 54–61) and at Dun Aengus and a number of other forts on or near the western and southern coasts of Ireland (Evans, 1966, p. 76f., pp. 118–121, 126, 129 and 131); back-terracing also appears in the second phase of a small multivallate promontory fort at Tower Point, St. Brides (Pembrokeshire) (Wainwright, 1971b). That the building tradition represented by such structures owes something to maritime connections with Brittany and even with southern France, is suggested also by the presence on at least one site in Gwynedd—Pen-y-Gaer, Llanaelhaearn (Caernarvonshire) (R.C.A.H.M. (Wales), 1960, No. 1057) of dry-stone ramparts strengthened back and front with successive revetments, built up from the original surface in the manner of the *Murus Duplex* of southern France (Soutou, 1962). This type of construction is well represented in the walled promontory forts and cashels of western and southern Ireland as well as at Worlebury (Somerset) (Dymond, 1902) and produces terraces in front of as well as behind the central portion of the rampart, as occurs at Pen-y-Gaer. Hamilton has drawn attention to the distribution of this *Murus Duplex* technique, with front as well as rear terracing, from the Alpine area through southern France to Spain and northwards to the western sides of Britain and Ireland (1966, 1968, pp. 45–52 and 1970), and there is a strong temptation to link it with the well-known diffusion of stone *chevaux de frise* in northern Spain and Portugal and on the western coasts of Ireland and Britain, lately studied by Hogg (1957a) and Harbison (1968 and 1971b).

Wales, too, has its *chevaux de frise*, and the association of these with the walled forts is clear enough. The best site is Pen-y-Gaer, Llanbedr-y-cennin (R.C.A.H.M. (Wales), 1956, No. 315), where the stone *chevaux de frise* are related to a primary ditchless walled rampart, to which outer banks and ditches were later added, but the other sites are in south-west Wales, and are there related to an extension of the walled fort complex. The ditchless walled fort of Carn Goch, Llangadog (Carmarthenshire), with gate and posterns of northwestern type, encloses an area of 25 acres (Pl. III) (Hogg, 1965, pp. 121 and 136) and is said formerly to have had stone *chevaux de frise*. What remains of the similar feature at the relatively small but strongly fortified Craig Gwrtheyrn, near Llandysul (Carmarthenshire) (Gardner, 1932) lies outside a barbican earthwork which is probably a later addition to the entrance of a walled and ditched bivallate fort (Fig. 11) and other groups of stone *chevaux de frise* have been reported at Carn Alw (Pembrokeshire) (Harbison, 1971b, p. 203) and Poll Carn, Treffgarne (Pembrokeshire) (Crossley, 1963, p. 188). Whether these peculiar obstacles are in themselves sufficient proof of migrations or even of cultural influences, reaching Britain or Ireland from the Iberian peninsula early in the Iron Age is perhaps open to doubt, in view of the hint provided by the discovery of timber stakes apparently planted for the same purpose at the Niederneundorf, Central Germany, Lausitz Culture fort, the Hallstatt "C" Koberstadt in the middle Rhineland, and the Fou de Verdun promontory fort in central France (Hawkes, 1971, Fig. 1c and Harbison, 1971b, pp. 214–216), that wooden *chevaux de frise* may once have been common in districts well provided with timber, and have been replaced by stone pillars only in areas where it was more convenient to use stone. In this connection the way in which the massive rampart of a very large hillfort at Castillo Viejo, Sequeros

(Salamanca) was revetted with stone posts alternating with panels of dry-stone walling, as a substitute for a timber post and panel revetment, is highly significant (Spindler, 1970). The tendency to revet ramparts or entrance passages with upright stone slabs, which is particularly well represented at Parc Cynog (Carmarthenshire) (De Quincey, 1969) and St. David's Head (Pembrokeshire) (Crossley, 1963, p. 174) and crops up to some degree in north-west Wales, as well as Brittany, Cornwall, Lancashire, and the far north of Scotland may also represent adaptation of a tradition of timber casing the immediate source of which may have been in lowland Britain. Nonetheless, it must be admitted that this community of structural traits along the western seaboards of Britain and Ireland, and the Continental analogues, do suggest some kind of contact, the degree of which, unfortunately, it is difficult to gauge owing to the extreme poverty of the associated objects which have so far been brought to light on the Welsh and Irish sites. We seem, in fact, to have in these traits, both in Wales and in Ireland, evidence of a separate Continental influence quite distinct from that in lowland Britain, which superimposed itself on a local Bronze Age tradition of settlement building, based on pastoralism and small units (p. 273 below).

In north-west Wales, though some of the walled forts which have been excavated have yielded finds connected with occupation in the Roman period or immediately before it, others like Conway Mountain and Pen y Gaer, Llanbedr-y-cennin, have produced little more than saddle querns, which at least show that they had a permanent population during part of the late prehistoric phase. Here, as on the small stone-built and usually ditchless forts of coastal Merionethshire, we seem to be dealing with communities which for long had no local supply of pottery. In the south-east, however, at St. David's Head and Moel Trigarn, the prehistoric finds are a little more varied and even include a little coarse pottery of Iron Age "A" affinity, at the latter site. But in general we have to base such views as we can form of the chronological position of the walled forts on the evidence for their relationship to the early hillforts of the Marches, particularly in areas where the two groups overlap. Thus, certain forts in the northern Marches, like Titterstone Clee, Caynham Camp, the Breiddin, Moel Hiraddug and Pen y Gorddyn Fawr, shared some of the characteristics of walled forts at some stage of their history, even though they combined these in some cases, with some of those of the early Marches forts, like inturned entrances and guard-chambers. At Caer Drewyn (Merionethshire) a fine walled fort, enclosing 8 acres, with back-terraces and ditchless, has two inturned entrances, one of which has at least one C-shaped guard-chamber. This fort must belong to roughly the same early phase as the second period of construction at Moel Hiraddug and yet it probably succeeded a small ditched fort. This sequence shows that the construction of a walled fort on the same site is a cultural phenomenon and not a simple matter of geological necessity (Gresham, 1967, pp. 144–148). If Gresham is right in suspecting C-shaped guard-chambers in the ruined inturned entrance at Moel Offrwm, the largest walled fort in west Merionethshire (1967, p. 142), there would be a strong suggestion that the walled fort tradition had developed at each end of the Bala Cleft by the end of the fifth century B.C., if not earlier, and this would be supported by the links between Periods II and III at Dinorben and the Caernarvonshire forts which have already been mentioned (p. 268 above). Consideration of the relationship of the north-western walled forts to ancient trackways, as defined by Gresham (1967, Figs 25 and 47) might suggest that the spread of their tradition to sites like Caer Drewyn, Craig Rhiwarth, the Breiddin and Titterstone Clee may have arisen from the movements of pastoralists who had evolved the tradition originally in the rocky regions of Gwynedd. Once established, however, this tradition seems to have persisted locally for centuries in north-west and south-west Wales. During this time, the massive wall round the large settlement on Garn Boduan in the Lleyn was rebuilt, largely on a different alignment (Hogg, 1960) and much the same kind of thing happened at Carn Fadrun (R.C.A.H.M. (Wales), 1964, No. 1650) and Conway Mountain (Griffiths and Hogg, 1956). Owing to the paucity of finds at the north-western sites so far explored one cannot fully define the exotic element in the population which their structural features suggest, and which may not have been much less than, and possibly of diverse origin from, that which we have argued was present in the early hillforts of the Marches. Indeed, such diversity may be at least as much the reason for the almost total dominance of the circular house in the walled forts of north-west and south-west Wales (Fig. 9) as re-emergence of the indigenous Bronze Age culture. One of the keys to this problem might be the excavation of one of the walled forts of south-west Wales (e.g., Craig Gwrtheyrn) where finds seem likely to be more abundant, for in this way we could perhaps establish more clearly the relationship of the larger walled forts to the numerous small enclosures of central and southern Wales, which seem more definitely to relate to the surviving Late Bronze Age population.

D. *The Earliest Hillforts in The South* (*c 400–200* B.C.)

We have already seen (p. 255 above) that though unfortified settlements on the South Wales seaboard have produced material belonging to the earliest phase of the Iron Age, there is very little evidence as yet for hillfort building in South Wales as early as this. Although it must be admitted that this may be partly due to the small scale of hillfort excavation in South Wales, compared with the central and northern Marches during the last forty years, we have already seen that the main focus of colonisation and large hillfort building during the Late Bronze Age and the first phase of the Early Iron Age was, in fact, in the latter area and that the concentration of the population in large hillforts may have arisen from the need for protection against raids from a warlike and unconquered Late Bronze Age enclave to the west (p. 253 above). At the same time we have noted the abundance in central and southern Wales of very small fortified enclosures, many of which are univallate (Fig. 5) and some of which may be early. We have already mentioned a small primary fort with rampart and ditch, enclosing a mere 1½ acres, at Caer Drewyn (p. 270 above) and the earliest Late Bronze Age fort at Ffridd Faldwyn only enclosed about 3 acres. Spurgeon has shown how numerous small univallate forts are in Montgomeryshire and described how small univallate enclosures were replaced by larger multivallate ones at Gaer Fawr, Guilsfield, Cefn Carnedd, Llandinam, Y Gaer, Trefeglwys and Cefn yr Allt, Berriew (1972). Further south, in Breknockshire, there is reason to think that the fine multivallate hill-fort at Pen-y-crug replaced a small univallate enclosure (Fig. 12) (Hogg, 1965, p. 145), Fennifach nearby is a small univallate hillfort with possible surface indications of a bastion near the entrance (Information from Mr. Kay), and the small univallate enclosure on Twyn Llechfaen yielded the writer coarse pottery which probably belongs to an early phase in the Iron Age (Savory, 1961 and 1971d). In Monmouthshire again, at Lodge Farm, Caerleon a large multi-vallate fort encloses a small univallate one which is presumably earlier (Savory, 1950a, p. 233) and at Llanmelin another multivallate hillfort was probably preceded by a smaller univallate enclosure (Hogg, 1965, p. 141). Finally, in Glamorgan, we have proof that a large univallate enclosure, apparently built in the later pre-Roman Iron Age, replaced a small univallate enclosure, without a ditch but with an internal revetment wall (Hogg, 1963). The only object associated with the fort in this case was a small bronze terret ring (so far unpublished) cast in one piece with a collar for fastening on a chariot pole rather than a yoke, which seems to relate to a Continental early La Tène form rather than to later British ones. Summerhouse, Boverton (Glamorganshire) is another example of a small univallate fort enclosed by a larger, multivallate one, and at Piercefield, St. Arvans (Monmouthshire) a small univallate fort is too close to a large multivallate site to be likely to be contemporary with it in construction (Savory, 1950a, pp. 233 and 235).

Unfortunately, we have insufficient information from scientific excavations to be able to judge what type of construction was typical of the earlier south Wales forts. At Twyn-y-gaer, Cwmyoy (Monmouthshire) we know that the primary rampart of a medium-sized univallate hillfort was of box type, dry-stone-revetted, and had been built before Herefordshire stamped ware had reached the site but probably when pottery of Iron Age "A" tradition was in use there (Information from L. A. Probert). At Castell Cogan, a small bivallate contour fort near the estuary of the Taf in Carmarthenshire, recent excavations appear to indicate that the rear face of the inner rampart was revetted with timber, presumably because it was timber-framed (Grealey et al., 1972). The pottery from the interior of this site, which contained at least two large circular timber-framed houses, is said to be a coarse ware like that from Coygan Camp, further west. At the latter site, however, a small bivallate promontory fort, the main rampart, revetted with dry-stone walling without and upright slabs within was apparently not built until the time when pottery of Silurian "Iron Age B" affinity was in use on the site (Wainwright, 1967a, pp. 28–44). At Pen Dinas, Aberystwyth, there is a long sequence of hillfort building, with later phases in which dry-stone revetted and ditched contour forts enclosing about 5 acres were built first on the southern and then on the northern hill and finally united to form one of the largest hillforts in west Wales. Since the single re-storable pot from this site is of imported Herefordshire stamped ware but apparently belongs to a late period of construction, the earliest of the stone forts here is likely to belong to an early phase in the local Iron Age (Forde *et al.*, 1963). But the various entrances constructed in all these phases show very little elaboration beyond moderate thickening or overlapping of the rampart terminals, of a sort associated with walled forts or small fortified enclosures of other types to be found in various parts of the interior of Wales; the same applies to the entrances at Coygan. Superficial examination of various medium-sized univallate hillforts in south and central Wales does not, indeed, suggest that deep inturning or guard-chamber construction was very widely adopted by their builders, any more than it was by the builders of walled forts. At Cwm Cefn-y-gaer, Llanddewi Ystradenny and Careg Wiber, Llandrindod (Radnorshire), at the Hillis Camp, Llanfilo (Brecknockshire) and Gaer Fawr, Trawscoed (Cardiganshire) there are deeply and sharply inturned entrances which may relate to the early phase of hillfort construction in the Marches, a small bivallate fort at West Ford Rings, Haycastle (Pembrokeshire) has paired guard-chambers in the entrance (Crossley, 1963, p.187) and the rare reports of probable or possible rectangular houses inside enclosures in west Wales (Fig. 10) may also reflect early influences from the great hillfort concentration of the Marches, but on present knowledge it is likely that most of the true hillforts in the interior of Wales which have univallate or bivallate defences belong like Castle Ditches, Llancarfan to a later horizon. In their place, during the first half of the Early Iron Age in Wales, must have stood some, at least, of the small embanked or walled homesteads, with circular dwellings, whose later development will be considered in the next chapter (p. 274 below). As in Ireland, the inhabitants of such homesteads must have represented, substantially, the descendants of the Bronze Age population.

IV. The Later Stages

A. The Localisation of the Hillfort Tradition in Wales (c 300 B.C.–A.D. 75)

We have seen that by the end of the first phase of the Early Iron Age three main settlement types were present in Wales: large and populous hillforts of Marches type, walled forts, and small, more or less defensively sited and enclosed homesteads. The distributions of these types, while differing overall, with an eastern, a north-western and a southern bias respectively, overlap con-siderably: in west Merionethshire, for example—a zone of contact between the first two groups—there are many walled forts which are so small that they are likely to have been occupied by only one family (Gresham, 1967, pp. 158–168), while on the other hand a few walled forts, some of them large, were built in the Upper Severn basin and in west Wales. At the same time, small enclosures, suitable for a few families only, are as common in the Upper Severn basin,

Brecknockshire and Glamorganshire as true hillforts (Figs 5–13). But these small enclosures prove, on closer examination, to vary a great deal in character. While some are in strong contour or promontory positions, with single or multiple ramparts which are sometimes quite formidable (Pl. IV and Fig. 16), others are in plateau or hill-slope positions and are so weakly embanked for much of the way round that they appear to have very little military value. This type of earthwork tends to be roughly circular in plan, and in parts of Pembrokeshire where it is particularly common (Pl. VII) it is often called a "rath", though this word is sometimes applied to true promontory forts (Grimes, 1964). Ring-works of this kind are the least known of all Welsh types of fortified settlement: hardly any at all have been excavated outside Pembrokeshire and even in that county the meagre results of most of the explorations e.g., at Trelissey, Knock and Merryborough (Thomas and Walker, 1959 and Crossley, 1964, 1965)— seemed to suggest occupation mainly in the Roman period. But at Walesland Rath, Wainwright (1971a) was able to show by means of complete excavation of a typical earthwork enclosing a mere half-acre that a weak dump rampart and ditch had already been built here by the end of the third century B.C. (as a C-14 date suggests), to enclose four peripheral ranges of timber buildings, 33 m, 30 m and 18 m long and 1·2 m–4·2 m wide and two or three circular huts, one of them roughly 9 m in diameter (Fig. 15). One of the entrances was dry-stone revetted and was flanked on one side by a clubbed rampart terminal which probably supported a look-out platform. The possible analogy with Hamilton's fort at Clickhimin, Shetland (1968), with its storeyed, peripheral half-timbered ranges and central circular stone-built hut cannot be established until more sites of this kind have been explored in south-west Britain. The use of part of the peripheral ranges for industrial purposes is suggested by the discovery of fragments of crucibles for bronze-working; though pastoralism must have been important the fragments of wooden ploughshares (not spear tips!) associated with a later, first century B.C.–first century A.D. phase on this site (Wainwright, 1971a, pp. 94–98) show that a mixed agriculture was practised.

In the light of Walesland, with its scanty, not very characteristic pottery, and of the primary, similarly "hill-slope" enclosure at Castle Ditches, Llancarfan (Glamorganshire) (p. 272 above), which could be roughly contemporary, we can see that many of the numerous small enclosures of south and central Wales could have been occupied during an intermediate, Early or Middle La Tène phase, when the apparent rarity, in most of this area, of large hillforts might, as already suggested, denote the existence of a culture of different origin to that which dominated the Marches of Wales. It is here that the widely-spaced concentric earthworks of Lady Fox (1952, 1958 and 1969) become significant, because though hardly any of them have been excavated in Wales their inner enclosures generally, in size and style of construction, resemble the simple plateau and hill-slope ring-works just discussed, with entrance elaboration rarely going beyond clubbing of the rampart terminals, perhaps to provide emplacements for look-outs or slingers. In fact, they seem to belong to the same larger complex as that which extends through south-western England into Ireland, with its innumerable "raths" and sites of various types with widely-spaced defences (O'Kelly, 1970 and Raftery, B., 1972): in Ireland, indeed, this tradition is now seen to have important links through hill-top ceremonial sites like Rathgall (see Raftery below pp. 339–357), Dún Ailinne (see Wailes, below, p. 330) and the Navan Rath, with the native culture of the Bronze Age and even the Late Neolithic. Though the points of divergence of these regions are well-known, there appears to be a common denominator, which includes resistance to the intrusive Continental elements of the final Bronze Age and Hallstatt periods, established in eastern Wessex and the Marches (p. 253 above) and survival of an "einzelhof" tradition of fortified settlements, often taking the form of a ring-work, dependent to a considerable extent upon the pastoralism natural to the damp western side of the British Isles. The surviving widely-spaced concentric enclosures of Wales, well represented by the Bulwarks, Llanmadoc (Glamorganshire), probably reflect little more than the accident of preservation of outer banks which formerly existed at many sites which now appear to be simple ring-works. At any rate they have virtually the same distribution (Fig. 13) and represent the need for an outer enclosure in which flocks and herds could be kept securely, when necessary, clear from the settlement and any adjoining cultivated fields.

There is certainly evidence that some ring-works and concentric sites were occupied down to the Roman conquest and beyond, as at Walesland and Summerhouses, Tythegston (Glamorganshire) (Davies, J., 1966 and 1967a) and the inner bank of the concentric hill-slope earthwork on Kilvey Hill (Glamorganshire) (Morris, 1968) does not seem to have been constructed until the second century A.D. or later. But the lack of pottery at the Bulwarks, Llanmadoc (Glamorganshire) (Davies, A. G., 1964) and the Castle Ditches, Llancarfan (Glamorganshire) ring-work may be due to another common characteristic of the Welsh and Irish Iron Ages, the widespread lack of local pottery industries during the Early and Middle La Tène periods and the dependence of a large part of Wales, at least, upon occasional imports of pottery from neighbouring regions. This aceramic phase accounts for the extreme poverty of the north-western walled forts and the absence of pottery from the row of at least four circular huts built behind the inner rampart of a promontory fort with widely spaced dump ramparts at Henllan (Cardiganshire) (Williams, 1945) (Fig. 14). Such promontory forts, evidently serving the same purpose as the concentric ring-works, are common on the Pembrokeshire and Gower coasts (Fig. 13); one of them, the Knave, Rhossili (Williams, 1939) was occupied long enough to receive a little Iron Age "B" pottery of Somerset affinity. The concentric enclosures of north-west Wales with their central hut-circles (Gresham, 1967, pp. 206–224 and R.C.A.H.M. (Wales), 1964, xcv–vii) probably represent an extension northwards of the southern group during the aceramic phase: one that was completely excavated—Llwyn-du Bach, Penygroes (Caernarvonshire)—proved to be aceramic (Bersu and Griffiths, 1949) but was mistakenly attributed to the

Dark Ages, partly on the strength of its relationship to ancient field systems which are not closely datable; the small group of double ring-works, with widely spaced ramparts, in south Lleyn (Fig. 13), to which Castell Odo belongs (Alcock, 1960 and R.C.A.H.M. (Wales), 1964, lxxvi–viii) probably also belong to this movement, for at the latter site the later phases, during which the concentric arrangement developed, were also aceramic. Here, however, the settlement was larger, and comprised several hut-circles.

The need to provide a temporary refuge for livestock in conditions of inter-tribal warfare would have been felt by the inhabitants of large hillforts in any part of Iron Age Britain where stock-raising was important. But with certain exceptions, like Danebury (Hampshire), where a concentric outer bank was apparently provided for the stalling of cattle (Cunliffe, 1972a) the main hillfort group of eastern Wessex and the west Midlands did not resort to annexed enclosures for this purpose. In the Marches, certainly, the much larger area sometimes comprised within the outer line of defence may be of this nature (Kenyon, 1942) and so may be the lateral annexe at Croft Ambrey (Stanford, 1967). But as one goes westwards in the Cambrian Massif the number of true hillforts, including large ones, which have had dependent enclosures added laterally or terminally, greatly increases and this probably reflects the necessarily much larger role played by stock-raising in the economy of the upland communities, whether they were surviving aborigines or newcomers who had adapted themselves (Fig. 13). Examples of large sites with terminal annexes are Castle Bank, Llansanffraid yn Elfael (Radnorshire) (Pl. V), Allt yr Esgair, Llangasty (Brecknockshire) (Savory, 1955b, p. 43f.), Moel Offrwm (Merionethshire) (Gresham, 1967, p. 142), Campswood (Monmouthshire) and Llanmelin. Several smaller forts with similar annexes exist in west and mid Wales. Good examples of lateral annexes are provided by Dinas Bran, Llangollen (Denbighshire) (Forde-Johnston, 1964), Cefn Carnedd, Llandinam (Montgomeryshire), where the original fort had already been enlarged and provided with multiple banks (Spurgeon, 1972, pp. 339–341), and Craig Gwrtheyrn (Carmarthenshire) (Fig. 11) where two lateral annexes, defended by dump ramparts seem to have been added after the original, walled fort had been provided with a barbican entrance. Again, smaller examples of lateral annexes exist in mid Wales—at Gaer Fawr and Gaer Fach in the Epynt, for example— and in west Wales, but there appear to be no examples in Glamorganshire. Among the walled forts of the north, dependent enclosures occur, as at Moel Hiraddug, where recent evidence hardly supports Houlder's idea (Houlder, 1961) that the innermost rampart is later than the outer ones, and Tre'r Ceiri (R.C.A.H.M. (Wales) 1960, No. 1056), where the annexe does not seem to have contained many huts. On the other hand the twice-added lateral annexes at Braich y Ddinas in the north-west (R.C.A.H.M. (Wales), 1956, No. 252) and Moel Trigarn in the south-west (Hogg, 1965, p. 142) all contain the sites of numerous dwellings: in the latter case St. Joseph has suggested (1961, p. 266) on the strength of an air-photograph that some of the hut-floors may be earlier than the inner rampart, and excavations would be necessary to determine whether the annexes here and on some other sites were originally free of houses.

Other features of Welsh hillforts which seem to belong to the phase of localisation and may be related to pastoralism, if not to local social conditions, are cross-banks and barbicans (Figs 8 and 13). The former appear at several small sites in west Wales (Savory, 1954a), as well as at the larger sites of Cefn Carnedd, Llandinam (Montgomeryshire) (Spurgeon, 1972, pp. 339–341) (where it is considered to be the latest feature of the site) and Hillis Camp, Llanfilo (Brecknockshire) (Savory, 1955b, p. 44). At Twyn y Gaer, Cwmyoy (Monmouthshire) the two cross-banks have been shown to be secondary. It is not yet clear whether such sub-divisions arise from a desire to separate the living quarters of the inhabitants from the temporary shelters of livestock, or to emphasise social distinctions among the former. Barbicans, as developed in some of the very large hillforts of Wessex and the Marches, appear military in purpose; in a simple form they are found at an early date; e.g., at Crickley Hill (Dixon 1972), but the elaborate structures at Old Oswestry (Varley, 1948, pp. 51 and 53), Burfa Camp, Evenjobb (Radnorshire), Cefn Carnedd (Montgomeryshire), and Moel Offrwm (Merionethshire) belong to a later phase of multiple "dump" ramparts as does the miniature one at Mynydd Bychan (Glamorganshire) (Fig. 18). In Wales itself the small but massive barbican at the large univallate hillfort on Merlin's Hill, Abergwili (Carmarthenshire) (Grealey, 1971) may be relatively early and is at least as military in character as that at Craig Gwrtheyrn (Fig. 11). But the small semicircular outworks in front of the simple entrances of some Pembrokeshire raths (Spurgeon, 1963 and Crossley, 1963, p. 175 and p. 193f.) may be pastoral in function and the small annexes flanking the passage leading up to the main entrance at the Gwernyfed Gaer (Brecknockshire) (Savory, 1958b) might be similarly explained.

An assessment of the general culture of the people who built the more specifically Welsh or western types of hillfort and fortified homestead is rendered difficult by the poverty of material from excavations in areas where, as we have seen, wooden and leather vessels largely replaced pottery, and ironwork, where it survives, tends to be in very poor condition. But we know now (Peacock, 1968) that the manufacture of pottery was already becoming industrialised in Britain during the La Tène period and that its distribution may not therefore coincide with that of other kinds of object or structure which the archaeologist may use to define cultural groups. Hence the distribution of Herefordshire stamped ware, manufactured near the Malvern Hills from the fourth to the second centuries B.C., to Twyn y Gaer, the Breiddin, Pen Dinas (Aberystwyth) and probably also to Ffridd Faldwyn (Montgomeryshire) and Twyn Llechfaen (Brecknockshire), which overlaps with that of a much more primitive ware, commonly referred to as "VCP", both spatially and temporally. The latter has been attributed by Gelling and Stanford (1967) to bake-ovens, but this attribution probably does not account for all the sherds of this ware, almost invariably small and difficult to restore, which have been found, not only in apparent association with Herefordshire stamped ware at Twyn y Gaer,

Croft Ambrey and the Breiddin, but far beyond the present range of the latter at Moel Hiraddug and Dinorben and even in north-west Wales. Whether or not this ware has Late Bronze Age antecedents in the Irish Channel area (Savory, 1970, p. 43, p. 47) it certainly had a long life both at Dinorben and at Croft Ambrey, though it is as yet too early to give judgment on the possibility apparently revived by recent discoveries at the Breiddin, that the manufacture of VCP was renewed in north Wales during the Dark Ages (Gardner and Savory, 1964, p. 193 and Savory, 1971b, p. 25: Musson, 1972) (p. 289 below). Perhaps the most significant point about "VCP" is its failure to appear, so far, in west or south Wales. Even in north-west Wales its appearances are so rare and dubious that we are forced to turn to metal-work as a possible means of cultural definition.

The recent discovery of an important hoard of insular La Tène art metal-work at Tal-y-llyn (Merionethshire) (Savory, 1964a, b, 1966, 1968b, 1971b, pp. 64–75) has emphasised the relative wealth of north Wales in fine Early Iron Age metal-work, much of it belonging to an early stage in the development of the insular art style. I have given my reasons elsewhere for deprecating the extreme position taken up by Fox in attributing all these works to importation from various parts of lowland Britain. Undoubtedly Fox was right to stress the significance of the Llyn Cerrig Bach deposit in relation to the ancient route connecting the Severn valley with Ireland through North Wales and Holy Island: one must connect it also with the nature of the walled fort group of the north-west as a partial extension of the large settlement tradition of the Marches. It is in fact likely that north-west Wales played a far more important part than south-west Scotland in founding the distinctive Ulster school of La Tène metal-work. But just as the structural features of the walled forts show direct influences from the Continent, as well as from the Marches, so does the metal-work, particularly at Tal-y-llyn, show a direct influence from the Continental Middle La Tène. In view of the probable mobility of La Tène metal-workers it would be wrong to insist that all the fine metal-work so far found in North Wales represented a local tradition. Some of its types are certainly southern English (if not inspired from the East Riding), but to think that the manufacture of much of it in north-west Wales is impossible because pottery was not made there is an error which can be refuted by considering northern Ireland, where the existence of a local La Tène metal-working school has always been admitted, although pottery is virtually non-existent there also, and taking note of the resources of north-west Wales in copper ores which were certainly used during the Bronze Age and were being exploited by the Romans within a remarkably short time after the conquest (Savory, 1965, pp. 188–191 and 1971b, pp. 64–68). No doubt large scale exploration of hillforts close to the likely mining areas—Moel Offrwm and Craig y Deryn in Merionethshire for example, or the numerous north Cardiganshire sites, including the interior of Pen Dinas (Aberystwyth) would throw light on this point. In any case the dates, ranging from the third to the first centuries B.C. to which the Cerrig-y-drudion bowl and choice pieces in the Tal-y-llyn and Moel Hiraddug hoards and the ritual deposit at Llyn Cerrig Bach can be assigned suggest that it is the walled fort group (Fig. 10) with which this metal-work should be brought into relation rather than the final phase during which a few sites in north-west Wales were fortified or refortified with multiple dump ramparts (Fig. 16).

B. The Spread of Multivallate Defences in Wales

The present appearance of many hillforts, large or small, in Wales and the Marches often owes most of all to developments during the last two centuries or so before the Roman conquest. Multiple closely-spaced dump ramparts, whether or not they replace earlier multivallate or bivallate defences of box or wall type, seem in general to represent the final phase of Early Iron Age military engineering. This can be seen not only at Old Oswestry but at several large hillforts on the Clwydian Range (Forde Johnston, 1965) where such ramparts seem to have replaced earlier univallate defences and a few such additions appear even in north-west Wales (Fig. 16) (Hogg, 1972a, p. 20). But in north Wales the chronology and cultural background of these developments remain obscure because apparently the whole area remained aceramic down to the Roman conquest. Recent excavations have thrown very little light on this problem, even if at Dinorben it is now possible to see that the phase, Period V, during which the great inner rampart was rebuilt with back-terracing and a sloping front and two outer banks and ditches of dump construction was early Roman, or more probably late pre-Roman in date (Gardner and Savory, 1964, pp. 91–95, Savory, 1971b, p. 30). Here, however, the appearance of multiple dump defences cannot be precisely equated with any new cultural group moving north-westwards from the Marches because the back-terracing of the main rampart reflects if anything a cultural influence from the opposite direction—from the walled forts of Gwynedd, in fact. Such terraces are hardly known elsewhere in the Marches, except possibly at the unexcavated Ivington Camp in Herefordshire (R.C.H.M. (England), 1934, pp. 131–133). In the south, on the other hand, a scatter of trivallate earthworks, many of them promontory forts, along the seaboard, have been interpreted by Hogg (1972a, p. 15) as the work of a fresh band of settlers. Here, however, there is another index of cultural change, in that during the second century B.C., as it seems, pottery again becomes relatively plentiful along the south-Wales seaboard and, once again this reflects contacts of some sort with the districts on the other side of the Severn estuary.

The pottery which has been described as "Western 2nd B", characterised by cylindrical and ovoid jars with everted rims often with relatively well-finished soapy surfaced ware and sometimes with tooled decoration forming zigzags, arcades, swags and other curvilinear motifs, tends to replace the traditional stamped ware of Herefordshire in the second century B.C. at Croft Ambrey and Midsummer Hill, and spreads to Twyn y Gaer, Cwmyoy (Monmouthshire) and Castle Ditches, Llancarfan (Glamorganshire) which, however, remained univallate camps. This pottery also appears, from an early stage of its development, at Llanmelin Camp (Monmouthshire) (Nash-Williams, 1933, pp. 291–307), which is bivallate, with dump ramparts, and at a similarly early stage at Coygan Camp in west Wales (Wainwright, 1967a, p. 133f.), which is also bivallate; here, indeed, its arrival appears to coincide with the first fortification of the site, on a small scale, with a main entrance which was too narrow to admit a vehicle and which shows no special elaboration. Turning to the group of sites with three or more closely sited dump ramparts, the best known of these is still the large promontory fort at Sudbrook (Monmouthshire), which was evidently related to the terminal of a ferry across the Bristol Channel (Nash-Williams, 1939). Here the subordinate role of the middle rampart, on a site which only has a slight elevation above the surrounding country and needs defence in depth (in this case 60 yd excluding a "counterscarp" bank probably formed by ditch clearance), is a striking feature. The nature of the pottery at this site suggests construction of the defences at a somewhat later date than Llanmelin, i.e., in the first century B.C., with occupation continuing down to the establishment of Belgic dynasties in Gloucestershire and north Somerset, the importation of wheel-turned pottery of Belgic tradition, and the Roman conquests. Unfortunately the entrance at this promontory site, which had suffered from erosion, was no longer available for study. The only other site of this period in Monmouthshire which has been explored is Coed y Bwnydd, a contour site north of Usk which is defended, on one side, by four dump ramparts and three ditches (Babbidge, 1970; Babbidge and Williams, 1971). Here, however, the absence of pottery or other finds of dating value concentrates interest on structural evidence which can at any rate be compared with that from neighbouring sites. The inner rampart north of the entrance was revetted internally with timber, but this no doubt corresponds to the double dry-stone revetment walls in the same position at Sudbrook, combined here too with a glacis front. There was evidence, moreover, for two periods of construction of the inner rampart south of the entrance and of huts behind the rampart which were generally circular and timber-framed, but included, in the first phase, a small rectangular structure interpreted as a granary.

Somewhat oddly, our main example of entrance elaboration, in the late phase, in south Wales, continues to be that revealed at a small fortified homestead, barely $\frac{1}{2}$-acre internally, at Mynydd Bychan, Llysworney (Glamorganshire) (Savory, 1954b, 1955a). For this small site, which in its first phase (Fig. 18) contained three or four timber-framed circular huts, was defended by three dump ramparts on its northern and possibly originally on its eastern side and had a double gateway defended on the south by a D-shaped bastion or platform of limestone blocks, high enough to need revetment with a timber palisade. The approaches to the gateway were further controlled by a miniature barbican, flanked by dry-stone walls which on the north joined the ends of the innermost and outermost ramparts and on the south ran out from the bastion, which was connected with the terminal of the innermost rampart by a bridge in front of the gateway. At some stage in the history of this little stronghold a further palisade had been constructed to bar the approach through the barbican. The pottery associated with this phase at Mynydd Bychan is very close to that found at Llanmelin and Sudbrook in its pre-Belgic phase. Should the occupants of this site be regarded as part of a fresh wave of settlers, arriving in the first century B.C. and responsible also for the multivallate coastal forts of Glamorganshire and the very large multi-vallate contour forts, with deeply inturned entrances at Llanblethian, very close to Mynydd Bychan, and at the Caerau, Llantrisant? It is surely dangerous, as late as this in the Early Iron Age, to regard pottery as an index of much more than the range of local industrial centres, like that which produced the Here-fordshire stamped ware, and it is important to note that small fortified home-steads like Mynydd Bychan are part of the native culture of south Wales, rather than that of the area to the east or south-east, from which new settlers might be presumed to have come. Moreover, as we have seen, the new pottery style is associated with the occupation of a large univallate hillfort at Castle Ditches, Llancarfan (Glamorganshire) and with bivallate forts at Llanmelin and Coygan. The supposed new settlers, moreover, would have done nothing to alter the circular-house tradition of south Wales, except possibly at Coed y Bwnydd: at Sudbrook the two rectangular hut-floors which Dr. Nash-Williams explored behind the rampart are far larger (60 ft × 40 ft) than the traditional rectangular post-hole structures of Herefordshire and their precise nature was not established. It seems more likely that the spread of trivallate fortification simply reflects changes in tactics in areas which were in contact with each other through trade-changes which called for adaptations in the lay-out of earthworks which were carried out on new sites, but not necessarily on old ones.

In the light of the excavations at Mynydd Bychan one can at least partially understand the entrance features at several other forts along the south Wales seaboard, such as a considerable broadening and flattening of one of the rampart terminals flanking the entrance at the large multivallate hillforts of Piercefield near Chepstow and Lodge Farm near Caerleon, for example, at the large univallate promontory fort at Woodreefe and at other promontory forts with lateral entrances at Llanboidy and Castle Lloyd (Laugharne) in Carmarthenshire (Savory, 1950a and 1954a). We must regard these features, and the barbican lay-outs associated in some cases, as the final stage of the developments which began as much as 500 years earlier in the Marches and west Midlands, but we cannot be sure that they were still regular practice as late as the actual Roman conquest period c A.D. 50–75. At Mynydd Bychan there was a second phase of occupation, continuing into the Roman period and perhaps into the early part of the second century A.D., in which the enclosure was divided into four yards by dry-stone walls in which there were three or four circular houses with dry-stone foundations and a quadrilateral building, constructed after the defences had become ruined (Fig. 18). The associated pottery consists largely of imported wheel-turned Belgic ware of the Roman conquest period, related to the "Glevum" ware found at Sudbrook, and may indicate that the reconstruction of the houses on the site belongs to the middle of the first century A.D. At Walesland Rath in Pembrokeshire (Wainwright, 1971a, p. 84), however, related pottery was associated with the second period of occupation in which the defences were reconstructed, not later than the first century B.C., but here there was certainly occupation from the late second to the fourth centuries A.D. and the "Belgic" ware may simply represent trading contacts in the latter part of the first century A.D.

V. The Roman Conquest and After

A. The Role of Hillforts in the Conquest Period

We have now seen how much archaeological perspectives have lengthened since the time when the evolution of hillfort architecture, at least in north Wales, could be seen very largely as a response to the pressure of Rome. It is clear that in reality that evolution was nearly complete when Roman armies arrived in the Welsh Marches and the question is rather whether we can in fact find structural changes at any sites, particularly evidence of slighting, which can be confidently attributed to Roman campaigns in Wales. At one time, indeed, it used to be held that the Romans had demolished the Period II rampart at Dinorben, which we now know to have been destroyed several centuries before the Roman invasion, and this meant that the reconstructions of Period III–V and the whole history of the second main entrance, with its guard-chambers, had to fall within the Roman period. But it is now clear (Gardner and Savory, 1964, pp. 27–29, p. 42 and pp. 91–92, and Savory, 1971b, p. 30) that the evidence on which this dating was based cannot be accepted and there is no reason to doubt that the final multivallate defences of Dinorben, with their enormous sloping-fronted, back-terraced main rampart, reflect a combination of ideas derived partly from the central Marches of Wales, partly from Irish Sea Province, in the immediately pre-Roman phase. There is no doubt, however, that this rampart was slighted at its western end (Gardner and Savory, 1964, pp. 38–41), and pottery and other objects of second as well as third and fourth century date have been found in layers which pass over the remains of the last rampart at Dinorben, both in relation to hut floors near the north-eastern entrance and in the south-western area, where the layers climb upwards over the remains of the rampart and could hardly represent material carried southwards by denudation from the interior of the fort (Savory, 1971b, p. 15). So far as this evidence goes, the question must remain open as to whether demolition was the result of inter-tribal warfare or one of several Roman campaigns known to have occurred in the first century A.D., and the same might be said of the evidence from Pen y Gorddyn Fawr and Caer y Twr (Holyhead) (Gardner, 1910, pp. 151–153 and 1934, p. 167). At the Breiddin, O'Neil believed that the prehistoric defences had been dismantled by the Romans (O'Neil, 1937, p. 96) but the evidence here is interpreted differently by Musson (1972, p. 266f.). What is certain, however, is that there is no evidence for occupation of the site in the early Roman period. At Ffridd Faldwyn, too, O'Neil thought that the site had been hastily refortified during the Roman conquest period (1942, p. 20 and p. 24f.). At the Gwernyfed Gaer, Aberllynfi (Brecknockshire) the writer thought that the inner ditch at the northern end of the site had been deliberately filled with rubble from the rampart (Savory, 1958b, pp. 57–59) and here again there was no sign of occupation after the conquest period. On the other hand he suspected demolition at the entrance of Mynydd Bychan (Glamorganshire) before a very early Roman phase of occupation (1954b, p. 95 and 1955a, pp. 18–20). At some other sites where there has been fairly extensive excavation, e.g., Pen Dinas (Aberystwyth), Twyn y Gaer (Cwmyoy) and Twyn Llechfaen (Breconshire) occupation seems to have ceased by the Roman conquest and never to have been resumed, but these must be contrasted with a large number of sites near the northern and southern coasts of Wales which either continued to be occupied after the conquest, or were reoccupied later (p. 284 below).

While concrete archaeological evidence of the effect of Roman arms upon Welsh hillforts thus remains scanty, Romanists have long sought to reconstruct the course of campaigns in Wales with the help of classical texts and the evidence of Roman military sites. Vague though Tacitus' descriptions of campaigns may be (Jarrett, M. G., 1969 and Webster and Dudley, 1965), they at least make it clear that the main resistance came from the Silures and the Ordovices, and that a hillfort was attacked when Caratacus met his final defeat in the territory of the latter in 51 A.D. The site of this hillfort is really quite unidentifiable and Cefn y Carnedd near Caersws certainly does not fit the circumstances described by Tacitus. The advocacy of this site by Webster and others seems to be bound up with a widespread belief among Romanists that the Ordovices controlled central Wales at the time of the Roman invasion. In fact, the classical sources for the geography of Wales (Jarrett and Mann, 1968) are so derivative, corrupt and conflicting that the best evidence for the location of the Ordovices is probably that of old Welsh place names and tradition, which puts them in north-west Wales. In this case, we cannot ignore the evidence we have already considered (p. 267 above) of a distinctive hillfort group in north-west Wales, with a marked natural frontier separating it from the continuous spread of hillforts through the upper Severn basin, which one would naturally attribute to the Cornovii, as Richmond, indeed, did (1963). These are two distinct cultures, but it is, of course, possible that the Ordovices had been extending their authority among the hill-folk in the territory of the Cornovii because the governing class of the latter had made peace with Rome, as the subsequent privileges of their *civitas* suggest, while on the other hand the Druids in Anglesey had become a focal point for popular resistance to Rome. It is not, however, a sound procedure to equate the extent of the original Silurian and Ordovician territories with the distribution of known Roman forts, on the assumption that these tribes resisted while the Deceangli, Cornovii and Demetae did not: Jarrett and Mann, indeed, even argue on this basis that the territory of the Silures must have extended to Cardigan Bay because of the line of Roman forts spaced out along the road from Brecon through Llandovery to Llanio, Trawscoed and Pennal (1968, p. 171)! It is surely equally arguable that the lay-out of Roman roads in Wales and the forts which are spaced out along them is designed to isolate the main masses of hostile native population from each other and that the forts in the central Marches which continued to be occupied after the opening phase of conquest were bases for operations which were normally conducted a good deal further west. In the light of all this, one must now consider the evidence for a very wide-spread backwardness in acceptance of Roman provincial culture in Wales, which is suggested by the evidence for continued or renewed occupation of hillforts.

B. Continued Occupation of Hillforts

Some years ago Dr. Grace Simpson reviewed the evidence for continuing activity at Welsh hillforts in the second century A.D., and even later, which could be related to the signs she saw of destruction of local auxiliary forts during the Antonine period, and a continuing need for a large garrison in Wales (1963, pp. 72–75, 1964a, pp. 212–220 and 1964b, pp. 97–113). Since then a number of sites, large and small, have been added to the long list of those which have produced evidence of some kind of activity after the conquest period. It is clear, however, that the nature of this activity varied greatly and that much of it cannot be used to prove resistance to Rome. Wainwright, in particular, has pointed out the danger of assuming that a few potsherds scattered through the topsoil necessarily mean anything more than the practice of muck-spreading from some nearby Romano-British farmyard, and proposes to reduce to nine the list of hillforts which can be certainly said to have been occupied, in that they have produced evidence of structures in use during the second, third or fourth centuries A.D. (1967a, p. 69). Even at the time, the list was perhaps unduly short, and now it would need to be considerably lengthened as a result of recent discoveries. Moreover, it can now be more profitably analysed from the point of view of chronology, and the type of structure that was occupied or built.

First of all, one must recognise that there are a few sites where native occupation of a sort continued in the first or second centuries A.D., with small roundhouses of the local Iron Age type still being used or even constructed. This is the case at Tre'r Ceiri and Braich y Ddinas in Caernarvonshire, while at Dinorben huts of this type seem to have been built in the second century A.D. on the platform formed by the destruction of the north-east rampart (Gardner and Savory, 1964, pp. 59 and 93). Bearing in mind the delays with which pottery of Romano-British types would find its way into remote native villages it is reasonable to assume that occupation on a varying scale did continue at some north Wales hillforts, with or without official permission, during the period when the area was a far from fully pacified military zone. On the south Wales seaboard, too, there is evidence of some activity at Llanmelin and

Sudbrook hillforts in the Flavian period, although the former site seems to have been abandoned thereafter and the same applies to the miniature hillfort at Mynydd Bychan near Cowbridge (Simpson, 1964a, p. 217f.). At Kilvey Hill near Swansea we have already noticed the evidence for a small concentric earthwork having been constructed in the second century (p. 275 above), and the evidence for continued occupation in the same period at the similar site known as Maendy Camp, Ystradyfodwg (Glamorganshire) (Simpson, 1964a, p. 218) should be seen in the same light. But there is now clear evidence along the south Wales seaboard for buildings constructed within hillforts, during the early Roman period, with rectangular plans, in timber or dry-stone, which mark a break from local prehistoric traditions and must relate to contemporary structures outside hillforts which have been classed with the simpler "villa" sites. Such is the succession of structures which J. L. Davies located behind the inner rampart on the west side of the Bulwarks, Porthkerry (Glamorganshire) (1968). The second of these was burnt down about the middle of the second century A.D. while the third was occupied in the late third and fourth centuries. The simple rectangular structures which succeeded the Early Iron Age roundhouses at the Whitton (Glamorganshire) villa site (Jarrett, 1965, 1967, 1968) probably indicate the background, as far as the Vale of Glamorgan goes. Here is evidence of Romanisation, which we now know took the form of the development of a considerable number of true villa sites, and we must suppose that the interiors of some large hillforts were adapted to agricultural uses by estates which centred on buildings of Roman type, sometimes built within the ruined defences. This appears to be the explanation of second–fourth century structures related to field systems with the large hillfort at Caer Dynnaf, Llanblethian (Pl. VIII) (J. L. Davies, 1967b), and the casual finds of potsherds of similar dates made within the defences at Castle Ditches, Llancarfan, Caerau, Ely and Llantrithyd. In Monmouthshire surface indications of a true villa, with hypocaust and other tiles, have recently been observed within the great hillfort of Gaer Fawr, Llangwm.

In west Wales the evidence of Walesland Rath (Wainwright, 1971a, pp. 101–103) has now come to show only a partial replacement of native by Roman building traditions in the second century A.D. on an old defended site, but at Cwmbrwyn and Trelissey, and probably at Castle Flemish, at a somewhat later date, the latter are fully established. It was remoteness rather than hostility to Rome that caused the backwardness of the Demetae, and we know now that the Roman fort at Carmarthen was soon replaced by a small town (Wilson, 1969, p. 270). We can see that the slight indications of continued occupation in the early Roman period at small defended homesteads like Knock and Merryborough raths (Crossley, 1964 and 1965) and the promontory forts at Buckspool and Bosherston in Pembrokeshire and Bishopston and High Penard in the Gower need mean no more than tolerated occupation in a pacified area, and the early finds from a destroyed earthwork of the same type at Barland Quarry in the same area can be explained in the same way (Savory, 1962).

The continued or renewed occupation at a few sites on the northern sea-board of Wales where the associated structures are sufficiently well-known suggests a smaller degree of Romanisation than in South Wales, in that the roundhouse seems to have remained the normal dwelling type: only at Tre'r Ceiri is there a suggestion that a sub-rectangular type of dry-stone-walled hut was gaining ground in the Roman period (Hogg, 1960, pp. 15–17), but even here and at Braich y Ddinas, where a few rectangular huts also appear, the nature of the settlement, as a large walled village on a high hill-top, is very different from that of the south Wales homesteads just mentioned. Whether this difference can be interpreted as part of a tradition of resistance to Rome, even of periodical rebellion, rather than the result of poverty or a different social organisation, will remain uncertain until more is known about the hillforts in the interior of Wales. As the map shows (Fig. 19) sites with solid evidence of occupation in the earlier centuries of Roman rule are at present almost confined to the northern and southern seaboard: we simply do not know, as yet, what happened at the hillforts further inland and we cannot judge what part they played in any rebellions against Roman rule in the second century. The evidence from Craig y Deryn hillfort in Merionethshire (Gresham, 1967, p. 144), the Giants Bank, Llanmerewig (Montgomeryshire) and the Burfa Camp, Evenjobb (Radnorshire) (Simpson, 1964a, pp. 216, 218) is too poorly documented to be significant and the single early Romano-British sherd from the upper filling of the inner ditch at Aberllynfi (Brecknockshire) is hardly evidence of continued occupation. But it may well be that any resis-tance was of a guerrilla nature, based upon the difficulties of the terrain rather than in well-fortified fixed positions: the usefulness of the hillfort was related to inter-tribal warfare, not to resistance to the Roman army.

C. Reoccupation of Hillforts in the Third and Fourth Century A.D.

Dinorben hillfort, Abergele, is the most extensively explored of several sites along the northern seaboard of Wales which have yielded evidence of con-siderable activity in the late third and fourth centuries A.D.—activity which in the past has been interpreted as the result of use by a local militia, enrolled to relieve regular units of the Roman army in the defence of western coasts against raiders from Ireland (Wheeler, 1922). Once again this activity seems to be of somewhat different quality to that which appears during the same period at certain sites in south Wales. The latter in fact can now be seen to be linked with continued occupation of peaceful farms in areas long given over to purely civil administration, though even here the existence of a fort of Saxon Shore type at Cardiff suggests that protection against sea-raiders may have become an important consideration for many Romano-British landowners, and their *coloni*, along the southern seaboard of Wales. The principal exception here is Coygan Camp, where intense activity, in the period *c* A.D. 270–300, centred on a rectangular hut of timber and dry-stone masonry, 23 ft × 11 ft, backed against the rampart, with various out-buildings (Wainwright, 1967a, pp. 45–70). The fact that for part of its occupation this hut was used by a counterfeiter of coins, who, apparently in the reign of Carinus, had cause suddenly to bury the incriminating evidence of his activities in a pit dug in the floor of the hut, suggests that the re-occupation of the secluded ruins of a small hillfort in this case was not due solely to the normal activities of an agricultural community; and the well-known bronze saucepan found long ago in the neighbouring cave bears witness, with its base remodelled in Celtic style as late as the second or even third century, to the long survival of La Tène traditions in this western region of *Britannia*, no doubt as part of the resistance to Roman influences maintained by the successors of the local Celtic metal-workers of the first century A.D., who went on making brooches, bucket escutcheons and other such things long after the demand for sword-sheaths and shield-fittings had gone. But the briefness of the re-occupation at Coygan shows that the historical circumstances were not the same as those which affected Dinorben and similar sites in north Wales.

At Dinorben (Gardner and Savory, 1964 and Savory, 1971b) an abundant coin list permits the establishment of quite definite chronological limits, between *c* A.D. 260 and *c* A.D. 360, for the renewed activity on the site; for these coins, with a few exceptions, did not come from hoards but were scattered very widely about a site covering 5 acres, in different parts of which a number of different structures were in use over a long period. The main structure seems to have been a large circular house, the outer wall of which was about 65 ft in diameter, while the weight of the roof was partly carried on an inner ring of supports and access was gained through a corridor framed by four massive posts, two of which were on the outer and two on the inner ring of supports. This represents a nobleman's residence comparable to those which were being built in the late Roman period in Scotland, Ireland and the Isle of Man (Gardner and Savory, 1964, pp. 103–106, Fig. 14). Although such a link with the architectural standards of chieftains who for the most part lay outside of Roman control might suggest some form of native resurgence within the Roman province, the abundant finds from the neighbourhood of the house suggest an affluent and even literate farming community on good terms with fully Romanised centres of habitation not far away at *Deva* and *Viroconium*. It is far more likely that this site was the headquarters of a large estate, belonging to a Romanised British nobleman who was forced to take shelter in an abandoned hillfort during the troubled times of the Gallic Empire because local garrisons could not protect him against Irish raiders than that anything in the nature of rebellion was involved; Boon may well be right in seeing a special relationship with the Roman garrisons at Cae'rhun and Segontium, perhaps based on a contract to supply the meat ration which had now become important for the semi-barbaric members of Roman auxiliary units (Savory, 1971b, p. 33f.), but he adds that in this case a change of garrison at the end of the Magnentian episode might be the reason for the apparently sudden cessation of activity at Dinorben not very long after A.D. 355. Two other North Wales sites which have not been excavated on any scale—Bwrdd Arthur (Anglesey) and Moel Fenlli (Denbighshire)—have yielded enough late Roman coins and pottery to casual prospection to suggest that these very large hillfort sites may have seen the same sort of re-occupation as Dinorben, while the evidence at Parciau (Anglesey), Dinas Dinlle (Caernarvonshire) and Tre'r Ceiri is much more shadowy. We cannot judge confidently, however, whether the survival of the timber-framed roundhouse, which was certainly typical of most of north-east Wales in the immediate pre-Roman phase, was characteristic of the same wide area in the third and fourth centuries A.D., although this is likely, and is hinted, in fact, by the nature of the hut within the small embanked enclosure, occupied in the second and third centuries A.D. which adjoined the Breiddin (Mont-gomeryshire) hillfort (O'Neil, 1937, pp. 107–112 and p. 123), and would correspond to the persistence of the circular plan among the stone-built dwellings of north-west Wales in the same period.

It is necessary at this point to rebut the implication made by a reviewer of the supplementary report on excavations at Dinorben, that post-hole arrange-ments recorded at Dinorben can be lightly reinterpreted by people who never visited the excavations, on the assumption that not a single hut-floor was ever stripped widely enough to establish its complete plan. Dinorben was certainly a peculiarly difficult site to excavate, not only because of its dense tree cover and the exigencies of an active quarry, but because all the dwellings had been constructed on platforms recessed into more or less steeply-sloping hill-sides and the talus upon which the down-slope part of the floors had been built had usually been eroded during the long period, lasting indeed until the mid-nineteenth century, when Dinorben was free of tree-cover. Nonetheless a wide area was cleared around the large Romano-Celtic roundhouse already referred to, and several of the smaller Early Iron Age hut floors were almost completely cleared, with a view to getting a complete plan; when this was not obtained, it was due to the fact that posts had been driven into made ground, subse-quently eroded, and not cut into the underlying sub-soil. In many cases hut hollows which were regularly circular were not completely explored because a section showed that they were too badly eroded to retain contemporary deposits: all too often all that remained was a shallow deposit, resting on the rock, in which late Roman material occurred. In the south-western area of the site a further difficulty was that there had already been extensive disturbances during Dr. Gardner's excavations of 1912–1922. It was therefore suggested with due caution in 1971 (Savory, 1971b, p. 18f.) that a large circular house, like that at the northern end of the site may have existed in this area also, to account for a gently curving line of large post-holes (*not* a straight line), near which fourth century coins and pottery had been found in abundance. But it has since been suggested that what really existed here was a continuous line of posts connected with staging built to reactivate the defence of the great inner rampart on the south side of the site, possibly with wooden towers at intervals, in line with what is now alleged to have happened at the Breiddin. Such an interpretation, on this chronological horizon, would revive Wheeler's idea of a late Roman militia, and it is now necessary to examine this possibility in a wider context.

At the Breiddin hillfort recent emergency excavations, not yet fully published, have revealed a long sequence of structural phases, with associated post-hole systems along the line of the main rampart. In the light of the similarly complicated sequence at Dinorben, this writer has every sympathy with the excavator in his problem of interpretation, bearing in mind the particular hazards of dealing with the collapsed rubble core of a dry-stone rampart, such as survives from the later phases at the Breiddin. He well remembers the difficulties here, being a survivor of the original excavation team of 1933–1935. The main rampart of dry-stone, apparently without timber-lacing, had been deliberately demolished at some time—O'Neil thought at the Roman conquest, Musson is inclined to think in late Roman times—and crude pottery now familiar under the name "VCP" was found, along with late Romano-British sherds, in the debris overlying the demolished rampart as well as in a layer contemporary with the rampart at the entrance. The recent excavations (Musson, 1972 and see below pp. 293 ff.) have produced similar "VCP", much of it in association with Malvernian stamped ware of the third century B.C., in a layer behind the rampart, but some in an area where the ruins of the rampart had been disturbed. Accordingly, Musson has been inclined to revive the idea that some "VCP" may be early Dark Age in date, and to use this possibility, combined with the presence of ordinary fourth century Romano-British pottery, to support the view that a system of large post-holes partly inserted into the ruins of the rampart might represent the framework and towers of a re-built rampart of the late fourth or early fifth centuries A.D. My own view, on personal observation, is that no distinction can be made between the "VCP" potsherds of Iron Age and alleged Dark Age date at the Breiddin, and that there is no convincing evidence for Dark Age "VCP" anywhere else in North Wales or the neighbouring counties of England. The *bête noire* here is the idea that demolitions of ramparts must necessarily be attributed to the Romans. But demolition of the stone rampart at the Breiddin could perfectly well have been due to tribal warfare in the second century B.C. and have been followed by the construction of timber buildings behind the ruined rampart, as at Walesland Rath, at a time when, as we find elsewhere in north Wales, pottery was not being used. A similar complicated sequence of post-holes immediately behind the inner rampart at Moel Hiraddug hillfort (Flintshire) prompted the excavator at one time (Davies, 1971, p. 8) to suggest a sub-Roman refortification, but here again the whole sequence will probably turn out in the end, to be prehistoric. The late Roman pottery at the Breiddin is said to be late fourth century in date and no coins were found during the excavations on this site. If there really was a late Roman refortification here, it would have been a good deal later than the reoccupation of Dinorben. The alleged late Roman timber staging at the two sites, then, would not have been of the same date. In fact the line of large post-holes, of early fourth century date, at Dinorben, was not found to continue south-eastwards along the heap of slaked lime from the burning of the Period II rampart, as it should have done if it had really been connected with a refortification of the main southern rampart in late Roman times; it was in fact on a curve which carried it into the disturbed occupation layer further north, where post-holes did not clearly show up (Savory, 1971b, p. 18f. Figs 6–7). At the same time it should be remembered that refortification of South Cadbury (Somerset) hillfort, which has doubtless provided the stimulus for speculation at the Breiddin and Moel Hiraddug, takes one well into the fifth century A.D. and is associated with the use of Dark Age import wares, such as are known from certain Welsh sites (Alcock, 1972c, pp. 174–180). Neither the Breiddin nor Dinorben have produced these wares and the class of late Roman flanged bowl at Dinorben which the writer was once inclined to regard as possibly very late fourth century or very early fifth (Gardner and Savory, 1964, p. 98f.) should probably be regarded as early fourth century (Savory, 1971b, p. 63). There is, in fact, no solid evidence for the refortification of any large hillfort in Wales in the late Roman period.

D. The Dark Age Forts of Wales

The fact that a number of hillforts in Wales and the Marches bear traditional names connected with the heroes of Old Welsh oral and literary tradition—Bwrdd Arddur, Caer Caradoc, Craig Gwtheyrn, Dinas Emrys, Moel Fenlli etc.—has led to speculation about the possibility of such sites in fact having been re-occupied in the fifth and sixth centuries A.D. We have just seen, however, that there is as yet no solid evidence of this and that the attempt to demonstrate that this happened arises from recent discoveries in the West Country, where it now seems that several large hillforts may have been refortified at one time or another during this period, as part of the resistance of sub-Roman Dumnonia to Saxon encroachment. It does not follow, however, that the historical circumstances were the same in Wales, which was largely cushioned against Saxon attack, down to the seventh century, by surviving sub-Roman communities in the west Midlands. The major preoccupation in Wales, during the fifth and sixth centuries, would generally have been with the Irish, who in fact established themselves at the beginning of this period in various parts of Wales, probably as a rule in the form of limited numbers of fighting men brought in to reinforce the garrison of late Roman Britain. But there is as yet no sign of actual refortification of Iron Age hillforts in the western parts of Wales. What we have instead is re-occupation, probably small-scale, of one site—Coygan Camp, attested by Dark Age "import ware" (Wainwright, 1967a, pp. 70–73, p. 157f.), and the construction of a series of small strongholds on sites not previously fortified or fortified on a different plan: Dinas Powys (Alcock, 1963a), Carreg y Llam near Nevin (Caernarvonshire) (Hogg, 1957b), Garn Boduan near Nevin (Caernarvonshire) (Hogg, 1960), Castell Degannwy (Caernarvonshire) (Alcock, 1967) and Dinas Emrys, Beddgelert (Caernarvonshire) (Savory, 1960). Among these sites Carreg y Llam and Garn Boduan represent the tradition of the late Romano-British and sub-

Roman enclosed hut-groups of north-west Wales, like Din Lligwy and Pant-y-saer with their roundhouses adapted to a more definitely defensive position (Alcock, 1971b, p. 216f., Fig. 17) and they no doubt belonged to the same sort of people—sub-Roman noblemen—as the other sites, where the house-type is not known or has changed to a sub-rectangular structure. Sites of this kind have very little to do with the true Early Iron Age fort tradition structurally, and even less socially, and it would be inappropriate to describe them in detail here. The true limits of our subject have already been passed.

13 | *Excavations at the Breiddin 1969–1973*

C. R. Musson

On behalf of the Rescue Archaeology Group

I. Introduction

Ever since the excavations of Bryan O'Neil in the early 1930s the Breiddin hillfort has held a special interest for students of Roman and post-Roman Britain. In his trenches at the hillfort entrance, O'Neil found 30 sherds of third century or fourth century Roman pottery, set in a thick occupation deposit behind the ruined Iron Age rampart. With it was some crude "native imitation pottery" which the excavator saw as an attempt to perpetuate the potting tradition after the supply of commercially produced Roman wares had finally died out. If O'Neil was right in this, the occupation could run on into the fifth century or even later, though his trenches were too small to give much idea of the extent and character of the resettlement.

At the other end of the time-scale the prehistoric levels produced not only Iron Age pottery but also a small fragment of socketed axe and half of an expanded terminal armlet of well known Late Bronze Age type. In the light of recent speculation about early hillfort origins these scraps took on a new significance. Could they, perhaps, be evidence not of cultural retardation in a geographically isolated area, but of a genuine Late Bronze Age occupation in the early first millennium B.C.?

The chance to test these questions came in 1969 when quarrying began to damage the defences at the southern tip of the hillfort. A rapidly assembled team carried out trial excavations for six weeks in October and November of that year, with unexpectedly encouraging results. A section through the inner rampart revealed at least two phases of construction, with three types of prehistoric pottery; and the area behind the rampart produced Roman pottery very similar to that found by O'Neil 400 m away to the north, as well as two substantial post-holes. The most revealing cutting, however, was a small test trench at the base of the hill-slopes some way behind the rampart, where a slight hollow suggested the possible existence of an ancient building-platform. From the filling of this hollow came a mixed bag of finds—an eighteenth century clay pipe, Roman and prehistoric pottery, and a finely preserved bronze pin with long straight shaft and flat nail-like head. Close parallels could be found in several Late Bronze Age contexts, most notably in the Heathery Burn Cave, County Durham, where the finds are traditionally dated to the mid-eighth century B.C. On the structural side, the same trench showed that, given damp conditions, traces of wattle and daub roundhouses could be detected in some detail, despite the unhelpful subsoil. The trench revealed parts of at least four successive houses, each about 7 m in diameter. If structural evidence of this kind could be recovered on the hill-slopes, it might also be found on the flatter areas of the summit ridge, or in the lee of the ramparts where it could be linked stratigraphically to the defences.

A major campaign of excavation was therefore financed by the Welsh office of the Department of the Environment, and carried out by the Rescue Archaeology Group during the winter months of 1970–1972. At the time of writing (early summer 1973) small investigations are still in progress to check contentious points and to collect additional radiocarbon samples. The following account is therefore tentative in some respects and conclusions which seem quite reasonable now may have to be modified, or qualified, as post-excavation work nears completion. In particular, some of the outstanding dating problems may be solved by further radiocarbon tests.

II. The Site, and Methods of Excavation

The site of the hillfort is shown in Fig. 1 and Pl. I. The Breiddin Hills are a striking and isolated group of sharp volcanic ridges, rising steeply from the southern bank of the River Severn west of Shrewsbury, just across the Welsh border into Montgomeryshire. The westernmost ridge, on which the hill-fort lies, is a single hogback of dolerite, with precipitous slopes overlooking the river valley and the Shropshire Plain to the north and east. The central ridge, lower and more broken, has a small double-banked settlement, trenched by O'Neil in the 1930s. The westernmost ridge, higher again and rising to several separate peaks, has two small hillforts along its 6 km length, both under a hectare in area, and neither yet excavated.

By contrast, the main hillfort encloses almost 30 hectares. The precise area is difficult to calculate since there are no artificial defences on the western side, the hillslope simply becoming more and more steep, with cliffs and scree-slopes falling precipitously to the valley below. On the east and round the ends of the ridge there are artificial defences, for the most part double but for a short distance north of the entrance, treble. Only the third bank has a ditch, the others consisting of stones and earth scraped together from uphill; over the years their capping of loose scree has collapsed down the slope so that they now appear as straggling lines of stonework half-lost amongst the under-growth and forestry. The distance between them is considerable, 50 m and more between the first and second, about half as much between the second and third. A single entrance track cuts diagonally across the hill-slope from the east, so that the arms which link the first and second ramparts form a gradually narrowing passageway nearly 80 m long, overlooked on the uphill side. At the entrance itself the inner rampart is slightly inturned on the northern side, though O'Neil's excavations suggested this may have been a fairly late innovation; his trenches were too limited to show the form of the gateway itself.

Within the ramparts the hillfort divides conveniently into two parts. North of the entrance the ground rises steeply to a narrow grassy ridge, capped by the distinctive eighteenth century monument known as Rodney's Pillar. Stone hut-circles were reported here in the nineteenth century, but none can now be seen and they may have been imaginary. Nor is there any sign of the small building platforms found in other Marches hillforts, such as Caer Caradoc above Church Stretton, or Midsummer Hill in Herefordshire. South of the entrance the land is more broken, with steep slopes and outcrops of rock between areas of flattish land quite suitable for building. On the west, sheltered by a massive knob of rock is a large natural pond, choked with marsh plants and fallen trees. The southern half of the interior, like the hill-slopes to the east, is smothered in Forestry Commission conifers.

The recent excavations were concentrated at the southern tip of the hill, beyond the main area of forestry. In the interior of the hillfort there were trial cuttings on the eastern slopes, and a single area-excavation on the summit ridge, about 35 m by 40 m. The two hand-dug excavations across the inner rampart were 10 m and 25 m wide, and there were subsidiary mechanical sections at two points on the end of the ridge where the threat from quarrying was most immediate.

The excavations occupied a professional team of six to eight people for thirteen months. The whole of the work was concentrated into the period from late September to early May, since experience in the exploratory season of 1969 had shown that colour changes in the soil could only be detected properly in damp conditions. The natural soil is lean and crumbly, with a dense scatter of loose stones which confuse and complicate the identification of archaeological features. Colour changes are absent, or barely detectable, until excavation reaches the level of bedrock or clean yellow subsoil, and stratification in the sense of distinctive layers superimposed upon one another hardly exists.

On such a site traditional methods of excavation would have been self-defeating. There were few, if any, detectable levels to be "followed", even in the rampart cuttings, and pits or post-holes in the interior could only be seen as vague concentrations of stone, scarcely distinguishable from the general scatter around and between them. The technique adopted was to remove a thickness of 2–10 cm of soil, leaving all projecting stones in place and marking the position of every find, however insignificant it seemed at the time. The resulting surface was then drawn, stone by stone, noting soil colour changes, if there were any, and numbering pits or post-holes which could already be clearly seen. This process was repeated up to ten times for a soil-depth of 30–60 cm, until all features had either been removed or could be seen as distinctive stone-groups or darker markings in the yellow subsoil. These could be dug as individual features, though the majority were still excavated in successive horizontal spits, rather than by the commoner method of half-sectioning. Every find was individually numbered and its position plotted on the appropriate spit-plan, so that it was located within a matter of a few centimetres in relation to the process of excavation as well as to objective site levels.

The record of an area in the interior thus consisted of up to ten or more overlay drawings on transparent plastic. Post-holes, pits and other features often only became clear at the lowest levels, but they could then be traced upwards through the overlay plans so that their true outline and profile could eventually be identified. The recovery of information therefore took place in two interlinked processes: meticulous "objective" recording at the time of excavation, during which some but not all of the archaeological features were detected; and constant re-examination of the drawings, especially at the end of excavation, so that the true outline of features could be recovered and additional ones identified. In the course of this re-examination finds allocated simply to a spit at the time of excavation could now be reassigned to individual features, so that few are likely to have been wrongly attributed even when the features in which they lay were unrecognised at the time of excavation.

Much the same pattern was followed in the rampart cuttings, though detectable changes in soil colour and structural features like rampart revetments gave occasional clues to the real slope of the deposits and hence to the most appropriate slope for the surface of each successive spit. Even on the ramparts, however, the analysis of stratification was to a large extent retrospective, since the colour of the soil or the character of the stone changed only indistinctly from one sweep of excavation to the next.

With these difficulties in mind, the uncertainties of the following account can perhaps be kept in perspective.

III. The Earliest Phase of Hillfort Construction

The earliest occupation of the hill-top is represented by a thin scatter of Late Neolithic flints, polished axe fragments, and pottery in the Ebbsfleet tradition. Barbed and tanged arrowheads and a perforated axe-hammer have also been picked up on the hill-top in the past. But the first phase of enclosure or defence almost certainly belongs to the ninth or eighth centuries b.c. The earliest rampart (Fig. 3, top) was a meagre bank less than a metre high, reinforced on the down-hill side by pairs of posts set in two lines no more than a metre apart. Every post within the excavated area had been burned. A charcoal sample from the base of one of them gave a radiocarbon date of 800 ± 41 b.c. The second rampart, perhaps no more than a repair, was scarcely more substantial. Another 30 cm or so of core material had been added, retained at the back by a line of boulders and at the front by posts set more deeply at intervals in a continuous foundation trench. The burning, in this case, was more sporadic. A charcoal sample, again from the bottom of a post-hole, gave a radiocarbon date of 828 ± 71 b.c.—not significantly different from the first.

It should be said immediately that this phasing is conjectural. The core material *seemed* to fall into two halves, the lower part generally lighter, with little sign of pre-rampart occupation, the upper part darker, with quantities of charcoal, burned bone and pottery. From the upper core, too, came a nail-headed bronze pin with swollen neck, an amber bead and a blue faience star-bead. The distinction between the fillings was never very clear, however, and it is possible that only a single rampart was involved, with a front revetment supported in the continuous foundation trench and internal timbering in the paired post-holes. Whatever the phasing, there appears to be no parallel in Britain for the closeness of the internal timbering, though many early hillforts, of course, have posts set at rather wider intervals in their defensive banks.

From sealed occupation deposits behind the rampart came a knob-headed pin and the plain bronze ring shown in Pl. II. Less well-stratified deposits nearby produced a socketed bronze hammer and a pair of tweezers too fragile for illustration. Of these objects only the hammer is a well-authenticated Late Bronze Age type, but unstratified levels in the interior of the hillfort produced the large nail-headed pin already mentioned in the introduction, a socketed knife (with *copper*, not *iron* rivets as stated in previous interim reports), a small un-looped spear-head (still undergoing conservation), the tip and half the hilt of a bronze sword, and a totally undamaged socketed axe with its carbonised willow shaft still in position. This was a remarkable find, since it gave the chance not only to date the axe but also to relate it chronologically to the earliest rampart phases. The resulting radiocarbon determination, 754 ± 50 b.c., leaves little doubt that the axe belongs to the same phase of activity as the early rampart.

Behind the rampart, the occupation soil in places reached a depth of 30 cm and there were occasional concentrations of stone which might have been pits or post-holes. At one point a small area of paving had survived beneath a large boulder, and there were two rectangular floor areas which may have been the remnants of buildings. The smaller was a patch of damaged but well-laid cobbling 2 m by 2·5 m, the larger a rectangle of darker soil, about 4 m by 3 m, within which there were several shallow pits or hearths. In neither case was there evidence for the wall and roof construction; in this respect, and in their general dimensions, they resemble the rectangular floor areas which characterise the last phase of occupation at Moel-y-Gaer, Flintshire, though the latter, of course, have yet to be dated.

Over six hundred sherds of coarse brown or black-faced pottery were recovered from the occupation deposits behind the rampart, and half as many again from unsealed deposits in the interior. In shape and fabric they seem to form a single group, dominated by short-necked situlate jars with fairly slack shoulders, globular or barrel-shape pots with round or internally bevelled rims, and open bowls with simple rounded or flattened rims. There were also two small but very fragmentary vessels with quite sharp carinations, and a slack-profiled jar in a rather finer fabric, with a slightly raised cordon on the shoulder. Apart from two circle-impressed sherds, one cabled rim and another with a possible finger-nail impression, this was the only sign of decoration. Found in isolation, much of this pottery would probably have been assigned to the earlier part of the Iron Age, but the radiocarbon date for the occupation soil (868 ± 64 b.c.) leaves little doubt that it can properly be called Late Bronze Age pottery.

Sites like Mam Tor, Ivinghoe Beacon and Dinorben have hinted at very early origins for some of our hillforts, but in no case could the Bronze Age objects or the early radiocarbon dates be tied with absolute certainty to the construction of the enclosing banks. The four dates at the Breiddin, on the other hand, leave little room for equivocation. It is even possible that the whole 30 hectares of the hill-top was enclosed at this early stage. There is no obvious place where the bank could turn back across the top of the hill to form a strong ridge-end fort, assuming that its purpose *was* defensive, and O'Neil recovered Late Bronze Age objects 400 m north of the present excavations. He also found a thin occupation layer and probably a post-hole beneath the later Iron Age rampart. Only further excavation, of course, could reveal the true extent of the earliest defence. In the current climate of opinion a Bronze Age hillfort will surprise no-one, but the potential size of the early settlement at the Breiddin raises questions beyond the scope of this brief account.

IV. The Iron Age Hillfort

The subsequent Iron Age occupation appears to fall into two phases, the earlier preceded by the construction of a new and more substantial rampart, stone-faced at front and back. Unfortunately a rampart of this kind is difficult to date by radiocarbon methods, since charcoal found within it could easily be derived from earlier levels; there were no acceptable samples in this case. Behind the new rampart there were two separate phases of occupation, one represented by rectangular buildings or yards set against the rear revetment, the other by circular buildings with wattle and daub walls set in shallow foundation trenches. The two are shown together in Fig. 3, centre. From the rectangular structure came stamped vesicular pottery imported from the Malverns, involuted bow-brooches unlikely to be earlier than mid third century B.C., and a distinctive coarse red ware known along the Welsh Marches as "VCP" (very coarse pottery). The roundhouses produced no clearly associated finds, except for rectangular clay loomweights and three ribbed bronze rings, as yet unparalleled. Finds which could have belonged to either phase included a blue glass bead with raised spiral decoration and a ring-headed iron linch-pin, neither likely to have been in use much before the first century B.C.

In the interior there was a well-defined roundhouse phase, contrasting strongly with a series of small rectangular buildings represented solely by their corner post-holes (Fig. 2). There was tenuous evidence to link the four-posted buildings with stamped pottery and VCP, but their relationship to the roundhouses was quite unclear. Behind the rampart, on the other hand, there seemed little doubt at the time of excavation that the roundhouses were later, and a first century B.C./first century A.D. date, in keeping with the glass bead and linch-pin, seemed quite probable.

The radiocarbon dates, however, contradict this reading of the evidence. Charcoal from a burned roundhouse wall gave a radiocarbon date of 479 ± 55 b.c., while one from a four-posted building in the interior produced a date of 238 ± 70 b.c. Until further samples can be tested, both from the roundhouses and the four-posted buildings, the relationship between the two must be left unsettled. This is an interesting example, however, of the way radiocarbon dates can re-open questions of observation and interpretation well after the site work has been completed and the main lines of explanation decided.

V. The Problem of a Late Roman Re-Defence

At the hillfort entrance in the 1930s, O'Neil found a deep occupation deposit containing a quantity of late Roman pottery. This had accumulated behind and perhaps on top of a stony layer which butted against the rear of the pre-historic rampart and which O'Neil interpreted as deliberate slighting of the Iron Age defences, presumably at the beginning of the Roman period.

In the recent excavations, 400 m to the south, a rather similar situation was found in both the main rampart cuttings. Here too there was a stony layer about 4 m wide immediately behind the Iron Age rampart. In the wider cutting the stones were densely packed and gave a distinct impression of being deliber-ately laid, perhaps in several levels. As the excavation progressed there seemed little doubt that this was a deliberate filling, either to produce a flat surface at much the same level as the top of the Iron Age rampart, or to provide a firmer footing on the relatively soft Iron Age deposits below. Throughout its depth it produced Roman pottery attributable, as a group, to the later fourth century A.D.

The levelling was removed in several spits, the surface being drawn stone by stone after each sweep of excavation. After the final spit had been removed, several groups of stones were left standing proud of the exposed Iron Age levels. They clearly belonged to post-holes similar to the two found in the exploratory excavations of 1969. Re-examination of the earlier spit-plans showed that some, though not all, could be traced with a fair degree of certainty into the body of the Roman levelling, and there seemed little doubt that they belonged to the same general phase of activity.

At first they made little sense, but as work progressed the number increased until they stretched out along the full length of the main rampart cutting. Some were ill-defined; others were only detected at quite a low level, after the Roman stonework and parts of the underlying Iron Age levels had been removed. Gradually, however, a pattern began to emerge. There was a particularly dense concentration near the point of their first discovery; one post-hole was demonstrably later than its neighbour, and another probably so. With this as the only guide, it was possible to subdivide the group as shown in Fig. 3, bottom, an initial four-post setting (dotted) being replaced by a larger rectangle of six posts, accompanied by pairs of posts running away on either side along the length of the rampart. Over 80% of the Roman pottery from the trench fell within the area of the four-post and six-post settings. There was also a heavily burned stone slab hearth, marked on the drawing by cross-hatching.

It is not difficult to see this as a major re-defence of the site, in two stages: first a simple four-posted watchtower; then a more sophisticated structure, with a six-post tower flanked on either side by a two-level sentry-walk. (There are reasons for suggesting this particular construction, but they are too complicated to go into here.) In front of this defence the top of the Iron Age bank would have projected as a more or less level platform about 6 m wide, with a vertical wall at the front facing onto the hill-slope—Roman sherds were found low in the stonefall in front of the rampart, one piece lying against the very foot of the Iron Age revetment. At this point, at least, the Iron Age revetment was still in a good state of repair in the late fourth century A.D.

Needless to say, such a defence is without parallel in British hillforts, which makes it all the more frustrating that the search for similar evidence in the narrower rampart cutting was inconclusive. Even so, presented as it is in Fig. 3 the pattern looks attractive and convincing. It is only prudent to point out, however, that this is not a totally "objective" presentation of the evidence. There were three, or perhaps four, post-holes which did not fit this pattern, and which have not been shown; on the evidence available, they could all have been prehistoric. Four of the twenty-one post-holes allocated to the more sophisticated phase of re-defence (those shown in fine hatching) were not found for one reason or another, and are inserted here as a matter of conjecture; two lay in an area which was bulldozed before excavation could be completed, another was destroyed or obscured by a narrow baulk between trenches, and a fourth lay under a massive tree root. In addition, five others appeared to have been damaged, two of them all but destroyed, by a wide and rather ill-defined "intrusion" which disturbed parts of the Iron Age rampart and some at least of the levels behind it (the lighter area in Fig. 3). From high in this intrusion—or perhaps, with hindsight, from *above* it—came several sherds of undoubted late Roman pottery. The intrusion and the re-defence overlapped, so that the two could hardly belong together; and since the post-holes were not detected until at or near the bottom of the disturbance, the intrusion seemed likely to be later than the re-defence, and hence potentially post-Roman.

This is still a plausible reading of the evidence, but there are two difficulties which cannot be glossed over. The intrusion, especially the lower parts of it, produced a quantity of VCP, indistinguishable from that found in the prehistoric levels and in pieces too large and numerous to be easily explained as rubbish survival. If the intrusion was post-Roman, so too should be the VCP.

This, in turn would imply a life-span for VCP of some eight centuries or more, from at least the middle of the Iron Age to the end of the Roman period or later. While not impossible, such a conclusion demands the most rigorous examination of the evidence. The second problem lay in the radiocarbon date for charcoal from the intrusion—not A.D. 400 or thereabouts, but 109 ± 105 b.c. The sample was small, and could easily have been residual from earlier occupations, but the dating of the intrusion seemed so important that even a dubious radiocarbon date was better than none at all.

Taken together, these objections were strong enough to prompt a search for alternative explanations, always, of course, in keeping with the same site observations. The stratification in this part of the excavation was very ill-defined. The intrusion itself was only recognised at a low level. Its existence is not in doubt, but it may not have penetrated to as high a level as has previously been assumed. If so, it could quite possibly be pre-Roman. This would explain both the VCP and the early radiocarbon date. The Roman pottery recovered from a high level (before the presence of the intrusion was actually recognised) must then have come from a later, undetected, disturbance, probably made during the construction of the fourth century re-defence.

While quite consistent with the site evidence, this leaves one problem unsolved—the post-holes of the re-defence appeared in some cases to have been *cut* by the intrusion. If the intrusion was prehistoric, the post-holes must be also. They might then be explained as four-posted buildings similar to those found in the interior, or as an otherwise unrecognised pre-Roman defence.

But the post-holes were not *certainly* cut by the intrusion; they were simply *not detected* until the intrusion had been removed. It is an open question whether post-holes filled with stones and black soil would have been visible in an intrusion containing exactly similar material. Fortunately there were radiocarbon samples from three of them, which can now be submitted for examination. If the results produce a Roman date, the pattern shown in Fig. 3 is proved beyond reasonable doubt. If not, the true extent of the re-defence will remain a matter of conjecture. Some, if not all of the post-holes in the area of the hypothetical watchtowers were undoubtedly Roman, since their packing stones penetrated well into the make-up of the Roman levelling; the concentration of Roman pottery at this point also argues strongly for a specific focus of Roman activity, though a sentry tower is clearly not the only acceptable explanation.

Until the extra radiocarbon tests are completed, therefore, the true extent of the Roman structures cannot be decided. It would certainly be futile to seek parallels for the style of the re-defence, or to make elaborate reconstructions of its timbering; and ill-defined traces of stone-founded buildings in the interior of the fort give little help in deciding the reason for the re-occupation, the identity of the new inhabitants, or the length of their stay. Whatever the uncertainties, there is little doubt that the Breiddin *was* substantially re-occupied, and very possibly re-defended, towards the end of the fourth century A.D. To this extent the present excavations have added significantly to the possibilities raised by O'Neil's excavations almost forty years ago.

Addendum, February 1975

Further radiocarbon dates have now been received:

A date of 1550 ± 100 b.c. suggests that the larger of the two rectangular floor areas behind the rampart (p. 297) belongs to the Late Neolithic/Early Bronze Age occupation, and not to the Late Bronze Age hillfort. The smaller cobbled area, however, was clearly related on stratigraphical evidence to the early rampart, and must date to the Late Bronze Age.

The original roundhouse date of 479 ± 55 b.c. (top of p. 299) is now supplemented by dates of 460 ± 100 b.c., 375 ± 63 b.c. and 320 ± 80 b.c. from other parts of the site. These confirm that the roundhouses are in a general sense earlier than the four-posted buildings, which now have dates of 294 ± 40 b.c., 240 ± 80 b.c., 238 ± 70 b.c. and (less well provenanced) 170 ± 70 b.c.

The samples from the supposedly late Roman post-holes behind the rampart (p. 301) produced a date of 172 ± 45 b.c., reinforcing the possibility that some of the post-holes attributed to the contentious "late Roman re-defence" might in fact belong to prehistoric four-posted buildings.

Renewed excavations in 1975 have confirmed, on clear stratigraphical evidence, that the roundhouses are earlier than the four-posted buildings (p. 299). They have also shown beyond doubt that the majority of the post-holes tentatively attributed to a "late Roman re-defence" on pp. 299–301 actually belong to four-posted buildings of the middle to later Iron Age, roughly aligned along the back of the rampart. The Roman levelling behind the rampart, however, remains intact, though there is growing evidence that the re-occupation may have begun in the later third century, rather a hundred years later as suggested on p. 299. At the time of writing (June 1975) the excavations are still in progress.

14 | Moel y Gaer (Rhosesmor) 1972–1973: An Area Excavation in the Interior

Graeme Guilbert

I. Introduction

In the past attempts have often been made to classify hillforts according to the nature of their site and setting and, although no clear chronological significance can be attached to such a classification, it can still remain a useful approach for the ease with which it enables the fieldworker to define his subject. W. J. Varley has written that "Your true contour work requires an isolated knoll with flattish top and steepish slopes all the way round" (Varley, 1948, p. 54) and this definition conveys precisely the character of Moel y Gaer, Rhosesmor (Flintshire SJ211691). It sits at the southern end of Halkyn Mountain, a ridge of millstone grit rising to its greatest height of 303 m O.D. within the hillfort, commanding vistas over Welsh mountains and Cheshire plainland. Moel y Gaer, then, is a contour fort and, as such, depends upon the strategic positioning of its ramparts for its defensive qualities. Excellent these are too, with the ground falling away on all sides, but never so steeply as to forbid access to the fertile lands and spring-line some 30 m below. But it is not with the defences that we are chiefly concerned here, nor with the environs that might have conditioned the choice of site. Our main concern is the successive settlements that occupied the hilltop and, therefore, it is one particular phrase in Varley's definition which draws our attention: the hill, he said, should have a "flattish top". This, above all, is the feature which has contributed most to the relevance of the present Moel y Gaer excavation. Very little of the 6 acre interior slopes to any excess and, as a result, terraced building platforms, so familiar in the hillforts of north-east Wales, are not to be seen at Moel y Gaer. Indeed, there was no need of them when most of the ground is good for building without adaptation. At so many of the excavated hillforts in the Northern Marches the rugged terrain dictated the settlement plan (e.g., Dinorben, Moel Hiraddug, Breiddin). By contrast, as we shall see, within the ramparts of Moel y Gaer the "prehistoric town-planner" had a far greater opportunity to express his ideals.

II. The Final Occupation

Today the site is common grazing land and is covered by gorse bushes and coarse, tussocky grass. Once this vegetation and the thin black humus had been stripped the surface of the archaeology was immediately revealed. There was no topsoil and the site seems to have been eroded very little since its abandonment so that the micro-contours of the modern ground surface mirrored those of the final phase occupation deposits. A layer of stone rubble, nowhere more than 10 cm in thickness, was all that existed to bear witness to the occupied areas. The continuity of this layer was broken by an apparently random distribution of undulating humps of pale brown, sandy soil. These humps divided the site into a series of fairly level areas within which detailed cleaning and recording revealed variations in the density of stone-cover. It is within this framework that approximately rectangular areas of relatively uniform stone density have been recognised (Fig. 1). The rectangles varied from c 10 m² to 18 m² in area. Although they were sometimes not easy to define with precision, the fact that this same basic size and shape recurred across the site indicates that we are dealing with a standardised unit of some kind, and this prompts their interpretation as the floor areas of rectangular buildings. They lay within and around larger, less-formalised stone-covered areas which contained burnt stones, potsherds and stone implements, and are probably to be regarded as outdoor yards. Lines of stones, crossing and bounding these yards, often delimited changes of stone density and these alignments are interpreted as the packing of shallow gullies which once held the base of a fence or windbreak. The stones themselves are best seen as a deliberate deposit rather than an occupation build-up, and it is clear that, in addition to examining their characteristics, some explanation of their purpose is required. This may best be tackled by relating the sequence of events which, in the excavator's view, led to the formation of the stone deposit as we see it today.

Once they had selected the positions of the yards and buildings these were scraped down to a relatively flat surface, the upcast material being dumped aside to form the humps of our excavation. The general consistency of this overburden suggests that some of the humps might have been turf stacks which implies an occupational hiatus between this settlement and those earlier ones described below. However, detailed analysis of soil samples must precede any categorical statement along these lines. The buildings and windbreaks could then have been erected and immediately afterwards the stones laid down to produce a durable but well-drained surface on top of the clayey subsoil. The variations in the density of the stone-cover were probably not deliberate but were the accidental result of working within separate units; for this reason it is necessary to postulate that the buildings and windbreaks were constructed before the hard-standing was deposited. The surface presented by the stones was generally fairly compact but nowhere very smooth. However, inside the rectangular buildings a padding of straw, rush matting or even timber floorboards could have provided a far more amenable living surface.

Throughout the excavation all finds were individually plotted (an easy task in the comparative poverty of a Welsh hillfort) but even so there is great difficulty in assigning artefacts to our final phase with any confidence. Occasionally domestic stone implements lay on the surface of the yards and in one particular instance a stone grinder and quern sat upright in a shallow hollow immediately outside one of the buildings (Pl. II). Since there is little variation in the form and fabric of pottery from beginning to end of the prehistoric occupation of Moel y Gaer, isolated sherds can never be confidently allocated for fear that they may be residual (except, of course, where they were found in post-holes of buildings of the earliest phase). It is only where there were groups of sherds in positions meaningful to our interpretation of the final phase that the pottery can be treated as significant. In Fig. 2 one of the yards is illustrated and the distribution of all potsherds is shown against a background of the rectangular floor areas and fence lines. This plan portrays several ways in which the accurate location of finds can be useful. The most immediate impression is that given by the clustering of potsherds in the yard outside each of the two buildings. The closely comparable situation of these two assemblages, combined with the fact that practically all of the constituent sherds lay on or were impressed into the surface of the "flooring" (rather than being incorporated in its make-up), is clear evidence for the contemporaneity of pottery and yard. Seen from the reverse point of view, the stratified position of the pottery can be used as evidence that the stones were a unitary deposit rather than an accumulation during an occupation. The individual groups of potsherds were quite plainly bounded by the fence lines, thereby demonstrating the validity of our interpretation of these features which must have been upstanding physical barriers to the movement of objects. This is clearly demonstrated by the northern cluster of sherds in Fig. 2. Finally, the pottery distribution may be used in a negative way to corroborate a previous suggestion. The relative lack of potsherds within the rectangular floor areas can be taken as evidence that the buildings were easily swept clean and thus our hypothetical matting or timber floors gain some credibility. Alternatively, of course, it can be argued that all the domestic activity took place out of doors and that the pottery lay where it was originally broken.

A subject which has not yet been discussed concerns the superstructures which accompanied these rectangular floor areas. Sealed underneath the final phase deposits were a great number of post-holes cut into the natural subsoil. The vast majority of these, without doubt, belonged to earlier circular and rectilinear buildings and the few post-holes which remain unallocated bear no relationship to the final period floors. It must be assumed, then, that these postulated buildings had no earth-fast foundations but were timber-framed huts constructed on sleeper-beams which sat directly on the ground surface. Such structures need not in themselves leave any archaeological trace except in exceptional soil conditions (as has been noted elsewhere (Alcock, 1965, p. 190)). As a result there is an almost total lack of comparable material from prehistoric excavations in Britain. The best parallel known to the author is the early Iron Age settlement site at All Cannings Cross (Wiltshire) where the excavator found "rectangular houses . . . and their adjacent yards" and where "post-holes were not necessary in the construction of the huts" (Cunnington, 1923, p. 58). Despite the fact that each building at All Cannings Cross had its own individual yard, the basic principle was similar to that at Moel y Gaer and, more important, the postulated buildings were comparable in size and in the lack of sunken foundations. Somewhat closer to home, the recognition at Midsummer Camp (Herefordshire) of a building which "used sleeper beams as the found-ation for a rectangular structure 15 ft × 12 ft" (Stanford, 1972a, p. 31) might also be seen as a parallel.

III. Post-Built Structures

Unlike the final phase, the earlier occupations left abundant post-holes, but no accompanying floor levels or occupation soils have survived. It might be thought that these deposits were destroyed when the site was reorganised at a later date, but their total absence underneath the "upcast humps" of our final phase suggests that they had already been eroded by that time. In view of this, the break in occupation which has already been postulated above becomes a little more credible. The structures depicted by the post-holes may be classified into three distinct categories which will be called post-ring round-houses, stake-wall round-houses and four-posters. It will be convenient to define the characteristics of each type in turn before discussing their spatial and chronological relationships.

A. Post-Ring Round-Houses

Twenty-two post-ring round-houses have been identified in whole or in part within the excavated area. They displayed a remarkable homogeneity of design, the main structural element being a circle of posts which most pro-bably held a ring-beam upon which a conical roof would have rested. The dia-meters of the post-rings varied from 4·3 m to 7·4 m and the number of posts from seven to thirteen, being almost invariably an odd number. The three largest rings were in fact oval rather than circular, but it will be convenient to call them all rings and to refer to all these buildings as round-houses. The reason for the oval post setting in the larger houses is somewhat obscure since, in terms of the distribution of roof thrusts, a circle ought to be structurally stronger. One might be excused for thinking that the larger the building the greater the need for the stability provided by a true circle. Only one of the post-ring round-houses has been found to possess any additional setting of sub-stantial uprights. This was in one of the oval buildings, where a semicircle of posts, open-side facing towards the house entrance, was centrally positioned

(Fig. 3). These timbers may have been intended to supplement the main ring of roof supports, but their close resemblance in plan and position to those encountered in an extant round-house in Italy might suggest otherwise. In the ethnographic parallel (Close-Brooks and Gibson, 1966, p. 350) the semi-circle served to support a series of two-tier bunks.

The position of the entrance into these round-houses was normally marked by a wider gap in the post-ring outside which a quartet of post-holes made up a roughly rectangular "porch" (Pl. III). In a recent study of round-houses it has been suggested that this four-post rectangle might equally well have been an internal lobby as an external porch (Avery and Close-Brooks, 1969, p. 350); or, to put it in a different way, the wall line of the house, being roughly concentric with the post-ring, might have terminated at either the outer or the inner pair of porch posts.

At Moel y Gaer there was very little evidence of the actual walls of the post-ring round-houses and, in fact, this was only found in one instance, where a narrow and shallow groove probably represented a slight bedding trench for the foot of a wattle and daub screen attached to the underside of the eaves (Fig. 4B). The groove barely penetrated the natural subsoil and was only found in this building because the soil conditions were particularly favourable. Even so, it could only be traced for about one fifth of the circuit and, in the remainder, was presumably not deep enough to penetrate the subsoil. Nevertheless, its identification is of great importance since it demonstrates that, in this instance at least, the wall-line was aligned on the inner porch posts. The evidence of one building from a total of twenty-two is clearly insufficient to allow any categorical generalisations but, bearing in mind the marked standardisation of the other features of the post-ring round-houses, it is not unreasonable to infer that each of the wall lines occupied a similar position. Judged on this basis the floor diameter of the post-ring round-houses ranged from 6·5 m to 11·5 m.

Even less can be said about the material of the walls, since all we know is that it has left no archaeological trace. We have already envisaged the idea of a wattle screen but must point out that such a wall may not have played any major loadbearing role. Unsupported by stakes penetrating into the ground, it is unlikely to have been capable of sustaining much of the lateral pressure exerted by a heavy turf or thatch roof. It should be noted that in the one example where this type of wall was attested the distance between post-ring and wall line was a mere 0·65 m so that very little of the roof would have projected beyond the main ring-beam (Fig. 4B) and we should imagine a relatively high wall which need only have been strong enough to withstand the elements. In many of the other post-ring round-houses it is inferred that this distance was as much as 2 m, and here something more substantial may have been necessary. At least two possibilities can be given here, neither of which need be represented in the archaeological record. A stout turf or cob wall sitting directly on the ground surface would have provided a fairly stable raft upon which the eaves could rest. Alternatively, a substantial wall of timbers could have been joined at the top by a second ring-beam and secured into a sleeper-beam at the base. Something very akin to this has recently been postulated for a large post-ring round-house excavated in an early hillfort on the Cotswolds (Dixon, 1973, p. 58).

A closer look at the individual post-holes reveals an interesting difference between those of the ring and the porch. The post-pits in which the roof supports were set were normally cylindrical and cut fairly precisely to the size of the timber they were made to hold (i.e., normally between 0·12—0·20 m in diameter). In other words the post-pits were "tailor made" for the posts and therefore required very little packing. By way of contrast, although the porch posts were not necessarily any bigger than those of the ring, their pits were often far larger than the timbers themselves and were frequently oval (Fig. 4B). There is no obvious reason for this since the posts did not always occupy the same position within the pits. The answer may lie in the different techniques involved in the construction of circular and rectangular buildings. (It must be remembered here that, although the round-house and its porch were parts of the same building, they were probably structural entities in their own right, tied together in a more or less superficial manner.) The choice of a central point and the marking out of a circle on the ground is a simple matter. Equally, the erection of a ring of posts on that circle is not difficult, especially since, in ring-beam construction, the precise spacing between uprights is not critical, so long as they are reasonably equidistant. The post-pits can therefore be confidently dug where required. The laying out of a rectangular structure is somewhat more complex. Since it is likely that all joinery would be completed at ground level before the building operation begins, the accurate positioning of the uprights is essential to the ease of erection. The post-pits might, in this case, be dug larger than strictly necessary in order to allow a certain amount of space within which the uprights can be manoeuvred until the structure has been "squared up". A parallel for the oval post-pits may be found at Shearplace Hill (Dorset) where, in their reconsideration of the excavated Round House A, Avery and Close-Brooks interpret similar features as indicating that "the exact position of the verticals was not easy for the designer to predict" (Avery and Close-Brooks, 1969, p. 349). Similarly, it should be noted that the post-pits for the rectangular four-posters at Moel y Gaer were rarely "tailor-made".

In some cases the oval post-pits served an additional purpose, each one containing two or even three contiguous timbers. This may be the result of a design involving separate uprights at the wall-end and for the porch structure. The building in Fig. 3 had three posts which may indicate a separate door-frame too; if so, the duplication in the outer post-holes might suggest doors at both front and back of the porch. Figure-eight shaped post-pits at the inner end of the porch were also found in several instances and were probably a variation of the same idea (Fig. 4A).

Of the internal arrangements relatively little detail survived. Central hearths, witnessed simply by reddened areas on the natural clay, were found in only seven post-ring round-houses. Even so, their apparent absence from the remaining buildings need mean nothing; the use of stone slab hearths, for example, might have prevented any scorching of the subsoil, and, if these slabs were later removed, they need leave no archaeological trace. In five of these round-houses clusters of stake-holes or small post-holes were found to either side of the hearth and may best be seen as uprights to support a cooking spit straddling the open fire (Pl. III and Fig. 3). Once again we may look to our ethnographic parallel near Rome for a comparable arrangement. There, a pair of posts set astride the hearth are pierced with holes for wooden pegs to support a cross bar from which a cooking pot can hang (Close-Brooks and Gibson, 1966, p. 350). Occasionally alignments of stake-holes suggest internal partitions. There were also some unallocated post-holes both inside and outside the buildings but these rarely fell into any repeated pattern. In a number of instances a small post-hole lay near, though slightly offset from, the centre of a round-house floor area (e.g. Fig. 4B) and, whilst they seem unlikely to represent central posts as such (i.e. to support the apex of the roof), they could perhaps have held temporary scaffolding poles employed during roof construction. Sometimes surplus post-holes appeared to form pairs but these were difficult to identify with confidence since they did not occur in a regular spatial relationship to the round-houses; besides which it is entirely likely that odd posts would have been erected, as domestic necessity demanded, both indoors and outdoors.

It is not difficult to find parallels in British prehistory for this basic style of round-house construction and many are listed elsewhere (Musson, 1970b, p. 270; Avery and Close-Brooks, 1969, p. 350). There are, in fact, several sites at which comparable buildings have been excavated in Wales: Llandegai, Caernarvonshire (Musson, 1970b, p. 276); Llwyn du Bach, Caernarvonshire (Bersu and Griffiths 1949); Henllan, Cardiganshire (Williams, 1945); Castell Cogan, Carmarthenshire (Grealey et al., 1972); Walesland Rath, Pembrokeshire (Wainwright, 1971a). What is very rare, though, is for a sufficiently large area to have been dug for the excavator to be able to identify a building "type". Indeed, taken on their own, it is unlikely that any one of the post-ring round-house plans at Moel y Gaer would be sufficiently distinctive to achieve any great esteem among prehistorians (with the possible exception of the oval building illustrated in Fig. 3). As a group, on the other hand, they exhibit such uniformity and such repetitive symmetry that their value must surpass that of any individually more grandiose structure. What we have here is a successful design which was repeated with little variation time and again.

B. Stake-Wall Round-Houses

The second type of round-house at Moel y Gaer displayed an even greater standardisation of ground plan. These, the stake-wall round-houses, were extremely simple in design with a wall of rammed stakes, only ever roughly circular, and never so precisely laid out as the post-rings (Fig. 5A). The internal diameters ranged from 5·6 m to 8·0 m. A gap in the wall line of about 2 m width marked the entrance which was formed by a pair of fairly well-founded posts averaging 0·20 m scantling (Fig. 5B). In four of the eleven excavated examples a second pair of post-holes, placed a short distance outside the door posts, probably represents a vestigial porch (Fig. 5A). In two of these instances the extra pair of posts were set in markedly oval post-pits and, in this respect, we might see a resemblance to the post-ring houses; as we might also in the fact that one of the stake-wall round-houses had figure-eight post-pits containing paired timbers (Fig. 5A). In most of these buildings there were other irregular and unpredictable gaps in the line of the stake-wall but this phenomenon is more than likely attributable to the weathering of the surrounding subsoil which had effectively backfilled the stake-holes and rendered them indetectable. We do not have to look far for parallels this time; about 55 kms to the south, recent excavations at the Breiddin (Montgomeryshire) have yielded very similar structures with stake-built walls whose diameters varied from 4·0 m to 7·0 m (Musson, 1970a, p. 218 and 1972, p. 266).

C. Rectilinear Post-Hole Buildings

Large scale excavations on Iron Age settlement sites frequently produce rectilinear post-built structures and Moel y Gaer also has its share of these. Of the thirteen such buildings totally excavated at Moel y Gaer, all but three were large four-post squares and oblongs. There were, in fact, two instances where adjacent four-posters could be paired to make larger rectangles but in neither case is the resultant "eight-poster" of very great symmetry bay to bay, and it may therefore be better to discount the possibility (Pl. VII). On the other hand, Dixon has given evidence that the posts of the so-called "longhouses" at Crickley Hill (Gloucestershire) were roof supports within a building whose walls lay some distance outside them (Dixon, 1973, p. 58). If this was also the case at Moel y Gaer, then the irregular spacing of the uprights need not have affected the symmetry of the walled area.

Unfortunately, the absence of floor levels once again limits the amount of information to be deduced from the structures. Thus it is not possible to establish whether the buildings had raised floors (as has often been suggested for similar structures), or whether these were at ground-level. The most remarkable characteristic of the Moel y Gaer four-posters was the size of the timber uprights and the depth of the post-pits in which they stood. Posts of up to 0·50 m in diameter sunk over 0·60 m below the ground surface are indeed quite massive when compared to the round-house porch posts (Pl. VIII). It is difficult to believe that they were intended to do the same job and yet on the face of it both might be taken to represent the corner posts of simple rectangular structures. It might be argued that the larger span of the four-posters, which ranged from 3·4 m × 2·4 m to 4·0 m × 4 m, required the stronger timbers but some of the porches measured up to 2 m × 3 m. The extra strength possessed by these huge timbers must surely have been specifically employed to cope with the strains of a very different style of building: a raised floor, or even a tall multiple-storey structure. The pair of adjacent four-posters (Pl. VII) nearest the rampart provide another shred of evidence in favour of the raised floor theory. This was the only part of the excavated area in which the slope of the ground exceeded 1 in 12, and yet no terracing was considered necessary even though it would have been quite a small task to undertake. It is therefore necessary to invoke a raised floor, unless, of course, the buildings were never anything more than byres.

When the Moel y Gaer four-posters are compared to those recorded on other sites it is clear that they number among the larger examples, their floor areas varying from 7·6 m² to 16·0 m². These figures are calculated on the assumption that the wall-line ran between the posts so as to allow comparison with the list of "Rectilinear Iron Age Post-Hole Plans in England" compiled by Stanford (1970, pp. 125–126). Although subsequent excavations have now made this list very incomplete, it does give a fair impression of the range of sizes found.

It is principally on account of the scale of the post-holes that the remaining three rectilinear post-built structures at Moel y Gaer differed from those described above. Timbers of up to 0·20 m diameter, founded in post-pits averaging 0·30 m in depth are more comparable with the round-house post-holes than those of the large four-posters. However, this was the only similarity between the three buildings which had widely differing floor areas. Two of them were simple four-post squares of 2·7 m² and 6·0 m², both of which can be paralleled from sites in Stanford's list. The third was a far more individual structure consisting of five posts, four of which made up a perfect 3·2 by 3·2 m square. The fifth lay outside the square and was placed asymmetrically to it, but must be associated since the size and filling of all five post-holes were identical and there were no other posts within several metres of this group. As usual there was no evidence of the floor or the wall-line and therefore any reconstruction of the building must be highly conjectural. However, it should be noted that amongst the group of large four-posters at the southern end of the excavation a "spare" large post-hole lay in a similar situation relative to one of the four-posters as that in the five-post building.

D. An Anomaly

One of the most noticeable characteristics of the post-ring round-house plans is their symmetry which is especially well illustrated by Figs 3 and 4A. There was, however, one post-ring on the site which was far less symmetrical. It consisted of seven relatively large, irregularly spaced post-holes forming an approximate circle of 7·4 m diameter. A large sub-rectangular pit of 3·6 m × 2·4 m lay eccentrically within the post-ring (Pl. VI). Although there is no proof that the pit and post-ring were contemporary, the close spatial relationship of two unique features amongst such standardisation is unlikely to be a coincidence. The pit, 1·5 m deep, was largely filled with stones, one of which was a broken quern. Unfortunately, there were no other finds and the purpose of the pit remains unproven. Equally, any reconstruction of the superstructure will be conjectural, for there is, of course, no proof as to whether the seven posts supported a roof or were a free-standing circle of uprights. The infeasibility of attaching a domestic function to this unparalleled structure compels the author to seek a less worldly interpretation. Can it be that, amongst the mundane, we have located a sanctuary?

IV. Structural Sequence and Settlement Plans

The settlement involving rectangular sleeper-beam buildings was clearly the latest on the site, for, had it been superseded, its recorded remains must have been extensively damaged. Moreover, any alteration or wholesale reconstruction of such a settlement would have rendered its earlier phases indetectable. It will therefore be evident that this settlement was, as we saw it, in its final form. By the same token, the length of the ultimate phase of occupation must remain a matter of pure conjecture.

The general character of the site at this time has already been postulated as one of buildings clustered around courtyards. Any attempt to study this settlement in its broader layout is necessarily weakened by the tenuous nature of the remains, which made the positive identification of *all* the buildings extremely difficult. Since, as we have seen, this normally depended upon *relative* stone densities, their recognition was particularly difficult near the limits of excavation. Indeed, had we chosen to sample the threatened area with trial trenches the significance of the stones would undoubtedly have been missed, and it should be stressed that inappropriate digging methods would have been nothing short of destructive. The value of this aspect of the excavation must lie in the detection of a fugitive style of building, and this may be directly attributed to one factor; namely, the large scale of open area excavation which allowed the study of variations in the stone-cover and provided the repeating pattern which suggested the interpretation of the buildings. Having made these points, the one general observation which does seem valid relates to the distribution of the occupied areas (Fig. 6). Relatively extensive tracts of perfectly good building land were covered by broad heaps of upcast material which could quite easily have been piled much higher over more limited areas. This might well be seen as the deliberate contrivance of open spaces within the settlement and, as such, reflects a lack of pressure upon the available land. Certainly the pattern was far less congested than those which had gone before.

The post-built structures cannot all have been contemporary since many overlap, but it is possible tentatively to divide them into two phases as shown in Figs 7 and 8. Some explanation of the observations and the ideas behind this interpretation must now be attempted.

In the matter of relationships between overlapping structures the general absence of associated floors has already been acknowledged, but we are fortunate that the chronology of the two types of round-house could be established in the one part of the excavation where any stratigraphy survived in connection with the post-built structures. One of the stake-wall round-houses was built on a slightly raised platform, some of whose material had filled in the tops of several previously blocked post-holes of an adjacent post-ring round-house. Clearly, in this instance, the stake-wall round-house must have been the later and, by implication, this one established relationship may be applied to the two types as a whole.

Reference to Fig. 7 will make it obvious that all of the post-ring round-houses cannot have been strictly coeval but, all the same, it must be allowed that their similarity of ground plan is a clear expression of their general contemporaneity. It will be noticed that the overlapping ones were concentrated along the eastern periphery of the excavated area which is, in fact, the axial ridge of the hill. The rampart lies some 50–60 m to the west and, whilst the intervening area was covered by post-ring round-houses, there were no instances of complete rebuilding in this zone. (There were sometimes clear signs of extensive repair—Fig. 4B). On the available evidence, the most appealing hypothesis would suggest that the post-ring round-house occupation began on the higher parts of the site and, as the population grew, additional houses were built whilst the original ones decayed and were replaced on the same plots. Thus we may see the post-ring round-house phase reaching maturity with a maximum of seventeen houses wholly or partly within our 3000 m².

Whilst every one of the stake-wall round-houses overlapped with a post-ring round-house, Fig. 8 illustrates that the former can all have coexisted. Similarly, each of the rectangular four-post structures, large or small, could have stood alongside the stake-wall round-houses since their distributions were mutually exclusive. In fact, the only point of debate arises from the varying dispositions of the larger four-posters. Those at the southern and western edges of the excavated area were organised in relatively formal grid patterns and those at the south conflicted with the post-ring round-houses, one of which demonstrably ante-dated a four-poster. Since the gridded groups seem likely to have belonged to the same unitary settlement plan, all of these four-posters may safely be assigned to a later period than the post-ring round-houses. The large four-posters in the northern half of the excavation neither conformed to the grid nor clashed with the post-ring round-houses and it is therefore conceivable that they were a part of the earlier settlement. Even so, the close similarity of these more loosely distributed four-posters to those in the grid prompts their attribution to the same phase plan. The two smallest four-posters each lay athwart the wall-line of a post-ring round-house and they too seem best allotted to the second phase.

In conclusion what we might envisage at Moel y Gaer is a sequence of occupation which ran as follows. The settlement began with a few post-ring round-houses on the ridge, and spread outwards until the pattern was one of closely packed round-houses, apparently without any organised system of thoroughfares among the buildings. It quite possibly originated as an unenclosed settlement (a *hohensiedlung* similar to that proposed on Mam Tor in Derbyshire (Coombs, 1971, p. 102)) consisting of several of the larger round-houses. As it evolved, the buildings became standardised at about 7 to 9 m in diameter and exhibited a certain degree of discipline in their regular south-easterly orientation towards the morning sun, but sheltered from the predominant south-westerly winds. It must have been at this stage that the "sanctuary" was constructed (unless it was earlier altogether), for it demonstrably antedated an overlapping stake-wall round-house but fits neatly in amongst the small post-ring buildings. It may have been only when this settlement had reached its maximum extent that the defences were first constructed, the precise line of the rampart being determined by the contours which seem to have permitted sufficient space behind the defences for a broad "intervallum trackway" (Fig. 7). A major rearrangement ensued, in which a new style of round-house construction was adopted even though size remained pretty much the same. The most significant reorganisation, however, was in terms of the settlement plan, for the constituent parts were laid out far more systematically. Separate zones within the hillfort were given over to specific types of building. In the area excavated (Fig. 8) the southern part was covered by a neat grid arrangement of four-posters, north of which two swaths of stake-wall round-houses, their entrances mostly facing east, were separated by a wide linear space occupied by a less organised zone of four-posters.

Bearing in mind the total absence of hearths in either four-posters or round-houses in this second phase at Moel y Gaer, it is not possible to deduce which type of building should be regarded as the dwellings. The discovery of hearths within the floor areas of similar rectangular buildings in the Central Marches has been taken as proof that they were occupied (Stanford, 1970, p. 111 and 1971, p. 47). However, Stanford is the first to suggest that not all of his buildings need have served the same purpose and he divides them into equal proportions as dwellings and granaries (Stanford, 1967, p. 32). He has also pointed out the apparent lack of round-houses in the excavated hillforts of that area (Stanford, 1972a, p. 32), but a very different picture emerges in the Northern Marches where round-houses have been found in every major excavation. Under these circumstances it may be best to regard the round-houses at Moel y Gaer as dwellings and the four-posters as storage units. This, at least, is a working hypothesis until further excavation provides the answer.

But, however that problem may resolve itself, one factor which is beyond dispute is the organisation behind this second settlement plan. We are surely witnessing the work of the "prehistoric town-planner" taking the opportunity to do away with the former *ad hoc* arrangements and to lay out a functional and disciplined "new-town". Here we may compare the excavated Herefordshire hillforts which show similar characteristics (Stanford, 1972a, p.32), as do the current excavations at Danebury, Hampshire, where the 1500 m² stripped in 1971 caused the excavator to comment that "it is impossible to resist the conclusion that this area of the hillfort had been carefully and regularly planned" (Cunliffe, 1972b). But the new set-up at Moel y Gaer was not to last very long before the site was abandoned and the best timbers removed, presumably for reuse where the community re-established itself (one wonders where in the vicinity this major settlement site is awaiting discovery). A hiatus of unknown length followed before a new occupation began, the principal characteristic of which was its timber-framed rectangular buildings.

A problem which arises at this point is that of the transition between the post-ring and stake-wall round-house phases. Should we suspect a break in the occupation of the hill, or is there a case for believing in continuity? The problem cannot be resolved conclusively, but the radical and wholesale change in round-house design possibly indicates more than a contact with other peoples, and suggests a culture-break if not necessarily a gap in time. Such a notion can only gain support from the apparent introduction of four-post rectangular structures at the same time. On the other hand, there was one exceptional round-house at Moel y Gaer which combined a stake-built wall with a post-ring (Pl. V) and, since it did not overlap with any other clearly defined structure, it is impossible to say to which phase it belonged. Its ring of roof supports was reconstructed at least once even though the timbers involved were considerably larger than those in most of the post-rings. The stake-wall, on the other hand, showed no sign of refurbishment. It is possible, then, that this building may have been in use during both phases of round-house settlement; originally with a post-ring and later, when a wall of stakes was added, the internal roof supports were retained to cope with the greater weight of the roof in the larger structure (its diameter was about 10·5 m). It is therefore incorporated in both phase plans. Unfortunately, only half of the house lay within the threatened area and that part excluded the entrance which, if it could be excavated, might go a long way towards establishing whether the different styles of round-house represent two phases of one period of occupation or whether they were separated in time.

The one thing of which we can feel fairly certain is that this summary should not necessarily be applied to the rest of the hillfort. Even three-quarters of an acre can be no more than a glimpse of arrangements inside a settlement eight times that size (Fig. 9). We have excavated a *consolidated sample* but, however extensive, it is only a sample and can take no account of the possibility that specialised areas existed within the successive settlements. In Phase 2 there may have been other zones for different types of buildings, for pits or even open spaces. Even so it would be wrong to argue that *selective sampling* across the site could provide any more complete a picture. That technique necessarily deals with a series of relatively small areas which may demonstrate the former existence of similar or different styles of structures at various points within the settlement, but cannot hope to uncover anything of its overall organisation. The variations within the Phase 2 settlement plan occurred over such broad areas that the conclusions stated in this interim report could not have been gained from even a slightly smaller excavation, and a larger one might have modified them further. Only total excavation can ultimately supply the information necessary for the study of settlement plans.

At the present time very few prehistoric settlement sites have been comprehensively excavated and surely it is here that the next decades of hillfort studies belong. It has often been said that structures can be treated as cultural fossils in the same way as portable artefacts and this could be equally true of the whole assemblage of structures. One of the characteristic features of the Greek and Roman civilisations, for instance, was their individual approach to the layout of a settlement, be it fort or town (Mumford, 1961, Chapters 6–8); yet it is only through our wide knowledge of these as extant or extensively excavated sites that this significance can be appreciated. The study of settlement planning in any period, historic or prehistoric, is of relevance not only as a source of structural information but also as a reflection of the underlying social order. If the full potential of this comparatively new facet of hillfort studies is to be adequately realised, maybe in future the excavator's ideal site should not, as so often in the past, display a multi-period palimpsest with successive settlement plans contributing to each other's confusion. Perhaps instead he will seek the site with a single phase of occupation where every post-hole has something to say and every building and open space can be acknowledged as a significant part of the whole pattern.

V. Artefacts

The extreme acidity of the subsoil at Moel y Gaer has removed all trace of any metalwork that might formerly have existed and hence deprived us of one of the principal aids to dating. Only pottery and stone implements survive and, of these, the former is more useful as a cultural determinant. It shows little variation being coarse and heavily gritted and the few sherds of any size have a slack profile with slightly everted or flat-topped rims which often bear finger-tip or finger-nail impressions. This description will be familiar to students of prehistory as that of early Iron Age pottery commonly found on settlement sites from the south-west to the north of England. Indeed, North Wales already has, in Castell Odo, a fortified site renowned for its finger-tip decorated wares (Alcock, 1961). Whilst stopping briefly to note recent suggestions that "axiomatic 'Iron Age' labels" for this style of pottery should be abandoned (Burgess, 1970, p. 214), there seems little point in pursuing Moel y Gaer's cultural affinities any further at this stage. We must turn back to the structures and hope that radio-carbon dating of charcoal collected from the post-holes will at least put Moel y Gaer into chronological perspective.

Acknowledgements

I am indebted to Professor Leslie Alcock who read my text and suggested many revisions and to my wife whose contributions are too many to enumerate.

Addendum

This preliminary report was written in the spring of 1973. Subsequently, a further *c.* 3200 m² has been excavated to complete the examination of the threatened area. This included two substantial areas of the defences which established that the Phase 1 post-ring round-house settlement was enclosed by a free-standing timber palisade and the Phase 2 stake-wall round-houses and four-poster grid by a timber-framed-and-laced rampart. The problem of the transition from Phase 1 to 2 remains unsolved, despite the completed excavation of the unique round-house with post-ring and stake-wall which can now be attributed to Phase 1 alone. There was a further period of timber-laced rampart building, but this could not be demonstrably linked to the final phase of occupation.

The following radio-carbon dates have been obtained:

620 ± 70 b.c. (HAR-606) from charcoal collected around the central hearth of a post-ring round-house sealed beneath the Phase 2 rampart.

580 ± 90 b.c. (HAR-604) from charcoal found in the packing of the bedding slot for the front posts of the Phase 2 rampart.

240 ± 80 b.c. (HAR-603) from a heap of burnt twigs which overlay a part of the four-poster grid and was covered by the final rampart.

15 | *Dún Ailinne: An Interim Report*

Bernard Wailes

This report is written following five seasons of excavation (1968–1972), and summarises the major conclusions to date, tentative though many of these must be. Progress reports have been published after each of the first four seasons (Wailes, 1969, 1970a, 1970b; Selkirk and Wailes, 1970; Wailes, 1971), and some detailed points covered in those reports will not be reiterated below here. However, although considerable work remains to be done at this site it seems possible at this stage to attempt a provisional interpretation, and a preliminary consideration of the relationship of this site to some other apparently similar ones*.

The work is being financed by the National Monuments Branch (Office of Public Works), Dublin, who have provided not only primary labour costs but also generous equipment and servicing; the University Museum (University of Pennsylvania) and the Bredin Foundation have also supplied generous financial assistance; the Ford Foundation, through its scheme of archaeological Field Training Grants programme, has also assisted greatly by providing financial support for a number of students to participate each year in the excavation. The excavators gratefully acknowledge the support of these bodies, the co-operation and assistance of Mr. Jack Thompson, the owner of the land; the many kindnesses of Mr. Jim Byrne of Kilcullen and the interest and assistance of many others in the neighbourhood.

I. Introduction

The site lies in Knockaulin townland, just south of Kilcullen, County Kildare. It is a rounded hill of slate and greywacke bedrock with a thin covering of glacial till. Since the bedrock lies obliquely to the surface it outcrops in roughly parallel ridges which the glacial till often does not cover fully. The occasional outcrops of bedrock clearly have been used in the relatively recent past as sources of building stone and/or road metalling: the inside edge of the

---

*Since this text was prepared in Spring 1973, two further reports have been published—*Wailes, 1973* and *1974*. In the former, reasons are given for reinterpreting as *one* phase (Iron Age phase 3) the two phases (Iron Age phases 3 and 4) given in this article.

enclosure ditch shows numerous larger and smaller quarries. The site itself is formed by a substantial bank and ditch encircling the hill. The only original entrance lies on the east side; all other gaps through the bank appear to be secondary—indeed nearly all lie either at the angles of surrounding fields or opposite the little quarries in the inner face of the ditch. It must be emphasised that the enclosing bank lies outside the ditch. The site does not constitute a normal hillfort, therefore; indeed morphologically perhaps one should regard it as a henge. Further inferences to support this seemingly unusual interpretation will be argued briefly later in this report.

The interior of the site had been divided into three unequal sectors at one time, as the lines of the demolished fences (hedges) clearly show. The western and smallest of these sectors covers the steepest side of the hill, which remains under bracken, furze and rough grass. The two larger sectors, including the summit of the hill, were cleared and put under improved grassland in the 1950s. The earliest known aerial photo of the site (Ó Ríordáin, 1953, Pl. 20) shows parallel cultivation ridges prior to the clearance of the 1950s. Much of the site, therefore, has been cultivated at least twice, so that the upper part of the present soil profile is a disturbed plough soil. Apart from the old fence lines and a small spring on the north slope the only visible features of the site were (1) a slightly irregular arc-shaped embankment, with internal quarry ditch; (2) an indistinct squarish low irregularity within the curve of the quarry ditch just mentioned and (3) a very low diffuse roughly circular mound immediately north-east of the first two features mentioned (see Fig. 1). The first two features have been noted by various writers and surveyors, who have proposed various interpretations of them (see below, p. 321); to the best of my knowledge, the low mound had not been noted prior to the start of our work in 1968.

II. Historical

This brief review of documentary evidence is included to indicate the main reason why this site was selected for excavation. I am most grateful to a number of people for assistance with the historical sources, notably Mr. Alfred P. Smyth, Dr. Frances O'Kane, Dr. Kathleen Hughes and Mr. Sean O'Nuallain. It must be emphasised that any errors in the account below must be attributed to myself.

The site name Aillinn (various alternative spellings) occurs from the eighth century A.D. in early Irish documentary sources, identified as one of the Royal residences of the Kings of Leinster. It is associated with Teamhair (Tara), Rath Croghan, Emain Macha (Navan Fort)—which are respectively the traditional seats of the High Kings of Ireland, the kings of Connaught and the kings of Ulster (Kenney, 1929, pp. 479–481). Although other royal sites are documented for Leinster (e.g., Dinn Riogh, Nas ni Riogh), the singling out of "Aillinn" alone for inclusion with Tara, Rath Croghan and Emain Macha indicate that it was a site of prime importance in protohistorical Ireland—in all probability the Leinster equivalent of the other three sites. In short "Aillinn" could be interpreted reasonably as *the* provincial "capital" of Leinster, with whatever actual function or functions this might imply.

The Hill of Allen, headquarters of the legendary Finn Mac Cumhal (Finn McCool), seemed a likely candidate for the "Aillinn" of the early documents. However, John O'Donovan, a field officer of the Ordnance Survey, resolved the question in 1837 by close consideration of the place-names, and concluded that "Aillinn" should be identified with Knockaulin. Indeed one could share O'Donovan's excitement even now in reading his letter of the fourth of December 1837, the day following that when he first visited the site— shortly after he had concluded his detailed consideration of the place-name evidence (O'Donovan, 1837, 30th November, 4th December). O'Donovan's identification has not been disputed since, to the best of my knowledge, and Knockaulin Hill remains identified as Dún Ailinne. Dún Ailinne supposedly was founded by Art Mesdelmond or by Senda Siothbhac (O'Donovan, 1837, pp. 46–47). Mr. Alfred Smyth, from his studies of the Leinster genealogy, informs me that both these individuals appear in the royal genealogy of Leinster and that both might be very roughly dated to the period around the birth of Christ. As far as this evidence goes, then, we have the suggestion that Dún Ailinne was the main royal site of Leinster, was founded in the pagan period and was the equivalent to (and probably at least partly contemporaneous with) Rath Croghan, Emain Macha and Tara. All these sites are celebrated as being abandoned in the early Christian period (Kenney: op. cit.) and it is often held that they were abandoned at the time of the conversion in the fifth century A.D. (de Paor and de Paor 1958, pp. 32, 48).

O'Donovan (1837, p. 120) identified the arc-shaped embankment and the squarish mound on the top of the hill as a round small fort enclosing a square one and interprets the latter as the monument Angus Ossory erected subsequent to the abandonment of the site. Camden (1789, p. 543) also interpreted the embankment as a "rath now destroyed". Others (e.g., Evans, 1966, p. 137) have suggested that a round Neolithic or Bronze Age cairn might be identified in these ambiguous remains. The low mound does not appear to have been noticed by any previous workers and certainly none of the traces of foundations, discovered in our excavation, were ever noticed—hardly surprising since they do not show on any of a number of aerial photographs taken at various times over the past 25 years.

It can be seen that no clear idea could be derived from documentary sources as to the nature of the site or the details of its function(s) other than that there was reason to believe it to have been of major importance in the Iron Age. On the other hand there was (and is) no reason to doubt this general, even vague, identification.

III. The Excavation

Work started in 1968 with caesium magnetometer survey of the whole site covering the top of the hill in particular detail*. This revealed one well-defined

---

* "Cesium magnetometer and Resitivity survey, Dún Ailinne, Ireland" MASCA Newsletter 4 no. 2, p. 3 (University Museum, University of Pennsylvania, Philadelphia, Pa., U.S.A.)

anomaly over the low mound mentioned above. In view of the subsequent discovery, through excavation, of the extreme variability and irregularity of the bedrock and its thin covering of unsorted glacial till, the lack of success in locating similar anomalies is hardly surprising. This is reinforced by the eventual discovery that the high magnetic anomaly over the low mound lay above a sizeable area of very intense burning of Iron Age phase 6.

Excavation commenced by stripping a large area centring on the low mound. With the lifting of the first sods blackened earth, containing burnt stone, charcoal, ash and considerable quantities of animal bone, could be seen immediately underneath. The discovery of small blue glass beads strongly suggested that a general "Iron Age" date was likely, and excavation proceeded on the assumption that the low mound was a central part of an Iron Age occupation of some sort. This initial view has been amply confirmed.

A. The Embankment

The arc-shaped embankment proves to lie over the Iron Age levels, separated from them by a well-developed and culturally sterile humus. Since it appears to have been regarded by Camden (op. cit.) as a feature of some antiquity (i.e., he gives no indication that it was thought to be of recent origin in his day) we may loosely regard this as "medieval"—i.e., post-Iron Age and pre-seventeenth century. There is no indication whatsoever that this bank, or its internal quarry ditch, were ever more extensive than they are today. It cannot be regarded as a ruined rath (ring-fort). Possibly it might be an unfinished ring-fort, but internal ditches appear to be a most unusual ring-fort feature. I know of no class of monument morphologically similar to this feature, and extensive excavation has yielded no structural or artefactual clue as to its function or its date. It appears to be entirely incidental to the use of the site as a "Royal site" of the pagan Iron Age.

The ambiguous squarish feature inside the arc of the embankment quarry ditch now seems likely to be due to the intersection of trenches 515 and 516 with trenches 217 and 517. The amorphous small mounds immediately to the north of this intersection are both very recent: one covered a late type of clay pipe, the other covered a late nineteenth century/early twentieth century mineral water bottle. The two large boulder erratics in this immediate area (Wailes, 1970a, Fig. 3) both lie close to the surface. Neither is embedded in the subsoil, nor indeed in the Iron Age levels. If they were connected originally with any Neolithic grave or tomb, they have been subsequently displaced.

B. The Bank and Ditch

The bank and ditch surrounding the site encloses an area of some 34 acres. Three cuttings (21, 22, 23, see Fig. 1) were made in 1968 to gain an initial impression of the construction. Cuttings 21 and 22 were made mechanically but finished manually, so that the main construction features cannot have escaped our attention. These two cuttings show that the bank was a simple dump construction and that the ditch silted in naturally. There is no indication of more than one phase of construction, nor of recutting or reuse. Cutting 23 was designed to test for the possibility of post-holes or a palisade trench on the inner lip of the ditch, as was found at the Rath na Riogh at Tara (O Ríordáin 1954, p. 13). No indication of any such structures was found. Cutting 24 demonstrated that there was a causeway of unexcavated bedrock interrupting the ditch at the main entrance to the east. This confirmed our suspicion that this entrance was, indeed, the only likely candidate for an original entrance.

It should be noted that there is, as yet, no date for the construction of the bank and ditch. They are only assumed, for the time being, to be most probably of the Iron Age.

C. Neolithic

From the first season of excavation numerous Neolithic artefacts have come both from the top soil and the Iron Age levels: leaf- and lozenge-shaped arrow heads, portions of ground-stone axes, fragments of shouldered bowls. From the first, therefore, it seemed highly likely that Neolithic material had been disturbed by Iron Age activity and incorporated into Iron Age levels. So far, only two features may be plausibly identified as Neolithic. Feature 281 is a trench, of open U-shaped form, cut across by Iron Age features and overlain by Iron Age occupation. It was packed with stones, haphazardly disposed, and does not appear to have been a palisade trench. Trench 281 has yielded a number of quartz flakes, a hollow scraper and a portion of a leaf-shaped arrow head; on the other hand it has so far produced no artefacts whatsoever of Iron Age type. Pit 293 was almost completely obliterated by Iron Age trench 514. However, enough of the fill remained intact on the northwest side to preserve *in situ* a large part of a Neolithic pot, including some very large sherds indeed. The proximity of these sherds and their size indicate that they are indeed *in situ*, and were not dug up and redeposited in the Iron Age. The pot is of "Linkardstown" general type, and most closely resembles the pot from Ballintruer Mor, County Wicklow—for which information I must thank Miss Ellen Prendergast of the National Museum of Ireland. As the Iron Age levels are progressively cleared, no doubt further Neolithic features will be identified, hopefully including some intact. At this point it is impossible to say anything coherent of the Neolithic activities at this site.

D. Iron Age—General

The succession of Iron Age activities on the site appears to have been more or less continuous. That is to say, there is no indication whatsoever of any hiatus during the Iron Age sequence. The last Iron Age phase blanketed much of the excavated area with a layer of burnt material, that layer which was revealed as soon as the sod was lifted. So, despite subsequent cultivation, much of the Iron Age levels remain untouched by the plough—an unusual and fortunate situation. The location of phases 5, 6 and 7 (see Fig. 4) means that over a large part of the site a stratigraphy thus can be observed. In the very limited area covered by the deposits of phases 5 and 6 quite a detailed stratigraphic sequence is evident. But outside the protection of these latest levels there is no stratigraphy save that of plough soil over subsoil. In these peripheral areas the "normal" situation obtains in which a sequence can be observed only by intersection of features or by the geometric inference of an apparent plan. Thus for example the annex or "entrance" at the south side (see Fig. 3, and see below under phase 2) can be fairly confidently assigned to phase 2 both on account of its intersection by the trenches 515, 516 of phase 3 and by its plan relationship to the main phase 2 structure. Feature 229, at the northwest of the excavated area, can be related at present to no phase.

The major Iron Age trenches all appear to have contained upright timbers originally: they were, in fact, palisade trenches. In only one case does rotted timber remain *in situ;* in all other cases timbers appear to have been extracted, presumably for subsequent reuse or to clear the area for a new phase of activity. As can be seen from Fig. 3 a number of recognisable post-sockets have been identified in the primary fill of these trenches. Feature 316, for example, shows an unusually well-preserved close setting of post-holes. For the main part, however, the original presence of timbers must be inferred by two methods. First, the primary fill of the trenches, where this survives sufficiently distinct from the secondary fill, often shows slight arcs as if it had originally been packed around timbers, and frequently contains vertical "packing stones". Second, there is no reason to suppose that these trenches could have fulfilled any other function: they are, in the main, far too small to have formed any useful enclosing function on their own as open ditches, and there is no trace whatever of banks, however small, either inside or outside them. One must conclude that the removal of timbers, very evident in the case of the few well-preserved post-holes, was in general sufficiently violent to destroy any coherent indication of the original packing of clay and stones around timbers.

The depth of the trenches may vary considerably. As work has progressed, it has become increasingly clear that this variation is due largely to the relative ease or difficulty of penetrating the highly variable subsoil and bedrock. The glacial till is easy enough to excavate, but is much shallower in some places than others. The bedrock can be highly friable and easily cut into but in other places may be exceedingly hard. Thus one may note on the eastern side of the phase 2 structure, in the vicinity of features 85, 315, and the western end of 316, that a ridge of hard bedrock lies close to the surface with no covering of glacial till. The two gaps in trench 513, on either side of the end of trench 316, are most likely due to the unwillingness of the builders to cut into this hard bedrock. Feature 315 seems most probably an attempt to remedy this weakness with an internal support. It seems quite feasible that the timber palisade continued across these gaps in the trench, the timbers being held upright by the weight and stability of the whole structure.

The first three Iron Age phases, then, are interpreted as circular palisade constructions, of differing sizes and complexity, but of basically the same mode of construction. The depth of the phase 2 trenches is appreciably greater than that of the phase 1 and 3 trenches, suggesting either a more solid or a considerably higher structure in that phase. The phase 4 large post-holes require little explanation: they clearly supported a series of separate and very large posts. No major construction seems to have taken place during phase 5, although it should be noted that excavation is insufficiently advanced to be certain of this. Phases 6 and 7 appear to be phases of deposition only: there are no indications of construction.

E. Iron Age, phase 1

A circular palisade trench approximately 22 m in diameter marks this phase. No other features can be assigned certainly to this phase as yet. This trench, feature 512, cannot be traced across the distance of some 4 m on the north-north-eastern part of the circumference. It would appear probable that this marks an entrance, but the truncation, on the west side of the gap of trench 512 by trench 514 makes the details unclear. The possibility of another entrance on the south side remains.

F. Iron Age, phase 2

This is the most remarkable of the Iron Age structures. The circular palisade trenches (60, 513, 514) are graded from the smallest inner one to the largest outside one. The closeness of these trenches would hardly permit viable "corridors" or "passageways." This proximity also is not consistent with a roof support: the distance between the outer and inner trenches is only 3·5 m, hardly too great a distance to span. The intermediate vertical support, such as would be provided by the palisade in trench 513, would be hardly necessary. As I have already suggested (Wailes, 1970b, p. 513) the close spacing and size grading of these three trenches is consistent with the notion that a super-structure, higher on the outside and lower on the inside, was supported by the timbers set in those trenches. Since there is an intermediate trench this must have played some functional role in supporting the superstructure. The whole arrangement might have supported two parapet walks, the outer higher than the inner, with the posts in trench 513 supporting the outer side of the inner parapet walk and the inner side of the outer one (see Fig. 5). Alternatively such platforms could be regarded as seats or stands for spectators viewing some ceremony or performance within the enclosure. There is no indication, at least as yet, of any substantial post-holes within the phase 2 structure that could possibly have supported a roof across the minimum diameter of 28·5 m. At present the evidence points to a "raked" timber structure around an open space. This triple circle is broken to the east-north-east by an entrance. The outer trench, 514, is broken for a greater distance than trenches 60 and 513. These two are broken by a gap of only 3·5 m between features 316 and 85.

Two linear palisade trenches, 278 and 314, flank this entranceway and run down the slope of the hill towards the main entrance through the bank and ditch that enclose the whole site. The extent of trenches 278 and 314 cannot be followed at present owing to the enclosing fence around the excavation area. One may note at this point that a slight linear depression leads up the hill from the original entrance through the bank and ditch towards the funnel formed by trenches 278 and 314 between the phase 2 entrance (see Fig. 1).

On the south side of the phase 2 structure trenches 513 and 514 join and end, leaving trench 60 to continue further only to break, leaving a gap 1·2 m wide immediately facing the equivalent gap between trenches 217 and 366. As a glance at Fig. 3 will show, these two latter trenches form a part of what appears to be a ground plan of a circular construction about 14·5 m internal diameter, that seems likely to form either an annexe or a second entrance to the main phase 2 structure. On the north-eastern side of this "annexe" there is a gap between trenches 355 and 518 on the north and 215 on the south. As this is an area of hard ridged bedrock, one cannot be certain whether this gap is deliberate or whether it is due only to the nature of the bedrock, in which case perhaps the palisade continued across the gap. However, the curious arrangement of stake holes between 520 and 514, outside (i.e., immediately east of) this gap, suggest some contemporaneous blocking structure. Here, one might draw attention to the curious similarity of plan between this pattern of stake holes and the pattern of stake holes within the "annexe", between trenches 217 and 515.

G. Iron Age, phase 3

Phase 3 is defined by a circular structure of two concentric palisade trenches, 515 and 516, which has a maximum and minimum diameter of 44 m and 37 m. Although this structure is not nearly as elaborate as that of phase 2, it neverthe-less shows quite a complex arrangement to the north-east. Here the outer trench, 516, terminates, leaving a gap about 3 m across, and features 434 and 428 serve to link the ends of 516 to the inner trench, 515. 428 and 434 continue inside the line of 515, and are flanked by features 475 and 476. Although trench 515 continues across this complex, the whole arrangement is suggestive of an elaborate entrance gateway. Although it is possible that there was an entrance through this structure on the southwest side, where it is incompletely excavated, the positioning of the 475/434/428/476 complex, and the breaking of trench 516, at a position very similar to that of the entrance of the preceding phase 2 structure, strongly suggests that the entrance of the phase 3 structure lay in this sector also.

Feature 42 was probably constructed at this time. It lies at the centre of the concentric circles formed by 515/516 and appears to have been used through the succeeding phase 4, also laid out on the same central point. The structure is a curious one. Superficially it is a small circular hut with an internal diameter of about 5 m. But while it is still not fully excavated, it is clear that there was intense and extensive burning on the floor: the extent of this burning, and the lack of any constructed hearth, indicate that feature 42 most probably was not a "hut" in any normal residential sense of the term. This impression receives further support from the curious series of pits arranged radially around the exterior of this hut. Some of these pits originally contained posts; the purpose of the others is not so clearly determinable. In plan, they suggest the possibility of a series of external buttresses. At any rate they are certainly not storage pits or rubbish pits.

It was thought at first that the large post-holes (Numbers 1–30) were a part of this phase. But subsequent excavation has shown that these holes were cut through the occupation surface that continues over the fill of feature 476 and adjoining areas of 515. It thus seems clear that, although these posts were arranged concentrically to trenches 515 and 516, they were erected at least slightly later. This precludes any possibility, as far as one can see at present, of postulating a roof structure for phase 3, since the span from trench 515 to the central hut (42) is some 15 m. This is certainly too great a distance for a single span beam without intermediate support. In the fill of trench 516, a little to the south of feature 428, a short La Tène C type sword was found. It is complete, but exceptionally heavily mineralised, as is all the iron from the site.

H. Iron Age, phase 4

The circle of large post-holes that define this phase are laid out on the same centre as the palisade trenches of the preceding phase. As already noted, the Iron Age phase 3 palisades had been dismantled, and the trenches filled in, before the post-holes for the Iron Age phase 4 structure were dug. The use of the same geometric centre for both phases suggests that the central "hut" (feature 42) was standing during both phases. The large posts were eventually removed at the end of Iron Age phase 5 (see below), and in no case does a clear impression of the original post remain in a hole—the extraction process always involved heavy disturbance of the primary fill. However, in almost every hole vertical stones remain, evidently the original "packing-stones" that wedged the post tightly upright. And in a few holes, a sufficient arc of the original primary fill remained intact to estimate the diameter of the post that had stood there. These posts appear to have been about 0·5 m in diameter (appreciably larger than a typical telegraph pole today).

The depth of the holes is usually about a metre below the excavated surface, so probably slightly more from the original ground surface at the time of construction. The posts could have stood to a considerable height, therefore. The distance between this circle of posts and the central "hut" is about 8·0 m, with no indication of intermediate holes of this phase. The likelihood of a roof is remote, therefore. There is no means of knowing whether or not lintels joined the tops of these large posts, as the contemporaneous ground surface below is too trampled to show any clear trace of "drip lines" from rainwater.

I. Iron Age, phase 5

While the phase 4 posts were still standing, intense burning took place around posts 1, 2, 29 and 30, on the eastern perimeter of the phase 4 circle (see Fig. 4). It is quite likely that the intense burning on the upper part of the floor level of the central "hut" (feature 42) is also of this phase. In this case the hut had been dismantled by this time, as the burning carries across the infilled wall-trench of the "hut". But there is no stratigraphic connection that can be made between the relatively small area of phase 5 burning and the "hut", despite every attempt in excavation.

Much of the phase 5 level remains to be excavated. In many places it can be subdivided into two separate phases of burning, but it is not yet clear whether the upper and lower phases of burning in one place can be connected with the same sequence in another place. There are a few pits or post-holes of this phase, but few of these have been fully excavated yet, and they show no coherent plan at present. Since the burning covers such a limited area, surrounding only a few posts of the circle, perhaps the burning was not intended to destroy the timbers, but represents some less easily identifiable intention. However, intense burning of this phase, around large standing timbers, is reminiscent of the burning of the outer timber wall of the "ceremonial" phase of Site B at Emain Macha (Selkirk and Waterman, 1970, p. 307). If, as seems likely at Emain Macha, the burning was intended to destroy the standing timbers, it was evidently unsuccessful at Dún Ailinne, as the timbers were still standing and had to be removed at the end of the phase, after the burning (or the two attempts at burning?). Perhaps experimental attempts were made to burn a few timbers, and when this proved unsuccessful, all timbers were extracted manually. This simpler explanation seems more likely.

J. Iron Age, phase 6

Once the circle of large posts had been removed and the sockets filled in, the area of burning of phase 5 was covered by a layer consisting mainly of redeposited glacial till. On the northern part of this was laid a "paving" of slate slabs, evidently freshly quarried from somewhere on the hill. This "paving" cannot have been a paving in the sense of a floor that was trodden upon, since it was not at all evenly laid, and not even the smallest projections show any signs of abrasion. It is possible that the redeposited till might have been to stifle the fire, but the "paving" can hardly have been for this purpose. There were patches of heavy burning on the surface of the phase 6 redeposited till, but these should be referred, perhaps, to the subsequent phase.

The holes of the phase 4/5 posts were all covered by the deposits of phase 6. Most could be identified before the level was removed, as the settling of the fill in the post-holes had resulted in subsidence of the covering layer. In several places, this subsidence was so pronounced that the covering layer of phase 6 had "pulled away" where local areas had sunk, rather like poorly-rolled pastry tearing away from the edge of the pie-dish as it sinks over the soft filling.

K. Iron Age, phase 7

Finally, a large area of the Iron Age "occupation" was covered by a layer of burnt material. This consisted of blackened earth and burnt stones, and contained considerable quantities of animal bones (see below, p. 331) indicative of feasting. The layer extends far enough to lie partly under the "medieval bank", and there is covered by the sterile humus formation upon which that bank was built. There is no doubt that phase 7 represents the latest Iron Age activities in this central area of the site, on the top of the hill.

The layer is lensed with very thin patches of humic material, which seem characteristic of the pattern of vegetation growth that invades bare earth in this climate over a period of a few months. Judging by the patchy growth of vegetation on excavation spoil dumps, I would estimate that the humus patches in this layer cannot represent growth periods of more than a year or two at the most. It appears, then, that phase 7 was a period of a few years during which periodic activities took place in this area, but in which there was no continual use. The accumulations of animal bones and evidence for fires both suggest that a part of these periodic activities must have included feasting.

L. Post-Iron Age

The "medieval embankment" has been discussed already (above, pp. 320–322). The lack of information precludes any useful further discussion here. The sporadic occurrence of lead musket balls and bottle glass of eighteenth or early nineteenth century date indicate only slight activity on the site. The hill is supposed to have been occupied by rebels during the 1798 uprising. Very numerous blank ·303 cartridge cases, fragments of late type clay pipe and two brass badges of the South Lancashires are evidence for British Army activities, probably during the period 1916–1921. There is local recollection of a British Army Unit temporarily under canvas on the hill at some stage during that period. In short, there seems to be no substantial occupation of the site after the Iron Age.

IV. Interpretation

I have already proposed that Dún Ailinne is interpreted best as a ceremonial site (Wailes, 1970b, pp. 515, 517; Wailes, 1971, p. 11). Clearly, the possibility of residential, domestic, industrial or even defensive occupation cannot be ruled out, since only a small area of the whole has been excavated, and that incompletely as yet. A "ceremonial" interpretation thus must rest, provisionally, upon the overall appearance of the site, the results of excavation to date, and the documentary sources.

A. The Site

The whole oval enclosure covers an area of some 40 acres: i.e., 40 acres from the outside of the bank—some 34 acres internally. It is formed by a substantial bank with an internal ditch. This arrangement does not suggest that the bank and ditch were intended primarily for defence. This is supported by the placing of this earthwork in relation to the relief of the hill as a whole: from the top of the hill only a small portion of the bank can be seen; indeed, even from the top of our 30 ft high photographic tower one cannot see the whole circumference. This would make the direction of defence almost impossible for a commander. Moreover, there is no sign that the single original entrance had any additional defensive works such as guard-houses, inturned bank, or the like, such as is frequently found in hillforts. An internal ditch might suggest that the earthwork was designed to keep something *in* the enclosure, rather than to keep something *out*, but what? If cattle, then the height of bank and depth of ditch are considerably in excess of the minimum requirement. On the other hand, one is forcibly reminded of henge monuments. The internal ditch at these sites is regarded as one argument for their non-defensive and so "ceremonial" nature, and this argument applies equally well to sites of other periods.

B. The Excavation to Date

As we have seen, little can be said of Iron Age phase 1. At present, however, there is no indication of any internal structure within the 22·0 m diameter circular palisade trench defining the phase. A roofed structure is highly unlikely, therefore, and so a residential purpose cannot be inferred. The elaborate and unusual structure of Iron Age phase 2 likewise cannot be argued to have been roofed, and the triple palisade trenches of the enclosure, whatever their purpose (see Figs 3, 5), certainly were not part of any residential structure(s) disposed around the interior of the external "wall". The "hut" (feature 42) is central to the double palisade trenches of Iron Age phase 3 and the circle of large posts of Iron Age phase 4. If all of these structures were contemporaneous, any roof would have required horizontal supports of 7 metres between the inner palisade trench and the large posts, and supports of 8 m between the large posts and the "buttresses" surrounding the "hut". These spans are extremely unlikely. But, in any case, the double palisade and the circle of large post-holes have been shown to be non-contemporaneous (see above, p. 327). The "hut" itself is sufficiently small (just over 5 m internal diameter) to have been spanned without internal supports, perhaps. But the heavy burning across much of its floor indicates that its purpose was non-residential. Moreover, the irregular holes that surround the exterior indicate some unusual function. Some of these appear to have contained timber uprights, others are ambiguous as to original function. Their disposition suggests some form of external bracing for the "hut"—a series of "buttresses", perhaps? At all events, feature 42 does not seem to have been residential/

domestic in purpose. The circle of large posts, Iron Age phase 4, cannot be a residential structure, and subsequent phases show little or no building at all. Turning from the structural evidence to that of other features, we note that there are no "hearths" suggestive of domestic cooking. Kathleen Hughes had suggested (1972, p. 32) that the extensive burning in the central "hut" might have been the result of *prolonged* burning. She points to the story of St. Brigit and the never-dying fire at the nearby early ecclesiastical site of Kildare and, in view of the pagan elements of Brigit (the goddess Brig), proposes that the never-dying fire *might* have been originally at the pagan sanctuary of Dún Ailinne, the story being transposed after the conversion to the Christian context of Kildare. There are several other areas of burning, but all of these are extensive, and some were very clearly so intensely hot as to oxidise the subsoil beneath to a depth of down to about 20 cm. It seems highly likely that some form of cooking was practised on the site, most evidently in the latest Iron Age phase (7). This level contains considerable quantities of animal bones, many of them clearly partly charred during cooking, and many showing "butchering" marks (including marks made in cutting cooked meat from the bone)[1]. But there remains no evidence for "domestic" cooking or catering having been practised. It must be remembered also that during Iron Age phase 7, from which the most extensive evidence of cooking comes, there is no evidence whatever that any structures were standing.

The artefactual evidence to date also appears to support a ceremonial rather than a residential interpretation. All the identifiable pottery from the excavation is Neolithic, although admittedly it would be difficult to insist, in the present state of knowledge of Irish Iron Age pottery, that absence of pottery should be taken as indicative of non-residential function! One would expect that a site of known social-political importance, as is Dún Ailinne, would be likely, if residential, to show evidence for metal-working, and perhaps other crafts such as enamelling and glass-working. Although some quantity of iron objects (including the La Tène "C" sword) has been found, there is not one piece of iron slag. Similarly, there is no indication whatever of bronze-working, despite the presence of various bronze artefacts. Again, the quite numerous glass beads and bracelets appear to have been imported to the site, to judge by the lack of any indication of glass-working there.

In sum, the excavated area, and the structures as known to date, all point to a ceremonial and non-residential function for the site. Residential or other use cannot be ruled out for areas of the site not yet investigated.

V. Discussion

A. Irish "Royal Sites"

I have pointed out briefly before the basic similarity of Dún Ailinne to the Rath na Riogh at Tara and to Emain Macha (Navan Fort) (Wailes, 1970a,

[1] I am indebted to Miss Robin Robertson for her painstaking analytical and experimental work on the bone material. This is not quite ready for publication at the time of writing.

pp. 89–90). All three have substantial external banks and internal ditches. The Rath na Riogh at Tara has not been excavated with the exception of small-scale work there during the late Professor Ó Ríordáin's work at the Rath of the Synods. This remains unpublished except for a brief account (Ó Ríordáin, 1954) in which it is stated that a cutting across the bank and ditch of the Rath na Riogh revealed a palisade ditch inside the main ditch (ibid. p. 13). There is no evidence as to date, but nothing to indicate a date other than the Iron Age date usually inferred from the documentary sources (see above, p. 320).

At Emain Macha[2] the earliest occupation of Site B was residential, and apparently of the Late Bronze Age or Early Iron Age (Selkirk and Waterman, 1970, pp. 305–306). But the subsequent large circular timber structure is interpreted as being probably ceremonial. This has four concentric circles of large post-holes, a central post-hole with a ramp, and an "ambulatory" or "corridor" leading to the centre from the west side. This structure was covered by a thick layer of stones while the inner timbers were still standing (ibid. pp. 306–307). The later, "ceremonial", phases at Emain Macha are decidely reminiscent of Dún Ailinne. The "ambulatory", though inside the structure, is a rather similar concept to the elaborate "funnel" entrance to Iron Age phase 2 structure at Dún Ailinne. The covering of stones, with timbers still standing, is repeated at Dún Ailinne in the timbers of Iron Age phase 4 being surrounded by the deposits of phase 6, after the burning of phase 5: this is far less spectacular and extensive at Dún Ailinne, but the parallel is striking. The massive circular timber structure itself is also, of course, generally similar at both sites, although the details are different. The chronology of the Emain Macha sequence appears to be earlier than that at Dún Ailinne (see Appendix: dating), but both fall into the appropriate period of the pagan Iron Age.

The substantial excavations, though still incomplete, of two of the known pagan "Royal sites" of Ireland shows, then, that the similarity of superficial appearance (henge-like, with roughly central feature) is continued in the similarity of the roughly central structures. I should conclude on a note of caution by pointing out that at neither site has the enclosing bank and ditch been shown to be contemporary with the "central" Iron Age structures. Since both sites have produced Neolithic material, a Neolithic date for the bank and ditch is plausible for either site; indeed, any late prehistoric or very early historic date remains possible. However, at both sites the bank and ditch are well-preserved and relatively little eroded, and at both sites the major known period of activity is the early Iron Age. These factors tend to favour an Iron Age rather than Neolithic date.

B. Celtic "Sanctuaries"

I do not propose to engage in an exhaustive comparative examination of known "sanctuaries" of the Iron Age in Celtic areas. Rather, I wish to draw

[2] The only available account of the "Navan Fort" excavations appeared in *Current Archaeology*, September 1970 (Selkirk and Waterman, 1970). This was particularly useful, as an equivalent article on Dún Ailinne (Selkirk and Wailes, 1970) immediately follows, in the same issue.

attention, simply, to some of the known and suspected examples of circular Celtic Iron Age structures that seem at least analogous in some way to Dún Ailinne (and to Emain Macha).

Although the "square-within-a-square" form of temple is best known, both from Romano-Celtic times and pre-Roman times there are also circular ones known. At Frilford a small horse-shoe shaped ditch enclosed six post-holes, disposed in two rows, with votive deposits of a plough-share, a sword and a shield (Ross, 1967, p. 45). The whole appears to be pre-Roman Iron Age. At Figsbury (Wiltshire) there is an inner ditch, about 100 ft within the outer one, but this inner ditch has no corresponding banks. The excavator suggested that it was an additional quarry ditch for the outer bank (which has an external ditch, in normal hillfort style (Cunnington, 1925, pp. 48–49). However, it seems an entirely unreasonable extra labour to take material an extra one hundred feet, when an internal ditch to the bank would have served the same purpose equally well. Mrs. Cunnington considered that both outer bank-and-ditch and inner ditch were constructed at the same time (ibid. pp. 48, 50), but in fact the inner ditch seems to be of considerably different construction, being markedly irregular in both plan and profiles. If it is contemporary with the enclosing bank-and-ditch, it seems likely that its purpose was quite different. This is supported, perhaps, by the discovery of human skeletal remains scattered with other finds in a layer of rubble and soil on the floor of this inner ditch (ibid. p. 51). The dating of the site is not very clear. Most datable pottery was Iron Age "A" (ibid. p. 50), but five Bronze Age sherds were also found, and there is a bronze sword said to come from the site, also (ibid.). In all, there seems to be a case for considering the possibility of some form of "ritual" site within the defences at Figsbury.

At Maiden Castle, Dorset, there is a circular Romano-British period hut close to the temple site. Wheeler remarks upon the apparently deliberately archaic nature of this hut. It lies upon an earlier, pre-Roman, hut that was situated at the end of the Iron Age "street" in this part of the site (Wheeler, 1943, pp. 74–77; P1. XX). The Iron Age hut seems a likely candidate for a "sanctuary" building of some sort. Other circular Iron Age and Roman period "ritual" constructions are given by Piggott (1968, pp. 64–70). In all, even without an complete cataloguing, it is possible to consider Dún Ailinne as an Iron Age "ceremonial" site within a general Celtic Iron Age context of at least roughly equivalent sites. The location of some of these within hillforts suggests that all hillforts may not have been entirely defensive/residential in nature. Some, at least, may also have combined "ceremonial" or "ritual" features.

C. Irish Hillforts

Returning to Ireland, and a wider consideration of the problem there, we must first note that the study of hillforts in Ireland, in any systematic way, is only just beginning. Barry Raftery (1972) has provided us with the first

serious attempt at this, and his opening remarks (ibid. p. 37) reveal clearly
the paucity of synthetic survey prior to his article. Moreover, in his concluding
remarks he makes it clear that even the basic field-work and identification of
sites is by no means complete: "since this paper was written the number of
hillforts recognised in Ireland has increased to almost fifty" (ibid. p. 55)[3].

We may legitimately ask why Irish hillforts should be so little known.
Perhaps the most important reason is the extreme richness of Ireland in extant
monuments, which has meant that some large classes of monument remain
inadequately studied so far. One must recall that there are in excess of 30 000
"ring-forts" in Ireland, covering a wide range of variation in size and form.
Doubtless they also cover a considerable range of both date and function.
But, at all events, they do indeed present a formidable task to the field-worker,
let alone the excavator. Yet, Ireland has a series of Ordnance Survey maps from
the 1840s onwards, which include, from the first editions, identified ancient
monuments. Again, there have been, and are, excellent field archaeologists
in Ireland. But their (legitimate) attention has been drawn rather by other
classes of monument than "forts" (ring-, hill- or other), so that there remains
a gap between the available published data (Ordnance Survey maps in various
editions and at various scales) and systematic archaeological synthesis from
this data, enlarged by further field-work.

It may still seem odd that such seemingly obvious monuments as hillforts
should remain so little known were it not for an aspect of them that remains
largely unremarked. This is that many of the visible ramparts are extremely
small. Indeed, the characteristic Irish field "fence" is frequently no smaller.
This consists, typically, of a small ditch, with a correspondingly low bank on
which grow bushes, the whole very similar to the equally characteristic English
"hedge". The vertical height from crest of bank to present bottom of ditch is
frequently not more than one metre. The published section of the enclosing
bank and ditch at Freestone Hill, County Kilkenny (Raftery, 1969, Figs 14–16)
appears to be quite typical. Obviously, this is not to deny that often massive
ramparts do exist at some sites. But "token" ramparts (if I might coin a tentative
term) are quite usual. It is also worth emphasising that some sites with massive
ramparts also have "token" ramparts. Thus Grianan Aileach, County Donegal,
has a massive inner rampart of stone and three concentric outer "token"
ramparts of (apparently) earth. Raftery (Raftery, B., 1972, p. 45) points out
that the central "cashel" was reconstructed in modern times, and describes
the outer ramparts as "very worn", thus quite rightly suggesting that the
contrast between them "may be quite exaggerated". He also suggests the
possibility that they may date to quite different phases of construction at different periods. However, the modern reconstruction used only the stone from the

---

[3] I am deeply grateful to Mr. Raftery for providing me with not only this published work, but also
for his kind permission to read his M.A. thesis, in University College (Dublin), on this subject.
These works form the indispensable basis for my suggestions below, augmented only marginally
by my own casual observations in the course of field-work directed, primarily, toward rather
different ends.

tumbled walls, rebuilt on the extant foundation courses, so that its present impressive thickness and height cannot be so very different from the original. The outer ramparts are eroded to some degree, of course, but to my eyes their present miniscule height and relative sharpness of profile suggests a very small original construction, rather than originally large banks now eroded almost to the point of disappearance as surface features. If Grianan Aileach is all of one period of construction, I would prefer to regard it as a strong cashel (dimensionally within the range of larger ring-forts) surrounded by concentric "token" ramparts.

I use Grianan Aileach to illustrate a point, although the site is not typical in its combination of the two types of rampart. This point is that very small ramparts cannot be considered as defensive in any way unless, of course, they *do* turn out to be substantial ramparts that have suffered very (I would say abnormally) heavy erosion. They may have served merely as footings for substantial timber palisades, but Freestone Hill shows no good evidence of this (Raftery, 1969, pp. 35–38). So, *if* these tiny ramparts cannot be regarded as defensive, they must be explained otherwise. They define areas, but not, it seems, in any way that would be physically inclusive or exclusive: cattle, for example, could hardly have been kept in or out, much less humans. So one should consider the likelihood that they served to define assembly areas, ceremonial or ritual areas, or the like.

If we eliminate the few large sites with external banks and internal ditches (such as Dún Ailinne and Emain Macha; see Raftery, 1972, p. 43) from serious consideration as *forts* in the defensive sense, and similarly eliminate sites with "token" ramparts, we shall be left with a reduced number of sites that are (a) substantially larger than ring-forts, however this distinction is to be made (see Raftery, B., 1972, pp. 37–39), (b) situated on hills or other naturally defensible places, and (c) have walls or ramparts that could seriously be considered as primarily defensive in purpose. Of these some, from the relatively small size of their innermost enclosure, could be regarded as essentially ring-forts with elaborate and extensive outer defences: Dún Aengus, on Inishmore (Aran, County Galway), is an example of this problem.

I cannot, at this point, offer anything approaching an exhaustive review of these sites, and must rest with the few specific examples cited above. But these do raise the question as to how many "hillforts" there are in Ireland that would be classified as such in the normal European and British terminology: large defensive enclosures that were supposedly (and in some cases demonstrably) centres of local or regional military significance (though note that this is not inconsistent with other functions as well). This suggests that the hillfort, in the conventional sense of the term, may have been a considerably less important element in Iron Age Ireland than it was in other approximately contemporary Celtic areas. Kathleen Hughes (1972, pp. 264–265), though speaking mainly of the early Christian and Viking periods rather than the pagan Iron Age, contrasts the documentary and archaeological evidence for warfare. She concludes that warfare does not appear to have included, regularly if at all, the siege and sacking of forts. One may wonder in what degree or kind Irish society differed from that of the Celts in Britain and continental Europe, that such a difference should be evident—sparser population? more fragmented political structure? simply a preference for more open warfare? *less* warfare? There is, however, considerable variation in the pattern of hillforts. For example, the Ordnance Survey *Map of Southern Britain in the Iron Age* shows a clear distinction between the Wessex area, with larger and relatively fewer hillforts, and the south-west with smaller but rather more densely distributed hillforts. Ireland, perhaps, then represents one end of a continuum rather than a distinctively different entity.

A complementary viewpoint might be that in Ireland, hill-top enclosures were (for whatever reason) less likely to be fortifications than in Britain and Europe, so that other functions (ceremonial?) might be more evident there than in the other areas, or have remained a more prominent feature in Ireland. At all events, I find that the term "hill-top enclosure" is more appropriate, since more neutral, than the term "hillfort" to describe many Irish sites. And certainly Dún Ailinne, and similar sites, is better so termed.

D. Other Parallels

If, then, we have the makings of a "class" of Celtic Iron Age "ceremonial sites", what are their longer-range connections, both in time and space? We have already noted, though far from completely, that there are not dissimilar features (circular timber "sanctuaries" or "temples") at other early Iron Age sites within the Celtic world of the time. But, if the enclosing banks and ditches are also Iron Age, both Emain Macha and Dún Ailinne, and Rath na Riogh at Tara also, have dominant major features that are reminiscent of "henge monuments". Indeed, in general terms one might say that the features that distinguish these Irish Iron Age sites from henges (apart from their date) is their considerable size, so that the internal circular timber structures are almost dwarfed by comparison.

An apparently obvious parallel is the Goloring, in the Koberner Wald of west Germany (Röder, 1948). This site is a circular earthwork about 200 m in diameter, with external bank and internal ditch. There is a slighter inner concentric earthwork of about half the diameter of the outer. The inner profile shows clearly that the interior of this inner earthwork is higher than the surrounding area, giving it something of the appearance of a "platform ring-fort", although this may be due to the relief of the land (ibid. Tafel 19) rising towards the centre of the site. Near the centre of the whole site there is a very large post-hole (see site plan ibid. Tafel 13; detail plan of central area Abb. 3; and section, Abb. 4). This is reminiscent of the large central post-hole of the "ceremonial" phase of Site B at Emain Macha (Selkirk and Waterman, 1970: plan on p. 306, text on p. 307). However, this large post-hole seems to have been the only structural timber feature at the Goloring, although it must be admitted that the excavation was not very extensive. Sherds of

Hunsrück-Eifel culture pottery indicate a probable Hallstatt D date, in the sixth century B.C., for the site (Röder, 1948, pp. 94–95).

The parallel of the henge-like earthwork is unmistakable, as Röder recognised explicitly in the title of his article. And much of the discussion in the article is taken up with possible parallels, most of which he finds in the henge monuments themselves, in Britain and Ireland. It is certainly chronologically possible, or so it would seem, that the Goloring could have influenced the Irish "Royal sites", particularly bearing in mind that the earlier C-14 age determinations for Emain Macha Site B are from the residential phase (see Appendix: dating). But the apparent lack of any internal timber circles at the Goloring suggest strongly that this feature should be derived elsewhere, if it is to be "derived" at all, and is not a regional (re-)invention of the Iron Age in Ireland.

A native Irish/British derivation seems inherently likely at present. First, there is the continuity of circular timber building in the islands from at least Late Neolithic times onward to the Iron Age. As we have seen, the earlier phases at Emain Macha were residential, and for that site one could argue for a purely "on-site" local transition from circular residential to circular ceremonial timber building. At any rate, the Hiberno-British circular building tradition through later prehistory serves as one obvious origin. Second, there is the problem of ceremonial use, however. Henge monuments do not appear to have been built, or rebuilt, after the Early Bronze Age at the latest. This is not to say that they may not have been used during the Bronze Age, but the paucity of identifiable Bronze Age sherds from henge sites does not commend such a suggestion, though it remains possible. The account of the curious monument at Coolhill, County Cork (Mahr, 1937, pp. 362–363), with what appears to have been a Bronze Age urn of some sort, tempts one to propose that site as a likely "gap-filler" between Early Bronze Age and Iron Age. But the circumstances of the discovery, and the unsatisfactory nature of the only extant drawing (no scale, apart from other ambiguities), do not permit the placing of any substantial weight here. The circular timber structure at Rathgall (Raftery, see below, p. 339 ff.) appears to be Late Bronze Age in date, and might be interpreted as a henge-like structure. And there are, of course, various barrow structures that echo henges—notably disc barrows. But these do not seem to date later than the latter part of the Early Bronze Age either.

On the whole, it is not possible to make a clear case in favour of continuity of tradition of henges or henge-type structures from Neolithic to Iron Age. Nevertheless, the henges seem far and away the best candidates as prototypes for the sites such as Dún Ailinne, despite the apparent chronological gap during much of the Bronze Age. Continental European prototypes are almost non-existent, and close parallels are quite lacking to date. Despite the lack of work on Irish henge monuments, they do exist, and so one can say that there is a well-defined British/Irish tradition of Neolithic circular ceremonial sites with external banks and internal ditches, and, in most excavated examples, interior timber structures.

Appendix: Radiocarbon Chronology

For the information of the reader, I append the radiocarbon dates presently (May 1973) available from Dún Ailinne and Emain Macha, with brief comment below.

Emain Macha (Smith, Pearson and Pilcher, 1970, pp. 287–288)

UB-188	Primary fill of enclosure ditch	680 b.c. ± 50	} "Domestic" or
UB-203	Phase 2 roundhouse	410 b.c. ± 45	"residential"
UB-187	Late in "domestic" phase	395 b.c. ± 50	phase
UB-186	Large post structure	465 b.c. ± 50	} "Ceremonial" phase
UB-202	Burning of large posts	265 b.c. ± 50	

Dún Ailinne (Stuckenrath and Mielke, 1973, pp. 399–400)

SI-982	Pit containing Food Vessel sherds	1270 b.c. ± 55
SI-984	Iron Age phase 2 palisade trench	250 b.c. ± 50
SI-983	Iron Age phase 2/3/4 occupation level	420 b.c. ± 85
SI-980	Iron Age phase 3 palisade trench	a.d. 50 ± 85
SI-978	Iron Age phase 3 palisade trench	a.d. 20 ± 85
SI-985	Iron Age phase 3 palisade trench	a.d. 195 ± 90
SI-987	Iron Age phase 4/5 post-hole	a.d. 95 ± 50
SI-986	Iron Age phase 4/5 post-hole	125 b.c. ± 80
SI-981	Iron Age phase 5/6/7 occupation level	540 b.c. ± 85
SI-979	Iron Age phase 5/6/7 occupation level	1 b.c. ± 80
SI-977	Iron Age phase 5/6/7 occupation level	215 b.c. ± 70

Comment

First, these age-determinations are cited as originally published, according to the 5568 ± 30 half-life. The main point of this comparison is the evidence for the two sites relatively; the translation into calendar years is less important for present purposes. Also, in view of the present uncertainty as to the best available "calibration table" to convert radiocarbon age-determinations into an approximate calendar year system, it seems unwise to propose any such "calendar years". In these terms, it is sufficient for the moment that both sites, recalibrated or not, appear to have been abandoned before the fifth century A.D. conversion of Ireland to Christianity.

The Emain Macha age-determinations are internally consistent, and appear to confirm the notion derived from the eight successive "domestic" phases (Selkirk and Waterman, 1970, p. 305) that the whole "domestic" or "residential" period was quite lengthy. The burning of the large posts (UB-202: the sample is small branches, probably kindling material) around the third century b.c. indicates a rather surprisingly early end to the timber "ceremonial" structure, and its covering by the large mound. However, this would not necessarily preclude its continued "sanctity", and use as (say) an assembly site.

The Dún Ailinne age-determinations are far less satisfactory. The "food-vessel" date seems reasonable enough, but the Iron Age determinations are internally inconsistent, even though they all lie within the general time-period considered likely from documentary and artefactual evidence. In view of the Neolithic artefacts re-deposited into Iron Age levels, it seems highly likely that "neolithic" charcoal might also be re-deposited. For this reason, I prefer to place more reliance upon the samples from the palisade trenches, even though it is impossible to tell whether they relate to the building or dismantling of a particular phase. SI-980, -978 and -985 "cluster" well enough, and suggest that Iron Age phase 3 might be "early a.d." in time. Until the next series of samples has been dated, I prefer to suggest no more than this. But it does seem likely that the abandonment of Dún Ailinne was considerably later than that of Emain Macha (Navan Fort).

16 | *Rathgall and Irish Hillfort Problems*

Barry Raftery

I. The Site

The hillfort of Rathgall lies on the end of a prominent east-west orientated shoulder of upland some 450 ft above sea level. Apart from the north and north-eastern sides, where the slopes are negligible, the ground falls sharply from the defensive ramparts. In the west, especially, the natural defences of the hill are added to by the presence at the foot of the slope, of soggy lowland, the site perhaps of a lake in prehistoric times. Despite its relatively low altitude the hillfort is well situated and possesses a wide view in every direction.

The present visible remains comprise four roughly concentric ramparts which crown the eminence (Fig. 1) and enclose a total area of 18 acres (Orpen, 1911). The innermost of the four enclosures consists of a polygonal wall of dry-stone masonry (Pl. I). It is irregularly built and in places bulges unevenly. Its preserved height varies from 1·50 m–2·50 m above the surface of the interior and the area enclosed has axes ranging from 44 m–46 m. The thickness of this wall varies surprisingly from a massive 8 m in the south to but a single metre in the north. A simple gap in the west forms the only entrance into this inner enclosure. In the south, remains of what appears to be a small rectangular chamber exist within the body of the wall.

At a distance varying from about 27 m to about 53 m outside this are the second and third ramparts which together form the main defensive element on the site. These banks are only 10 m–12 m apart and clearly constitute a single defensive concept. The innermost of the two is a massive structure towering at times as much as 5 or 6 m above ground level on the outside. Due to the heavy vegetation cover the nature of construction of this bank is not evident. The outermost of these two lines of defence, however, is of stone, but is for much of its circumference in a state of considerable ruin, its height rarely exceeding one metre.

It is not altogether clear how many of the gaps which occur in these two ramparts are original entrances. Certainly, when in use there were at least five entries through the great second rampart and at least three through the lesser (outer) third bank. These openings are clearly indicated in several instances by large granite slabs which line them. Indeed, in the case of the western entrance through the second rampart the slabs assume almost megalithic proportions.

This entrance in the west is the only one in the second bank which remains open today. All the others have been sealed off by a stone wall built along the inner face of this rampart. This wall resembles in construction that of the inner enclosure. Though built against an earlier rampart, which is generally circular in plan, the facing wall is nonetheless built on the same polygonal principle as the innermost wall. In addition, its consistent height and the almost complete absence of collapsed material along its base suggest strongly that it is of no great antiquity.

The outermost enclosure is largely circular in plan but it departs from its natural line to form a slight bulge in the south-west. It is uncertain whether this bulge is an original feature. The diameter of the area enclosed by the outermost bank is approximately 310 m. This rampart has been completely removed for a considerable part of its original circuit in the north-east. Elsewhere it is densely overgrown and has in places been considerably modified when it was adapted as a field boundary. Its original appearance is therefore a matter of some uncertainty.

II. The Excavation

Excavation to date has been concentrated in two main areas (Raftery, 1970a; 1971). First, the entire surface of the central enclosure has been investigated as well as a sizeable area immediately to the east of it; second, excavation has taken place on the south-eastern slopes of the hill beyond the outermost rampart.

Most of the excavated area is devoid of useful stratigraphy. There appears to have been intensive cultivation in fairly recent times and this has caused a uniform layer of undifferentiated brown humus, averaging 30 cm–40 cm in thickness, to form almost everywhere on the site. No structural features show up in this level but thousands of artefacts ranging widely in date occur together emphasising the total destruction of any archaeological layers which may have existed. This brown material rests directly on the yellow subsoil and only when the latter has been reached by excavation is it possible to recognise features such as post-holes, pits or bedding trenches. Owing to this lack of stratigraphy, therefore, it is difficult in most cases to establish with any degree of confidence the relationship between the various structural features revealed on the site.

One fact which was early revealed by the excavation was the late date of the polygonal wall of the inner enclosure. The foundation stones of this wall were seen to lie but a few centimetres under the surface sod; in fact, in places they seemed almost to be resting on it. Prehistoric layers existed under the basal stones of this wall and it is highly probable that it was not built earlier than the Medieval period and may, indeed, be considerably later.

So far the excavation has demonstrated that three principal phases of human activity are present on the site. Only the earliest of these (that of the Late Bronze Age) is clearly represented by both structural remains and artefacts. The later periods (Iron Age and Medieval) are, as yet, present in the archaeological record for the most part only in terms of objects discovered.

A. The Late Bronze Age House Complex

The overwhelming mass of material from the site belongs to the earliest phase. The focus of the Late Bronze Age settlement seems to have been a large circular house surrounded by a boundary ditch dug roughly concentrically with it (Fig. 2; Pl. I). The house was 15 m in diameter. Its wall must have consisted of timber uprights which stood in a bedding trench dug into the subsoil to a depth of from 15–25 cm. The packing stones which kept these wall posts in position were still *in situ* in places around the outer edge of the trench, though of the timbers themselves only some patches of carbonised wood in the grey fill of the trench remained. The entrance was a simple gap on the east side of the house, originally flanked by large posts. A small, internal, porch-like feature was formed by the inward turning of the walls of the house. This formed two short parallel stretches of timbering each 1 m long and ending originally in a second pair of doorposts (the southern portion of the entrance has subsequently been obliterated by a later pit).

Within the house on either side of the entrance, extending for a short distance from each of the inner doorposts, an arc of presumably continuous vertical beams ran concentric with the outer wall. In each case the bedding trench which held these timbers ends in a single deep post-hole. The curve of the southward-running of the two arcs of timbers was continued for about one quarter of the circumference of the house by a series of free-standing uprights placed at intervals of 50 cm to 75 cm.

To roof a building of this size a considerable number of substantial beams would be required. Many post-holes came to light in the interior of the house, but it is difficult to discern any obvious pattern among them. Two roughly parallel rows of post-holes leading inwards from the entrance might suggest the former presence of a passageway of some sort about 6 m in length. It might also be put forward tentatively that a hexagonal supporting framework of timber beams existed 2 to 3 m in from the wall and that further uprights were concentrated towards the centre of the house. But these must have been replaced and added to during the occupation of the dwelling so that the picture presented is one of general confusion. Apart from a small fire-reddened area in the north-eastern portion of the house, no indications of a hearth came to light.

Several carelessly dug hollows found within the area of the house may perhaps be interpreted as rubbish disposal pits because of their irregular appearance and the domestic refuse which came from them. A pit found near the centre of the house, however, had a significance different from that and indeed different from any other pit on the site.

This pit had been carefully dug; it was oval in plan and measured 1·75 m by 1·25 m. It was 40 cm deep. The sides and base of the pit were found to be covered by a dense, black, carbonised substance which could be interpreted as the remains of a former lining of organic material. A very large boulder was found lying directly on the black layer. The boulder had been specially selected so that it almost completely filled the pit. To finish the final sealing of the pit required only the packing of a clean, yellow sandy soil around the edges of the stone until only the upper portion of the latter was visible above the present level of the subsoil.

It is obvious that the pit had been deliberately and carefully filled in. There was no sign that it had ever fulfilled any practical function. No silting or any other material of similar type was present. Lying in the black layer under the boulder a small, penannular ring of gold was discovered (Pl. II:3) and a tiny scatter of burnt human bones clustered in its immediate vicinity.

The notion that the gold ring was simply lost here may be rejected. The suggestion that this large pit was dug and sealed with such care merely to hide a single tiny ring is also unlikely. It seems to the writer that the only possible conclusion is that the ring represents a careful deposit made in compliance with some religious or ritual motivation. The most likely explanation, therefore, is that this is a foundation deposit contemporary with the building of the circular house and if this is acceptable, a date for the construction of the house in the Dowris Phase of the Late Bronze Age is indicated.

The large number of pits and post-holes which occur around the outside of this house very probably form part of the general domestic complex. Detailed analysis of the post-hole depths and their filling material has not as yet been attempted and no clear pattern emerges on superficial examination. Some could be eave-supports, some might indicate the existence of small structures external to the house. Around the southern perimeter of the house an arc of post-holes concentric with the wall could represent the remains of an outer veranda or passageway. In the south-west a small square formed by a group of stake-holes might be construed as marking the former presence of some sort of wooden stand or rack.

Little can be said about the pits. With one exception they were dug casually and probably represent receptacles for the disposal of domestic refuse similar to those found within the house. The single exception is a large, deep, funnel-shaped pit found a short distance outside the entrance to the house in the east. It was 1·60 m deep and its sides and bottom were smooth and regular. Traces of a wickerwork basket which had formerly lined this pit could be recognised. This had been renewed at least once and possibly twice. This pit was without doubt a storage pit and it is likely that grain supplies for the occupants of the roundhouse were kept here. When finally abandoned as a storage pit it degenerated into a rubbish dump and many hundreds of potsherds of varying type as well as bone fragments and other occupation refuse were found in it. After a period of disuse, when the process of silting was allowed to advance in the pit, a large number of stones, some of considerable size, were piled in, filling it completely.

The habitation complex described above was surrounded by a fosse which ran 8 m to 10 m outside the house and which enclosed a circular area some 35 m in diameter. The fosse had been dug into the hard subsoil with varying degrees of care and precision. The initial intention clearly was to produce a fosse of V-shaped cross-section, but because of the many natural boulders and perhaps also the hard nature of the subsoil, the V-profile was not adhered to for much of its circumference. The depth of the ditch in the subsoil varied to a surprising extent from a maximum of 1·50 m in the north to as little as 50 cm in the south. At three points very large boulders were left *in situ* in the base of the ditch, thus rendering ineffective any meagre defensive significance it might have had. No portion of the ditch was left undug to form a causeway; it is probable that a timber bridge was laid across it, possibly at the constricted portion opposite the entrance to the house in the east.

A low earthen bank seems to have existed outside the fosse. For almost its entire circumference it lies under the much later stone wall and obviously served as a guide-line for the builders of the latter structure. The bank can be seen, however, as a prominent hump running across the entrance to the stone enclosure in the west and emerges again from under the wall for a short distance in the north-east and east though excavation has shown that it is incomplete here. After the first season's excavation at Rathgall this bank was taken to be an integral part of the ditched enclosure but this is now not certain: the bank diverges considerably from the ditch in the south and west. Further excavation is necessary to ascertain its function and its relationship, if any, to the fosse inside it.

B. Sunken Hearths

A series of sunken hearths of varying sizes was an interesting feature of the Late Bronze Age settlement. These have not yet all been fully excavated but it appears that as many as nine exist. Inside the ditched enclosure six hearths occurred, all but one of these being in the north east. These are large, oval or rectangular in shape, and were dug to a depth of 40 or 50 cm into the subsoil. None is associated with a house structure. In several cases, however, the existing post-hole arrangments show that canopy-like roofs formerly gave some shelter from the elements. One had a large pit set at each of the two corners of one end and several had traces of a former basketry lining similar to that found partially preserved in the large storage pit described above.

The outer bedding trench of the large circular house had been dug into one of these hearths so that the latter clearly belongs to an earlier phase of occupation on the site. The gap in time between the abandonment of the hearth and the construction of the house does not, however, appear to have been great, so that it is possible to consider them all as belonging in general to the same cultural group.

It is not certain whether the hearths were used for domestic purposes only or whether some, at least, of them may not have also served in connection with the bronze-working attested on the site (see below, p. 346). Bones and potsherds discovered in several suggest normal domestic use but clay mould fragments found in one hearth could be taken to infer the more specialised use related to bronze-working.

Finds

Many artefacts were found in the brown humus scattered over the entire area of the ditched enclosure. Most of these are Late Bronze Age in date. Coarse potsherds (Fig. 5) form the overwhelming bulk of the objects found and the great number of these—now in the region of 5000—suggests habitation on a considerable scale. Some of this pottery may belong to an iron-using phase; the bulk of it, however, almost certainly can be referred to the earliest period of occupation on the site. The ware is crude, the forms for the most part comprise flat-bottomed, bucket-shaped pots, often with a row of pin-prick perforations under the rim, though several small bowls are also represented. Ornament is uncommon. It consists in the main of thumb-nail impressions, incised zig-zags, hatched triangles, oblique strokes on flattened rim surfaces and in one case a pot was decorated with an overall pattern of closely-spaced, vertical strokes obviously produced by a toothed implement of some kind. In this report it is of considerable interest that an object of just this type was found almost on the bottom of the ditch surrounding the circular house. This was a small, saw-like artefact of slate, some 4·7 cm in length, which would have been exactly suited for marking pottery. Finally, several of the pots were embellished by the addition of cordons, D-shaped in cross-section, applied separately to the outer surface of the pot a short distance below the rim. Two such cordon fragments, discovered in 1969, were erroneously described in the first preliminary report as belonging to that class of pottery known as cordoned ware (Raftery, 1970a, p. 54).

Saddle querns and stone rubbers from the site show that land in the vicinity was cultivated. A solid bronze bar toggle of north European type found in the north-eastern part of the enclosure has important chronological and cultural implications; it appears to be an import from the *Nordischer Kreis* where objects of this type are dated to Montelius Period V or VI. This date agrees substantially with the date suggested above for the penannular gold ring from inside the house.

Although for much of its circumference the fill of the ditch was without finds a great concentration of artefacts came from its eastern part where a dense black organic soil was encountered in which were a large number of potsherds and clay mould fragments, some bracelet fragments, a saddle quern, glass beads and a bronze conical rivet of the distinctive type found commonly on Irish bronze cauldrons of the Late Bronze Age.

C. The Workshop Area

The most significant aspect of this dark layer with its concentration of domestic refuse was that it had not come from the circular house inside the ditch but rather had fallen into the ditch from an occupation layer immediately outside it. A portion of the innermost wall was removed here in 1970 and investigation under it and to the east of the ditch revealed the presence of an undisturbed habitation layer. It became apparent that this was associated with a large timber building of uncertain shape which had stood immediately outside the ditch. Hundreds of clay mould fragments (Fig. 4) were found in the western end of this structure and it became clear that the edifice which once stood here was a workshop or smithy where the manufacture of bronze implements was conducted on a scale of intensity considerably above that of the ordinary needs of a farming community.

Excavation was resumed here in 1972 and was largely concentrated in the general vicinity of the workshop. A further stretch of the stone wall was removed and it became evident that extensive occupation levels existed all around the outer, eastern perimeter of the circular ditch. A stratigraphical sequence of exceptional complexity was unearthed in this area which has not yet been analysed in any detail. Superficially, three principal stages of Late Bronze Age activity seem present on the site, none, however, being separated from the other by any great interval of time.

A large number of post-holes has thus far been brought to light in the area of the workshop but it has still not been possible to reconstruct either the size or the plan of the putative structure. It seems that much rebuilding and renewal of posts took place, leaving a confused and on the surface unintelligible mass of post-holes.

Elsewhere there were also haphazard concentrations of post-holes suggesting the former presence of further buildings but again there is uncertainty as to the original appearance of such structures. In one area it was possible to recognise traces of a small rectangular edifice with approximate dimensions of 3·50 m × 2·75 m. This cannot have been a structure of any great significance. The post-holes which held the wall uprights were of unimpressive proportions. They had been sunk into a shallow and irregular trench and the original building would appear to have been a flimsy one, possibly of wattle construction.

A further interesting feature discovered during 1972 partly under the late wall and immediately east of the large circular ditch, described above, was a second circular ditch, shallower than the first one and enclosing a lesser area than the former but otherwise very similar to it. This second ditch, which has as yet been only partially investigated, is about 1 m wide and somewhat less than this in depth and encloses an area approximately 16 m in diameter. Since the above was written, further excavation has been conducted here, and it has been revealed that the ditch enclosed a burial complex belonging to the Late Bronze Age phase of activity on the site.

Finds

Occupation levels in the general area of the workshop produced a very large quantity of finds. Apart from the great number of coarse potsherds the most numerous artefacts from this portion of the site were the broken fragments of clay moulds, many hundreds of which were unearthed (Fig. 4). In many instances the pieces were large enough to allow the nature of the objects cast to be identified and it could be seen that weapons and bladed implements were the predominant forms. In addition, objects of bronze, lignite, stone, glass, amber and gold were discovered, these forming an interesting and important body of associated material. It seems evident that the wealth of the occupants of Late Bronze Age Rathgall was considerable.

Among the bronzes the principal finds included a small, socketed gouge, a tanged punch, portion of the blade of an axehead, a fragment of what appears to be a chain-link and a perforated disc which may belong to that group of objects known as *phalerae*. The mould fragments indicate, of course, that a large body of varied bronze implements were once present on the site.

As objects of personal adornment several incomplete bracelets of jet or lignite were found and more than thirty glass beads which, in addition to the forty or so glass beads found in previous years' excavation, constitutes the biggest single body of Late Bronze Age glass material from Ireland. The beads are normally either dark green or dark blue in colour and several are decorated with a series of concentric-circle motifs. Some tend towards a sub-triangular form though the majority are circular. A number of small amber fragments were also discovered which can best be interpreted as portion of a bead of this material.

Stone objects consisted of several whetstones, a small perforated disc resembling somewhat a button in appearance, some pieces of shale bracelets and four rectangular saddle quern rubbers which complement the large number of actual saddle querns discovered during the excavations.

Among the more interesting discoveries in 1972 were the four gold objects, all found in the vicinity of the workshop. These included a hollow gold bead of roughly biconical form (Pl. II : 1), its shape not unlike that of the contemporary amber beads; a small penannular ring made up of a bronze core covered over with thin gold foil (Pl. II : 4); a short length of finely twisted gold wire at one extremity of which are attached two tiny gold rings (Pl. II : 2); and a composite bead or pendant of gold and glass (Pl. II : 5a and b).

This last is the major find from the site. It is an object of great beauty and advanced technological expertise, eloquent testimony to the wealth and stature of the Rathgall community of artisans.

The object is formed of a short cylinder of gold, 1·3 cm in length, with its ends finely hammered to form minute flanges. A bead of dark green colour has been mounted on the centre of this and this is turn is flanked on either side by a raised, convex rib of gold. Added to each end of the cylinder are tiny, delicate loops of gold wire, twisted to an incredible degree of fineness and held in place by the end-flanges.

D. *Iron Smelting*

The evidence for bronze-working at Rathgall is thus positive and it is, therefore, interesting to note that iron-working also took place there. This manifested itself in the form of a small oval pit measuring 50 cm by 40 cm and about 25 cm deep. It had been dug into the fill of the ditch round the large circular house at a time when the ditch had become completely filled up with refuse and silted material. A large quantity of waste products from the smelting process was scattered around the pit, amounting in all to as much as 30 or 40 lb weight of slag. The chronological position of the iron-working within the occupational sequence at Rathgall is as yet uncertain, especially since there seems no reliable way of estimating the length of time required to fill the ditch completely. Dr. R. F. Tylecote, of the Department of Metallurgy in the University of Newcastle-upon-Tyne, has examined some slag samples from Rathgall and in a preliminary note to the writer he comments on the very primitive nature of the smelting. An as yet unpublished C-14 determination of a.d. 265 ± 70 for charcoal from the smelting pit, recently obtained by courtesy of the Smithsonian Institute, has indicated a date for the ironworking unrelated to the Late Bronze Age activity on the site.

E. *Late Occupation*

Apart from the probable early evidence of iron-working on the site indications of a fully developed Iron Age culture at Rathgall are so far meagre in the extreme. The main defensive ramparts could conceivably be Iron Age in date but this has not yet been tested by excavation. In view of the great paucity of Iron Age finds after four years' excavation it must be admitted that this becomes increasingly unlikely. A heavily corroded and damaged bronze object has come to light which might belong to the ring-headed or ibex-headed group of pins. The general chronological and cultural significance of the pottery is somewhat ambiguous (see below) but seems at this site to be essentially a Late Bronze Age phenomenon.

Only one object stands out as belonging certainly to the sub-La Tène Iron Age period. This is a bronze strap-tag decorated with an openwork triskele and engraved palmette design. The writer has suggested elsewhere that this bronze might be dated to the early centuries A.D. (Raftery, 1970b) and in this object at least there is definite evidence of some Iron Age presence on the site.

Whatever the nature of this Iron Age activity, however, a long period of time elapsed before Rathgall was once again the focus of human attention. The presence of medieval occupants in the thirteenth and fourteenth centuries A.D. is shown by the many green-glazed potsherds from the site, while silver coins of English monarchs Edward I and Edward III provide useful fixed chronological points.

A series of shallow rectilinear trenches which occurred all over the excavated area was referred to by the writer in the first preliminary report as possibly being the remains of medieval houses. This appears now to be unlikely. Although green-glazed potsherds were found in the brown filling material of several of these trenches, the shank of a clay pipe firmly embedded in the base of one would appear to give a more accurate indication of date, and it now seems probable that these trenches may be related to spade cultivation of comparatively recent times.

F. Outside Settlement

An aerial photograph of the hillfort and surrounding area taken by Dr. J. K. St. Joseph in 1965 revealed a series of curiously regular circular areas of vegetation in a large field immediately to the north of the outer hillfort rampart (Raftery, 1970a, Pl. X). The vegetation had been cleared in the process of land reclamation soon after the photo was taken so that in Autumn, 1971, when initial investigation took place here, there was no surface evidence whatever to indicate the former presence of these circles. A series of exploratory cuttings was laid out in order to try to establish whether these rings were of natural or artificial origin. It was soon discovered that they were entirely natural. Completely by chance, however, evidence of considerable human activity, almost certainly contemporary with the earliest settlement on the hill-top, came to light and in Spring, 1972, further excavation took place here.

The first indication of prehistoric habitation to be encountered consisted of the foundation-trench of a hut, D-shaped in plan (Pl. III). The dimensions of this structure were modest—its maximum internal width was 2·40 m. A pit and two shallow post-holes were the only features found in the interior of the hut. The doorway, which was a narrow gap 50 cm wide in the south-west, had been carefully constructed (Pl. IV). The gap was flanked by two deep post-holes, with a thin, narrow groove (presumably for a threshold beam) running between them.

Coarse pottery of the type so common in the main excavation area on the summit was found in the bedding trench and elsewhere in the immediate vicinity of the building.

Not far from this hut a second interesting complex came to light. This consisted of a concentration of pits and post-holes clustered around a central, carefully dug, ditch which was penannular in plan (Fig. 3; Pl. V). This enclosed an area some 3·50 m in diameter. The ditch was flat-bottomed and had a fairly constant depth of 50 cm. A narrow causeway leading to the interior was left undug in the south-east. But in the north a large, natural boulder, left *in situ* by the builders, formed an obstacle almost filling the ditch and showing it to have fulfilled no obvious practical function. Inside this curious enclosure a mass of small post- or stake-holes which do not form an immediately recognisable pattern was encountered.

A considerable number of pits of varying shape and depth clustered irregularly around the ditch, particularly in the vicinity of the entrance. Practically all of these produced coarse pottery and a small number of clay mould fragments also came to light. Near the ditch, part of a barbed-and-tanged chert lance-head was found and in a post-hole an almost square whetstone or burnisher was discovered.

One pair of large, rectangular pits deserves special mention. They were roughly equal in size, measuring about 1·50 m in length and 1 m to 1·25 m in width and were dug to a depth of 35 cm and 40 cm respectively. One pit had been dug partly across the other. The earlier of the two had originally been lined with some organic material, now indicated by a black, carbonised layer covering the sides and base. In each corner there was a substantial post-hole, suggesting that the pit had been covered formerly by a canopy-like roofing. The pit is thus strikingly similar in construction to one of the hearths found inside the ditched enclosure on the hill-top.

These two pits were almost entirely filled with a tight packing of medium-sized stones, two of which proved to be broken, discarded saddle querns. Many of these stones were cracked and reddened by intense heat. These pits may represent the remains of former hearths or ovens, though in each case charcoal was conspicuously lacking.

As well as the various pits a large number of post-holes also came to light in this area; these were concentrated around the penannular ditch but formed no clear pattern. The holes were at times quite large and deep and must have held posts of substantial size. It does not seem possible to see in these post-holes the remains of any normal structure and it is likely that originally a series of large free-standing posts surrounded the small ditched enclosure. A shallow, sunken hearth occurred among the post-holes to the north-east of the penannular ditch.

The function of this whole complex is, of course, a matter for speculation; inevitably, lacking any logical explanation for the various features described, religious or ritual considerations come to the fore. May we think of this, perhaps, as a shrine of some sort ? At Frilford, Berkshire, in England a comparable penannular ditched enclosure (of Iron Age date) was interpreted in such a way and was, indeed, overlain by a Romano-British rotunda (Harding, 1972, p. 61ff., Fig. 8).

Some 30 m to the north-east of the penannular ditch a second ditched enclosure was discovered (Pl. VI). The latter formed an almost geometrically regular circle enclosing an area 4·50 m in diameter. The trench was dug with exceptional care to a depth of 75 cm to 80 cm and had steeply sloping, almost vertical, sides and a flat bottom. Three post-holes forming a line in the base of the ditch occurred at one point which could, perhaps, have supported a bridge or gang-plank of some sort across the ditch into the interior.

A pit of moderate size, three post-holes and a number of minor depressions occurred in the level area within the ditch. Some coarse potsherds came from the pit and, perhaps significantly, a small amount of burnt human bones was found in the fill of the central post-hole and scattered in its vicinity. In the fill of the ditch coarse potsherds were also found and immediately outside it a single, small lump of waste bronze came to light.

The use to which this structure with its ring ditch was put is also conjectural.

But the exceptional care which evidently went into the excavation of the ditch, the lack of evidence of any obvious secular function which it might have served and above all the presence of human bones, all urge the possibility that this site could, like that described earlier, be viewed as having served some religious or ceremonial function.

A number of pits occurred outside this circular ditch. Cuttings elsewhere on the hill-slope revealed widespread evidence of land use in the form of pits, post-holes and scattered finds so that extensive human activity over a wide area of the hill-slope is indicated.

III. Discussion

In recent years hillfort research in Ireland has made considerable advances due mainly to intensive field survey and to large-scale excavation at five major sites. Much new information has come to light since the writer's initial attempt in 1969 to summarise what was then known about Irish hillforts (Raftery, 1972) and although large gaps still exist in our knowledge important new concepts regarding the place of the hillfort in early Irish society are beginning to emerge.

Rathgall must be considered significant in these new developments. At this site the most extensive and best documented settlement so far uncovered is that dating to the Late Bronze Age and it seems fair to say that during that period Rathgall was at least a substantial, permanently occupied village and its status may even have approached that of a small township. It is not yet certain whether this settlement was defended or not. However, in view of the minimal evidence of Iron Age occupation thus far brought to light and the general unlikelihood that the massive enclosing ramparts are of medieval origin the notion that the first hillfort at Rathgall may have been constructed by the Late Bronze Age metal-workers is at least a possibility worthy of consideration.

A number of questions are thus posed by the Rathgall excavation which have a considerable bearing on the hillfort problem as a whole in Ireland. Of these, the most pressing is the matter of the earliest evidence for hillfort construction in Ireland and the problem of their ultimate origins.

The possibility of the existence of a Late Bronze Age hillfort at Rathgall, as yet unproven, is interesting in view of the growing body of opinion in Britain that hillforts there were already being constructed in the earlier part of the last millennium B.C. (e.g., Mackie, 1969b; Savory, 1971a; Savory, 1971b; for comment on Dinorben evidence, however, see Alcock, 1972 d; Gelling, 1972; Savory, *vide supra*, p. 273 ff.) The difficulties of relating Late Bronze Age hill-top settlements to the surrounding hillfort defences are, however, acute and it should be pointed out that it has been established in several instances where the two occur together that they are, in fact, unrelated (e.g., Alcock, 1972c, pp. 114–118).

In Ireland, apart from Rathgall, similarly early settlement may have occurred at Emain Macha (Navan Fort), County Armagh. Here excavation has revealed a complicated sequence of settlement on the hill-top and it is evident that the site was inhabited fairly continuously and for a long period of time (Selkirk and Waterman, 1970). A series of C-14 determinations suggests that settlement at Navan Fort may have begun as early as the seventh century B.C. (*Radiocarbon*, 12, 1970, pp. 287–288)[1] and, indeed, a fragment of a bronze socketed sickle discovered during the excavation implies contact with Late Bronze Age cultural traditions—although it seems that from a very early stage iron-working was carried on at the site.

At Navan Fort, therefore, as at Rathgall, settlement in the first half of the last millennium B.C. is attested, but as at the Wicklow site it cannot be related to the great earthen rampart which encloses it. Indeed, at the Armagh site it is highly possible that the latter enclosure belongs to a later Iron Age phase when the hill-top had become a centre of exceptional importance.

Apart from the two hillforts referred to above, where occupation in the first half of the last pre-Christian millennium occurs but which cannot be positively related to the actual period of hillfort construction, there is but one hillfort in Ireland where detailed investigation of the banked enclosure has been carried out and where it might be argued that the first defence to be erected was built by people with a Late Bronze Age cultural background. This important site is on Cathedral Hill at Downpatrick, County Down (Proudfoot, 1954; 1956).

Attention was drawn to the site by the discovery of two hoards of Late Bronze Age gold objects found buried in shallow pits on the hill-top (Proudfoot, 1955; 1957). The trial excavations which took place were mainly concentrated on the fortification which surrounds the hill where, according to the excavator, successive phases of constructional development could be recognised. It is the earliest of these which are of interest here.

The sequence of habitation began with a clearly discernible pre-hillfort level considered to be contemporary with the deposition of the gold objects. This was represented in the stratigraphy by a thick layer of organic material which contained many sherds of coarse pottery and which directly underlay the earliest rampart.

Referring to the first fortification at Downpatrick the excavator states that "the pre-bank phase of occupation ended when the site was strongly defended by the digging of a steep-sided ditch or fosse . . ." (Proudfoot, 1956, p. 65) and further, he writes: "during the occupation of the hill-top by people using coarse pottery of 'flat-rimmed' type a ditch more than ten feet wide and eight feet deep had been dug" (Proudfoot, 1954, p. 100). Elsewhere it is stated that pottery of "flat-rimmed ware" type was found in the ditch (Proudfoot, 1954, p. 99; but see the apparently contradictory statements here regarding the relationship of pre-bank pottery to that in the ditch).

The conclusions to be drawn from the two preliminary reports suggest that

[1] The C-14 determinations are referred to without comment as it is not considered apposite here to enter into a discussion on the merits or otherwise of radiocarbon as a means of acquiring meaningful absolute dates.

the period of pre-bank occupation continued right up to the construction of
the fort and it is strongly implied that there was little, if any, change between
the pre-fort population and the actual fort-builders. Each group, it seems, used
coarse pottery, and no material evidence of any exotic influences could be
detected.

It can be seen, therefore, that some grounds exist for considering the primary
hillfort at Downpatrick as being a product of Late Bronze Age peoples who first
lived in an open settlement, then, as a response to some feeling of insecurity,
defended themselves by digging a deep ditch around the hill, piling the earth
behind it and facing the bank thus formed with a stout timber palisade. If this
should prove correct, and further excavation is urgently required at this key
site, then Downpatrick could be considered as so far the earliest established
hillfort in Ireland.

The presence of coarse pottery at the County Down site is interesting, for
rough, handmade wares of various kinds have been recovered from most hillfort
excavations in Ireland. It is, of course, unwise to over-emphasise the significance of this type of pottery for its relationship to the hillfort is not always
clear and on its own it cannot be dated, but its constant appearance at hillfort
excavations seems more than coincidence. Moreover, at a number of sites
this pottery is securely dated. At Rathgall, for instance, an eighth–seventh
century B.C. date is likely while, at both Navan Fort and Downpatrick coarse
wares may be equally early in date. At the opposite extreme the Kilkenny hillfort
of Freestone Hill has produced similar wares associated with Roman bronzes of
the fourth century A.D. (Raftery, 1969, pp. 86–96). At other sites this pottery is
found in chronologically uncertain levels but at all events a long and, it seems,
continuous life for the coarse ware is indicated. Among major hillforts excavated this pottery is so far significantly absent only at Dún Ailinne.

The presence of coarse pottery at many hillfort sites, its basically unchanging
form over many centuries, the complete absence of imported Iron Age wares
of diagnostic type, allied to the hints at direct continuity from pre-hillfort to
hillfort times at Downpatrick, urge reconsideration of the view widely held
that the hillfort in Ireland must by its very existence be taken to denote military works erected by invading Iron Age groups. On the contrary it could be
argued that some, at least, of our earliest hillforts were a response by native
population groups to insecure and politically unstable times. It is even possible
that the very insecurity which caused the indigenous people to build hillforts
was caused by the presence of small bands of intruders who themselves were
perhaps hillfort builders and who brought with them the knowledge of the
new metal, iron.

It is clear, at all events, that Late Bronze Age people lived on hill-tops. It
is possible that in some cases they defended these hill-tops and that hillfort
construction may have begun in Ireland before the middle of the last millennium
B.C. Archaeological excavation shows, however, that hillfort occupation
certainly occurred during the sub-La Tène Iron Age, although it is to be noted
that the concentration of Iron Age material in the northern two-thirds of

Ireland is not reflected in any significant way in the hillfort distribution. Objects of insular La Tène type possibly dating to the last few centuries B.C. have been recovered from a small number of hillforts. These include in the east of the country, the iron sword from Dún Ailinne (Wailes, 1970a, 88), the safety pin *fibulae* (Jope, 1962, p. 26)—and perhaps the Lough na Shade trumpet? (Megaw, 1970, p. 147)—from Emain Macha. In the west the principal La Tène object is the bronze *fibula*, recently referred to by Harbison, found "in the interior of the wall of Dún Aengus, by boys who were rooting for rabbits" (Harbison, 1971b, p. 205; Jope, 1962, Fig. 2:5).

In the early centuries of our era hillforts were, it seems, important centres of population and in the archaeological remains recovered from sites of this period extensive evidence of strong influences emanating from the nearby provincial Roman world are clearly discernible. C-14 determinations for the recently discovered hillfort at Armagh town suggest occupation at this time (*Radiocarbon*, 13, 1971, pp. 103–104). At Freestone Hill, County Kilkenny, a coin of Constantine II and other provincial bronzes were found as well as a tinned bronze mount held to be Roman in form but whose decoration is entirely native (Raftery, 1969, pp. 62–72; with regard to the mount from Freestone Hill, however, see Raftery, 1970b, p. 209, footnote 40). A bronze strap-tag from Rathgall was interpreted by the present writer in a similar way and a suggested date in the second century A.D. was put forward for its manufacture (Raftery, 1970b, pp. 200–211). At Clogher, County Tyrone, as well as a bronze "toilet implement" and some possible Roman pottery, an Omega pin, possibly of first or second century date and a Nauheim type brooch fragment were found[2]. The Dún Ailinne excavations have also brought to light bronze *fibulae* of Roman type[3] and finally the openwork bronze brooches from Emain Macha have been considered by Jope as belonging to this general chronological context (1962, pp. 34–37). He saw the provincial Roman divided-bow brooches as prototypes for the Irish-made objects, though it could be argued that a comparison with the openwork handles of southern British mirrors is an equally valid one [compare, for instance, the Colchester mirror-handle (Fox, C., 1958, Fig. 51) with the Somerset, County Galway brooch (Raftery, 1960, pp. 2–5].

It cannot be stated when hillforts in general were abandoned, though it is probable that the majority were deserted by the middle of the first millennium A.D. With the coming of Christianity, sites like Tara and Emain Macha at least, inextricably linked with what would have been considered dark, pagan practices, would have been evacuated rapidly. Some hillforts undoubtedly continued in occupation, however. Pottery of E-ware type and a bronze penannular brooch from Clogher and souterrain ware from Downpatrick (Proudfoot, 1954, p. 99) show continued use after A.D. 500 and the historical

---

[2] I am indebted to Mr. Richard Warner, Assistant Keeper, Ulster Museum, Belfast, for this information.
[3] I am indebted to Dr. Bernard Wailes, Associate Professor, Department of Anthropology, University of Pennsylvania, for this information.

sources record the destruction of Grianan Aileach in Donegal in 1101 (A.F.M. *sub anno* 1101). Finally, reoccupation of a number of hillforts took place in Medieval times. This has been demonstrated both at Rathgall and at Downpatrick, but it cannot have been more than a relatively short-lived phase at particular sites in response probably to specific local events.

The foregoing brief survey of the archaeological evidence for dating Irish hillforts shows that little more than a start has been made in the establishment of a coherent chronological framework for the hillfort series in the country. The ultimate beginnings of hillfort development must still be considered obscure, although Late Bronze Age origins are becoming ever more probable. A concentration of activity in the early centuries A.D. is hinted at: the period between these two extremes is unclear. In view of the Downpatrick evidence and the suggestions which have been made regarding the coarse pottery, it is important to note that all the Iron Age metal-work found in hillforts is of native manufacture. While at all times outside influences can be recognised, the essential insularity of the material Iron Age culture as recovered by excavation cannot be denied. In no instance has an imported foreign assemblage been recognised.

Viewed structurally the same basic insularity can be detected in the Irish hillforts. The number of such monuments now known in this country is almost sixty. On the basis of superficially observed ground plans a threefold typological division was suggested by the writer in 1969 (Raftery, 1972). These comprised Class I, univallate forts (Pl. VII), Class II, multivallate forts with widely-spaced ramparts (Pls VIII, IX) and Class III, in land promontory forts (Pl. X). It was observed that Class I forts had a generally eastern distribution while Class II forts were found mainly in the west of the country. The extent to which these apparent concentrations might represent cultural groupings was considered and the possibility of seeing the hillfort distribution as reflecting the presence of immigrant peoples was discussed without, however, any firm conclusions being reached (Raftery, 1972, p. 48ff.).

The archaeological evidence tends to stress the native rather than the exotic contribution to the development of the Irish hillfort. Apart from the apparent novelty of the actual hillfort itself as a type there is little in plan or construction which compels of necessity their attribution to intrusive forces. Their very simplicity is striking, especially in the unelaborate entrances. At no Irish hillfort has an inturned entrance been recognised. A considerable variety of types within the suggested tripartite division is evident, too, in size and construction, and indeed, on these grounds the dangers of over-emphasising the significance of the distribution map should be guarded against in the still tentative state of our research. The extent to which multivallate sites are also multi-period constructions is unknown, the extent to which forts with internal ditches should be grouped as a separate class distinct from the other univallate types is problematical and indeed the extent to which a 2-acre fort and a 40-acre fort are functionally distinct remains unresolved.

Our knowledge of hillforts in the eastern part of the country is more extensive than is our knowledge of such structures in the west, because of the concentration of excavation in the former area. In the west only the somewhat enigmatic structure at Cahercommaun has been investigated archaeologically although the chronological conclusions reached by the excavator for that site have been queried elsewhere by the writer (1972, p. 51ff.) Moreover, this site, though sharing, some attributes with the western multivallate series, fits uneasily, it seems within the hillfort class and on the whole owes more to ring-fort than hillfort traditions.

The *fibula* from Dún Aengus, if one can assume it to have been lost by the builders of the fort, is an Iron Age type and dates perhaps to the last century B.C.; it is however certainly Irish in manufacture. The cultural significance of the *chevaux-de-frise* defence at the same site is a matter which at the time of writing remains unresolved.

Apart from a small number of examples of *chevaux-de-frise* defences in northern and western Britain, the principal occurrence of this defensive construction is in Iberia. The Irish examples (of which there are four in the extreme west of the country) have been traditionally regarded as in some way a product of Iberian influences. A more recent view expressed by Dr. Peter Harbison, however, considers both the insular and the Iberian series as being derived from a common central European source, the prototypes there being timber examples of Hallstatt C date. The Irish *chevaux-de-frise* is seen by Harbison as having arrived in the country ultimately from the Continent but through Britain (Harbison, 1971b, pp. 195–225).

Dr. Harbison is, of course, perfectly correct in pointing out that *chevaux-de-frise* defences of timber *may* once have been widespread in Europe. But until more than a single example in the supposed area of origin has come to light and until it can be shown more convincingly that the *chevaux-de-frise* of stone is of necessity later than that of wood then the question must remain open. If outside influences are to be sought, an Iberian source for the Irish *chevaux-de-frise* idea is still every bit as likely as is a British/central European one.

Thus, in the case of Class I and Class II hillforts, no really conclusive statements can be made regarding their origins on the basis of their structural features. Two exceptional sites in the north-east of Ireland belonging to Class III, however, call for special comment. These are the County Antrim inland promontory forts of Lurigethan and Knockdhu (Evans, 1966, p. 49). Although included by the writer in the same category as the vastly smaller Kerry site of Caherconree (Pl. X) (Lynch, 1899, p. 5ff.) it is clear that the latter resembles the Antrim examples only in so far as all share a common promontory situation. In Ireland the two north-eastern forts certainly stand alone among the inland structures.

Apart from their promontory situation and their exceptional size, it is the nature of their fortifications which differentiates them from other hillforts. For both at Lurigethan and Knockdhu the defences consist of a series of banks and ditches set contiguously without any space between each line of obstruction.

This closely-spaced multivallation, entirely distinct from the type of multi-vallation which characterises the forts of Class II plan, is absent from other Irish hillforts, with the possible exception of Clogher, where closely spaced multivallation of a sort occurs around part of the circumference of the defences.

The Antrim forts are so similar to one another that they must be viewed as belonging in the same cultural and chronological context. Can we see them as beach-head sites built by warlike intruders of south British or north-west French origin? Could they have been constructed by peoples moving up the Irish sea, peoples who perhaps were also responsible for the fortification of the coastal promontory at Loughshinny, north of Dublin, a monument very like the Antrim forts in both size and defensive detail (Pl. XI)? (Townland: Drumanagh, O.S. half-inch 13, 0 273562). Interesting possibilities are raised by this speculation, for in north-west France it was the Veneti who guarded their promontory settlements with closely-spaced, multivallate defences, who had trading links with the western islands and who almost certainly settled in the Cornish peninsula of Britain in the last century B.C. It is possible that these people also came to Ireland[4] and brought with them the notion of closely-spaced multivallation. Ó Ríordáin's statement referring to the discovery of a Roman sherd at Loughshinny (now, unfortunately, apparently lost) is of great interest in such a context (Ó Ríordáin, 1953, p. 17).

The whole question of the relations between the hillforts in general and the coastal promontory forts is brought to the fore by this discussion. Few positive statements can be made regarding the coastal structures, however, though it may be significant that closely-spaced multivallation occurs amongst them with some frequency. It is thus possible that these forts, in conjunction with the two Antrim sites referred to above, form a group of fortified settlements generally distinct from the main hillfort series. They may represent intrusions by individual Iron Age groups in the last century B.C., possibly from the Venetic area of north-west France arriving via southern Britain.

In conclusion, it can be seen that as hillfort research advances, so the problems requiring solution multiply. The evidence from excavation in most cases does not demonstrate positively the presence of implanted Iron Age cultures. Structurally, the same is true apart from the occurrence of closely-spaced multivallation and the possible significance of the *chevaux-de-frise* defences.

Excavation is not sufficiently advanced to allow generalisations with regard to the use to which the enclosed areas were put, but in most cases domestic settlement of a permanent nature can be deduced. It may be argued that some hillforts such, for instance, as Caherconree, County Kerry, could never have been settled permanently, but this is by no means certain.

In the cases of both Dún Ailinne and Emain Macha, excavation has revealed the former presence of an elaborate series of circular timber-built structures on the respective hill-tops (for Emain Macha, see Selkirk and Waterman, 1970; for Dún Ailinne, see above, pp. 330–331). At Dún Ailinne

---

[4] A similar possibility was considered by M. J. O'Kelly from observation of structural details uncovered in the ramparts of two County Cork promontory forts (O'Kelly, 1952, pp. 25–59).

and in the later structural phases at Emain Macha evidence of normal residential use of the sites seems to be scanty and the possibility is strong that both these major monuments derived their importance more from their function as centres of ceremony or assembly than as actual settled habitations. The presence of internal ditches at both and the importance attributed to both in the literary sources lends further emphasis to this hypothesis. Taken in conjunction with the as yet unexcavated enclosure at Tara, it seems that sites with internal ditches were exceptional royal centres the significance of which may have been basically non-military.

Figures

(Arranged in Chapter Sequence)

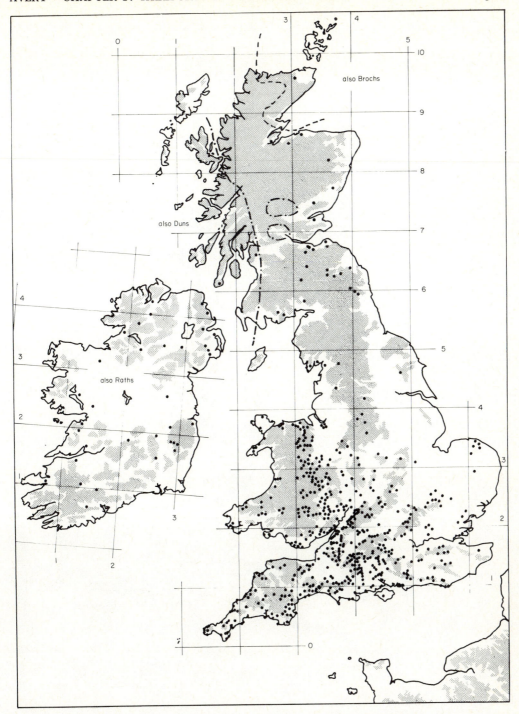

Fig. 1. Major forts (3 acres and over) plotted individually and also generalised distributions of fortlets (brochs, duns and raths). After B. Raftery (1972, p. 41), Feachem (1966, p. 78), Rivet (1966, map at back) and Ordnance Survey gazetteer to the map of Southern Britain in the Iron Age, with additions. English and Irish grid lines at 100 km intervals; land above 800 ft marked.

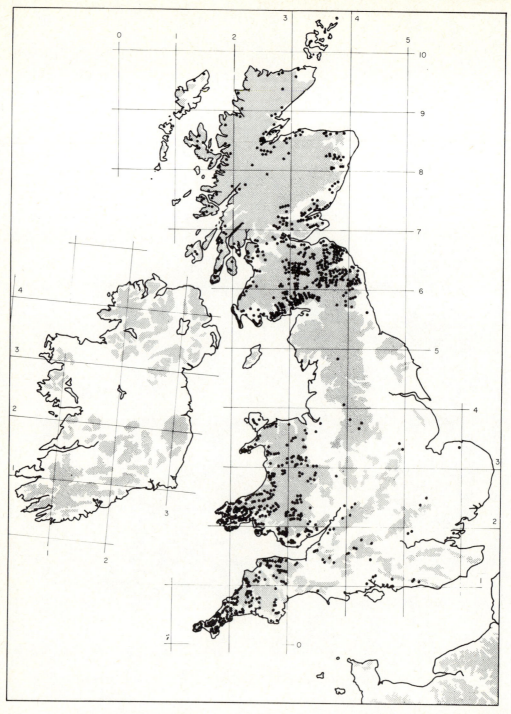

FIG. 2. Minor forts (under 3 acres), after Rivet (1966, map at back) and Ordnance Survey gazetteer
to the map of Southern Britain in the Iron Age, with additions.

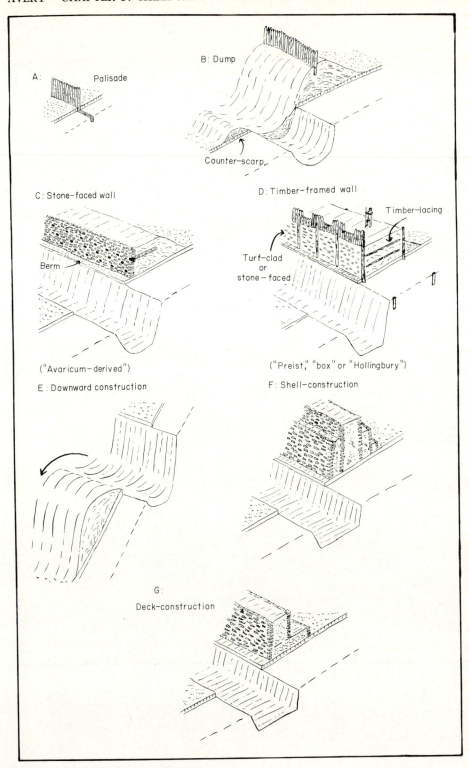

FIG. 3. Constructional techniques in hillfort ramparts.

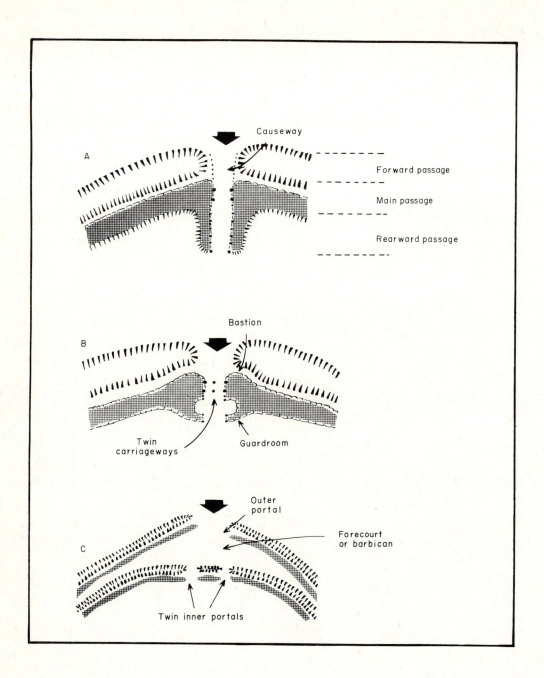

FIG. 4. Terminology of hillfort entrance structures.

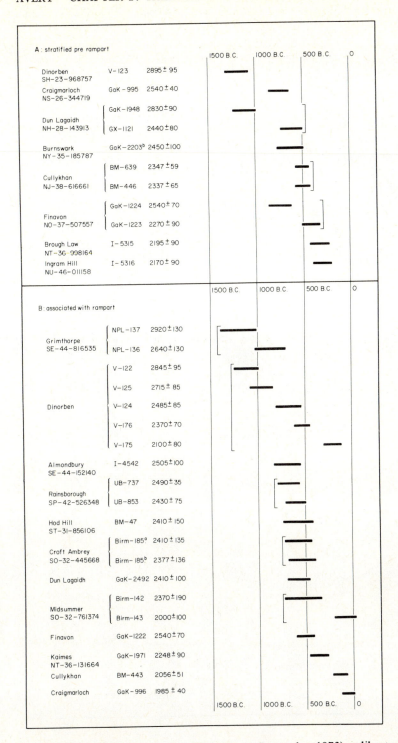

FIG. 5. Radiocarbon counts for hillforts (as at September 1973), calibrated after Damon, Long and Wallick (1972). Data given are site, grid reference, laboratory number, radiocarbon years before present (conventional 5568 ½-life) and diagram showing likely range of each calibrated date (from plus one standard deviation to minus one standard deviation).

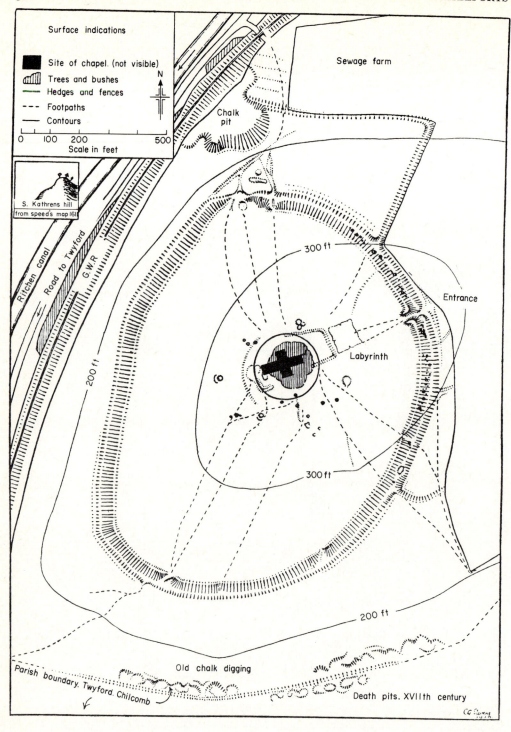

FIG. 1. Map of St. Catharine's Hill, Winchester, 1925–1928. From C. G. Stevens, *SCH* Fig. 1; scale and lettering standardised.

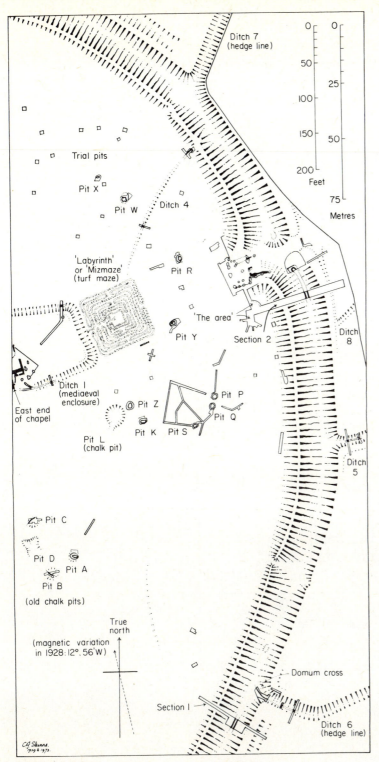

Ditch 7
(hedge line)

0
50
100
150
200
Feet

0
25
50
75
Metres

Trial pits

Pit X

Pit W   Ditch 4

'Labyrinth'
or 'Mizmaze'
(turf maze)

Pit R

'The area'

Pit Y

Section 2

Ditch 8

Ditch I
(mediaeval
enclosure)

East end
of chapel

Pit Z   Pit P

Pit Q

Pit K   Pit S

Pit L
(chalk pit)

Ditch
5

Pit C

Pit D

Pit A

Pit B

(old chalk pits)

True
north

(magnetic variation
in 1928: 12°. 56'W)

Domum cross

Section I

Ditch 6
(hedge line)

C.G Stevens.
1929 & 1973.

FIG. 2. St. Catharine's Hill: plan showing the Iron Age excavation, 1927–1928. From C. G. Stevens, *SCH* Fig. 36; scales and lettering standardised.

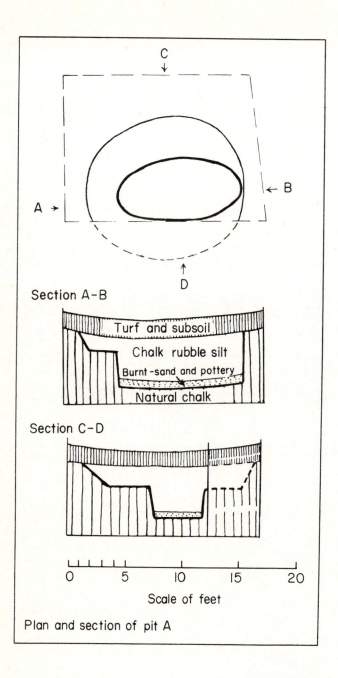

Section A–B

Turf and subsoil

Chalk rubble silt

Burnt-sand and pottery

Natural chalk

Section C–D

0   5   10   15   20

Scale of feet

Plan and section of pit A

Fig. 3. St. Catharine's Hill: plan and sections of Pit A. From C. G. Stevens, *SCH* Figs. 9 and 36, with plan re-drawn and scale and lettering standardised.

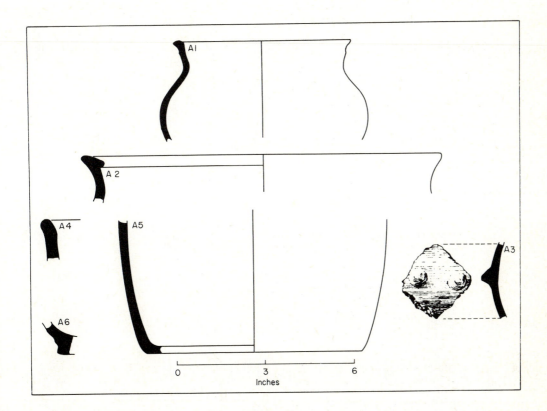

FIG. 4. St. Catharine's Hill: pottery from Pit A. From C. G. Stevens, *SCH* Fig. 10; scale and lettering standardised.

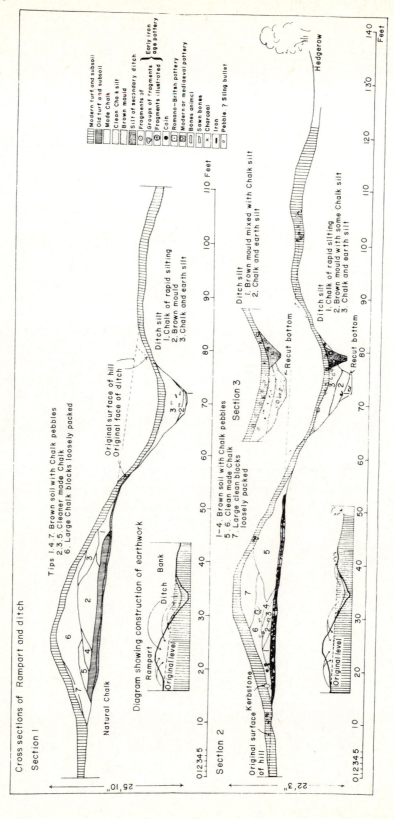

FIG. 5. St. Catharine's Hill: sections 1 and 2–3 through the defences, with diagrams showing dump construction of rampart. From C. G. Stevens, *SCH* Fig. 4; scale and lettering standardised.

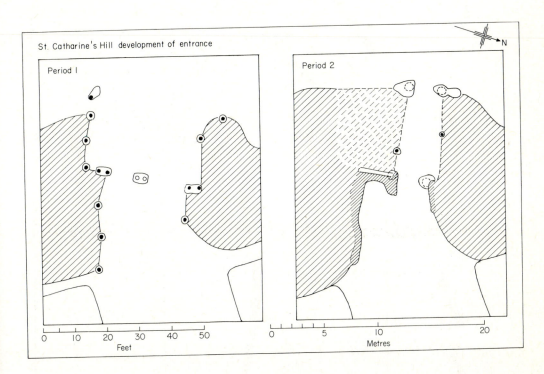

St. Catharine's Hill development of entrance

Period 1

Period 2

N

0 10 20 30 40 50
Feet

0 5 10 20
Metres

FIG. 6. St. Catharine's Hill: the original and the reconstructed entrance, drawn by Professor B. Cunliffe to show his proposed re-interpretation. His Periods 1 and 2 correspond to Periods A and C in *SCH*.

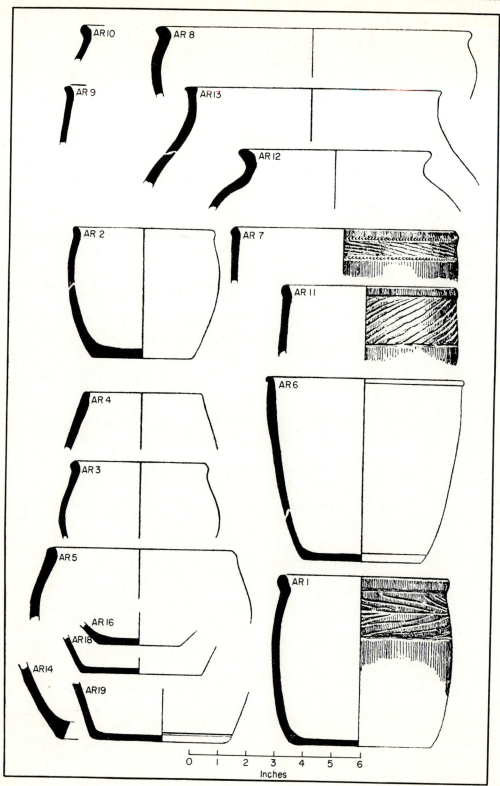

FIG. 7. St. Catharine's Hill: pottery from the "Area" (see Fig. 2) directly ensuing on the entrance reconstruction (Fig. 6). From C. G. Stevens, *SCH* Fig. 13; scale and lettering standardised.

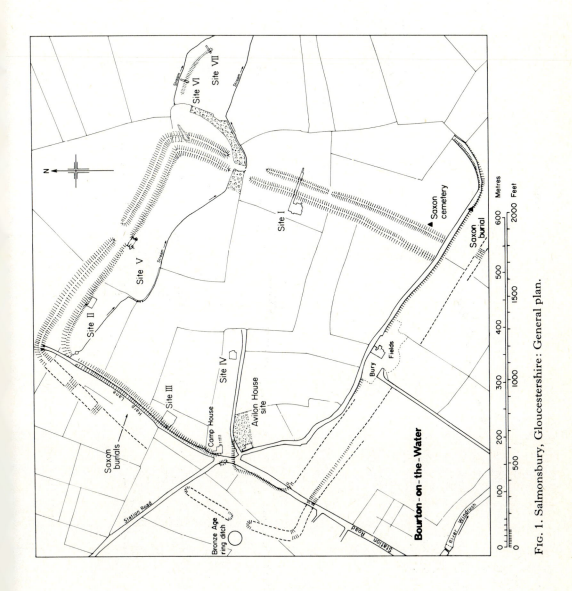

Fig. 1. Salmonsbury, Gloucestershire: General plan.

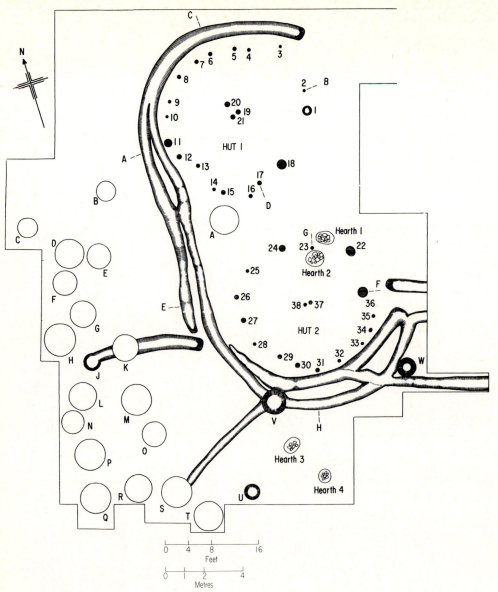

FIG. 2. Salmonsbury, Gloucestershire: Site I. Plan of huts and pits. Iron Age Period I.

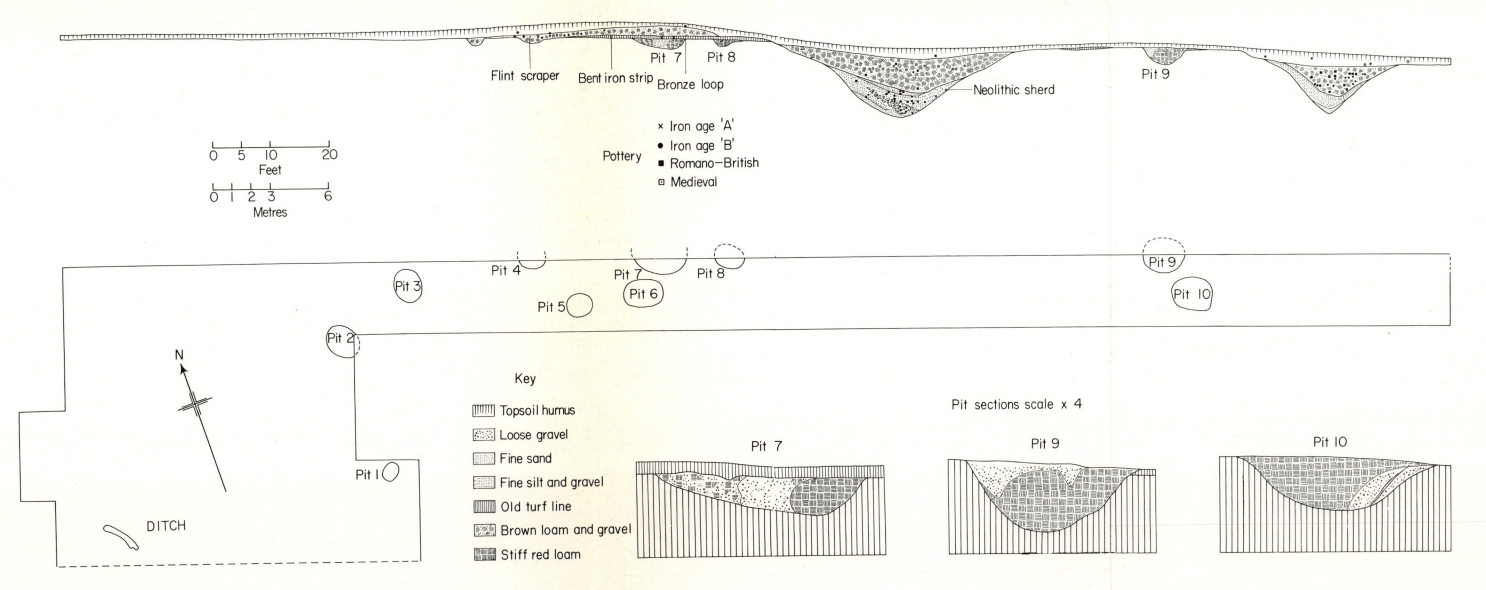

Flint scraper   Bent iron strip   Bronze loop   Pit 7   Pit 8   Neolithic sherd   Pit 9

Pottery
× Iron age 'A'
● Iron age 'B'
■ Romano−British
▫ Medieval

0 5 10   20
Feet

0 1 2 3   6
Metres

N

Pit 3   Pit 4   Pit 7   Pit 8   Pit 9   Pit 10
Pit 5   Pit 6
Pit 2
Pit 1

Key

▥ Topsoil humus
▒ Loose gravel
▤ Fine sand
▦ Fine silt and gravel
▥ Old turf line
▨ Brown loam and gravel
▦ Stiff red loam

Pit sections scale x 4

Pit 7   Pit 9   Pit 10

DITCH

Fig. 3. Salmonsbury, Gloucestershire: Site I. Section through the ramparts and ditches, Iron Age Period I; and plan and sections of pits, late Neolithic.

[Facing page 374]

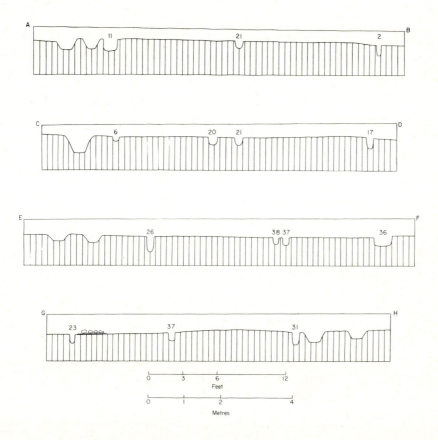

Fig. 4. Salmonsbury, Gloucestershire: Site I. Sections through hut 1 (A–B and C–D) and hut 2 (E–F and G–H).

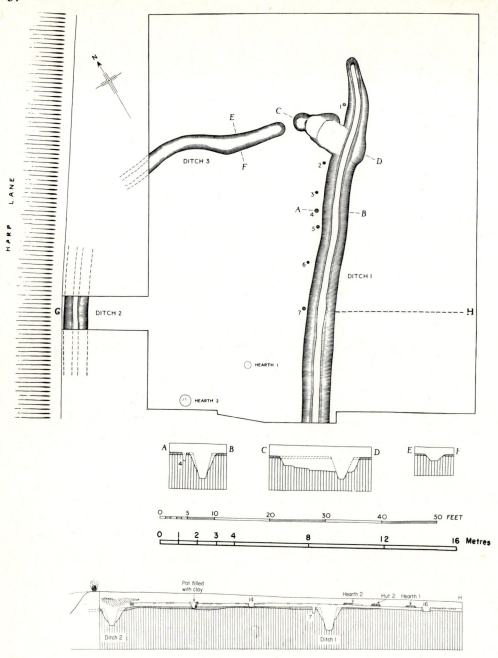

Fig. 5. Salmonsbury, Gloucestershire: Site III. Plan of ditches. Iron Age Period II, phase i: section of ditches and paving. Iron Age Period II, phases i and ii. Hearths 1 and 2 and Hut 2 east of Ditch 1 refer to features shown on Fig. 6.

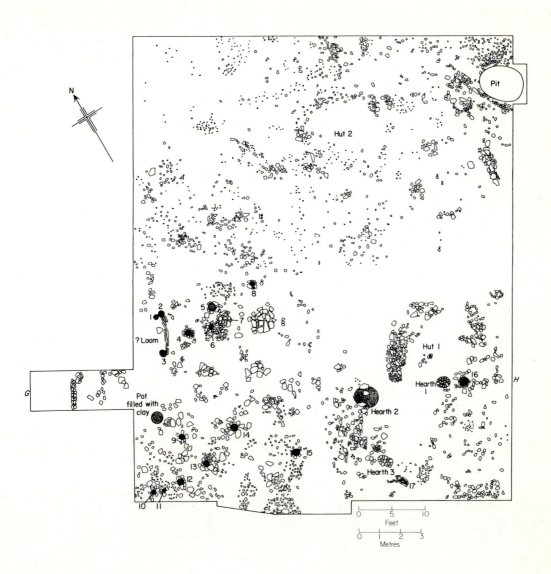

FIG. 6. Salmonsbury, Gloucestershire: Site III. Plan of huts and other structures. Iron Age Period II, phase ii.

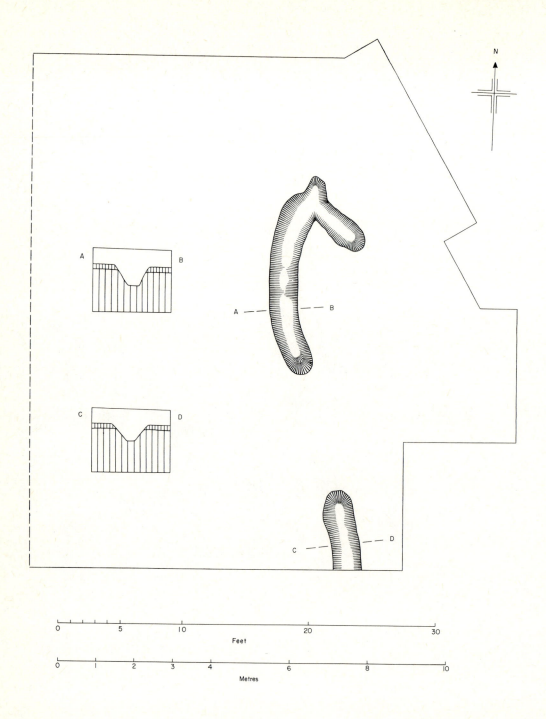

FIG. 7. Salmonsbury, Gloucestershire: Site IV. Plan and sections of late Neolithic and Early Bronze Age ditches.

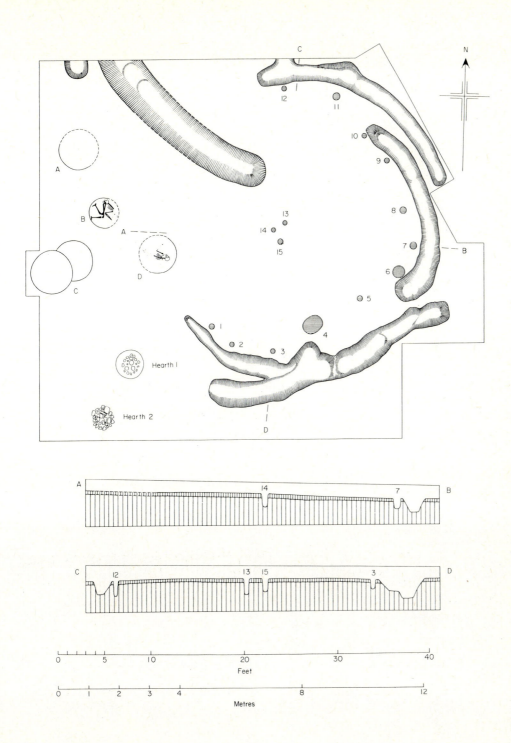

Fɪɢ. 8. Salmonsbury, Gloucestershire: Site IV. Plan of hut and pits. Iron Age Period I.

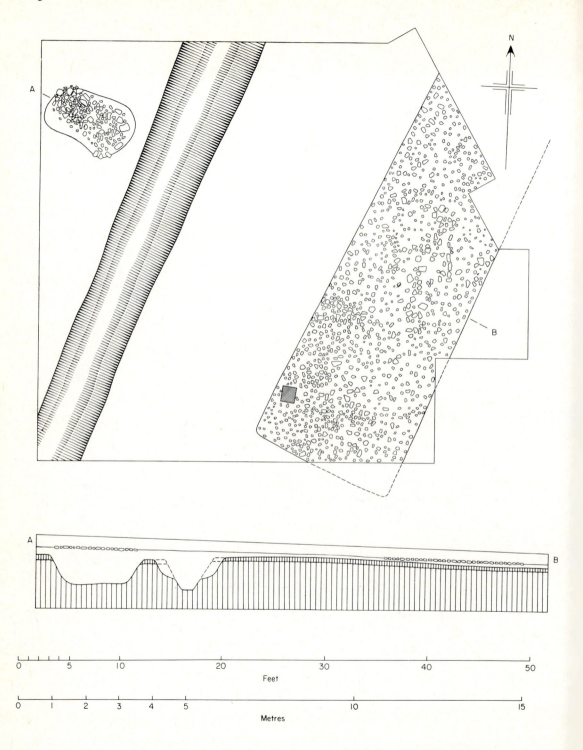

FIG. 9. Salmonsbury, Gloucestershire: Site IV. Plan of Romano-British structures.

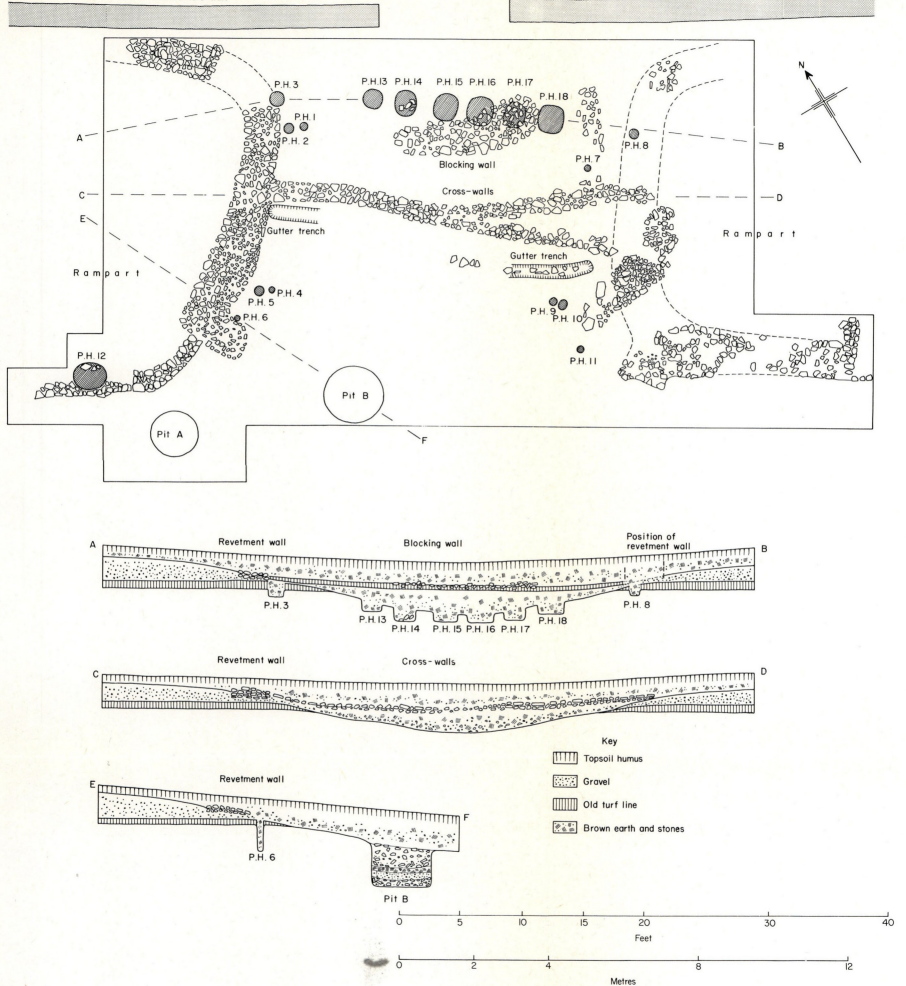

Modern field wall

P.H. 3
P.H.13 P.H.14 P.H.15 P.H.16 P.H.17
P.H.18
P.H. 8
P.H. 1
P.H. 2
Blocking wall
P.H. 7
Cross-walls
A ——— B
C ——— D
E
Gutter trench
Gutter trench
Rampart
Rampart
P.H. 4
P.H. 5
P.H. 6
P.H. 9
P.H. 10
P.H. 11
P.H. 12
Pit B
Pit A
F
N

A   Revetment wall   Blocking wall   Position of   B
                                                    revetment wall
P.H. 3   P.H. 8
P.H. 13
P.H. 14 P.H. 15 P.H. 16 P.H. 17   P.H. 18

C   Revetment wall   Cross-walls   D

E   Revetment wall
                                F
P.H. 6
Pit B

Key

⊞ Topsoil humus
∷ Gravel
▥ Old turf line
▨ Brown earth and stones

0   5   10   15   20   30   40
Feet

0   2   4   8   12
Metres

Fig. 10. Salmonsbury, Gloucestershire: Site V. Plan and sections of north-east inner rampart
and entrance, Iron Age Period I, phases i and ii; and cross-walls, Roman period.

[Facing page 380]

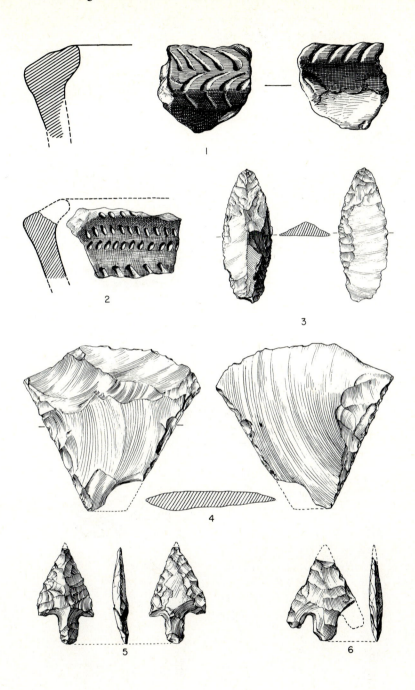

Fig. 11. Salmonsbury, Gloucestershire: late Neolithic and Early Bronze Age finds. Scale: 1–2, ½; 3–6, ⅟₁.

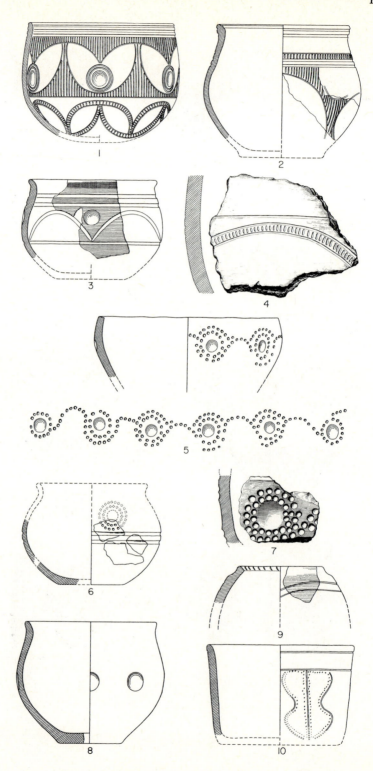

Fig. 12. Salmonsbury, Gloucestershire: Western Second B pottery with curvilinear decoration. Period I. Scale: 1–3, 5–6, and 8–10, $\frac{1}{4}$; 4 and 7, $\frac{1}{2}$.

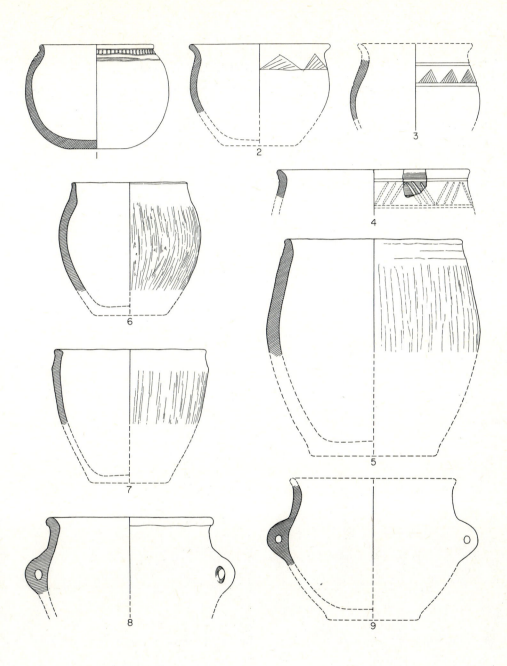

FIG. 13. Salmonsbury, Gloucestershire: Western Second B pottery with linear decoration, and handled pots. Period I. Scale: ¼.

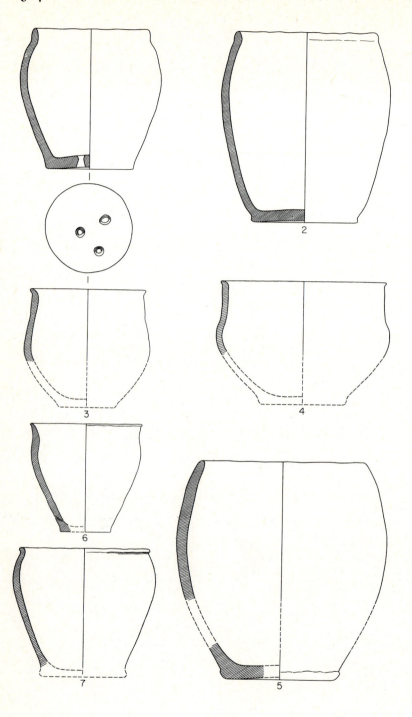

FIG. 14. Salmonsbury, Gloucestershire: Western Second B pottery, plain wares. Period I. Scale: ¼.

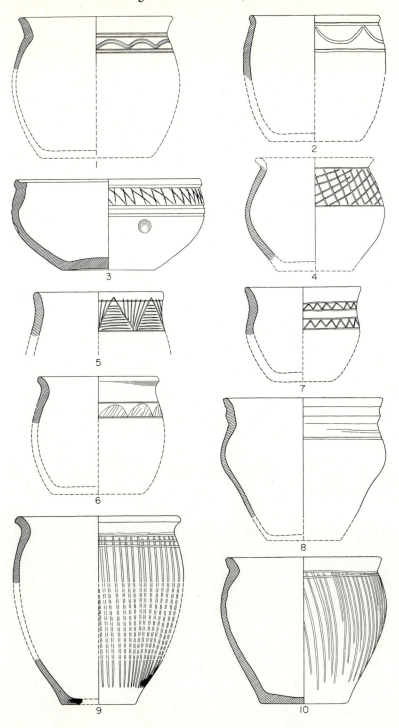

FIG. 15. Salmonsbury, Gloucestershire: Western Second B pottery. Period II. Scale: ¼.

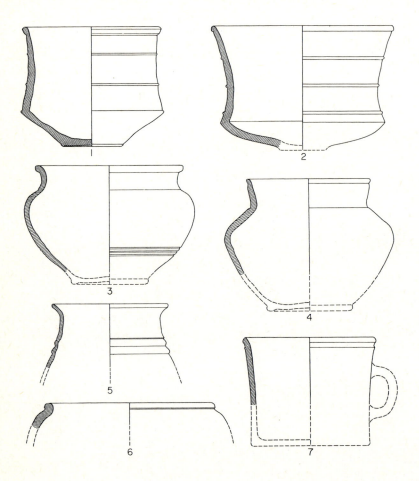

FIG. 16. Salmonsbury, Gloucestershire: Western Third C pottery. Period II, phase i. Site III. Scale: ¼.

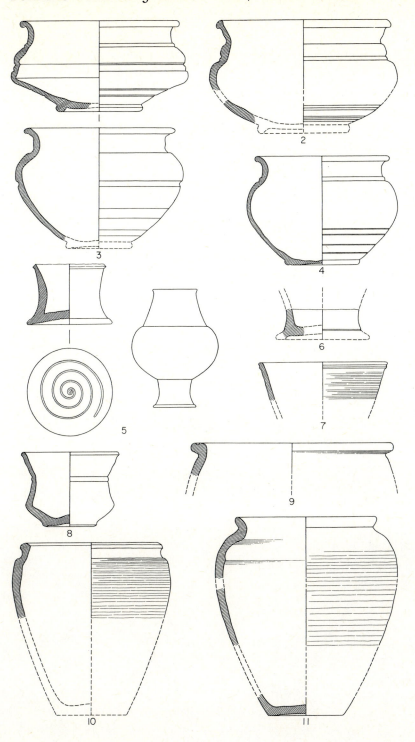

FIG. 17. Salmonsbury, Gloucestershire: Western Third C pottery. Period II, phase ii. Site III, below paving. Scale: ¼.

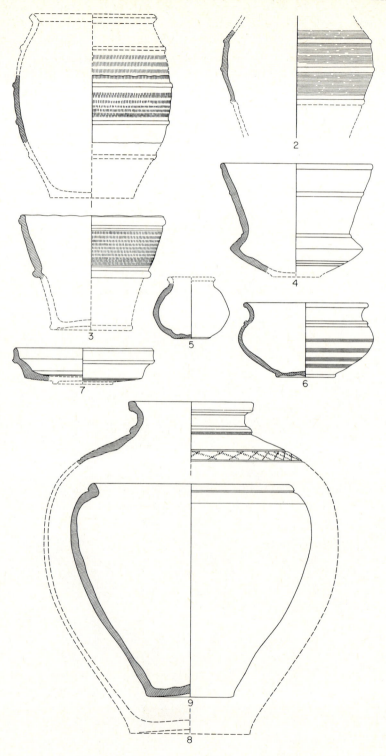

FIG. 18. Salmonsbury, Gloucestershire: Western Third C pottery. Period II, phase ii. 1–6, Site III, on paving; 7–9, Site IV. Scale: $\frac{1}{4}$.

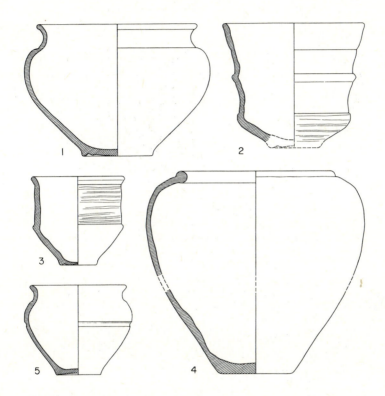

Fig. 19. Salmonsbury, Gloucestershire: Romanised Belgic pottery. Period II, phase ii. Site III, pit 1. Scale: ¼.

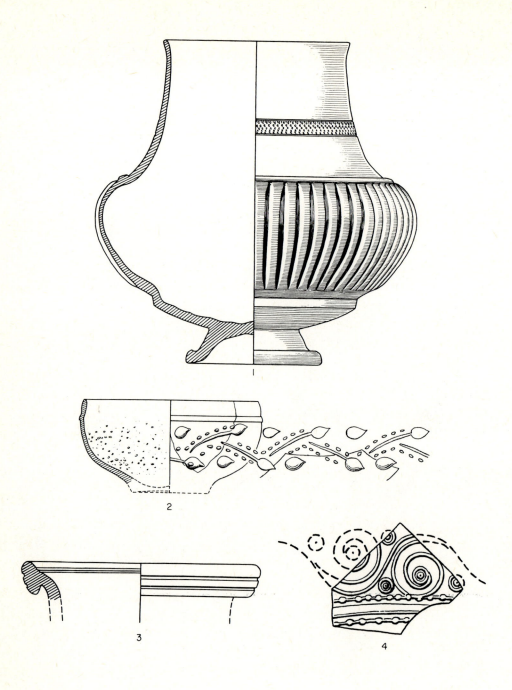

FIG. 20. Salmonsbury, Gloucestershire: imported Gallo-Belgic and early Roman pottery. Period II. Site III. Scale: 1–3, $\frac{1}{2}$; 4, $\frac{1}{1}$.

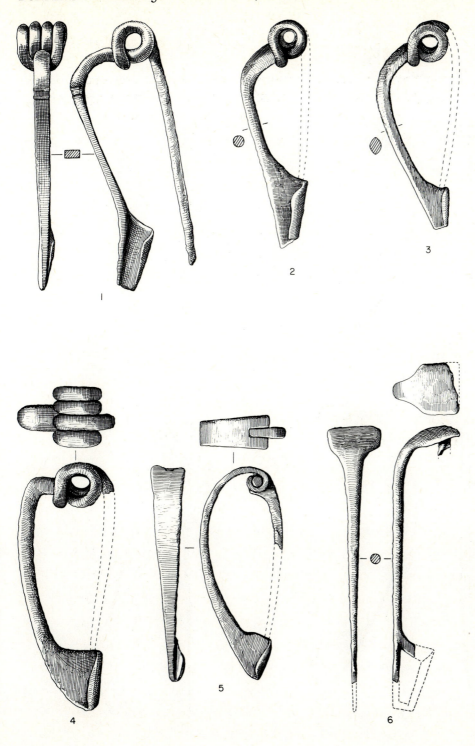

FIG. 21. Salmonsbury, Gloucestershire: brooches or iron. Period II. Scale: $\frac{1}{1}$.

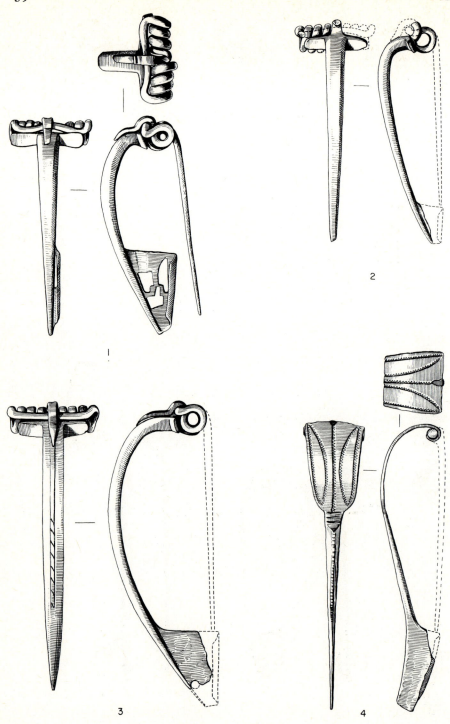

Fig. 22. Salmonsbury, Gloucestershire: brooches of bronze. Period II. Scale: $\frac{1}{1}$.

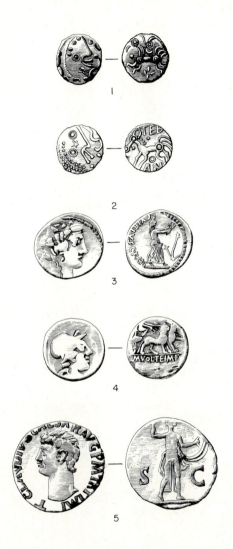

Fig. 23. Salmonsbury, Gloucestershire: coins. Scale: $\frac{1}{1}$.

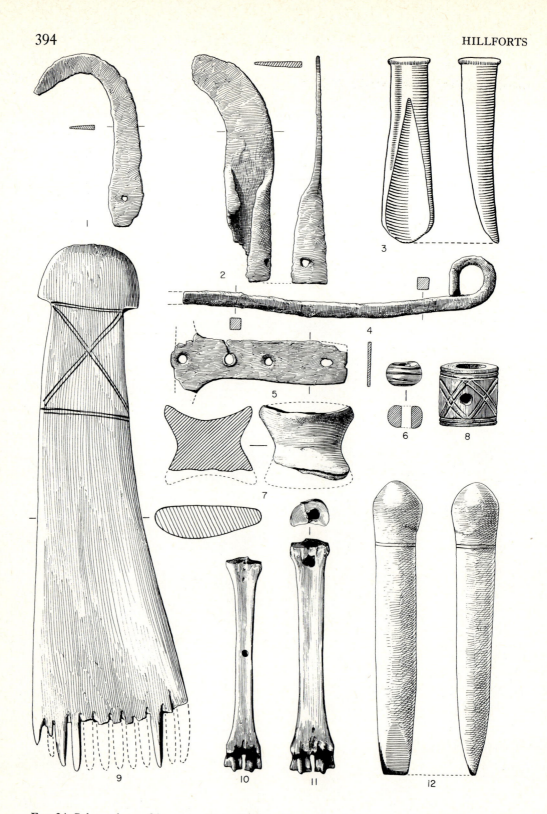

FIG. 24. Salmonsbury, Gloucestershire: objects of iron, glass, baked clay, antler and bone. Period I. Scale: 1–5, 8 and 10–11, $\frac{1}{2}$; 6–7, 9 and 12, $\frac{1}{1}$.

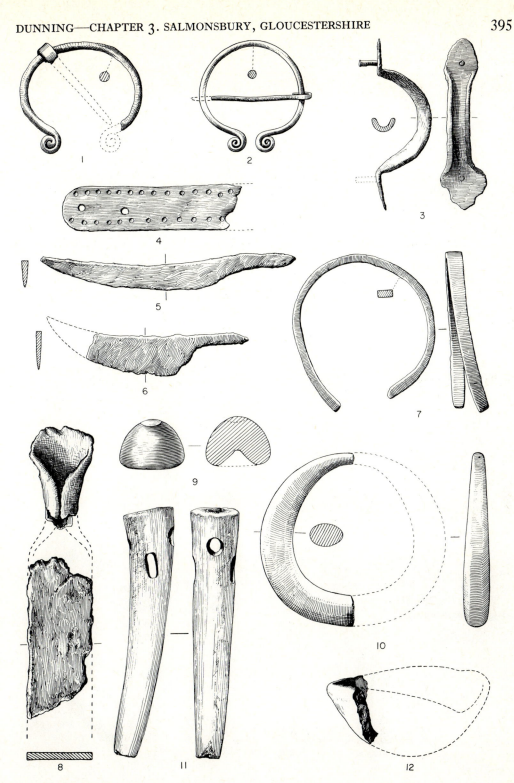

FIG. 25. Salmonsbury, Gloucestershire: objects of bronze, iron, glass, antler, bone and baked clay. Period II, phase i. Site III, ditch 1 and below paving. Scale: 1–2, 4 and 9–10, $\frac{1}{1}$; 3, 5–8 and 11–12, $\frac{1}{2}$.

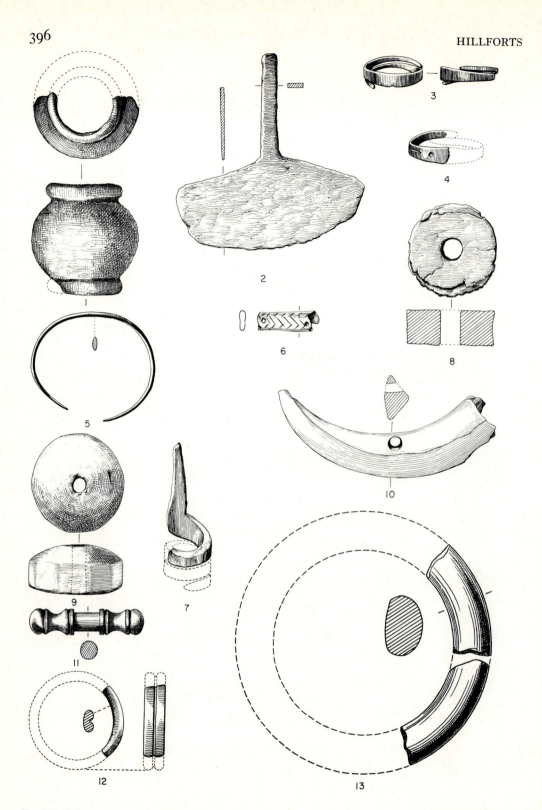

FIG. 26. Salmonsbury, Gloucestershire: objects of bronze, iron, lead, stone, bone and shale. Period II, phase ii, on paving. Scale: 1, 3–8, 10–11 and 13, $\frac{1}{1}$; 2, 9 and 12, $\frac{1}{2}$.

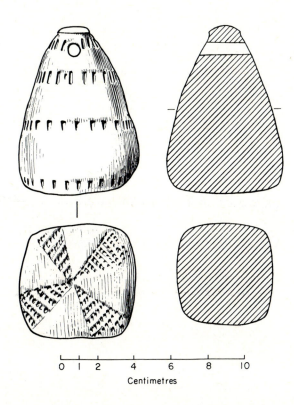

FIG. 27. Decorated pyramid of stone. Garden of Avilon house, Bourton-on-the-Water, Gloucestershire. Scale: ½.

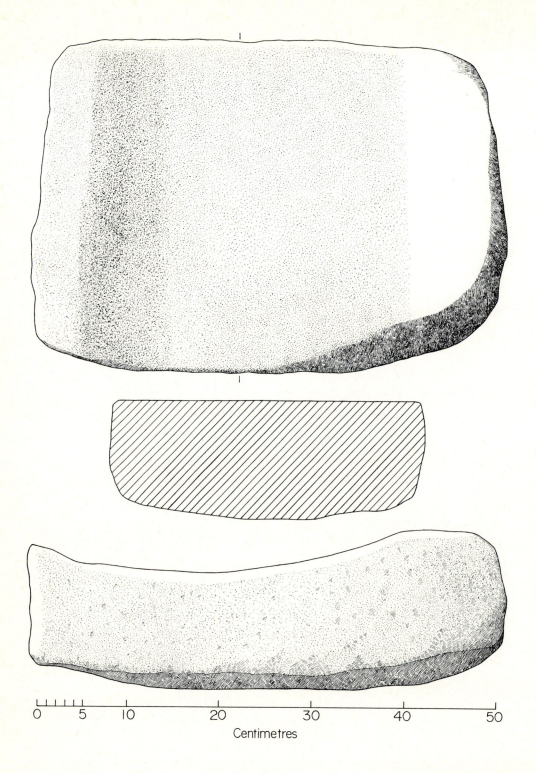

Fɪɢ. 28. Saddle quern. Period I. Camp House, Bourton-on-the-Water, Gloucestershire. Scale: ¼.

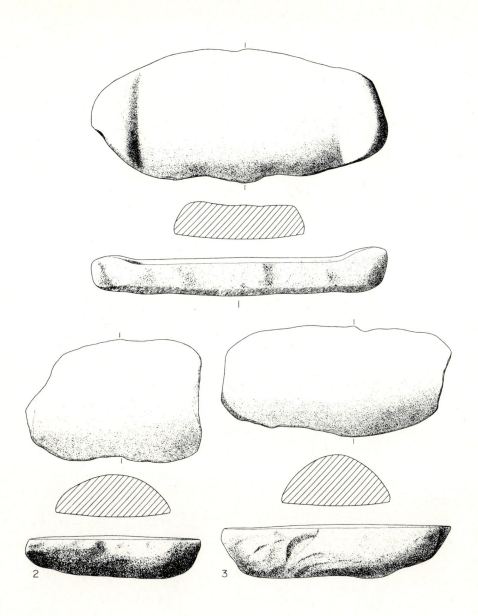

FIG. 29. Salmonsbury, Gloucestershire: rubbers for saddle querns. 1, Period I. Site III, pit L;
2, Period I. Site III, pit M; 3, Period II, phase ii. Site III, below paving. Scale: $\frac{1}{3}$.

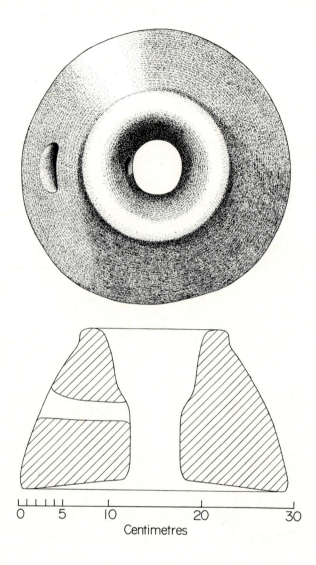

FIG. 30. Salmonsbury, Gloucestershire: upper stone of rotary quern. Scale: ¼.

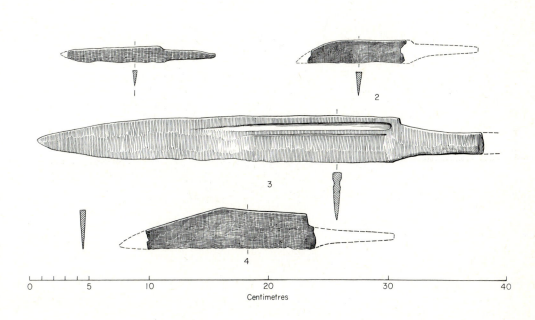

FIG. 31. Anglo-Saxon knives and seax of iron, Bourton-on-the-Water, Gloucestershire. 1, Bourton cemetery; 2, south bank of annexe; 3–4, Harp Lane. Scale: ⅓.

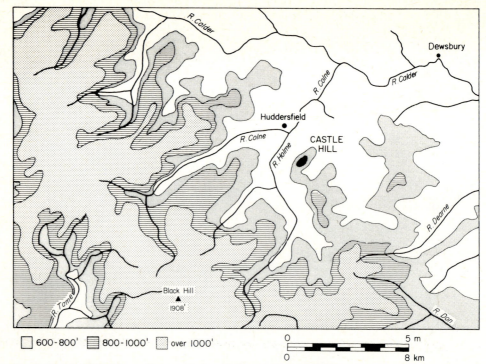

FIG. 1. Castle Hill, Almondbury: site in relation to the central Pennines.

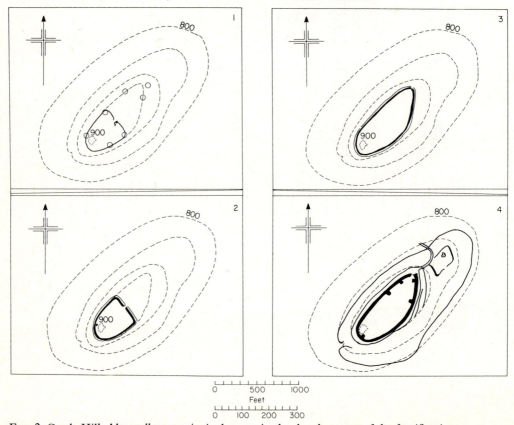

FIG. 2. Castle Hill, Almondbury: principal stages in the development of the fortifications.

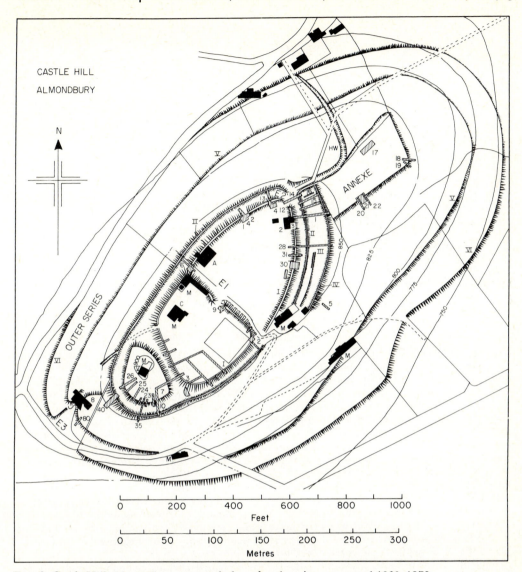

Fɪɢ. 3. Castle Hill, Almondbury: general plan, showing sites excavated 1939–1972.

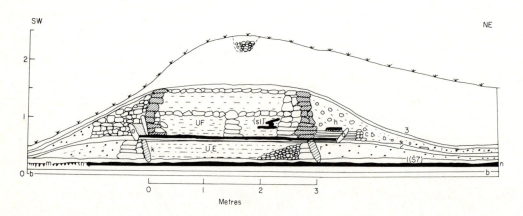

FIG. 4. Castle Hill, Almondbury. A section through the Inner Rampart, Site 35. This particular section is one of the principal keys to the entire stratigraphy. Resting on the bedrock (b) there is an original land-surface with Pennine Maglemosian flints (m) on part of which rests a Late Neolithic floor (n), radiocarbon dated by (S.7) to 2151 b.c. ± 85, covered by a soil-profile (1) accumulated during the first interregnum (Deposit 3). On top of this rests the remains of the bank of the Univallate Enclosure (U.E.), 3.5 m wide, lying between two inclined slabs (k and r) supporting a front and rear revetment enclosing a false-clay core. The remains of this bank were levelled off and the upper surface developed a soil-profile (2) in the second interregnum. Over part of this land surface there was then placed a floor, made up of humus, charcoal and calcined comminuted bone, 3·5 m wide, 6 cms thick, resting between two inclined slabs (O—O) which we regard as a hut-floor belonging to the Open Settlement (Deposit 6). On top of this in turn the Inner Rampart of the Univallate Fortlet (U.F.) was built. The outer and inner revetments are shaded. Immediately inside the inner revetment is a laid clay floor supported on the outside by a dwarf cobbled wall (c).

On top of this laid clay floor was a slabstone hearth, resting on cobbles and yielding a pottery group. Just inside the inner face of the inner revetment is a pile of burnt timber, (shown in solid black) the lower log (S.1) radiocarbon dated to 590 b.c. ± 95.

Piled up against the outer face of the outer revetment which is patinated on the outside, proving it lay exposed to weather for some time, is a large quantity of roughly dressed stone which we regard as an extension to the original rampart, belonging to either the Bivallate fort, or more probably, the final Multivallate fort. Over the whole surface of everything that lies below is the land-surface of the third interregnum (3) on top of which is the accumulated debris of the medieval occupation, not shown in the drawing.

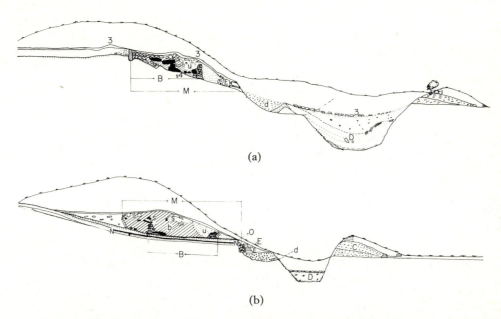

(a)

(b)

Fig. 5. Castle Hill, Almondbury. (a) Section through the Inner and Second Ramparts at Site 28. N.B. The stone-revetted, timber-laced rampart, 4·1 m wide, radiocarbon dated by S.4 to 555 b.c. ± 90, is heat-transformed (not exceeding 600°C) in shaded areas, unburnt in area (u); it belongs to the Bivallate Fort, Inner rampart (B). Outside it lay a sloping berm and a ditch, the surviving half marked (d). Later, a new outer revetment was built on the edge of the original berm at (E), and a new deeper ditch was cut through the outer half of the earlier one (D). These later additions belong to the Multivallate Fort (M). Charcoal and timber fragments lie in the middle filling of the later ditch above tumbled revetment stones. All the prehistoric ruins were overlain by land-surface (3) belonging to the Great Interregnum. A similar sandstill surface formed across the ditch which was slabbed off at this level in the medieval period. The counterscarp was a wedge of clay and shale tips resting against a stone kerb on the outer face. All earlier ramparts were overlain with medieval banks (details not shown).

(b) Section through the Inner and Second Ramparts at Site 1. Resting on the original land surface is a Late Neolithic Floor (N—N) covered by the soil profile accumulated in the first interregnum, on top of which is a hut-floor ending at O, belonging presumably to the Open Settlement. This is succeeded by the rampart of the Bivallate Fort within the limits shown (B), partly burned (b), partly unburned (u), with berm and part of original narrow ditch (d). The partly blocked up ditch was then made to carry an added rampart (E) outside which was a new ditch (D) and a counterscarp (C). The bottom half of Ditch D contained material from the burnt rampart core above. All prehistoric remains were covered by land-surface (3) of the Great Interregnum. The upper part of the Inner Rampart, the ditch and the counterscarp belong to the medieval structures not shown in detail.

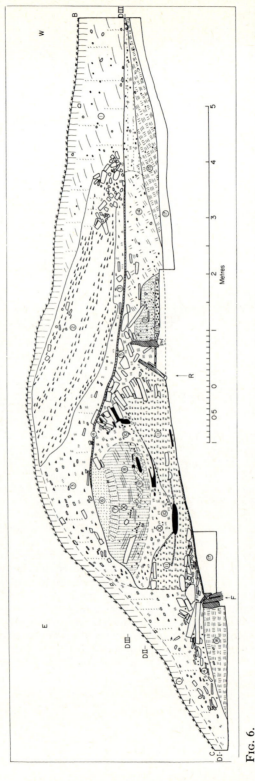

Fig. 6.
Castle Hill, Almondbury, 1970.   Site 31.   South section.   1. Post-Norman silt and soil profile.   2. Norman shale tip.   3. Norman light brown shaley clay.   4. Orange stained layer.
5. Stoney tumble.   6–10. Burnt rampart material.   6. Orange-brown clayey earth.   7. Light, friable, purplish-red clay.   8. Loose, bright orange earth.   9. Grey-black timber-stained earth.
10. Thick dark red-brown shaley clay.   11 Light brown shaley clay, more compact towards bottom.   12. Dark brown clayey earth with charcoal.   13. Much charcoal in stiff brown earth.
14. Thick grey orange-stained clay with rubble.   15. Stiff yellow clay with some charcoal.   16. Stiff yellow clay.   17. Thick yellow-brown shaley clay, natural, over Elland shale beds.
Burnt timbers indicated in solid black.   ⊗ = Thermoluminescent dating samples.   F and R indicate front and rear revetments of rampart of bivallate fortification, with stone revetment of
multivallate phase above.

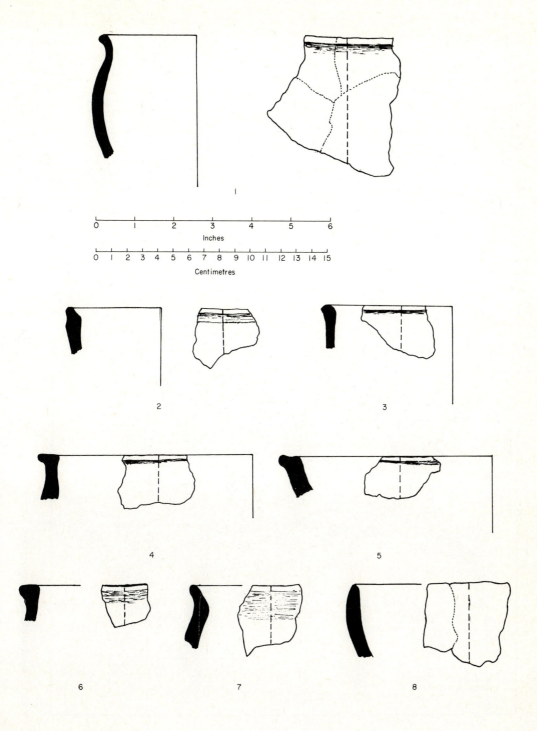

Fɪɢ. 7. Castle Hill, Almondbury: pottery.

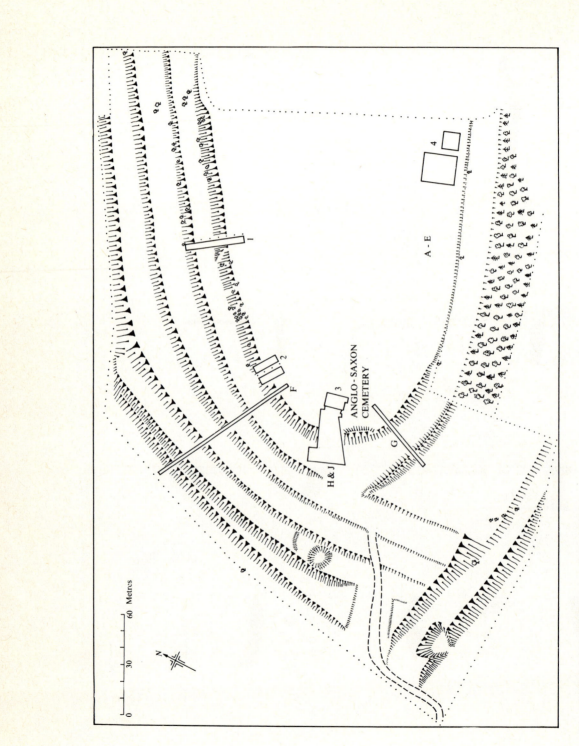

FIG. 1. Blewburton Hill: general site plan.

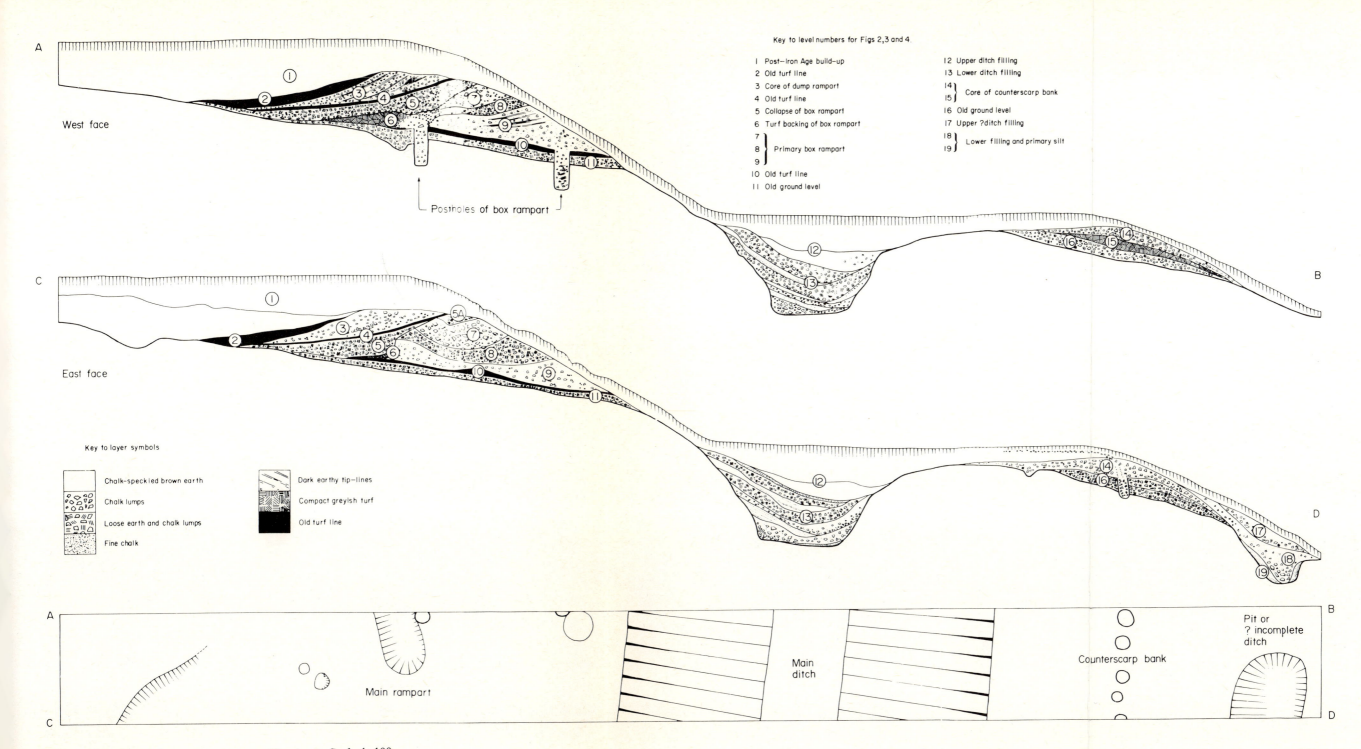

West face

Posthotes of box rampart

East face

Key to level numbers for Figs 2,3 and 4.

1   Post—Iron Age build-up
2   Old turf line
3   Core of dump rampart
4   Old turf line
5   Collapse of box rampart
6   Turf backing of box rampart
7
8   } Primary box rampart
9
10 Old turf line
11 Old ground level

12 Upper ditch filling
13 Lower ditch filling
14
15 } Core of counterscarp bank
16 Old ground level
17 Upper ?ditch filling
18
19 } Lower filling and primary silt

Key to layer symbols

Chalk-speckled brown earth

Chalk lumps

Loose earth and chalk lumps

Fine chalk

Dark earthy tip-lines

Compact greyish turf

Old turf line

Main rampart

Main ditch

Counterscarp bank

Pit or ? incomplete ditch

FIG. 2. Blewburton Hill: plan and sections of Cutting 1. **Scale 1:100.**

[*Facing page 408*]

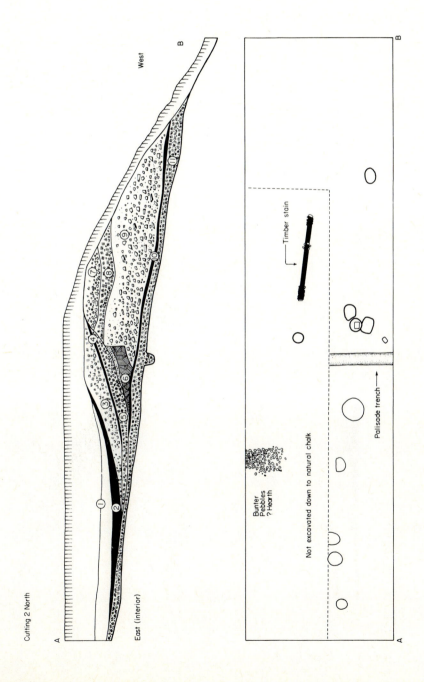

Fɪɢ. 3. Blewburton Hill: plan and section of Cutting 2 (north). Scale 1:100.

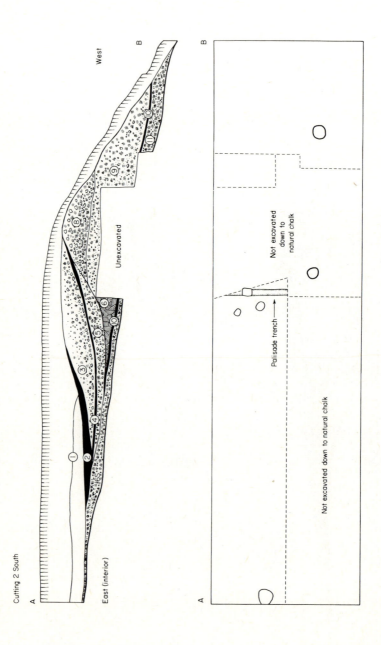

Cutting 2 South

A

West

B

East (interior)

Unexcavated

B

Not excavated down to natural chalk

Palisade trench

Not excavated down to natural chalk

A

Fig. 4. Blewburton Hill: plan and section of Cutting 2 (south). Scale 1:100.

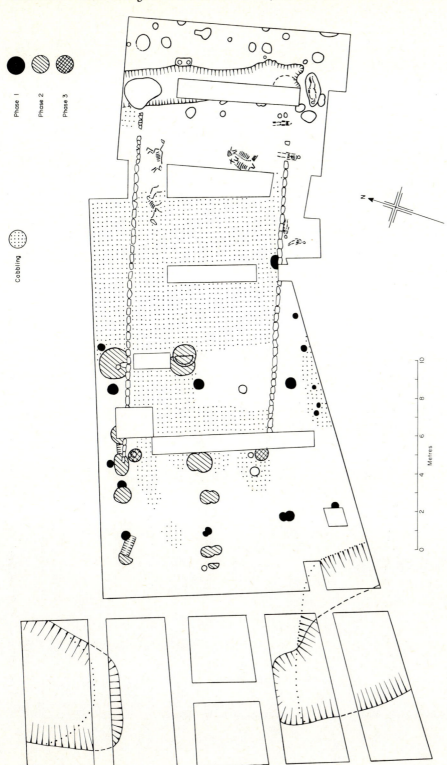

Phase 1

Phase 2

Phase 3

Cobbling

N

Metres

10 8 6 4 2 0

FIG. 5. Blewburton Hill: plan of western entrance, Cutting 3.

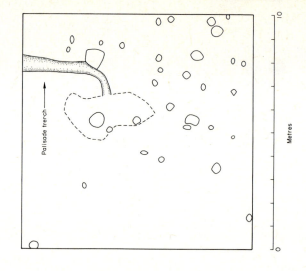

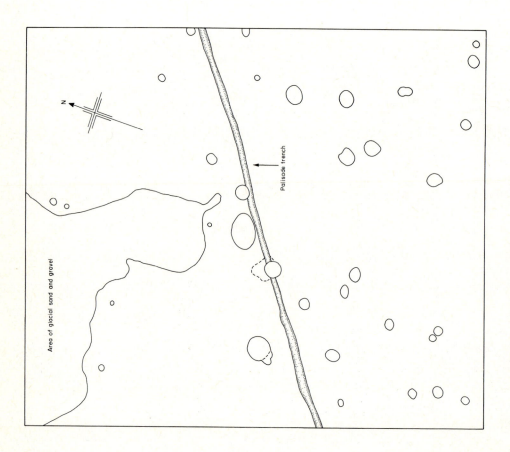

Fig. 6. Blewburton Hill: plan of interior, Cutting 4.

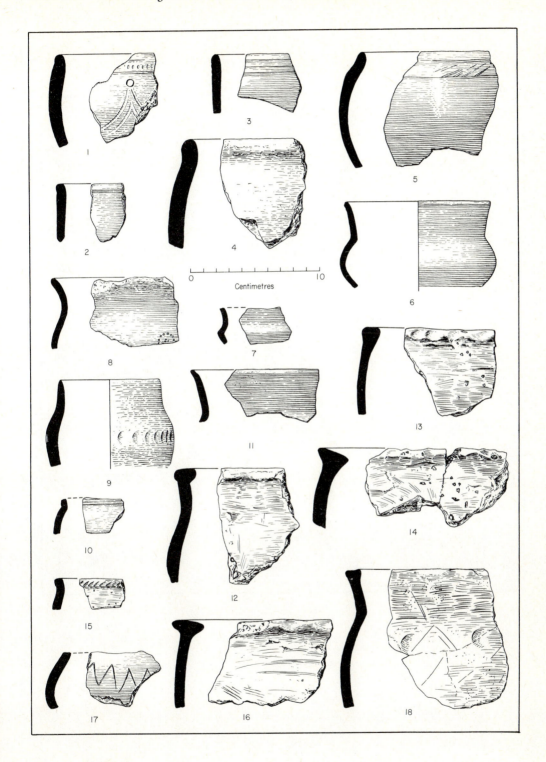

Fig. 7. Blewburton Hill: pottery.

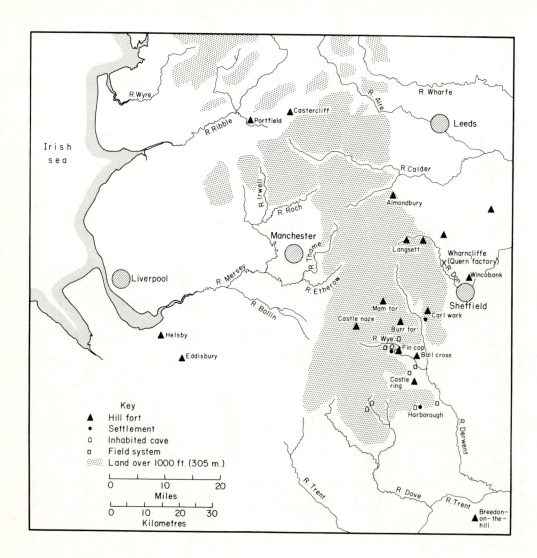

FIG. 1. The Southern Pennines in the Iron Age.

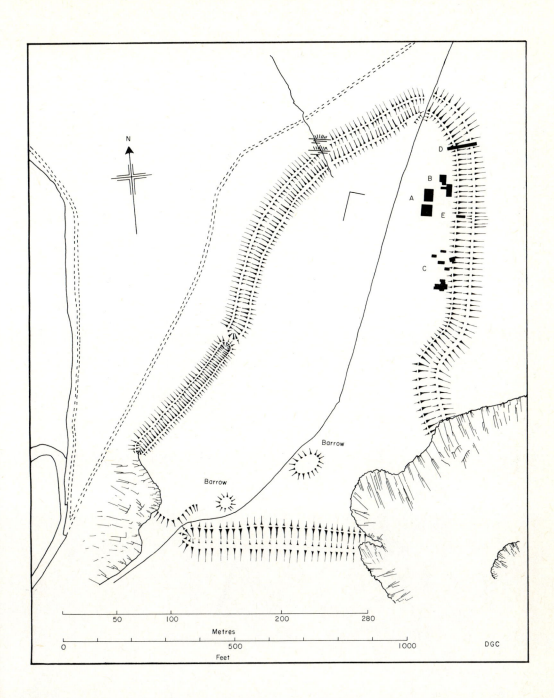

FIG. 2. Mam Tor: general site plan.

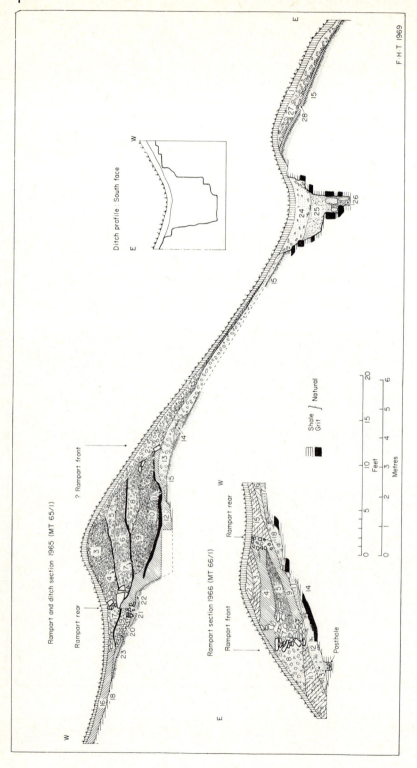

Fig. 3. Mam Tor: section across defences, 1965/66 (areas D and E are shown on Fig. 2).

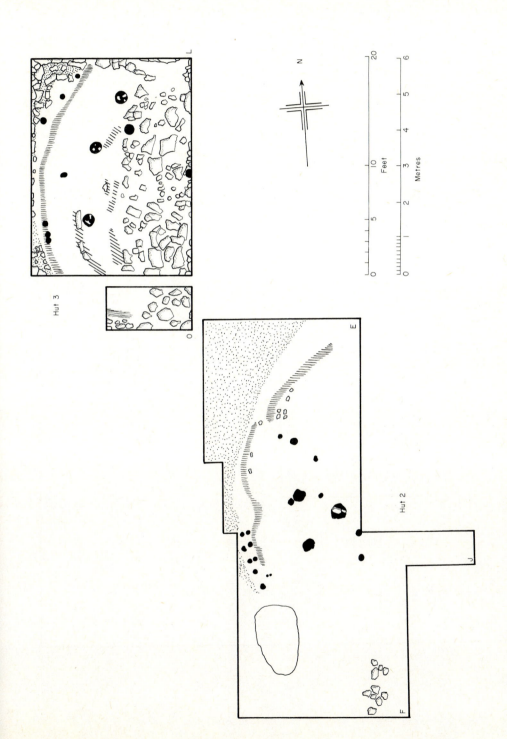

Fig. 4. Mam Tor: plan of huts 2 and 3 (area B shown on Fig. 2).

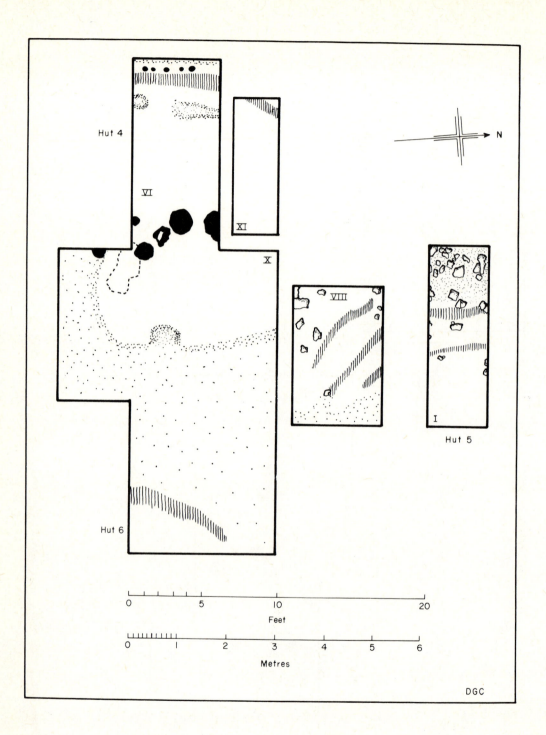

FIG. 5. Mam Tor: plan of huts 4, 5 and 6 (area C shown on Fig. 2).

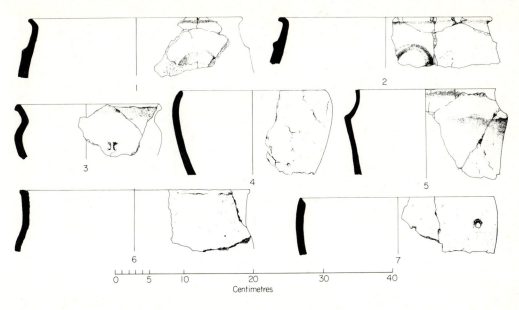

FIG. 6. Mam Tor: pottery (i).

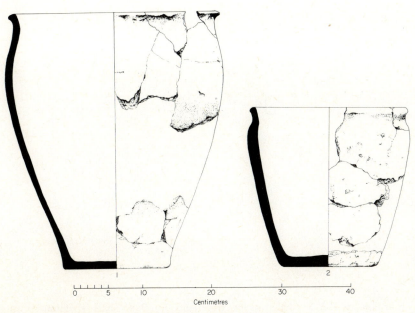

FIG. 7. Mam Tor: pottery (ii) found together in hut 4.

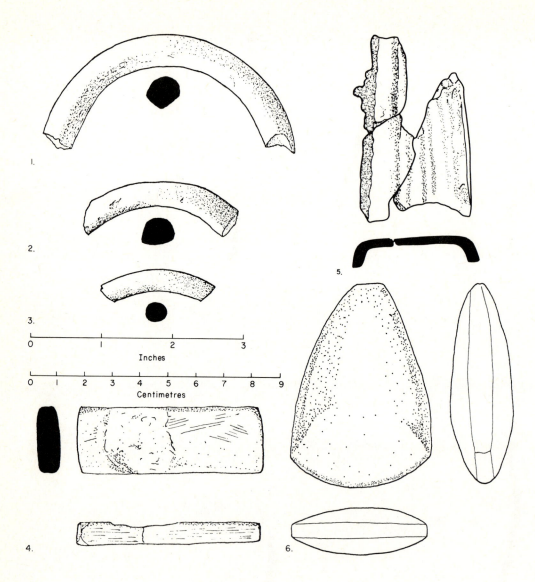

FIG. 8. Mam Tor: other objects. 1, 2, 3: Shale bracelet fragments, hut 3. 4: Shale whetstone from magnetometer anomaly. 5: Bronze socketed axe, hut 4. 6: Polished stone axe, hut 3.

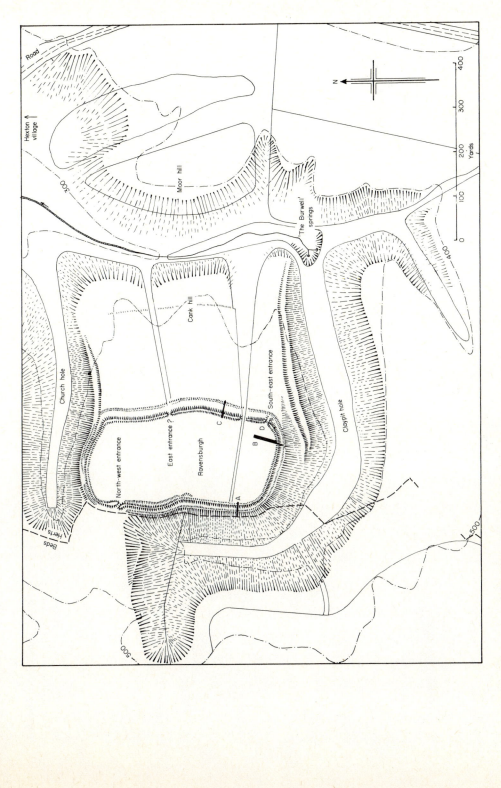

FIG. 1. Ravensburgh Castle: general site plan.

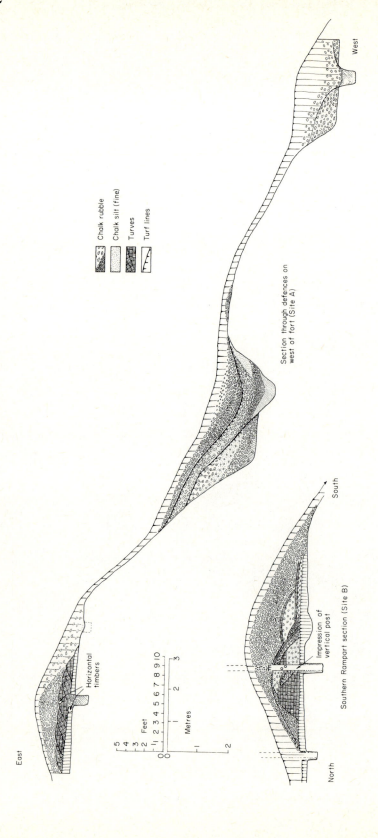

FIG. 2. Ravensburgh Castle: section through defences on west side of fort (Site A). Section through southern rampart (Site B).

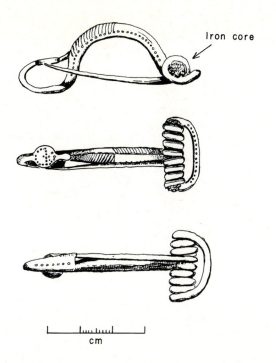

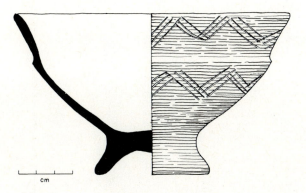

Fig. 3. Ravensburgh Castle: La Tène 1b brooch and "angular" bowl.

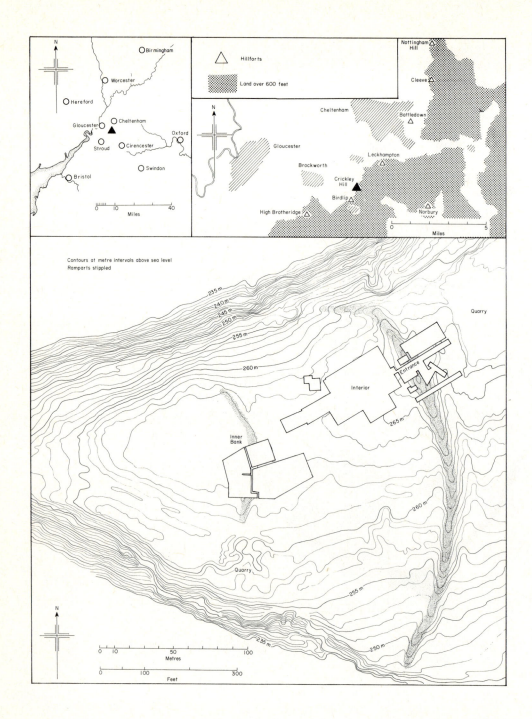

Fig. 1. Crickley Hill: location map and general site plan.

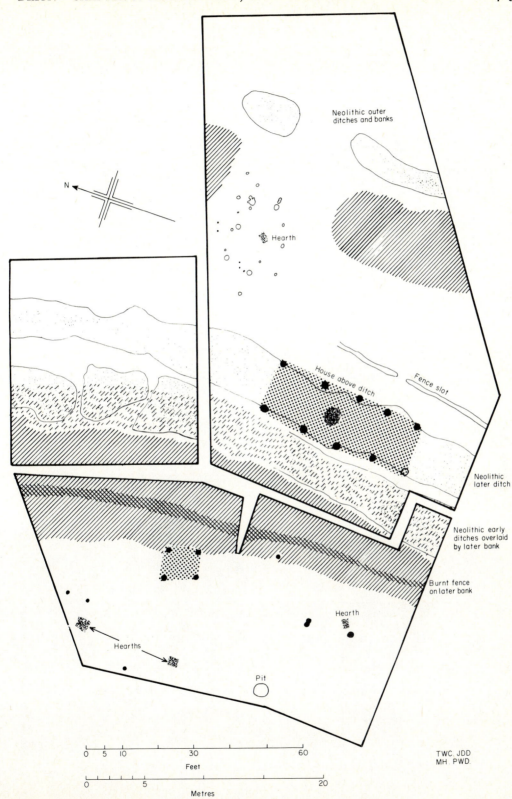

Fig. 2. Crickley Hill: the inner bank, block plan.

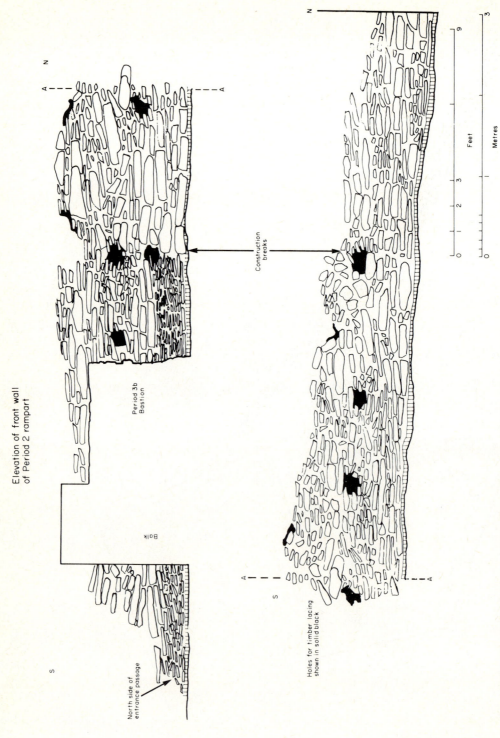

Elevation of front wall
of Period 2 rampart

FIG. 3. Crickley Hill: elevation of front wall of period 2 rampart.

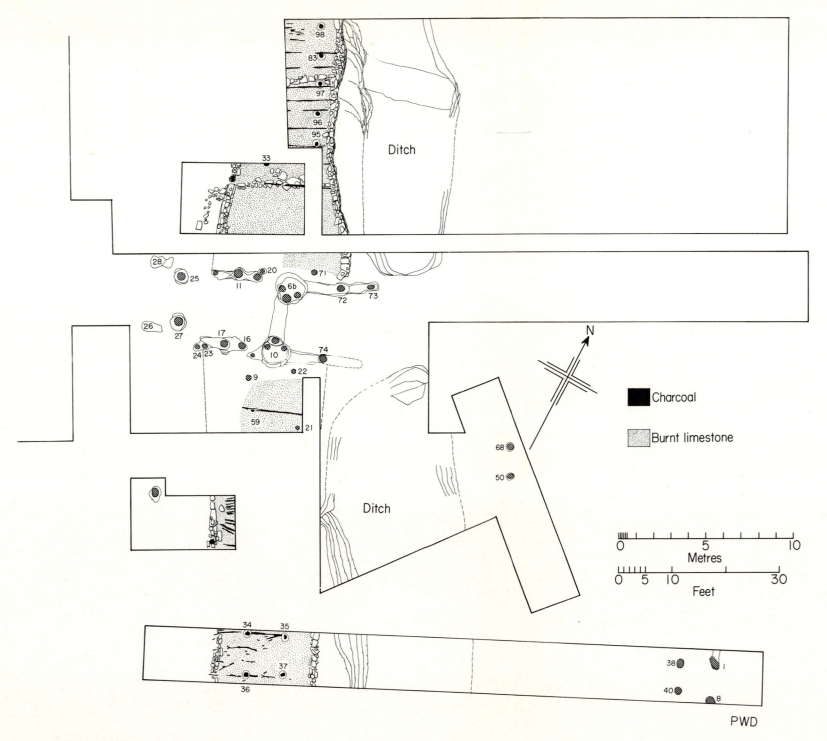

Ditch

Ditch

N

Charcoal

Burnt limestone

5
0   Metres   10

0   5   10   30
        Feet

PWD

Fɪɢ. 4. Crickley Hill: the entrance, Period 2.

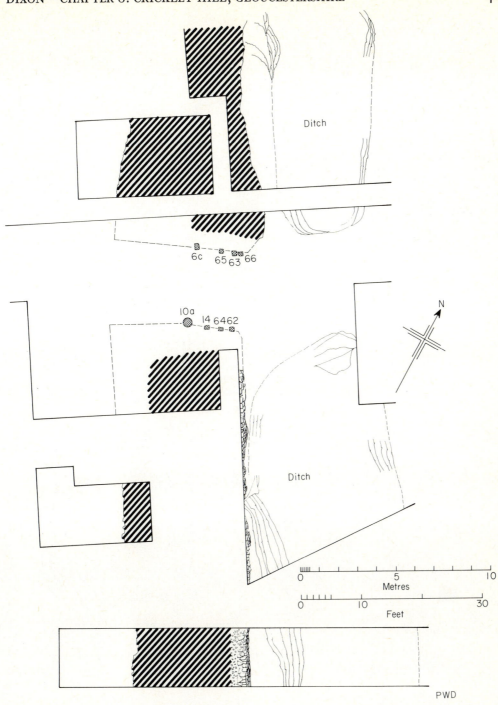

Fɪɢ. 5. Crickley Hill: the entrance, period 3a.

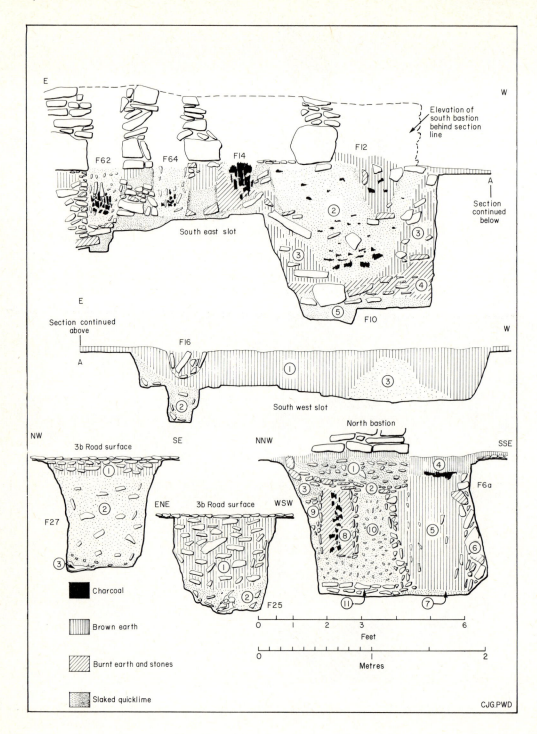

FIG. 6. Crickley Hill: post-holes in the entrance passage.

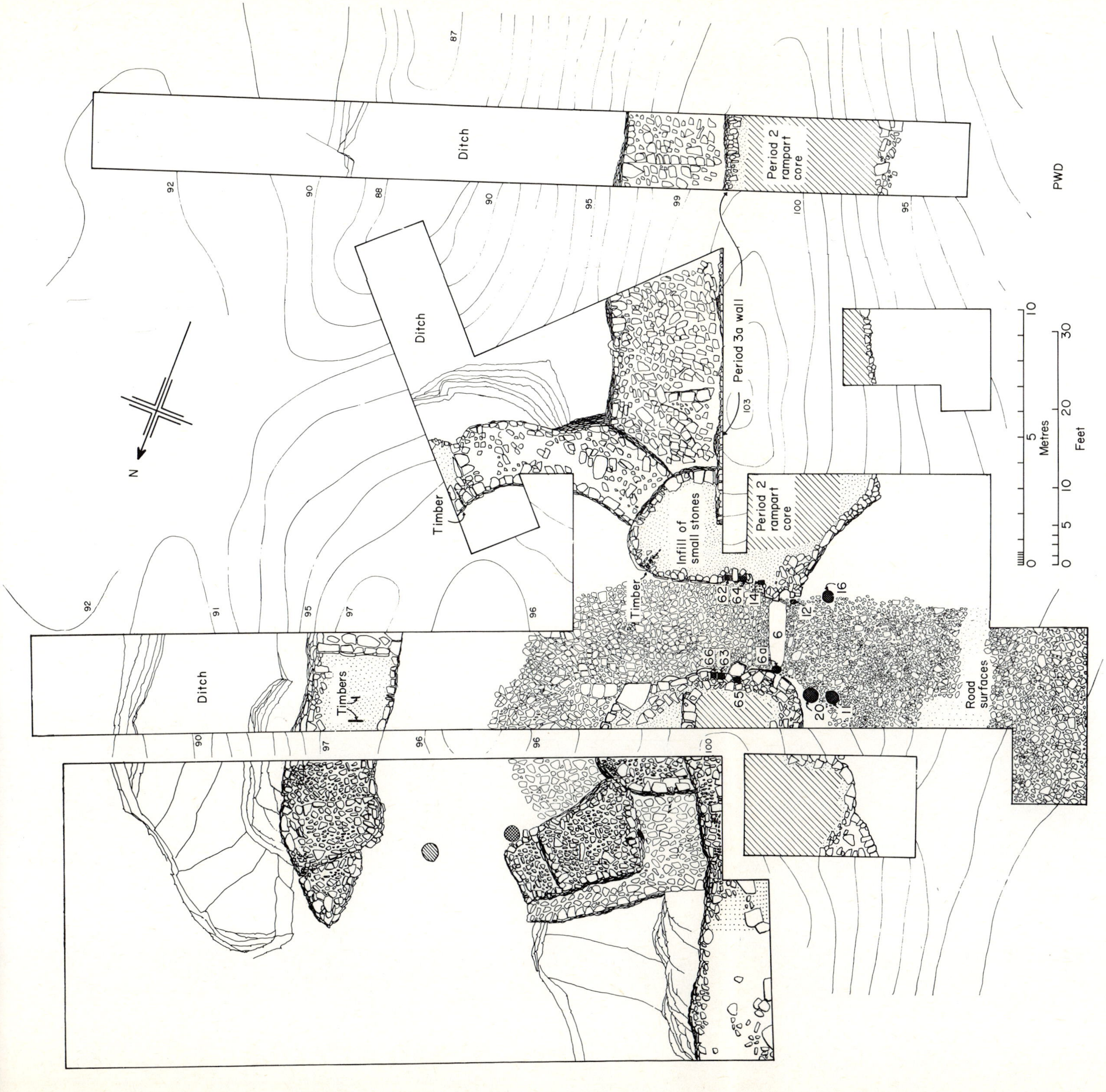

FIG. 7. Crickley Hill: the entrance, period 3b.

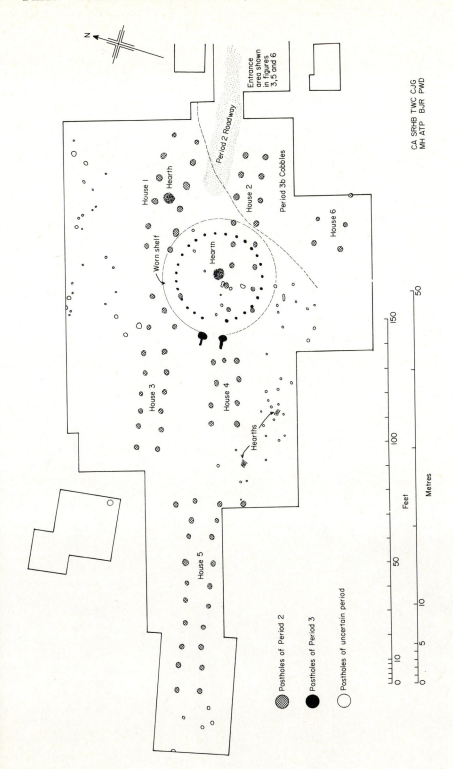

Fig. 8. Crickley Hill: the interior.

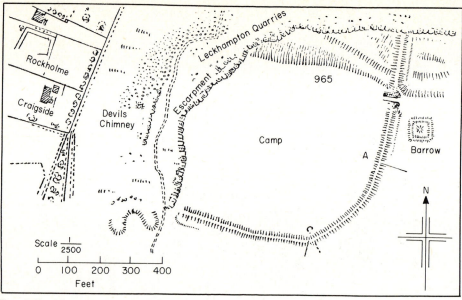

FIG. 1. Leckhampton: general site plan.

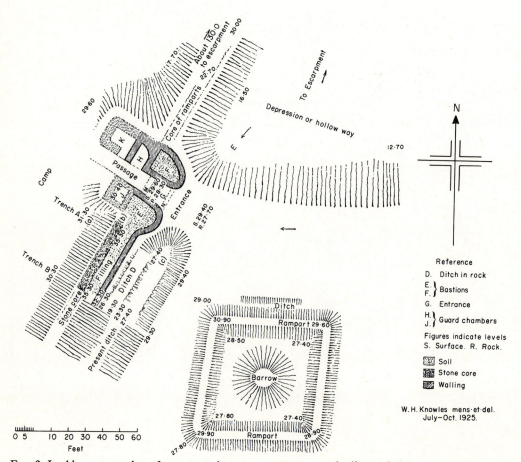

FIG. 2. Leckhampton: plan of structures in eastern entrance, and adjacent barrow.

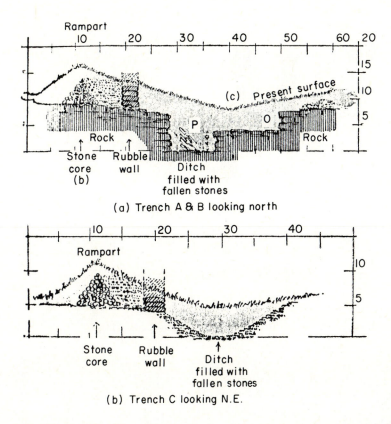

(a) Trench A & B looking north

(b) Trench C looking N.E.

Fig. 3. Leckhampton: sections across defences, 1925: (a) north face of trenches A and B; (b) northeast face of trench C.

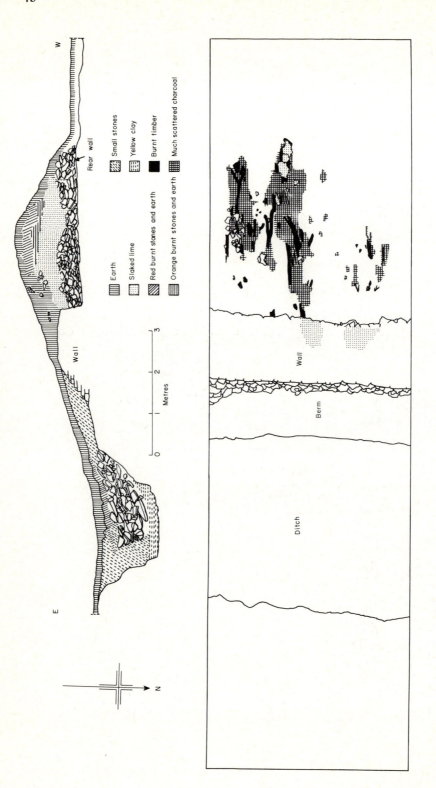

Fig. 4. Leckhampton: plan and section of Cutting 5, 1970.

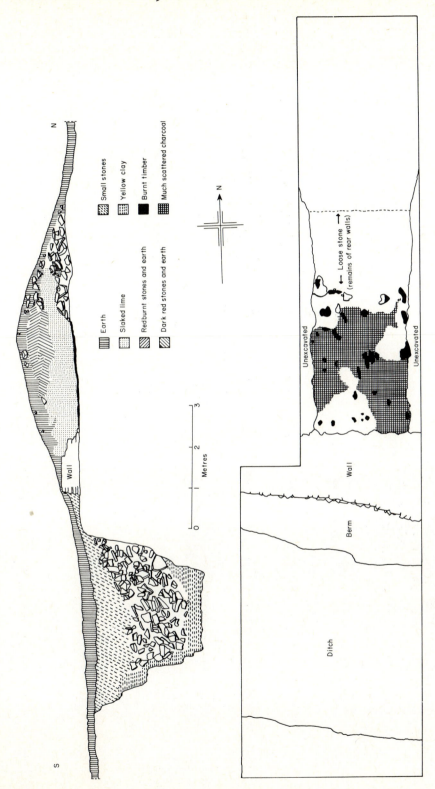

Fig. 5. Leckhampton; plan and section of Cutting 2, 1969.

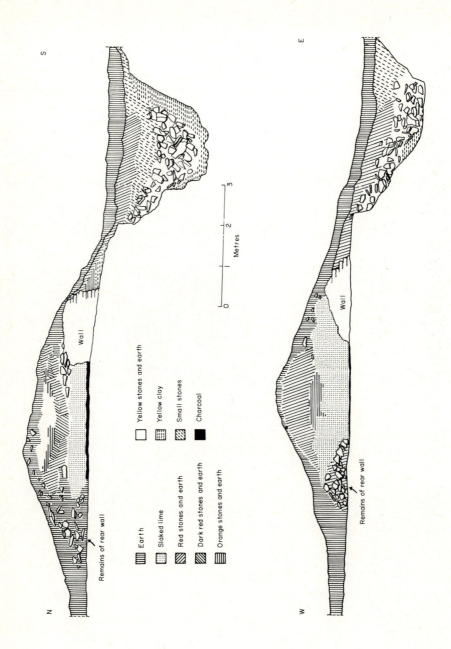

Fig. 6. Leckhampton: sections across Cutting 2, 1969 (upper section) and Cutting 5, 1970 (lower section).

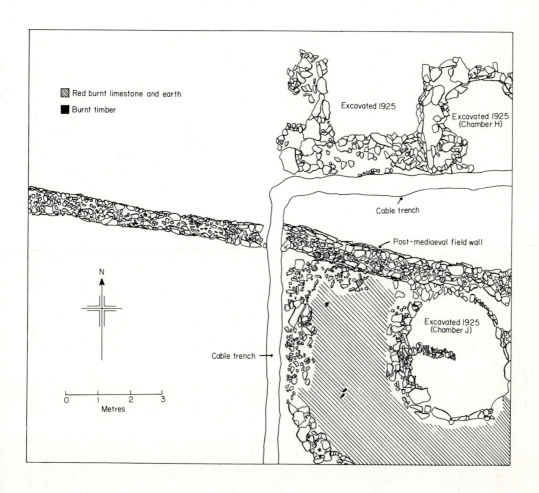

Fig. 7. Leckhampton: plan of Cutting 4, 1970.

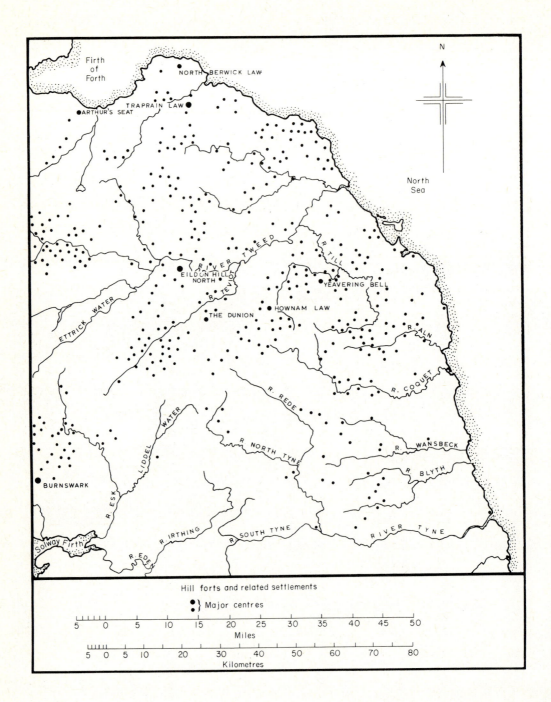

FIG. 1. Hillforts and related settlements in the Tyne-Forth region.

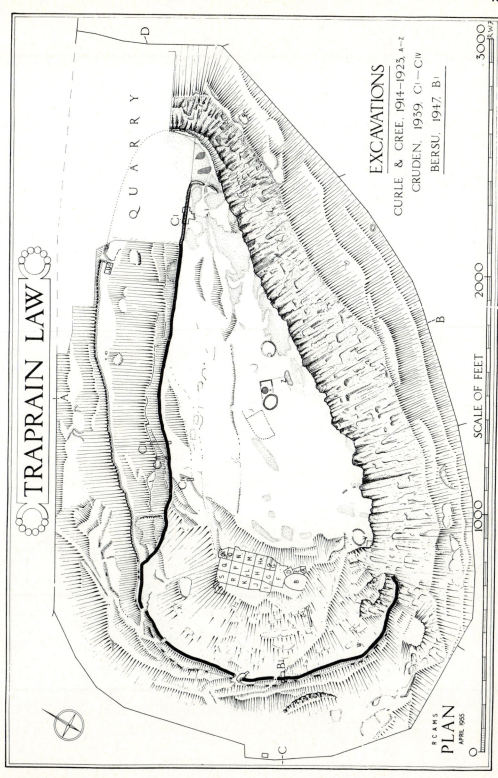

FIG. 2. Traprain Law: general site plan (from R. W. Feachem, 1956a).

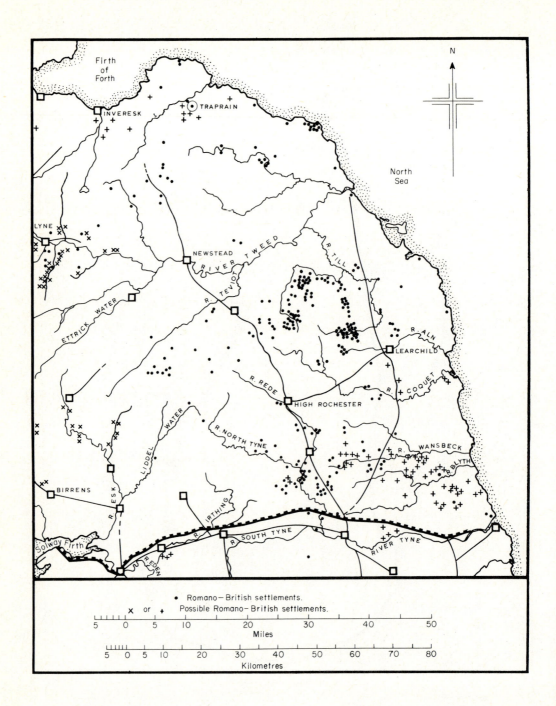

FIG. 3. Romano-British settlements in the Tyne-Forth region.

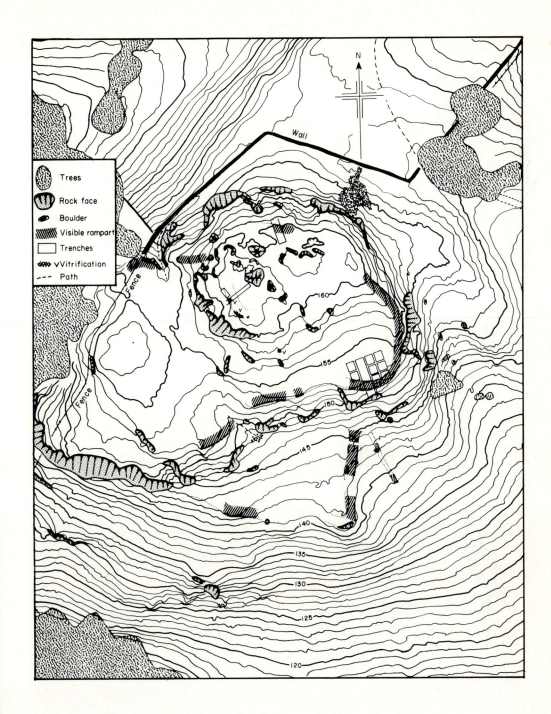

FIG. 1. Sheep Hill, Dunbartonshire: photogrammetric plan. Contours in metres above mean sea level: Scale 1:1200.

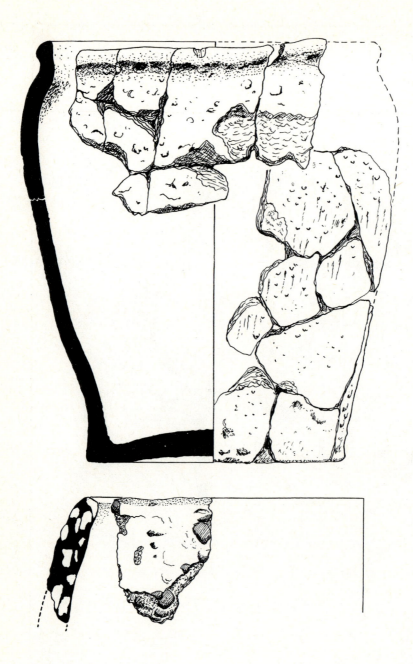

FIG. 2. Sheep Hill, Dunbartonshire: pottery. Scale 1:2.

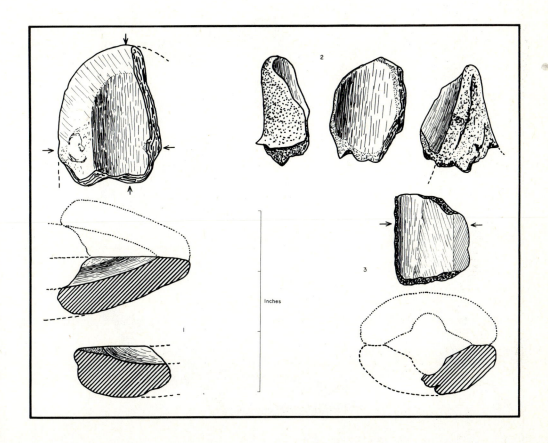

FIG. 3. Sheep Hill, Dunbartonshire: fragments of moulds.

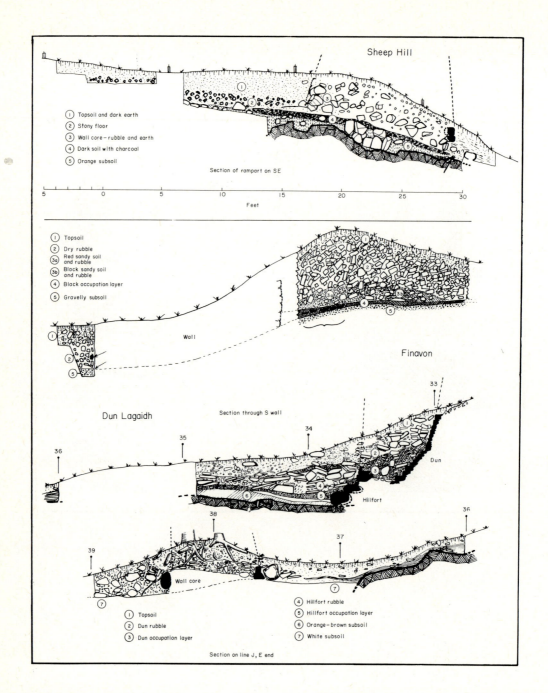

Sheep Hill

① Topsoil and dark earth
② Stony floor
③ Wall core – rubble and earth
④ Dark soil with charcoal
⑤ Orange subsoil

Section of rampart on SE

5   0   5   10   15   20   25   30

Feet

① Topsoil
② Dry rubble
③a Red sandy soil and rubble
③b Black sandy soil and rubble
④ Black occupation layer
⑤ Gravelly subsoil

Wall

Finavon

Section through S wall

Dun Lagaidh

Dun

Hillfort

Wall core

① Topsoil
② Dun rubble
③ Dun occupation layer

④ Hillfort rubble
⑤ Hillfort occupation layer
⑥ Orange–brown subsoil
⑦ White subsoil

Section on line J, E end

FIG. 4. Sections of the deposits at Sheep Hill, Dunbartonshire, Finavon, Angus and Dun Lagaidh, Ross and Cromarty.

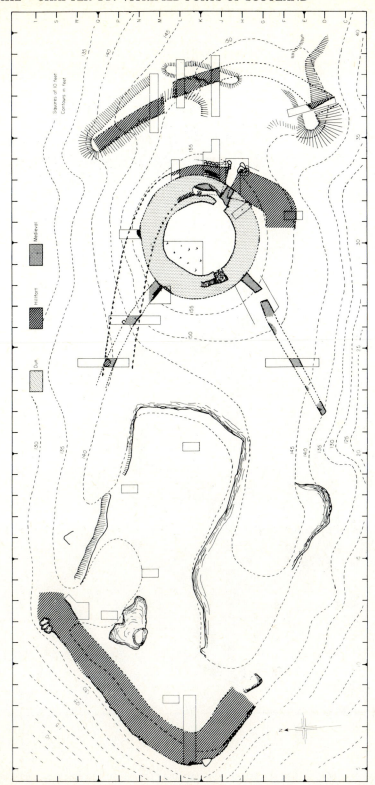

FIG. 5. Dun Lagaidh, Ross and Cromarty, general site plan. Contours in feet above sea level. Scale 1:545.

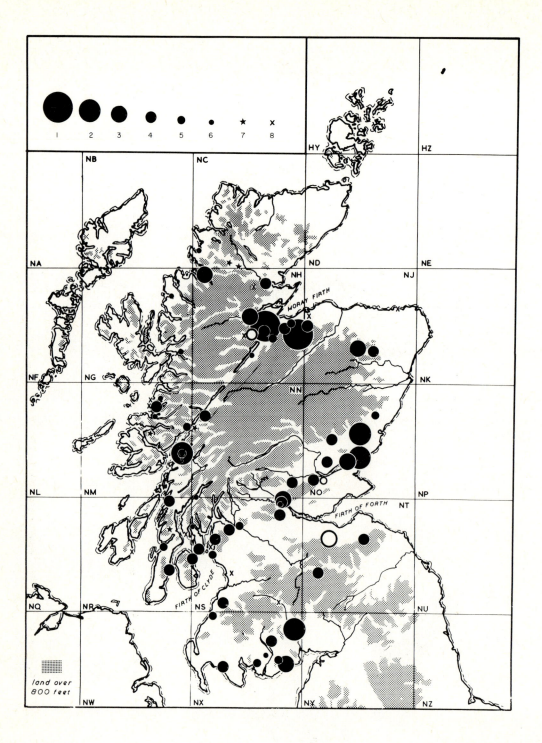

FIG. 6. Map of timber-framed forts in Scotland. The symbols represent the size groups given in the Appendix.

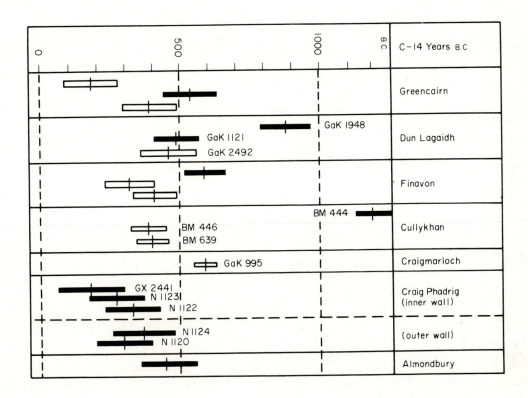

FIG. 7. Chart of radiocarbon dates for timber-framed forts in Scotland.

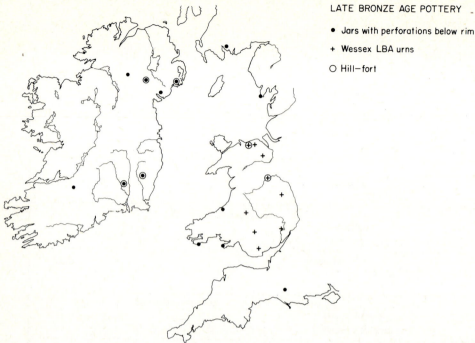

Savory Fig. 1. Distribution of Late Bronze Age pottery in Wales and Ireland.

LATE BRONZE AGE POTTERY

- • Jars with perforations below rim
- + Wessex LBA urns
- ○ Hill—fort

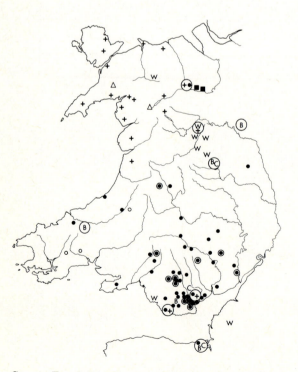

Savory Fig. 2. Distribution of Late Bronze Age metal-work.

LATE BRONZE AGE METALWORK

- + "Late" palstaves
- △ N. Wales sickles
- ○ Socketed axes with 2 mouth mouldings
- • "S. Wales" axes
- W Wilburton types
- B Broadward types
- C Carp's tongue types
- ◯ Hoards
- ■ Northern socketed axes

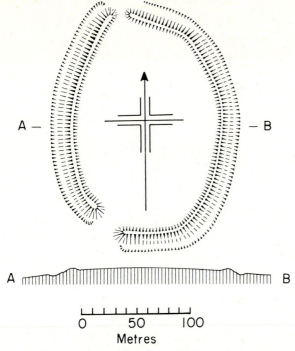

FIG. 3. Beacon Ring, Montgomeryshire: general site plan.

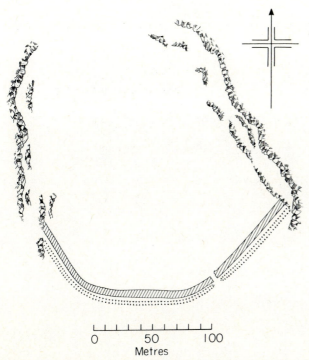

FIG. 4. The first drystone rampart (= Period II) at Dinorben, Denbighshire.

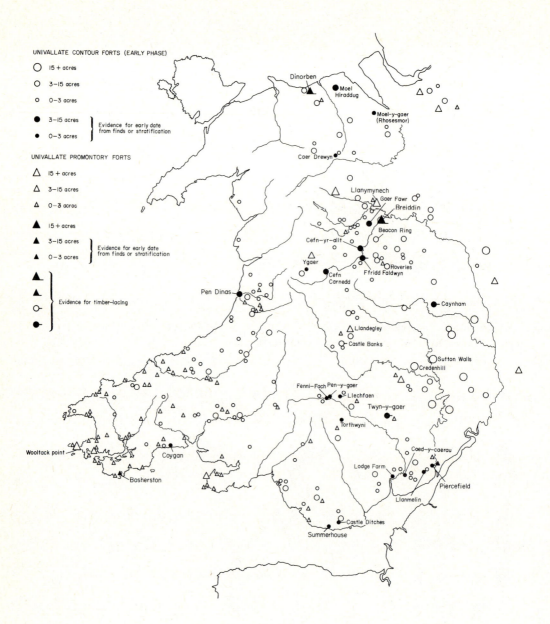

FIG. 5. Distribution of Univallate forts in Wales.

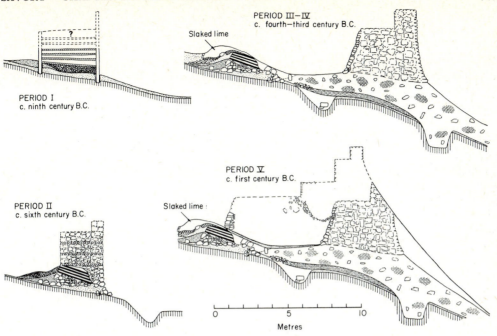

PERIOD I
c. ninth century B.C.

PERIOD II
c. sixth century B.C.

PERIOD III—IV
c. fourth—third century B.C.

Slaked lime

PERIOD V
c. first century B.C.

Slaked lime

0   5   10

Metres

FIG. 6. Dinorben, Denbighshire: suggested structural sequence for main south-western rampart.

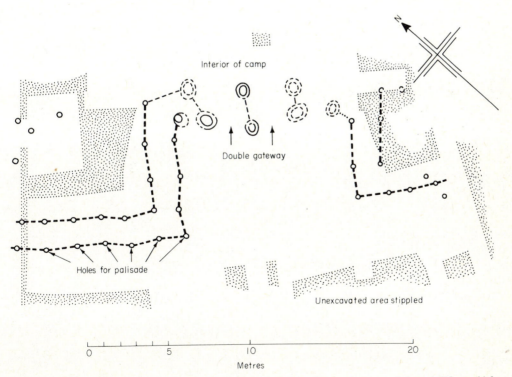

Interior of camp

Double gateway

Holes for palisade

Unexcavated area stippled

0   5   10   20

Metres

FIG. 7. Ffridd Faldwyn, Montgomeryshire; plan of earliest entrance of first hillfort. (After Grimes.)

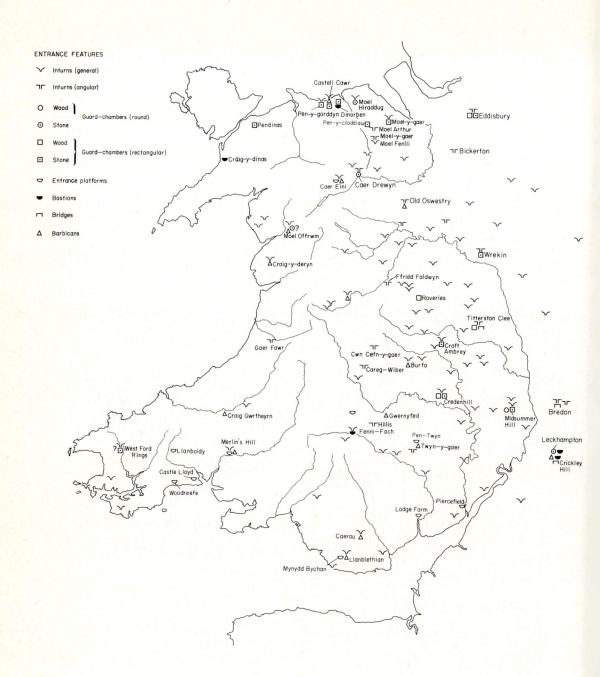

FIG. 8. Map of entrance features in Welsh hillforts.

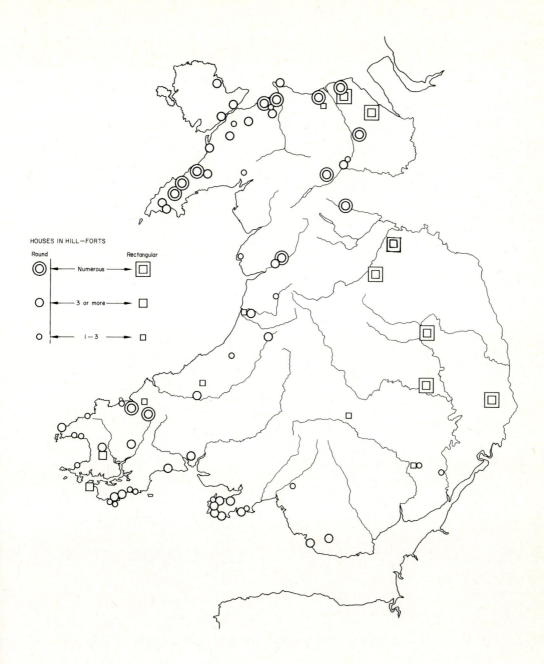

FIG. 9. Distribution of houses in Welsh hillforts.

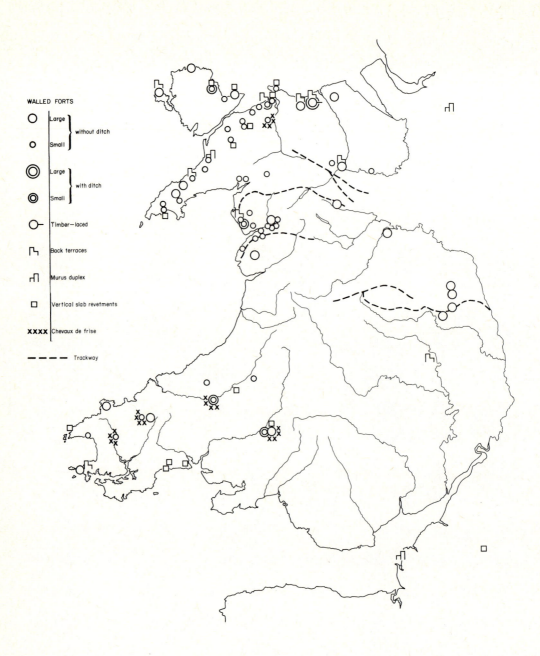

Fig. 10. Distribution of walled forts in Wales.

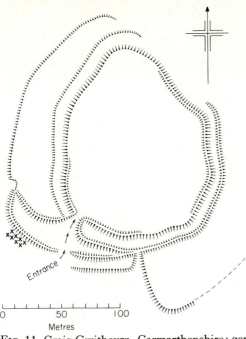

FIG. 11. Craig Gwitheyrn, Carmarthenshire: general site plan. (After Willoughby Gardner.)

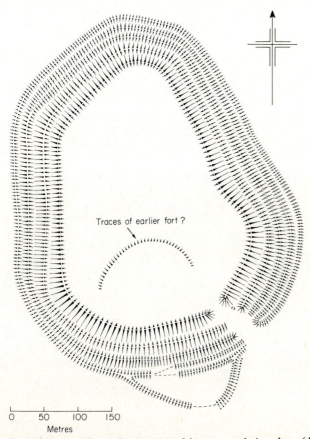

FIG. 12. Pen-y-Crug, Brecnockonshire: general site plan. (After Hogg.)

Fɪɢ. 13. Map of pastoralism in Wales.

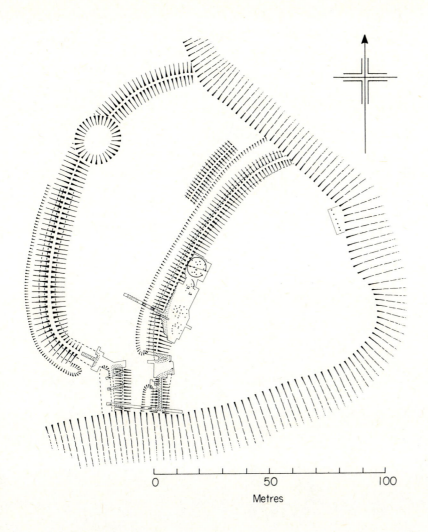

Fig. 14. Caeran Henllan, Cardiganshire: general site plan. (After Audrey Williams.)

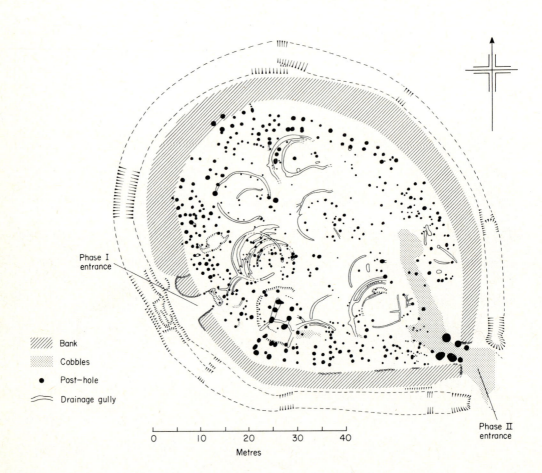

Phase I
entrance

Phase II
entrance

Bank

Cobbles

Post—hole

Drainage gully

0   10   20   30   40

Metres

Fig. 15. Walesland Rath, Pembrokeshire: reconstructed plan of phases. (After Wainwright.)

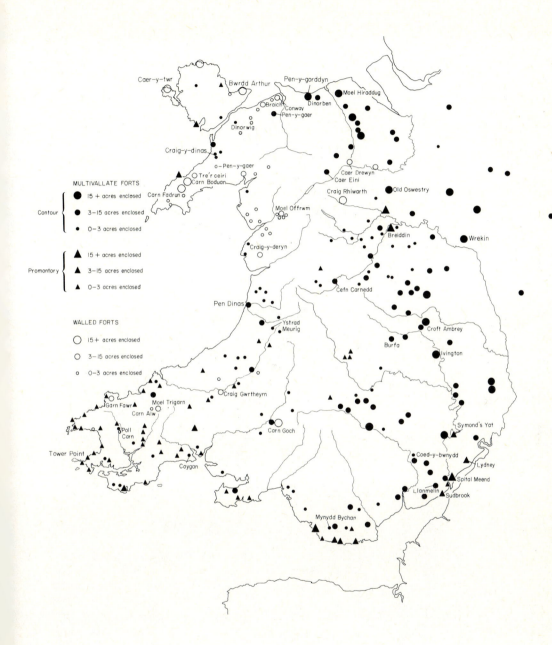

FIG. 16. Distribution of Multivallate forts in Wales.

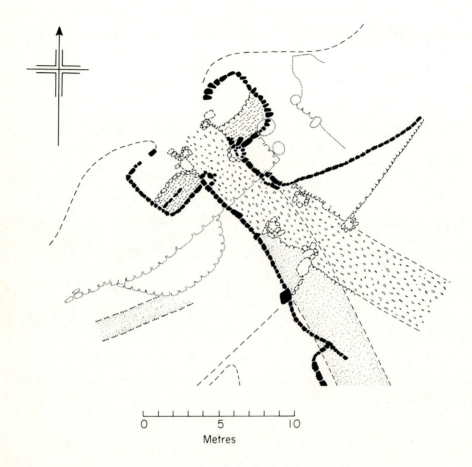

Fig. 17. Dinorben, Denbighshire: plan of south-east entrance.

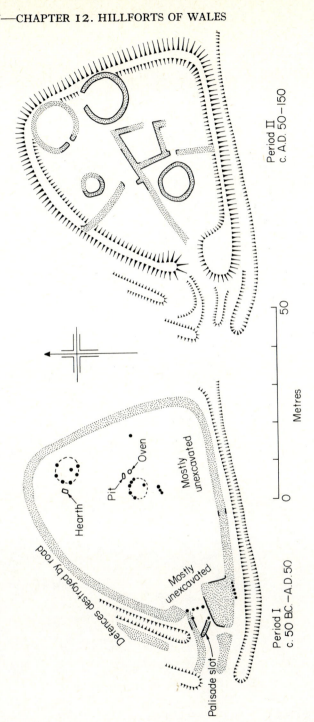

Fig. 18. Mynydd Bychan, Glamorgan: plan of Periods I and II.

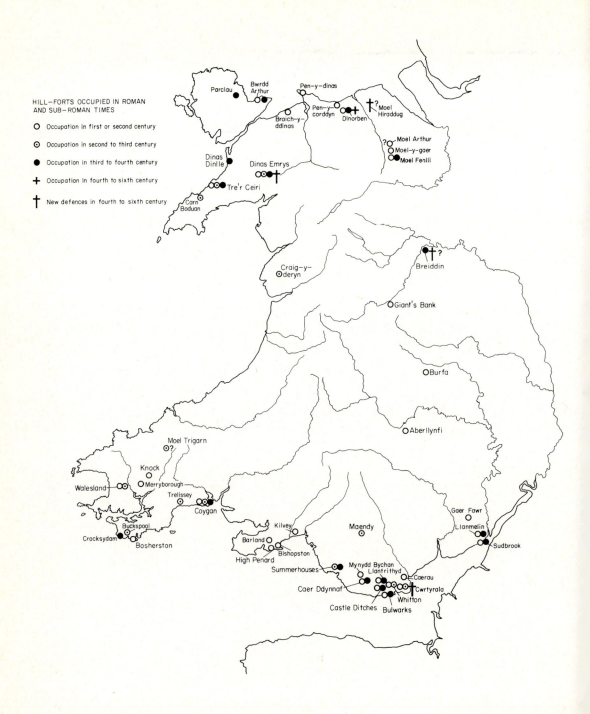

FIG. 19. Distribution of hillforts occupied in Roman and sub-Roman times.

FIG. 1. The Breiddin: general site plan, with the excavations at the southern tip of the hill.

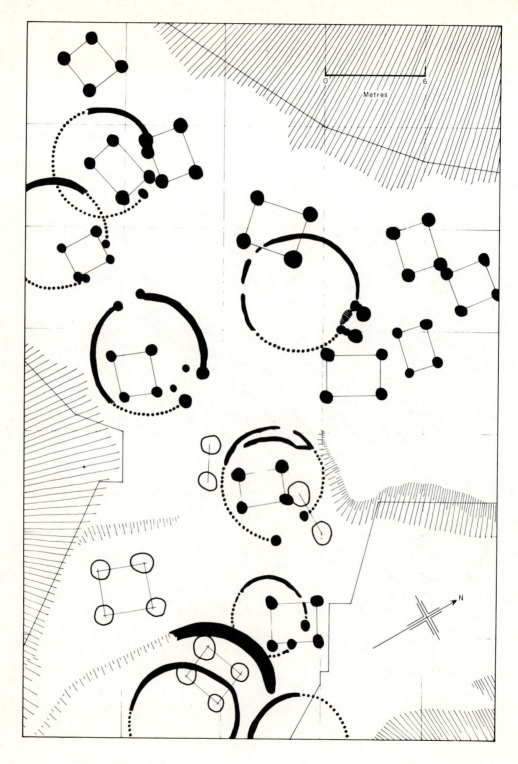

Fig. 2. The Breiddin: plan of Iron Age structures in the interior.

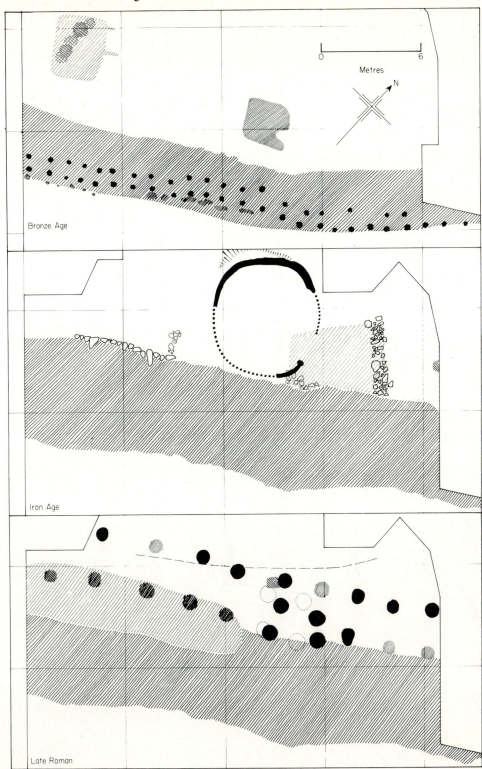

FIG. 3. The Breiddin: the main rampart cutting.

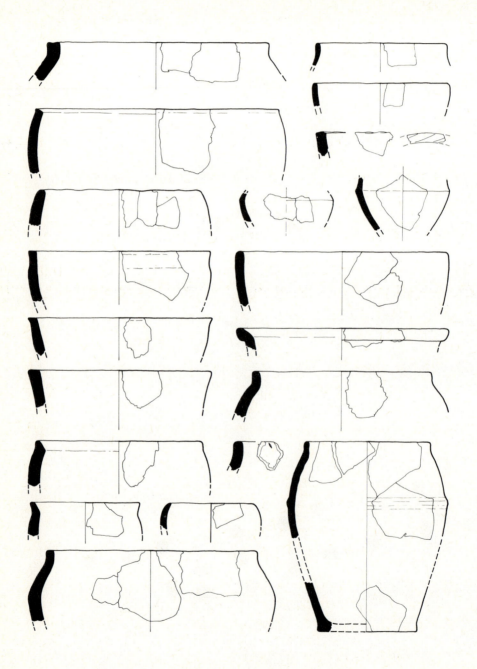

Fig. 4. The Breiddin: pottery associated with the Late Bronze Age occupation. Scale 1:4.

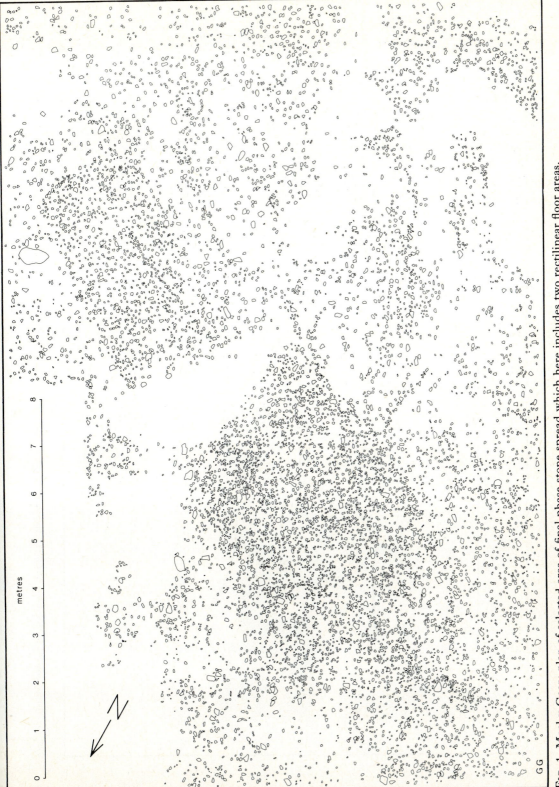

FIG. 1. Moel y Gaer: plan of selected area of final phase stone spread which here includes two rectilinear floor areas.

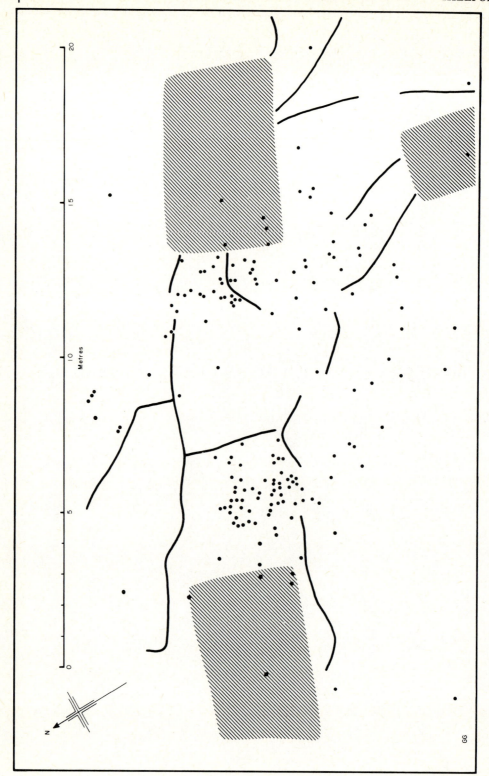

Fig. 2. Moel y Gaer: sketch plan of one of the final phase yards. Floor areas (hatched) with fence lines and pot sherd distribution (see p. 305).

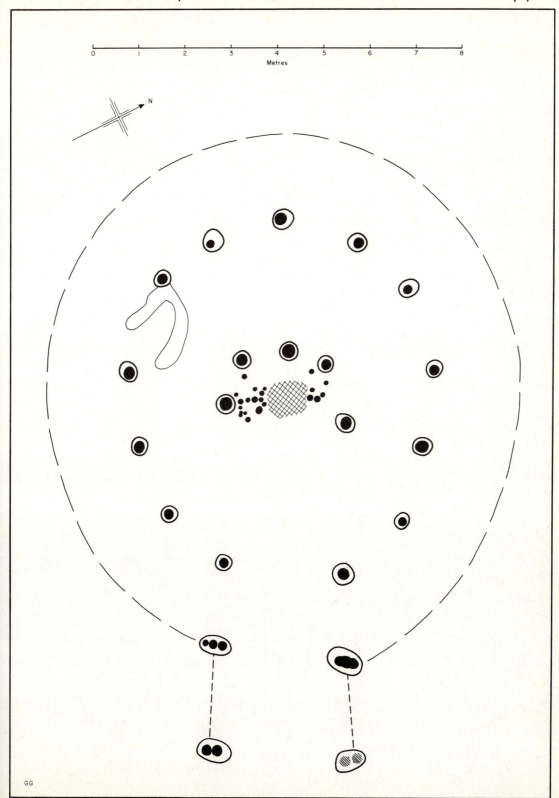

Fig. 3. Moel y Gaer: a typically symmetrical post-ring round-house. Hearth cross-hatched. Conjectural position of wall inserted as dashed line.

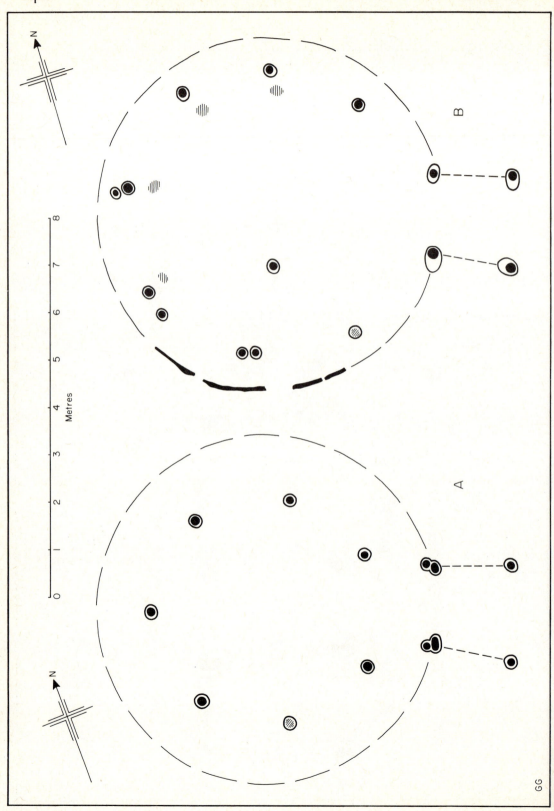

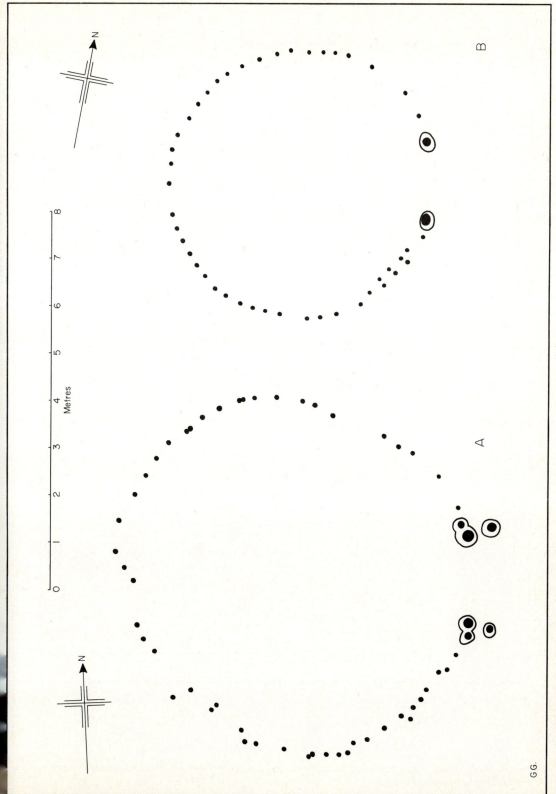

FIG. 5. Moel y Gaer: two stake-wall round-houses.

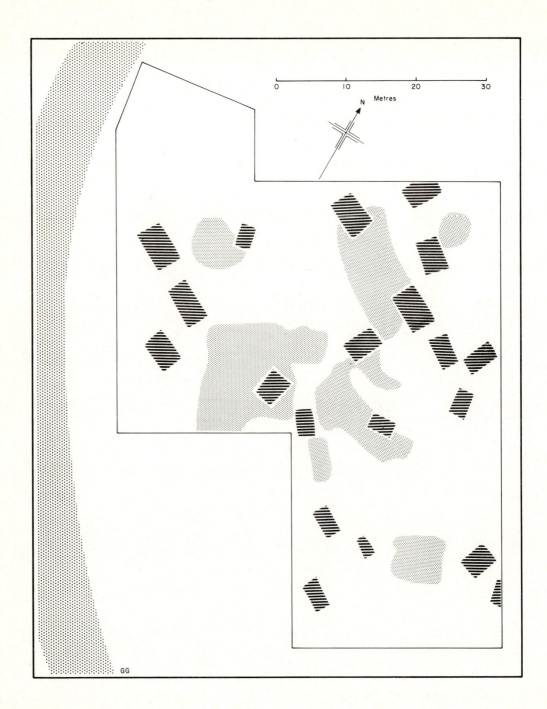

Fig. 6. Moel y Gaer: sketch plan of final phase. Rectangular floors hatched, yard areas stippled. Stippled area to west is rampart.

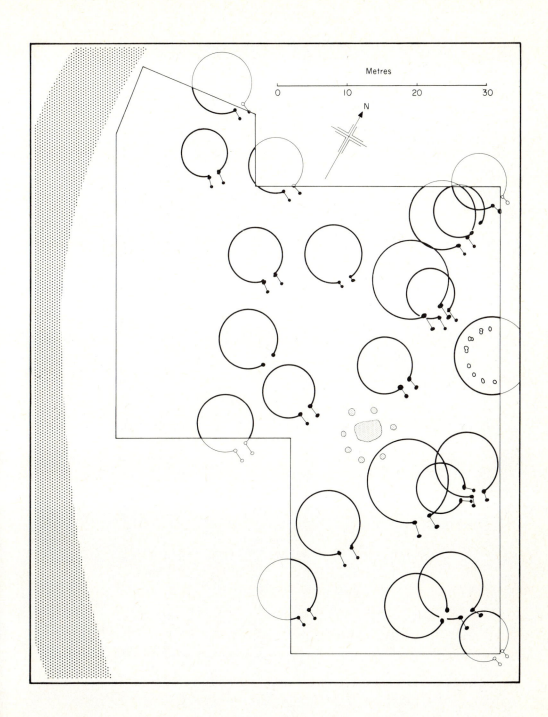

FIG. 7. Moel y Gaer: sketch plan of post-ring round-houses. Strippled area is rampart.

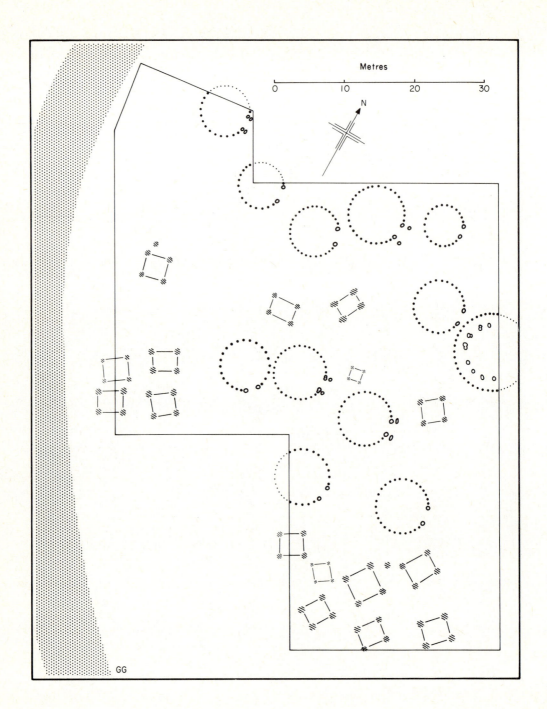

FIG. 8. Moel y Gaer: sketch plan of stake-wall round-houses and four-posters. Stippled area is rampart.

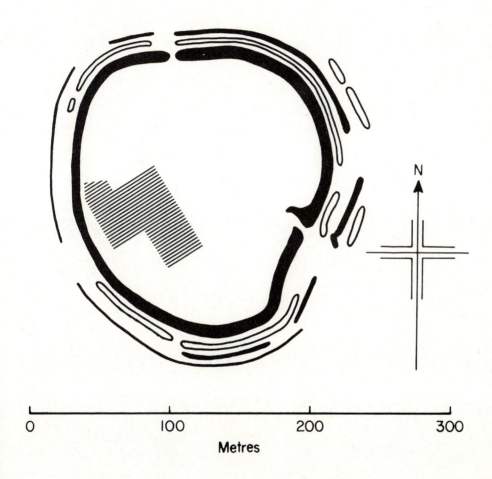

FIG. 9. Moel y Gaer: sketch plan of the earthworks with excavated area shaded.

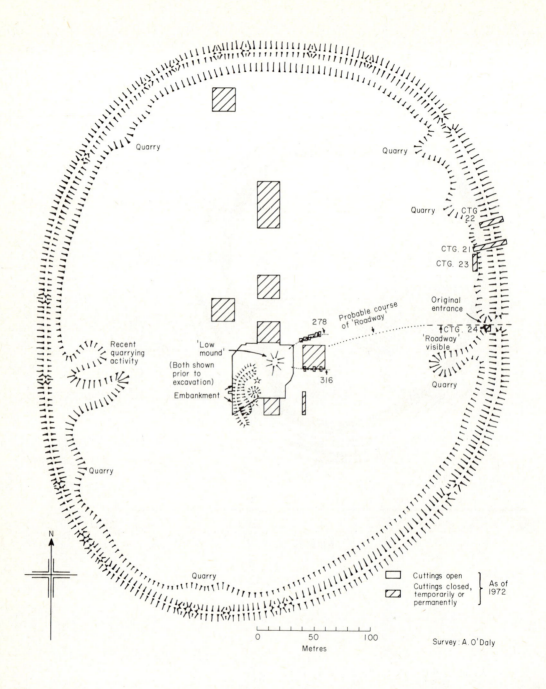

Fig. 1. Dún Ailinne: general site plan, 1972.

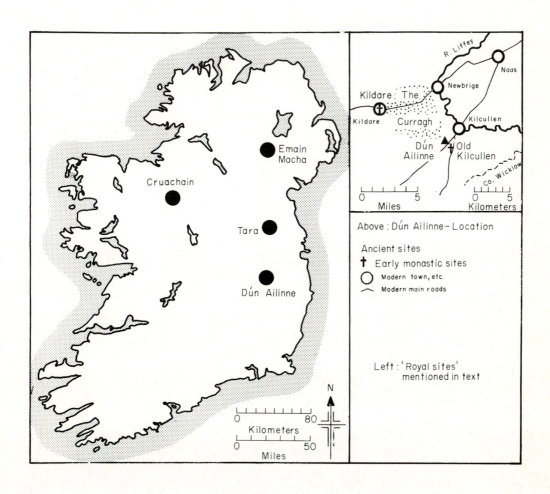

FIG. 2. Dún Ailinne: location map, and Royal Sites in Ireland.

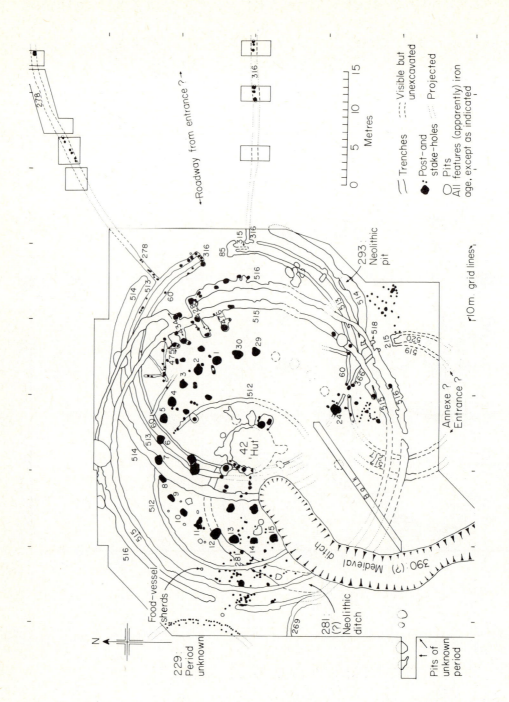

FIG. 3. Dún Ailinne 1972: detailed plan of central area.

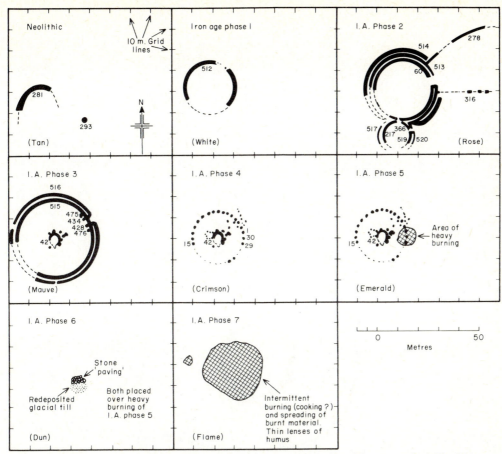

FIG. 4. Dún Ailinne: main identifiable phases, August, 1972. (See Note at end of Ch. 15.)

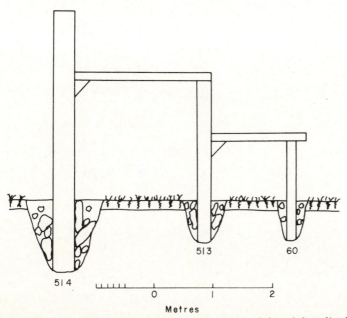

FIG. 5. Dún Ailinne: a suggested reconstruction of the triple palisade trenches of Iron Age phase 2.

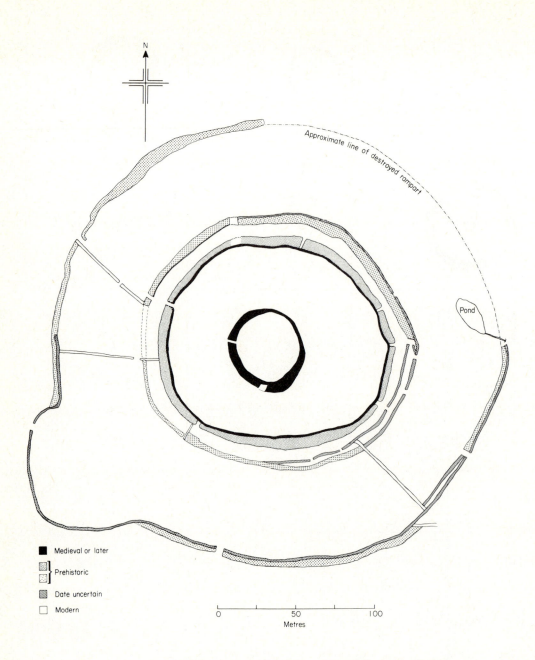

FIG. 1. Rathgall: general site plan.

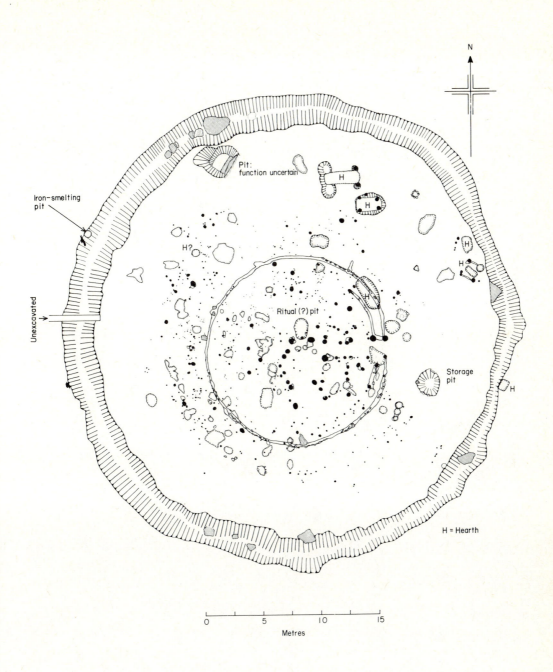

FIG. 2. Rathgall: plan of the central habitation complex.

FIG. 3. Rathgall : plan of penannular ditch and post-hole complex on southern slope outside hillfort.

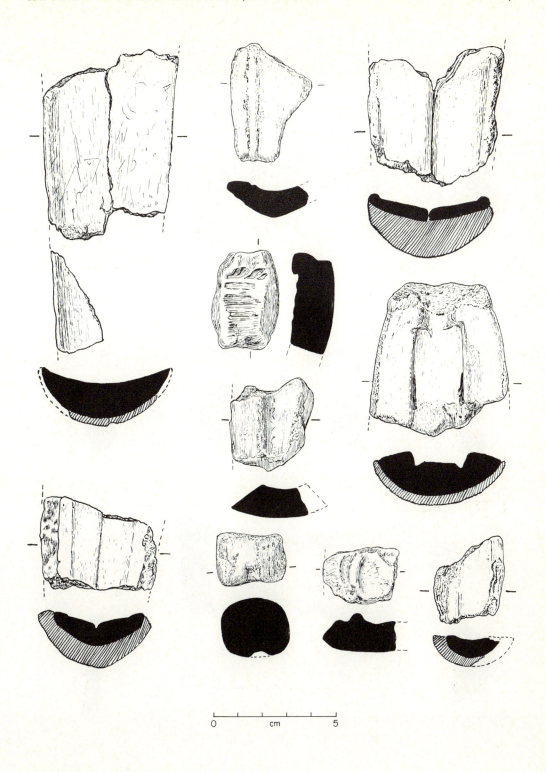

Fig. 4. Rathgall: clay mould fragments.

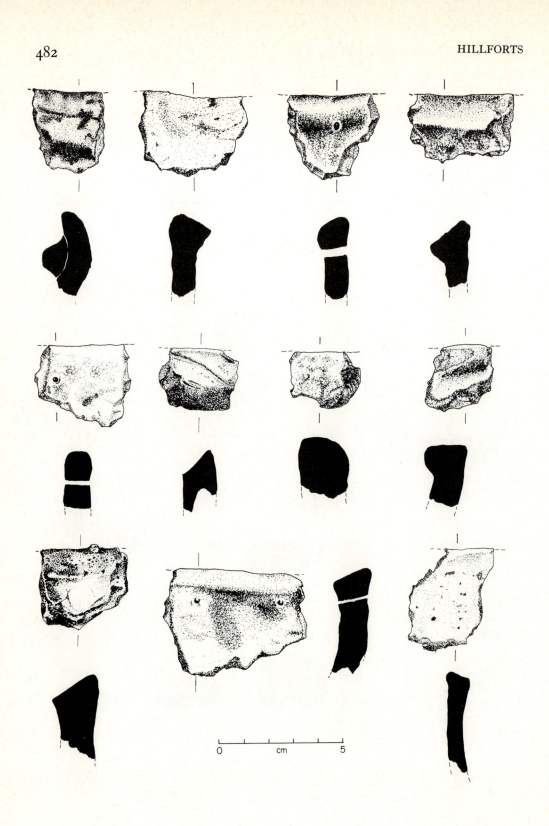

FIG. 5. Rathgall: rim sherds of coarse pottery.

Plates

(Arranged in Chapter Sequence)

Pl. I. St. Catharine's Hill, Winchester in December, 1916. Taken from WSW, on the river Itchen near St. Cross, by the headmaster M. J. Rendall, who later gave it to the author as lantern-slide.

Pl. II. St. Catharine's Hill: east face of Section 2 through the defences, August 1928, before being widened from 4 ft to 8 ft (*SCH* Pl. II, 2).

Pl. III. St. Catharine's Hill: north side of entrance, seen from east, in course of excavation, August, 1927. (Photograph not used in *SCH*.)

Pl. I. Salmonsbury, Gloucestershire: Site I. section of inner rampart with pits below old turf-line.

Pl. II. Salmonsbury, Gloucestershire: Revetment wall in inner rampart, near north-east entrance.

Pl. III. Salmonsbury, Gloucestershire: Site I. Hut I from the south. Period I.

Pl. IV. Salmonsbury, Gloucestershire: Site III. Crouched burial in pit B. Period I.

Pl. V. Salmonsbury, Gloucestershire: Site III. Belgic ditch I from the south. Period II, phase i.

Pl. VI. Salmonsbury, Gloucestershire: Belgic hut I from the south. Period II, phase ii.

Pl. VII. Salmonsbury, Gloucestershire: Site V. north-east entrance from the east.

Pl. VIII. Salmonsbury, Gloucestershire: Site V. north-east entrance from the west.

Pl. IX. Salmonsbury, Gloucestershire: Site III. *Terra nigra* vessel from ditch i. Period II, phase i. Scale ¼.

Pl. X. Salmonsbury, Gloucestershire: Site III. Bronze toilet set found on paving. Period II, phase ii. Scale: ⅟₁.

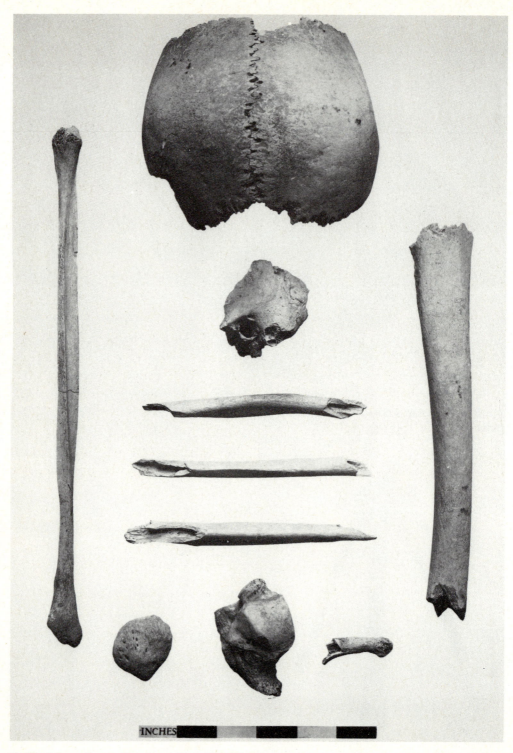

Pl. XI. Salmonsbury, Gloucestershire: Site III. Dissembled bones of young woman from make-up of paving. Period II, phase ii.

Pl. I. Inner rampart. Site 30, Castle Hill, Almondbury. Inner face (a) medieval shale bank, (b) collapsed revetment, multivallate fort (both totally unaffected by burning).

Pl. II. Transverse section. (a) Boundary slabs of inner face, (b) collapsed inner face, (c) base of rampart, clay with timber inserts (unburned), (d) upper part of rampart (fire-reddened and charred timbers).

Pl. I. Blewburton Hill from the west.

Pl. II. Blewburton Hill: Cutting F, 1948, looking west.

Pl. III. Blewburton Hill: Cutting 1, looking north.

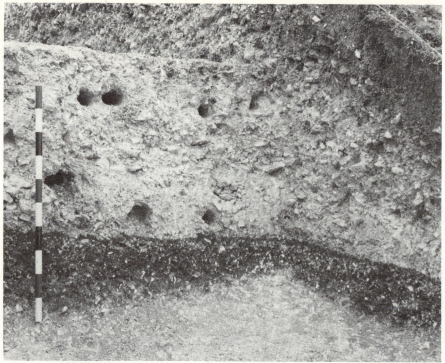

Pl. IV. Blewburton Hill: Cutting 2 (South), showing cavities of timber-laced rampart.

Pl. V. Blewburton Hill: Cutting 2 (South), showing cavities of timber-laced rampart.

Pl. VI. Blewburton Hill: Cutting 2 (South), stains of horizontal timbers from vertically above.

Pl. VII. Blewburton Hill: Cutting 2 (North), showing normal, "negative" and hollow (filled with plaster) post-holes.

Pl. VIII. Blewburton Hill: western entrance with horse-burials, 1949.

Pl. IX. Blewburton Hill: horse-burials in western entrance, Cutting 3.

Pl. I. Ravensburgh Castle: air view looking south, 1971. Arrows indicate the location of the site.

Pl. II. Ravensburgh Castle: from the west: drawn by W. Stukeley in July, 1724.

Pl. III. Ravensburgh Castle: section through southern rampart from interior.

Pl. IV. Ravensburgh Castle: south-east entrance. The causeway built over the filled-in ditch is between the two figures.

Pl. I. Crickley Hill: Period 2 entrance from the south.

Pl. II. Crickley Hill: interior from the south-east showing roundhouse and initial stages of clearance of the longhouses.

Pl. I. Sheep Hill, Dunbartonshire: fragments of moulds.

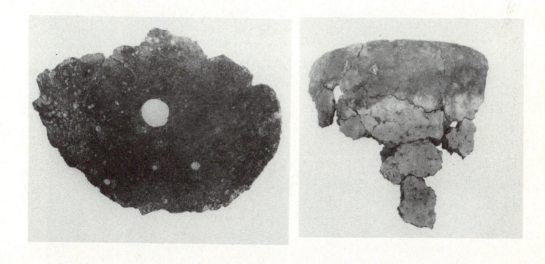

Pl. II. Dun Lagaidh, Ross and
Cromarty: bronze "razor".

Pl. III. Dun Mor Vaul broch,
Tiree: Dunagoil ware vessel.

Pl. IV. Dun Lagaidh, Ross and Cromarty: general view from the west.

Pl. V. Abernethy, Perthshire: beam sockets in interior face of fort wall.

Pl. VI. Dun Lagaidh, Ross and Cromarty: beam sockets (arrowed) and vitrification.

Pl. VII. Dun Lagaidh, Ross and Cromarty: hillfort gateway with dun wall in background.

Pl. VIII. Dun Lagaidh, Ross and Cromarty: dun wall overlying stump of hillfort wall.

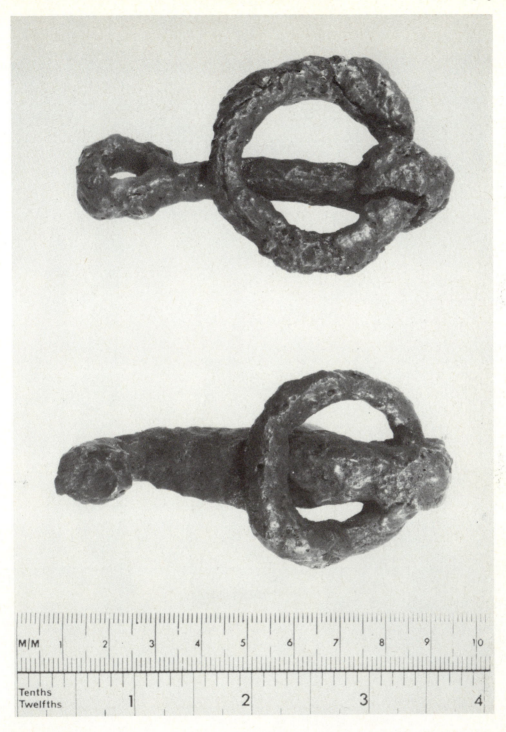

Pl. IX. Dun Lagaidh, Ross and Cromarty: bridle-bit from dun.

Pl. X. Dun Lagaidh, Ross and Cromarty: riveted bronze fragments from dun. Scale × 2.

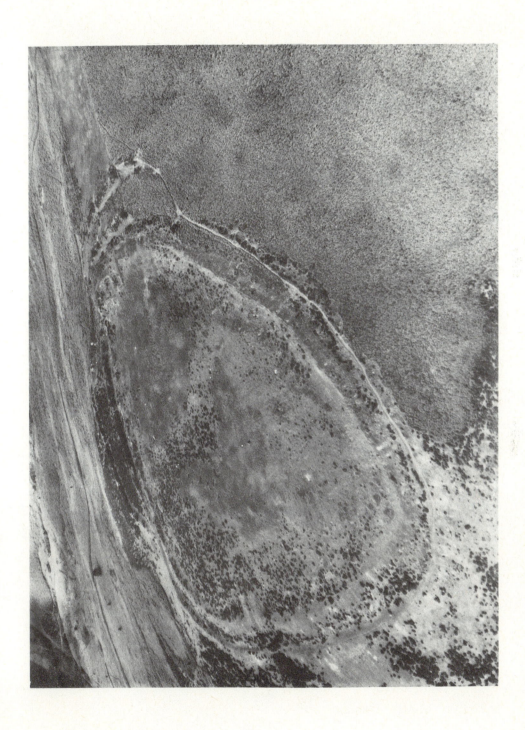

Pl. I. Moel y Gaer, Llanbedr, Denbighshire.

Pl. II. Beacon Ring, Trelystan, Montgomeryshire.

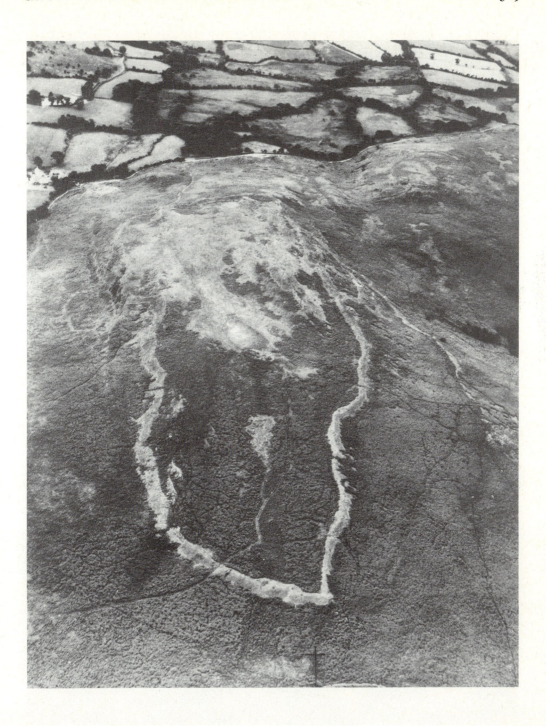

Pl. III. Carn Goch, Llangadog, Carmarthenshire.

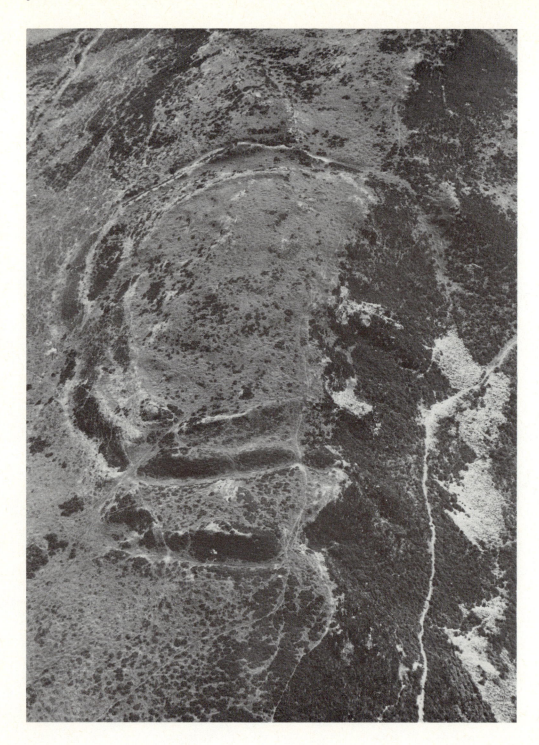

Pl. IV. Ystrad Meurig, Cardiganshire.

Pl. V. Castle Bank, Llansanffraid-yn-Elfael, Radnorshire.

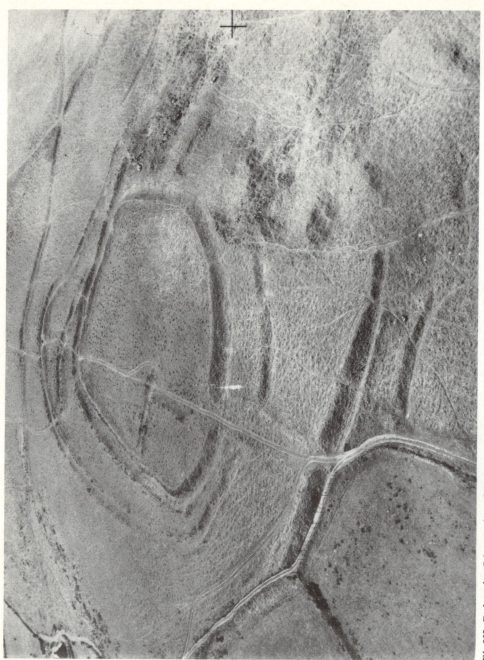

Pl. VI. Bulwarks, Llanmadoc, Glamorganshire.

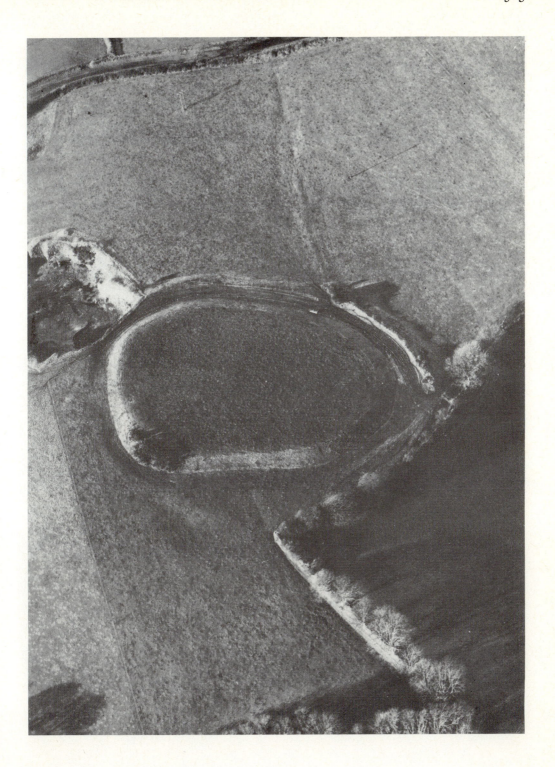

Pl. VII. Vaynor Gaer, Llawhaden, Pembrokeshire.

Pl. VIII. Caer Ddynnaf, Llanblethian, Glamorganshire.

Pl. I. The Breiddin Hills from the east.

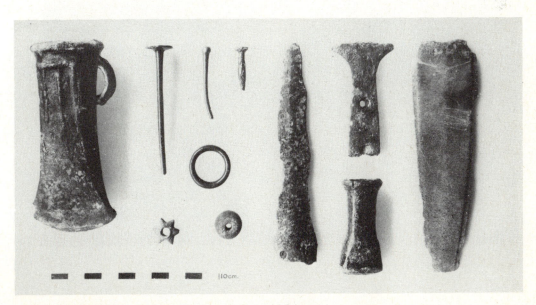

Pl. II. The Breiddin: objects of bronze, amber and faience.

Pl. I. Moel y Gaer: air-view from the south-west. Photo: G. D. B. Jones.

Pl. II. Moel y Gaer: stone pestle and quern *in situ* in one of the yards belonging to the final occupation. Scale 30 cm.

Pl. III. Moel y Gaer: the largest of the post-ring round-houses with four post porch in foreground. Scales 2 m.

Pl. IV. Moel y Gaer: segment of round-house overlain by final phase deposits with rectangular floor area accentuated by differential cleaning. Scales 2 m.

Pl. V. Moel y Gaer: same area as above, with stake-wall and post-ring of underlying round-house fully exposed. Scales 2 m.

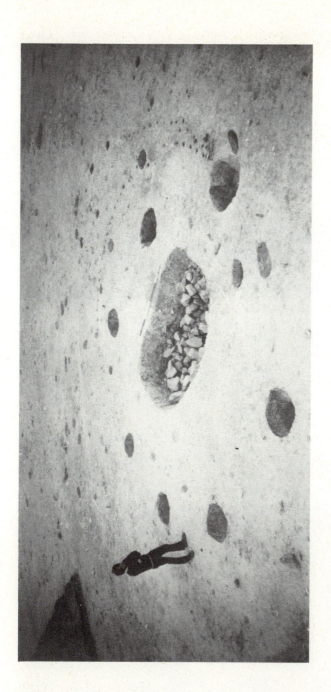

Pl. VI. Moel y Gaer: large sub-rectangular pit surrounded by seven-post circle (see p. 311). Scales 2 m.

Pl. VII. Moel y Gaer: a pair of four-posters. Scales 2 m.

Pl. VIII. Moel y Gaer: a four-poster post-hole with stone packing *in situ* around excavated post-pipe. Scale 30 cm.

Pl. I. Dun Ailinne, Kilcullen, Co. Kildare: air photograph. Photo: Leo Swan.

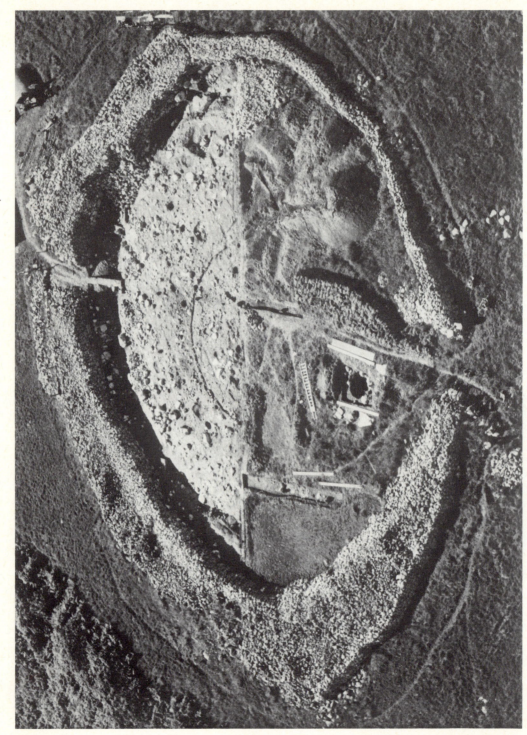

Pl. I. Rathgall: the inner enclosure partly excavated. Photo: Leo Swan.

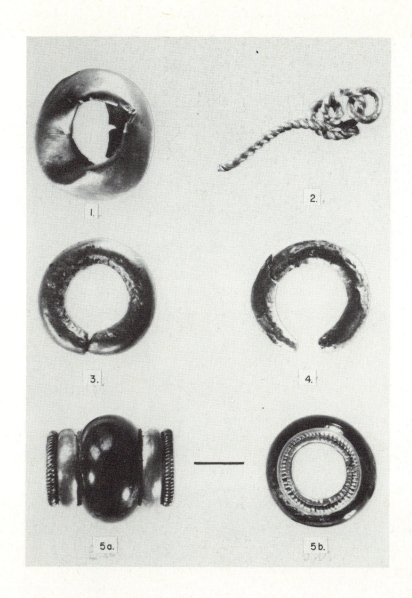

Pl. II. Rathgall: objects of gold. Scale: approx. 3:1.

Pl. III. Rathgall: hut site on southern slope outside hillfort.

Pl. IV. Rathgall: detail of entrance features of hut-site.

Pl. V. Rathgall: penannular ditch and post-hole complex on southern slope outside hillfort.

Pl. VI. Rathgall: circular ditch on southern slope outside hillfort.

Pl. VII. Dunmurry Hill, Co. Kildare: class I, univallate hillfort. Photo: J. K. St. Joseph, Cambridge University Collection.

Pl. VIII. Mooghaun, Co. Clare: class II, multivallate hillfort. Photo: D. D. C. Pochin-Mould.

Pl. IX. Cashel Fort, Co. Cork: class II, multivallate hillfort. Photo: D. D. C. Pochin-Mould.

Pl. X. Caherconree, Co. Kerry: class III, inland promontory fort. Photo: D. D. C. Pochin-Mould.

Pl. XI. Loughshinny, Co. Dublin: coastal promontory fort. Photo: J. K. St. Joseph, Cambridge University Collection.

Bibliography

Abercromby, J. (1912). *The Bronze Age Pottery of Great Britain and Ireland*, 2 vols.

Akerman, J. Y. (1867). "Account of Researches in Anglo-Saxon Cemeteries at Filkins and at Broughton Poggs, Oxfordshire", *Archaeologia*, **37**, 140–146.

Alcock, L. (1960). "Castell Odo: An Embanked Settlement on Mynydd Ystum, Caernarvonshire", *Archaeologia Cambrensis*, **109**, 78–135.

Alcock, L. (1961). "The Winged Objects in the Llyn Fawr Hoard", *Antiquity*, **35**, 149–151.

Alcock, L. (1963a). *Dinas Powys*. University of Wales Press, Cardiff.

Alcock, L. (1963b). "Pottery and Settlements in Wales and the March, A.D. 400–700". In *Culture and Environment* (Essays in Honour of Sir Cyril Fox) (I. Ll. Foster and L. Alcock, eds), pp. 281–302.

Alcock, L. (1965). "Hillforts in Wales and the Marches", *Antiquity*, **39**, 184–195.

Alcock, L. (1967). "Excavations at Degannwy Castle, Caernarvonshire, 1961–6", *Archaeological Journal*, **124**, 190–200.

Alcock, L. (1968). "Cadbury Castle, 1967", *Antiquity*, **42**, 47–51.

Alcock, L. (1969). "Excavations at South Cadbury Castle, 1968: A Summary Report", *Ant. J.*, **49**, 30–40.

Alcock, L. (1970a). "South Cadbury Excavations, 1969", *Antiquity*, **44**, 46–49.

Alcock, L. (1970b). "Excavations at South Cadbury Castle, 1969", *Ant. J.*, **50**, 14–25.

Alcock, L. (1971a). "Excavations at South Cadbury Castle, 1970: A Summary Report", *Ant. J.*, **51**, 1–7.

Alcock, L. (1971b). *Arthur's Britain*. Penguin Books, London.

Alcock, L. (1972a). "The Irish Sea Zone in the Pre-Roman Iron Age", In *The Iron Age in the Irish Sea Province* (C. Thomas, ed.), pp. 99–108. C.B.A., London.

Alcock, L. (1972b). "Excavations at Cadbury-Camelot, 1966–70", *Antiquity*, **46**, 29–38.

Alcock, L. (1972c). *By South Cadbury is that Camelot*. Thames and Hudson, London.

Alcock, L. (1972d). "Review of Savory: Excavations at Dinorben, 1965–9", *Antiquity*, **46**, 330–331.

Alcock, L. and Jones, G.R.J. (1962) "Settlement Patterns in Celtic Britain", *Antiquity*, **36**, 51–55.

Allcroft, H. (1908). *Earthwork of England*.

Allen, D.F. (1958). "The Origins of Coinage in Britain: A Reappraisal". In *Problems of the Iron Age in Southern Britain* (S.S. Frere, ed.), pp. 97–308. C.B.A., London.

Allen, D.F. (1961). "A Study of the Dobunnic Coinage". In Clifford (1961), pp. 75–149.

Allen D.F. (1963). *Sylloge of Coins of the British Isles: The Coins of the Coritani*. London.

Allen, D. F. (1967). "Iron Currency Bars in Britain", *Proc. Prehist. Soc.*, **33**, 307–335.

Allen, D. F. (1968). "The Celtic Coins". In Richmond (1968), 43–57.

Anderson, James (1779). "An Account of Ancient Monuments and Fortifications in the Highlands of Scotland", *Archaeologia*, **5**, 24–66.

Anderson, J. (1883). *Scotland in Pagan Times, Vol. 2. The Iron Age*. Edinburgh.

Anthony, I. E. (1958). *The Iron Age Camp at Poston, Herefordshire*. The Woolhope Club, Hereford.

Applebaum, S. (1954). "The Agriculture of the British Early Iron Age as Exemplified at Figheldean Down, Wiltshire", *Proc. Prehist. Soc.*, **20**, 103–114.

Armitage, E. S. and Montgomerie, D. H. (1912). "Ancient Earthworks", *V.C.H. Yorkshire*, **II**, 1–71.

Avery, D. M. E. (1973). "British la Tène Decorated Pottery: An Outline", *Études Celtiques*, **13**, 522–551.

Avery, D. M. E. (forthcoming). "Caesar and Cassivellaunus". In *Archaeology into History*, Vol. 2 (C. F. C. and S. C. Hawkes, eds). Dent, London.

Avery, D. M. E., and Close-Brooks, J. (1969). "Shearplace Hill, Sydling St Nicholas, House A: A Suggested Reinterpretation", *Proc. Prehist. Soc.* **35**, 345–351.

Avery, D. M. E., Sutton, J. E. G. and Banks, J. W. (1967). "Rainsborough, Northants, England: Excavations 1961–5", *Proc. Prehist. Soc.*, **33,** 207–306.

Babbidge, A. V. (1970). *Archaeology in Wales*, **10,** 12.
Babbidge, A. V. and Williams, E. (1971). *Archaeology in Wales*, **11,** 12–13.
Balcarres, A., Allcroft, A. H. *et al.* (1910). *Scheme for Recording Ancient Defensive Earthworks and Fortified Enclosures.* Congress of Archaeological Societies in Union with the Society of Antiquaries of London, Taunton.
Barlow, E. and Robertson, A. (1974). "The Dun Lagaidh Hoard of Short Cross Sterlings", *Glasgow Arch. Journ.* **3,** 78–81.
Barton, K. L. (1962). "Settlements of the Early Iron Age and Pagan Saxon Periods at Linford, Essex". *Trans. Essex Arch. Soc.*, 3rd series, **1,** 57–104.
Bateman, T. (1848). *Vestiges of the Antiquities of Derbyshire.*
Bateson, J. D. (1973). "Roman Material from Ireland: A Re-consideration", *Proc. Royal Irish Academy*, **73C,** 21–97.
Behn, F. (1936). *Urgeschichte von Starkenburg.* Mainz.
Behrens, G. (1912). "Neue Funde aus dem Kastell Mainz", *Mainzer Zeitschrift*, **7,** 82–109.
Benoît, F. (1945). *L'Art primitif Méditerranéen de la Vallée du Rhone: la Sculpture.* Éditions d'Art et d'Histoire, Paris.
Benton, S. (1931). "The Excavation of the Sculptor's Cave, Covesea, Morayshire", *Proc. Soc. Ant. Scot.*, **65** (1930–1931), 177–216.
Bersu, G. (1940). "Excavations at Little Woodbury, Wiltshire", *Proc. Prehist. Soc.*, **6,** 30–111.
Bersu, G. (1945). *Das Wittnauer Horn im Kanton Aargau.* Monographien zur Ur-und-frühgeschichte der Schweiz, Bd. 1V.
Bersu, G. (1946). "A Hill-Fort in Switzerland", *Antiquity* **20,** 4–8.
Bersu, G. (1948). *Scot. Reg. Group* (C.B.A.), 2nd Report, p. 5.
Bersu, G. and Griffiths, W. E. (1949). "Concentric Circles at Llwyn-du-Bach, Penygroes, Caernarvonshire", *Archaeologia Cambrensis*, **100,** 173–206.
Bevan-Evans, M. (1963). *Archaeology in Wales*, **3,** 6.
Bevan-Evans, M. (1964). *Archaeology in Wales*, **4,** 7.
Biddle, M. (1970). "Excavations at Winchester, 1969: Eighth Interim Report", *Ant. J.* **50,** 277–326.
Biddle, M. and B. K. (1970). "Metres, Areas and Robbing", *World Arch.*, **I,** 208–219.
Binchy, D. A. (1970). *Celtic and Anglo-Saxon Kingship*, O'Donnell Lectures for 1967–1968. Oxford.
Birchall, A. (1965). "The Aylesford-Swarling Culture: The Problem of the Belgae Reconsidered", *Proc. Prehist. Soc.*, **31,** 241–367.
Blundell, J. D. and Longworth, I. H. (1957). "A Bronze Age Hoard from Portfield Farm, Whalley, Lancashire", *British Museum Quarterly*, **XXXII,** Nos. 1–2, 8–14.
Bonney, D. (1972). "Early Boundaries in Wessex". In *Archaeology and the Landscape* (P. J. Fowler, ed.), pp. 168–186. London.
Boon, G. C. (1969). "Belgic and Roman Silchester: The Excavations of 1954–8 with an Excursus on the Early History of Calleva", *Archaeologia*, **102,** 1–81.
Bowen, E. G. and Gresham, C. A. (1967). *History of Merioneth*, *Vol. I.*, Dolgellau, 1967.
Bowen, H. C. (1961). *Ancient Fields.* British Association for the Advancement of Science.
Bowen, H. C. (1966). "Romano-British Rural Settlements in Dorset and Wiltshire, I: Origins and Types of Settlement". In *Rural Settlement in Roman Britain* (A. C. Thomas, ed.), pp. 43–53. C.B.A., London.
Bowen, H. C. (1967). "Corn Storage in Antiquity", *Antiquity*, **41,** 214–216.
Bowen, H. C. (1969). "The Celtic Background". In *The Roman Villa in Britain.* (A. L. F. Rivet, ed.), pp. 1–48. London.
Bowen, H. C. (1972). "Air Photography: Some Implications in the South of England". In *Archaeology and the Landscape* (P. J. Fowler, ed.), pp. 38–49. London.
Bradford, J. S. P. (1940). "The Excavation of Cherbury Camp, 1939", *Oxoniensia*, **5,** 13–20.
Bradford, J. S. P. (1942). "An Early Iron Age Site on Blewburton Hill, Berks.", *Berks. Arch. J.*, **46,** 97–104.
Bradley, R. (1968). "The South Oxfordshire Grim's Ditch and its Significance", *Oxoniensia*, **33,** 1–13.
Bradley, R. (1971a). "Stock-raising and the Origins of the Hillfort on the South Downs", *Ant. J.*, **51,** 8–29.

Bradley, R. (1971b). "A Field Survey of the Chichester Entrenchments". In Cunliffe (1971b), pp. 17–36.

Bradley, R. (1971c). "Economic Change in the Growth of Early Hillforts". In *The Iron Age and its Hill-forts* (M. Jesson and D. Hill, eds), pp. 71–83. Southampton University Archaeological Society, Southampton.

Brailsford, J. W. (1948). "Excavations at Little Woodbury, Wiltshire (1938–39), Part II", *Proc. Prehist. Soc.*, **14**, 1–18.

Brailsford, J. W. (1958). "Early Iron Age C in Wessex", *Proc. Prehist. Soc.*, **24**, 101–119.

Breeze, D. J. and Dobson, B. (1972). "Hadrian's Wall: Some Problems", *Britannia*, **3**, 182–208.

Bren, J. (1971). "The Present State of Research into the Problems of Celtic Oppida in Central Europe", *Bulletin of the University of London, Institute of Archaeology*, **10**, 13–22.

Bretz-Mahler, D. (1961). "Musée d'Epernay: Catalogue de la Céramique des Cimetières de l'Epoque de la Tène I", *Mémoires de la Societé d'Agriculture, Commerce, Sciences et Arts de la Marne* (Châlons-sur-Marne) (1961), 8–60.

Bretz-Mahler, D. (1971). *La Civilisation de la Tène I en Champagne: le Faciès marnien.* 23° supplement to *Gallia*. Paris.

Brewster, T. C. M. (1963). *The Excavation of Staple Howe* (Published privately, Malton, Yorks.).

Britton, D. and Longworth, I. H. (1968). "Late Bronze Age Finds in the Heathery Burn Cave, Co. Durham", *Inventaria Archaeologia.* 9th set, G.B. 55.

Brodribb, A. C. C., Hands, A. R. and Walker, D. R. (1972). *Excavations at Shakenoak, Vol. III.*

Brothwell, D. R. (1961). "Cannibalism in Early Britain", *Antiquity*, **35**, 304–307.

Brothwell, D. R., Bishop, A. C. and Woolley, A. R. (1974). "Vitrified Forts in Scotland: A Problem in Interpretation and Primitive Technology", *Journ. Arch. Science*, **I**, 101–107.

Bulleid, A., (1958). *The Lake Villages of Somerset*, 5th edition. Glastonbury Antiquarian Society.

Bulleid, A. and Gray, H. St. G. (1911). *The Glastonbury Lake Village, Vol. I.*

Bulleid, A. and Gray, H. St. G. (1917). *The Glastonbury Lake Village, Vol. II.*

Bulleid, A. and Gray, H. St. G. (1948). *The Meare Lake Village, Vol. I.*

Bulleid, A. and Gray, H. St. G. (1953). *The Meare Lake Village, Vol. II.* See also Cotton (1966).

Burgess, C. B. (1968a). "The Later Bronze Age in the British Isles and North-western France", *Arch. J.* **125**, 1–45.

Burgess, C. B. (1968b). *Bronze Age Metalwork in Northern England, c.* 1000 to 700 *B.C.*, Oriel Press, Newcastle upon Tyne.

Burgess, C. B. (1970). "The Bronze Age", *Current Arch.*, **19**, 208–15.

Burleigh, R. and Switzur, V. R. (1973). "The Radiocarbon Calendar Recalibrated Too Soon?", *Antiquity*, **47**, 309–17.

Burley, E. (1956). "A Catalogue and Survey of the Metalwork from Traprain Law", *Proc. Soc. Ant. Scot.* **89**, 118–226.

Burrow, E. (1919). *Ancient Camps . . . of Gloucestershire.*

Burrow, E. J. *et al.* (1925). "Excavations on Leckhampton Hill, Cheltenham", *Trans. Bristol and Gloucester Arch. Soc.*, **47**, 81–112.

Burstow, G. P. and Holleyman, G. A. (1964). "Excavations at Ranscombe Camp, 1959–60", *Sussex Arch. Coll.*, **102**, 55–67.

Bushe-Fox, J. P. (1915). *Excavations at Hengistbury Head, Hampshire, in* 1911–12. Society of Antiquaries, Research Report No. 3.

Bushe-Fox, J. P. (1949). *Fourth Report on the Excavation of the Roman Fort at Richborough, Kent.* Society of Antiquaries, Research Report No. 16.

Calder, C. S. T. and Steer, K. A. (1949). "Dun Lagaidh and Four Other Prehistoric Monuments in the Ullapool area", *Proc. Soc. Ant. Scot.*, **83** (1948–1949), pp. 68–76.

Camden, W. (1587). *Britannia*, 2nd ed.

Camden, W. (1789). *Britannia*, translated from the edition of 1607 by R. Gough, 3 vols.

Chadwick, S. (1958). "Early Iron Age Enclosures on Longbridge Deverill Cow Down, Wiltshire". In *Problems of the Iron Age in Southern Britain* (S. S. Frere, ed.), pp. 18–20. C.B.A., London.

Champion, S. (1971a). "The Hillforts of the Cotswold Scarp, with Special Reference to Recent Excavations", *Proc. Cheltenham Nat. Field Club*, 18–23.

Champion, S. (1971b). "Excavations at Leckhampton Hill, 1969–70 Interim Report", *Trans. Bristol and Gloucester Arch. Soc.*, **90**, 5–21.

Champion, T. (1971). "The End of the Irish Bronze Age", *North Munster Antiquarian Journal*, **14**, 17–24.

Childe, V. G. (1933). "Excavations at Castlelaw Fort, Midlothian", *Proc. Soc. Ant. Scot.*, **67** (1932–1933), 362–88.

Childe, V. G. (1935a). *The Prehistory of Scotland*. Edinburgh.

Childe, V. G. (1935b). "Excavation of the Vitrified Fort of Finavon, Angus", *Proc. Soc. Ant. Scot.*, **69** (1934–1935), 49–80.

Childe, V. G. (1936). "Supplementary Excavations at the Vitrified Fort of Finavon", *Proc. Soc. Ant. Scot.*, **70**, (1935–1936), 347–52.

Childe, V. G. (1940). *Prehistoric Communities of the British Isles*. London and Edinburgh.

Childe, V. G. (1946). *Scotland before the Scots*. Edinburgh.

Childe, V. G. and Thorneycroft, W. (1938a). "The Vitrified Fort at Rahoy, Morvern, Argyll", *Proc. Soc. Ant. Scot.*, **72** (1937–1938), 23–43.

Childe, V. G. and Thorneycroft, W. (1938b). "The Experimental Production of the Phenomena Distinctive of Vitrified Forts", *Proc. Soc. Ant. Scot.*, **72** (1937–1938), 44–55.

Chitty, L. F. C. (1937). "How did the Hill-fort Builders Reach the Breiddin? A Tentative Explanation", *Archaeologia Cambrensis*, **92,** 129–150.

Christison, D. (1889). "The Duns and Forts of Lorne, Nether Lochaber, and the Neighbourhood", *Proc. Soc. Ant. Scot.*, **23** (1888–1889), 368–434.

Christison, D. (1898). *Early Fortifications in Scotland*, Rhind Lectures for 1894. Edinburgh and London.

Christison, D. and Anderson, J. (1899). "On the Recently Excavated Fort on Castle Law, Abernethy, Perthshire", *Proc. Soc. Ant. Scot.*, **33** (1898–1899), 13–33.

Christison, D. and Ross, T. (1905). "Report on the Society's Excavations on the Poltalloch Estate, Argyll in 1904–5", *Proc. Soc. Ant. Scot.*, **39**, (1904–1905), 259–322.

Clark, J. G. D. (1934). "Derivative Forms of the *petit tranchet* in Britain", *Arch. J.*, **91,** 32–58.

Clark, J. G. D. (1952). *Prehistoric Europe: the Economic Basis*. Methuen, London.

Clark, J. G. D. and Fell, C. I. (1953), "The Early Iron Age at Micklemoor Hill, West Harling, Norfolk, and its Pottery", *Proc. Prehist. Soc.*, **19,** 1–40.

Clarke, D. L. (1968). *Analytical Archaeology*. London.

Clarke, D. L. (1970). *Beaker Pottery of Great Britain and Ireland*, 2 vols. Cambridge.

Clarke, D. L. (1972). "A Provisional Model of an Iron Age Society and its Settlement System". In *Models in Archaeology* (D. L. Clarke, ed.), pp. 801–869.

Clarke, D. V. (1970). "Bone Dice and the Scottish Iron Age", *Proc. Prehist. Soc.*, **36,** 214–232.

Clarke, D. V. (1971). "Small Finds in the Atlantic Province: Problems of Approach", *Scottish Arch. Forum*, 22–54.

Clarke, R. R. (1954). "The Early Iron Age Treasure from Snettisham, Norfolk", *Proc. Prehist. Soc.*, **20,** 27–86.

Clay, R. C. C. (1924). "An Early Iron Age Site on Fyfield Bavant Down", *Wilts. Arch. Mag.*, **42,** 457–496.

Clay, R. C. C. (1925–7). "Swallowcliffe Down", *Wilts. Arch. Mag.*, **43** (1925), 59–93; (1927), 540–547.

Clifford, E. M. (1930). "A Prehistoric and Roman Site at Barnwood near Gloucester", *Trans. Bristol and Gloucester Arch. Soc.*, **52,** 201–254.

Clifford, E. M. (1934). "An Early Iron Age Site and Finds at Barnwood, Gloucester", *Trans. Bristol and Gloucester Arch. Soc.*, **56,** 227–235.

Clifford, E. M. (1937). "The Earthworks at Rodborough, Amberley and Minchinhampton, Gloucestershire", *Trans. Bristol and Gloucester Arch. Soc.*, **59,** 287–308.

Clifford, E. M. (1961). *Bagendon, a Belgic Oppidum*. Cambridge.

Close-Brooks, J. and Gibson, S. (1966). "A Round Hut Near Rome", *Proc. Prehist. Soc.*, **32,** 349–352.

Clutterbuck, T. (1817). *History of Hertfordshire*, Vol. 3.

Coblenz, W. (1966). "Zür Frage der befestigten Siedlungen der Lausitzer Kultur", *Actes du VIIe Congrès International des Sciences Préhistoriques et Protohistoriques*, pp. 715–719. Prague.

Coles, J. M. (1959). "Scottish Swan's Neck Sunflower Pins", *Proc. Soc. Ant. Scot.*, **92** (1958–1959), 1–9.

Coles, J. M. (1960). "Scottish Late Bronze Age Metalwork", *Proc. Soc. Ant. Scot.*, **93** (1959–1960), 16–134.

Coles, J. M. (1969). "Scottish Early Bronze Age Metalwork", *Proc. Soc. Ant. Scot.*, **101** (1968–1969), 70–72.

Collingwood, R. G. and Richmond, I. (1969). *The Archaeology of Roman Britain*. Methuen, London.

Collins, A. E. P. (1947). "Excavations on Blewburton Hill, 1947", *Berks. Arch. J.*, **50**, 4–29.

Collins, A. E. P. (1952). "Excavations on Blewburton Hill, 1948–49", *Berks. Arch. J.*, **53**, 21–64.

Collins, A. E. P. and F. J. (1959). "Excavations on Blewburton Hill, Berks, 1953", *Berks. Arch. J.*, **57**, 52–73.

Collis, J. (1968). "Excavations at Owslebury, Hants: An Interim Report", *Ant. J.*, **48**, 18–31.

Collis, J. (1970). "Excavations at Owslebury, Hants: A Second Interim Report", *Ant. J.*, **50**, 246–261.

Collis, J. (1973). "Manching Reviewed", *Antiquity*, **47**, 280–283.

Colvin, H. M. (1959). "An Iron Age Hillfort at Dover ?", *Antiquity*, **33**, 125–127.

Coombs, D. G. (1967). "Mam Tor, 1967", *Derbyshire Arch. J.*, **87**, 158–159.

Coombs, D. G. (1971). "Mam Tor: A Bronze Age Hillfort ?", *Current Arch.*, **27**, 100–102.

Corcoran, J. X. W. P. (1952). "Tankards and Tankard Handles of the British Early Iron Age", *Proc. Prehist. Soc.*, **18**, 85–102.

Cotton, Mrs. M. A. (1947). "Excavations at Silchester 1938–9", *Archaeologia*, **92**, 121–167.

Cotton, Mrs. M. A. (1954). "British Camps with Timber-Laced Ramparts", *Arch. J.*, **111**, 26–105.

Cotton, Mrs. M. A. (1957). "Appendix: Muri Gallici". In Wheeler and Richardson (1957), 159–216.

Cotton, Mrs. M. A. (1958). "Observations on the Classification of Hill-Forts in Southern England". In *Problems of the Iron Age in Southern Britain* (S. S. Frere, ed.), pp. 61–68. C.B.A., London.

Cotton, Mrs. M. A. (1959) "Cornish Cliff Castles: A Survey", *Proc. West Cornwall Field Club*, **2**(3) (1958–1959), 113–121.

Cotton, Mrs. M. A. (1961). "The Pre-Belgic Iron Age Cultures of Gloucestershire". In Clifford (1961), 22–42.

Cotton, Mrs. M. A. (1962). "Berkshire Hillforts", *Berks. Arch. J.*, **60**, 30–52.

Cotton, Mrs. M. A. (1966). *The Meare Lake Village, Vol. III*.

Cotton, M. A. and Frere, S. S. (1968). "Ivinghoe Beacon Excavations, 1963–5", *Records of Bucks*, **18**, 187–260.

Cowen, J. D. (1951). "The Earliest Bronze Swords in Britain and their Origins on the Continent of Europe", *Proc. Prehist. Soc.*, **17**, 195–213.

Cowen, J. D. (1967). "The Hallstatt Sword of Bronze: On the Continent and in Britain", *Proc. Prehist. Soc.*, **33**, 377–454.

Cowen, J. D. (1971). "A Striking Maritime Distribution Pattern", *Proc. Prehist. Soc.*, **37**, 154–166.

Cram, C. L. (1967). "Report on the Animal Bones from Hockwold". In Salway (1967), 75–80.

Crawford, O. G. S. (1924). *Air Survey and Archaeology*. Ordnance Survey Professional Paper No. 7. H.M.S.O.

Crawford, O. G. S. (1928). *Air Survey and Archaeology*. Ordnance Survey Professional Papers, new series, No. 7 (second edition). H.M.S.O.

Crawford, O. G. S. and Keiller, A. (1928). *Wessex from the Air*. Oxford.

Cree, J. E. (1923). "Excavations on Traprain Law", *Proc. Soc. Ant. Scot.*, **57** (1922–1923), 180–225.

Cree, J. E. (1924). "Excavations on Traprain Law", *Proc. Soc. Ant. Scot.*, **58** (1923–1924), 241–285.

Cree, J. E. and Curle, A. O. (1921). "Excavations on Traprain Law", *Proc. Soc. Ant. Scot.*, **55** (1920–1921), 153–206.

Cree, J. E. and Curle, A. O. (1922). "Account of the Excavations on Traprain Law . . . in 1921", *Proc. Soc. Ant. Scot.*, **56** (1921–1922), 189–259.

Crittall, E. (1973). *A History of Wiltshire, Vol. I, part 2*. Victoria County Histories, Oxford.

Cross, T. P. and Slover, C. H. (1973). *Ancient Irish Tales*, 2nd edition, with revised bibliography by C. W. Dunn. Dublin.

Crossley, D. W. (1963). "List of Hill-Forts and other Earthworks in Pembrokeshire", *Bulletin of the Board of Celtic Studies*, **20**, 171–205.

Crossley, D. W. (1964). "Excavations at Merryborough Camp, Wiston, a Pembrokeshire Protected Enclosure, 1963", *Bulletin of the Board of Celtic Studies*, **21**, 105–118.

Crossley, D. W. (1965). "Excavations at Knock Rath, Clarbeston, 1962", *Bulletin of the Board of Celtic Studies*, **21**, 264–275.

Cruden, S. H. (1940). "The Ramparts of Traprain Law: Excavations in 1939", *Proc. Soc. Ant. Scot.*, **74**, (1939–1940), 48–59.

Cunliffe, B. (1964). *Winchester Excavations*, 1949–1960, *I*. Mus. and Lib. Committee, City of Winchester.

Cunliffe, B. (1966). "Stoke Clump, Hollingbury, and the Early pre-Roman Iron Age in Sussex", *Sussex Arch. Coll.*, **104**, 109–20.

Cunliffe, B. (1968). "Excavations at Eldon's Seat, Encombe, Dorset", *Proc. Prehist. Soc.*, **34**, 191–237.

Cunliffe, B. (1970). "Danebury", *Current Arch.*, **18**, 191–3.

Cunliffe, B. (1971a). "Danebury, Hampshire: First Interim Report on the Excavation, 1969–1970", *Ant. J.*, **51**, 240–252.

Cunliffe, B. (1971b). *Excavations at Fishbourne* 1961–1969, *Vol. I.*, *The Site*. Society of Antiquaries Research Report No. 26. Oxford.

Cunliffe, B. (1971c). "Aspects of Hill-Forts and Their Cultural Environments". In *The Iron Age and its Hill-forts* (M. Jesson and D. Hill, eds), pp. 53–69. Southampton University Archaeological Society, Southampton.

Cunliffe, B. (1972a). "Danebury", *Current Arch.*, **30**, 177–183.

Cunliffe, B. (1972b). *Archaeological Excavations* 1971, pp. 48–50. H.M.S.O.

Cunliffe, B. (1973). "The Early Pre-Roman Iron Age, *c.* 650–*c.* 400 B.C." In *A History of Wiltshire*, *Vol. I. pt.* 2 (E. Crittall ed.), pp. 407–438.

Cunliffe, B. and Phillipson, D. W. (1968). "Excavations at Eldon's Seat, Encombe, Dorset, England", *Proc. Prehist. Soc.*, **34**, 191–237.

Cunnington, M. E. (1908). "Olivers Camp, Devizes", *Wilts. Arch. Mag.*, **35**, 408–444.

Cunnington, M. E. (1909). "Notes on a Late Celtic Rubbish Heap near Oare", *Wilts. Arch. Mag.*, **36, 125**–139.

Cunnington, M. E. (1912). "A Late Celtic Inhabited Site at All Cannings Cross Farm", *Wilts. Arch. Mag.*, **37**, 526–538.

Cunnington, M. E. (1913). "Casterley Camp Excavations", *Wilts. Arch. Mag.*, **38,** 53–105.

Cunnington, M. E. (1917). "Lidbury Camp", *Wilts. Arch. Mag.*, **40,** 12–36.

Cunnington, M. E. (1923). *The Early Iron Age Inhabited Site at All Cannings Cross Farm near Devizes, Wiltshire.*

Cunnington, M. E. (1925). "Figsbury Rings. An Account of Excavations in 1924", *Wilts. Arch. Mag.*, **43,** 48–58.

Cunnington, M. E. (1932). "Chisbury Camp", *Wilts. Arch. Mag.*, **46,** 4–7.

Cunnington, M. E. (1933). "Excavations in Yarnbury Castle Camp, 1932", *Wilts. Arch. Mag.*, **46,** 198–213.

Curle, A. O. (1914). "Report on the Excavation, in September 1913, of a Vitrified Fort at Rockcliffe, Dalbeattie, known as the Mote of Mark", *Proc. Soc. Ant. Scot.*, **48** (1913–1914), 125–168.

Curle, A. O. (1915). "Excavations on Traprain Law", *Proc. Soc. Ant. Scot.*, **49**, (1914–1915), 139–202.

Curle, A. O. (1920). "Excavations on Traprain Law", *Proc. Soc. Ant. Scot.*, **54** (1919–1920), 54–123.

Curle, A. O. (1923). *The Traprain Treasure*. Glasgow.

Curle, A. O. (1941). "An Account of the Partial Excavation of a "Wag" or Galleried Building at Forse, in the Parish of Latheron, Caithness", *Proc. Soc. Ant. Scot.*, **75** (1940–1941), 23–39.

Curle, A. O. (1948). "The 'Wag' of Forse, Caithness", *Proc. Soc. Ant. Scot.*, **82** (1947–1948), 275–283.

Curle, A. O. and Cree, J. E. (1916). "Excavations on Traprain Law", *Proc. Soc. Ant. Scot.*, **50** (1915–1916), 64–144.

Curwen, E. C. (1929). "Excavations in the Trundle, Goodwood, 1928", *Sussex Arch. Coll.*, **70**, 33–85.

Curwen, E. C. (1931). "Excavations in the Trundle: Second Season 1930", *Sussex Arch. Coll.*, **72**, 100–150.

Curwen, E. C. (1932). "Excavations at Hollingbury Camp, Sussex", *Ant. J.*, **12**, 1–16.

Curwen, E. C. (1937). *The Archaeology of Sussex*, 1st edition. London.

Curwen, E. C. (1954). *The Archaeology of Sussex*, 2nd edition. Methuen, London.

Curwen, E. and Curwen, E. C. (1927). "Excavations in the Caburn, near Lewes", *Sussex Arch. Coll.*, **68**, 1–56.

Curwen, E. and Hawkes, C. F. C. (1931). "Prehistoric Remains from Kingston Buci", *Sussex Arch. Coll.*, **72**, 185–217.

Curwen, E. C. and Williamson, R. P. R. (1931). "The Date of Cissbury Camp", *Ant. J.*, **11**, 14–36.

Damon, P. E., Long, A. and Wallick, E. I. (1972). "Dendrochronologic Calibration of the Carbon-14 Time Scale". In *Proceedings of the Eighth International Radiocarbon Dating Conference, New Zealand* Vol. I. (T. A. Rafter and T. Grant-Taylor, eds), pp. A29–A43.

Dastugue, J. (1971). "Merri:—Camp de Biere", *Gallia Préhistoire*, **14**, 336.

Davies, A. G. (1964). "The Excavation at The Bulwark, Llanmadoc, Glam.", *Bulletin of the Board of Celtic Studies*, **21**, 100–104.

Davies, J. L. (1966). *Archaeology in Wales*, **6,** 7.

Davies, J. L. (1967a). *Archaeology in Wales*, **7,** 7.

Davies, J. L. (1967b). "Recent Archaeological Discovery and Excavation in Glamorgan: Late Iron Age and Roman Periods", *Morgannwg*, **11,** 75–78.

Davies, J. L. (1969). *Archaeology in Wales*, **9,** 9ff.

Davies, J. L. (1970). *Archaeology in Wales*, **10,** 9ff.

Davies, J. L. (1971). *Archaeology in Wales*, **11,** 8ff.

Davies, J. L. and Bevan Evans, M. (1969). *Archaeology in Wales*, **9,** 9–10.

Déchelette, J. (1910). *Manuel d'Archéologie Préhistorique, Celtique et Gallo-Romaine, Vol. II, part I: Age du Bronze*. Picard, Paris.

Déchelette, J. (1913). *Manuel d'Archéologie Préhistorique, Celtique et Gallo-Romaine: Vol. II, part 2: Premier Age du Fer ou Époque de Hallstatt*. Picard, Paris.

Déchelette, J. (1914). *Manuel d'Archéologie Préhistorique, Celtique et Gallo-Romaine: Vol. II, part 3: Second Age du Fer, ou Époque de La Tène*. Picard, Paris.

Déchelette, J. (1927). *Manuel d'Archéologie Préhistorique, Celtique et Gallo-Romaine. Vol. IV: Second Age du Fer ou Époque de La Tène*. Picard, Paris.

Dehn, W. (1958). "Die Heuneburg an der oberen Donau und ihre Wehranlagen". In *Neue Ausgrabungen in Deutschland* (W. Krämer, ed.), pp. 127–146.

Dehn, W. (1961). "Zangentore an Spätkeltischen Oppida", *Pamatký Archeologičke*, **52,** 390–396.

Dehn, W. (1962). "Aperçu sur les oppida d'Allemagne de la fin de l'époque celtique", *Celticum*, **3,** 328–386.

de Navarro, J. M. (1972). *The Finds from the Site of La Tène; I: Scabbards and the Swords found in them*, 2 vols. Oxford.

de Paor, M. and L. (1958). *Early Christian Ireland*. Thames and Hudson, London.

de Quincey, A. B. (1969). "A Promontory Fort at Parc Cynog, Carmarthenshire", *Archaeologia Cambrensis*, **118,** 73–85.

Dewar, H. S. L. and Godwin, H. (1963). "Archaeological Discoveries in the Raised Bogs of the Somerset Levels, England", *Proc. Prehist. Soc.*, **29,** 17–49.

Dixon, P. W. (1969). *Excavations at Crickley Hill*. Annual Report of Gloucestershire College, Cheltenham.

Dixon, P. W. (1970). *Excavations at Crickley Hill*. Annual Report of Gloucestershire College, Cheltenham.

Dixon, P. W. (1971). *Excavations at Crickley Hill*. Annual Report of Gloucestershire College, Cheltenham

Dixon, P. W. (1972). "Crickley Hill, 1969–1971", *Antiquity*, **46,** 49–52.

Dixon, P. W. (1973). "Longhouse and Roundhouse at Crickley Hill", *Antiquity*, **47,** 56–9.

Downman, E. A. (1910). *Some Ancient Earthworks of Hertfordshire*. Guildhall Library Ms 2584. 913.42.

Dryden, H. (1886). "Hunsbury, or Danes Camp, and the Discoveries there", *Associated Architectural Societies, Reports and Papers: Northampton Architectural Society*, **18** (1885–1886), 53–61 (pub. Williamson, Lincoln).

Dudley, D. and Jope, E. M. (1965). "An Iron Age Cist-burial with Two Brooches from Trevone, North Cornwall", *Cornish Arch.*, **4,** 18–23.

Dudley, D. R. and Webster, G. (1965). *The Roman Conquest of Britain, A.D.* 43–57. London.

Dunning, G. C. (1931). "Salmonsbury Camp, Gloucestershire", *Antiquity*, **5,** 489–491.

Dunning, G. C. (1932a). "Bronze Age Settlements and a Saxon Hut near Bourton-on-the-Water, Gloucestershire", *Ant. J.*, **12,** 279–293.

Dunning, G. C. (1932b). "On the La Tène II Brooches of Britain". In Wheeler and Wheeler (1932), 69–71.

Dunning, G. C. (1934a). "The Swan's Neck and Ring-Headed Pins of the Early Iron Age in Britain", *Arch. J.*, **91,** 269–295.

Dunning, G. C. (1934b). "Excavations at Salmonsbury Camp, Bourton-on-the-Water", *Proc. 1st. International Congress of Prehistoric and Protohistoric Sciences*, p. 273. London.

Dunning, G. C. (1937). "A Beaker from Bourton-on-the-Water, Gloucestershire", *Proc. Prehist. Soc.* **3,** 163–164.

Dunning, G. C. and Ogilvie, J. D. (1967). "A Belgic Burial-Group at Sholden, near Deal", *Arch. Cantiana*, **82,** 221–226.

Dyer, J. (1961). "Dray's Ditches, Bedfordshire, and Early Iron Age Territorial Boundaries in the Eastern Chilterns", *Ant. J.*, **41,** 32–43.

Dyer, J. (1962). "Ravensburgh Castle: Observations on its Construction", *Bedfords. Arch. J.*, **1**, 77–78.

Dymond, C. W. (1902). *Worlebury: An Ancient Stronghold in the County of Somerset*. Weston-super-Mare.

Dymond, C. W. and Tomkins, H. G. (1886). *Worlebury: An Ancient Stronghold in the County of Somerset* (privately printed).

Edeine, B. (1965). "Sur une tour interne du rampart protohistorique du Camp de Bierre Commune de Merri (Orne)," *Bulletin de la Société Préhistorique Française*, **62**, 262–270.

Edwards, A. J. H. (1935). "Rock-Carvings on Traprain Law", *Proc. Soc. Ant. Scot.*, **69** (1934–1935), 122–127.

Eichholz, D. E. (1972). "How Long did Vespasian Serve in Britain?", *Britannia*, **3**, 149–163.

Eóban, G. (1964). "The Later Bronze Age in Ireland in the light of Recent Research", *Proc. Prehist. Soc.*, **30**, 268–351.

Eóban, G. (1965). *Catalogue of Irish Bronze Swords*. Dublin.

Ettlinger, E. and Simonett, C. (1952). *Römische Keramik aus dem Schutthügel von Vindonissa*.

Evans, A. J. (1890). "On a Late-Celtic Urnfield at Aylesford, Kent", *Archaeologia*, **52**, 315–388.

Evans, E. E. (1966). *Prehistoric and Early Christian Ireland*. Batsford, London.

Evans, J. (1881). *The Ancient Bronze Implements, Weapons and Ornaments of Great Britain and Ireland*.

Evens, E. D., Smith, I. F. and Wallis, F. S. (1972). "The Petrological Identification of Stone Implements from South-Western England", *Proc. Prehist. Soc.*, **38**, 235–275.

Evison, V. I. (1961). "The Saxon Objects from Northolt Manor, Middlesex", *Medieval Arch.*, **5**, 226–230.

Evison, V. I. (1964). "A Decorated Seax from the Thames at Keen Edge Ferry", *Berks. Arch. J.*, **61**, 28–36.

Feachem, R. W. F. (1956a). "The Fortifications on Traprain Law", *Proc. Soc. Ant. Scot.*, **89** (1955–1956), 284–289.

Feachem, R. W. F. (1956b). "Fortifications". In *The Problem of the Picts* (F. T. Wainwright, ed.), pp. 66–86.

Feachem, R. W. F. (1963). *A Guide to Prehistoric Scotland*. London.

Feachem, R. W. F. (1966). "The Hill-Forts of Northern Britain". In *The Iron Age in Northern Britain* (A. L. F. Rivet, ed.), pp. 59–87. Edinburgh.

Feachem, R. W. F. (1971). "Unfinished Hill-forts". In *The Iron Age and Its Hillforts* (M. Jesson and D. Hill, eds), pp. 19–39.

Feachem, R. W. F. (1973). "Ancient Agriculture in the Highland of Britain", *Proc. Prehist. Soc.* **39**, 332–353.

Fell, C. I. (1936). "The Hunsbury Hill-Fort, Northants", *Arch. J.*, **93**, 57–100.

Fell, C. I. (1961). "The Coarse Pottery at Bagendon". In Clifford (1961), 212–257.

Filip, J. (1962). *Celtic Civilisation and its Heritage* (trans. R. F. Samsour). Czechoslovak Academy of Sciences.

Forde, C. D. (1937a). "Excavations at Pen Dinas Hill Fort, Cardiganshire. Third Season, 1936", *Bulletin of the Board of Celtic Studies*, **8**, 378–380.

Forde, C. D. (1937b). "Excavations on Pen Dinas, Cardiganshire, 1937", *Bulletin of The Board of Celtic Studies*, **9**, 85–88.

Forde, C. D. (1938). "Excavations at Pen Dinas, Cardiganshire, 1937", *Ant. J.*, **18**, 77–81.

Forde, C. D., Griffiths, W. E., Hogg, A. H. A. and Houlder, C. H. (1963). "Excavations at Pen Dinas, Aberystwyth", *Archaeologia Cambrensis*, **112**, 125–153.

Forde-Johnston, J. (1962a). "Early's Hill, Pontesbury and related Hillforts in England and Wales", *Arch. J.*, **119**, 66–91.

Forde-Johnston, J. (1962b). "The Iron Age Hillforts of Lancashire and Cheshire", *Trans. Lancs. and Cheshire Ant. Soc.*, **72**, 9–46.

Forde-Johnston, J. (1964). "Fieldwork on the Hillforts of North Wales", *Flintshire Historical Society Publications*, **21**, 1–20.

Forde-Johnston, J. (1965). "The Hill-forts of the Clwyds", *Archaeologia Cambrensis*, **114**, 146–178.

Forde-Johnston, J. (1966). "The Dudsbury Barrow and Vessels with Shoulder Grooves in Dorset and Wiltshire", *Proc. Dorset Nat. Hist. and Arch. Soc.*, **87**, 126–141.

Foster, I.LL. and Alcock, L. (1963). *Culture and Environment* (Essays in Honour of Sir Cyril Fox). London.

Foster, I.LL. and Daniel, G. (1965). *Prehistoric and Early Wales*. London.

Fowler, E. (1960). "The Origins and Development of the Penannular Brooch in Europe", *Proc. Prehist. Soc.*, **26**, 149–177. See also Burley, E.

Fowler, E. (1963). "Celtic Metalwork of the Fifth and Sixth Centuries A.D.", *Arch. J.*, **120**, 98–160.

Fowler, E. (1962). *Field Survey in British Archaeology*. C.B.A., London.

Fowler, M. J. (1953). "The Typology of Brooches of the Iron Age in Wessex", *Arch. J.*, **110**, 88–105.

Fowler, P. J. (1964). "Cross-Dykes on the Ebble-Nadder Ridge", *Wilts. Arch. Mag.*, **59**, 46–57.

Fowler, P. J. (1971). "Hillforts A.D. 400–700". In *The Iron Age and Its Hillforts* (M. Jesson and D. Hill, eds), pp. 203–213.

Fowler, P. J. (1972). *Archaeology and the Landscape* (Essays for L. V. Grinsell). London.

Fowler, P. J., Gardner, K. S. and Rahtz, P. A. (1970). *Cadbury Congresbury, Somerset*, 1968 (Dept. of Extra-Mural Studies, Bristol University).

Fox, Lady A. F. (1952). "Hill-Slope and Related Earthworks in South-West England and South Wales", *Arch. J.*, **109**, 1–22.

Fox, Lady A. F. (1958). "Southwestern Hillforts". In *Problems of the Iron Age in Southern Britain* (S. S. Frere, ed.), pp. 35–60.

Fox, Lady A. F. (1964). *South-West England*. Thames and Hudson, London.

Fox, Lady A. F. (1969). "Prehistoric and Roman Settlement in Devon and West Somerset", *Proc. Devon Arch. Soc.*, **27**, 37–48.

Fox, A. and Ravenhill, W. D. (1972). "The Roman Fort at Nanstallon, Cornwall", *Britannia*, **3**, 56–111.

Fox, C. F. (1923). *The Archaeology of the Cambridge Region*.

Fox, C. F. (1927). *Archaeologia Cambrensis*, **82**, 67–112.

Fox, C. F. (1946). *A Find of the Early Iron Age from Llyn Cerrig Bach, Anglesey*. National Museum of Wales, Cardiff.

Fox, C. F. (1955). *Offa's Dyke*. British Academy, London.

Fox, C. F. (1958). *Pattern and Purpose: Early Celtic Art in Britain*. National Museum of Wales, Cardiff.

Fox, C. F. (1959). *The Personality of Britain*, 4th edition, new impression. National Museum of Wales, Cardiff.

Fox, C. F. and Hemp, W. J. (1926). "Two Unrecorded Hill-forts on Llanymynech Hill, Montgomeryshire, and Blodwell Rock, Shropshire, and their Relation to Offa's Dyke", *Archaeologia Cambrensis*, **81**, 395–400.

Frere, S. S. (1958a). *Problems of the Iron Age in Southern Britain*. Papers given at a C.B.A. Conference, December 1958, University of London Institute of Archaeology Occasional Paper No. 11.

Frere, S. S. (1958b). "Some Problems of the Later Iron Age". In *Problems of the Iron Age in Southern Britain* (S. S. Frere, ed.), pp. 84–92.

Frere, S. S. (1967). *Britannia: A History of Roman Britain*. London.

Frey, O-H. (1969). *Marburger Beitrage zur Archaologie der Kelten*, Festschrift für W. Dehn; *Fundberichte aus Hessen*, Beiheft I, 1969. Habelt, Bonn.

Gardner, W. (1910). "Pen-y-Corddyn, Near Abergele", *Archaeologia Cambrensis*, **65**, 79–156.

Gardner, W. (1926). "The Native Hill-forts in North Wales and their Defences", *Archaeologia Cambrensis.*, **81**, 221–282.

Gardner, W. (1932). "Craig Gwrtheyrn Hill Fort, Llanfihangel ar Arth, Carmarthenshire", *Archaeologia Cambrensis*, **87**, 144–150.

Gardner, W. (1934). "Caer y Twr, A Hillfort on Holy Island, Anglesey", *Archaeologia Cambrensis*, **89**, 156–173.

Gardner, W. and Savory, H. N. (1964). *Dinorben, a Hill-fort Occupied in Early Iron Age and Roman Times*, National Museum of Wales, Cardiff.

Gelling, P. S. (1972). "The Hill-fort on South Barrule and its Position in the Manx Iron Age". In *Prehistoric Man in Wales and the West* (F. Lynch and C. B. Burgess, eds), pp. 285–292. Adams and Dart, Bath.

Gelling, P. S. and Stanford, S. (1967). "Dark Age Pottery or Iron Age Ovens ?", *Trans. Birmingham Arch. Soc.*, **82**, 77–91.

Giot, P-R. (1952). "Quelques stèles gauloises gravées ou inscrites", *Annales de Bretagne*, **59**, 213–220.

Giot, P-R. (1960). *Brittany*. Thames and Hudson, London.

Giot, P-R and Briard, J. (1969). "Les Retranchements du Cap d'Erquy: Fouilles de 1968 au fossé de Pleine-Garenne", *Annales de Bretagne*, **76**, 21–36.

Giot, P-R., Briard, J. and Avery, M. (1968). "Les Retranchements du Cap d'Erquy: Fouilles de 1968 au fossé Catuélan", *Annales de Bretagne*, **75**, 67–84.

Godwin, H. (1956). *History of the British Flora*. Cambridge.

Gomme, G. L. (1907). *Index of Archaeological Papers* 1665–1890. London.

Gordon, A. S. R. (1940). "The Excavation of Gurnard's Head, an Iron Age Cliff Castle in Western Cornwall", *Arch. J.*, **97**, 96–111.

Göse, E. (1950). "Gefässtypen der römischen Keramik im Rheinland", *Bonner Jahrbücher*, Beiheft I.

Gould, I. C. (1902). "Mam Tor near Castleton", *Derbyshire Arch. and Nat. Hist. Soc.*, **24**, 27–31.

Gray, J. W. and Brewer, G. W. S. (1904). "Evidence of Ancient Occupation on Cleeve Hill, Gloucs." *Proc. Cheltenham Nat. Field Club*, **15**, 49–57.

Grealey, S. (1971). "The Hill Fort on Merlin's Hill, Abergwili, Carmarthenshire", *Carmarthenshire Antiquary*, **7**, 98–101.

Grealey, S., Jones, G. D. B. and Little, J. H. (1972). "Excavations at Castell Cogan, 1971: An Interim Report", *Carmarthenshire Antiquary*, **8**, 17–22.

Greene, D. (1972). "The Chariot as Described in Irish Literature". In *The Iron Age in the Irish Sea Province* (A. C. Thomas, ed.), pp. 59–73.

Greene, K. T. (1972). *Guide to Pre-Flavian Fine Wares, c. A.D. 40–70*. Department of Archaeology, University College, Cardiff.

Greig, C. (1970). "Excavations at Cullykhan, Banff", *Aberdeen University Review*, **43**, 274–283.

Greig, C. (1971). "Excavations at Cullykhan, Castle Point, Troup, Banffshire", *Scottish Arch. Forum.*, **3**, 15–21.

Greig, C. (1972). "Cullykhan", *Current Arch.*, **32**, 227–231.

Grenier, A. (1945). *Les Gaulois*. Paris.

Gresham, C. A. (1967). "Prehistoric Times: Hill-forts". In *History of Merioneth*, Vol. I (E. G. Bowen and C. A. Gresham, eds), pp. 129–172. Merioneth Historical and Record Society, Dolgellau.

Griffiths, W. E. and Hogg, A. H. A. (1956). "The Hill-fort on Conway Mountains, Caernarvonshire", *Archaeologia Cambrensis*, **105**, 49–80.

Grimes, W. F. (1945). "Maiden Castle", *Antiquity*, **19**, 6–10.

Grimes, W. F. (1951a). *The Prehistory of Wales*. National Museum of Wales, Cardiff.

Grimes, W. F. (1951b). "The Jurassic Way across England". In *Aspects of Archaeology in Britain and Beyond* (W. F. Grimes, ed.), pp. 144–171.

Grimes, W. F. (1952). "Art of British Iron Age Pottery", *Proc. Prehist. Soc.* **18**, 160–175.

Grimes, W. F. (1964). "The Problem of the Raths of Pembrokeshire". In *The Land of Dyfed in Early Times* (D. Moore, ed.), pp. 17–18. Cambrian Archaeological Association, Cardiff.

Grundy, G. B. (1936). *Saxon Charters of Gloucestershire*.

Hamilton, J. R. C. (1966). "The Origin and Development of Iron Age Forts in Western Britain". In *VIIᵉ Congrès International des Sciences Préhistoriques et Protohistoriques*, Vol. 2, pp. 846–849. Prague.

Hamilton, J. R. C. (1968). *Excavations at Clickhimin, Shetland*. H.M.S.O., Edinburgh.

Hamilton, J. R. C. (1970). *The Brochs of Mousa and Clickhimin*. H.M.S.O., Edinburgh.

Hamlin, A. (1966). "Early Iron Age Sites at Stanton Harcourt", *Oxoniensia*, **31**, 1–27.

Harbison, P. (1968). "Castros with *chevaux-de-frise* in Spain and Portugal", *Madrider Mitteilungen*, **9**, 116–147.

Harbison, P. (1969). "The Chariot of Celtic Funerary Tradition". In *Marburger Beiträge zur Archäologie der Kelten* (O-H. Frey, ed.), pp. 34–58.

Harbison, P. (1971a). "The Old Irish 'Chariot'", *Antiquity*, **45**, 171–177.

Harbison, P. (1971b). "Wooden and Stone *Chevaux-de-frise* in Central and Western Europe", *Proc. Prehist. Soc.*, **37**, 195–225.

Harcourt, L. V. (1848). "On Celtic Antiquities near Chichester", *Sussex Arch. Coll.*, **I**, 149–159.

Harden, D. B. (1937). "Excavations on Grim's Dyke, North Oxfordshire", *Oxoniensia*, **2**, 74–92.

Harding, D. W. (1967). "Blewburton", *Current Arch.*, **4**, 83–85.

Harding, D. W. (1970). "The 'New' Iron Age", *Current. Arch.*, **20**, 235–239.

Harding, D. W. (1972). *The Iron Age in the Upper Thames Basin*. Clarendon Press, Oxford.

Harding, D. W. and Blake, I. M. (1963). "An Early Iron Age Settlement in Dorset", *Antiquity*, **37,** 63–64.

Hartley, B. R. (1956). "The Wandlebury Iron Age Hillfort: Excavations of 1955–1956", *Proc. Cambridge Antiquarian Soc.*, **50,** 1–28.

Hawkes, C. F. C. (1931). "Hillforts", *Antiquity*, **5,** 60–97.

Hawkes, C. F. C. (1936a). "The Excavations at Buckland Rings, Lymington, 1935", *Proc. Hampshire Field Club*, **13,** 124–164.

Hawkes, C. F. C. (1936b). "The Twyford Down Village, the Abandonment of St. Catharine's Hill, and the First Settlement of Winchester", *Proc. Hampshire Field Club*, **13,** 208–212.

Hawkes, C. F. C. (1939a). "The Excavations at Quarley Hill, 1938", *Proc. Hampshire Field Club*, **14,** 136–194.

Hawkes, C. F. C. (1939b). "The Caburn Pottery and its Implications", *Sussex Arch. Coll.*, **80,** 217–262.

Hawkes, C. F. C. (1939c). "The Pottery from Castle Hill, Newhaven", *Sussex Arch. Coll.*, **80,** 269–292.

Hawkes, C. F. C. (1956). "Hampshire and the British Iron Age, 1905–55", *Proc. Hampshire Field Club*, **20** (in honour of Frank Warren), 14–22.

Hawkes, C. F. C. (1958). "The ABC of the British Iron Age". In *Problems of the Iron Age in Southern Britain* (S. S. Frere, ed., pp. 1–16).

Hawkes, C. F. C. (1959). "The ABC of the British Iron Age", *Antiquity*, **33,** 170–182.

Hawkes, C. F. C. (1961). "The Western Third C Culture and the Belgic Dobunni". In Clifford (1961), 43–67.

Hawkes, C. F. C. (1962). "Early Iron Age Pottery from Linford, Essex". In Barton (1962), 83–87.

Hawkes, C. F. C. (1971). "Fence, Wall, Dump, from Troy to Hod". In *The Iron Age and its Hillforts* (M. Jesson and D. Hill, eds), pp. 5–18. Southampton University Archaeological Society, Southampton.

Hawkes, C. F. C. (1972), "Europe and England: Fact and Fog", *Helinium*, **12** (2), 105–116.

Hawkes, C. F. C. (1973). "Cumulative Celticity in pre-Roman Britain", *Études Celtiques*, **13** (2), 607–628.

Hawkes, S. C. (1958). "Early Iron Age Enclosures on Longbridge Deverill Cow Down, Wiltshire". In *Problems of the Iron Age in Southern Britain* (S. S. Frere, ed.), pp. 18–20.

Hawkes, C. F. C. and Dunning, G. C. (1930), "The Belgae of Gaul and Britain", *Arch. J.*, **87,** 150–335.

Hawkes, C. F. C. and Hull, M. R. (1947). *Camulodunum*. Society of Antiquaries Research Report No. 14.

Hawkes, C. F. C., Myres, J. N. L. and Stevens, C. G. (1930). *St. Catharine's Hill, Winchester*. Hampshire Field Club and Archaeological Society, Winchester.

Hawkes, C. F. C. and Smith, M. A. (1957). "On some Buckets and Cauldrons of the Bronze and Early Iron Ages", *Ant. J.*, **37,** 131–198.

Hawkes, J. (1940). "The Excavations at Balksbury, 1939", *Proc. Hampshire Field Club*, **14,** 338–345

Hawley, W. (1926). "Further Excavations on Park Brow", *Archaeologia*, **76,** 30–40.

Haworth, R. (1971). "The Horse Harness of the Irish Early Iron Age", *Ulster J. Arch.*, **34,** 26–49.

Helbaek, H. (1952). "Early Crops in Southern England". *Proc. Prehist. Soc.*, **18,** 194–233.

Hemp, W. J. (1928). "A La Tène Shield from Moel Hiraddug, Flintshire", *Archaeologia Cambrensis*, **83,** 253–284.

Hencken, T. C. (1938). "The Excavation of the Iron Age Camp on Bredon Hill, Gloucestershire", *Arch. J.*, **95,** 1–111.

Hermet, F. (1934). *La Graufesenque*.

Hodgson, G. W. I. (1968). "A Comparative Account of the Animal Remains from Corstopitum and the Iron Age Site of Catcote, near Hartlepool, Co. Durham", *Arch. Aeliana*, **46,** 127–162.

Hodson, F. R. (1962). "Some Pottery from Eastbourne, the 'Marnians' and the pre-Roman Iron Age in Southern Britain", *Proc. Prehist. Soc.*, **28,** 140–155.

Hodson, F. R. (1964a). "La Tène Chronology, Continental and British", *Bulletin of the University of London, Institute of Archaeology*, **4,** 123–141.

Hodson, F. R. (1964b). Cultural Grouping within the British pre-Roman Iron Age", *Proc. Prehist. Soc.*, **30,** 99–110.

Hodson, F. R. (1968). *The La Tène Cemetery at Münsingen-Rain, Acta Bernensia* V. Bern.

Hogg, A. H. A. (1951). "The Votadini", In *Aspects of Archaeology in Britain and Beyond* (W. F. Grimes, ed.), pp. 200–220. London.

Hogg, A. H. A. (1957a). "Four Spanish Hill-forts", *Antiquity*, **31**, 25–33.

Hogg, A. H. A. (1957b). "A Fortified Round Hut at Carreg-y-llam, near Nevin", *Archaeologia Cambrensis*, **106**, 46–55.

Hogg, A. H. A. (1958). "The Secondary Iron Age in Britain", *Antiquity*, **32**, 189–190.

Hogg, A. H. A. (1960). "Garn Boduan and Tre'r Ceiri", *Arch. J.*, **117**, 1–39.

Hogg, A. H. A. (1962). "A List of Hill-forts in Cardiganshire", *Bulletin of the Board of Celtic Studies*, **19**, 354–366.

Hogg, A. H. A. (1963). *Archaeology in Wales*, **3**, 7.

Hogg, A. H. A. (1964). "The Iron Age". In *Inventory of Caernarvonshire, Vol. III, West*, R.C.A.H.M (Wales and Mon.), lxx–lxxxi.

Hogg, A. H. A. (1965). "Early Iron Age Wales". In *Prehistoric and Early Wales* (I. Ll. Foster and G. E. Daniel, eds), pp. 109–150. Routledge and Kegan Paul, London.

Hogg, A. H. A. (1969). "A Sample of French Hill-forts", *Antiquity*, **43**, 260–273.

Hogg, A. H. A. (1971). "Some Applications of Surface Fieldwork". In *The Iron Age and its Hill-forts* (M. Jesson and D. Hill, eds), pp. 105–125. Southampton University Archaeological Society, Southampton.

Hogg, A. H. A. (1972a). "Hill-forts in the Coastal Area of Wales". In *The Iron Age in the Irish Sea Province* (A. C. Thomas, ed.), pp. 11–23.

Hogg, A. H. A. (1972b). "The Size-Distribution of Hill-forts in Wales and the Marches". In *Prehistoric Man in Wales and the West* (F. Lynch and C. B. Burgess, eds.), pp. 293–305. Adams and Dart, Bath.

Hooley, R. W. (1927). "Hallstatt Pottery from Winchester", *Proc. Hampshire Field Club*, **10**, 63–68.

Hooley, R. W. and Dunning, G. C. (1929). "Excavation of an Early Iron Age Village on Worthy Down, Winchester", *Proc. Hampshire Field Club*, **10**, 178–195.

Houben, P. (1839). *Das Grabfeld von Xanten*.

Houlder, C. H. (1961). "Rescue Excavations at Moel Hiraddug. I, Excavations in 1954–1955", *Publications of the Flintshire Historical Society*, **19**, 1–20.

Hughes, K. (1972). *Early Christian Ireland: Introduction to the Sources*. Hodder and Stoughton, London.

Hull, E. (1907). "Observations of Classical Writers on the Habits of the Celtic Nations, as Illustrated from Irish Records", *The Celtic Review*, **3** (1906–1907), 62–76 and 138–154.

Hull, M. R. (1958). *Roman Colchester*. Society of Antiquaries Research Report No. 20.

Hull, M. R. (1961). "The Brooches at Bagendon". In Clifford (1961), 167–185.

Irving, G. V. (1857). "On the Camps at Cissbury and High Down, Sussex", *Journal of the Archaeological Association*, **13**, 274–293.

Jackson, K. H. (1955). "The Britons in Southern Scotland", *Antiquity*, **29**, 79.

Jackson, K. H. (1964). *The Oldest Irish Tradition: A Window on the Iron Age*. Rede Lecture, 1964. Cambridge.

Jacobsthal, P. (1944). *Early Celtic Art*, 2 vols. Oxford.

Jarman, M., Fagg, A. and Higgs, E. S. (1968). "Appendix A: Animal Remains". In Stead (1968), 182–189.

Jarrett, M. G. (1965). "The Roman Villa at Whitton, Glamorgan: Excavations of 1965", *Morgannwg*, **9**, 91–95.

Jarrett, M. G. (1966). "The Roman Villa at Whitton, Glamorgan: Second Interim Report", *Morgannwg*, **10**, 59–63.

Jarrett, M. G. (1967). "The Roman Villa at Whitton, Glamorgan: Excavations of 1967", *Morgannwg*, **11**, 78–81.

Jarrett, M. G. (1968). "The Roman Villa at Whitton: Excavations of 1968", *Morgannwg*, **12**, 101–104.

Jarrett, M. G. (1969). *The Roman Frontier in Wales*. University of Wales, Cardiff.

Jarrett, M. G. and Mann, J. C. (1968). "The Tribes of Wales", *Welsh History Review*, **4**, 161–171.

Jesson, M. and Hill, D. (1971). *The Iron Age and its Hillforts*. University of Southampton, Monograph series No. 1, Southampton.

Jewell, P. A. (1963). "Cattle from British archaeological sites". In *Man and Cattle* (A. E. Mourant and F. E. Zeuner, eds), pp. 80–91.

Jobey, G. (1964). "Enclosed Stone-built settlements in North Northumberland", *Arch. Aeliana*, **42**, 41–64.

Jobey, G. (1965). "Hill-forts and Related Settlements in Northumberland", *Arch. Aeliana*, series 4, **43**, 21–64.

Jobey, G. (1966a). "Homesteads and Settlements in the Frontier Area". In *Rural Settlement in Roman Britain* (A. C. Thomas, ed.), pp. 1–14. C.B.A. Research Report No. 7, London.

Jobey, G. (1966b). "A Field Survey in Northumberland". In *The Iron Age in Northern Britain* (A. L. F. Rivet, ed.), pp. 89–110.

Jobey, G. (1968). "A Radiocarbon Date for the Palisaded Settlement at Huckhoe", *Arch. Aeliana*, **46**, 293–295.

Jobey, G. (1970). *Discovery and Excavation in Scotland*, **21**.

Joffroy, R. (1954). *Le Trésor de Vix*, Monuments et Mémoires Piot, vol. XLVIII-i.

Joffroy, R. (1960). *L'Oppidum de Vix et la civilisation Hallstattienne finale dans l'Est de la France*.

Jones, G. D. B. and Thompson, F. H. (1965). "Excavations at Mam Tor and Brough on Navis", *Derbyshire Arch. J.*, **85**, 123–125.

Jones, G. R. J. (1961). "Settlement Patterns in Anglo-Saxon England", *Antiquity*, **35**, 221–232.

Jope, E. M. (1954). "An Iron Age Decorated Sword-Scabbard from the River Bann at Toome", *Ulster J. Arch.*, **17**, 81–91.

Jope, E. M. (1955). "Chariotry and Paired Draught in Ireland during the Early Iron Age: The Evidence of Some Horse Bridle-Bits", *Ulster J. Arch.*, **18**, 37–44.

Jope, E. M. (1961). "Daggers of the Early Iron Age in Britain", *Proc. Prehist. Soc.*, **27**, 307–343.

Jope, E. M. (1962). "Iron Age Brooches in Ireland: A Summary", *Ulster J. Arch.*, **24/25** (1961–1962), 25–38.

Jope, E. M. and Wilson, B. C. S. (1957). "A Burial Group of the First Century A.D. from Loughey", *Ulster J. Arch.*, **20**, 73–95.

Jullian, C. (1926). *Histoire de la Gaule* (Paris, in 8 volumes, pub. 1920–1926).

Kendrick, T. D. and Hawkes, C. F. C. (1932). *Archaeology in England and Wales*, 1914–1931. Methuen, London.

Kenney, J. F. (1929). *Sources for the Early History of Ireland*, Vol. I. New York.

Kent, J. (1951). "Coin Evidence and the Evacuation of Hadrian's Wall", *Trans. Cumberland and Westmorland Arch. Soc.*, series 2, **51**, 4–15.

Kenyon, K. M. (1942). "Excavations at the Wrekin, Shropshire, 1939", *Arch. J.*, **99**, 99–109.

Kenyon, K. M. (1950). "Excavations at Breedon-on-the-Hill, Leicestershire, 1946", *Trans. Leicestershire Arch. and Hist. Soc.*, **26**, 17–82.

Kenyon, K. M. (1952). "A Survey of the Evidence Concerning the Chronology and Origins of Iron Age 'A' in Southern and Midland Britain". *Eighth Annual Report of the London University Institute of Archaeology*, pp. 29–78.

Kenyon, K. M. (1953). "Excavations at Sutton Walls, Herefordshire, 1948–1951", *Arch. J.*, **110**, 1–87.

Kimmig, W. and Gersbach, E. (1971). "Die Grabungen auf der Heuneburg, 1966–1969", *Germania*, **49**, 21–91.

King, D. G. (1961). "Bury Wood Camp; Report on Excavations, 1959", *Wilts. Arch. Mag.*, **58**, 40–47.

King, D. G. (1962). "Bury Wood Camp; Report on Excavations, 1960", *Wilts. Arch. Mag.*, **58**, 185–208.

King, D. G. (1967). "Bury Wood Camp: Excavations in the Area of the S.W. Opening", *Wilts. Arch. Mag.*, **62**, 1–15.

King, D. G. (1969). "Bury Wood Camp: Excavations in the N.E. and N.W. Areas", *Wilts. Arch. Mag.*, **64**, 21–50.

King, E. (1812). "A Description of Antiquities discovered on Hagbourn Hill", *Archaeologia*, **17**, 348–349.

Knorr, R. (1912). *Die Terra Sigillata Gefässe von Aislingen*. Reprinted in Ulbert, G. (1959).

Knorr, R. (1919). *Töpfen und Fabriken verzierter Terra Sigillata des ersten Jahrhunderts*.

Knorr, R. (1952). *Terra Sigillata Gefässe des ersten Jahrhunderts mit Töpfernamen*.

Krämer, W. (1958a). *Neue Ausgrabungen im Deutschland*. Römisch-Germanische Kommission des Deutschen Archäologischen Instituts, Berlin.

Krämer, W. (1958b). "Manching, ein vindelikisches Oppidum an der Donau". In *Neue Ausgrabungen im Deutschland* (W. Krämer, ed.), pp. 175–202.

Krämer, W. (1960). "The *Oppidum* of Manching", *Antiquity*, **34**, 191–200.

Krämer, W. (1962). "Manching II. Zu den Ausgrabungen in den Jahren 1957 bis 1961", *Germania*, **40,** 293–317.

Krämer, W., and Schubert, F. (1970). *Die Ausgrabungen in Manching*, 1955–1961, Vol. I. Römisch-Germanische Kommission.

Lacaille, A. D. and Grimes, W. F. (1961). "The Prehistory of Caldey: Part 2", *Archaeologia Cambrensis*, **110,** 30–70.

Lane, H. C. (1969). "Markland Grips Iron Age Promontory Fort", *Derbyshire Arch. J.*, **89,** 59–67.

Lane-Fox, A. (1869a). "An Examination into the Character and Probable Origin of the Hillforts of Sussex", *Archaeologia*, **42,** 27–52.

Lane-Fox, A. (1869b). "Further Remarks on the Hillforts of Sussex: Being an Account of Excavations in the Forts at Cissbury and Highdown", *Archaeologia*, **42,** 53–76.

Lane-Fox, A. (1881). "Excavations at Mount Caburn Camp, near Lewes, Conducted in September and October 1877, and July 1878", *Archaeologia*, **46,** 432–495.

Langmaid, N. (1971). "Norton Fitzwarren", *Current Arch.*, **28,** 116–120.

Lasfarques, J. (1972). "Une Industrie Lyonnaise", *Archéologia*, **50,** 17.

Leechman, M. H. (1962). *The Vitrified fort of Dunagoil* (unpublished M.A. Thesis, University of Edinburgh).

Lewis, M. J. T. (1966). *Temples in Roman Britain*. Cambridge.

Libby, W. F. (1970). "Radiocarbon Dating", *Phil Trans. Roy. Soc. Lond.*, sec. A, **249,** No. 1193, 1–10.

Liddell, D. (1930). "Report on the Excavations at Hembury Fort, First Season, 1930", *Proc. Devon Arch. Exploration Soc.*, **1** (pt. 2), 40–63.

Liddell, D. (1931). "Report on the Excavations at Hembury Fort, Devon, Second Season, 1931", *Proc. Devon Arch. Exploration Soc.*, **1** (pt. 3), 90–120.

Liddell, D. (1932). "Report on the Excavations at Hembury Fort, Third Season, 1932", *Proc. Devon Arch. Exploration Soc.*, **1** (pt. 4), 162–190.

Liddell, D. (1933). "Excavations at Meon Hill", *Proc. Hampshire Field Club*, **12,** 127–162.

Liddell, D. (1935a). "Report on the Excavations at Hembury Fort, Fourth and Fifth Seasons, 1934 and 1935", *Proc. Devon Arch. Exploration Soc.*, **2** (Pt. 3), 135–175.

Liddell, D. (1935b). "Report of the Hampshire Field Club's Excavations at Meon Hill, Second Season, 1933", *Proc. Hampshire Field Club*, **13,** 7–54.

Longworth, I. H. (1968). "A Bronze-age Hoard from Portfield Farm, Whalley, Lancashire", *British Museum Quarterly*, **32,** 1–2, 8–14.

Louis, M. and Taffanel, O. and J. (1958). *Le Premier Age du Fer Languedocien*, 2 ème Partie. Institut International d'Etudes ligures, Bordighera-Montpellier.

Lynch, F. (1970). *Prehistoric Anglesey*. Anglesey Antiquarian Society, Llangefni.

Lynch, P. J. (1899). "Caherconree, County Kerry", *J. Royal Soc. Ant. Ireland*, **9,** 5–17.

Lynch, F. and Burgess, C. (1972). *Prehistoric Man in Wales and the West* (Essays in Honour of Lily F. Chitty). Bath.

McKerrell, H. (1971). "Some Aspects of the Accuracy of C-14 Dating", *Scottish Arch. Forum*, **3,** 73–84.

MacKie, E. W. (1963). "A Dwelling Site of the Earlier Iron Age at Ballevullin, Tiree", *Proc. Soc. Ant. Scot.*, **XCVI** (1962–1963), 155–183.

MacKie, E. W. (1965). "The Origin and Development of the Broch and Wheelhouse Building Cultures of the Scottish Iron Age", *Proc. Prehist. Soc.*, **31,** 93–146.

MacKie, E. W. (1968). *Second Interim Report on the Lochbroom Excavation*. University of Glasgow.

MacKie, E. W. (1969a). "Timber-laced and Vitrified Forts: Causes of Vitrification", *Glasgow Arch. J.*, **I,** 69–71.

MacKie, E. W. (1969b). "Radiocarbon Dates and the Scottish Iron Age", *Antiquity*, **43,** 15–26.

MacKie, E. W. (1970). "The Scottish 'Iron Age': A Revision Article on the Final Prehistoric Age in Scotland", *Scott. Hist. Rev.*, **49,** 1–32.

MacKie, E. W. (1971a). "English Migrants and Scottish Brochs", *Glasgow Arch. J.*, **2,** 39–71.

MacKie, E. W. (1971b). "Thoughts on Radiocarbon Dating", *Antiquity*, **45,** 197–200.

MacKie, E. W. (1971c). "Some Aspects of the Transition from the Bronze to Iron—Using Periods in Scotland", *Scottish Arch. Forum*, **3,** 55–72.

MacKie, E. W. (1975). "The Brochs of Scotland". In *Recent work in Rural Archaeology* (P. J. Fowler, ed.). Bath.

Mahr, A. (1937). "New Aspects and Problems in Irish prehistory", *Proc. Prehist. Soc.*, **3**, 261–436.

Manby, T. G. (1963). "Early Iron Age Pottery from Melbourne, South Derbyshire", *Derbyshire Arch. J.*, **83**, 100–101.

Mann, J. (1971). "Early Fourth Century Re-organisation of Hadrian's Wall", *Roman Seminar Papers*, No. 3. Newcastle.

Mann, L. M. (1925). "Note on the Results of the Exploration of the Fort at Dunagoil", *Trans. Bute Nat. Hist. Soc.* **9**, 56–60.

Mann, L. and Marshall, J. N. (1915). "Excavations at Dunagoil", *Trans. Bute Nat. Hist. Soc.*, **8** (1914–1915), 42–49 and 68–86.

Manning, W. H. (1972). "Iron-work Hoards in Iron Age and Roman Britain", *Britannia*, **3**, 224–250.

Mattingly, H. and Sydenham, E. A. (1923). *Roman Imperial Coinage, I.*

Maxwell, G. (1969). "Duns and Forts—A Note on Some Iron Age Monuments of the Atlantic Province", *Scottish Arch. Forum*, **1**, 41–52.

Mayet, F. (1971). "La Céramique à 'Parois Fines' de Conimbriga", *Actas do II Congresso Nacional de Arqueologia*, Coimtra, Vol. 2, 445–449.

Meaney, A. L. and Hawkes, S. C. (1970). *Two Anglo-Saxon Cemeteries at Winnall, Winchester, Hampshire.* Society for Medieval Archaeology Monograph Series No. 4.

Megaw, J. V. S. (1966). "The Vix Burial", *Antiquity*, **40**, 38–44.

Megaw, J. V. S. (1970). *Art of the European Iron Age.* Adams and Dart, Bath.

Meyer, A. B. (1885). *Gurina im Obergailthal, Kärnthen.*

M'Hardy, A. B. (1906). "On Vitrified Forts, with Results of Experiments as to the Probable Manner in which their Vitrification may have been Produced", *Proc. Soc. Ant. Scot.*, **40** (1905–1906), 136–150.

Michael, H. N. and Ralph, E. K. (1972). "Discussion of Radiocarbon Dates Obtained from Precisely Dated Sequoia and Bristlecone Pine Samples". In *Proceedings of the Eighth International Radiocarbon Dating Conference* (T. A. Rafter and T. Grant-Taylor, eds), Vol. I, pp. A.11–A.27.

Morris, B. (1968). "The Excavation at Kilvey Hill", *Gower*, **19**, 22–24.

Mourant, A. E. and Zeuner, F. E. (1963). *Man and Cattle.* Royal Anthropological Institute, Occasional paper No. 18.

Müller-Wille, M. and Vierck, H. (1971). "Pferdegrab und Pferdeopfer im frühen Mittelalter", *Berichten van de Rijksdienst voor het Oudheidkundig Bodemonderzoek*, **20-21** (1970–1971), 119–248.

Mumford, L. (1961). *The City in History.* Secker and Warburg, London.

Murray-Threipland, L. (1943). "Excavations in Brittany, 1939", *Arch. J.*, **100**, 128–149.

Murray-Threipland, L. (1956). "An Excavation at St. Mawgan-in-Pyder, N. Cornwall", *Arch. J.*, **113**, 33–81.

Musson, C. R. (1970a). "The Breiddin 1969", *Current Arch.*, **19**, 215–218.

Musson, C. R. (1970b). "House-plans and Prehistory", *Current Arch.*, **21**, 267–277.

Musson, C. R. (1971). *Archaeology in Wales*, **11**, 13–15.

Musson, C. R. (1972). "Two Winters at the Breiddin", *Current Arch.*, **33**, 263–267.

Nan Kivell, R. de C. (1926). "Objects found during Excavations on the Romano-British Site at Cold Kitchen Hill, Brixton Deverill", *Wilts. Arch. Mag.*, **43**, 389–394.

Nash-Williams, V. E. (1933), "An Early Iron Age Hill-fort at Llanmelin, near Caerwent, Monmouthshire", *Archaeologia Cambrensis*, **88**, 237–346.

Nash-Williams, V. E. (1939). "An Early Iron Age Coastal Camp at Sudbrook, near the Severn Tunnel, Monmouthshire", *Archaeologia Cambrensis*, **94**, 42–79.

Nash-Williams, V. E. and Savory, H. N. (1949). "List of Hill-forts and other Earthworks in Wales. I. Glamorgan", *Bulletin of the Board of Celtic Studies*, **13**, 152f.

Neish, J. and Stuart, J. (1860). "Reference Notes to Plan and Views of Ancient Remains on the Summit of the Laws, Forfarshire", *Proc. Soc. Ant. Scot.* **3** (1859–1860), 440–454.

Newcomb, R. M. (1970). "The Spatial Distribution Pattern of Hillforts in West Penwith", *Cornish Arch.*, **9**, 47–52.

Newton, R. G. (1971). "A Preliminary Examination of a Suggestion that pieces of Strongly Coloured Glass were Articles of Trade in the Iron Age in Britain", *Archaeometry*, **13**, 11–16.

O'Donovan, J. (1837). *Ordnance Survey Letters, Kildare, Vol. II.* Ordnance Survey Office, Phoenix Park, Dublin.

O'Kelly, M. J. (1952). "Three Promontory Forts in Co. Cork", *Proc. Royal Irish Academy*, **55**, 25–59.

O'Kelly, M. J. (1970). "Problems of Irish Ring-Forts". In *The Irish Sea Province in Archaeology and History* (D. Moore, ed.), pp. 50–55. Cambrian Archaeological Association, Cardiff.

Oliva Prat, M. (1970). *Ullastret, Giua de las Excavaciones y su Musei*. Diputación Provincial, Gerona

O'Neil, B. H. St. J. (1934). "Excavation at Titterstone Clee Hill Camp, Shropshire", *Ant. J.*, **14**, 13–32.

O'Neil, B. H. St. J. (1937). "Excavations at Breiddin Hill Camp, Montgomeryshire, 1933–35", *Archaeologia Cambrensis*, **92**, 86–128.

O'Neil, B. H. St. J. (1942). "Excavations at Ffridd Faldwyn Camp, Montgomery, 1937–39", *Archaeologia Cambrensis*, **97**, 1–57.

O'Neil, H. E. (1934). "Excavation of a Romano-British Building at Bourton-on-the-Water", *Trans. Bristol and Gloucester Arch. Soc.* **56**, 99–128.

O'Neil, H. E. (1935). "Roman Finds in Bourton-on-the-Water", *Trans. Bristol and Gloucester Arch. Soc.*, **57**, 234–247.

O'Neil, H. E. (1961). "Saxon Burials in the Fosse Way at Bourton-on-the-Water, Gloucestershire", *Proc. Cotteswold Naturalists' Field Club*, **33**, 166–169.

O'Neil, H. E. (1966). "Archaeological Observations on the Jurassic Way in Northern Oxfordshire and the Cotswolds", *Proc. Cotteswold Naturalists' Field Club*, **35**, 42–48.

O'Neil, H. E. (1968). "The Roman Settlement on the Fosse Way at Bourton-on-the-Water, Gloucestershire", *Trans. Bristol and Gloucester Arch. Soc.*, **87**, 29–55.

Ordnance Survey (1962). *Map of Southern Britain in the Iron Age*. Chessington, Surrey.

O'Riordain, S. P. (1953). *Antiquities of the Irish Countryside*. Methuen, London.

O'Riordain, S. P. (1954). *Tara: The Monuments on the Hill*. Dundalgan Press, Dundalk.

Orpen, G. H. (1911). "Rathgall, Co. Wicklow", *J. Royal Soc. Ant. Ireland*. **41**, 138–150.

Ottaway, B. and Ottaway, J. H. (1972). "The Suess Calibration Curve and Archaeological Dating", *Nature*, **239**, 512–513.

Overbeck, F. and Happach, H. (1957). "Das Alter der Grenzhorizont norddeutscher Hochmoore nach Radiocarbon-Datierungen", *Flora*, **144**, Pt. 3, 335–402.

Peacock, D. P. S. (1967). "Romano-British Pottery Production in the Malvern District of Worcestershire", *Trans. Worcestershire Arch. Soc.*, **3**, series I, 15–28.

Peacock, D. P. S. (1968). "A Petrological Study of Certain Iron Age Pottery from Western England", *Proc. Prehist. Soc.*, **34**, 414–426.

Peacock, D. P. S. (1969). "A Contribution to the Study of Glastonbury Ware from Southwestern Britain", *Ant. J.*, **49**, 41–61.

Peacock, D. P. S. and Thomas, A. C. (1967). "Class 'E' Imported Post-Roman Pottery: A Suggested Origin", *Cornish Arch.*, **6**, 35–46.

Penney, S. (1974). *Iron Age Bone and Antler-Working Techniques, with Special Reference to Meare and Glastonbury* (unpublished B.A. dissertation, Queen's University, Belfast).

Pennington, R. (1877). *Notes on the Barrows and Bone Caves of Derbyshire*.

Pennington, W. (1969). *The History of British Vegetation*.

Perry, B. T. (1969). "Iron Age Enclosures and Settlements on the Hampshire Chalklands", *Arch. J.*, **126**, 29–43.

Petch, J. A. (1923). *Early Man in the District of Huddersfield*. Tolson Memorial Museum Handbook, p. 3.

Pič, J. L. and Déchelette, J. (1906). *Le Hradischt de Stredonitz*.

Piggott, C. M. (1946). "The Late Bronze Age Razors of the British Isles", *Proc. Prehist. Soc.*, **12**, 121–141.

Piggott, C. M. (1960). "The Excavations at Hownam Rings, Roxburghshire, 1948", *Proc. Soc. Ant. Scot.*, **82**, (1947–1948), 193–224.

Piggott, C. M. (1952). "The Excavations at Bonchester Hill, 1950", *Proc. Soc. Ant. Scot.*, **84** (1949–1950), 113–136.

Piggott, S. (1931). "Ladle Hill—An Unfinished Hillfort", *Antiquity*, **5**, 474–485.

Piggott, S. (1950). "Swords and Scabbards of the British Early Iron Age", *Proc. Prehist. Soc.*, **16**, 1–28.

Piggott, S. (1953a). "Three Metal-Work Hoards of the Roman Period from Southern Scotland", *Proc. Soc. Ant. Scot.*, **87** (1952–1953), 1–50.

Piggott, S. (1953b). "A Late Bronze Age Hoard from Peeblesshire", *Proc. Soc. Ant. Scot.*, **87**, 1952–1953, 175–186.

Piggott, S. (1958). "Native Economies . . .". In *Roman and Native in North Britain* (I. A. Richmond, ed.), pp. 1–27. Nelson, Edinburgh.

Piggott, S. (1959). "Traders and Metalworkers". In *The Prehistoric Peoples of Scotland* (S. Piggott, ed.), pp. 73–103. Edinburgh.

Piggott, S. (1965). *Ancient Europe*. Edinburgh.

Piggott, S. (1966). "A Scheme for the Scottish Iron Age". In *The Iron Age in Northern Britain* (A. L. F. Rivet, ed.), pp. 1–15, Edinburgh.

Piggott, S. (1968). *The Druids*. Thames and Hudson, London.

Piggott, S. (1970). *Neolithic Cultures of the British Isles*. Cambridge.

Piggott, S. and Piggott, C. M. (1940). "Excavations at Rams Hill, Uffington, Berks.", *Ant. J.*, **20**, 465–80.

Piggott, S. and Piggott, C. M. (1952). "Excavations at Castle Law, Glencorse, and at Craig's Quarry, Dirleton, 1948–9", *Proc. Soc. Ant. Scot.*, **86** (1951–1952), 191–195.

Pitt-Rivers, A. H. L. F. (1888). *Excavations in Cranborne Chase*, Vol. II, pp. 233–253.

Pollard, S. H. M. (1966). "Neolithic and Dark Age Settlements on High Peak, Sidmouth, Devon", *Proc. Devon Arch. Exploration Soc.*, **23**, 35–59.

Powell, T. G. E. (1933). "Oxenton Hill Camp", *Trans. Bristol and Gloucester Arch. Soc.*, **55**, 383–384.

Powell, T. G. E. (1958). *The Celts*. Thames and Hudson, London.

Powell, T. G. E. (1963). "Excavations at Skelmore Heads near Ulverston, 1957 and 1959", *Trans. Cumberland and Westmorland Arch. Soc.*, **63**, 1–30.

Preston, F. L. (1954). "The Hill Forts of the Peak", *Derbyshire Arch. J.*, **74**, 1–31.

Proudfoot, V. B. (1954). "Excavations at the Cathedral Hill, Downpatrick, Co. Down, 1953", *Ulster J. Arch.*, **17**, 97–102.

Proudfoot, V. B. (1955). *The Downpatrick Gold Find*. Belfast.

Proudfoot, V. B. (1956). "Excavations at Cathedral Hill, Downpatrick, Co. Down, 1954", *Ulster J. Arch.*, **19**, 57–72.

Proudfoot, V. B. (1957). "A Second Gold Find from Downpatrick", *Ulster J. Arch.*, **20**, 70–72.

Proudfoot, V. B. (1961). "The Economy of the Irish Rath", *Medieval Arch.*, **5**, 94–122.

Proudfoot, V. B. (1970). "Irish Raths and Cashels: Some Notes on Chronology, Origins and Survivals", *Ulster J. Arch.*, **33**, 37–48.

Quilling, F. (1903). *Die Nauheimer Funde*.

Radford, C. A. R. (1951). "Report on the Excavations at Castle Dore", *J. Royal Inst. Cornwall*, new series 1. Appendix as separate vol. (1951).

Radford, C. A. R. (1952). "Prehistoric Settlements on Dartmoor and the Cornish Moors", *Proc. Prehist. Soc.*, **18**, 55–84.

Radford, C. A. R. (1970). "The Later Pre-Conquest Boroughs and their Defences", *Medieval Arch.*, **14**, 82–103.

Radley, J. and Radford, L. (1969). "Iron Age Pottery from Brassington Common", *Derbyshire Arch. J.*, **89**, 121–122.

Rafter, T. A. and Grant-Taylor, T. (1972). *Proceedings of the Eighth International Radiocarbon Dating Conference, New Zealand*. Royal Society of New Zealand, Wellington.

Raftery, B. (1969). "Freestone Hill, Co. Kilkenny: An Iron Age Hillfort and Bronze Age Cairn", *Proc. Royal Irish Academy*, **68**, section C, 1–108.

Raftery, B. (1970a). "The Rathgall Hillfort, County Wicklow", *Antiquity*, **44**, 51–54.

Raftery, B. (1970b). "A Decorated Strap-end from Rathgall, Co. Wicklow", *J. Royal Soc. Ant. Ireland*, **100**, 200–211.

Raftery, B. (1971). "Rathgall, Co. Wicklow: 1970 excavations", *Antiquity*, **45**, 296–298.

Raftery, B. (1972). "Irish hill-forts". In *The Iron Age in the Irish Sea Province* (A. C. Thomas, ed.), pp. 37–58. C.B.A. Research Report No. 9, London.

Raftery, B. (1973). "Rathgall: A Late Bronze Age Burial in Ireland", *Antiquity*, **47**, 293–295.

Raftery, J. (1960). "A Hoard of the Early Iron Age", *J. Royal Soc. Ant. Ireland*, **90**, 2–5.

Raftery, J. (1972). "Iron Age and Irish Sea: Problems for Research", In *The Iron Age in the Irish Sea Province* (A. C. Thomas, ed.), pp. 1–10.

Rahtz, P. A. (1961). "Second Interim Report on Excavations at Hog Cliff Hill, Maiden Newton", *Proc. Dorset Nat. Hist. and Arch. Soc.*, **82**, 83.

Rahtz, P. and ApSimon, A. M. (1962). "Excavations at Shearplace Hill, Sydling St. Nicholas, Dorset, England", *Proc. Prehist. Soc.*, **28**, 289–328.

Rahtz, P. and Fowler, P. J. (1972). "Somerset A.D. 400–700". In *Archaeology and the Landscape* (P. J. Fowler, ed.), pp. 187–221.

Rahtz, P. A., and Musty, J. W. G. (1960). "Excavations at Old Sarum, 1957", *Wilts. Arch. Mag.*, **57**, 353–370.

Ralph, E. K., Michael, H. N. and Han, M. C. (1973). "Radiocarbon dates and reality", *MASCA Newsletter*, **9**, No. 1, 1–18. (Univ. Museum, Univ. of Pennsylvania).

R.C.A.H.M. (Scotland) (1914). *Fifth Report and Inventory of Monuments and Constructions in Galloway*, 2 vols. Edinburgh.

R.C.A.H.M. (Scotland) (1920). *Seventh Report with Inventory of Monuments and Constructions in the County of Dumfries*. Edinburgh.

R.C.A.H.M. (Scotland) (1956). *Inventory of the Ancient and Historical Monuments of Roxburghshire*. Edinburgh.

R.C.A.H.M. (Scotland) (1963). *Stirlingshire: An Inventory of the Ancient Monuments*. Edinburgh.

R.C.A.H.M. (Scotland) (1967). *Peebles-shire: An Inventory of the Ancient Monuments*. Edinburgh.

R.C.A.H.M. (Scotland) (1972). *Argyll: An Inventory of the Ancient Monuments. Vol. 7: Kintyre*. Edinburgh.

R.C.A.H.M. (Wales and Mon.) (1956). *Inventory of the Ancient Monuments in Caernarvonshire, Vol. I*. H.M.S.O., London.

R.C.A.H.M. (Wales and Mon.) (1960). *Inventory of the Ancient Monuments in Caernarvonshire, Vol. II*. H.M.S.O., London.

R.C.A.H.M. (Wales and Mon.) (1964). *Inventory of the Ancient Monuments in Caernarvonshire, Vol. III*. H.M.S.O., London.

R.C.H.M. (England) (1910). *Inventory of the Historical Monuments in Hertfordshire*. H.M.S.O., London.

R.C.H.M. (England) (1934). *Inventory of the Historical Monuments of Herefordshire, III*. H.M.S.O., London.

R.C.H.M. (England) (1970a). *Inventory of the County of Dorset, Vol. II, South-East*. H.M.S.O., London.

R.C.H.M. (England) (1970b). *Inventory of the County of Dorset, Vol. III, Central Dorset*. H.M.S.O., London.

R.C.H.M. (England) (1972). *Inventory of the County of Dorset, IV, North Dorset*. H.M.S.O., London.

Rennie, D. M. (1959). "The Excavation of an Earthwork on Rodborough Common in 1954–1955", *Trans. Bristol and Gloucester Arch. Soc.*, **78**, 24–43.

Reynolds, P. J. (1967). "An Experiment in Iron Age Agriculture", *Trans. Bristol and Gloucester Arch. Soc.*, **86**, 60–73.

Rhodes, P. P. (1950). "The Celtic Field Systems on the Berkshire Downs", *Oxoniensia*, **15**, 1–28.

Rice-Holmes, T. (1907). *Ancient Britain and the Invasions of Julius Caesar*. Oxford.

Richardson, K. M. (1951). "The Excavation of Iron Age Villages on Boscombe Down West", *Wilts. Arch. Mag.*, **54**, 123–168.

Richmond, I. A. (1925). *Huddersfield in Roman Times*.

Richmond, I. A. (1958). *Roman and Native in North Britain*.

Richmond, I. A. (1962). "The Earliest Roman Occupation of Gloucester", *Trans. Bristol and Gloucester Arch. Soc.*, **81**, 14–16.

Richmond, I. A. (1968). *Hod Hill, Vol. 2, Excavations Carried out Between 1951 and 1958*. British Museum.

Richmond, I. A. and Crawford, O. G. S. (1949). "The British Section of the Ravenna Cosmography" *Archaeologia*, **93**, 1–50.

Ritchie, A. (1970). "Palisaded Sites in North Britain", *Scottish Arch. Forum. Edinburgh*, 48–67.

Ritchie, G. and A. (1971). "Metalworkers". In *Who are the Scots?* (G. Menzies, ed.). Glasgow.

Ritterling, E. (1913). "Das Frührömische Lager bei Hofheim im Taunus", *Annalen des Vereins für Nassauische Altertumskunde*, 40.

Rivet, A. L. F. (1958a). "Some of the Problems of Hillforts". In *Problems of the Iron Age in Southern Britain* (S. S. Frere, ed.), pp. 29–34.

Rivet, A. L. F. (1958b). *Town and Country in Roman Britain*. Hutchinson, London.

Rivet, A. L. F. (1962). *Map of Southern Britain in the Iron Age*. Ordnance Survey, London.

Rivet, A. L. F. (1966). *The Iron Age in Northern Britain*. Edinburgh University Press.

Rivet, A. L. F. (1969a). *The Roman Villa in Britain*. London.

Rivet, A. L. F. (1969b). "Social and Economic Aspects". In *The Roman Villa in Britain* (A. L. F. Rivet, ed.), pp. 173–216.

Rivet, A. L. F. (1971). "Hillforts in Action". In *The Iron Age and Its Hillforts* (M. Jesson and D. Hill, eds), pp. 189–202.

Robertson, A. (1970). "Roman Finds from Non-Roman Sites in Scotland", *Britannia*, **I**, 198–226.

Roder, J. (1948). "Der Goloring: Ein eisenzeitliches Heiligtum vom Hengecharakter im Koberner Wald", *Bonner Jahrbücher*, **148**, 81–132.

Ross, A. (1967). *Pagan Celtic Britain*. Routledge and Kegan Paul, London.

Roth, H. L. (1918). "Studies in Primitive Looms, Part IV (Conclusions)", *J. Royal Anth. Inst.*, **48**, 103–145.

Rowntree, A. (1931). *History of Scarborough*.

Roy, W. (1793). *The Military Antiquities of the Romans in Britain*. Society of Antiquaries of London.

Russell, V. (1971). *West Penwith Survey*. Cornwall Arch. Soc.

St. Joseph, J. K. S. (1961). "Aerial Reconnaissance in Wales", *Antiquity*, **35**, 263–274.

Salway, P. (1967). "Excavations at Hockwold-cum-Wilton, Norfolk, 1961–1962", *Proc. Cambridge Antiquarian Soc.*, **60**, 39–80.

Saunders, A. (1961). "Excavations at Castle Gotha, St. Austell, Cornwall, Interim Report", *Proc. West Cornwall Field Club*, **2** (1960–1961), 216–220.

Saunders, C. (1972). "The Pre-Belgic Iron Age in the Central and Western Chilterns", *Arch. J.*, **128**, 1–30.

Savory, H. N. (1937). "An Early Iron Age Site at Long Wittenham, Berks.", *Oxoniensia*, **2**, 1–11.

Savory, H. N. (1939). "Early Man: IV:—Early Iron Age". In *Victoria County History of Oxfordshire* Vol. I. (L. F. Salzmann, ed.), pp. 251–261.

Savory, H. N. (1949). "List of Hill-forts and other Earthworks in Wales, I, Glamorgan", *Bulletin of the Board of Celtic Studies*, **13**, 152–161.

Savory, H. N. (1950a). "List of Hill-forts and other Earthworks in Wales, II, Monmouthshire", *Bulletin of the Board of Celtic Studies*, **13**, 231–238.

Savory, H. N. (1950b). "List of Hill-forts and other Earthworks in Wales, III, Brecknockshire", *Bulletin of the Board of Celtic Studies*, **14**, 69–75.

Savory, H. N. (1952a). "List of Hill-forts and other Earthworks in Wales, IV, Radnorshire", *Bulletin of the Board of Celtic Studies*, **15**, 73–80.

Savory, H. N. (1952b). "An Ancient Settlement on Merthyr Mawr Warren", *Trans. Cardiff Naturalists' Soc.*, **82**, 42f.

Savory, H. N. (1953). "List of Hill-forts and other Earthworks in Wales and Monmouthshire: Additions and Corrections to Sections I–III", *Bulletin of the Board of Celtic Studies*, **15**, 228–231.

Savory, H. N. (1954a). "List of Hill-forts and other Earthworks in Wales, V, Carmarthenshire", *Bulletin of the Board of Celtic Studies*, **16**, 54–69.

Savory, H. N. (1954b). "The Excavation of an Early Iron Age Fortified Settlement on Mynydd Bychan, Llysworney (Glam.), 1949–50: Part I", *Archaeologia Cambrensis*, **103**, 85–108.

Savory, H. N. (1955a). "The Excavation of an Early Iron Age Fortified Settlement on Mynydd Bychan, Llysworney (Glam.), 1949–50: Part II", *Archaeologia Cambrensis*, **104**, 14–51.

Savory, H. N. (1955b). "Prehistoric Brecknock", *Brycheiniog*, **I**, 79–125.

Savory, H. N. (1958a). "The Late Bronze Age in Wales: Some New Discoveries and New Interpretations", *Archaeologia Cambrensis*, **107**, 3–63.

Savory, H. N. (1958b). "Excavations at an Early Iron Age Hill-fort and a Romano-British Iron-Smelting Place at Gwernyfed Park, Aberllynfi, in 1951", *Brycheiniog*, **4**, 53–71.

Savory, H. N. (1960). "Excavations at Dinas Emrys, Beddgelert, Caernarvonshire, 1954–56", *Archaeologia Cambrensis*, **109**, 13–77.

Savory, H. N. (1961). "Twyn-llechfaen Hill-fort Excavations, 1959", *Bulletin of the Board of Celtic Studies*, **19**, 173–176.

Savory, H. N. (1962). "Recent Archaeological Excavation and Discovery in Glamorgan: Prehistoric Periods", *Morgannwg*, **6**, 95–97.

Savory, H. N. (1964a). "The Tal-y-Llyn Hoard", *Antiquity*, **38**, 18–31.

Savory, H. N. (1964b). "A New Hoard of La Tène Metalwork from Merionethshire", *Bulletin of the Board of Celtic Studies*, **20**, 449–475.

Savory, H. N. (1965). "The Guilsford Hoard", *Bulletin of the Board of Celtic Studies*, **21**, 179–94.

Savory, H. N. (1966). "Further Notes on the Tal-y-Llyn (Mer.) Hoard", *Bulletin of the Board of Celtic Studies*, **22**, 88–103.

Savory, H. N. (1967). "The Bronze Age Pottery from the Lesser Garth Cave", *Trans. Cardiff Naturalists' Soc.*, **93**, 34–36.

Savory, H. N. (1968a). "The Prehistoric Material (from Dan-yr-Ogof Caves)", *Archaeologia Cambrensis*, **117**, 34–40.

Savory, H. N. (1968b). *Early Iron Age Art in Wales*. National Museum of Wales, Cardiff.

Savory, H. N. (1969). "The Excavation of the Marlborough Grange Barrow, Llanblethian (Glam.), 1967", *Archaeologia Cambrensis*, **118**, 49–72.

Savory, H. N. (1970). "The Later Prehistoric Migrations Across the Irish Sea". In *The Irish Sea Province in Archaeology and History* (D. Moore, ed.), pp. 38–49. Cambrian Archaeological Association, Cardiff.

Savory, H. N. (1971a). "A Welsh Late Bronze Age Hillfort", *Antiquity*, **45**, 251–261.

Savory, H. N. (1971b). *Excavations at Dinorben, 1965–9*. National Museum of Wales, Cardiff.

Savory, H. N. (1971c). "Excavations at Dinorben Hill Fort, Abergele, 1961–9", *Trans. Denbighshire Hist. Soc.*, **20**, 9–30.

Savory, H. N. (1971d). "Prehistoric Brecknock", *Brycheiniog*, **15**, 3–22.

SCH. *Saint Catharine's Hill, Winchester:* Vol. XI of the Hampshire Field Club's *Proceedings* (Winchester, 1930), by C. F. C. Hawkes, J. N. L. Myres and C. G. Stevens; completed 25 November 1929; indexed by the Rev. A. Snell.

Schubert, H. R. (1957). *History of the British Iron and Steel Industry*. London.

Schwappach, F. (1969). "Stempelverzierte Keramik von Armorica". In *Marburger Beiträge zur Archäologie der Kelten* (O. H. Frey, ed.), pp. 213–287.

Selkirk, A. and Wailes, B. (1970). "Dún Ailinne", *Current Arch.*, **22**, 308–311.

Selkirk, A. and Waterman, D. (1970). "Navan Fort", *Current Arch.*, **22**, 304–308.

Shepard, A. O. (1956). *Ceramics for the Archaeologist*. Carnegie Institute of Washington, D.C., publication 609.

Simpson, D. D. A. (1971). "Kaimes Hill-fort, Midlothian", *Glasgow Arch. J.*, **2**, 7–28.

Simpson, G. (1963). "Caerleon and the Roman Forts in Wales in the Second Century A.D. Part 2— Southern Wales", *Archaeologia Cambrensis*, **112**, 13–76.

Simpson, G. (1964a). "The hill-forts of Wales and their Relation to Roman Britain: A Recension". In Gardner and Savory (1964), 209–20.

Simpson, G. (1964b). *Britons and the Roman Army*. Gregg, London.

Singer, C., Holmyard, E. J., Hall, A. R. and Williams, T. I. (1956). *A History of Technology*, Vol. 2, *the Mediterranean Civilisation and Middle Ages: c.* 700 *B.C.–A.D.* 1500. Oxford.

Small, A. (1969). "Burghead", *Scottish Arch. Forum*. **I**, 61–68.

Small, A. (1971). "Craig Phadrig: Interim Report on 1971 Excavation", *Univ. Dundee Dept. Geog. Occ. Papers*, **I**.

Smith, A. H. (1964). *Place-Names of Gloucestershire*. English Place-Names Society, Vol. XXXVIII.

Smith, I. F. (1968). "Report on Late Neolithic Pits at Cam, Gloucestershire", *Trans. Bristol and Gloucester Arch. Soc.*, **87**, 14–28.

Smith, I. F. (1972). "Ring-ditches in Eastern and Central Gloucestershire". In *Archaeology and the Landscape* (P. J. Fowler, ed.), pp. 157–167.

Smith, M. A. (1959). "Some Somerset Hoards and their Place in the Bronze Age of Southern Britain", *Proc. Prehist. Soc.*, **25**, 144–187.

Smith, R. A. (1909a). "Harborough Cave, near Brassington", *J. Derbyshire Arch. and Nat. Hist. Soc.*, **31**, 97–114.

Smith, R. A. (1909b). "On a Late Celtic Mirror found at Desborough, Northants, and other Mirrors of the Period", *Archaeologia*, **61**, 329–346.

Smith, R. A. (1925). *Guide to Early Iron Age Antiquities*. British Museum.

Smith, R. A. (1926). "Park Brow, The Finds and Foreign Parallels", *Archaeologia*, **76**, 14–29.

Smith, R. A. (1927). "Pre-Roman Remains at Scarborough", *Archaeologia*, **77**, 179–200.

Smith, A. G., Pearson, G. W. and Pilcher, J. R. (1970). "Belfast Radiocarbon Dates I", *Radiocarbon*, **12**, No. I, 285–290.

Soutou, A. (1962). "Le Castellum gabale du Roc de la Fare", *Gallia*, **20**, 333–348.

Spratling, M. (1970). "The Smiths of South Cadbury", *Current Arch.* **22**, 188–191.

Spindler, K. (1970). "Eine eisenzeitliche Befestigung mit Steinfoster von Castillo Viejo", *Madrider Mitteilungen*, **11**, 110–112.

Spurgeon, C. J. (1963). "Two Pembrokeshire Earthworks", *Archaeologia Cambrensis*, **112**, 154–158.

Spurgeon, C. J. (1969). *Archaeology in Wales*, **9**, 12f.

Spurgeon, C. J. (1972). "Enclosures of Iron Age Type in the Upper Severn Basin". In *Prehistoric Man in Wales and the West* (F. Lynch and C. B. Burgess, eds), pp. 321–344. Adams and Dart, Bath.

Stanford, S. C. (1967). "Croft Ambrey: Some Interim Conclusions", *Trans. Woolhope Nat. Field Club*, **39**, 31–39.

Stanford, S. C. (1970). "Credenhill Camp—an Iron Age Hillfort Capital", *Arch. J.*, **127**, 82–129.

Stanford, S. C. (1971). "Invention, Adoption and Imposition". In *The Iron Age and its Hillforts* (M. Jesson and D. Hill, eds), pp. 41–52. Southampton University Archaeological Society, Southampton.

Stanford, S. C. (1972a). "Welsh Border Hillforts". In *The Iron Age in the Irish Sea Province* (A. C. Thomas, ed.), pp. 25–36. C.B.A. Research Report No. 9, London.

Stanford, S. C. (1972b). "The Function and Population of Hill-forts in the Central Marches". In *Prehistoric Man in Wales and the West* (F. Lynch and C. Burgess, eds), pp. 307–319. Adams and Dart, Bath.

Stanford, S. C. (1974). *Croft Ambrey* (published privately).

Stanley, J. (1954). "An Iron Age Fort at Ball Cross Farm, Bakewell", *J. Derbyshire Arch. and Nat. Hist. Soc.*, **74**, 85–99.

Stead, I. M. (1965a). *The La Tène Cultures of Eastern Yorkshire*, Yorkshire Philosophical Society, York.

Stead, I. M. (1965b). "The Celtic Chariot", *Antiquity*, **39**, 259–265.

Stead, I. M. (1967). "A La Tène Burial at Welwyn Garden City", *Archaeologia*, **101**, 1–62.

Stead, I. M. (1968). "An Iron Age Hill Fort at Grimthorpe, Yorkshire, England", *Proc. Prehist. Soc.*, **34**, 148–190.

Stead, I. M. (1972). "Yorkshire Before the Romans: Some Recent Discoveries". In *Soldier and Civilian in Roman Yorkshire* (R. M. Butler, ed.), pp. 21–43.

Stead, W. H. and Bevan-Evans, M. (1961). *Archaeology in Wales*, **1**, 4.

Stead, W. H. and Bevan-Evans, M. (1962). *Archaeology in Wales*, **2**, 5.

Steer, K. A. (1956). "The Early Iron Age homestead at West Plean", *Proc. Soc. Ant. Scot.*, **89** (1955–1956), 227–249.

Steer, K. A. (1958). "The Severan Reorganisation". In *Roman and Native in North Britain* (I. A. Richmond, ed.), pp. 91–111.

Steer, K. A. (1964). "John Horsley and the Antonine Wall", *Arch. Aeliana*, **42**, 1–40.

Stevens, C. E. (1966). "The Social and Economic Aspects of Rural Settlement". In *Rural Settlement in Roman Britain* (A. C. Thomas, ed.), pp. 108–128.

Stevenson, R. B. K. (1951). "The Nuclear Fort of Dalmahoy, Midlothian and Other Dark Age capitals", *Proc. Soc. Ant. Scot.*, **83** (1948–1949), 186–197.

Stevenson, R. B. K. (1956). "Native Bangles and Roman Glass", *Proc. Soc. Ant. Scot.*, **88** (1954–1956), 208–221.

Stevenson, R. B. K. (1966). "Metalwork and Some Other Objects in Scotland and Their Cultural Affinities". In *The Iron Age in Northern Britain* (A. L. F. Rivet, ed.), pp. 17–44. Edinburgh.

Stevenson, R. B. K. (1971). "Note on a Mould from Craig Phadrig". In Small (1971), 49–51.

Stuart, J. D. M. and Birkbeck, J. M. (1936). "A Celtic Village on Twyford Down", *Proc. Hampshire Field Club*, **13**, pt. 2, 188–207.

Stuart, P. (1962). "Gewoon Aardewerk uit de Romeinse Legerplaats en de Bijbehorende Grafvelden te Nijmegen", *Oudheidkundige Mededeelingen*, **43**, Supplement.

Stuckenrath, R. and Mielke, J. E. (1973). "Smithsonian Institution Radiocarbon Measurements VIII", *Radiocarbon*, **15**, No. 2, 388–424.

Stukeley, W. (1776). *Itinerarium Curiosum*, 1776.

Suess, H. E. (1970a). "Bristlecone Pine Calibration of the Radiocarbon Time Scale 5200 B.C. to the Present". In *Nobel Symposium* 12: *Radio-carbon Variations and Absolute Chronology* (I. U. Olsson, ed.), pp. 303–309. Stockholm.

Suess, H. E. (1970b). "The Three Causes of the Secular C-14 Fluctuations: Their Amplitudes and Time Constants". In *Nobel Symposium* 12: *Radio-Carbon Variations and Absolute Chronology* (I. U. Olsson, ed.), pp. 595–605. Stockholm.

Switsur, V. R. (1973). "The Radiocarbon Calendar Recalibrated", *Antiquity*, **47**, 131–137.

Taffanel, O. and J. (1960). "Deux tombes de cavaliers du Ier Age du Fer a Mailhac (Aude)", *Gallia*, **20**, 3–32.

Taverner, F. (1640). *History of the Antiquities of Hexton* (c. 1640). British Museum Add. Ms. 6223.

Thomas, A. C. (1961). "The Animal Art of the Scottish Iron Age and its Origins", *Arch. J.*, **118**, 14–64.

Thomas, A. C. (1966a). *Rural Settlement in Roman Britain*. Council for British Archaeology, Research Report 7.

Thomas, A. C. (1966b). "The Character and Origins of Roman Dumnonia". In *Rural Settlement in Roman Britain* (A. C. Thomas, ed.), pp. 74–98.

Thomas, A. C. (1968). "The Evidence from North Britain". In *Christianity in Britain*, 300–700 *A.D.* (M. W. Barley and P. Hanson, eds), pp. 93–121.

Thomas, A. C. (1972). *The Iron Age in the Irish Sea Province*. Council for British Archaeology, Research Report 9.

Thomas, N. (1958). "Excavations at Callow Hill, Glympton and Stonesfield, Oxon.", *Oxoniensia*, **22**, 1–10.

Thomas, N. (1960). *A Guide to Prehistoric England*. Batsford, London.

Thomas, W. G. and Walker, R. F. (1959). "Excavations at Trelissey, Pembrokeshire, 1950–1", *Bulletin of the Board of Celtic Studies*, **18**, 295–303.

Tierney, J. J. (1960). "The Celtic Ethnography of Posidonius", *Proc. Royal Irish Academy*, **60C**, 189–275.

Torbrügge, W. and Uenze, H. P. (1968). *Bilder Zur Vorgeschichte Bayerns*. Thorbecke Verlag, Konstanz.

Tratman, E. K. (1970). "The Glastonbury Lake Village: A Reconsideration", *Proc. Bristol Univ. Spelaeological Soc.*, **12**(2), 143–167.

Tristram, E. (1915). "Mam Tor Earthwork", *J. Derbyshire Arch. and Nat. Hist Soc.*, **37**, 87–90.

Trow-Smith, R. (1957). *A History of British Livestock Husbandry to 1700*. London.

Turnbull, L. (1963). *Late Fourth Century Pottery in Northern Britain* (unpublished B.A. Dissertation, Newcastle upon Tyne).

Turner, E. (1850). "On the Military Earthworks of the Southdown, with a More Enlarged Account of Cissbury", *Sussex Arch. Coll.*, **3**, 173–184.

Turner, J. (1965). "A Contribution to the History of Forest Clearance", *Proc. Royal Soc.*, **B161**, 343–354.

Tylecote, R. F. (1962). *Metallurgy in Archaeology*. London.

Ulbert, G. (1959). *Die römischen Donau Kastelle Aislingen und Burghöfe*. Limesforschungen, I.

Varley, W. (1935). "Maiden Castle, Bickerton: Preliminary Excavations, 1934", *Annals of Archaeology and Anthropology, University of Liverpool*, **22**, 97–110.

Varley, W. (1936). "Further Excavations at Maiden Castle, Bickerton, 1935", *Annals of Archaeology and Anthropology, University of Liverpool*, **23**, 101–112.

Varley, W. (1940). *Prehistoric Cheshire*. Cheshire Rural Community Council, Chester.

Varley, W. (1948). "The Hillforts of the Welsh Marches", *Arch. J.*, **105**, 41–66.

Varley, W. (1952). "Excavations of the Castle Ditch, Eddisbury, 1935–38", *Trans. Hist. Soc. Lancs. and Cheshire*, **102**, 1–68.

Varley, W. (1963). *Cheshire Before the Romans*.

Vermeulen, W. (1932). *Een Romeinsch Grafveld op de Hunnerberg te Nijmegen*.

Viré, A. (1909). "31 ième Rapport mensuel de la Commission d'études des encientes préhistoriques", *Bulletin de la Société Préhistorique Française*, **6**, 408–416.

Wacher, J. S. (1964). "Excavations at Breedon on the Hill, Leicestershire, 1957", *Ant. J.*, **44**, 122–142.

Wailes, B. (1969). "Excavations at Dún Ailinne, Co. Kildare, Ireland: 1968", *Expedition*, **II**, No. 2, 2–5.

Wailes, B. (1970a). "Excavations at Dún Ailinne, Co. Kildare: 1968–9 Interim Report", *J. Royal Soc. Ant. Ireland*, **100**, pt. I, 79–90.

Wailes, B. (1970b). "Excavation at Dún Ailinne, near Kilcullen, 1970", *J. Co. Kildare Arch. Soc.*, **XIV**, No. 5, 507–517.

Wailes, B. (1971). "Excavation at Dún Ailinne, near Kilcullen, 1970", *J. Co. Kildare Arch. Soc.*, **XV**, No. I, 5–11.

Wailes, B. (1973). "Excavation at Dún Ailinne, near Kilcullen, 1973", *J. Co. Kildare Arch. Soc.* **XV**, No. 3, 234–42.

Wailes, B. (1974). "Excavation at Dún Ailinne, near Kilcullen, 1974", *J. Co. Kildare Arch. Soc.* **XV**, No. 4.

Wainwright, F. T. (1956). *The Problem of the Picts.* Edinburgh and London.

Wainwright, F. T. (1963). *The Souterrains of Pictland.* London.

Wainwright, G. J. (1967a). *Coygan Camp: A Prehistoric, Romano-British and Dark Age Settlement in Carmarthenshire.* Cambrian Archaeological Association, Cardiff.

Wainwright, G. J. (1967b). "The Excavation of an Iron Age Hillfort on Bathampton Down, Somerset", *Trans. Bristol and Gloucester. Arch. Soc.,* **86,** 42–59.

Wainwright, G. J. (1968). "The Excavation of a Durotrigian Farmstead near Tollard Royal in Cranborne Chase, Southern England", *Proc. Prehist. Soc.,* **34,** 102–147.

Wainwright, G. J. (1969). "The Excavation of Balksbury Camp, Andover, Hants.", *Proc. Hampshire Field Club,* **26,** 21–55.

Wainwright, G. J. (1971a). "Excavation of a Fortified Settlement at Walesland Rath, Pembs.", *Britannia,* **2,** 48–108.

Wainwright, G. J. (1971b). "Excavations at Tower Point, St. Brides, Pembrokeshire", *Archaeologia Cambrensis,* **120,** 84–90.

Wainwright, G. and Spratling, M. (1973). "The Iron Age Settlement of Gussage All Saints", *Antiquity,* **47,** 109–130.

Ward, J. (1889). "Recent Diggings at Harborough Rocks, Derbyshire", *Reliquary,* **3,** 216–230.

Ward Perkins, J. B. (1939a). "Iron Age Metal Horses' Bits of the British Isles", *Proc. Prehist. Soc.,* **5,** 173–192.

Ward Perkins, J. B. (1939b). "Excavations on Oldbury Hill, Ightham, 1938", *Arch. Cantiana,* **51,** 137–181.

Ward Perkins, J. B. (1944). "Excavations on the Iron Age Hillfort of Oldbury, near Ightham, Kent", *Archaeologia,* **90,** 127–176.

Wardman, A. M. (1972). *The Early La Tène Brooches of the British Isles* (unpublished B.A. Thesis, Queen's University of Belfast).

Warner, R. B. (1973). "The Excavations at Clogher and their Context", *Clogher Record* (pub. Cumann Seanchais Chlochair; Clogher, Co. Tyrone), **8** (1973), 5–12.

Watson, G. R. (1968). "Christianity in the Roman Army". In *Christianity in Britain,* 300–700 *A.D.* (M. W. Barley and P. P. C. Hanson, eds), p. 53. Leicester.

Webster, G. A. (1958). "The Roman Military Advance under Ostorius Scapula", *Arch. J.,* **115,** 49–98.

Webster, G. A. (1970). "The Military Situation in Britain between A.D. 43 and 71", *Britannia,* **I,** 179–197.

Webster, G. and Dudley, D. R. (1965). *The Roman Conquest of Britain.* Batsford, London.

Wedderburn, L. M. McL. (1973). *Excavations at Greencairn, Cairnton of Balbegno, Fettercairn, Angus.* Dundee Mus. and Art Gallery, Occ. Papers in Archaeology, No. I.

Wheeler, R. E. M. (1922). "Roman and Native in Wales: An Imperial Frontier Problem", *Trans. Hon. Soc. of Cymmrodorion* (1920–1921), 40–96.

Wheeler, R. E. M. (1925). *Prehistoric and Roman Wales.* Clarendon Press, Oxford.

Wheeler, R. E. M. (1929). "'Old England', Brentford", *Antiquity,* **3,** 20–32.

Wheeler, R. E. M. (1936). "The Excavation of Maiden Castle, Dorset: Second Interim Report", *Ant. J.,* **16,** 265–283.

Wheeler, R. E. M. (1943). *Maiden Castle, Dorset.* Society of Antiquaries, Research Report No. 12.

Wheeler, R. E. M. (1953). 'An Early Iron Age "Beach Head" at Lulworth, Dorset", *Ant. J.,* **33,** 1–13.

Wheeler, R. E. M. (1954). *The Stanwick Fortifications.* Society of Antiquaries, Research Report No. 17.

Wheeler, R. E. M. and Richardson, K. M. (1957). *Hill-forts of Northern France.* Society of Antiquaries, London.

Wheeler, R. E. M. and Wheeler, T. V. (1932). *Report on the Excavation of the Prehistoric, Roman and Post-Roman Site in Lydney Park, Gloucestershire.* Society of Antiquaries, Research Report No. 9.

Wheeler, R. E. M. and Wheeler, T. V. (1936). *Verulamium: A Belgic and Two Roman Cities.* Society of Antiquaries, Research Report No. 11.

Whitley, M. (1943). "Excavations at Chalbury Camp, Dorset, 1939", *Ant. J.,* **23,** 98–121.

Whybrow, C. (1967). "Some Multivallate Hillforts on Exmoor and in North Devon", *Proc. Devon Arch. Soc.,* **25,** 1–18.

Williams, A. (1939). "Excavations at the Knave Promontory Fort, Rhossili, Glamorgan", *Archaeologia Cambrensis*, **94,** 210–219.

Williams, A. (1945). "A Promontory Fort at Henllan, Cards.", *Archaeologia Cambrensis*, **98,** 226–240.

Williams, A. (1950). "Excavations at Allard's Quarry, Marnhull", *Proc. Dorset Nat. Hist and Arch. Soc.*, **72,** 20–75.

Williams, A. (1951). "Excavations at Beard Mill, Stanton Harcourt, Oxon., 1944", *Oxoniensia*, **16,** 5–22.

Williams-Freeman, J. P. (1915). *Field Archaeology as Illustrated by Hampshire.*

Wilson, A. E. (1938). "Excavations in the Ramparts and Gateway of The Caburn, August–October, 1937", *Sussex Arch. Coll.*, **79,** 169–194.

Wilson, A. E. (1939). "Excavations in the Caburn, 1938", *Sussex Arch. Coll.*, **80,** 193–213.

Wilson, A. E. (1940). "Report on the Excavations on Highdown Hill, Sussex, August 1939", *Sussex Arch. Coll.*, **81,** 173–203.

Wilson, A. E. (1950). "Excavations at Highdown Hill, 1947", *Sussex Arch. Coll.*, **89,** 163–178.

Wilson, D. R. (1969). "Roman Britain in 1969: Sites Explored", *Britannia*, **I,** 269–305.

Winbolt, S. E. (1932). *The Chilterns and the Thames Valley.*

Wolseley, G. R. and Smith, R. A. (1924). "Discoveries near Cissbury", *Ant. J.*, **4,** 347–359.

Wolseley, G. R. (1926). "Prehistoric and Roman Settlements on Park Brow", *Archaeologia*, **76,** 1–13.

Woodhead, T. A. (1924). *History of the Vegetation of the Southern Pennines.*

Worsfold, F. H. (1943). "A Report on the Late Bronze Age Site Excavated at Minnis Bay, Birchington, Kent, 1938–40", *Proc. Prehist. Soc.*, **9,** 28–47.

Wray, D. A. *et al.* (1930). *The Geology of the Country Around Huddersfield and Halifax.*

Young, A. (1966). "The Sequence of Hebridean Pottery". In *The Iron Age in Northern Britain* (A. L. F. Rivet, ed.), pp. 45–58.

Young, A. and Richardson, K. M. (1955). "Report on the Excavations at Blackbury Castle", *Proc. Devon Arch. Exploration Soc.*, **5** (1954–1955), 43–67.

Author Index

(Numbers in italic refer to pages where references are listed in the Bibliography.)

Subject Index

A

Abbey Craig, Stirlingshire, 234
Aberllynfi, Brecknockshire, 286
Abernethy, Perthshire, 20, 57, 209, 216, 227, 232, 234
        culture, 30–31, 32, 195, 230, 231
Adabrock-type bronzes, 193, 196, 220
air-photography, 61, 239, 276
Aislingen, 105
All Cannings Cross, Wiltshire, 27, 30, 31, 61, 65, 66, 68, 69, 71, 252, 261, 306
Allt yr Esgair, Brecknockshire, 276
Almondbury, Castle Hill, Yorkshire, 119–131, 151, 247
animal burials, 170
        see also horse-burials.
An Knap, Arran, 234
annexed enclosures, 6, 9, 76–77, 121, 125, 263, 276–277
Ardelve, Ross and Cromarty, 235
Ardifuar, Argyllshire, 218
Arisaig, Inverness-shire, 234
Armorica, 6, 7, 33, 45, 94, 113, 242
Arras culture, 126, 128
Arthur's Seat, Edinburgh, 191
Auldhill, Ayrshire, 234
Avaricum, 14

B

back-terracing, 14–15, 268–269, 270, 279, 282
Bagendon, Gloucestershire, 40, 41, 57, 99, 100, 101, 106, 107, 114, 118
Balksbury, Hampshire, 21, 57
Ball Cross, Derbyshire, 14, 151
Ballevullin, Tiree, 149
Ballintruer Mor, Co. Wicklow, 323
banquettes, see back-terracing
barbicans, 6, 18, 59, 72, 269, 276, 277, 280–281
bards, 49
Bard's Castle, Wester Ross, 235
Barland Quarry, 285
Barnwood, Gloucestershire, 113
Barry Hill, Perthshire, 229, 234
bastions, 17, 166–172, 175, 179, 180, 181, 184, 254, 255, 264–265, 268, 272, 280

Bathampton Camp, Somerset, 11, 21, 36, 37, 57
Battlesbury, Wiltshire, 17
Beacon Ring, Montgomeryshire, 264
beads, 23, 244, 297, 298–299, 331, 344, 346
Belgae, 60, 74, 78, 85, 86, 88, 98, 99, 100, 101, 107, 111, 112, 114, 115, 118, 142, 146, 154, 156, 158, 181, 182, 280, 281–282.
Belgic invasion hypothesis, 32, 41–42, 74
Benderloch, Argyllshire, 222, 227, 233, 243
berms, 5, 15, 124, 135, 153, 155, 163, 170, 181
Bignan, Morbihan, 94
Bindon Hill, Dorset, 12, 57, 249
bird, bronze, 69
"Bishopsland" phase, 251
Bishop's Loch crannog, Lanarkshire, 229
Bishopston, Glamorganshire, 285
bivallation, 4, 5, 15, 17 18,, 31, 32, 33, 34, 37, 40, 76, 80, 121, 122, 123, 124, 125, 126, 127, 130, 136, 156, 239, 257, 258, 261, 262, 269, 272, 273, 274, 280, 281
Blackburn Mill hoard, Roxburghshire, 201
Blackbury Castle, Devon, 18, 57
Blewburton Hill, Berkshire, 11, 13, 16, 17, 36, 42, 133–146, 258
Boscombe Down West, Wiltshire, 26, 27, 71
Bosherston, Pembrokeshire, 252, 256, 285
boundary ditches, 6, 24, 28, 54
box-ramparts, *see* wall-ramparts
bracelets, 151, 219, 229, 331, 346
Braes, Stirlingshire, 234
Braich y Ddinas, Caernarvonshire, 257, 268, 276, 284, 286
Brassington Common, Derbyshire, 150
Bredon Hill, Gloucestershire, 17, 18, 19, 23, 57, 91, 180–181, 182, 187, 189
Breedon Hill, Leicestershire, 152
Breiddin, Montgomeryshire, 21, 150, 193, 238, 240, 244, 246, 248, 249, 250, 252, 253, 259, 260, 261, 262, 263, 268, 270, 271, 277, 278, 282, 288–290, 293–302, 303, 310
Brigantes, 119, 121, 130, 131
"Broadwood" group bronzes, 250
brochs, 3, 32, 182, 189, 209, 213, 214, 222, 223, 227, 228, 229
Bromfield, Shropshire, 248, 249